BARRON'S

OFFICER CANDIDATE SCHOOL TESTS

2ND EDITION

Rod Powers
1st SGT., USAF (Retired)

About the Author

Rod Powers is a retired Air Force first sergeant with 23 years of active duty service. As a first sergeant for 11 years, and as a guide for the About.com United States Military career information site, he has provided assistance to thousands of people about career opportunities in the United States armed forces. Powers currently resides in Daytona Beach, Florida.

Dedication

To Mom, who didn't live to see the completion of this book; and to Katie, Shilynn, and Joy, without whose help I might not have made it, either. My "three amigos" helped to get me through the toughest experience of my entire life.

Acknowledgments

The author would like to thank the recruiting commands of the United States Air Force, Navy, Coast Guard, Marine Corps, and Army for their invaluable assistance. Special thanks go to the Federal Aviation Administration and NASA for information and illustrations about flight. And I would especially like to thank my agent, Barb Doyen, and Barron's for helping me through the tough times and for not allowing me to give up. Without you, this book would not have been possible. Finally, to Autumn McLeod, assistant extraordinaire, for her hard work in getting this revision into final shape.

All inquiries should be addressed to:
Barron's Educational Series, Inc.
250 Wireless Boulevard
Hauppauge, New York 11788
www.barronseduc.com

Library of Congress Catalog Card No.: 2012947547

ISBN: 978-1-4380-0035-0

Printed in the United States of America
9 8 7 6 5 4 3 2 1

Table of Contents

So, You Want to Be an Officer?

CHAPTER 1

A piece of paper makes you an officer, a radio makes you a commander.

—General Omar Bradley

More precisely, you must be interested in becoming a commissioned officer in one of the branches of the United States Armed Forces. Otherwise, you presumably wouldn't be reading this book. After all, that's what this book is all about—becoming a commissioned officer by way of Officer Candidate School (OCS), Officer Candidate Course (OCC), or Officer Training School (OTS).

What's the difference? Actually, there's not much difference between the three, other than the name. The Air Force calls its program to turn college graduates into commissioned officers Officer Training School; the Army, Navy, and Coast Guard call their schools Officer Candidate Schools. The Marine Corps sends applicants to their Officer Candidate Course, which (among other officer courses) is conducted at their Officer Candidates School. A rifle by any other name would shoot as straight.

In these modern times, there are many more people who wish to become a commissioned officer in the U.S. military than the services are allowed to accept (Congress tells the military services how many commissioned officers they can have on active duty at any given time). As a result, the selection process for OCS/OTS/OCC has become very selective.

Technically, the selection rate for OCS/OTS/OCC hovers between 50 and 65 percent. Sounds easy, right? At least half, probably more, of those who apply get accepted. What's absent from the equation is that the services employ military officer recruiters whose primary job is to get rid of candidates who are not competitive before they even begin the official application process. For every four officer applicants who walk into a recruiter's office, three get turned away because their college grade point average, criminal history, or officer candidate test results simply don't make the grade. Of the 25 percent who actually get to submit an application, the selection board chooses about half. That means the real-world selection rate is about 12.5 percent.

Assuming an applicant is medically qualified, and doesn't have a significant criminal background (see Chapter 2), the two most important factors used for selection for OCS/OTS/OCC are college GPA and OCS/OTS/OCC selection test results.

We can't do much to help you with your GPA. That's between you, your college, and your professors. What we *can* do is help you prepare for the selection tests used by the five branches of the Armed Forces for selection to attend OCS/OTS/OCC.

Obviously, you're interested in becoming an officer. But do you know what an "officer" in the military is? Most people with no military experience don't.

MILITARY RANK STRUCTURE

Let's get technical here for a second. There are actually three categories of "officers" in the United States military. There are noncommissioned officers (petty officers in the Navy and Coast Guard), warrant officers, and commissioned officers. Within each of the categories are ranks, that each have a corresponding "pay grade" (E-1 through E-9 for enlisted, W-1 through W-5 for warrant officers, and O-1 through O-10 for officers). The pay grade is used to determine how much a military member is paid, and whether or not he or she outranks other military members. This is necessary because the services often use different rank titles for the same pay grade. For example, in the Air Force, a staff sergeant is a noncommissioned officer in the pay grade of E-5. In the Army, a staff sergeant is a noncommissioned officer with the pay grade of E-6. In the Air Force, Army, and Marine Corps, an O-3 has the rank of captain. However, in the Navy and Coast Guard, one doesn't achieve the rank of captain until one becomes an O-6 (although in the Navy and Coast Guard, it's customary to address the person in charge of a ship as "Captain," regardless of rank).

Commissioned Officer Rank

	Army/Air Force/Marines	Navy/ Coast Guard
O-1	 Second Lieutenant (Gold Bar)	 Ensign
O-2	 First Lieutenant (Silver Bar)	 Lieutenant Junior Grade (JG)
O-3	 Captain (Silver Bars)	 Lieutenant
O-4	 Major (Gold Leaf)	 Lieutenant Commander
O-5	 Lieutenant Colonel (Silver Leaf)	 Commander (CDR)

	Army/Air Force/Marines	Navy/ Coast Guard
O-6	 Colonel	 Captain
O-7	 Brigadier General	 Rear Admiral (lower half)
O-8	 Major General	 Rear Admiral (upper half)
O-9	 Lieutenant General	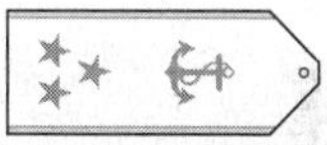 Vice Admiral
O-10	 General	 Admiral

Note: The Navy also uses Air Force/Army/Marine style rank on the collar.

Warrant Officer Rank

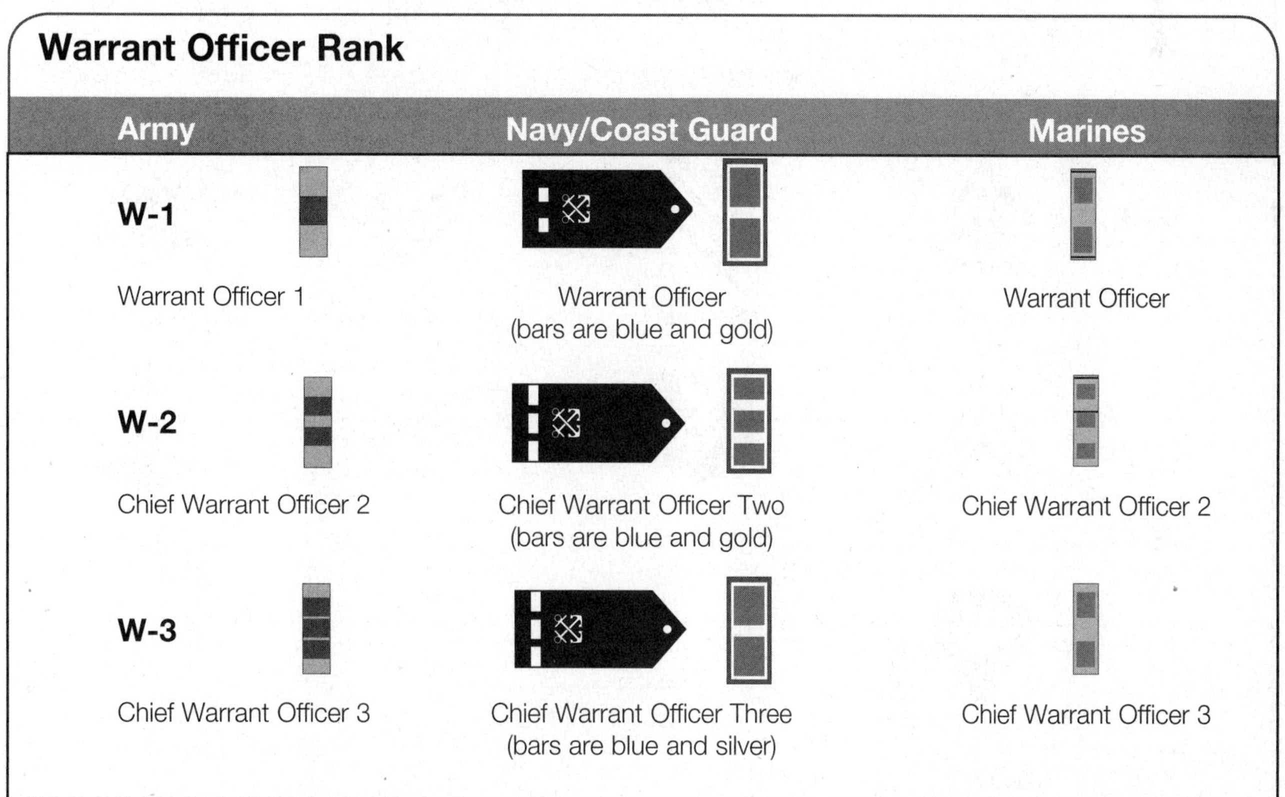

Army		Navy/Coast Guard	Marines
W-1	Warrant Officer 1	Warrant Officer (bars are blue and gold)	Warrant Officer
W-2	Chief Warrant Officer 2	Chief Warrant Officer Two (bars are blue and gold)	Chief Warrant Officer 2
W-3	Chief Warrant Officer 3	Chief Warrant Officer Three (bars are blue and silver)	Chief Warrant Officer 3

	Army	Navy/Coast Guard	Marines
W-4	Chief Warrant Officer 4	Chief Warrant Officer 4 (bars are blue and silver)	Chief Warrant Officer 4
W-5	Chief Warrant Officer 5	Chief Warrant Officer 5 (bars are blue and silver)	Chief Warrant Officer 5

Note: The Air Force does not have Warrant Officers.

Enlisted Rank Chart

	Army	Navy/Coast Guard	Air Force	Marine Corps
E-1	No insignia Private	Seaman Recruit	No insignia Airman Basic	No insignia Private
E-2	Private	Seaman Apprentice	Airman	Private First Class
E-3	Private First Class	Seaman	Airman First Class	Lance Corporal
E-4	Corporal Specialist	Petty Officer Third Class	Senior Airman	Corporal

	Army	Navy/Coast Guard	Air Force	Marine Corps
E-5	Sergeant	Petty Officer Second Class	Staff Sergeant	Sergeant
E-6	Staff Sergeant	Petty Officer First Class	Technical Sergeant	Staff Sergeant
E-7	Sergeant First Class	Chief Petty Officer	Master Sergeant	Gunnery Sergeant
		(Collar & Cap)	First Sergeant (Master Sergeant)	
E-8	Master Sergeant	Senior Chief Petty Officer	Senior Master Sergeant	Master Sergeant
	First Sergeant	(Collar & Cap)	First Sergeant (Senior Master Sergeant)	First Sergeant
E-9	Sergeant Major	Master Chief Petty Officer	Chief Master Sergeant	Master Gunnery Sergeant

	Army	Navy/Coast Guard	Air Force	Marine Corps
E-9	Command Sergeant Major	(Collar & Cap)	First Sergeant	Sergeant Major
			Command Chief Master Sergeant	
Special Pay Grade	Sgt. Major of the Army	Master Chief Petty Officer of the Navy	Chief Master Sergeant of the Air Force	Sgt. Major of the Marine Corps
		(Collar & Cap)		

Just to complicate matters further, in the Navy and Coast Guard, the term "rate" is used instead of "rank" when denoting enlisted personnel. To avoid confusion, we'll use the term "rank" in this chapter, regardless of service branch, even though it may not be technically correct in some cases.

Within each category (enlisted, warrant officers, commissioned officers), members take rank and precedence over each other based on pay grade. An E-7 in the Navy would outrank an E-4 in the Coast Guard. Warrant officers outrank all enlisted personnel, and commissioned officers outrank all warrant officers and enlisted personnel. So, a brand new O-1, straight out of OCS/OTS/OCC, would outrank an E-9 who had 30 years in the military (however, any such commissioned officer who didn't heed the wisdom and experience of this seasoned Noncommissioned Officer/Petty Officer would likely find his/her career cut short).

OFFICERS, WARRANTS, AND ENLISTED—THE DIFFERENCES

Commissioned Officers

Commissioned officers are the top brass. Their primary function is to provide overall management and leadership in their area of responsibility. Commissioned officers do not specialize to the extent that enlisted members and warrant officers do (with certain exceptions such as pilots, doctors, nurses, and lawyers). Let's take, for example, an intelligence officer. An enlisted member assigned to an intelligence career field will have a specific specialty, such as translator/linguist, intelligence analyst, or imagery analyst. Unless that enlisted member retrains, he will remain an intelligence analyst or imagery analyst for his entire career. The commissioned officer, however, is designated as a member of the Intelligence Branch. He can start his career in charge of soldiers performing imagery analysis, then move to a section in charge of general intelligence analysis, then maybe lead a platoon of ground surveillance systems specialists, etc. As he moves up the ranks, he gets more and more experience in the different areas of his branch, and is responsible for commanding more and more troops. All of this has the primary purpose of (ultimately) generating an experienced officer who can command an entire company, battalion, or division. The Army has an interesting program called the Branch Detail Program. Some branches, such as infantry and armor, have a greater need for junior officers than other branches, but a lesser need for mid-level officers. Conversely, other branches, such as intelligence and transportation, need fewer junior officers, but require more mid-level officers. The Army solves this program by "detailing" new second lieutenants from their primary branch to one of these shortage branches. After two or three years, when these officers are about ready to be promoted to captain (O-3), they are returned to their primary branch.

Active duty commissioned officers must have a minimum of a four-year bachelor's degree, except for the Army, who will commission a current enlisted member (not a civilian applicant) with 90 credit hours. However, those active duty enlisted soldiers who are commissioned without a bachelor's degree must complete a degree within one year of commissioning, or they will revert to enlisted status, or be required to separate. The Army National Guard also only requires 90 credit hours for commissioning (the Air National Guard requires a bachelor's degree).

As commissioned officers move up the ranks, if they want to get promoted, they will have to earn a master's degree. Commissioned officers are commissioned through specific commissioning programs, such as one of the military academies (Naval Academy, Air Force Academy, Military Academy, and the Coast Guard Academy), ROTC (Reserve Officer Training Corps), OCS, OTS, or OCC. More details about commissioning opportunities are discussed later in this chapter.

The Navy and Marine Corps have special commissioned officers called Limited Duty Officers (LDOs). Enlisted members (Navy) and warrant officers (from both services) can be appointed as a Limited Duty Officer based on extensive experience and outstanding performance in their specialties. As the name implies, LDOs have a limited scope of duties, and generally their promotion and assignment opportunities are significantly more limited than Unrestricted Line Officers. LDOs are not required to have college degrees, nor are they required to attend OCS/OCC/ROTC, or a service academy.

Warrant Officers

Warrant Officers are very highly trained specialists. This is where they differ from commissioned officers. Unlike commissioned officers, warrant officers remain in their primary specialty to provide specialized knowledge, instruction, and leadership to enlisted members and commissioned officers alike.

Warrant officers will be quick to tell you that they are commissioned. By law, warrant officers in the pay grades of W-2 and above receive a commission, just as do other officers (except noncommissioned/petty officers). However, for clarity, we will continue to refer to officers in the "O" pay grades as "commissioned officers," and officers in the "W" pay grades as "warrant officers."

With few exceptions, one must be an enlisted member with several years of experience, be recommended by his or her commander, and pass a selection board to become a warrant officer.

The Air Force is the only service that does not have warrant officers. The Air Force eliminated their warrant officer positions when Congress created the grades of E-8 and E-9 in the late 1950s. The other services elected to retain the warrant ranks, and shifted the emphasis from a promotion opportunity for E-7s to a highly selective system for highly-skilled technicians.

There are five separate warrant ranks. Warrant officers outrank all enlisted members.

Warrant officers are not required to have college degrees (they are selected primarily based upon technical skills and experience), but many of them do.

Enlisted Personnel

Enlisted members are the backbone of the military. They perform the actual hands-on jobs that the services need to get done in order to accomplish their missions. Enlisted members are "specialists." They are trained to perform specific tasks related to their military specialty. As enlisted personnel progress up the ranks (there are nine enlisted pay grades), they assume more responsibility and provide direct supervision to their subordinates.

Enlisted personnel in certain grades have special status. In the Army, Air Force, and Marine Corps, these members are known as noncommissioned officers, or NCOs. In the Navy and Coast Guard, NCOs (E-4 and above) are petty officers. In the Marine Corps, NCO status begins at the grade of E-4 (corporal).

In the Army and Air Force, enlisted personnel in the grades of E-5 through E-9 are NCOs. However, some Army E-4s are laterally promoted to "corporal," and are considered NCOs (there's no pay increase for this, just an increase in status and authority).

There is an additional special status within the NCO/petty officer ranks. In the Army and Air Force, personnel in the grades of E-7 to E-9 are known as senior NCOs. In the Marine Corps, those in the grades of E-6 through E-9 are known as staff NCOs. In the Navy and Coast Guard, enlisted members in the grades of E-7 to E-9 are chief petty officers.

The following example is not an exact analogy, since it's not possible to accurately compare the military to a civilian company or corporation. However, it may help the layman visualize the differences between enlisted, warrant officers, and commissioned officers.

Think of the enlisted member as the worker in a civilian company. The enlisted are the ones who perform the majority of the "hands-on" work. Within this worker group, NCOs (Army, Air Force, and Marines) and petty officers (Navy and Coast Guard) are the foremen and line supervisors. They perform the job, but also provide direct supervision to the other workers. Senior NCOs (Army, Air Force, and Marines) and chief petty officers (Navy and Coast Guard) are assistant managers who came up through the ranks of the corporation. They are valuable as managers because of their many years of experience, but will never make it to the Board of Directors. Commissioned officers are the managers of the company. They have broad areas of responsibility for the management, organization, and efficiency of various departments of the corporation. Senior commissioned officers (generals and admirals) are the board of directors. Warrant Officers can be thought of as the experienced technical specialists the company hires to perform highly-specialized functions.

Differences in Pay

Commissioned officers have a greater degree of responsibility than enlisted members and warrant officers and therefore receive more pay.

The below charts show the average monthly salaries for military members in calendar year 2012. The figures include base pay, average housing allowance, average food allowance, and tax advantage (because housing and food allowances are not taxable). The charts do not include special pays such as combat zone pay, flight pay, hazardous duty pay, sea pay, submarine duty pay, etc.

2012 Base Pay for Enlisted Members

Pay-Grade	Less-than-2	Over-2	Over-3	Over-4	Over-6
E-9	—	—	—	—	—
E-8	—	—	—	—	—
E-7	2,680	2,925	3,037	3,185	3,301
E-6	2,318	2,550	2,663	2,772	2,885
E-5	2,124	2,266	2,375	2,487	2,662
E-4	1,946	2,046	2,157	2,267	2,364
E-3	1,758	1,868	1,981	1,981	1,981
E-2	1,671	1,671	1,671	1,671	1,671
E-1	1,491	1,491	1,491	1,491	1,491

Pay-Grade	Over-8	Over-10	Over-12	Over-14	Over-16
E-9	4,709	4,816	4,905	5,109	—
E-8	3,855	4,026	4,131	4,258	4,394
E-7	3,499	3,611	3,811	3,977	4,090
E-6	3,143	3,244	3,437	3,496	3,540
E-5	2,845	2,994	3,013	3,013	3,013
E-4	2,364	2,364	2,364	2,364	2,364
E-3	1,981	1,981	1,981	1,981	1,981
E-2	1,671	1,671	1,671	1,671	1,671
E-1	1,491	1,491	1,491	1,491	1,491

Pay-Grade	Over-18	Over-20	Over-22	Over-24	Over-26
E-9	5,268	5,523	5,740	5,968	6,315
E-8	4,641	4,767	4,980	5,098	5,390
E-7	4,209	4,256	4,412	4,496	4,816
E-6	3,590	3,590	3,590	3,590	3,590
E-5	3,013	3,013	3,013	3,013	3,013
E-4	2,364	2,364	2,364	2,364	2,364
E-3	1,981	1,981	1,981	1,981	1,981
E-2	1,671	1,671	1,671	1,671	1,671
E-1	1,491	1,491	1,491	1,491	1,491

2012 Base Pay for Warrant Officers

Pay-Grade	Less-than-2	Over-2	Over-3	Over-4	Over-6
W-5	—	—	—	—	—
W-4	3,897	4,191	4,313	4,431	4,635
W-3	3,558	3,707	3,859	3,908	4,069
W-2	3,130	3,309	3,465	3,578	3,677
W-1	2,763	2,991	3,142	3,240	3,500

Pay-Grade	Over-8	Over-10	Over-12	Over-14	Over-16
W-5	—	—	—	—	—
W-4	4,837	5,040	5,349	5,618	5,875
W-3	4,382	4,709	4,863	5,041	5,224
W-2	4,124	4,281	4,436	4,625	4,773
W-1	3,806	3,944	4,135	4,325	4,473

Pay-Grade	Over-18	Over-20	Over-22	Over-24	Over-26
W-5	—	6,931	7,282	7,543	7,834
W-4	6,084	6,288	6,590	6,836	7,118
W-3	5,553	5,775	5,909	6,051	6,243
W-2	4,908	5,067	5,173	5,257	5,257
W-1	4,610	4,777	4,777	4,777	4,777

2012 Base Pay for Commissioned Officers

Pay-Grade	Less-than-2	Over-2	Over-3	Over-4	Over-6
O-10	—	—	—	—	—
O-9	—	—	—	—	—
O-8	9,683	10,001	10,210	10,270	10,532
O-7	8,046	8,419	8,592	8,730	8,979
O-6	5,963	6,551	6,982	6,982	7,008
O-5	4,972	5,600	5,988	6,061	6,303
O-4	4,290	4,965	5,296	5,371	5,678
O-3	3,771	4,275	4,614	5,031	5,272
O-2	3,258	3,711	4,274	4,418	4,509
O-1	2,828	2,944	3,559	3,559	3,559

Pay-Grade	Over-8	Over-10	Over-12	Over-14	Over-16
O-10	—	—	—	—	—
O-9	—	—	—	—	—
O-8	10,971	11,072	11,489	11,609	11,968
O-7	9,224	9,510	9,793	10,077	10,971
O-6	7,308	7,349	7,349	7,765	8,504
O-5	6,447	6,766	6,999	7,300	7,761
O-4	6,008	6,417	6,738	6,960	7,088
O-3	5,536	5,707	5,989	6,135	6,135
O-2	4,509	4,509	4,509	4,509	4,509
O-1	3,559	3,559	3,559	3,559	3,559

Pay-Grade	Over-18	Over-20	Over-22	Over-24	Over-26
O-10	—	15,647	15,723	16,050	16,620
O-9	—	13,686	13,883	14,167	14,664
O-8	12,488	12,966	13,287	13,287	13,287
O-7	11,725	11,725	11,725	11,725	11,785
O-6	8,937	9,371	9,617	9,866	10,351
O-5	7,982	8,199	8,446	8,446	8,446
O-4	7,162	7,162	7,162	7,162	7,162
O-3	6,136	6,136	6,136	6,136	6,136
O-2	4,509	4,509	4,509	4,509	4,509
O-1	3,559	3,559	3,559	3,559	3,559

2012 Base Pay for Commissioned Officers with Enlisted Experience

Pay-Grade	Less-than-2	Over-2	Over-3	Over-4	Over-6
O-3E	—	—	—	5,030	5,272
O-2E	—	—	—	4,418	4,509
O-1E	—	—	—	3,557	3,800

Pay-Grade	Over-8	Over-10	Over-12	Over-14	Over-16
O-3E	5,536	5,708	5,989	6,226	6,363
O-2E	4,653	4,896	5,083	5,222	5,222
O-1E	3,940	4,084	4,226	4,418	4,418

Pay-Grade	Over-18	Over-20	Over-22	Over-24	Over-26
O-3E	6,548	6,548	6,548	6,548	6,548
O-2E	5,222	5,222	5,222	5,222	5,222
O-1E	4,418	4,418	4,418	4,418	4,418

PATHWAYS TO A COMMISSION

There are several ways to become a commissioned officer in the United States Military Services. You can attend one of the service academies, participate in the Reserve Officer Training Corps (ROTC) while in college, or even join the military as an enlisted member and apply for one of a number of enlisted commissioning programs.

Service Academies

Everyone's heard of "West Point." The U.S. Military Academy (the official name of the Army's service academy) at West Point, New York has turned out such famous generals as Douglas McArthur and George Patton. However, all of the services (except the Marine Corps) operate their own service academies. The Navy's academy is often referred to as "Annapolis" because it is located in the city of Annapolis, Maryland. The Air Force Academy is located in Colorado Springs, Colorado. The Coast Guard operates their academy in New London, Connecticut. Marine Corps officer candidates attend the U.S. Naval Academy (they're designated as USMC cadets in their junior year, and attend special Marine Corps subject matter classes).

The academies offer a complete four-year college education for free. Additionally, cadets are paid during the four years they attend the school. Upon graduation, cadets are commissioned in the pay grade of O-1 for their specific service. Sounds great, huh? So why doesn't everyone do it?

The catch is that, of all the commissioning programs, the service academies are the most selective. From 6,000–16,000 people apply each year, and only 1,000–1,500 are selected. It's almost as hard to get into a service academy as it is to get accepted to Harvard or Yale. In most cases, one must be nominated by a congressman to even apply. One's high school academic record, community involvement, and athletic ability must clearly surpass that of one's contemporaries. All in all, the academies can be a hard nut to crack for the vast majority of high school or junior college graduates.

ROTC/Marine Corps PLC

The Reserve Officer Training Program (ROTC) and Marine Corps Platoon Leader's Course (PLC) are offered at most colleges and universities in the United States. There are two-year, three-year, and four-year programs, but only the last two years (junior and senior year of college) are necessary to obtain a commission. Basically, these are programs whereby college students attend military-sponsored classes and training events while going to college, in addition to their normal course load (although most colleges grant credit for any ROTC/PLC courses attended). In addition to military courses, students attend military events (such as field training) during the summer months. PLC is kind of a cross between ROTC and OCC (see below). Members attend the same course as OCC, but it is broken up into phases, and the cadets attend these phases while still enrolled as students in college. In addition to PLC, Marine candidates can attend Navy ROTC under a program called the "Marine Option."

The services even offer scholarships to selected ROTC/PLC participants, in exchange for a commitment to join the military upon college graduation. It's not necessary to be selected for the scholarship program in order to participate or be offered a commission, however. On the other hand, participation in ROTC/PLC does not guarantee a commission. Upon completion of the program, the military services are free to grant a commission, or not, depending on the student's performance in the program. With that said, the services get the vast majority (about 65 percent) of their commissioned officers from the ROTC/PLC programs.

OCS/OTS/OCC

ROTC/PLC spreads out the potential officer's training (part time) over a period of years. The services' OCS/OCC/OTS programs, on the other hand, are designed for those college graduates who wish to get the training all at once after graduation from college. It's an ideal program for those who were not lucky/good enough to be offered a position at a service academy and did not/could not participate in college ROTC or Marine Corps PLC. Officers commissioned through OCS/OTS/OCC are often called "90-Day Wonders" in the military, because that used to be the length of the school for the Army and Navy during World War II. Currently, the course runs between 10 and 17 weeks, depending on the service.

Each branch of service operates its own specific officer training program. The Army's OCS is located at Fort Benning, Georgia. The Air Force runs their Officer Training School at Maxwell Air Force Base in Alabama. The Navy's OCS program is at Pensacola, Florida. The Marine Corps conducts their course at Quantico,

Virginia, and the Coast Guard OCS program is co-located with their service academy at New London, Connecticut. Additionally, individual states operate their own OCS programs under a coordinated national curriculum for members of the Army National Guard. Detailed information about OCS/OTS/OCC and selection requirements can be found in Chapter 2.

Direct Appointment

Doctors, lawyers, and chaplains in the military are "special" officers that (in the view of the military services) don't require as rigorous military training. As such, the military services conduct a two-week "mini-OCS" for these candidates. The course teaches the basics—how to wear the uniform, appearance standards, basic marching, rank recognition, etc. Of course, to be eligible, one must be a qualified doctor, lawyer, or clergyman.

Enlisted to Officer Programs

Each of the services offers various programs for enlisted members to seek a commission. Some of these programs are as simple as obtaining a college degree in one's own off-duty time, then applying for OCS/OCC/OTS. Other programs offer a chance for enlisted members to attend college full-time, while still receiving their enlisted pay and benefits. Enlisted members are eligible to apply to attend the service academies without a congressional nomination (although the selection criteria are still just as tough). For junior enlisted members with a superior record who may need a little help with academy academics, the services even operate preparatory schools to help prepare selected members for the tough academic standards of the respective service academy. In most of the active duty services, enlisted members can apply for an early transfer to the Reserves to attend ROTC, leading to a commission.

OFFICER PROMOTIONS

The legal basis for commissioned officer promotions is contained in Title 10, United States Code (USC). This law prescribes strength and grade authorizations, promotion list components, promotion procedures, and separation procedures resulting from non-selection. In short, Congress tells the military how many commissioned officers they can have in each pay grade at any given time, and what these officers need to do (as minimum requirements) to be promoted

It's impossible for all of the services to be exactly the same when it comes to commissioned officer promotion opportunities. Changes in authorizations, losses, and promotions to the next higher grade create fluctuations in promotion opportunities in each of the branches. However, the Department of Defense (DOD) requires that promotion opportunities for commissioned officers be approximately the same for all of the services, when possible, within constraints of available promotion positions.

The chart below is derived from DOD Instruction 1320.13. It shows the point where commissioned officers (in any of the services) can expect to be promoted (assuming they are selected for promotion), based upon their time in service. The minimum time in grade for promotion is set by federal law.

Promote to:	Time in Service	Minimum Time in Grade Required by Law	Promotion Opportunity
O-2	18 months	18 months	Fully qualified (nearly 100 percent)
O-3	4 years	2 years	Fully qualified (nearly 100 percent)
O-4	10 years	3 years	Best qualified (80 percent)
O-5	16 years	3 years	Best qualified (70 percent)
O-6	22 years	3 years	Best qualified (50 percent)

The chart above shows promotion opportunity rates for "in the zone" promotion.

Commissioned officers are recommended for promotion by their commanders, and are selected by centralized (service-wide) promotion boards. The boards make promotion determinations based on the content of the officers' promotion records. The promotion records contain information such as source of commission, current and previous assignment information, level of responsibility, performance (fitness) reports from supervisors and commanders, disciplinary actions, and medals and decorations.

There are basically three promotion opportunities: Below-the-Zone, In-the-Zone, and Above-the-Zone. Below-the-Zone only applies for promotion to the rank of O-4 to O-6. One year before they would normally be eligible for In-the-Zone consideration, up to 10 percent of those recommended can be promoted to Below-the-Zone.

Most officers are selected for promotion In-the-Zone. Those not selected In-the-Zone have one more chance, a year later—Above-the-Zone (the selection rate for Above-the-Zone is extremely small —around three percent). Those "passed over" for Above-the-Zone must usually separate or retire (if eligible for retirement).

The two most significant factors in an officer's promotion records are inarguably their fitness report(s) and level of responsibility in their current and past assignments. Because of this, many people consider the officer promotion system to be very political in nature. A "blah" fitness report can result in being passed over. Lack of current or previous assignments that had significant degrees of responsibility can also result in not being selected.

General/Flag officers (O-7 and above) are the most political of all. These officers are nominated for promotion by the President (usually based on recommendations from the service secretaries), and confirmed by Congress.

Officer Candidate School (OCS), Officer Candidate Course (OCC), and Officer Training School (OTS)

CHAPTER 2

All of us want people who are making our service the career of first choice. That is really what we want. We do not want people who have failed to get into here or were disappointed there.

—Maj. Gen. Arthur Denaro

As mentioned in Chapter 1, all five of the services have programs designed to turn selected college graduates into commissioned officers. The programs are known as Officer Training School in the Air Force, Officer Candidate Course in the Marine Corps, and Officer Candidate School in the Army, Navy, and Coast Guard.

OVERVIEW

Army

Army Officer Candidate School (OCS) is a 12-week program, located at Fort Benning, Georgia, that graduates commissioned officers in the United States Army.

The Army established their OCS in 1941 to provide infantry officers for World War II. Through all the years since, OCS has remained an important commissioning source for the Army, commissioning over 800 brand-spanking-new lieutenants annually. An additional 650 Army National Guard candidates train there and at other locations each summer.

Interestingly enough, the Army is the only service that requires OCS candidates to attend enlisted basic training before attending OCS (the other services incorporate "basic training" into their OTS/OCS/OCC programs).

Following enlisted basic training, candidates attend the 12-week OCS course where they receive rigorous training in skills that provide the foundation for Army leadership. The training consists of classroom and field training in various subjects such as leadership principles, drill and ceremonies, weapons, Army tactics, combat support and staff functions, land navigation, and communications. Cadets are required to give several oral presentations throughout the course to help them develop their communicative abilities.

After successfully completing OCS, new officers attend a six-week, branch-immaterial Basic Officer Leadership Course (BOLC) where they learn skills important on the battlefield to officers of all branches. After this, they generally go directly to the Officer Basic Course (OBC) for their designated branch, where they receive classroom and hands-on training in career-specific skills. New OBC graduates usually begin their Army officer careers as platoon leaders in the rank of second lieutenant and are stationed at installations around the world.

New Army second lieutenants are commissioned in the Combat Arms, Combat Support, or Combat Service Support branches:

COMBAT ARMS

- Infantry
- Armor
- Field Artillery
- Air Defense Artillery
- Aviation
- Special Forces (additional selection process required)
- Corps of Engineers

COMBAT SUPPORT

- Signal Corps
- Military Police Corps
- Military Intelligence Corps
- Civil Affairs
- Chemical Corps

COMBAT SERVICE SUPPORT

- Adjutant General Corps
- Finance Corps
- Medical Service Corps (additional selection process required)
- Ordnance
- Transportation Corps
- Quartermaster Corps

Air Force

The Air Force did not become a separate service from the Army until 1947. However, their officer training school has roots that precede that major reorganization of the military services. Originally established in 1941 at Lackland Air Force Base (then part of Kelly Field), in San Antonio, Texas, the mission of the Air Corps Replacement Training Center (Air Crew) was to provide a cadre of rated officers (pilots, navigators, and bombardiers) to the Army Air Corps. In April 1942, a separate "officer training school" was established in Miami Beach, Florida to train non-rated officers for the Army Air Corps.

OTS for the Air Force is presently located at Maxwell Air Force Base, Alabama, and provides a 12-week basic officer training course programmed to commission 1,000 Air Force officers annually (which is about 20 percent of total Air Force commissions).

Air Force OTS is an intense course that instructs in the primary areas of physical fitness, communications skills, leadership and management, professional military knowledge, defense studies, discipline, military justice, and Air Force values. Upon graduation, cadets are commissioned as second lieutenants in the Air Force and attend technical training related to their officer specialty. After technical training, officers are stationed at various Air Force bases throughout the world.

New Air Force second lieutenants are commissioned into one of the following Air Force Specialty Fields:

- Pilot Field
- Navigator Field
- Space, Missile, and Command and Control Field
- Intelligence Field
- Weather Field
- Operations Support Field
- Logistics Field
- Security Forces Field
- Civil Engineer Field
- Communications Field
- Services Field
- Public Affairs Field
- Mission Support Field
- Manpower Field
- Scientific Research Field
- Developmental Engineering Field
- Acquisitions Field
- Contracting Field
- Finance Field
- Special Investigations Field

Navy

Navy Officer Candidate School is one of five officer training schools located at Naval Station Newport in Rhode Island. The 12-week OCS course is designed to give you a working knowledge of the Navy, afloat and ashore, and to prepare you to assume the responsibilities of a Naval Officer. As with the other services, Navy OCS is extremely demanding, morally, mentally, and physically. Mental training involves memorization of military knowledge (chain of command, code of conduct, general orders of a sentry, etc.). Students participate in a variety of academic courses that include naval engineering, customs and courtesies, military justice, discipline, leadership, naval history, navigation, seamanship, damage control, management, decision-making, as well as submarine, surface, and air warfare tactics.

Physical training begins almost immediately upon arrival at Navy OCS, and consists of running programs augmented by calisthenics, as well as aquatic programs. Graduates of Navy OCS attend technical training at a Navy specialty school to learn their specific job before reporting to their first assignment in the fleet.

New naval ensigns are commissioned into one of the following Navy Officer Designators:

- Surface Warfare
- Submarine Warfare
- Special Operations
- Naval Aviation
- Naval Flight Officer
- Aviation Maintenance
- Special Duty Officer (Cryptology)
- Special Duty Officer (Intelligence)
- Special Duty Officer (Public Affairs)
- Special Duty Officer (Oceanography)
- Supply Corps
- Civil Engineer Corps

Marine Corps

To become a Marine Corps officer through the Officer Candidates School program, prospective candidates attend their initial training course in Quantico, Virginia.

There are two types of students at Marine Corps OCS—those in the Platoon Leaders Class (PLC) and those in the Officer Candidate Class (OCC). PLC students can be freshmen, sophomores, juniors, or seniors in college who have not yet received their degree, while OCC candidates have already earned their bachelor's degree from college.

The OCC classes are conducted three times a year, in January, June, and October. OCC candidates are put through the rigors in one 10-week course, whereas PLC students evolve through two six-week training courses or a combined 10-week course, both of which are conducted at OCS during the summer.

PLC and OCC class sizes are typically 250 to 300 students, broken into four to six platoons. The platoons train in a physically demanding environment where sleep deprivation, military tasks, and memorization are constantly forced on candidates to test their ability to handle stress.

Fifty percent of the Marines' OCS training involves leadership evaluation, 25 percent is academic, and 25 percent is physical fitness.

Once OCC training is completed, the candidates are commissioned as second lieutenants in the Marine Corps. From there, the newly commissioned officers attend another six months of rigorous training at The Basic School (TBS), also located at Quantico. The Basic School is a strict learning environment where officers learn how to lead Marines in peacetime and war. After TBS, the new Marines officers head to their Military Occupational Specialty (MOS) school to learn their specific job in the Marine Corps. From there, they enter the fleet.

New Marine Corps second lieutenants are commissioned into one of the following fields:

- Personnel and Administration
- Intelligence
- Infantry
- Logistics
- Command and Control
- Field Artillery
- Engineering and Construction
- Tanks and Amphibious Assault Vehicles
- Supply
- Financial Management
- Motor Transport
- Public Affairs
- Corrections (law enforcement)
- Aircraft Maintenance
- Aviation Logistics
- Air Command and Control
- Pilots and Naval Flight Officers

Coast Guard

The United States Coast Guard's OCS program is located concurrent with the Coast Guard Academy in New London, Connecticut. OCS is a rigorous 17-week course of instruction that prepares candidates to serve effectively as officers in the United States Coast Guard. In addition to indoctrinating students into a military lifestyle, OCS also provides a wide range of highly technical information necessary for performing the duties of a Coast Guard officer.

The United States Coast Guard is not part of the Department of Defense. In peacetime, the Coast Guard falls under the Department of Homeland Security. During times of armed conflict, the President of the United States has the authority to order all or part of the Coast Guard under the command of the Department of the Navy. The Coast Guard is the smallest of America's armed forces, with only about 5,900 commissioned officers (compare that to the Navy, that has about 54,000 commissioned officers). As such, competition for a Coast Guard commission is tough. The Coast Guard only commissions about 300 new officers per year.

Academics are taught in the areas of Coast Guard orientation, leadership, management, military and maritime law, seamanship, navigation, and professional military subjects. The course includes practical training in the areas of ship maneuvering, tracking surface contacts, damage control, gunnery, law enforcement, and communications.

Graduates of the program receive a commission in the Coast Guard at the rank of ensign. Graduates may be assigned to a ship, flight training, a staff job, or an operations ashore billet.

New Coast Guard ensigns are commissioned into one of the following specialties:

- Aviation
- Civil Engineering
- Civil Rights
- Communications Management
- Environmental Protection
- Finance & Supply
- Industrial Management
- Intelligence
- Legal Assistance
- Merchant Marine Safety
- Military Readiness
- Engineering
- Personnel
- Port Safety and Law Enforcement
- Public Affairs
- Research and Development

SERVICE COMMITMENTS

The military services need to get their money's worth when they train a new commissioned officer. Therefore, there are minimum periods that the officer is required to serve after completing OCS/OTS/OCC:

Army – Three years
Air Force – Four years
Navy – Four years
Marine Corps – Three and one-half years
Coast Guard – Three years

There may be additional service commitments due to specialty training. For example, Naval Propulsion Officers incur a five-year service commitment. Pilots in the Air Force incur a 10-year service commitment and Navy/Marine Corps pilots must service a minimum of eight years following flight training. Air Force navigators, as well as Navy/Marine Corps flight officers, are committed for six years.

QUALIFICATIONS

OCS/OTS/OCC programs are very competitive. As military recruiting and retention have been on the upswing for the past several years, the competition for one of the relatively few slots keeps getting tougher and tougher. Most applicants will find they are not competitive unless they have a college grade point average of at least 3.1. Additionally, the ideal candidate has a sustained record of athletic and community involvement.

Citizenship

Federal law requires that all commissioned officers in the United States Armed Forces be United States citizens.

Age

Under federal law, the maximum age for an active duty commission is age 35. However, the law allows each of the branches to set their own maximum commission ages (up to the limit authorized by law), based on the individual service's particular needs.

- **Army:** 19½ to 29 years of age (waivers may be granted up to 34 years of age). For helicopter pilots, must not have reached their 30th birthday as of the date they enter flight training. Applicants for the Army National Guard must be able to complete the commissioning program prior to reaching age 40.
- **Air Force:** 18 to 35. Pilots and navigators must be commissioned and enter flight training prior to age 30.
- **Navy:** 19 to 35. Several Navy occupations have stricter limits. Nuclear officers must be between the ages of 19 and 27. Aviators must be between the ages of 19 and 26 at the time they enter flight training.
- **Marine Corps:** 18 to 30 years of age. Waivers can be granted up to age 35 in certain cases. Aviators must be between the ages of 19 and 26 at the time they enter flight training.
- **Coast Guard:** 21 to 36 years of age. Waivers may be granted in limited instances.

Education

As previously mentioned, in most cases OCS/OTS/OCC applicants must have a bachelor's degree (except for those who apply during their senior year in college). The Army will allow an enlisted applicant to apply for OCS with only 90 college credits. The Army National Guard will accept OCS applicants (from both enlisted and civilians) with only 90 college credits. To be competitive, applicants should have a college GPA of 3.1 or above.

Vision

Distant visual acuity of any degree that does not correct with spectacle lenses to 20/20 in one eye and 20/100 in the other eye is disqualifying.

Near visual acuity of any degree that does not correct to 20/40 in the better eye is likewise disqualifying.

Aviation candidates have stricter requirements:

- **Army:** To enter Army helicopter flight training, the applicant can have vision no worse than 20/50 (correctable to 20/20) in each eye.
- **Air Force:** To become a pilot, the candidate's vision can be no worse than 20/70 (correctable with glasses to 20/20) in each eye. To enter navigator training, the candidate can have vision no worse than 20/200 in each eye (also must be correctable to 20/20).
- **Navy/Marine Corps:** To become a pilot in the Navy or Marine Corps, an applicant's uncorrected vision can be no worse than 20/100 (correctable to 20/20) in each eye.
- **Coast Guard:** Coast Guard aviation applicants can have vision no worse than 20/50 in either eye (correctable to 20/20).

Height

Applicants to join any of the military services must be between 60 and 80 inches (males) and between 58 and 80 inches (females). Aviators who fly in ejection-seat aircraft may have stricter limits, depending on the capabilities and restrictions of the ejection seat/airframe.

Weight

Each of the services has their own individual weight standards:

Initial Accession Weight Chart–Army Males

Height (Inches)	Minimum weight (any Age)	Age 17-20	Age 21-27	Age 28-39	Age 40+
60	100	139	141	143	146
61	102	144	146	148	151
62	103	148	150	153	156
63	104	153	155	158	161
64	105	158	160	163	166
65	106	163	165	168	171
66	107	168	170	173	177
67	111	174	176	179	182
68	115	179	181	184	187
69	119	184	186	189	193
70	123	189	192	195	199
71	127	194	197	201	204
72	131	200	203	206	210
73	135	205	208	212	216
74	139	211	214	218	222
75	143	217	220	224	228
76	147	223	226	230	234
77	151	229	232	236	240
78	153	235	238	242	247
79	159	241	244	248	253
80	166	247	250	255	259

If a male exceeds the weight shown in the chart above, his body fat will be measured per the method described in Army Regulation 600-9, *Weight Management Program.*

Army male applicants who exceed the following body fat limits are disqualified:

Age 17–20: 24%
Age 21–27: 26%
Age 28–39: 28%

Initial Accession Weight Chart–Army Females

Height (Inches)	Minimum weight (any Age)	Age 17-20	Age 21-27	Age 28-39	Age 40+
58	90	112	115	119	122
59	92	116	119	123	126
60	94	120	123	127	130
61	96	124	127	131	135
62	98	129	132	137	139
63	100	133	137	141	144
64	102	137	141	145	148
65	104	141	145	149	153
66	106	146	150	154	158
67	109	149	154	159	162
68	112	154	159	164	167
69	115	158	163	168	172
70	118	163	168	173	177
71	122	167	172	177	182
72	125	172	177	183	188
73	128	177	182	188	193
74	130	183	189	194	198
75	133	188	194	200	204
76	136	194	200	206	209
77	139	199	205	211	215
78	141	204	210	216	220
79	144	209	215	222	226
80	147	214	220	227	232

If a female exceeds these weights, her percent body fat will be measured by the method described in Army Regulation 600-9, *Weight Management Program.*

Army female applicants who exceed the following body fat limits are disqualified:

Age 17–20: 30%
Age 21–27: 32%
Age 28–39: 34%

Initial Accession Weight Chart–Air Force Males/Females

Height	Maximum Weight	Minimum Weight
58	131	91
59	136	94
60	141	97
61	145	100
62	150	104
63	155	107
64	160	110
65	165	114
66	170	117
67	175	121
68	180	125
69	186	128
70	191	132
71	197	136
72	202	140
73	208	144
74	214	148
75	220	152
76	225	156
77	231	160
78	237	164
79	244	168
80	250	173

If the individual exceeds the MAXIMUM weight in the chart above, he/she will be required to undergo a bodyfat measurement test. In order to qualify for enlistment, a male age 29 or less must have no more than 20 percent body fat. A male 30 years or older can have no more than 24 percent body fat. A female age 29 or less must have no more than 28 percent body fat. A female 30 years or older can have no more than 32 percent body fat.

Initial Accession Weight Chart–Navy Males

Height	Navy Weight Standard	Minimum Weight
58	132	98
59	137	99
60	142	100
61	147	102
62	152	103
63	157	104
64	162	105
65	167	106
66	172	107
67	177	111
68	182	115
69	188	119
70	192	123
71	196	127
72	201	131
73	206	135
74	211	139
75	216	143
76	221	147
77	226	151
78	231	153

Only applicants not meeting the Navy weight standard for their height will be measured for body fat percentage. Male applicants who exceed 23 percent body fat are disqualified. Body fat measurements are performed according to the instructions contained in OPNAV Instruction 611.1G, *Physical Readiness program.*

Initial Accession Weight Chart–Navy Females

Height	Navy Weight Standard	Minimum Weight
58	134	90
59	138	92
60	142	94
61	145	96
62	149	98
63	152	100
64	156	102
65	160	104
66	163	106
67	167	109
68	170	112
69	174	115
70	177	118
71	181	122
72	185	125
73	188	128
74	192	132
75	195	136
76	199	139
77	203	143
78	206	147

Only applicants not meeting the Navy weight standard for their height will be measured for body fat percentage. Female applicants who exceed 34 percent body fat are disqualified. Body Fat Measurements are performed according to the instructions contained in OPNAV Instruction 611.1G, *Physical Readiness Program.*

Initial Accession Weight Chart–Marine Corps Males

Height	Minimum Weight	Maximum Weight
64	105	160
65	106	165
66	107	170
67	111	175
68	115	181
69	119	186
70	123	192
71	127	197
72	131	203
73	135	209
74	139	214
75	143	219
76	147	225
77	151	230
78	153	235

Applicants who exceed the weight listed on the above chart are measured for body fat. The Marine Corps body fat limit for male applicants is 18 percent. The procedures to measure body fat can be found in Marine Corps Order (MCO) 6100.12, *Marine Corps Physical Fitness Test and Body Fat Composition Manual.*

Initial Accession Weight Chart–Marine Corps Females

Height	Minimum Weight	Maximum Weight
58	90	121
59	92	123
60	94	125
61	96	127
62	98	130
63	100	134
64	102	138
65	104	142
66	106	147
67	109	151
68	112	156
69	115	160
70	118	165
71	122	170
72	125	175
73	128	180

Applicants who exceed the weight listed on the above chart are measured for body fat. The Marine Corps body fat limit for female applicants is 26 percent. The procedures to measure body fat can be found in Marine Corps Order (MCO) 6100.12, *Marine Corps Physical Fitness Test and Body Fat Composition Manual.*

COAST GUARD

The Coast Guard is the only service that includes "frame size" in their weight chart. In order to determine maximum allowable weight, you must first determine the individual's "frame size code" by measuring the circumference of his or her wrist.

For males, using a cloth tape measure on the wrist of the dominant hand, fingers extended and apart, measure all the way around at the point where there are two "knobs" just above the hand. Be sure the tape goes across both wrist bones ("knobs").

A. Under 6¼ inches
B. 6¼ to under 6½
C. 6½ to under 6¾
D. 6¾ to under 7
E. 7 to under 7¼
F. 7¼ to under 7½
G. 7½ to under 7¾
H. 7¾ to under 8
J. 8 to under 8¼
K. 8¼ to under 8½
L. 8½ to under 8¾
M. Greater than 8¾

Initial Accession Weight Chart–Coast Guard Males

Height	Frame Size Code											
	A	B	C	D	E	F	G	H	J	K	L	M
60	140	144	148	152	160	159	163	167	171	175	179	183
61	144	148	152	156	160	164	167	171	175	179	183	187
62	148	152	156	160	164	168	172	176	179	183	187	191
63	152	156	160	164	168	172	176	180	184	188	191	195
64	157	160	164	168	172	176	180	184	188	192	196	200
65	161	165	169	172	176	180	184	188	192	196	200	204
66	165	169	173	177	181	184	188	192	196	200	204	208
67	169	173	177	181	185	189	193	196	200	204	208	212
68	173	177	181	185	189	193	197	201	205	208	212	216
69	177	181	185	189	193	197	201	205	209	213	216	220
70	182	185	189	193	197	201	205	209	213	217	221	225
71	186	190	194	197	201	205	209	213	217	221	225	229
72	190	194	198	202	206	209	213	217	221	225	229	233
73	194	198	202	206	210	214	218	221	225	229	233	237
74	198	202	206	210	214	218	222	226	230	233	237	241
75	202	206	210	214	218	222	226	230	234	238	242	245
76	207	210	214	216	222	226	230	234	238	242	248	250
77	211	215	219	222	226	230	234	238	242	246	250	254
78	215	219	223	227	231	234	238	242	246	250	254	258
79	219	223	227	231	235	239	243	246	250	254	258	262
80	223	227	231	235	239	243	247	251	255	258	262	266

A member who exceeds the maximum allowable weight on the chart above is measured for body fat, using the procedures outlined in Coast Guard Commandant Instruction (COMDTINST) M1028-C, *Allowable Weight Standards for the Health and Well-Being of Coast Guard Military Personnel.*

Male body-fat limits are:

- Age less than 30: 23 percent
- Age 30 to 35: 25 percent

Initial Accession Weight Chart–Coast Guard Females

Height	Frame Size Code											
	N	P	Q	R	S	T	U	V	W	X	Y	Z
58	122	126	130	134	137	141	145	149	152	156	160	164
59	125	129	133	137	140	144	148	152	155	159	163	167
60	128	132	136	140	143	147	151	155	158	162	166	170
61	131	135	139	142	146	150	154	157	161	165	169	172
62	134	138	142	145	149	153	157	160	164	168	172	175
63	137	141	145	148	152	156	160	163	167	171	175	178
64	140	144	147	151	155	159	162	166	170	174	177	181
65	143	147	150	154	158	162	165	169	173	177	180	184
66	146	150	153	157	161	165	168	172	176	180	183	187
67	149	152	156	160	164	167	171	175	179	182	186	190
68	152	155	159	163	167	170	174	178	182	185	189	193
69	155	158	162	166	170	173	177	181	185	188	192	196
70	157	161	165	169	172	176	180	184	188	191	195	199
71	160	164	168	172	175	179	183	187	190	194	198	202
72	163	167	171	175	178	182	186	190	193	197	201	205
73	166	170	174	178	181	185	189	193	196	200	204	208
74	169	173	177	180	184	188	192	195	199	203	207	210
75	172	176	180	183	187	191	195	198	202	206	210	213
76	175	179	183	186	190	194	198	201	205	209	213	216
77	178	182	185	189	193	197	200	204	208	212	215	219
78	181	185	188	192	196	200	203	207	211	215	218	222
79	184	188	191	195	199	203	206	210	214	218	221	225
80	187	190	194	198	202	206	209	213	217	220	224	228

For females, using a cloth tape measure on the wrist of the dominant hand, fingers extended and apart, measure all the way around at the point where there are two "knobs" just above the hand. Be sure the tape goes across both bones ("knobs").

N. Under 5¼ inches
P. 5¼ to under 5½
Q. 5½ to under 5¾
R. 5¾ to under 6
S. 6 to under 6¼
T. 6¼ to under 6½
U. 6½ to under 6¾
V. 6¾ to under 7
W. 7 to under 7¼
X. 7¼ to under 7½
Y. 7½ to under 7¾
Z. Greater than 7¾

A member who exceeds the maximum allowable weight on the chart above is measured for body fat, using the procedures outlined in Coast Guard Commandant Instruction (COMDTINST) M1028-C, *Allowable Weight Standards for the Health and Well-Being of Coast Guard Military Personnel.*

Female body-fat limits are:

- Age less than 30: 33 percent
- Age 30 to 35: 35 percent

Drug/Alcohol History

The United States Military does not condone the illegal or improper use of drugs or alcohol. It is DOD's stated position that illegal drug use and abuse of alcohol:

- ✔ Is against the law.
- ✔ Violates the high standards of behavior and performance expected of a member of the United States Armed Forces.
- ✔ Is damaging to physical, mental, and psychological health.
- ✔ Jeopardizes the safety of the individual and others.
- ✔ Is fundamentally wrong, destructive to organizational effectiveness, and totally incompatible with service as a member of the U.S. Military.
- ✔ Is likely to result in criminal prosecution and discharge under other than honorable conditions.

All applicants are carefully screened concerning drug and alcohol involvement. As a minimum, you can expect the recruiter to ask:

- ✔ "Have you ever used drugs?"
- ✔ "Have you been charged with or convicted of a drug or drug-related offense?"
- ✔ "Have you ever been psychologically or physically dependent upon any drug or alcohol?"
- ✔ "Have you ever trafficked, sold, or traded in illegal drugs for profit?"

If the answer to either of the last two questions is yes, then you can expect to be ineligible for a commission. If the answer to either of the first two questions is yes, then you can expect to have to complete a drug abuse screening form, detailing the specific circumstances of your drug usage. The military service will then make a determination as to whether or not your previous drug usage is a bar to service in that particular branch of the military. In most cases, a person who *experimented* with marijuana in the past will be allowed to apply. Usage considered to be more than experimentation is a bar to joining the military. An "experimenter" is defined as:

> *...one who has illegally, wrongfully, or improperly used any narcotic substance, marijuana, or dangerous drug, for reasons of curiosity, peer pressure, or other similar reason. The exact number of times drugs were used, is not necessarily as important as determining the category of use and the impact of the drug use on the user's lifestyle, the intent of the user, the circumstances of use, and the psychological makeup of the user. An individual whose drug experimentation/use has resulted in some form of medical, psychiatric, or psychological treatment; a conviction or adverse juvenile adjudication; or loss of employment does not fall within the limits of this category. For administrative purposes, determination of the category should be within the*

judgment of either the district or recruiting station commanding officer, aided by medical, legal, and moral advice, with information as available from investigative sources.

While not a hard and fast rule, one can expect that any admitted use of marijuana over ten or so times, or any admitted use of hard drugs, will be disqualifying, and require a waiver.

In any case:

✔ ***Dependency*** on illegal drugs is disqualifying.
✔ Any history of drug use is ***potentially*** disqualifying.
✔ Any history of ***dependency*** on alcohol is disqualifying.

Criminal History

Commissioned officers must be above reproach. Therefore, any conviction of a felony, or any misdemeanor involving moral turpitude, are disqualifying for a commission. It's important to note here—for military accession purposes—there's no such thing as an expunged or sealed criminal record. Federal law requires one to report every arrest and conviction as part of the military application process. Failure to do so is a felony in itself. The military is not as concerned with the ultimate disposition of a criminal case as they are with the evidence of whether or not the individual actually committed the offense in the first place.

While not an all-inclusive list, the following are examples of criminal offenses that are rarely (if ever) waived:

- Aggravated assault: With a dangerous weapon, intentionally inflicting great bodily harm, with intent to commit a felony
- Arson
- Attempting to commit a felony
- Bribery
- Burglary
- Carnal knowledge of a child under 16
- Carrying a concealed firearm or unlawful carrying of a firearm
- Carrying a concealed weapon (other than a firearm), possession of brass knuckles
- Child pornography offenses
- Conspiring to commit a felony
- Criminal libel
- Draft evasion
- Drugs: Use, possession, trafficking, sale, or manufacture of an illegal or illicit drug (except for marijuana use or possession)
- DUI/DWUI/DWI (driving under the influence, while intoxicated, or impaired by drugs or alcohol)
- Embezzlement
- Extortion
- Forgery: Knowingly uttering or passing forged instrument
- Indecent acts or liberties with a child under 16, molestation
- Grand larceny
- Grand theft
- Housebreaking
- Indecent assault
- Involuntary manslaughter
- Kidnapping, abduction

- Leaving the scene of an accident (hit-and-run) involving personal injury
- Lewd, licentious, or lascivious behavior
- Looting
- Mail or electronic emissions matters: Abstracting, destroying, obstructing, opening, secreting, stealing, or taking
- Maiming or disfiguring
- Manslaughter
- Murder
- Negligent homicide
- Perjury
- Public record: Altering, concealing, destroying, mutilating, obliterating, or removing
- Rape
- Riot
- Robbery
- Sedition or soliciting to commit sedition
- Selling, leasing, or transferring a weapon to a minor or unauthorized individual
- Sexual harassment

Medical Standards

DOD sets the overall general medical standards for enlistment or accession. However, while DOD sets the overall standards, each of the military services is allowed to individually waive the standards, depending upon the particular needs of the service. If the examining military medical official disqualifies an applicant, the official will usually make a recommendation about whether or not he/she recommends that the service waive the disqualification. The doctor normally makes this recommendation based upon his/her professional opinion as to whether the precise nature of the medical disqualification will significantly interfere with the proper performance of military duties (either now or in the future). The waiver request is then considered by medical officials assigned to the individual service. If the examining medical official recommends a waiver, the chances of receiving the waiver from the service concerned is pretty good (although still not a certainty). If the military doctor does not recommend a waiver, the chances of receiving an approved medical waiver are slim.

OCS/OTS Examinations

CHAPTER 3

Ability will never catch up with the demand for it.

—Malcolm Forbes

For those wishing to join one of the five U.S. military branches as an enlisted member, studying for the entrance examination is relatively simple. The Armed Services Vocational Aptitude Battery (ASVAB) is the standard test used for enlistment by all the services. Applicants for OCS/OCC or OTS don't have it as easy. Each of the services has different tests for their officer school candidate applicants.

TESTS USED BY THE VARIOUS BRANCHES

The test used for Air Force OTS applicants is the Air Force Officer Qualifying Test (AFOQT). The Army uses portions of the ASVAB test to determine whether or not one qualifies for OCS attendance. Army applicants who don't have a bachelor's degree (usually current enlisted or Army National Guard applicants) must achieve a qualifying score on the ASVAB portion and have qualifying Scholastic Aptitude Test (SAT) or American College Test (ACT) scores. The Marine Corps give candidates a choice: they can either qualify with SAT or ACT scores, or they can qualify with scores taken from a portion of the ASVAB. The Navy uses scores from the Aviation Selection Test Battery (ASTB), or portions thereof, depending on whether or not the candidate is interested in becoming an aviator. The Coast Guard requires a minimum qualifying score on a portion of the ASVAB and qualifying scores on the SAT or ACT. Marine Corps and Coast Guard aviation candidates are required to complete the ASTB.

Air Force Officer Qualifying Test (AFOQT)

The AFOQT is comprised of 12 subtests with 480 questions. The good news is that 220 of these questions are in a subtest called self-description inventory, which have no right or wrong answer and are not used in calculating your test scores. Additionally, the rotated blocks and hidden figures subtests are not used in computing the pilot and navigator composite scores.

The 12 subtests are:

Verbal Analogies: This subtest measures ability to reason and see relationships between words. See Chapter 5 for more information and practice questions (25 questions/8 minutes).

Arithmetic Reasoning: This subtest measures general reasoning. It is concerned with one's ability to arrive at solutions to problems. See Chapter 8 for more information and practice questions (25 questions/29 minutes).

Word Knowledge: This subtest measures verbal comprehension involving the ability to understand written language. See Chapter 5 for more information and practice questions (25 questions/5 minutes).

Mathematics Knowledge: This subtest measures functional ability in using learned mathematical relationships. See Chapter 7 for more information and practice questions (25 questions/22 minutes).

Instrument Comprehension: This subtest measures ability to determine the position of an airplane in flight from reading instruments. See Chapter 11 for more information and practice questions (20 questions/6 minutes).

Block Counting: This subtest measures ability to "see into" a three-dimensional stack of blocks and determine how many pieces are touched by certain numbered blocks. See Chapter 11 for more information and practice questions (20 questions/3 minutes).

Table Reading: This subtest measures ability to read tables quickly and accurately. See Chapter 6 for more information and practice questions (40 questions/7 minutes).

Aviation Information: This subtest measures knowledge of general aeronautical concepts and terminology (past and current). See Chapter 11 for more information and practice questions (20 questions/8 minutes).

Rotated Blocks: This subtest measures spatial aptitude, that is, ability to visualize and mentally manipulate objects in space. See Chapter 11 for more information and practice questions (15 questions/13 minutes).

General Science: This subtest measures verbal comprehension in the area of science. See Chapter 9 for more information and practice questions (20 questions/10 minutes).

Hidden Figures: This subtest measures perceptual reasoning using visual imagery and short-term memory. See Chapter 11 for more information and practice questions (15 questions/8 minutes).

Self-Description Inventory: This subtest is used to gather statistical information concerning Air Force officer applicants. The questions have no right or wrong answers and are not used in the scoring or selection process (280 questions/40 minutes).

The scores from the subtests result in five composite scores:

Pilot

This composite score measures some of the knowledge and abilities considered necessary for successful completion of pilot training. The Pilot composite includes subtests that measure quantitative ability, the ability to determine aircraft attitude from instruments, knowledge of aeronautical concepts, and perceptual speed. This composite score is derived from the number of test questions answered correctly on the Arithmetic Reasoning, Math Knowledge, Instrument Comprehension, Table Reading, and Aviation Information subtests of the AFOQT.

Navigator-Technical

This composite score measures some of the knowledge and abilities considered necessary for successful completion of navigator training. The Navigator-Technical composite shares some subtests with the Pilot composite, with the exception that measures of ability to determine aircraft attitude and knowledge of aeronautical concepts are not included. However, subtests are added measuring verbal aptitude, some spatial abilities, perceptual speed, and knowledge of general science. This composite score is derived from the number of test questions answered correctly on the Verbal Analogies, Arithmetic Reasoning, Math Knowledge, Block Counting, Table Reading, and General Science subtests of the AFOQT.

Academic Aptitude

This composite score measures verbal and quantitative knowledge and abilities. The Academic Aptitude composite combines all subtests that make up the Verbal and Quantitative composites. This composite score is derived from the number of test questions answered correctly on the Verbal Analogies, Arithmetic Reasoning, Word Knowledge, and Math Knowledge subtests of the AFOQT.

Verbal

This composite score measures verbal knowledge and abilities. The Verbal composite has subtests that measure the ability to reason and recognize relationships among words and the ability to understand synonyms. This composite score is derived from the number of test questions answered correctly on the Verbal Analogies and Word Knowledge subtests of the AFOQT.

Quantitative

This composite score measures quantitative knowledge and abilities. The Quantitative composite shares subtests with the Navigator-Technical composite discussed above, and has subtests that measure the ability to understand and reason with arithmetic relationships and to use mathematical terms, formulas, and relationships. This composite score is derived from the number of test questions answered correctly on the Arithmetic Reasoning and Math Knowledge Subtests of the AFOQT.

The composite scores are each reported as a percentile score. A percentile score indicates how an individual's test performance compares to a normative reference group. A normative reference group consists of a group of examinees with demographic and aptitude characteristics representative of those who are taking the test. The number of test questions answered correctly by an examinee is compared to the scores of those in the normative reference group and the results are reported on a 1 to 99 scale. For example, an individual with a percentile score of 50 has a score equal to or better than 50% of those in the normative reference group, an individual with a percentile score of 75 has a score equal to or better than 75% of those in the normative reference group, etc.

An individual can take the AFOQT a maximum of two times in a lifetime, with a minimum interval of six months between test administrations. Waivers to take the test a third time are granted to individuals who have completed significant training since the previous administration if the training impacts the skills being measured by the test (college-level math and English courses, private pilot's license, etc.).

Scores to qualify for Air Force OTS are relatively low: for pilot positions, minimum scores of 25 in the pilot composite, and 10 in the navigator composite are required. Additionally, the combined pilot and navigator composite scores must total 50.

Navigator applicants require a pilot score of 10, a navigator score of 25, with a combined pilot and navigator score of 50.

All OTS candidates require a verbal score of 15, and a minimum quantitative score of 10.

Don't let these minimum scores fool you, however. OTS selection is competitive, which means that applicants are competing with other applicants for a limited number of slots. Average AFOQT composite scores for those who have been selected in recent years are as follows:

Pilot: 69.18
Navigator-Technical: 70.14
Academic: 63.84
Verbal: 60.04
Quantitative: 61.02

Army Officer Candidate School Test

Candidates for Army OCS must achieve a qualifying score on the GT, or General Technical Army composite score that is derived from the Verbal Expression and Arithmetic Reasoning subtests of the ASVAB. In addition to a qualifying GT composite score, current enlisted and Army National Guard applicants who do not possess a bachelor's degree at the time of application must achieve a minimum score of 850 on the SAT, or a score of 19 on the ACT.

The ASVAB is the test taken by all applicants wishing to enlist in the United States Military (see *Barron's ASVAB, 10th Edition*, for complete information).

The Army is the only service that requires officer candidates to enlist and go through basic training before they can actually attend OCS. That means applicants must achieve a minimum AFQT (Armed Forces Qualification Test) score of 31 to be qualified for enlistment. Additionally, to qualify for OCS, applicants must achieve a minimum score of 110 on the Army's GT composite.

There are four basic versions of the ASVAB: (1) a paper version that is given to high school seniors under a cooperative program between the Department of Defense and Department of Education; (2) a paper version that can be taken for purposes of joining the military; (3) a paper version that can be taken by those currently in the military, called the Armed Forces Classification Test; and (4) a computerized version, known as the CAT-ASVAB, or Computer Adaptive Testing ASVAB. Over 85 percent of those who join the military take the CAT-ASVAB, so that is the version we'll discuss here.

The ASVAB is comprised of 10 subtests. The subtests are as follows:

General Science: This is a subtest of knowledge measuring the physical and biological sciences. The subtest consists of 16 questions to be answered in 8 minutes.

Arithmetic Reasoning: This is a subtest measuring ability to solve arithmetic word problems. The subtest consists of 16 questions to be answered in 39 minutes.

Word Knowledge: This is a subtest measuring ability to select the correct meaning of words presented in context and to identify the best synonym for a given word. This subtest has 16 questions to be answered in 8 minutes.

Paragraph Comprehension: This is a subtest measuring ability to obtain information from written passages. The subtest consists of 11 questions to be answered in 22 minutes.

Automotive Information: This subtest measures one's general knowledge of automobiles and vehicle maintenance. The subtest consists of 11 questions that must be answered in 6 minutes.

Mathematics Knowledge: This is a subtest measuring knowledge of high school mathematics principles. The subtest consists of 16 questions to be answered in 18 minutes.

Mechanical Comprehension: This is a subtest measuring knowledge of mechanical and physical principles and ability to visualize how illustrated objects work. This subtest has 20 questions to be answered in 19 minutes.

Electronics Information: This is a subtest to measure knowledge of electricity and electronics. This subtest consists of 16 questions to be answered in 8 minutes.

Shop Information: This is a subtest measuring knowledge of shop terminology and tool use. This subtest has 11 questions that must be answered in 5 minutes.

Assembling Objects: This is a subtest measuring ability to picture how an object will look when its parts are mentally put together. It consists of 16 questions to be answered in 9 minutes.

There is no way for one to take only part of the ASVAB, but applicants for Army OCS should concentrate their study efforts on those subtests of the ASVAB that are used to comprise the Army's GT composite score and the overall AFQT score.

AFQT Score

Like the AFOQT composite scores used by the Air Force, the AFQT score is a "percentile score." That means, for example, that an individual with an AFQT score of 50 has a score equal to or better than 50% of those in the normative reference group who took the test previously to establish the "norms."

The AFQT score is determined from the following subtests of the ASVAB:

Arithmetic Reasoning: See Chapter 8 for complete information and practice questions.

Word Knowledge: See Chapter 5 for complete information and practice questions.

Paragraph Comprehension: See Chapter 6 for complete information and practice questions.

Mathematics Knowledge: See Chapter 7 for complete information and practice questions.

The Army's GT Composite Score

As mentioned previously, the Army requires a minimum score of 110 in the GT (General Technical) composite score area.

Of the four ASVAB subtests used to determine AFQT score, three of those subsets are also used to compute the Army's GT composite score: Paragraph Comprehension, Word Knowledge, and Arithmetic Reasoning.

Marine Corps Officer Candidate School Test

The Marine Corps uses one of three methods to determine OCC qualification: SAT/ACT scores, a portion of the ASVAB, or the Navy/Marine Corps Aviation Selection Test Battery (ASTB).

SAT/ACT: Except for aviation candidates, one may qualify for Marine Corps OCC based on their SAT or ACT scores. To qualify, one must achieve a minimum combined score of 1,000 on the verbal and math sections of the SAT, or a combined math and verbal score of 45 on the ACT.

The Marine Corps GT Composite Score: The Marine Corps GT composite score composite is the same as the Army GT score components: Paragraph Comprehension, Word Knowledge, and Arithmetic Reasoning. The minimum qualifying GT score is 115 for Marine Corps OCS.

Marine Corps Aviation Candidates: Marine Corps aviation candidates must take the Navy/Marine Corps Aviation Test Battery (ASTB). See Navy Officer Candidate School Test, below, for complete information. Marine Corps aviation candidates require the following minimum scores:

For Pilot:	For Naval Flight Officer (NFO):
AQR: 4	AQR: 4
PFAR: 6	FOFAR: 6

COAST GUARD REQUIREMENTS

SAT/ACT: Coast Guard OCS candidates require a minimum combined verbal and math score of 1,000 on the SAT, or a verbal and math score of 21 on the ACT.

The Coast Guard GT Composite Score: Coast Guard OCS applicants must also achieve a qualifying score on the GT composite of the ASVAB. The Coast Guard GT composite score is the same as the Army and Marine Corps GT score components: Paragraph Comprehension, Word Knowledge, and Arithmetic Reasoning. Coast Guard applicants require a minimum GT score of 109.

Coast Guard Aviation Candidates: As with the Marine Corps and Navy, aviation candidates must take the Aviation Selection Test Battery (ASTB). For more information, see the Navy Officer Candidate School Test information below. Coast Guard aviation candidates require the following minimum scores:

AQR: 4
PFAR: 6

Navy Officer Candidate School Test

The U.S. Navy and Marine Corps Aviation Selection Test Battery (ASTB) was developed primarily to predict the success of students in aviation officer training programs. The Navy, Marine Corps, and Coast Guard use various subtests from the complete test battery as a primary selection instrument for their aviation programs. Portions of the test are also used by the Navy as selection criteria for Officer Candidate School (OCS).The test contains six subtests with 176 questions.

The test is administered in a paper format, but at many sites it can be administered on a computer through a web-based system called APEX.NET. There are three versions of the test—Form 3, Form 4, and Form 5. Each version of the test contains different questions, but all three versions have the same format, subtests, and number of questions.

ASTB Subtests

The subtests are as follows:

Math Skills Test (MST): The math skills assessed by the MST include arithmetic and algebra, with some geometry. The assessments include both equations and word problems. Some items require solving for variables, others are time and distance problems, and some problems require the estimation of simple probabilities. Skills assessed include basic arithmetic operations, solving for variables, fractions, roots, exponents, and the calculation of angles, area, and perimeter of geometric shapes. This subtest has 30 questions that must be answered in 25 minutes. See Chapters 7 and 8 for more information and practice questions.

Reading Skills Test (RST): The RST measures your reading comprehension level and basic vocabulary knowledge. Reading comprehension items require ASTB examinees to extract meaning from text passages. Each item requires the examinee to determine which of the response options can be inferred from the passage itself. Vocabulary questions measure your ability to select the correct meaning of words presented in context and to identify the best synonym for a given word. The RST section consists of 27 questions that must be answered in 25 minutes. See Chapters 5 and 6 for more information and practice questions.

Mechanical Comprehension Test (MCT): Items contained within the mechanical comprehension portion of the ASTB include topics that would typically be found in an introductory high school physics course and the application of these topics within a variety of situations. The questions in this portion of the test gauge examinees' knowledge of principles related to gases and liquids, and their understanding of the ways in which these properties affect pressure, volume, and velocity. The subtest also includes questions that relate to the components and performance of engines, principles of electricity, gears, weight distribution, and the operation of simple machines, such as pulleys and fulcrums. This subtest is comprised of 30 questions that must be answered in 15 minutes. See Chapter 10 for more information and practice questions.

Spatial Apperception Test (SAT): These items evaluate an examinee's ability to match external and internal views of an aircraft based on visual cues regarding its direction and orientation relative to the ground. Each item consists of a view from inside the cockpit that the examinee must match to one of five external views. The SAT measures your ability to visualize the orientation of objects in three-dimensional space. The subtest has 25 questions that must be answered in 10 minutes. See Chapter 11 for more information and practice questions.

Aviation and Nautical Information Test (ANIT): This subtest assesses your familiarity with aviation history, nautical terminology and procedures, and aviation-related concepts such as aircraft components, aerodynamic principles, and flight rules and regulations. There are 30 questions on this subtest that must be answered in 15 minutes. See Chapter 11 for more information and practice questions.

Aviation Supplemental Test (AST): The final subtest of the ASTB will typically contain a variety of items that are similar in format and content to the items in the preceding subtests. On this subtest you may see questions that you've already answered on the previous subtests; you may see questions that are only slightly changed from previous questions you answered on the other subtests; or you may see questions that are entirely different, but drawn from the same subject matter areas as the previous subtests. The results of this subtest are fed into a proprietary algorithm that affects the composite scores used for pilot and flight officer selections (AQR, PFAR, and FOFAR, explained below). "Proprietary" means that the Navy will not disclose exactly how it's done. There are 34 questions that must be answered in 25 minutes.

ASTB Scores

The subtests of the ASTB are used to calculate four separate composite scores. The Navy will not release the exact formulas used to generate the scores, but the following guidance should be helpful:

Academic Qualifications Rating (AQR): This score is affected by performance on all subtests, but the strongest influence is made by the Math Skills Test. The AQR ranges from 1 to 9 and is used to predict academic performance in Aviation Preflight Indoctrination (API) and primary phase ground school.

Pilot Flight Aptitude Rating (PFAR): This score is affected by performance on all subtests, but the greatest contribution is made by the Aviation & Nautical Information and Spatial Apperception Tests. The PFAR ranges from 1 to 9 and is used to predict primary flight performance for Student Naval Aviators (pilots).

Flight Officer Flight Aptitude Rating (FOFAR): This score is affected by performance on all subtests, but the strongest influence is made by the Math Skills Test. This score ranges from 1 to 9 and is used to predict primary flight performance for Student Naval Flight Officers (navigators).

Officer Aptitude Rating (OAR): This score is affected by performance on the first three subtests: Math Skills, Reading Comprehension, and Mechanical Comprehension. This score ranges from 20 to 80 with a mean of 50. The score is used to predict academic performance in Navy Officer Candidate School. To qualify for OCS, all candidates require a minimum OAR of 40.

The minimum scores to become a Navy pilot are:

AQR: 3
PFAR: 4

The minimum score requirements to qualify as a Navy flight officer are:

AQR: 3
FOFAR: 4

Non-Aviation Applicants

Navy non-aviation applications are not required to take the entire test, but the Navy highly encourages them to do so. However, if desired, non-aviation applicants may take only those portions of the test that are used to comprise the Officer Aptitude Rating (Math Skills, Reading Comprehension, and Mechanical Comprehension).

Examinees who take only the OAR portion will receive only one score, the OAR, which is used to predict academic performance in Navy Officer Candidate School.

Applicants who have taken only the OAR portion of the ASTB may take the remaining portions to obtain a complete set of scores. Examinees must take the remaining portions within 90 days of the initial test, and the test date of the SAT, ANIT, and AST will become the official test date for the complete exam. The test merge will count as only one attempt against the examinee's three-test lifetime limit (see re-testing, below).

RETESTING

Air Force Officers Qualifying Test

AFOQT scores are valid for life. Current Air Force policy allows applicants to test twice on the AFOQT (one retest). The minimum retest interval is six months, but a retest may occur after several years. Additional retests can be and are granted, but require a waiver. Only the latest scores (not the highest) are used.

Armed Services Vocational Aptitude Battery

ASVAB tests are valid for two years. Retests are generally only authorized when (1) the scores are too low to qualify for enlistment/accession, (2) the scores are expired (two years), or (3) something unusual happened during the test (sickness, broken air conditioning, etc.) that negatively affected the test results.

When a retest is authorized, a minimum 30-day period is required before the retest, and a minimum 180-day period is required for the second and subsequent retests.

Aviation Selection Test Battery

You may only retake the battery three times. After the first time, you're required to wait at least 30 days before taking it again (i.e., you can't take it until the 31st day after your first test). After the second time, you're required to wait at least 90 days before taking it for the last time (i.e., you can't take it until the 91st day after your second test).

If you take a retest too early or if you take a retest using a form that you've already taken, the scoring computer will consider it an illegal test. An illegal test is counted as one of the three tests you may take in your lifetime, even though the score is not counted as a valid score.

Regardless of whether your retest scores are higher than those of a previous test, only the most recent scores are considered for program eligibility.

The Art of Test-Taking

CHAPTER 4

Seeing much, suffering much, and studying much, are the three pillars of learning.

—Benjamin Disraeli

Have you ever heard someone say, "I'm just not any good at taking tests?" I've probably heard that a thousand times in my Air Force career. The truth is, however, that those who are good at taking tests are the ones who've taken a little extra time to learn proper test-taking strategies.

PAPER TESTS

At this time, there is no computerized version of the AFOQT. All Air Force OTS candidates must take a pencil-and-paper version of the test. Most candidates who take the ASTB take a paper version of the exam, but some Navy and Marine Corps testing sites have access to a computerized version of the test on a restricted Internet site. For Army (and non-aviation Marine Corps/Coast Guard) candidates, where the ASVAB is the testing medium, you may have a choice of taking the paper-based ASVAB or the computerized ASVAB (although the services are moving away from the paper-based ASVAB). Fully, 80 to 85 percent of those who take the ASVAB today take the computerized version.

There are two primary advantages of the paper-based tests. First, the paper tests allow you to skip questions you're not sure about and then come back to them later (if there is time). This can be helpful when you're trying to get as many questions answered as possible.

The second, I hesitate to call an advantage. The paper-based tests allow you to go back and change your answers. This is generally not a good idea, unless you are 100 percent sure that you are changing it to the correct answer because you originally misread the question or have some other reason to absolutely know that you're changing it to the correct answer. Several years ago, the Air Force Senior Noncommissioned Officers Academy (SNCOA) conducted a study of Air Force multiple-choice tests. The study found that when SNCOA students changed an answer on a test, they changed it from a correct answer to an incorrect answer 72 percent of the time. When in doubt, your first instinct often turns out to be the correct one.

A major disadvantage of paper-based tests is that there is a real danger of mistakenly answering the wrong questions on the wrong lines. In other words, if you're not paying attention, it's easy to mark the answer for question #20 in the answer space for question #21, etc. If you don't catch this error right away, you can lose a lot of time having to go back and correct your answers.

Remember, the paper-based tests are machine–scored. To ensure the scoring machine properly records your answer, you must make sure you mark the answer sheet correctly by completely shading in the answer block. Don't circle the answer, don't put a check mark, and don't draw a smiley face. If you have to erase, make sure you erase completely.

COMPUTERIZED TESTS

If you're applying for a commission in the Army, Coast Guard, or Marine Corps (non-aviation), chances are you'll be taking the computerized ASVAB, officially known as Computerized Adaptive Testing, or the CAT-ASVAB.

The CAT-ASVAB consists of 145 questions in 10 subtests. Currently, the time limit to take this test is 154 minutes. Even though only certain subtests of the ASVAB are used for commissioned officer qualifications for the Army, Coast Guard, and Marine Corps, one must take the entire test.

Unlike the paper versions, you cannot skip questions or change answers on the computerized ASVAB. The CAT-ASVAB adapts or changes in relation to your ability. The initial question presented within a subtest will be of average or middle-range ability. If you answer correctly, the next question will be more difficult. If the first question presented is answered incorrectly, the second item will be less difficult. Questions will continue to be presented based on previous responses until your level of ability is determined. Once this has been established, all questions presented will be at this level of difficulty. The result is that you are presented with questions that match your ability level, and you are not called upon to answer questions that are too easy or too difficult.

Unlike the paper versions, the computerized ASVAB scores are not based on "number correct." Instead, harder questions are granted more points than easier questions. The computer then uses formulas that equate the CAT-ASVAB raw scores to the paper versions. The result is that both scores become equivalent (although, in actual practice, most people seem to score slightly higher on the CAT-ASVAB).

The computerized (Internet) version of the ASTB is not adaptive. In other words, the questions are presented in the same order as they are on the paper version of the test and they carry the same scoring weight, whether they are considered hard or easy.

MULTIPLE–CHOICE TESTS

Developing a test in the military is almost an exact science. Test questions are created by subject matter experts and then the test is validated by testing psychologists. Because of this consistency in test development, there are certain rules you can follow when taking a military test that can help you to score higher.

Directions

This sounds obvious, but make sure you read the directions carefully. Don't make assumptions about what the directions are going to say. Each subtest has its own directions, and some subtests may have different directions for different areas of the subtests.

Marking Your Answers

As mentioned before, when taking the paper-based tests, be careful how you mark your answer sheet. Stray marks, incompletely shaded areas, and incomplete erasers can cause the scoring machine to incorrectly read your answer sheet. When this happens, it's rare that the machine will give you a higher score. The usual result is a lower score than what you would have otherwise achieved.

Marking the Right Answer to the Right Question

It's embarrassing how often this has happened to those taking paper-based tests. You'll be humming right along, doing pretty well, and then suddenly you realize that you skipped an answer space 20 questions ago, and every question afterward has been recorded in the wrong space. You must then waste valuable time going back to erase and remark those last 20 questions.

After you mark the answer on your answer sheet, go back and look at the question number and then look at your answer sheet again to ensure that you answered the question in the correct space. This extra half-second effort can save you from having a minor stroke when you're three questions away from finishing the test.

Understand the Question

Read the question carefully to make sure you understand what it is asking. One question may ask, "What would be a good title for the above passage?" and another question may ask, "What would ***not*** be a good title for the above passage?"

Read All the Answer Choices

Always read all of the answer choices before selecting an answer. The instructions generally state to select the "most correct" or "best possible" answer. Test developers will often place a "distracter," or almost-correct choice, before the "most correct" choice. Sometimes there are several choices that are reasonably or somewhat correct, but only one of the choices will be the "most correct."

Key Words

Absolute words, such as *never, none, nothing, nobody, all, always, everyone, everybody, only,* and *any* are often contained in choices that are the wrong answers. Choices that contain these words are generally too broad and are difficult to defend.

Limiting words, such as *usually, few, some, many, often, generally, sometimes, possible,* and *occasionally* often indicate a correct answer.

Frequency

Just because "B" was the correct answer for the last four questions doesn't mean that "B" won't be the correct answer for the next question. Answer choices are truly randomized and sometimes the dice do roll sevens several times in a row.

Eliminate Wrong Choices

Sometimes one or more of the answer choices are obviously incorrect. It's often helpful to read through all the choices and eliminate the ones that are wrong. If you eliminate all but one, that's obviously the correct answer. If you eliminate all but two, then you only have to decide between two choices to determine the correct answer.

Skipping Questions

This is possible on the paper versions of the tests only. On the CAT-ASVAB and computerized version of the ASTB, it's impossible to skip questions because each question must be answered before the next question is presented on the computer screen. On the paper versions, it's possible to skip the harder questions and then return to them when you complete the remaining questions of the subtests. Sometimes a person will get a mental block on a certain question; putting it on the back burner for a while can clear it up. When you skip a question, go ahead and shade in any answer on your answer sheet (to keep you from getting out of sequence), and then circle the number in your test booklet to remind yourself to take another look at the question, if you have time.

Guessing Is Okay

There are no penalties for wrong answers. If you absolutely have no idea what the correct answer is, select a choice anyway. This way, you still have a one in four (or one in five) chance of getting the correct answer. If you leave the answer blank, you have zero chance.

When making an "educated guess," try to eliminate any obviously incorrect choices first. Look for the "key words" (described above) to increase your chances of guessing correctly. Usually, if two choices have conflicting meanings, one of them is probably correct. Conversely, if two choices have almost identical meanings, then both of them are probably wrong.

STUDY HABITS

Presumably, your goal is to score well on one of the military officer candidate school/officer training school examinations. Otherwise you probably wouldn't have spent the money on this book. However, you can't do it with this book (or any other OCS/OTS/OCC Test Preparation Guide) alone. If you want to score well, you have to study. Efficient study habits are the key to successful test preparation.

Develop Your Vocabulary

Two of the most significant parts of all of the OCS/OCC/OTS tests are word knowledge and reading comprehension. Additionally, your ability to read and understand questions is an essential skill. Every time you see or hear a word you don't understand, write it down and make a note of where you saw or heard the word and in what context the word was used. Later, when you have a chance, look the word up in a dictionary, making sure you completely understand its meaning.

Periodically review your word list, and try to use the words in conversation whenever possible. Using this technique, you will quickly build your vocabulary, which will not only help you on the tests, but will be beneficial to you in your everyday life.

Practice Basic Math Skills

You can't use a calculator on any of the tests. All of the math questions are designed to be solved using a pencil and scratch paper. If you need to count on your fingers and toes to compute that 5 + 6 = 11, you're going to lose valuable time.

Study Schedule

Develop a study schedule and stick to it. You should set aside a MINIMUM of 30 minutes of uninterrupted study time each day. Studies have shown that the average person retains information more efficiently if he/she studies uninterrupted for extended periods of time, once a day, rather than studying for several short sessions each day.

Eliminate Distractions

Study in a well-lit, quiet area. Turn off the radio and TV. If you live with others, make a deal with them to leave you alone during your scheduled study periods.

Concentrate on Your Weak Areas

This may seem obvious, but it's a trap that many people fall into. It takes less effort to read about or study areas you have an interest in or knowledge of than to study areas that you lack interest in, or are confused by. Because of this, we sometimes choose the path of least resistance, and subconsciously devote too much study time to areas that are easiest for us. This is a mistake. Why waste time studying areas of the tests you already know you will probably do well in?

Stay in Shape

Students who are in good physical condition have an advantage over those who are not. It's a well-established fact that good physical health improves the ability of the mind to function smoothly and efficiently. Besides, when you finally get to OCS/OCC/OTS, there will be several huge drill instructors waiting for you who will be happy to give you extra attention if you show up as a couch potato.

USING PRACTICE TESTS

If used correctly, the practice tests in this book can be valuable study aids. However, it will do you no good to simply study the questions presented in this book. Military tests are highly controlled materials and no author of a military test study guide has access to the actual questions that appear on the test. The best that we can do is to present questions that are *similar* to those you will see on the actual test.

Too many people purchase study guides, and then waste valuable time studying only the questions. When they take the official examination, they often become upset because none of the questions they studied appeared on the actual test. The fact of the matter is that if a publisher ever did (through devious means) get their hands on actual test material and then published it, the military would immediately declare the test to be "compromised," and it would be replaced with a backup version with different questions.

The practice tests in this guide have two primary purposes:

1. **To determine your weak areas.** Use the practice tests to determine areas you need to improve on. Then, using the appropriate study habits (see above), bone up on those areas using relevant study materials (such as high school or college textbooks).
2. **Test Familiarization.** The practice tests can give you a good idea of how the military tests are structured and the type of questions that are asked. This can help you to feel more comfortable when you take the actual exam, and can increase your test-taking speed. You won't have to waste time trying to figure out how a question works, which means you will have more time available for answering the questions.

Read the subject review chapters and answer the example questions at the end of each chapter. This will give you a good idea of the areas you need to concentrate on.

When taking the practice tests, try to simulate the actual testing environment. Eliminate distractions, take the entire exam at one time, time yourself, and don't allow anyone to interrupt you. Once you complete the test, check your answers to see what areas you need to spend more time brushing up on.

Using the practice tests as a self-assessment tool can help you to significantly improve your scores on the actual examination.

On Test Day

- Get a good night's sleep the night before the test. Last-minute cramming is unlikely to improve your score, and is likely to make you tired which, in turn, can cause you to make mistakes.
- Eat a light meal before taking the test. Having a little fuel in your body can help you concentrate, but too much can make you feel drowsy.
- Reschedule the test if you're sick, injured, or have any other unusual reason that would negatively affect your ability to concentrate on the test.
- Bring a watch to help you keep track of how much time there is remaining for each subtest. If you're taking the CAT-ASVAB, there is a timer on the computer screen.
- Wear comfortable clothes. Include a sweater or a jacket that can be added or removed, depending on the room temperature.
- Arrive on time! Better yet, arrive with five or ten minutes to spare. Military tests are very structured and the examiners will lock the door at the designated testing time. In the military there is a saying: "If you're on time, that means you're five minutes too late." If you're not sure about the test location or how to get there, do a trial run a day or two before.
- Don't drink too much liquid before the test. Time spent going to the bathroom is valuable time lost that could be spent answering questions.

Word Knowledge

The first two years of college are vocabulary lessons. The second two years are spent learning who to ask and where to look it up.

—Bill Austin

You cannot be an effective leader if you cannot communicate effectively. This is one of the reasons that the military requires commissioned officers to have a college degree.

The military takes its use of words seriously. For example, enlisted Air Force and Army members no longer eat in a chow hall, as they did in years past. Today, they eat in the "Enlisted Dining Facility." Military parents don't drop their kids off at daycare. Their children attend the "Child Development Center." That $9,000 hammer that everyone read about several years ago was a "Material Penetrating Impact Device" (MPID).

Seriously, the military services expect their officers to have a superior knowledge of vocabulary. Military officers spend a significant amount of time reading, writing, and speaking. If one of your subordinates does something exceptional, and you cannot adequately write a citation that will justify the award of a medal, you're not an effective leader, even if you can shoot a rifle or fly a plane. If you cannot decipher a regulation or understand your instructions from a higher-headquarters message, your career as an officer is going to be short-lived.

IMPROVING YOUR VOCABULARY

Vocabulary literally means "all the words in a language." Now, the military doesn't expect its officers to memorize the dictionary, but they do expect officers to be able to communicate effectively, and that means having a broad vocabulary.

Reading

There is no better way to improve your vocabulary than reading. Research has shown that people who read for enjoyment possess a significantly broader vocabulary than those who dislike reading. Additionally, it's not necessary to read the most difficult books. In fact, you'll have better success if you choose books that are just a little bit more difficult than your current reading level. If you choose books that are significantly beyond your current capability, chances are you will get discouraged and quit reading.

You should read books and articles that contain just one or two new words per page. Your goal is to not get bogged down with new words, but rather to slowly and steadily increase your scope of word knowledge.

While reading, it is often possible to puzzle out the meaning of a new word by evaluating the context in which the word is used. Take, for example, the following passage:

> "It had been three days since the ship-wreck, and Tammy was unable to find food, nor much drinkable water. At this point, she would do anything to get off that wretched island."

We can derive several important clues about the meaning of the word *wretched* based on the context used in the passage. Obviously, Tammy is not having a very good time, nor does she find the island to be a very pleasant environment. Therefore, we can surmise that *wretched* has something to do with unpleasantness. Checking our handy pocket dictionary confirms our guess:

adj. **wretch·ed·er, wretch·ed·est**

1. In a deplorable state of distress or misfortune; miserable: "the wretched prisoners huddling in the stinking cages" (George Orwell).
2. Characterized by or attended with misery or woe: a *wretched life.*
3. Of a poor or mean character; dismal: *a wretched building.*
4. Contemptible; despicable: *wretched treatment of the patients.*
5. Of very inferior quality: *wretched prose.*

While reading for the purpose of broadening your vocabulary, it is very useful to have easy access to a pocket dictionary. While context can give you some clues about the meaning of a word, a dictionary is useful to help confirm your conjectures.

Parts of a Word

Most words in the English language are created from building blocks called prefixes, roots, and suffixes. These basic groups generally have the same meaning, regardless of what word they are a part of. Knowing the primary root words, prefixes, and suffixes used in the English language can dramatically improve your chances of puzzling out the meaning of an unfamiliar word, even if the sentence context provides few clues. Not all words contain a prefix, root, or suffix. Some words contain all three, and many words in the English language contain at least one.

Word Roots

Word roots are syllables that form the main part of a word and its meaning. A word root may be the word itself, such as the word *flex,* or it may be an element from which many words can be formed, as in the example *brev,* meaning short. It can even be both, such as with *micro,* which means small.

A studied knowledge of common word roots can significantly increase one's vocabulary. As we'll see shortly, word roots used in conjunction with prefixes and suffixes can result in a vast array of different words.

Prefixes

Prefixes (when used) come at the beginning of a word. When used at the beginning of a word, a prefix changes the meaning of the word. Take, for example, the word *social.* In itself, one of the meanings of the word is *to be disposed to mix in friendly converse,* or *companionable.* However, if we add the prefix *anti,* which means against, we change the entire meaning of the original word. *Antisocial* describes *a person who is antagonistic toward or disrespectful of others.* If we know the meaning of the word *social,* and if we know that the prefix *anti* means against, then we know the definition of the word *antisocial.*

Sometimes a prefix is also a word root. It's a prefix if it's at the front of the word and changes the meaning of another correct word. It's considered a word root if it's contained anyway in the word, but isn't changing the meaning of another "stand-alone" word. Take the word root/prefix *inter,* for example. It's both a word root (as in *interrupt*) and a prefix (as in *international*). Don't let this bother you. The important thing is that both word roots and prefixes can give you important clues as to the definition of a word.

The following chart contains some of the common roots and prefixes that form the basis of many English words:

Common Prefixes

Root/Prefix	Definition	Examples
a/n	without, not	abyss, anhydrous
a	on	afire, ashore
act	do	activity, react
anti	opposite of, against	antibody, antisocial
bene	good, well	benefactor, benevolent
bio	living matter, life	biography, biology
cent	hundred, hundredth	centennial, centimeter
dia	through, apart	diabetes, dialog
endo	within, inside	endocrine, endogamy
geo	earth, soil, global	geography, geology
hydr/o	liquid, water	hydrate, hydrophobia
max	greatest	maximal, maximize
neo	new, recent	neoclassic, neonatal
pel	drive, force	compel, expel
put	think	computer, dispute
re	again, back	rewind, rebound
san	health	sane, sanitary
sta	stand	stable, stagnant
tact	touch	contact, tactile
uni	one, single	unicycle, unilateral
vid	see	evident
zo/o	animal life	zoology

Suffixes

A suffix is just the opposite of a prefix in that it goes onto the end of a word. Like prefixes, suffixes also change the meaning of a word. Take, for example, the word *child*. A child is a human being, not yet of adult age. When we say, "That woman has a beautiful *child*," we are complimenting her on the appearance of her offspring. However, if we add the suffix *less*, which means "not having" to the word *child*, the resultant word is *childless* and means something totally different. We could now say, "It's too bad she has to go through life *childless*," meaning she doesn't, and won't ever, have any children.

It's entirely possible to have a word containing both a prefix and a suffix. The main definition of the word *break* is to divide into pieces (usually through violent or unintentional actions). If we add the suffix *able*, meaning "capable of," we form the new word, *breakable*. We would then be describing an item that breaks easily, or is capable of breaking. However, if we now add the prefix *un*, which means "not," our end result is the word *unbreakable*, and we're describing an item that can't be broken.

The chart below shows some of the most common suffixes used in the English language:

Common Suffixes

Suffix	Definition	Examples
-able or -ible	capable of	likeable
-age	action or result	brokerage
-al	characterized by	national
-ance	instance of an action	maintenance
-ation	action or process	generation
-en	made of	golden
-ful	full of	peaceful
-ic	consisting of	alcoholic
-ical	possessing a quality of	statistical
-ion	result of an act or process	election
-ish	relating to	foolish
-ism	act or practice	materialism
-ist	characteristic of	fascist
-ity	quality of	relativity
-less	not having	childless
-let	small	booklet
-man	relating to humans	airman
-ment	action or process	enjoyment
-ness	possessing a quality	likeness
-or	a person who does a thing	moderator
-ous	having	dangerous
-y	quality of	freely

Definitions

As mentioned before, a handy pocket dictionary can be a valuable tool if you wish to increase the scope of your vocabulary. We've all met people who made a New Year's resolution to learn one new word per day and use it in conversation. While some of these people may turn out to be boring at New Year's Eve parties, they employ this method because it's been shown to work. Use your handy pocket dictionary to look up a couple of random new words per day, and then make a point to use them in conversation during that day. This helps to reinforce the proper meaning of the word, and helps you to remember the correct context when used in a sentence.

Homonyms

Any serious student of languages will tell you that English is one of the hardest languages to learn. Ever wonder why we have to teach our own language to native speakers throughout almost the entire spectrum of public schooling? From kindergarten to high school, we teach our children their native language. A large part of the reason is that English grammar contains all kinds of strange rules, and exceptions that contradict the rules. One strange facet of the English language, found in almost no other language, is homonyms. Homonyms are words that sound the same, but are spelled differently and have completely different meanings. *Two* is not the same as *to*, which is not the same as *too*.

The chart below shows some common homonyms that sometimes result in confusion. Using your pocket dictionary to look up the definitions of these words is a good practice.

Common Homonyms

ad add	brake break	dam damn	gnu knew new	mail male	straight strait
aid aide	bus buss	days daze	hail hale	marry merry	team teem
affect effect	but butt	dear deer	hangar hanger	marshal martial	threw through
allowed aloud	buy by bye	dew do due	hay hey	meat meet mete	vain vane vein
ant aunt	capital capitol	discreet discrete	high hi	morning mourning	vary very
ascent assent	carat caret carrot karat	elicit illicit	holey holy wholly	mustard mustered	wail wale whale
aye eye I	cell sell sale	faint feint	incite insight	patience patients	wait weight

bail bale	sear seer sere	fair fare	it's its	peace piece	weather whether
bare bear	chili chilly	feat feet	knight night	peak peek pique	you're your
baron barren	cites sights sites	flour flower	know no	racket racquet	wear where
be bee	Claus clause claws	for fore four	lessen lesson	real reel	their there they're
beat beet	colonel kernel	foul fowl	lightening lightning	right rite write	
boar boor bore	council counsel	gait gate	made maid	sew so sow	

Synonyms and Antonyms

A synonym is a word that has the same meaning or nearly the same meaning as another word. For example, *brawny* is a synonym of the word *strong*, since they mean nearly the same thing. An antonym, on the other hand, is a word that means the opposite or nearly the opposite of another word. *Weak* would be an antonym of *strong*.

Your best resource to study synonyms and antonyms is a dictionary. However, your handy pocket dictionary probably won't work. You'll need a full-sized desktop dictionary. Many dictionary entries will include the abbreviation *syn*, which stands for synonym. The words that follow this definition are recognized synonyms of the word. Likewise, there may be an entry abbreviated *ant*. This stands for antonym, and the words that follow will be antonyms of the word.

Verbal Analogies

The Air Force is the only service that tests its officer candidates on their ability to solve verbal analogies. So, if you're planning on seeking your commission in the Army, Navy, Marine Corps, or Coast Guard, you can ignore this section. If, however, you have your sights set on becoming an Air Force officer, you'll need to demonstrate your ability to reason, in addition to demonstrating your vocabulary level and knowledge of word meanings.

Verbal analogies test your ability to determine relationships between words. In order to do so, you're not only going to need knowledge of the word meanings and the ideas that they represent, but you'll also be required to use a degree of logic to determine how the subject words relate to each other.

There are two basic types of verbal analogy questions used on the AFOQT. The first type of question contains three capitalized words in the stem. This is followed by five one-word choices. Your task is to find the choice that most closely relates to the third capitalized word in the stem, in the same way that the first two capitalized words relate to each other:

DOG is to PUPPY as LION is to

(A) kitten
(B) cat
(C) lioness
(D) cub
(E) dog

In this case, the correct answer would be (D) *cub.* A baby dog is referred to as a puppy. Therefore the relationship between the second capitalized word is the infant or baby form of the first capitalized word. A lion's offspring are called cubs, and represents the same relationship to a lion as puppies relate to dogs.

In the second type of verbal analogy question asked on the AFOQT, only the first pair of capitalized words appears in the stem, followed by pairs of words in the answer options:

DOG is to PUPPY as

(A) cub is to lion
(B) lion is to cub
(C) cat is to lion
(D) man is to boy
(E) woman is to baby

Again, the correct answer would be (B) *lion is to cub.* Some of the other relationships are nearly the same, but answer (B) is the closest, as the relationship in the stem represents adult and baby animals. While choices (D) and (E) are close, they do not approach the same level of relationship as represented in option (B).

A common trap in verbal analogies is to mistake the proper order of the relationship. Answer (A), *cub is to lion,* is in the exact opposite order as the relationship shown in the stem, *DOG is to PUPPY.*

Answer Sheet for Practice Questions

1 Ⓐ Ⓑ Ⓒ Ⓓ	18 Ⓐ Ⓑ Ⓒ Ⓓ	35 Ⓐ Ⓑ Ⓒ Ⓓ Ⓔ	51 Ⓐ Ⓑ Ⓒ Ⓓ Ⓔ
2 Ⓐ Ⓑ Ⓒ Ⓓ	19 Ⓐ Ⓑ Ⓒ Ⓓ	36 Ⓐ Ⓑ Ⓒ Ⓓ Ⓔ	52 Ⓐ Ⓑ Ⓒ Ⓓ Ⓔ
3 Ⓐ Ⓑ Ⓒ Ⓓ	20 Ⓐ Ⓑ Ⓒ Ⓓ	37 Ⓐ Ⓑ Ⓒ Ⓓ Ⓔ	53 Ⓐ Ⓑ Ⓒ Ⓓ Ⓔ
4 Ⓐ Ⓑ Ⓒ Ⓓ	21 Ⓐ Ⓑ Ⓒ Ⓓ Ⓔ	38 Ⓐ Ⓑ Ⓒ Ⓓ Ⓔ	54 Ⓐ Ⓑ Ⓒ Ⓓ Ⓔ
5 Ⓐ Ⓑ Ⓒ Ⓓ	22 Ⓐ Ⓑ Ⓒ Ⓓ Ⓔ	39 Ⓐ Ⓑ Ⓒ Ⓓ Ⓔ	55 Ⓐ Ⓑ Ⓒ Ⓓ Ⓔ
6 Ⓐ Ⓑ Ⓒ Ⓓ	23 Ⓐ Ⓑ Ⓒ Ⓓ Ⓔ	40 Ⓐ Ⓑ Ⓒ Ⓓ Ⓔ	56 Ⓐ Ⓑ Ⓒ Ⓓ Ⓔ
7 Ⓐ Ⓑ Ⓒ Ⓓ	24 Ⓐ Ⓑ Ⓒ Ⓓ Ⓔ	41 Ⓐ Ⓑ Ⓒ Ⓓ Ⓔ	57 Ⓐ Ⓑ Ⓒ Ⓓ Ⓔ
8 Ⓐ Ⓑ Ⓒ Ⓓ	25 Ⓐ Ⓑ Ⓒ Ⓓ Ⓔ	42 Ⓐ Ⓑ Ⓒ Ⓓ Ⓔ	58 Ⓐ Ⓑ Ⓒ Ⓓ Ⓔ
9 Ⓐ Ⓑ Ⓒ Ⓓ	26 Ⓐ Ⓑ Ⓒ Ⓓ Ⓔ	43 Ⓐ Ⓑ Ⓒ Ⓓ Ⓔ	59 Ⓐ Ⓑ Ⓒ Ⓓ Ⓔ
10 Ⓐ Ⓑ Ⓒ Ⓓ	27 Ⓐ Ⓑ Ⓒ Ⓓ Ⓔ	44 Ⓐ Ⓑ Ⓒ Ⓓ Ⓔ	60 Ⓐ Ⓑ Ⓒ Ⓓ Ⓔ
11 Ⓐ Ⓑ Ⓒ Ⓓ	28 Ⓐ Ⓑ Ⓒ Ⓓ Ⓔ	45 Ⓐ Ⓑ Ⓒ Ⓓ Ⓔ	61 Ⓐ Ⓑ Ⓒ Ⓓ Ⓔ
12 Ⓐ Ⓑ Ⓒ Ⓓ	29 Ⓐ Ⓑ Ⓒ Ⓓ Ⓔ	46 Ⓐ Ⓑ Ⓒ Ⓓ Ⓔ	62 Ⓐ Ⓑ Ⓒ Ⓓ Ⓔ
13 Ⓐ Ⓑ Ⓒ Ⓓ	30 Ⓐ Ⓑ Ⓒ Ⓓ Ⓔ	47 Ⓐ Ⓑ Ⓒ Ⓓ Ⓔ	63 Ⓐ Ⓑ Ⓒ Ⓓ Ⓔ
14 Ⓐ Ⓑ Ⓒ Ⓓ	31 Ⓐ Ⓑ Ⓒ Ⓓ Ⓔ	48 Ⓐ Ⓑ Ⓒ Ⓓ Ⓔ	64 Ⓐ Ⓑ Ⓒ Ⓓ Ⓔ
15 Ⓐ Ⓑ Ⓒ Ⓓ	32 Ⓐ Ⓑ Ⓒ Ⓓ Ⓔ	49 Ⓐ Ⓑ Ⓒ Ⓓ Ⓔ	65 Ⓐ Ⓑ Ⓒ Ⓓ Ⓔ
16 Ⓐ Ⓑ Ⓒ Ⓓ	33 Ⓐ Ⓑ Ⓒ Ⓓ Ⓔ	50 Ⓐ Ⓑ Ⓒ Ⓓ Ⓔ	66 Ⓐ Ⓑ Ⓒ Ⓓ Ⓔ
17 Ⓐ Ⓑ Ⓒ Ⓓ	34 Ⓐ Ⓑ Ⓒ Ⓓ Ⓔ		

Practice Questions

All of the services' officer qualifying tests contain questions that measure the candidate's word knowledge. Additionally, for those wishing to become Air Force officers, applicants are measured on their ability to solve verbal analogies.

Directions: Each of the following questions includes an underlined word. Your task is to decide which of the four choices *most nearly means* the same as the underlined word.

1. Adduce most nearly means:
   (A) cite as proof
   (B) inflexible
   (C) destroy
   (D) operate

2. Fastidious most nearly means:
   (A) taxing
   (B) purposeful
   (C) meticulous
   (D) missed

3. Our plan was to educe as much data from the prisoner as possible.
   (A) file
   (B) verify
   (C) examine
   (D) elicit

4. Palpable most nearly means:
   (A) obvious
   (B) regard
   (C) forces
   (D) ingenious

5. Gendarme most nearly means:
   (A) placement
   (B) relevant
   (C) destroyed
   (D) police

6. Due to the recent budget report, it was an auspicious time to ask for a raise in his salary.
   (A) inappropriate
   (B) mediocre
   (C) favorable
   (D) tentative

7. Gambol most nearly means:
   (A) relax
   (B) leap playfully
   (C) game
   (D) malnutrition

8. Hirsute most nearly means:
   (A) hairy
   (B) observant
   (C) scientist
   (D) medical

9. Assignation most nearly means:
   (A) travel
   (B) train
   (C) murder
   (D) appointment

10. Joy and hope are emotions indigenous to the human mind. — I. Taylor.
    (A) poor
    (B) native
    (C) positive
    (D) reliable

11. Delirious most nearly means:
    (A) deranged
    (B) behaved
    (C) starved
    (D) religious

12. Rapport most nearly means:
    (A) hypnotized
    (B) religious
    (C) harmony
    (D) timed

13. Taking that shortcut was the result of great forethought.

    (A) coincidence
    (B) deliberation
    (C) mediation
    (D) tactics

14. Subsidy most nearly means:

    (A) account
    (B) reliance
    (C) memorize
    (D) aid

15. Homophone most nearly means:

    (A) winter
    (B) geography
    (C) pale
    (D) homonym

16. His monologue tends to exasperate most audiences.

    (A) amuse
    (B) infuriate
    (C) bore
    (D) excite

17. Pattern most nearly means:

    (A) replication
    (B) reliance
    (C) pigmy
    (D) austere

18. Lexicon most nearly means:

    (A) prevent
    (B) book
    (C) dictionary
    (D) discussion

19. The reasoning behind his conclusion was obvious.

    (A) opinion
    (B) deduction
    (C) relationship
    (D) morale

20. Macadamize most nearly means:

    (A) cook
    (B) shrink
    (C) pave
    (D) enlarge

Directions: Choose the word that *most nearly means* the same as the CAPITALIZED word.

21. EXHAUST

    (A) pedicure
    (B) energize
    (C) revive
    (D) memorize
    (E) bankrupt

22. EMBROILMENT

    (A) cook
    (B) taxidermy
    (C) suffer
    (D) controversy
    (E) periodic

23. MESSIEURS

    (A) gentlemen
    (B) extol
    (C) maintain
    (D) automobiles
    (E) plan

24. NEFARIOUS

    (A) reliable
    (B) argument
    (C) wicked
    (D) famous
    (E) expert

25. OBSTREPEROUS
    (A) hinder
    (B) porous
    (C) partake
    (D) boisterous
    (E) quiet

26. CONSOLE
    (A) comfort
    (B) depress
    (C) invigorate
    (D) paint
    (E) mixture

27. COLLOQUY
    (A) prize
    (B) agreement
    (C) tenacity
    (D) velour
    (E) conversation

28. NEUROTIC
    (A) mishandle
    (B) easygoing
    (C) psychiatrist
    (D) overwrought
    (E) exotic

29. OBLIGATION
    (A) sedition
    (B) responsibility
    (C) ungratefulness
    (D) disobedience
    (E) endure

30. CONTEMPORANEOUS
    (A) simultaneous
    (B) hateful
    (C) religious
    (D) pitiful
    (E) traveling

31. SPECIALTY
    (A) entertainment
    (B) mirror
    (C) occupation
    (D) sideline
    (E) reliance

32. COQUETTE
    (A) tragedy
    (B) boredom
    (C) flirt
    (D) mistake
    (E) coy

33. DECLAMATORY
    (A) legislation
    (B) disconnect
    (C) talk
    (D) resource
    (E) monetary

34. DILATORY
    (A) inaction
    (B) delaying
    (C) amusing
    (D) period
    (E) troublesome

35. HUMILIATE
    (A) temperate
    (B) lazy
    (C) rely
    (D) fortify
    (E) embarrass

36. TOLERANCE
    (A) recording
    (B) mercilessness
    (C) painful
    (D) fortitude
    (E) maximum

37. TELEMETRY
    (A) transmission
    (B) focus
    (C) precision
    (D) enhancement
    (E) space

38. PERSUASIVE
    (A) questionable
    (B) enhancement
    (C) religious
    (D) influential
    (E) acceleration

39. DILETTANTE
    (A) play
    (B) physician
    (C) amateur
    (D) lady
    (E) purpose

40. EFFERVESCE
    (A) slackness
    (B) distortion
    (C) eloquent
    (D) liability
    (E) bubble

Directions: Each of the following questions consists of a pair of CAPITALIZED words and a third CAPITALIZED word that is related to one of the choices in the same manner that the first capitalized word is related to the second capitalized word. Your task is to select the choice that is *most similar* in relationship to the third capitalized word, with the same relationship as the first pair of capitalized words.

41. GLOVE is to HAND as HAT is to
    (A) face
    (B) head
    (C) fingers
    (D) foot
    (E) mirror

42. TEMPERATURE is to COLD as RUNNING is to
    (A) fast
    (B) walk
    (C) operate
    (D) skip
    (E) jog

43. SQUIRREL is to TREE as GOPHER is to
    (A) bush
    (B) cave
    (C) forest
    (D) ground
    (E) water

44. MIXTURE is to INDIVIDUAL as PERPLEX is to
    (A) confuse
    (B) enlighten
    (C) refuse
    (D) befuddle
    (E) confound

45. HAMBURGER is to CATTLE as BACON is to
    (A) ducks
    (B) beef
    (C) pigs
    (D) lambs
    (E) fowl

46. DRIVE is to DROVE as THROW is to
    (A) throwed
    (B) throwing
    (C) thrower
    (D) threw
    (E) toss

47. CREATE is to DESTROY as NATURAL is to
    (A) artificial
    (B) climate
    (C) enormous
    (D) sunlight
    (E) beach

48. LOS ANGELES is to CALIFORNIA as OMAHA is to
    (A) New Mexico
    (B) Idaho
    (C) West Virginia
    (D) Nebraska
    (E) Washington

49. XXI is to XXIX as 21 is to

(A) 29
(B) 30
(C) 31
(D) 32
(E) 33

50. CARPENTER is to HAMMER as COOK is to

(A) spatula
(B) pot
(C) stove
(D) oven
(E) apron

51. RELINQUISH is to TALK as OCTOPUS is to

(A) swim
(B) run
(C) flown
(D) book
(E) jump

52. BEHAVE is to CANDY as DISOBEY is to

(A) disruption
(B) spanking
(C) error
(D) situation
(E) requirement

53. BRAIN is to THOUGHT as CLOCK is to

(A) night
(B) day
(C) tick
(D) noon
(E) wall

Directions: Each of the following questions consists of a pair of CAPITALIZED words. Your task is to select the response that shows a relationship that is *most similar* to the relationship of the two CAPITALIZED words.

54. BARN is to COW as

(A) house is to person
(B) tailor is to cloth
(C) mother is to daughter
(D) minister is to congregation
(E) library is to book

55. CAR is to TRAVEL as

(A) train is to whistle
(B) mountain is to sea
(C) fork is to eat
(D) meat is to potatoes
(E) life is to death

56. PILOT is to CONDUCTOR as

(A) January is to February
(B) soldier is to teacher
(C) bark is to tree
(D) tailor is to cloth
(E) water is to drink

57. CAMERA is to PICTURE as

(A) green is to leaf
(B) gardener is to grass
(C) hay is to barn
(D) good is to evil
(E) oven is to cake

58. BRAVE is to FEARLESS as
    (A) cool is to cold
    (B) hot is to cold
    (C) radiator is to heat
    (D) rain is to weather
    (E) run is to walk

59. CANADA is to the UNITED STATES as
    (A) California is to New York
    (B) The United States is to Mexico
    (C) Alaska is to Canada
    (D) Brazil is to Korea
    (E) Maine is to Texas

60. GOLF BALL is to HOLE as
    (A) singer is to song
    (B) jack is to tire
    (C) football is to goal line
    (D) cook is to soup
    (E) Marine is to firearm

61. SURGEON is to SCALPEL as
    (A) cook is to knife
    (B) fireman is to hose
    (C) programmer is to computer
    (D) musician is to trumpet
    (E) author is to pen

62. FRAME is to PAINTING as
    (A) book is to page
    (B) honey is to bee
    (C) fence is to yard
    (D) sweater is to woman
    (E) park is to ranger

63. CYLINDER is to ICE CREAM CONE as
    (A) circle is to wheel
    (B) rectangle is to dollar bill
    (C) triangle is to pyramid
    (D) sandwich is to square
    (E) battery is to cylinder

64. MARCH is to WALK as
    (A) sprint is to run
    (B) fly is to swim
    (C) drive is to walk
    (D) patience is to upset
    (E) study is to read

65. ACQUIT is to BLAME as
    (A) orange is to red
    (B) life is to death
    (C) May is to June
    (D) book is to read
    (E) cigarette is to smoke

66. CHOCOLATE is to CAKE as
    (A) pie is to dessert
    (B) pocket is to pants
    (C) pain is to discomfort
    (D) potato is to soup
    (E) he is to she

Answer Key

1. A	16. B	31. C	46. D	61. A
2. C	17. A	32. C	47. A	62. C
3. D	18. C	33. C	48. D	63. C
4. A	19. B	34. B	49. A	64. E
5. D	20. C	35. E	50. A	65. B
6. C	21. E	36. D	51. D	66. D
7. B	22. D	37. A	52. B	
8. A	23. A	38. D	53. C	
9. D	24. C	39. C	54. A	
10. B	25. D	40. E	55. C	
11. A	26. A	41. B	56. B	
12. C	27. E	42. A	57. E	
13. B	28. D	43. D	58. A	
14. D	29. B	44. B	59. B	
15. D	30. A	45. C	60. C	

Answer Explanations

1. **(A) proof.** *Adduce* means "to cite as an example or proof in an argument."
2. **(C) meticulous.** *Fastidious* means "careful in all details; meticulous."
3. **(D) elicit.** *Educe* means "to draw or bring out."
4. **(A) obvious.** An example would be, "There was a palpable sense of expectation that the plane would crash."
5. **(D) police.** In continental Europe, particularly in France, a gendarme is a uniformed and armed police officer.
6. **(C) favorable.** *Auspicious* means "attended by favorable circumstances."
7. **(B) leaping.** *Gambol* means "playful leaping or frisking."
8. **(A) hairy.** *Hirsute* means "covered with hair or fur; hairy."
9. **(D) appointment.** An example would be, "The assignation was set for 11:00 P.M."
10. **(B) native.** *Indigenous* means "native to an area" or "innate; intrinsic." This quote uses the second meaning.
11. **(A) deranged.** An example would be, "He was hospitalized when he became delirious."
12. **(C) harmony.** An example would be, "When Bill and Suzie talked, they were in complete rapport."
13. **(B) deliberation.** The definition of *forethought* is "planning beforehand."
14. **(D) aid.** An example would be, "The youth group was able to operate because of a government subsidy."
15. **(D) homonym.** Both words mean "a word agreeing in sound with, but different in meaning from, another."
16. **(B) infuriate.** *Exasperate* means "to make very angry or impatient; annoy greatly."
17. **(A) replication.** An example would be, "I wish to pattern my life after yours."

18. **(C) dictionary.** *Lexicon* means "a word book with language and definitions." *Lexicography* is the task of making dictionaries, and a *lexicographer* is a person who makes dictionaries.
19. **(B) deduction.** *Reasoning* means "the basis or motive for an action, decision, or conviction."
20. **(C) pave.** *Macadamize* means "to cover or pave, as a path or roadway, with small broken stones."
21. **(E) bankrupt**. *Exhaust* means to drain of resources or properties.
22. **(D) controversy.** *Embroilment* means "a dispute between sides holding opposing views."
23. **(A) gentlemen.** *Messieurs* (the plural of *Monsieur*) is a form of polite address for a group of men in a French-speaking area.
24. **(C) wicked.** *Nefarious* means "wicked or evil to the extreme."
25. **(D) boisterous.** *Obstreperous* means "noisily and stubbornly defiant, or aggressively boisterous."
26. **(A) comfort.** *Console* means "to allay the sorrow or grief of."
27. **(E) conversation.** A *colloquy* is a conversation, especially a formal one.
28. **(D) overwrought.** *Neurotic* means "prone to emotional upset."
29. **(B) responsibility.** *Obligation* means "a moral contract, such as a duty."
30. **(A) simultaneous.** *Contemporaneous* means "living, occurring, or existing at the same time."
31. **(C) occupation.** *Specialty* means "a special pursuit, occupation, aptitude, or skill."
32. **(C) flirt.** A *coquette* is a woman who makes teasing sexual or romantic overtures.
33. **(C) talk.** *Declamatory* means "a full and formal style of utterance."
34. **(B) delaying.** *Dilatory* means "tending to delay."
35. **(E) embarrass.** *Humiliate* means "to lower the pride or dignity of a person."
36. **(D) fortitude.** *Tolerance* means "the capacity to endure hardship or pain."
37. **(A) transmission.** *Telemetry* is the science of automatically measuring and transmitting data remotely.
38. **(D) influential.** *Persuasive* means "tending to induce an action or belief."
39. **(C) amateur.** A *dilettante* is a dabbler in an art or a field of knowledge.
40. **(E) bubble**. *Effervesce* means "to emit small bubbles of gas, as a carbonated or fermenting liquid."
41. **(B) head.** As a glove is worn on the hand, and a hat is worn on the head.
42. **(A) fast.** As cold would be a measurement of temperature, fast would be a measurement of running.
43. **(D) ground.** As squirrels live in trees, gophers live in the ground.
44. **(B) enlighten.** As individual is an antonym of mixture, enlighten is an antonym of perplex.
45. **(C) pigs.** As hamburger is a meat made from cattle, bacon is a meat product made from pigs.
46. **(D) threw**. As drove is the past tense of drive, threw is the past tense of throw.
47. **(A) artificial.** As destroy is an antonym of create, artificial is an antonym of natural.
48. **(D) Nebraska.** As Los Angeles is a city located in California, Omaha is a city located in the state of Nebraska.

49. **(A) 29.** XXI are the Roman numerals for 21 and XXIX are the Roman numerals for 29.
50. **(A) spatula.** As a hammer is a small tool used by a carpenter, a spatula is a small tool used by a cook.
51. **(D) book.** As relinquish and talk are both verbs, octopus and book are both nouns.
52. **(B) spanking.** As candy would be a reward for behaving, spanking may be a punishment for disobeying.
53. **(C) tick.** As a brain thinks, a clock ticks.
54. **(A) house is to person.** As a cow lives in a barn, a person lives in a house.
55. **(C) fork is to eat**. As a car is used for the purpose of travel, a fork is used for the purpose of eating.
56. **(B) soldier is to teacher.** Pilot, conductor, soldier, and teacher are all occupations.
57. **(E) oven is to cake.** Just as a camera produces a picture, an oven produces a cake.
58. **(A) cool is to cold.** Fearless is a degree of brave, just as cold is a degree of cool.
59. **(B) the United States is to Mexico.** As Canada is a country north of the United States (another country), the United States is a country north of the country of Mexico.
60. **(C) football is to goal line.** As the golf ball enters the hole to score, the football passes the goal line to score.
61. **(A) cook is to knife**. As a surgeon uses a scalpel to cut doing his/her job, a cook uses a knife to cut as he/she prepares food.
62. **(C) fence is to yard.** As a frame surrounds a painting, a fence surrounds a yard.
63. **(C) triangle is to pyramid.** As an ice cream cone is a shape and is hollow, a pyramid is a shape and is hollow.
64. **(E) study is to read.** As marching is a more organized way of walking, studying is a more organized way of reading.
65. **(B) life is to death.** As blame is an antonym of acquit, death is an antonym of life.
66. **(D) potato is to soup.** As chocolate is a type of cake, so potato is a type of soup.

Reading Comprehension

CHAPTER 6

Education...has produced a vast population able to read but unable to distinguish what is worth reading.

—G.M. Trevelyan

Unsurprisingly, the military services not only want their commissioned officers to "read well" and be "well-read," but they also require them to be able to understand what they are reading. This is what is meant by "comprehension." Reading is only the first step in the process. You must then think about what you've read to make sure you understand what the writer is trying to convey.

While this may sound simple, miscommunication is the leading cause of almost every major military accident or battlefield disaster.

Military officers process an enormous amount of written communication. A former Air Force Vice Chief of Staff once commented that he had looked at 13,000 pieces of paper in a five-day period. If you can't read and understand what you read as a commissioned officer in the military, you can't function adequately as a leader.

All of the services, with the exception of the Air Force, include reading comprehension as part of their officer qualification tests. The Air Force eliminated the reading comprehension subtest in its latest revision of the AFOQT. However, if you wish to become a pilot or navigator in the Air Force, you must score well on the Table Reading subtest that measures your ability to quickly and accurately read tables.

For non-aviation candidates, the Army, Coast Guard, and Marine Corps use the Paragraph Comprehension subtest of the ASVAB as one of the components used in computing the overall General Technical (GT) score that is required for OCS/OCC selection. The Navy evaluates reading comprehension in the Reading Skills Test and the Aviation Supplemental Test of the ASTB. The latter also applies to aviation candidates of the Coast Guard and Marine Corps.

READING TO UNDERSTAND

Understanding what you read is a practiced art. The more you read, the better you get at it. Those who read for enjoyment often score better on reading comprehension tests than those who only read when they have to.

Reading comprehension involves several skills that anyone can develop with practice. To thoroughly understand what you read, you must develop the ability to recognize the main idea, recall details, make inferences, recognize and understand cause/effect relationships, compare relationships, and paraphrase and summarize passages and paragraphs.

The Main Idea

This is the most important part of a paragraph or passage. The main idea is the primary theme or idea that the writer wants the reader to understand. In many cases, the main idea is obvious. In other cases, the main idea may be implied by the writer, rather than stated directly.

Main Points

Quite often the main point of the paragraph or passage will be contained in the first sentence. Sometimes the main point is rephrased or summarized in the last sentence of the passage. For example, in the following passage, the main idea is stated in the first sentence:

> Effective time management is the most important trait of an efficient operation. Time management is about controlling the use of the most valuable (and undervalued) resource—time. The absence of time management is characterized by last–minute rushes to meet deadlines, meetings that are either double–booked or achieve nothing, days that seem somehow to slip unproductively by, and crises that loom unexpected from nowhere. This sort of environment leads to inordinate stress and performance degradation. Because personal time management is a management process, it must be planned, monitored, and regularly reviewed.

The main point is stated clearly in the very first sentence: "Effective time management is the most important trait of an efficient operation." The sentences that follow are sub-points that help to clarify and emphasize the main point of the paragraph.

Sometimes, however, the main point isn't found in the first sentence. Suppose we rewrote the passage thusly:

> The absence of time management is characterized by last–minute rushes to meet deadlines, meetings that are either double–booked or achieve nothing, days that seem somehow to slip unproductively by, and crises that loom unexpected from nowhere. This sort of environment leads to inordinate stress and performance degradation. Time management is about controlling the use of the most valuable (and undervalued) resource—time. Because personal time management is a management process, it must be planned, monitored, and regularly reviewed. Effective time management is the most important trait of an efficient operation.

The main point of the passage remains the same, but it isn't stated until the last sentence.

Often the main idea is implied:

> The plane landed at 4 P.M. As the door opened, the crowd burst into a long, noisy demonstration. The waiting mob surged against the police guard lines. Women were screaming. Teenagers were yelling for autographs or souvenirs. The visitor smiled and waved at his fans.

The main point of this passage isn't quite as clear as in the previous examples. However, it's obvious from the information provided that some popular person, hero, or famous personality is being welcomed enthusiastically at an airport.

When looking for the main idea on reading comprehension tests, it often helps to ask the following questions:

- ✔ Who or what is this paragraph about?
- ✔ What aspect of this subject is the author talking about?
- ✔ What is the author trying to get across about this aspect of the subject?

In addition, look for signal words in the passage. Signal words like *again, also, as well as, furthermore, moreover,* and *significantly* may call your attention to the main idea.

Sub-Points

Usually a paragraph or passage doesn't consist of only one point. The author may have several points (in addition to the main point) that he wishes to convey. Generally, these "sub-points" consist of facts, statistics, or clarifying descriptions that help the reader more clearly understand the main point.

In our example, the sub-points help to clarify the main point by providing information concerning the consequences of inefficient time management. The absence of time management leads to unproductivity, which results in a degradation of performance and an increase in stress.

Details

Many reading comprehension questions test your ability to quickly find details within a given passage. The details can be found in the sub-points. In providing details, the author may give examples to illustrate the point, or facts or statistics to support the point. The author may break down a number of major points into smaller categories to make it easier to understand. Or, the writer may compare two or more ideas, showing how they are similar or how they are different.

> For the purpose of drill, Air Force organizations are divided into elements, flights, squadrons, groups, and wings. The "rule of two" applies, i.e., an element must consist of at least two people, a flight must consist of at least two elements, and so on. Usually, an element consists of between 8 and 10 people, and a flight has 6 or 8 elements. Drill consists of certain movements by which the flight or squadron is moved in an orderly manner from one formation to another or from one place to another.

Notice how the writer uses the second, third, and fourth sentences to explain in detail how Air Force organizations are divided for the purposes of drill. These explanations are *supporting details.*

Analyzing

If the reading comprehension questions on the officer selection tests simply asked one to scan a passage and find the main point or supporting details, it would be a pretty simple test. No such luck—the services go beyond that. In order to properly answer many of the questions on the tests, you'll be required to analyze what you've read.

Analyzing is more complex than simply finding the main points, sub-points, and supporting details. In order to analyze, you'll need to be able to draw conclusions about what you've read and understand the similarities and differences of the ideas presented in the passage.

Paraphrasing

Paraphrasing means rewriting the passage in your own words. This is often useful when trying to understand a complex idea. Of course, you won't have time to rewrite every paragraph you'll see on the officer selection tests, but doing so as practice when you study for the tests can help you develop the ability to paraphrase mentally.

> Common acts of courtesy among all military personnel aid in maintaining discipline and promoting the smooth conduct of affairs in the military establishment. When courtesy falters within a unit, discipline ceases to function, and accomplishing the mission is endangered.

If we paraphrased the above passage, we might rewrite it like this: "In order to get the job done, it's important to remember that common courtesy in the military is important. Common courtesy helps to smooth things along. When it's lacking, there can be serious consequences."

Putting it in your own words can help you to understand the main idea that can, in turn, make it easier to discern information that may not be directly stated. It can also be helpful in making inferences and drawing conclusions from the information provided.

Finding Information

Sometimes a question will ask you to provide an answer that is based on the information in the passage, but is not clearly evident.

> In June 2004, the city counsel passed a resolution requiring all residents to paint their address numbers on their homes using a bright color. This was to assist firemen, police, and paramedics in finding an address during an emergency. In August, 300 residences were randomly sampled and it was found that 150 had complied with the new ordinance.

EXAMPLE

According to the above passage, what percentage of the randomly sampled residences had complied with the new ordinance?

(A) 10 percent
(B) 20 percent
(C) 50 percent
(D) 60 percent

The correct answer is (C) 50 percent. The author didn't specifically say that 50 percent had complied, but she included enough information in the passage so that you can calculate it on your own.

Drawing Implications

Sometimes you'll be required to draw conclusions or recognize logical implications based on the information provided. In answering this type of reading comprehension question, you'll need to go beyond the obvious. You'll have to look deep into what the author says to look for logical implications based on the information provided.

> One of the main reasons motorcyclists are killed in crashes is because the motorcycle itself provides virtually no protection in a crash. For example, approximately 80 percent of reported motorcycle crashes result in injury or death; the comparable figure for automobiles is about 20 percent.

EXAMPLE

Safe motorcycle riding means:

(A) always wear a helmet
(B) using premium gas
(C) selecting the most expensive motorcycle
(D) always ride with a buddy

The correct answer is (A) always wear a helmet. While the author didn't specifically state this in the passage, we can infer the correct answer because the author gives the reason for fatalities as virtually no protection. By providing a small degree of protection (a helmet), we've made a logical conclusion based on the information provided in the passage.

READING TABLES

While the AFOQT no longer has a subtest to measure reading comprehension, Air Force pilot and navigator applicants are tested on their ability to quickly and accurately find data on tables. If you're applying for a commission in the Army, Navy, Marine Corps, or Coast Guard, or if you have no interest in becoming a pilot or navigator in the Air Force, you can ignore this portion of the chapter and the table-reading practice questions that follow.

This portion of the AFOQT is actually pretty easy. All you have to do is to read the table, and find the requested information. The difficulty is that this is a "speed test." There are 40 questions and you only have 7 minutes to answer them (or at least answer as many as you can).

Take the table below, for example:

Y Value	X Value −3	−2	−1	0	+1	+2	+3
+3	19	20	23	25	26	28	30
+2	20	22	25	28	29	30	32
+1	22	25	28	31	33	34	35
0	25	26	27	28	29	30	31
−1	27	28	30	32	33	34	35
−2	28	30	31	32	33	35	36
−3	30	32	33	35	38	39	40

The values shown horizontally are the "X Values," while the values displayed vertically are the "Y Values." You are presented with the two values (example X = +1, Y = −1), and you find the number that intersects the two values. In this case, the correct answer would be 33.

Answer Sheet for Practice Questions

1 Ⓐ Ⓑ Ⓒ Ⓓ Ⓔ	14 Ⓐ Ⓑ Ⓒ Ⓓ Ⓔ	27 Ⓐ Ⓑ Ⓒ Ⓓ	40 Ⓐ Ⓑ Ⓒ Ⓓ
2 Ⓐ Ⓑ Ⓒ Ⓓ Ⓔ	15 Ⓐ Ⓑ Ⓒ Ⓓ Ⓔ	28 Ⓐ Ⓑ Ⓒ Ⓓ	41 Ⓐ Ⓑ Ⓒ Ⓓ
3 Ⓐ Ⓑ Ⓒ Ⓓ Ⓔ	16 Ⓐ Ⓑ Ⓒ Ⓓ	29 Ⓐ Ⓑ Ⓒ Ⓓ	42 Ⓐ Ⓑ Ⓒ Ⓓ Ⓔ
4 Ⓐ Ⓑ Ⓒ Ⓓ Ⓔ	17 Ⓐ Ⓑ Ⓒ Ⓓ	30 Ⓐ Ⓑ Ⓒ Ⓓ	43 Ⓐ Ⓑ Ⓒ Ⓓ Ⓔ
5 Ⓐ Ⓑ Ⓒ Ⓓ Ⓔ	18 Ⓐ Ⓑ Ⓒ Ⓓ	31 Ⓐ Ⓑ Ⓒ Ⓓ	44 Ⓐ Ⓑ Ⓒ Ⓓ Ⓔ
6 Ⓐ Ⓑ Ⓒ Ⓓ Ⓔ	19 Ⓐ Ⓑ Ⓒ Ⓓ	32 Ⓐ Ⓑ Ⓒ Ⓓ	45 Ⓐ Ⓑ Ⓒ Ⓓ Ⓔ
7 Ⓐ Ⓑ Ⓒ Ⓓ Ⓔ	20 Ⓐ Ⓑ Ⓒ Ⓓ	33 Ⓐ Ⓑ Ⓒ Ⓓ	46 Ⓐ Ⓑ Ⓒ Ⓓ Ⓔ
8 Ⓐ Ⓑ Ⓒ Ⓓ Ⓔ	21 Ⓐ Ⓑ Ⓒ Ⓓ	34 Ⓐ Ⓑ Ⓒ Ⓓ	47 Ⓐ Ⓑ Ⓒ Ⓓ Ⓔ
9 Ⓐ Ⓑ Ⓒ Ⓓ Ⓔ	22 Ⓐ Ⓑ Ⓒ Ⓓ	35 Ⓐ Ⓑ Ⓒ Ⓓ	48 Ⓐ Ⓑ Ⓒ Ⓓ Ⓔ
10 Ⓐ Ⓑ Ⓒ Ⓓ Ⓔ	23 Ⓐ Ⓑ Ⓒ Ⓓ	36 Ⓐ Ⓑ Ⓒ Ⓓ	49 Ⓐ Ⓑ Ⓒ Ⓓ Ⓔ
11 Ⓐ Ⓑ Ⓒ Ⓓ Ⓔ	24 Ⓐ Ⓑ Ⓒ Ⓓ	37 Ⓐ Ⓑ Ⓒ Ⓓ	50 Ⓐ Ⓑ Ⓒ Ⓓ Ⓔ
12 Ⓐ Ⓑ Ⓒ Ⓓ Ⓔ	25 Ⓐ Ⓑ Ⓒ Ⓓ	38 Ⓐ Ⓑ Ⓒ Ⓓ	51 Ⓐ Ⓑ Ⓒ Ⓓ Ⓔ
13 Ⓐ Ⓑ Ⓒ Ⓓ Ⓔ	26 Ⓐ Ⓑ Ⓒ Ⓓ	39 Ⓐ Ⓑ Ⓒ Ⓓ	

Practice Questions

Directions: Questions 1–15 have five possible answers. Read the paragraph and choose the answer that is the most correct, based on the information given in the passage.

1. Every four years, just after the Presidential election, the "United States Government Policy and Supporting Positions" is published. It is commonly known as the Plum Book and is alternately published by the House and Senate. The Plum Book is a listing of over 9,000 civil service leadership and support positions (filled and vacant) in the legislative and executive branches of the Federal Government that may be subject to noncompetitive appointments. These positions include agency heads and their immediate subordinates, policy executives and advisors, and aides who report to these officials. Many positions have duties that support administration policies and programs. The people holding these positions usually have a close and confidential relationship with the agency head or other key officials.

   According to the paragraph above, if the United States Senate published the Plum Book in 2004, which branch of the Federal Government would publish the book in the year 2012?

   (A) the House
   (B) the Senate
   (C) the White House
   (D) Congress
   (E) the Executive Branch

2. Performance awards may be given only to career employees, and are for performance during the previous appraisal period. The agency head or designee makes awards following a recommendation by the Performance Review Board. An executive may be awarded lump-sum payment between 5% and 20% of basic pay. Total award payments in an agency are limited to 10% of the aggregate amount of basic pay paid to career appointees as of the end of the previous fiscal year; an alternative formula is provided for small agencies.

   According to the paragraph above, employees may be rewarded

   (A) for making suggestions that increase company profits.
   (B) for participating on the Performance Review Board.
   (C) for projected future performance.
   (D) for past performance.
   (E) only to executives.

3. To have a healthy body, you must give it all the nutrients it needs to grow and develop. But how do you do that? First of all, you need to understand that there are no good or bad foods. Foods supply nutrients your body needs to grow, have energy, and stay healthy, and all foods can be part of a healthy diet. A healthy diet includes grain products, vegetables, fruits, low-fat milk products, lean meats, fish, poultry, and dry beans. Choose fewer foods that are high in salt, sugar, or saturated fat. The fats from meat, milk, and milk products are the main sources of saturated fats in most diets. Many bakery products are also sources of saturated fats. Vegetable oils supply smaller amounts of saturated fat. For example, non-fat milk, lean meat, and low-fat cheese have lower saturated fat than fatty meat, whole milk, and regular cheese. It's the total amount and types of foods you eat over several days that make up a healthy or unhealthy diet. So eat a variety of foods to get the energy, protein, vitamins, minerals, and fiber you need for good health.

   Based on the information in the paragraph above, a healthy diet includes many food products. Which of the following food products are bad for you?

   (A) vegetable oils
   (B) lean meats
   (C) dry beans
   (D) fruits
   (E) none of the above

4. LASIK is a surgical procedure intended to reduce a person's dependency on glasses or contact lenses. LASIK stands for Laser-Assisted *In Situ* Keratomileusis and is a procedure that permanently changes the shape of the cornea, the clear covering of the front of the eye, using an excimer laser. A knife, called a *microkeratome*, is used to cut a flap in the cornea. A "hinge" is left at one end of this flap. The flap is folded back revealing the stroma, the middle section of the cornea. Pulses from a computer-controlled laser vaporize a portion of the stroma and the flap is replaced.

   Which of the following statements is not supported by information in the paragraph above?

   (A) LASIK eliminates the need for glasses or contact lenses.
   (B) The LASIK procedure involves surgery.
   (C) A laser is used to change the shape of the cornea.
   (D) A *microkeratome* is a small scalpel.
   (E) The cornea is the clear covering of the front of the eye.

Questions 5–8 should be answered based on the information in the following paragraph:

The younger the child, the trickier using medicine is. Children under two years shouldn't be given any over-the-counter drug without a doctor's OK. Your pediatrician can tell you how much of a common drug, like acetaminophen (Tylenol), is safe for babies. Prescription drugs, also, can work differently in children than adults. Some barbiturates, for example, which make adults feel sluggish will make a child hyperactive. Amphetamines, which stimulate adults, can calm children. When giving any drug to a child, watch closely for side effects. If you're not happy with what's happening with your child, don't assume that everything's OK. Always be suspicious. It's better to make the extra calls to the doctor or nurse practitioner than to have a bad reaction to a drug. And before parents dole out OTC drugs, they should consider whether they're truly necessary. Americans love to medicate—perhaps too much. A study published in the October 1994 issue of the *Journal of the American Medical Association* found that more than half of all mothers surveyed had given their 3-year-olds an OTC medication in the previous month. Not every cold needs medicine. Common viruses run their course in seven to 10 days with or without medication. While some OTC medications can sometimes make children more comfortable and help them eat and rest better, others may trigger allergic reactions or changes for the worse in sleeping, eating, and behavior. Antibiotics, available by prescription, don't work at all on cold viruses.

5. A common problem in America is

(A) overmedication.
(B) parents don't heed the advice of their doctors.
(C) OTC drugs don't require a prescription.
(D) cost of prescription medication.
(E) hyperactive children.

6. When in doubt about giving a child medication, it's best to

(A) speak with a pharmacist.
(B) call the doctor or nurse practitioner.
(C) read the label closely.
(D) research the side-effects.
(E) avoid giving medications entirely.

7. Another word for *acetaminophen* would be

   (A) the common cold.
   (B) antibiotic.
   (C) Tylenol.
   (D) amphetamine.
   (E) barbiturate.

8. Which of the following statements is *not* true?

   (A) Older children are harder to medicate than younger children.
   (B) Antibiotics will not cure a cold.
   (C) Always be distrustful when giving children medication.
   (D) Drugs work differently in children than they do in adults.
   (E) OTC medicines can sometimes make children more comfortable.

Questions 9–12 should be answered based on the information in the following paragraph:

Massachusetts soils vary widely in color and in character. Broadly speaking, the uplands contain an abundance of mineral matter, while more or less organic matter is present in the lowlands. The western region is hilly and is separated by the Connecticut River Valley from a central upland plateau region which slopes to the Atlantic coast. Except on Cape Cod where there are long stretches of sandy, treeless flats, almost all of the land was originally covered with dense forests. Even after the forests were cleared or thinned, however, the soil did not yield readily to cultivation by the early farmers, and their skill and patience were taxed heavily before it became productive. The most arable soil is found in the broad Connecticut Valley in the west-central part of Massachusetts. Rich alluvial deposits are found in the fertile river valleys. On the whole, Massachusetts soils yield profitably when production is carried on under modern procedures. Even the sandy soils on Cape Cod have been made extremely fruitful when farmed by skillful agriculturists. In fact, Cape Cod and the South Shore produce the biggest cranberry crop in the world.

9. It can be inferred from this paragraph that

   (A) Massachusetts has no beaches.
   (B) farming is a hard business in Massachusetts.
   (C) the state is heavily populated with trees.
   (D) the soil of Massachusetts is the same consistency throughout the state.
   (E) Boston is the capital city of the state.

10. A good title for this paragraph might be

   (A) "Farming in Massachusetts."
   (B) "Massachusetts Geography."
   (C) "Early Farming Successes."
   (D) "Massachusetts—The Bay State."
   (E) "The Soil of Massachusetts."

11. In the second sentence of the paragraph, the word *abundance* means __________ .

(A) plentitude
(B) enjoyment
(C) distribution
(D) quantity
(E) ampleness

12. The Connecticut River Valley

(A) has the worst soil in the state.
(B) is the hilliest region in the state.
(C) divides the eastern and western regions of the state.
(D) was the first part of the state settled by early farmers.
(E) has soil that is reddish-brown in color.

Questions 13–15 should be answered based on the information in the following paragraph:

Prolific inventor Thomas Alva Edison (1847–1931) has had a profound impact on modern life. In his lifetime, the "Wizard of Menlo Park" patented 1,093 inventions, including the phonograph, the kinetograph (a motion picture camera), and the kinetoscope (a motion picture viewer). Edison managed to become not only a renowned inventor, but also a prominent manufacturer and businessman through the merchandising of his inventions.

13. A *kinetoscope* is used to

(A) take pictures.
(B) view movies.
(C) listen to music.
(D) manage business affairs.
(E) patent inventions.

14. Thomas Edison died at the age of __________ .

(A) 64
(B) 74
(C) 84
(D) 94
(E) 42

15. The word *renowned* (in the third sentence) means __________ .

(A) blind
(B) substantial
(C) brilliant
(D) impoverished
(E) famous

Directions: Questions 16–18 have four possible answers. Read the paragraph and choose the answer that best answers the question or completes the statement.

16. Leadership is an art, and leaders must work to perfect this art by developing a leadership style that capitalizes on their particular individual strengths. While an individual may exhibit a personalized leadership style, leaders must be flexible because methods, ideas, or techniques effective in one situation may not be effective in another.

    This paragraph best supports the idea that

    (A) leaders should be amenable to different techniques.
    (B) good leaders must be experienced.
    (C) unusual leadership styles are ineffective.
    (D) leaders are born, not made.

17. The Supreme Court consists of the Chief Justice of the United States and such number of Associate Justices as may be fixed by Congress. The number of Associate Justices is currently fixed at eight (28 U. S. C. §1). Power to nominate the Justices is vested in the President of the United States, and appointments are made with the advice and consent of the Senate.

    The Supreme Court

    (A) consists of justices nominated by Congress.
    (B) has nine justices.
    (C) was established by Article 2 of the Constitution.
    (D) rotates the duty of Chief Justice.

Questions 18–20 should be answered based on the information in the following paragraph:

Each year, alcohol-related crashes in the United States cost about $51 billion. Male drivers involved in fatal motor vehicle crashes are almost twice as likely as female drivers to be intoxicated with a blood alcohol concentration (BAC) of 0.08% or greater. A BAC of 0.08% is equal to or greater than the legal limit in most states. At all levels of blood alcohol concentration, the risk of being involved in a crash is greater for young people than for older people. In 2003, 25% of drivers ages 15 to 20 who died in motor vehicle crashes had been drinking alcohol. Young men ages 18 to 20 (under the legal drinking age) reported driving while impaired almost as frequently as men ages 21 to 34.

18. Most states have a BAC limit of __________ .

    (A) .08% or less
    (B) .08% or greater
    (C) .08%
    (D) 0.01%

19. Most drunk drivers involved in fatal crashes are __________ .

(A) underaged drinkers
(B) senior citizens
(C) women
(D) men

20. Underaged drinkers are

(A) more likely to drive drunk than those 21 to 34 years old.
(B) less likely to drive drunk than those 21 to 34 years old.
(C) just as likely to drive drunk as those who are 21 to 34 years old.
(D) not subject to DWI laws.

Directions: Questions 21–27 have four possible answers. Each question is composed of a sentence in which one word is omitted. Choose the answer that contains the word that would best complete the sentence.

21. Motivation is not something that happens __________; it is part of the total workplace environment and takes time.

(A) endlessly
(B) purposely
(C) overnight
(D) eventually

22. The aroma of the meal was so __________, I couldn't keep my mouth from watering.

(A) enticing
(B) unpalatable
(C) intemperate
(D) malignant

23. Outside the Washington Beltway—working in state government, city halls, and local offices —a __________ generation of leaders is taking shape.

(A) kinetic
(B) lonely
(C) fresh
(D) proclivity

24. The grass grew so __________ that Ron was forced to cut it twice a week.

(A) tediously
(B) reluctantly
(C) deliberately
(D) expeditiously

25. Because the project required so many __________ steps, the deadline was extended for two weeks.

    (A) intricate
    (B) simple
    (C) future
    (D) ingenious

26. The Japanese, always pressed for room on their island empire, have long been masters at __________ space.

    (A) manufacturing
    (B) utilizing
    (C) monopolizing
    (D) selling

27. Edwin Hubble was the first to study the relationship between the distances to galaxies and the __________ at which they are moving away from us.

    (A) method
    (B) velocity
    (C) semblance
    (D) flagrant

Directions: Questions 28–32 have four possible answers. Each question is composed of a sentence in which two words are missing. Choose the answer that contains the words that would best complete the sentence.

28. The man was too ________ to fit ________ in the airline seat.

    (A) bald .... correctly
    (B) fat .... neatly
    (C) tall .... comfortably
    (D) relaxed .... fully

29. When _______ a wheat crop, the farmer must correctly estimate the profit from the anticipated _______.

    (A) watering .... tax
    (B) watering .... yield
    (C) planning .... tax
    (D) planning .... yield

30. She was _______ of her boss manipulating her into performing tasks that were not on the _______ description.

    (A) upset .... narrative
    (B) tired .... job
    (C) angry .... job
    (D) cross .... narrative

31. The _______ of a good teacher is her ability to communicate _______ with her students.

    (A) hallmark .... effectively
    (B) hallmark .... desperately
    (C) complications .... effectively
    (D) complications .... desperately

32. Fishing in the large pond _______ his house was one of Bob's favorite _______.

    (A) on .... pursuits
    (B) in .... scenes
    (C) behind .... pastimes
    (D) under .... stories

Directions: Questions 33–40 have four possible answers. Within the passage there is one word that is incorrectly used. First, determine the word in the passage that is not used correctly, then select the answer that contains the word which, if used, would best convey the intended message.

33. The Falkland Islands, located about 300 miles off the southern tip of Argentina, were a British possession for 150 years when they was invaded by Argentine forces on April 2, 1982. The previous year, the 1,800 Falkland Islanders, mostly English-speaking sheep farmers, had voted in a referendum to remain British.

    (A) were
    (B) prior
    (C) stay
    (D) property

34. On April 8, 1974, Hank Aaron of the Atlanta Braves hit his 715th career home run, surpassing Babe Ruth's legendary record. However, as an African-American player who had communicated death threats during his pursuit of one of baseball's most distinguished records, the achievement was bittersweet.

    (A) advancement
    (B) famous
    (C) definite
    (D) received

35. Spiro Agnew, President Richard M. Nixon's first co-president, was one of the nation's most outspoken critics of the antiwar and counterculture movements of the late 1960s and early 1970s.

    (A) policy
    (B) reserve
    (C) vice
    (D) time

36. This year, instead of giving your mother something she shouldn't need for Mother's Day, you should give her something she can really use.

    (A) really
    (B) besides
    (C) regardless
    (D) doesn't

37. Once you have found the home of your choice, you may think that your shopping days are over. Actually, only the last phase has been completed. Next comes finding a mortgage and payment terms that fit your budget. Where you shop and what you look for are important.

    (A) first
    (B) when
    (C) receipts
    (D) house

38. The professional is an expert with specialized knowledge and skill in a significant field of human endeavor. Only by abbreviated education and experience is this expertise acquired. It is the basis of objective standards of professional competence for separating the profession from laymen and measuring the relative competence of its members.

    (A) subjective
    (B) prolonged
    (C) expertise
    (D) comparative

39. The U.S. Constitution establishes the basic principle of civilian control of the Armed Forces. As Commander-in-Chief (CINC), the President has the final word of suggestive authority; however, as head of the executive branch, he is subject to the "checks and balances" system of the legislative and judicial branches.

    (A) court
    (B) makes
    (C) command
    (D) procedure

40. It is the universal custom to display flags only from sunrise to sunset on buildings and stationary flagstaffs in the open. However, when a patriotic effect is desired, the flag may be furled 24 hours a day if properly illuminated during the hours of darkness.

    (A) holiday
    (B) makeshift
    (C) displayed
    (D) nighttime

41. Simple things like saying "please" and "thank you" help the organization run more smoothly because people respond more enthusiastically when asked in a direct manner to do something. They also appreciate knowing their efforts are recognized when told "thank you."

    (A) courteous
    (B) allow
    (C) directive
    (D) observing

Directions: Questions 42–47 each have five possible answers. You must find the entry that occurs as the intersection of the row and the column corresponding to the X value and Y value given.

	X Value						
Y Value	**–3**	**–2**	**–1**	**0**	**+1**	**+2**	**+3**
+3	19	20	23	25	26	28	30
+2	20	22	25	28	29	30	32
+1	22	25	28	31	33	34	35
0	25	26	27	28	29	30	31
–1	27	28	30	32	33	34	35
–2	28	30	31	32	33	35	36
–3	30	32	33	35	38	39	40

42. X = –1, Y = –1

    (A) 27
    (B) 28
    (C) 29
    (D) 30
    (E) 31

43. X = +3, Y = 0

    (A) 31
    (B) 32
    (C) 33
    (D) 34
    (E) 35

44. X = –2, Y = +2
   (A) 28
   (B) 29
   (C) 22
   (D) 23
   (E) 24

	X Value					
Y Value	**40**	**50**	**60**	**70**	**80**	**90**
40	$2,173.40	$1,492.92	$72.96	$520.39	$20.33	$753.92
50	$7,777.20	$432.96	$82.21	$327.80	$992.37	$67.32
60	$429.44	$4,932.30	$881.73	$223.79	$8,423.40	$7.40
70	$6,127.01	$783.99	$103.93	$72.44	$832.40	$3,042.31
80	$1.97	$732.44	$2.07	$44.90	$1,073.40	$223.80
90	$423.39	$77.32	$99.01	$8,420.00	$629.07	$3.72

45. X = 80, Y = 60
   (A) $103.93
   (B) $8,423.40
   (C) $992.37
   (D) $7.40
   (E) $881.73

46. X = 60, Y = 90
   (A) $881.73
   (B) $8,420.00
   (C) $992.37
   (D) $1.97
   (E) $99.01

47. X = 50, Y = 70
   (A) $732.44
   (B) $783.99
   (C) $881.73
   (D) $327.80
   (E) $72.44

Directions: Questions 48–51 each have five possible answers. Use the "Hours to Zero BAC for Men" and the "Hours to Zero BAC for Women" charts below to answer the questions.

Hours to Zero BAC for Men

Number of Drinks	100	120	140	160	180	200	220	240
15	**35**	**29**	**24**	**22**	**19**	**17**	**16**	**14**
14	32	27	23	20	17.5	16	15	13
13	30	25	21	19	16	15	14	12
12	28	23	20	17	15	13.5	13	11
11	25	21	18	16	14	12	12	10
10	23	19	16	14	12.5	11	11	9.5
9	21.5	18	15	13.5	11.5	10.5	10	9
8	19	16	13.5	12	10	9	9	8
7	17	14	12	10.5	9	8	8	7
6	14	12	10	9	8	7	6.5	5
5	12	10	8.5	7.5	6.5	5	5.5	5
4	9.5	8	7	6	5.5	5	4.5	4
3	7	6	5	4.5	4	3.5	3.5	3
2	3	4	3.5	3	3	2.5	2	2
1	2.5	2	2	2	1.5	1	1	1

Weight in Pounds

Hours to Zero BAC for Women

Number of Drinks	100	120	140	160	180	200	220	240
15	**42**	**35**	**30**	**26**	**23**	**21**	**19**	**17**
14	39	32	28	24.5	22	19	17.5	16
13	37	30	26	23	20	18	16	15
12	34	28	24	21	19	16.5	15	13.5
11	31	25	22	19	17	15	14	12
10	28	23	20	17.5	16	14	12.5	11
9	26	21.5	18.5	16	14.5	13	11.5	10.5
8	23	19	16.5	14.5	13	11.5	10.5	9.5
7	20	17	14.5	12.5	11.5	10	9	8
6	17.5	14	12.5	11	9.5	8.5	7.5	7
5	14.5	12	10.5	9	8	7	6.5	6
4	12	9.5	8.5	7	7	5.5	5	4.5
3	9	7	6.5	5.5	5	4.5	4	3.5
2	6	3	4	3.5	3	3	2.5	1.5
1	3	2.5	2	2	1.5	1.5	1.5	1

Weight in Pounds

48. A 200–pound man who consumes six drinks would have to wait how many hours before his blood alcohol content returned to zero?

(A) 5 hours
(B) 6 hours
(C) 7 hours
(D) 8 hours
(E) 9 hours

49. A 160–pound woman who consumes four drinks would have to wait how many hours before her blood alcohol content returned to zero?

(A) 7 hours
(B) 3 hours
(C) 8 hours
(D) 20 hours
(E) 12.5 hours

50. If it requires 19 hours for a 120–pound man to achieve a blood alcohol content level of zero, how many drinks has the man had?

(A) 15
(B) 12
(C) 6
(D) 10
(E) 7

51. A woman has 11 drinks and it takes her 15 hours to achieve a blood alcohol content level of zero. How much does the woman weigh?

(A) 180 pounds
(B) 200 pounds
(C) 120 pounds
(D) 140 pounds
(E) 160 pounds

Answer Key

1. B	11. A	21. C	31. A	41. A	51. B
2. D	12. C	22. A	32. C	42. D	
3. E	13. B	23. C	33. A	43. A	
4. A	14. C	24. D	34. D	44. C	
5. A	15. E	25. A	35. C	45. B	
6. B	16. A	26. B	36. D	46. E	
7. C	17. B	27. B	37. A	47. B	
8. A	18. A	28. C	38. B	48. C	
9. B	19. D	29. D	39. C	49. A	
10. E	20. B	30. B	40. C	50. D	

Answer Explanations

1. **(B) the Senate.** The Plum Book is published every four years, alternating between the House and the Senate. If the Senate published the book in 2004, the House would publish it in 2008, and it would again be the Senate's turn in 2012.
2. **(D) for past performance.** The first sentence states that performance awards are for performance during the previous appraisal period.
3. **(E) none of the above.** The passage specifically states that there are no good or bad foods. A healthy diet is made up of the total amount and types of foods eaten over several days.
4. **(A) LASIK eliminates the need for glasses or contact lenses.** This statement is not supported by the information in the passage. The first sentence in the paragraph indicates that the procedure *reduces* the dependency on glass or contacts, but does not state that the dependency is totally eliminated.
5. **(A) over-medication.** The eleventh sentence in the passage alludes that Americans probably medicate too much.
6. **(B) call the doctor or nurse practitioner.** The passage states that it's better to make the extra calls than to have a bad reaction to a drug.
7. **(C) Tylenol.** The word is defined in the third sentence.
8. **(A) older children are harder to medicate than younger children.** The first sentence states that it is trickier medicating a younger child than an older one.
9. **(B) farming is a hard business in Massachusetts.** The last portion of the passage discusses the need for modern farming techniques and skilled farmers in order to make the soil productive.
10. **(E) "The Soil of Massachusetts."** The primary theme of the passage is the soil characteristics of the state.
11. **(A) plentitude.** The sentence states that there is a lot of mineral matter in the uplands of the state.
12. **(C) divides the eastern and western region of the state.** This is discussed in the third sentence of the paragraph.
13. **(B) view movies.** This is explained in the second sentence of the passage.
14. **(C) 84.** Thomas Edison was born in 1847 and died in 1931.
15. **(E) famous.** *Renowned* means "well-known."

16. **(A) leaders should be amenable to different techniques.** The primary theme of the passage is that leadership is an art, and leaders must be flexible enough to use different techniques in different situations.
17. **(B) has nine justices.** The court consists of a Chief Justice and Associate Justices, currently set by law at eight.
18. **(A) .08% or less.** The passage states that a person with a BAC of .08% exceeds the legal limit in most states, meaning that the legal limit in most states is set at .08% or less.
19. **(D) men.** While young drivers are involved in more crashes than older people, the passage states that men are more likely to be involved in *fatal crashes* than women.
20. **(B) less likely to drive drunk than those 21 to 34 years old.** The last sentence states that under-aged drinkers drive intoxicated *almost* as much as those 21 to 34 years old.
21. **(C) overnight.** The sentence describes the fact that motivation is not something that happens quickly.
22. **(A) enticing.** The word *enticing* means "arousing," and best completes the meaning of the sentence.
23. **(C) fresh.** The word *fresh* in this context means "new," which best completes the meaning of the sentence.
24. **(D) expeditiously**. The word *expeditiously* means "quickly," which best completes the meaning of the sentence.
25. **(A) intricate.** The word *intricate* means "complicated or exacting," which best completes the meaning of the sentence.
26. **(B) utilizing.** The word *utilizing* means "making use of," which best completes the meaning of the sentence.
27. **(B) velocity.** The word *velocity* means "speed," which best completes the meaning of the sentence.
28. **(C) tall . . . comfortably.** This is the only two–word combination which, when applied to the sentence, correctly conveys the intended meaning.
29. **(D) planning . . . yield.** This is the only two–word combination which, when applied to the sentence, correctly conveys the intended meaning.
30. **(B) tired . . . job.** The other word combinations, if used, would result in a sentence which is not grammatically correct.
31. **(A) hallmark . . . effectively**. This is the only two–word combination, which, when applied to the sentence, correctly conveys the intended meaning.
32. **(C) behind . . . pastimes.** This is the only two–word combination, which, when applied to the sentence, correctly conveys the intended meaning.
33. **(A) were.** The sentence "…when they ***was*** invaded by Argentine forces…" is grammatically incorrect.
34. **(D) received.** Hank Aaron didn't make death threats, but he received several during his career.
35. **(C) vice.** Agnew was the "vice president," not the "co-president."
36. **(D) doesn't.** One gives someone something they can use, not something they don't need.
37. **(A) first.** Finding the home is the first phase of the process, not the last.
38. **(B) prolonged.** Extensive education and experience are required in order to become a professional.

39. **(C) command.** The president has the final word of command authority as CINC.
40. **(C) displayed.** The word "furled" is incorrectly used in the statement.
41. **(A) courteous.** The word "direct" is incorrectly used in the sentence.
42. **(D) 30.**

Y Value	X Value −3	−2	−1	0	+1	+2	+3
+3	19	20	23	25	26	28	30
+2	20	22	25	28	29	30	32
+1	22	25	28	31	33	34	35
0	25	26	27	28	29	30	31
−1	27	28	**30**	32	33	34	35
−2	28	30	31	32	33	35	36
−3	30	32	33	35	38	39	40

43. **(A) 31.**

Y Value	X Value −3	−2	−1	0	+1	+2	+3
+3	19	20	23	25	26	28	30
+2	20	22	25	28	29	30	32
+1	22	25	28	31	33	34	35
0	25	26	27	28	29	30	**31**
−1	27	28	30	32	33	34	35
−2	28	30	31	32	33	35	36
−3	30	32	33	35	38	39	40

44. **(C) 22.**

Y Value	X Value −3	−2	−1	0	+1	+2	+3
+3	19	20	23	25	26	28	30
+2	20	**22**	25	28	29	30	32
+1	22	25	28	31	33	34	35
0	25	26	27	28	29	30	31
−1	27	28	30	32	33	34	35
−2	28	30	31	32	33	35	36
−3	30	32	33	35	38	39	40

45. **(B) $8,423.40.**

Y Value	X Value					
	40	50	60	70	80	90
40	$2,173.40	$1,492.92	$72.96	$520.39	$20.33	$753.92
50	$7,777.20	$432.96	$82.21	$327.80	$992.37	$67.32
60	$429.44	$4,932.30	$881.73	$223.79	**$8,423.40**	$7.40
70	$6,127.01	$783.99	$103.93	$72.44	$832.40	$3,042.31
80	$1.97	$732.44	$2.07	$44.90	$1,073.40	$223.80
90	$423.39	$77.32	$99.01	$8,420.00	$629.07	$3.72

46. **(E) $99.01.**

Y Value	X Value					
	40	50	60	70	80	90
40	$2,173.40	$1,492.92	$72.96	$520.39	$20.33	$753.92
50	$7,777.20	$432.96	$82.21	$327.80	$992.37	$67.32
60	$429.44	$4,932.30	$881.73	$223.79	$8,423.40	$7.40
70	$6,127.01	$783.99	$103.93	$72.44	$832.40	$3,042.31
80	$1.97	$732.44	$2.07	$44.90	$1,073.40	$223.80
90	$423.39	$77.32	**$99.01**	$8,420.00	$629.07	$3.72

47. **(B) $783.99.**

Y Value	X Value					
	40	50	60	70	80	90
40	$2,173.40	$1,492.92	$72.96	$520.39	$20.33	$753.92
50	$7,777.20	$432.96	$82.21	$327.80	$992.37	$67.32
60	$429.44	$4,932.30	$881.73	$223.79	$8,423.40	$7.40
70	$6,127.01	**$783.99**	$103.93	$72.44	$832.40	$3,042.31
80	$1.97	$732.44	$2.07	$44.90	$1,073.40	$223.80
90	$423.39	$77.32	$99.01	$8,420.00	$629.07	$3.72

48. **(C) 7 hours.** On the BAC chart for men, the number *6* on the left side of the chart and the number *200* on the bottom of the chart intersect at the number *7*.
49. **(A) 7 hours.** On the BAC chart for women, the number *4* on the left side of the chart and the number *160* on the bottom of the chart, intersect on the number *7*.
50. **(D) 10 drinks.** On the bottom of the chart for men, locate *120*. Follow that column up until you find the number *19*. The number intersects on the row (left side of the chart) for *10*.
51. **(B) 200 pounds.** Locate the row that corresponds to *11* on the left side of the chart for women. Next, follow the row over to the column that contains the number *15*. This intersects the column for *200* (bottom of the chart).

Mathematics Knowledge

CHAPTER 7

Do not worry about your problems with mathematics. I assure you mine are far greater.

—Albert Einstein

If you want to score well on OTS and OCS/OCC examinations, you need to have a solid grasp of basic mathematics. You don't need to be a mathematical physicist—the military doesn't have a great need for those (actually, there is a need, but that's a totally separate commissioning program). You should know basic high-school and junior college level mathematics, including fractions, decimals, and percents, as well as basic algebra and geometry.

The ASTB and the AFOQT are the only officer candidate tests that directly ask mathematical knowledge-type questions. However, applicants for all services will use basic math skills to solve arithmetic reasoning (word problem) questions that are contained on all the tests (see Chapter 8).

If you're applying for OTS, OCC, or OCS, you've presumably graduated (or are close to graduating) from college, so our math review here will be very basic. If you're weak in math, the practice questions should help you determine those areas you need to concentrate more study time on, and then it's time to dig out those old college math textbooks (or visit the library) to brush up on your basics.

BASIC MATH REVIEW

Basic Terms

Math has its own vocabulary. For example, a mathematical *operation* is the process of combining two or more whole numbers. A *whole number* is a number such as 1, 2, 3, or 4. A *fraction*, on the other hand, is a portion of a whole number, such as $\frac{3}{4}$, $\frac{1}{2}$, or $\frac{1}{3}$. A whole number combined with a fraction, such as $3\frac{3}{4}$, is called a *mixed number*. In math, there are two types of operations: addition and multiplication. Subtraction and division are called *inverse operations*. When we perform addition, the answer is called the *sum*. When we subtract, the answer is the *remainder*. When we multiply in mathematics, the answer is called the *product*. Conversely, when we divide, the answer is the *quotient*.

EXAMPLE

Which of the following problems would result in a product of 24?

(A) 12 + 12
(B) 48 ÷ 2
(C) 12 × 2
(D) 26 − 2

The correct answer would be (C), because a *product* is a result of multiplication.

A *prime number* is a whole number that can be divided evenly by itself and by 1, but cannot be divided evenly by any other whole number. Examples of prime numbers are 2, 3, 5, 7, 11, and 13. A *composite number*, conversely, is a whole number that can be divided evenly by itself and by 1, and also by at least one other whole number. Examples of composite numbers are 4, 6, 8, 10, 15, and 27.

A *numerator* is the number above the divisor line of a fraction. For example, "3" is the numerator of the fraction $\frac{3}{4}$. A *denominator* is the number below the divisor line in a fraction. For example, "4" is the denominator in the fraction $\frac{3}{4}$.

Factors are numbers that can be multiplied to result in a whole number. For example, the factors of the number 6 are 2 and 3, because $2 \times 3 = 6$.

Exponents are an easier way to express repeated factors in multiplication. While 3×3 equals 9, the answer can also be written as 3^2. The small "2" is called an *exponent.* $3 \times 3 \times 3$ can be expressed as 3^3. When the exponent is a "2," we often say that the number is *squared.* 3^2 can be referred to as "3 squared." When the exponent is a "3," we say that the number is *cubed.* 3^3 is "3 cubed." Another way to refer to exponents is by the term *power.* 3^2 is "3 raised to the second power," or "3 to the second power." 3^3 is "3 raised to the third power," or "3 to the third power."

The *reciprocal* of a number is a number that, when multiplied by the original number, yields a product of 1. For example, the reciprocal of the number 3 is $\frac{1}{3}$, because $3 \times \frac{1}{3} = 1$. The easiest way to find the reciprocal of a number is to divide 1 by that number. $1 \div 2$ is $\frac{1}{2}$, so the reciprocal of 2 is $\frac{1}{2}$. $1 \div \frac{1}{2} = 2$, so the reciprocal of $\frac{1}{2}$ is 2.

Order of Operations

In math, there is a set order that problems are worked or solved in order to arrive at the correct answer. Look at the following example:

$$5 \times 2 + 3 =$$

If we multiply 5×2 (10), then add 3, we arrive at the answer 13. However, if we perform the addition first, $2 + 3$ (5), then multiply it by 5, we arrive at an entirely different answer (25). So, which is correct?

The proper order to solve a mathematical problem is:

1. Do any work contained in parentheses first.
2. Next, perform all multiplications and divisions (from left to right) in the problem.
3. Finally, do additions and subtractions.

If we take the problem $(4 \times 3) \times 3 - 6 \times (9 \div 3) =$ we would solve it thusly:

$$(12) \times 3 - 6 \times (3) =$$

$$36 - 18 = 18$$

Fractions

A fraction is a part of a whole number. Visualize a cake that has been cut into five equal pieces. Each piece represents $\frac{1}{5}$ of the total cake. If you ate two pieces, you would have consumed $\frac{2}{5}$ of the cake. As we mentioned before, the number written on top of the divisor line is called the *numerator*, and the number written below the divisor line is called the *denominator*.

We can also think of fractions as the result of multiplication. For example, the fraction $\frac{3}{5}$ is the same as $3 \times \frac{1}{5}$. Conversely, a fraction also represents a product of division. $\frac{3}{5}$ is the same as $3 \div 5$. Finally, a fraction can be thought of as a ratio, which is a comparison of two quantities. If I invested one dollar in a lottery ticket, and you invested two dollars, the ratio of my investment compared to yours would be 1:2, or, if expressed as a fraction, $\frac{1}{2}$ (I invested one-half of what you invested).

Converting and Simplifying Fractions

When we perform mathematical operations on fractions, we often wind up with large fractions that can be *simplified.* This is also known as reducing a fraction to its lowest terms. When we simplify a fraction, we convert the fraction such that the numerator and denominator can't be divided by the same whole number (other than the number 1). Take, for example, the fraction $\frac{3}{9}$. Both the "3" and the "9" can be evenly divided by a whole number (3). To simplify the fraction, we divide each part by that number (3), and we arrive at the simplified fraction of $\frac{1}{3}$.

Fractions that have a numerator that is larger than the denominator are called *improper fractions.* For example, $\frac{9}{4}$ is an improper fraction. To convert an improper fraction to proper terms, we change it to a whole number (if possible), or a mixed number (which is a whole number and a fraction). In order to do so, simply divide the numerator by the denominator. In the above example, if we divided 9 by 4, the quotient would be "2", with $\frac{1}{4}$ left over. Therefore, the proper mixed number would be $2\frac{1}{4}$.

Conversely, we can convert the mixed number back into an improper fraction (this is necessary if we wish to multiply or divide the mixed number—we'll discuss that a little later). First, multiply the whole number by the denominator. Next, add the result to the numerator. So, $2 \times 4 = 8$. Add 8 to the 1 in the numerator, and the sum is 9, so the fraction converts to $\frac{9}{4}$.

Adding and Subtracting Fractions

In order to add and subtract fractions, they must have the same denominator. If that's the case, the process is simple. You simply add or subtract the numerators: $\frac{1}{5} + \frac{3}{5} = \frac{4}{5}$, and $\frac{3}{7} - \frac{1}{7} = \frac{2}{7}$.

If the fractions you wish to add or subtract have different denominators, you must convert the fraction(s) so that they still have the same value, but all share the same denominator (this is called finding the *common denominator*). Depending on the fractions involved, this process can be easy or it can be difficult.

Take, for example, the fraction $\frac{3}{5}$. This fraction could also be expressed as $\frac{6}{10}$, or $\frac{12}{20}$, or $\frac{24}{40}$. All of these fractions have the same value as $\frac{3}{5}$, so $\frac{3}{5}$ can be converted to any of these fractions and still retain the same value.

In the problem $\frac{3}{5} + \frac{4}{15} = ?$, we can easily convert the fractions so that they share the same common denominator, because one of the denominators (15) can be evenly divided by the other denominator (5). $15 \div 5 = 3$. Multiply the denominator and the numerator of the fraction $\frac{3}{5}$ by 3, and we get $\frac{9}{15}$. Now, the denominators in both of our fractions are the same, and they can be added.

$$\frac{9}{15} + \frac{4}{15} = \frac{13}{15}.$$

You can use this method any time one denominator will divide evenly into the other denominator. But what if that's not the case? In the problem $\frac{1}{2} + \frac{2}{3} = ?$, neither denominator will divide evenly into the other. In simple problems like this, we can arrive at a common denominator by multiplying both denominators together. $2 \times 3 = 6$, so a common denominator for these fractions would be "6." Now, to convert the fractions, divide the number 6 by the denominator of the fraction, then multiply the numerator by the result:

For the fraction $\frac{1}{2}$, $6 \div 2 = 3$: multiply that by the numerator (1), and we arrive at the equivalent fraction of $\frac{3}{6}$.

For the fraction $\frac{2}{3}$, $6 \div 3 = 2$: multiply that by the numerator (2) and we arrive at the equivalent fraction of $\frac{4}{6}$. We can now add the fractions together:

$$\frac{3}{6} + \frac{4}{6} = \frac{7}{6}.$$

This fraction can then be *simplified* to $1\frac{1}{6}$.

Unfortunately, this method is rather cumbersome if you are adding more than two fractions together, because you can arrive at a very large common denominator. In the problem, $\frac{5}{9} + \frac{2}{3} + \frac{17}{18} = ?$, if we multiplied the denominators together we would arrive at a common denominator of 486. The problem would then convert to $\frac{270}{486} + \frac{324}{486} + \frac{459}{486} = \frac{1053}{486}$. Ouch! There's got to be an easier way, right?

There is! A simple way to find the common denominator when adding or subtracting multiple fractions is to take the largest denominator, then multiply it by whole numbers, starting with 1, 2, 3, 4, etc., until you find a number that the other denominators will divide into evenly.

In the problem $\frac{5}{9} + \frac{2}{3} + \frac{17}{18} = ?$, we select the largest denominator (18) and begin multiplying it by whole numbers. We find that $2 \times 18 = 36$, and the other two denominators (9 and 3) will both divide evenly into that number. So, our common denominator is 36. Let's convert the fractions:

$\frac{5}{9}$: $36 \div 9 = 4$. $4 \times 5 = 20$. So, $\frac{5}{9}$ converts to $\frac{20}{36}$.

$\frac{2}{3}$: $36 \div 3 = 12$. $2 \times 12 = 24$. $\frac{2}{3}$ converts to $\frac{24}{36}$.

$\frac{17}{18}$: $36 \div 18 = 2$. $2 \times 17 = 34$. $\frac{17}{18}$ converts to $\frac{34}{36}$.

Our problem converts to $\frac{20}{36} + \frac{24}{36} + \frac{34}{36} = \frac{78}{36}$. We can simplify this to $2\frac{6}{36}$, and further simplify that to $2\frac{1}{6}$.

Mixed numbers can be added and subtracted either by converting the mixed numbers to improper fractions, then adding or subtracting the fractions normally, or by adding or subtracting the fractions and adding or subtracting the whole numbers separately (Note: The latter doesn't work when multiplying or dividing fractions; we'll talk about this shortly).

$2\frac{1}{8} + 4\frac{3}{8} = (2 + 4) + (\frac{1}{8} + \frac{3}{8}) = 6\frac{4}{8}$. The $\frac{4}{8}$ can be simplified to $\frac{1}{2}$, resulting in the answer of $6\frac{1}{2}$.

Alternatively, we can solve it this way: $2\frac{1}{8} + 4\frac{3}{8} = \frac{17}{8} + \frac{35}{8} = \frac{52}{8}$. Converting the $\frac{52}{8}$ to a mixed number gives us $6\frac{2}{8}$ or $6\frac{1}{2}$.

Multiplying Fractions

Multiplying fractions is simple: we simply multiply the numerators by one another, and then we multiply the denominators by one another.

$\frac{3}{4} \times \frac{5}{7} \times \frac{1}{2} = \frac{15}{56}$. Since there are no whole numbers that will divide into both 15 and 56 equally, this is as far as the fraction can be reduced.

When multiplying a mixed number, first change the mixed number into an improper fraction, and then perform the multiplication:

$$2\frac{1}{4} \times \frac{1}{3} = \frac{9}{4} \times \frac{1}{3}$$

$$\frac{9}{4} \times \frac{1}{3} = \frac{9}{12}$$

This fraction can be simplified to $\frac{3}{4}$.

Dividing Fractions

We divide fractions using the same procedures as multiplying fractions except before we perform the operation, we must invert the second term (the fraction after the division sign).

$\frac{1}{2} \div \frac{1}{3}$ is the same as $\frac{1}{2} \times \frac{3}{1}$.

$\frac{1}{2} \times \frac{3}{1} = \frac{3}{2}$, which can be simplified to $1\frac{1}{2}$.

Decimals

A decimal is a special kind of fraction. The denominators in a decimal fraction are always the power of ten. The first place to the right of the decimal is 10^1 or "10." The second place is 10^2 or "100," etc.:

$0.5 = \frac{5}{10}$

$0.05 = \frac{5}{100}$

$0.005 = \frac{5}{1{,}000}$

$0.0005 = \frac{5}{10{,}000}$

Converting Decimals to Fractions

Remember, every decimal is a fraction in which the denominator is a power of 10. So 0.7 would convert to $\frac{7}{10}$. 3.05 would covert to $3\frac{5}{100}$, etc.

Converting Fractions to Decimals

This is a little more complicated. To convert a fraction to a decimal you divide the numerator by the denominator. For example, to covert $\frac{1}{5}$ to a decimal, you would divide 1 by 5 (1 ÷ 5). Below are some examples of common fractions converted to decimals:

$\frac{1}{2} = .50$

$\frac{1}{4} = .25$

$\frac{1}{5} = .20$

$\frac{4}{5} = .80$

$\frac{1}{3} = .33333333$ (and on)

$\frac{3}{4} = .75$

$\frac{3}{5} = .60$

$\frac{1}{8} = .125$

Adding and Subtracting Decimals

To add or subtract decimals, line up the numbers so that the decimal points are directly under and on top of one another, then simply add or subtract as normal. For example, 1.5 + .008 + 3.06 would line up as follows:

$$\begin{array}{r} 1.5 \\ .008 \\ \underline{3.06} \\ 4.568 \end{array}$$

If it helps, you can add zeros to keep the decimals lined up:

$$\begin{array}{r} 1.500 \\ 0.008 \\ \underline{3.060} \\ 4.568 \end{array}$$

Multiplying Decimals

You multiply a decimal just as if it were a whole number, except you must then determine where to place the decimal point in your answer. First count the number of decimal places to the right of the decimal point for each number. Next, add those numbers together. For example, in the problem $.25 \times .655$, there are two decimals places in the first number to the right of the decimal point, and three decimal places in the second number, so the sum of decimal places would be five.

Now, multiply the numbers as if they were whole numbers:

$$25 \times 655 = 16{,}375.$$

Next, in order to correctly place the decimal, count over five spaces from the right and place the decimal there. In this case, our answer would be .16375.

One more example:

$$40 \times 1.5.$$

In this case, the sum of our decimal places is one. Multiply $40 \times 15 = 600$ and move the decimal one place to the right. Our answer is 60.

Dividing Decimals

The method we use to divide decimals depends on whether we are dividing a decimal number by a whole number or if we are dividing a decimal number by another decimal number.

DIVIDING A DECIMAL BY A WHOLE NUMBER

The first step is to convert the decimal to a whole number by moving the decimal place to the right, while taking note of how many places you move it. For example, in the problem $2.6 \div 13$, convert 2.6 to 26 by moving the decimal one space to the right. Next, perform the division as if both were whole numbers ($26 \div 13 = 2$). Finally, remembering that we moved the decimal one place to the right at the beginning of the operation, we must now place the decimal one place to the left in our result. So, the answer "2" becomes ".2."

DIVIDING A DECIMAL BY ANOTHER DECIMAL

In this type of problem, first move the decimal in the divisor (the number that is being divided into the other number) enough places to the right to make it a whole number, making note of how many places you moved the decimal. Then, move the decimal in the dividend (the number being divided into) the same number of places. For example, .25 ÷ .05 becomes 25 ÷ 5. In this problem, there are no further steps to perform. The answer is 5.

However, what if the divisor is longer than the dividend, such as in the problem, 2.5 ÷ .005? In this case, move the decimal in the divisor the appropriate number of places to make it a whole number (in this case, three places), then move the decimal in the dividend the same number of places, adding zeroes as necessary. So, 2.5 ÷ .005 becomes 2,500 ÷ 5.

If the dividend is longer than the divisor, such as in the problem 0.155 ÷ 0.5, then you move the decimal in the divisor the number of places necessary to convert it to a whole number, and move the decimal in the dividend the same number of places. So, 0.155 ÷ 0.5 becomes 1.55 ÷ 5, and can be divided using the rules above for dividing decimals by whole numbers.

Percentages

A percent is a decimal fraction based on one–hundredths. For example, 5% is actually $\frac{5}{100}$ or .05 (all three numbers represent the same thing). To convert a percentage to a decimal, simply move the decimal point two places to the left of the whole percentage number. 50% becomes 0.5, 25% becomes .25, etc. To convert a percentage to a fraction, make the percent number the numerator, and 100 the denominator. 25% becomes $\frac{25}{100}$, 75% becomes $\frac{75}{100}$, and so on.

To convert a decimal to a percentage, move the decimal point two places to the right. In other words, .75 becomes 75%, .085 becomes 8.5%, and 9.5 would be 950%.

Let's say we wish to discover 17% of 250. First, convert the 17% to a decimal (.17), and then perform the multiplication: .17 × 250 = 42.5.

Ratios

A ratio is simply a way to make a comparison between two things. For example, if we shared a house, and I paid three times the household expenses that you paid, the ratio of my expenses to yours could be expressed by using the ratio 3:1. If I spent three dollars for every two dollars you spent, we could express it with the ratio 3:2.

Rounding

Sometimes dividing a fraction will result in repeated decimals. $\frac{1}{3}$ converts to .333333333 (with the 3s running on forever). In such cases, it's customary to round the decimal off to the nearest hundredth. So, $\frac{1}{3}$ would convert to .33.

Some math problems will require you to round off a number in order to arrive at an answer to the problem. The general rule to rounding is to first decide at what decimal place you wish to round to (nearest tenth, nearest hundredth, etc.), then look at the number to the right of that place. Round up for numbers 5 and greater, and round down for numbers 4 or less.

EXAMPLE

Rounded off to the nearest hundredth:

4.578972 = 4.58
9.5338 = 9.53
6.588394 = 6.59

Rounded off to the nearest tenth:

4.5789972 = 4.6
9.5338 = 9.5
6.588394 = 6.6

Squares and Roots

The square of a number is the number multiplied by itself. In other words, the square of 5 is 5 × 5, which equals 25, so the square of 5 is 25. We designate a square of a number with a superscript "2." For example, $5^2 = 5 \times 5$, or 25.

The *square root,* on the other hand, is two equal numbers that, when multiplied together, give that number. 5 is the square root of 25 because 5 × 5 = 25.

The square root is usually depicted with a symbol called the *radical sign* ($\sqrt{\ }$). So $\sqrt{25} = 5$ because $5 \times 5 = 25$.

Basic Algebra

According to the American Heritage Dictionary, *algebra* is "a branch of mathematics in which symbols, usually letters of the alphabet, represent numbers or members of a specified set and are used to represent quantities and to express general relationships that hold for all members of the set."

Whew! No wonder so many people begin to sweat when they merely hear the word *algebra.* In actuality, however, algebra is just a way to simplify complex mathematical problems into equations that can then be simplified and more easily solved.

When we attempt to solve an algebraic equation, we are usually looking for one or more unknowns. If you go to the store to buy apples, and one pound of apples costs $3.00, how much would you have to spend to buy three pounds?

We can express (and solve) this problem by using simple algebra. x (the unknown) is equal to three times the cost of a single pound, or, $x = 3 \times \$3.00$. By completing the math, we find that $x = \$9.00$.

Equations

Algebraic equations are mathematical expressions in which both sides are equal. It's obvious that 6 = 6. It's also obvious that 3 + 3 = 6, or 4 + 2 = 10 – 4. In all of these examples, the quantities are the same on both sides of the equal sign.

But, in algebra, the equation always includes one or more variables (unknowns) and we have to try to discern what those unknown variables are equal to. To help us solve for the unknown variable, we can use certain rules to simplify the equation.

1. **You may evaluate any parentheses, exponents, multiplications, divisions, additions, and subtractions in the usual order of operations (see above).**

   $(7 - 2)x + 3 = 14$. Using the order of operations, we perform the operations contained in parenthesis, first, so the equation becomes $5x + 3 = 14$.

2. **You may combine like terms. This means you can combine like variables.**

   $2x + 4x$ can be combined to be $6x$. $2a \times 6a$ can be combined to be $12a^2$.

   Variables are "like" when they have the same letter and are raised to the same power. We can combine $x + x$ into $2x$, for example, but $x^2 + x$ cannot be combined into x^3. We can multiply (or divide) the same variables with different powers, however, simply by adding or subtracting the exponents. x^2 times $x = x^3$, and $x^3 \div x^2 = x$.

3. **You may add or subtract any value to both sides of the equation (you have to add or subtract the same value to both sides in order to keep the equation equal).**

   In the equation $7x + 2 = 14$, we can subtract 2 from both sides of the equation ($7x + 2 - 2 = 14 - 2$. This would simplify to $7x = 12$). Remember that subtraction of any number is the exact same as adding the negative value of that number.

4. **You may multiply or divide both sides of the equation with any number except zero. Again, you have to multiply or divide by the same value on both sides to keep the equation equal.**

   In the example $7x = 14$, we need to eliminate the 7 times x on the left side of the equation, so it would make sense to divide both sides by 7. $\frac{7x}{7} = \frac{14}{7}$, or $x = 2$.

EXAMPLE

Let's try an example using the above rules for simplification:

Solve the equation $3x + 5x - 12 = x + 3$

First, let's combine the like terms "3x" and "5x"

$8x - 12 = x + 3$

Now, let's get rid of that pesky − 12 on the left side of the equation by adding a positive 12 to both sides.

$3x + 5x - 12 + 12 = x + 3 + 12$

Again combining the like terms gives us:

$8x = x + 15$

Now we need to eliminate the x on the right side of the equation, so we subtract x from both sides.

$8x - x = x - x + 15$

Once again combining the like terms gives us:

$7x = 15$

We need to know the value of x (or 1 times x, which is the same thing), so we eliminate the 7 multiplier by dividing both sides by 7.

$7x \div 7 = 15 \div 7$

$x = 2\frac{1}{7}$

Factoring

You may be presented with a multiplication answer and be asked to find the original multipliers. In algebra, this is known as *factoring*.

EXAMPLE

Let's factor $9x^3 + 3xy$.

The first step is to find the highest common factor. This means we must find the highest common expression that will divide into all of the terms.

The highest number that will factor into the coefficients 9 and 3 is 3 (3 will factor into 9 three times and into 3 one time).

The highest expression that will factor into x^3 and xy is x (x will factor into x^3 three times and xy one time). The variable y is not contained in the first term, so it cannot be used as a common factor.

So, the highest common factor is $3x$. We divide that into the expression to find the remaining factor: $(9x^3 + 3xy) \div 3x$. Our result is $3x(3x^2 + y)$.

Now, let's factor the expression $x^2 - 16$:

Note that this expression contains the square of one number (x) minus the square of another number (16 is the square of 4). To factor this type of expression the first step is to find the square root of the first term and place it to the left of two empty parentheses.

The square root of x^2 is x, so we would write $(x)(x)$.

Now, find the square root of the second term, and place it on the left side inside the parentheses. The square root of 16 is 4, so we would write $(x\ 4)(x\ 4)$.

Finally, because the 16 is a negative number (remember the expression was "minus" 16), and because we remember in multiplication that a negative number multiplied by a positive number results in a negative number, we place a "+" between the terms in the first parenthesis and a "–" between the terms of the second parentheses:

$(x + 4)(x - 4)$.

So, the factors of the expression $x^2 - 16$ are $(x+4)$, $(x-4)$.

EXAMPLE

One final example—factoring a *quadratic trinomial*. This is an expression in the form of $ax^2 + bx + c$, where a, b, and c are numbers (a cannot equal zero), and x is the "unknown." The factors of a quadratic trinomial always results in two pair of terms, with the terms in each pair separated by a plus or minus sign.

Let's factor the quadratic trinomial $x^2 - 12x + 20$.

The first step is to find the factors of the first trinomial. We can see that the factors of x^2 are x and x. We'll place them at the left of the two pair of parentheses:

$(x\ )\ (x\ )$

Now note that the last trinomial has a plus sign. This tells us that both of the resulting factors of the trinomial are going to be either plus or minus (two pluses result in a positive number and two negatives result in a positive number). But, because the second trinomial has a minus sign, both factors must also have a minus sign.

$(x -)\ (x -)$

Next we find the factors of the third trinomial (20) which, when combined (added or subtracted), also give us the number in the second trinomial (12). 2×10 is equal to 20, and $2 + 10$ is equal to 12. So, the factors are 2 and 10. Because we know that the factors must have minus signs, the factors are actually –2 and –10.

$(x-2)\ (x-10)$.

So, the factors of $x^2 - 12x + 20$ are $x-2$, $x-10$.

Quadratic Equations

A quadratic equation is a problem that includes the square of an unknown number, and no other term in the equation has an exponent higher than the unknown. The following would be examples of a quadratic equation:

EXAMPLE

$y^2 + 3y = 7$
$x^2 - x = 14$
$y^2 = x-y$

Normally, when we attempt to solve algebraic expressions, we try to simplify the equation by getting all the variables on one side. But, quadratic equations are solved in a different way.

To solve a quadratic equation, we factor it and set the factors equal to zero.

Let's try to solve the equation $x^2 = 8x + 20$.

First, let's get all the terms on the left side of the equation, leaving the right side equal to zero.

$x^2 - 8x - 20 = (8x - 8x) + (20 - 20)$

$x^2 - 8x - 20 = 0$

Now, let's factor it:

$(x - 10)\ (x + 2) = 0$

Next we set each factor equal to zero and solve them as individual equations:

$x - 10 = 0$, and $x + 2 = 0$

$x = 10$, $x = -2$

To make sure we're correct, we'll plug the numbers back into the original equation

$x^2 = 8x + 20$ (with $x = 10$)	$x^2 = 8x + 20$ (with $x = -2$)
$10^2 = 8(10) + 20$	$(-2)^2 = 8(-2) + 20$
$100 = 80 + 20$	$4 = -16 + 20$
$100 = 100$	$4 = 4$

So, the solution to the quadratic equation $x^2 = 8x + 20$ is $x = 10, -2$.

Inequalities

In algebra, a variable (unknown) is not always equal to a number. Sometimes the variable is *not* equal to a number. This is known as an inequality. In an inequality, the first number must be either greater or less than the second number.

In solving inequalities, you need to remember the following rules:

- ✔ Negative numbers are less than zero (they are also less than positive numbers).
- ✔ Zero is less than positive numbers (and also greater than negative numbers).
- ✔ Positive numbers are greater than zero (and also greater than negative numbers).

In *normal* algebra, the equal sign is used to compare expressions, indicating that both sides of the equation are the same. Special symbols are used to indicate inequalities. These symbols are:

$>$ indicates "greater than." For example, the number 4 is greater than 2 or $4 > 2$.

$<$ indicates "less than." For example, the number 2 is less than 4, or $2 < 4$.

$\geq$ indicates "greater than or equal to." For example, x is greater than or equal to 5, or $x \geq 5$.

$\leq$ indicates "less than or equal to." For example, x is less than or equal to 5, or $x \leq 5$.

$\neq$ indicates "not equal to." For example, 6 is not equal to 3, or $6 \neq 3$.

We solve inequalities the same way we solve other algebra problems (by simplifying), with one important exception: if you multiply or divide both sides of an inequality by a negative number, you must reverse the inequality symbol.

For example, in the inequality, $4x > -x$, if we divided both sides by $-x$, the result would be: $-3x < 1$.

Geometry Review

Geometry is the mathematics of the properties, measurement, and relationships of points, lines, angles, surfaces, and solids. When solving geometry problems, we use a combination of basic mathematics and algebra.

Like other disciplines of math, geometry has its own vocabulary:

Angles

When two lines intersect, they form an angle. The point where the lines intersect is called the *vertex*. Angles can be designated in one of three ways:

Angle B. The angle is designated a letter at the point of the vertex.

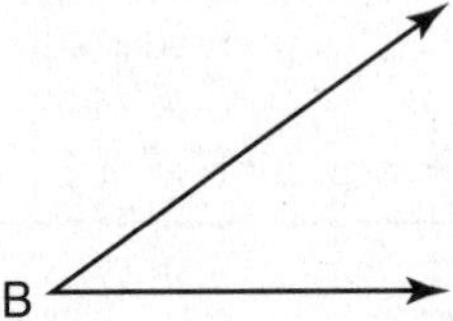

Angle ABC. The angle is designated by letters naming all of the lines that intersect to form the angle. The vertex is always the middle letter.

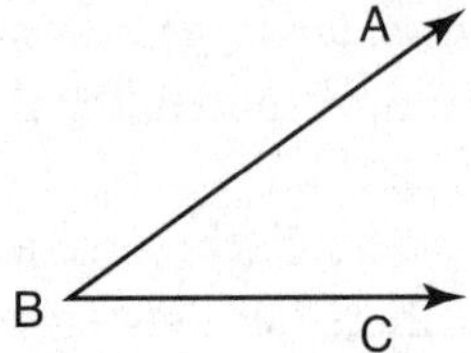

Angle 2. The angle is designated by a number marked on the inside of the angle.

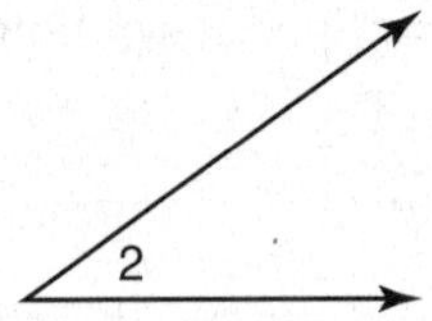

Measuring Angles
Angles are measured in degrees (°). Degrees are further broken down into minutes (′) and seconds(″). A tool called a protractor is often used to measure angles.

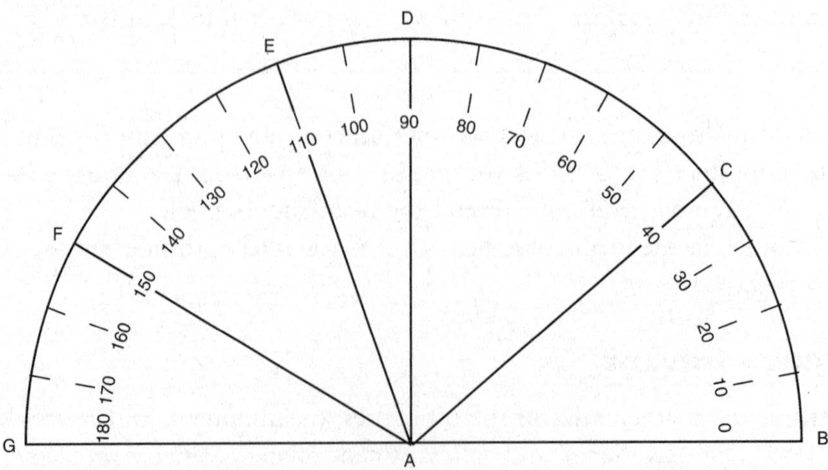

Straight Angle: An angle of 180 degrees.

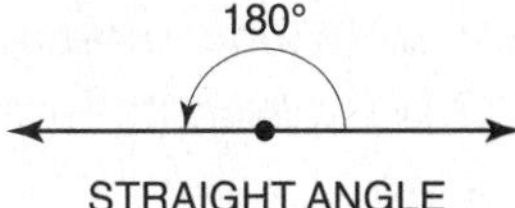

STRAIGHT ANGLE

Right Angle: An angle of 90 degrees.

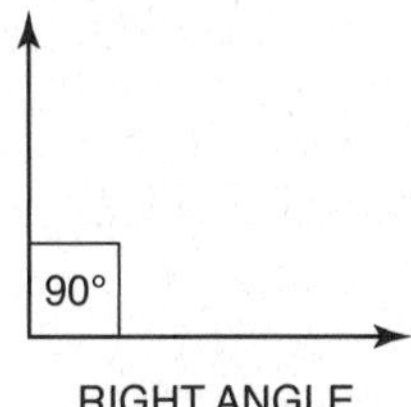

RIGHT ANGLE

Obtuse Angle: An angle of more than 90 degrees but less than 180 degrees.

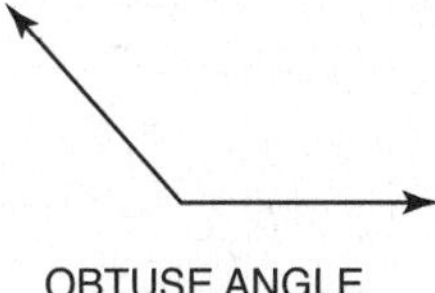

OBTUSE ANGLE

Acute Angle: An angle of more than 0 degrees but less than 90 degrees.

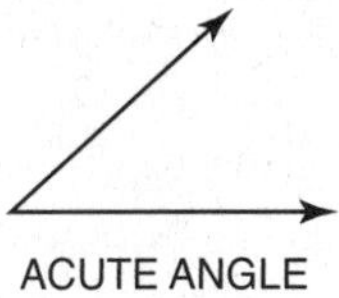

ACUTE ANGLE

Complementary Angles: Two angles whose sum is 90 degrees.

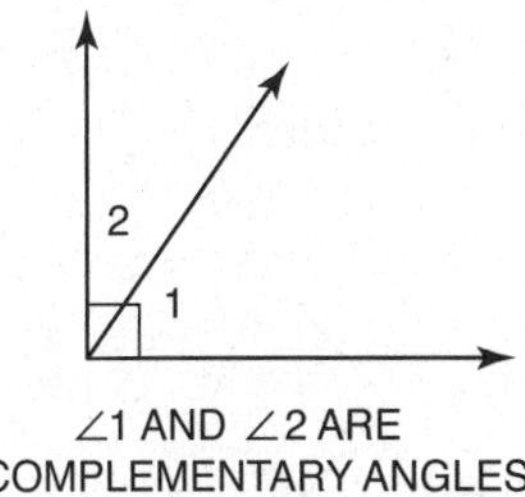

∠1 AND ∠2 ARE
COMPLEMENTARY ANGLES

Supplementary Angles: Two angles whose sum is 180 degrees.

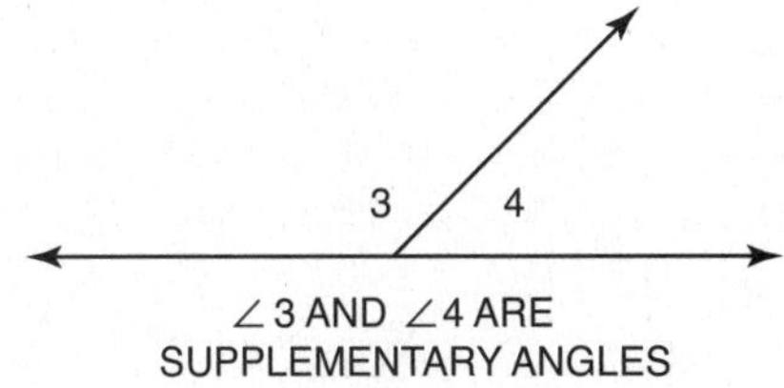

∠3 AND ∠4 ARE
SUPPLEMENTARY ANGLES

Lines

There are two basic types of lines: parallel and perpendicular. *Parallel lines* are two lines that are equally distant from one another at every point along the line. *Perpendicular lines* are two lines that intersect to form a right angle.

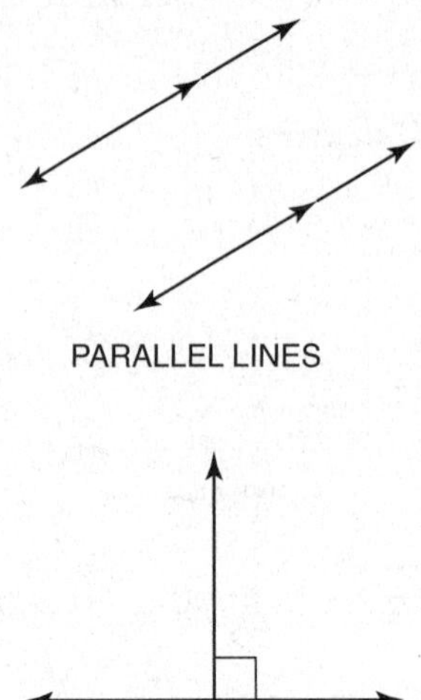

PARALLEL LINES

PERPENDICULAR LINES

Polygons

A *polygon* is a closed-in shape, made up of three or more straight lines. There are several types of polygons:

Triangle: A polygon with three sides.

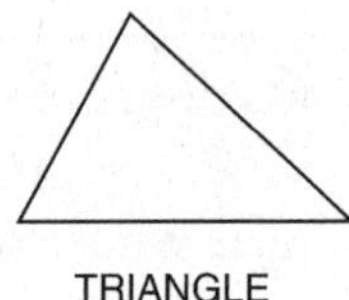

TRIANGLE

Quadrilateral: A polygon with four sides.

QUADRILATERAL

Pentagon: A polygon with five sides.

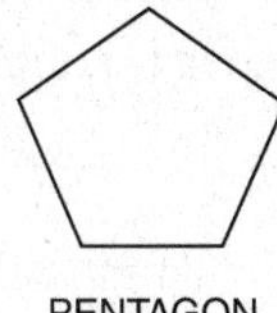

PENTAGON

Hexagon: A polygon with six sides.

HEXAGON

Octagon: A polygon with eight sides.

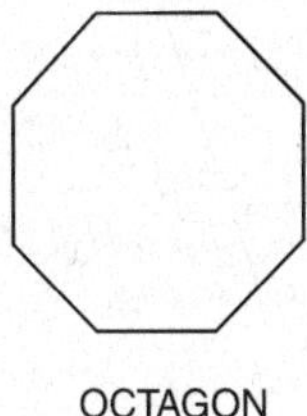

OCTAGON

Decagon: A polygon with ten sides.

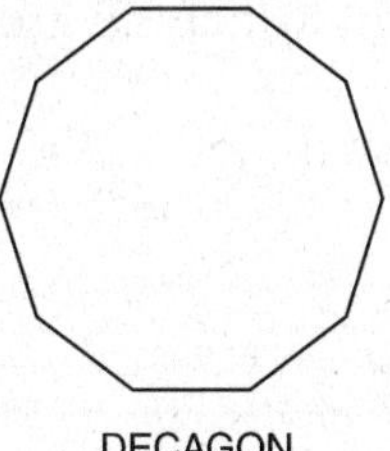

DECAGON

Triangles

We can see from the definition above that a triangle is a polygon with three sides. An additional feature of a triangle is that it contains a sum of 180 degrees. Triangles are classified in several ways:

Equilateral Triangle: A triangle in which all three sides and all three angles are equal. In an equilateral triangle, the angles of all three sides are 60 degrees each.

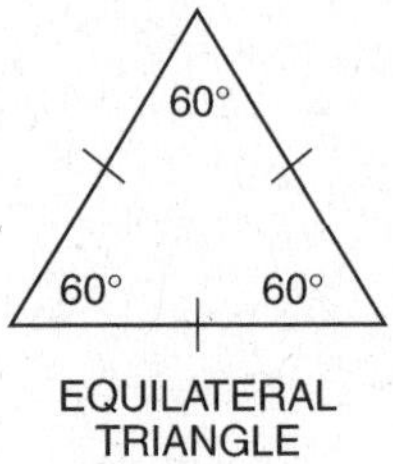

EQUILATERAL TRIANGLE

Isosceles Triangle: A triangle in which two of the sides have equal length, and whose opposing sides have equal angles.

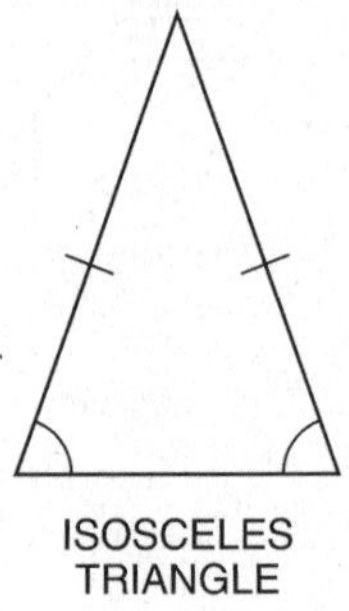
ISOSCELES TRIANGLE

Scalene Triangle: A triangle in which all three sides and all three angles are unequal.

SCALENE TRIANGLE

Acute Triangle: A triangle in which all three angles are less than 90 degrees.

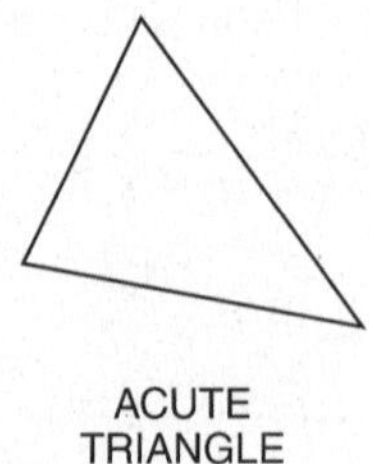
ACUTE TRIANGLE

Obtuse Triangle: A triangle in which one of the angles is greater than 90 degrees.

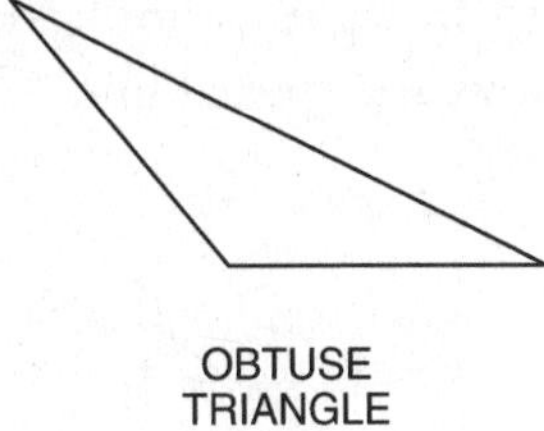

OBTUSE TRIANGLE

Right Triangle: A triangle with a 90-degree (right) angle. We call the longest side of a right triangle the *hypotenuse.* The other two sides are called *legs.*

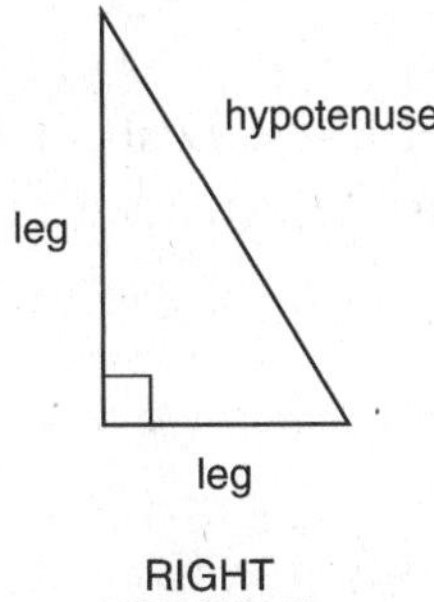

RIGHT TRIANGLE

Concurrent Triangles: Triangles that are identical. Both triangles are equal to each other in line length and angles.

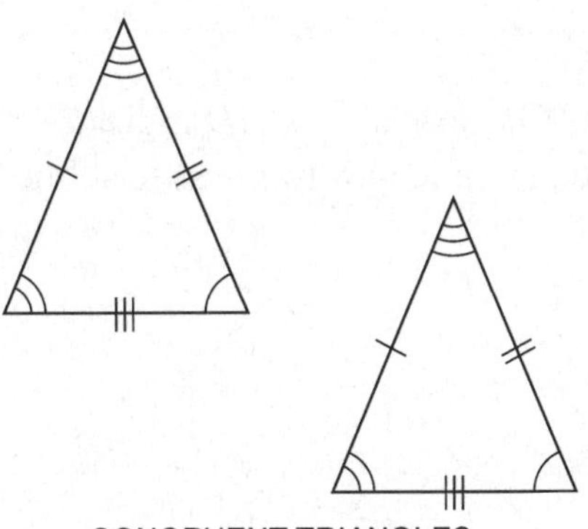

CONGRUENT TRIANGLES

Similar Triangles: Triangles that have the same shape but not the same size. The angles of the triangles are identical, however.

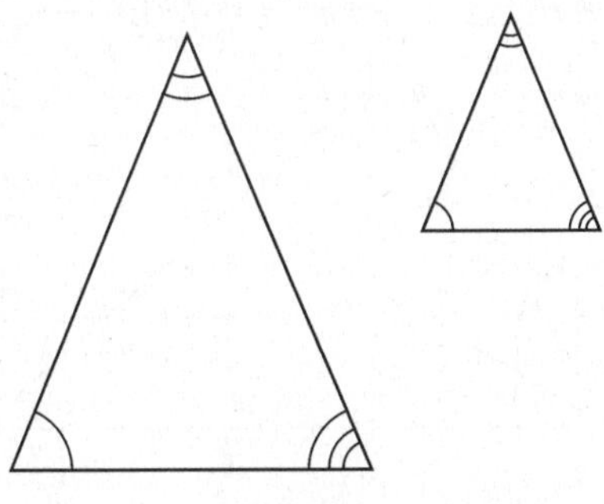

SIMILAR TRIANGLES

Special Lines

Special lines are often used with triangles to indicate altitudes, medians, and angle bisectors. In the illustration below, the special line *BD* indicates an altitude (height) of the triangle:

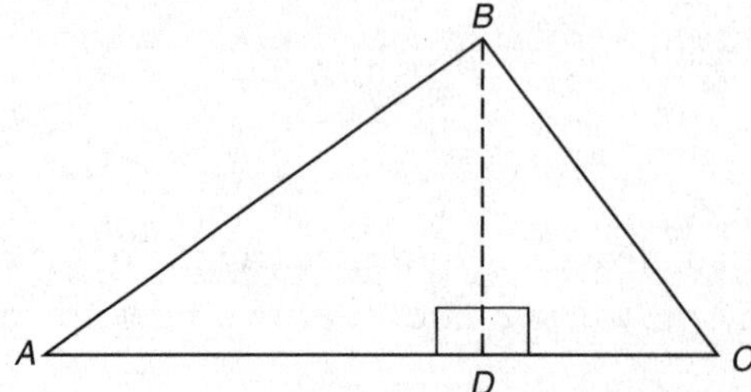

In the below example, the special line *CD* also indicates an altitude. In this case, however, the special line *AD* must be extended in order for the lines to meet at a right angle.

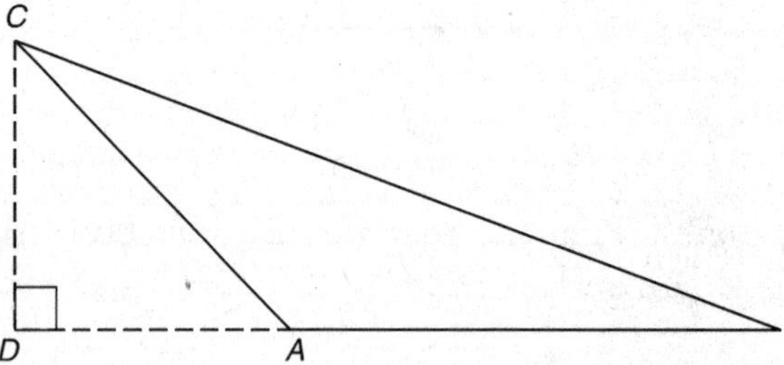

In the following example, the special line *AD* indicates the median, assuming that the special lines *CD* are equal in length to the special line *BD*:

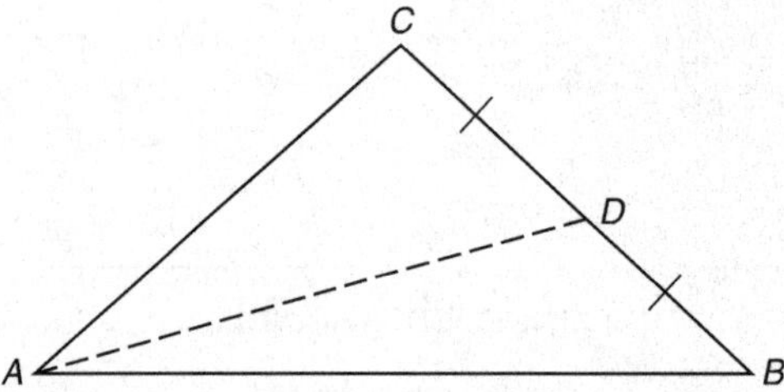

In the next illustration, the special line *AD* indicates an angle bisector of angle *A*, assuming Angle 1 and Angle 2 are equal.

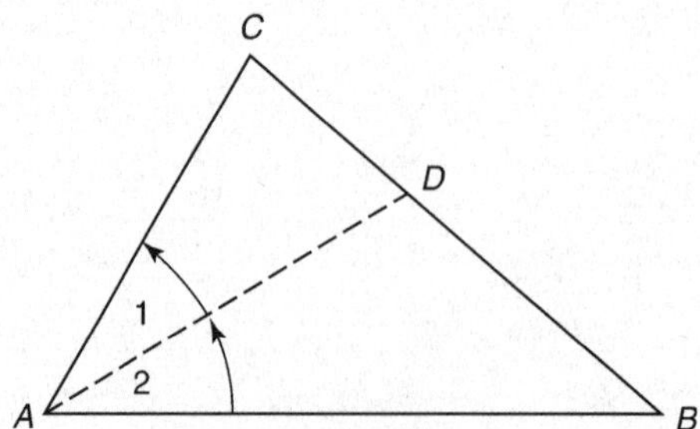

Quadrilaterals

Recall from the definition above that a quadrilateral is a polygon with four sides. All quadrilaterals contain angles whose sum measures 360 degrees. Quadrilaterals are classified in several ways:

Parallelogram: A quadrilateral whose opposing sides are parallel to each other. The other two opposite sides and the angles are also equal.

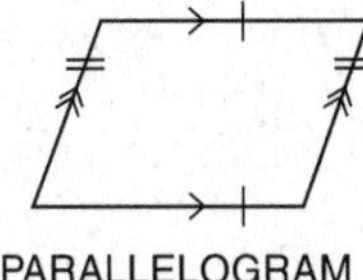

PARALLELOGRAM

Rectangle: Same as a parallelogram, but all the angles are right (90-degree) angles.

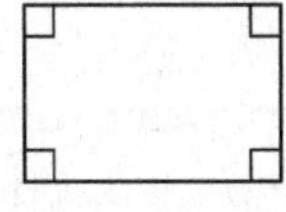

RECTANGLE

Square: Same as a rectangle, but all four sides are equal in length.

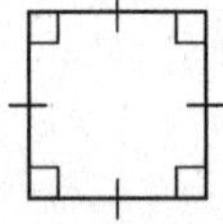

SQUARE

Rhombus: Same as a parallelogram, but all four sides are equal in length.

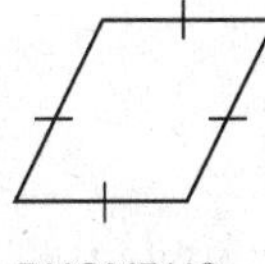

RHOMBUS

Trapezoid: A quadrilateral that has two sides parallel and two sides that are not.

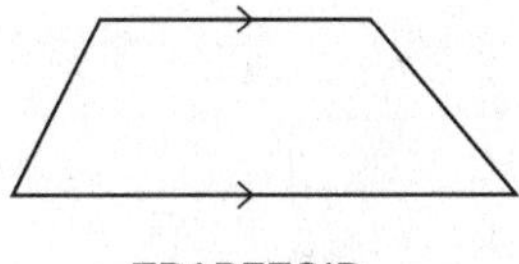

TRAPEZOID

Circles

A circle is a closed line containing 360 degrees. All points on the line are an equal distance from the center. The length around a circle (perimeter) is known as the *circumference.* A straight line drawn from one point of the circumference to another point, passing through the center, is called the *diameter.* A straight line drawn from the center to the circumference is called the *radius.* The radius is $\frac{1}{2}$ of the diameter.

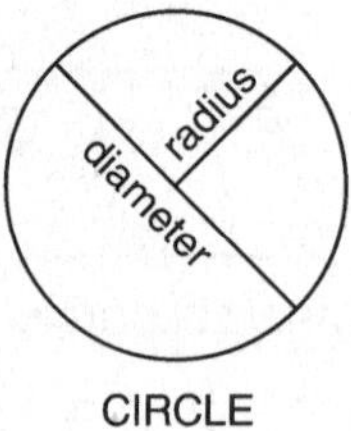

CIRCLE

Perimeters

The perimeter of a polygon is simply the sum of the length of all the sides. For example, look at the following hexagon (six-sided polygon):

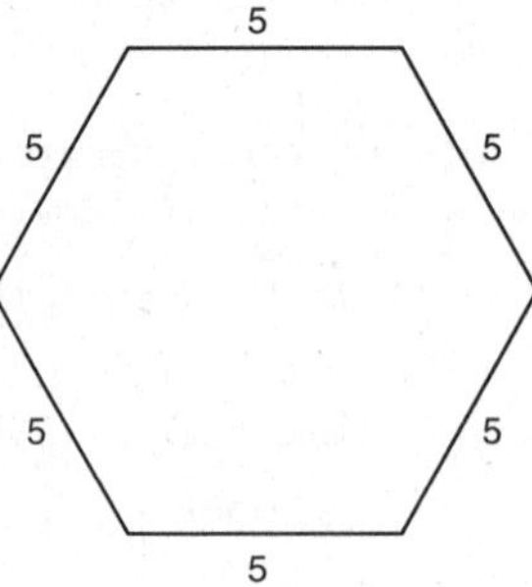

There are six sides to the shape, each measuring 5 inches. So, the perimeter of this example would be 5 + 5 + 5 + 5 + 5 + 5, or 6 × 5 (30 inches).

Pythagorean Theorem

Recall that the long line in a right triangle is called the *hypotenuse* and the other two lines are called *legs.* The Pythagorean Theorem states that the square of the hypotenuse (the long line) is equal to the sum of the square of the legs. We can express this mathematically with the equation: $c^2 = a^2 + b^2$ (c is the hypotenuse and a, b are the legs of the triangle).

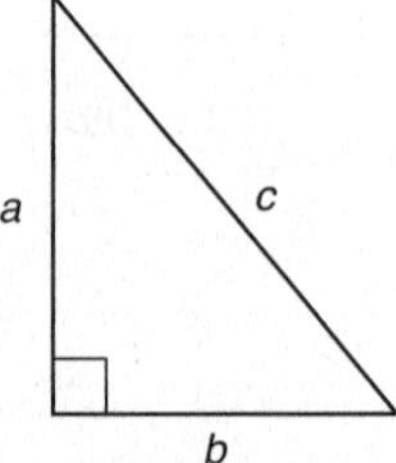

Thus, if we know the length of the two legs, we can discern the length of the hypotenuse, or if we know the length of one leg and the length of the hypotenuse, we can compute the length of the other leg simply by plugging in the numbers and solving the equation.

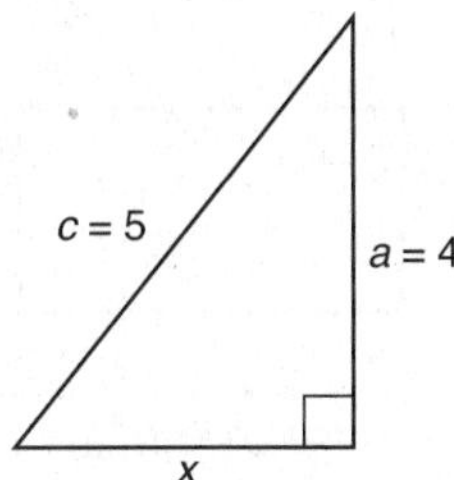

From the illustration above, we can see that the length of this right triangle's hypotenuse is 5, and that the length of the right leg is 4. Using the Pythagorean Theorem, we can discover the length of the other leg (x):

$$c^2 = a^2 + b^2$$

$$5^2 = 4^2 + x^2$$

$$5^2 - 4^2 = 4^2 - 4^2 + x^2$$

$$25 - 16 = x^2$$

$$9 = x^2$$

$$\sqrt{9} = \sqrt{x^2}$$

$$3 = x$$

Diameter of a Circle

The diameter of a circle is referred to as the *circumference.* To determine the diameter of a circle we use the number pi, which is designated by the Greek letter π. In math, we substitute either $3\frac{1}{7}$ or $\frac{22}{7}$ or 3.14 for *pi.*

The circumference of a circle is *pi* times the diameter. Remember that the diameter of a circle is twice the radius, so we can also say that the circumference of the circle is equal to *pi* times twice the radius. As a mathematical equation, we can express this as $C = (\pi)d$ or as $C = (\pi)2r$.

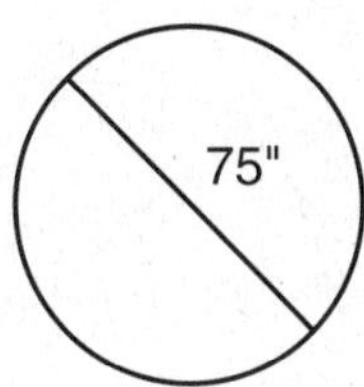

The circle above has a diameter of 75 inches. From that information we can compute the circumference:

$$C = (\pi)d$$
$$C = 3.14 \times 75$$
$$C = 235.5$$

The circumference of the above circle is $235\frac{1}{2}$ inches.

Area

Area is the space that is enclosed inside of the perimeter of a polygon.

Rectangles. To calculate the area of a rectangle we multiply the length times the width.

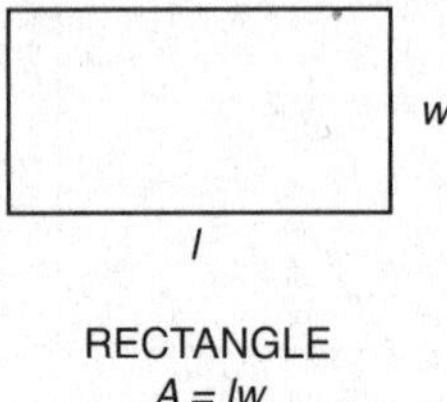

RECTANGLE
$A = lw$

Squares. Recall that a square is simply a rectangle whose sides are all of equal length. Therefore, the formula length times width still works, or more simply, the length of one side squared.

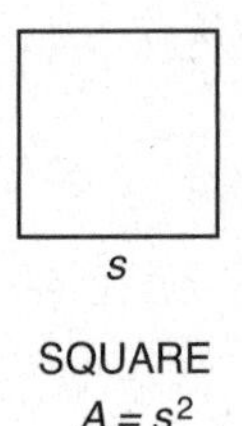

SQUARE
$A = s^2$

Parallelogram. To find the area of a parallelogram, we multiply the length of the base times the height.

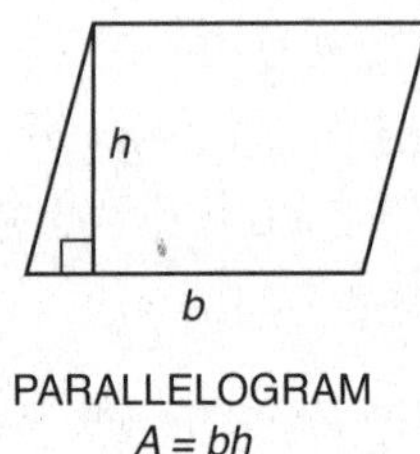

PARALLELOGRAM
$A = bh$

Triangles. The area of a triangle is determined by multiplying one-half of the base length by the height of the triangle.

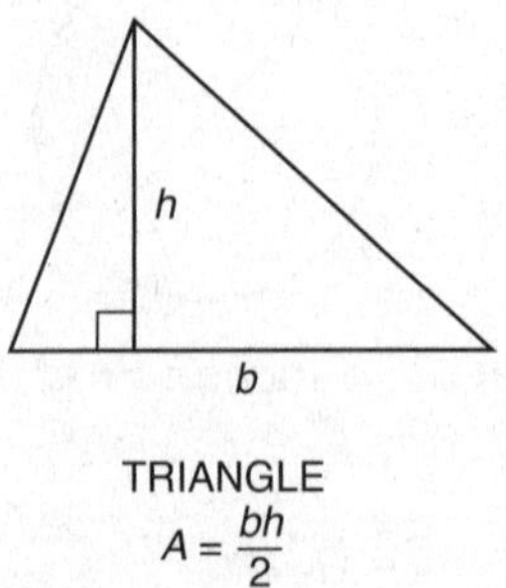

TRIANGLE
$A = \frac{bh}{2}$

Circles. The area of a circle is determined by multiplying *pi* by the square of the radius. This can be expressed mathematically by the formula $A = (\pi)r^2$.

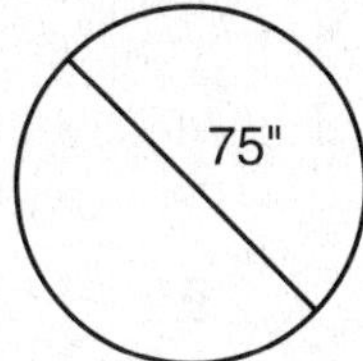

Recall that the radius is $\frac{1}{2}$ of the diameter. So, in the above example, the radius of the circle would be 37.5 inches. To find the area of this circle:

$$A = (\pi)r^2.$$
$$A = 3.14 \times 37.5^2$$
$$A = 3.14 \times 1{,}406.25$$
$$A = 4{,}415.63 \text{ square inches}$$

Volume. What area is to polygons, volume is to solid (three-dimensional) objects. A solid figure consists of a flat base and height.

Rectangular Solids. This is a solid that has a specific length, width, and height. To determine the volume we multiply the length times the width times the height.

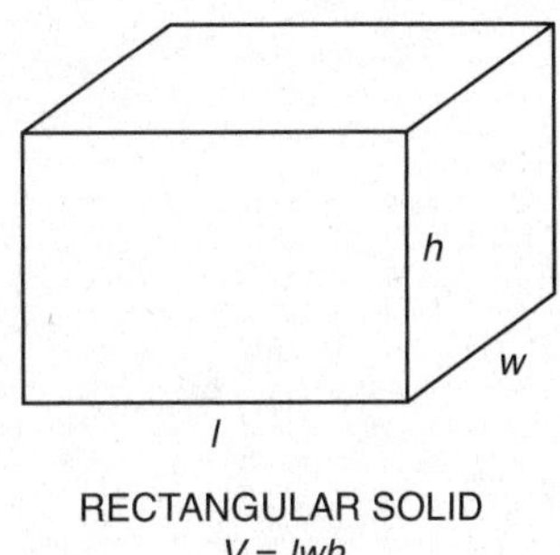

RECTANGULAR SOLID
$V = lwh$

Cube. A cube solid is the same as a rectangular solid except the length, width, and height are all equal. Therefore, we can shorten the formula (length times height times width) to simply one side "cubed" (raised to the 3rd power).

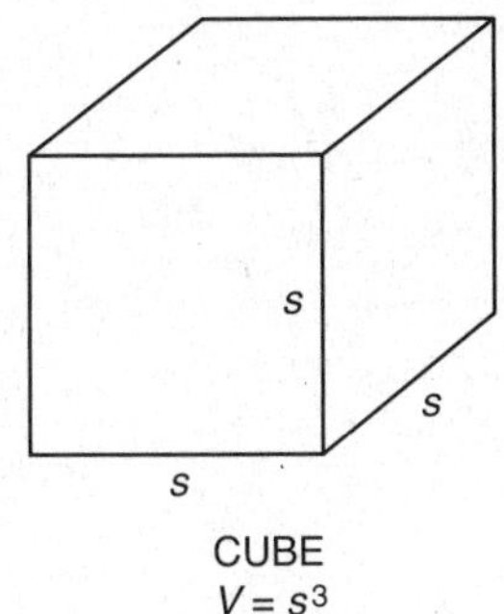

CUBE
$V = s^3$

Cylinders. A cylinder is a solid in which both bases are circles in parallel planes (think of a soda can). We can determine the volume of a cylinder by multiplying the area of its base by the height.

Remember, the area of a circle (the base of a cylinder) is computed by the formula $A = (\pi)r^2$. So, the formula to determine the volume of a cylinder can be expressed as $V = (\pi)r^2h$.

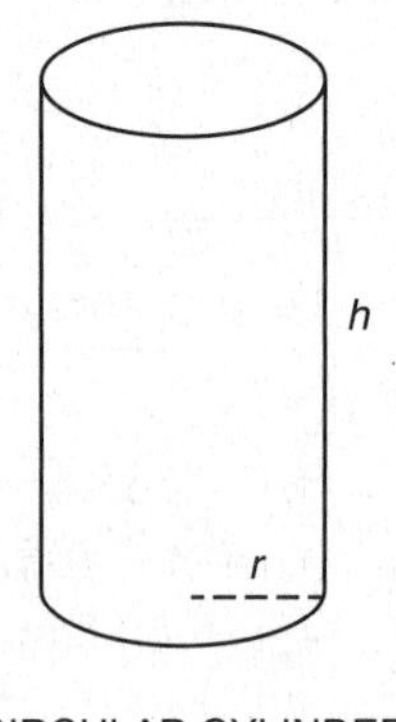

CIRCULAR CYLINDER
$V = \pi r^2 h$

Answer Sheet for Practice Questions

1 Ⓐ Ⓑ Ⓒ Ⓓ Ⓔ
2 Ⓐ Ⓑ Ⓒ Ⓓ Ⓔ
3 Ⓐ Ⓑ Ⓒ Ⓓ Ⓔ
4 Ⓐ Ⓑ Ⓒ Ⓓ Ⓔ
5 Ⓐ Ⓑ Ⓒ Ⓓ Ⓔ
6 Ⓐ Ⓑ Ⓒ Ⓓ Ⓔ
7 Ⓐ Ⓑ Ⓒ Ⓓ Ⓔ
8 Ⓐ Ⓑ Ⓒ Ⓓ Ⓔ
9 Ⓐ Ⓑ Ⓒ Ⓓ Ⓔ
10 Ⓐ Ⓑ Ⓒ Ⓓ Ⓔ
11 Ⓐ Ⓑ Ⓒ Ⓓ Ⓔ
12 Ⓐ Ⓑ Ⓒ Ⓓ Ⓔ
13 Ⓐ Ⓑ Ⓒ Ⓓ Ⓔ
14 Ⓐ Ⓑ Ⓒ Ⓓ Ⓔ
15 Ⓐ Ⓑ Ⓒ Ⓓ Ⓔ
16 Ⓐ Ⓑ Ⓒ Ⓓ Ⓔ
17 Ⓐ Ⓑ Ⓒ Ⓓ Ⓔ
18 Ⓐ Ⓑ Ⓒ Ⓓ Ⓔ
19 Ⓐ Ⓑ Ⓒ Ⓓ Ⓔ
20 Ⓐ Ⓑ Ⓒ Ⓓ Ⓔ
21 Ⓐ Ⓑ Ⓒ Ⓓ Ⓔ
22 Ⓐ Ⓑ Ⓒ Ⓓ Ⓔ
23 Ⓐ Ⓑ Ⓒ Ⓓ Ⓔ
24 Ⓐ Ⓑ Ⓒ Ⓓ Ⓔ
25 Ⓐ Ⓑ Ⓒ Ⓓ Ⓔ
26 Ⓐ Ⓑ Ⓒ Ⓓ Ⓔ
27 Ⓐ Ⓑ Ⓒ Ⓓ Ⓔ
28 Ⓐ Ⓑ Ⓒ Ⓓ Ⓔ
29 Ⓐ Ⓑ Ⓒ Ⓓ Ⓔ
30 Ⓐ Ⓑ Ⓒ Ⓓ Ⓔ
31 Ⓐ Ⓑ Ⓒ Ⓓ Ⓔ
32 Ⓐ Ⓑ Ⓒ Ⓓ Ⓔ
33 Ⓐ Ⓑ Ⓒ Ⓓ Ⓔ
34 Ⓐ Ⓑ Ⓒ Ⓓ Ⓔ
35 Ⓐ Ⓑ Ⓒ Ⓓ Ⓔ
36 Ⓐ Ⓑ Ⓒ Ⓓ Ⓔ
37 Ⓐ Ⓑ Ⓒ Ⓓ Ⓔ
38 Ⓐ Ⓑ Ⓒ Ⓓ Ⓔ
39 Ⓐ Ⓑ Ⓒ Ⓓ Ⓔ
40 Ⓐ Ⓑ Ⓒ Ⓓ Ⓔ
41 Ⓐ Ⓑ Ⓒ Ⓓ Ⓔ
42 Ⓐ Ⓑ Ⓒ Ⓓ Ⓔ
43 Ⓐ Ⓑ Ⓒ Ⓓ Ⓔ
44 Ⓐ Ⓑ Ⓒ Ⓓ Ⓔ
45 Ⓐ Ⓑ Ⓒ Ⓓ Ⓔ
46 Ⓐ Ⓑ Ⓒ Ⓓ Ⓔ
47 Ⓐ Ⓑ Ⓒ Ⓓ Ⓔ
48 Ⓐ Ⓑ Ⓒ Ⓓ Ⓔ
49 Ⓐ Ⓑ Ⓒ Ⓓ Ⓔ
50 Ⓐ Ⓑ Ⓒ Ⓓ Ⓔ
51 Ⓐ Ⓑ Ⓒ Ⓓ Ⓔ
52 Ⓐ Ⓑ Ⓒ Ⓓ Ⓔ
53 Ⓐ Ⓑ Ⓒ Ⓓ Ⓔ
54 Ⓐ Ⓑ Ⓒ Ⓓ Ⓔ
55 Ⓐ Ⓑ Ⓒ Ⓓ Ⓔ
56 Ⓐ Ⓑ Ⓒ Ⓓ Ⓔ
57 Ⓐ Ⓑ Ⓒ Ⓓ Ⓔ
58 Ⓐ Ⓑ Ⓒ Ⓓ Ⓔ
59 Ⓐ Ⓑ Ⓒ Ⓓ Ⓔ
60 Ⓐ Ⓑ Ⓒ Ⓓ Ⓔ
61 Ⓐ Ⓑ Ⓒ Ⓓ Ⓔ

Practice Questions

1. $(\sqrt{2} - \sqrt{3})^2 =$
   (A) $5 - 2\sqrt{6}$
   (B) $5 - \sqrt{6}$
   (C) $1 - 2\sqrt{6}$
   (D) $1 - \sqrt{2}$
   (E) 1

2. Which of the following is greater than $\frac{1}{2}$?
   (A) $\frac{2}{5}$
   (B) $\frac{4}{7}$
   (C) $\frac{4}{9}$
   (D) $\frac{5}{11}$
   (E) $\frac{6}{13}$

3. What is the average (arithmetic mean) of all the multiples of ten from 10 to 190 inclusive?
   (A) 90
   (B) 95
   (C) 100
   (D) 105
   (E) 110

4. If $x \neq 0$, which of the following <u>must</u> be greater than x?
   I $2x\ 2n$
   II x^2
   III $2 - x$
   (A) I only
   (B) II only
   (C) III only
   (D) I and II only
   (E) none of the above

5. $\sqrt{5}$ percent of $5\sqrt{5}$ =
   (A) 0.05
   (B) 0.25
   (C) 0.5
   (D) 2.5
   (E) 25

6. If $pqr = 1$, $rst = 0$, and $spr = 0$, which of the following <u>must</u> be zero?
   (A) p
   (B) q
   (C) r
   (D) s
   (E) t

7. What is the square root of 22,500?
   (A) 100
   (B) 125
   (C) 150
   (D) 175
   (E) 200

8. If $f(x) = x^2 - 3$, where x is an integer, which of the following could be a value of $f(x)$?
   (A) 6
   (B) 0
   (C) –6
   (D) 6 or –6
   (E) all of the above

9. Which of the following equations is incorrect?
   (A) $5x + 6 = 14$
   (B) $\sqrt{5} \times \sqrt{10} = \sqrt{(5 \times 10)}$
   (C) $\sqrt{5} + \sqrt{6} = \sqrt{(5+6)}$
   (D) All of the above are correct.
   (E) All of the above are incorrect.

10. If $f(x) = |(x^2 - 50)|$, what is the value of $f(-5)$?

(A) 75
(B) 25
(C) 0
(D) –25
(E) –75

11. In mathematics, the slope of a line is generally referred to by what letter?

(A) x
(B) y
(C) a
(D) b
(E) m

12. $\frac{3}{8} + 4\frac{2}{5} + 3\frac{1}{2} =$

(A) $8\frac{11}{40}$
(B) $8\frac{7}{8}$
(C) $7\frac{1}{2}$
(D) $7\frac{1}{3}$
(E) $9\frac{1}{2}$

13. If $f(x) = (x + 2) \div (x–2)$ for all integers except $x = 2$, which of the following has the greatest value?

(A) $f(-1)$
(B) $f(0)$
(C) $f(1)$
(D) $f(3)$
(E) $f(4)$

14. If x is an even integer, which of the following cannot be odd?

(A) $x + 3$
(B) $3x$
(C) $x^2 - 1$
(D) (A) and (B) are correct.
(E) (A), (B), and (C) are correct.

15. $2\frac{1}{4} \div 2\frac{4}{7} =$

(A) $1\frac{5}{8}$
(B) $1\frac{1}{2}$
(C) $\frac{1}{4}$
(D) $\frac{1}{2}$
(E) $\frac{7}{8}$

16. $-1\frac{1}{2} \div -\frac{3}{4} =$

(A) 2
(B) –2
(C) 1
(D) –1
(E) $\frac{1}{2}$

17. Which of the following is an improper fraction?

(A) $\frac{5}{10}$
(B) $\frac{20}{800}$
(C) $\frac{66}{55}$
(D) $\frac{85}{90}$
(E) all of the above

18. Which of the following numbers is the smallest?

(A) $\frac{35}{50}$
(B) $\frac{7}{10}$
(C) $\frac{1}{2}$
(D) $\frac{3}{5}$
(E) both (A) and (B)

19. Convert 35°C to Fahrenheit (F). The formula to convert Centigrade to Fahrenheit is F=9/5C + 32.

    (A) 90°F
    (B) 95°F
    (C) 100°F
    (D) 105°F
    (E) 110°F

20. Convert 122°F to Centigrade.

    (A) 40°C
    (B) 45°C
    (C) 50°C
    (D) 55°C
    (E) 60°C

21. 1 hour 30 minutes + 3 hours 40 minutes + 2 hours 45 minutes =

    (A) 6 hours 45 minutes
    (B) 6 hours 55 minutes
    (C) 7 hours 50 minutes
    (D) 7 hours 55 minutes
    (E) 8 hours 3 minutes

22. What is the length of the line segment in the *x-y* plane with end points at (–2,–2) and (2,3)?

    (A) 3
    (B) $\sqrt{31}$
    (C) $\sqrt{41}$
    (D) 7
    (E) 9

23. If $n^2 = 12$, then $n^4 =$

    (A) 16
    (B) 24
    (C) 36
    (D) 72
    (E) 144

24. What is the square root of 2,500?

    (A) 20
    (B) 30
    (C) 40
    (D) 50
    (E) 60

25. Which of the following equations is <u>incorrect?</u>

    (A) $\sqrt{5} + \sqrt{3} = \sqrt{5+3}$
    (B) $\sqrt{5} \times \sqrt{3} = \sqrt{5 \times 3}$
    (C) $\sqrt{5} \times \sqrt{25} = \sqrt{5 \times 5}$
    (D) All are correct.
    (E) All are incorrect.

26. What is the median of the following group of numbers?

    4 6 8 10 12 14 16

    (A) 4
    (B) 16
    (C) 11
    (D) 12
    (E) 10

27. What is the median of the following group of numbers?

    8 10 12 14 16 18

    (A) 12
    (B) 14
    (C) 13
    (D) 8
    (E) 18

28. What is the average of the following group of numbers:

    45.12, 55, 60.3, 92? (Round your answer to the nearest hundredth.)

    (A) 35.30
    (B) 63.11
    (C) 59.55
    (D) 28.00
    (E) 35.90

29. $(5.5 \times 10^5)(3.7 \times 10^{-3}) =$

(A) 2.035×10^{-15}
(B) 2.035×10^4
(C) 2.035×10^3
(D) 2.035×10^{-8}
(E) 2.035×10^8

30. $(4.2 \times 10^{-6}) \div (2.1 \times 10^{-3})$

(A) 2×10^{-9}
(B) 2×10^{-3}
(C) 2×10^3
(D) $2 \div 10^9$
(E) $2 \div 10^{-18}$

31. "Percent" means

(A) "per decimal."
(B) "per fraction."
(C) "per thousandth."
(D) "per 100 parts."
(E) "per portion."

32. .7 =

(A) 7%
(B) 70%
(C) 700%
(D) .7%
(E) 7000%

33. $\frac{4}{25} =$

(A) 5%
(B) 40%
(C) 16%
(D) .25%
(E) $\frac{1}{4}$

34. What number is equal to 35% of 14?

(A) .4
(B) 4.9
(C) 40
(D) 45
(E) 55

35. 33 is 12% of

(A) 200
(B) 275
(C) 300
(D) 350
(E) 375

36. $x = y - (50/y)$, where x and y are both > 0. If the value of y is doubled in the equation, the value of x will

(A) decrease.
(B) stay the same.
(C) increase fourfold.
(D) double.
(E) increase to more than double.

37. Find the number that is six less than $\frac{1}{9}$ of 45.

(A) 1
(B) 2
(C) 0
(D) –1
(E) –2

38. $\frac{x}{5} = \frac{7}{6}$

(A) $4\frac{1}{2}$
(B) $5\frac{1}{3}$
(C) $5\frac{5}{6}$
(D) $6\frac{1}{3}$
(E) $6\frac{1}{2}$

39. Which of the following could be a solution of the equation $|x| = |4x - 3|$?

(A) –1
(B) –0.6
(C) 0
(D) 0.6
(E) 1.5

40. Which of the following could not be the lengths of the sides of a right-angled triangle?

(A) 3, 4, 5
(B) 5, 12, 13
(C) 8, 15, 17
(D) 12, 15, 18
(E) 9, 12, 15

41. $4(2x - 1) = 20$

(A) 2
(B) 3
(C) 4
(D) 5
(E) 6

42. Simplify the following: $2x(3xy + y)$

(A) $6x^2y + 2xy$
(B) $6x^3 + xy$
(C) $3x^3y$
(D) $x^2 - xy$
(E) $2xy - y$

43. Which of the following values of x would make the following inequality true?

$3x - 14 \leq 3$

(A) 2
(B) 7
(C) 8
(D) 9
(E) 10

44. Which of the following is the reciprocal of $\frac{1}{6}$?

(A) 1
(B) 3
(C) 6
(D) $\frac{1}{3}$
(E) $\frac{1}{2}$

45. Simplify the following:

$(2a + 6 \times 2)(3a + 3) + a$

(A) $8a^2 + 38a$
(B) $8a^3 + 38$
(C) $6a^2 + 43a + 36$
(D) $4a^2 + 23a - 6$
(E) $6a - 23$

46. $x^2 - x = 42$

(A) $x = 7, -6$
(B) $x = 9, -4$
(C) $x = 8, -3$
(D) $x = 6, -1$
(E) $x = 5, -2$

47. $3x + 2y = 3$ and $x = 3y - 10$

(A) $x = -3, y = 1$
(B) $x = 4, y = -2$
(C) $x = -2, y = -1$
(D) $x = 1, y = -1$
(E) $x = -1, y = 3$

48. $7x(4x + 2) = 0$

(A) 0, –4
(B) 0, 4
(C) $0, -\frac{1}{2}$
(D) $0, -\frac{1}{14}$
(E) 0, – 2

49. How many faces does a cube have?

(A) 4
(B) 5
(C) 6
(D) 7
(E) 8

50. An acute angle is defined as

(A) an angle of 180 degrees.
(B) an angle greater than 90 degrees.
(C) an angle of 90 degrees.
(D) an angle less than 90 degrees.
(E) an angle less than 180 degrees.

51. How many connected lines must an object have to be considered a polygon?

    (A) 2 or more
    (B) 3 or more
    (C) 4 or more
    (D) 5 or more
    (E) one or more

52. Calculate the perimeter of the triangle below.

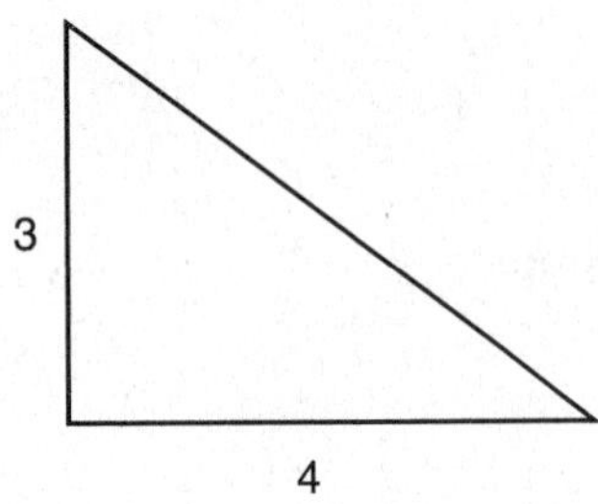

    (A) 7
    (B) 8
    (C) 9
    (D) 10
    (E) 12

53. What is the perimeter of a pentagon where all sides measure 3 feet?

    (A) 5 ft
    (B) 10 ft
    (C) 15 ft
    (D) 20 ft
    (E) 25 ft

54. What is the perimeter of the window pictured below?

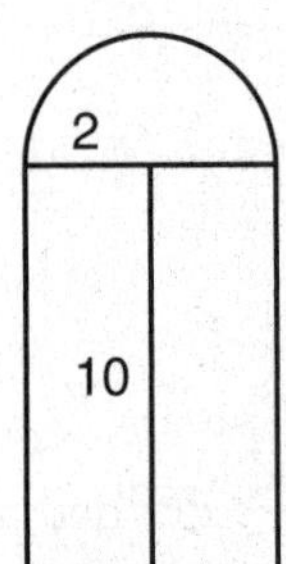

    (A) 14.25
    (B) 24.7
    (C) 36.14
    (D) $10 + 2\pi$
    (E) 30.28

55. Find the perimeter of the following parallelogram.

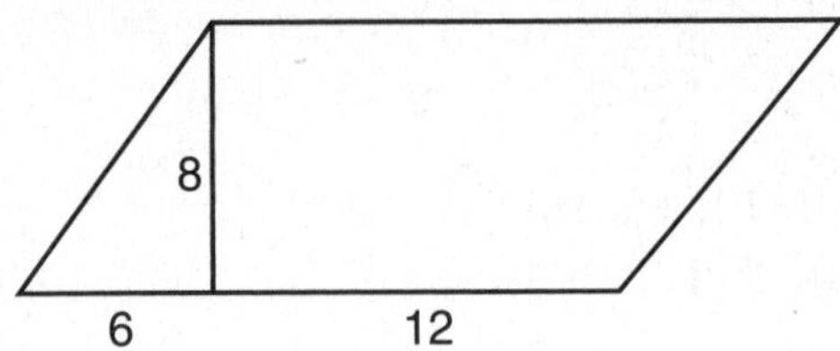

    (A) 52
    (B) 56
    (C) 60
    (D) 63
    (E) 65

56. What is the perimeter of a square that has sides measuring 6 feet?

    (A) 12 feet
    (B) 24 feet
    (C) 36 feet
    (D) 48 feet
    (E) 50 feet

57. A circle has a radius of 8 inches. What is the circumference of the circle?

    (A) 28.34
    (B) 30.5
    (C) 30
    (D) 45.5
    (E) 50.24

58. A rectangle is 8 feet long by 10 feet wide. What is its area?

    (A) 18 square feet
    (B) 36 square feet
    (C) 80 square feet
    (D) 88 square feet
    (E) $8\pi + 12$

59. What is the area of the diagram pictured below?

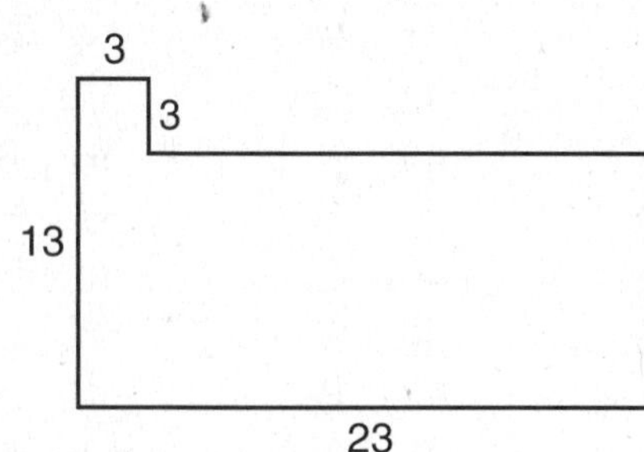

(A) 215
(B) 220
(C) 229
(D) 239
(E) 246

60. Calculate the area of a circle that measures 10 feet in diameter.

(A) $78\frac{1}{2}$ square feet
(B) 80 square feet
(C) $83\frac{1}{4}$ square feet
(D) 92 square feet
(E) $95\frac{1}{2}$ square feet

61. A solid rectangle has a length of 9 inches, a width of 3 inches, and a height of 12 inches. What is its volume?

(A) 24 cubic inches
(B) 39 cubic inches
(C) 42 cubic inches
(D) 324 cubic inches
(E) 336 cubic inches

Answer Key

1. A	14. B	27. C	40. D	53. C
2. B	15. E	28. B	41. B	54. E
3. C	16. A	29. C	42. A	55. B
4. E	17. C	30. B	43. A	56. B
5. B	18. C	31. D	44. C	57. E
6. D	19. B	32. B	45. C	58. C
7. C	20. C	33. C	46. A	59. D
8. A	21. D	34. B	47. E	60. A
9. C	22. C	35. B	48. C	61. D
10. B	23. E	36. E	49. C	
11. E	24. D	37. D	50. D	
12. A	25. A	38. C	51. B	
13. D	26. E	39. D	52. E	

Answer Explanations

1. **(A) $5 - 2\sqrt{6}$.**
   $(\sqrt{2} - \sqrt{3})^2 =$
   Expand as for $(a + b)^2$
   $(\sqrt{2} - \sqrt{3})(\sqrt{2} - \sqrt{3})$
   $= 2 - 2(\sqrt{2} + \sqrt{3}) + 3$
   $= 5 - 2\sqrt{6}$
2. **(B) $\frac{4}{7}$.** An easy way to check if a fraction is greater than $\frac{1}{2}$ is to double the numerator and check if the result is greater than the denominator. If we double the numerator in the fraction $\frac{4}{7}$, we get the number 8, which is greater than the 7 in the denominator.
3. **(C) 100.** One method of solving this problem would be to add all the multiples of 10 in the series (10 + 20 + 30 .... + 190), and then divide by the total number of terms (19).
   However, the average of an evenly spaced series of numbers is equal to the value of the middle term. In other words, it's the average of the two middle terms, if there is an even number of terms. The middle term out of the 19 numbers is the tenth term in the series (100).
4. **(E) none of the above.** While x is not equal to zero, it could be a positive or negative number, or it could be a fraction. Thus, none of the choices <u>must</u> be greater than x.
5. **(B) 0.25.** The equation can be written as $(\sqrt{5/100}) \times 5\sqrt{5} = x$.
   $x = 5 \times 5/100$
   $x = 0.25$
6. **(D) s.** If $pqr = 1$, then none of these variables can be equal to zero. Therefore, since p and r cannot be equal to zero, s must be equal to zero to make the third equation work. In the second equation ($rst = 0$), either s or t must be equal to zero, but there is not enough information to state that both s and t must be equal to zero.

7. **(C) 150.** A square root is a number that when multiplied by itself, results in the root number. In this case, $150 \times 150 = 22{,}500$.
8. **(A) 6.** Answer (A) is correct because when $x = 3$, $f(x) = 6$.
   Answer (B) is incorrect because to make $f(x) = 0$, x^2 would have to equal 3. But 3 is not the square of an integer.
   Answer (C) is incorrect because to make $f(x) = 0$, x^2 would have to be –3 but squares cannot be negative.
9. **(C)** $\sqrt{5}+\sqrt{6}=\sqrt{(5+6)}$**.** When adding square roots, you cannot combine unlike radicals.
10. **(B) 25.** If $x = -5$, then $(x^2 - 50) = 25 - 50 = -25$. But the sign $|x|$ means the absolute value of x. Absolute values are always positive. $|-25| = 25$
11. **(E)** ***m*.** Slope is a number that represents how steeply a line slants. The letter m is often used to stand for a line's slope.
12. **(A)** $8\frac{11}{40}$**.** The first step is to convert the mixed numbers into fractions. $\frac{3}{8}$ is already a fraction. $4\frac{2}{5}$ converts to $\frac{20}{5} + \frac{2}{5}\left(\frac{22}{5}\right)$. $3\frac{1}{2}$ converts to $\frac{6}{2} + \frac{1}{2}\left(\frac{7}{2}\right)$.
    Our problem now looks like $\frac{3}{8} + \frac{22}{5} + \frac{7}{2}$.
    Now we must find the least common denominator. In this case it's 40. We convert $\frac{3}{8}$ to $\frac{15}{40}$, $\frac{22}{5}$ to $\frac{176}{40}$ and $\frac{7}{2}$ to $\frac{140}{40}$. Now, perform the addition.
    $$\frac{15}{40} + \frac{176}{40} + \frac{140}{40} = \frac{331}{40}.$$
    We can simplify the fraction as $8\frac{11}{40}$.
13. **(D)** ***f*(3).** The easiest way to solve this problem is by substituting the possible answers into the expression, and then solve.
    $f(x) = (x + 2) \div (x - 2)$
    $a - f(-1) = (-1 + 2) / (-1 - 2) = 1 / -3 = -\frac{1}{3}$
    $b - f(0) = (0 + 2) / (0 - 2) = 2 / -2 = -1$
    $c - f(1) = (1 + 2) / (1 - 2) = 3 / -1 = -3$
    $d - f(3) = (3 + 2) / (3 - 2) = 5 / 1 = 5$
    $e - f(4) = (4 + 2) / (4 - 2) = 6 / 2 = 3$
14. **(B) 3*x*.** Answer (A) is incorrect because an even integer plus an odd integer will always result in an odd integer.
    Answer (B) is correct: odd times even will result in even.
    Answer (C) is incorrect because even though a square number is even, subtracting an odd number from an even number results in an odd number.
15. **(E)** $\frac{7}{8}$**.** To divide a fraction, we invert the second fraction, then multiply $\frac{9}{4} \times \frac{7}{18} = \frac{63}{72}$. This fraction will reduce to $\frac{7}{8}$.
16. **(A) 2.** When you multiply or divide two negative numbers, the result is always a positive number. Converting $1\frac{1}{2}$ to an improper fraction gives us $\frac{3}{2} \div \frac{3}{4}$. Invert the second fraction and multiply: $\frac{3}{2} \times \frac{4}{3} = \frac{12}{6}$, which simplifies to 2.

17. **(C) $\frac{66}{55}$.** An improper fraction is a fraction in which the top number (numerator) is larger than the bottom number (denominator).
18. **(C) $\frac{1}{2}$.** To solve this problem, we must first find the lowest common denominator and then convert the fractions. In this case, the lowest common denominator is 50. $\frac{35}{50}$ remains the same. $\frac{7}{10}$ converts to $\frac{35}{50}$. $\frac{1}{2}$ converts to $\frac{25}{50}$. $\frac{3}{5}$ converts to $\frac{35}{50}$. $\frac{25}{50}\left(\frac{1}{2}\right)$ is the smallest fraction.
19. **(B) 95°F.** $F = \frac{9}{5}C + 32$. Substitute "C" with 35.

    $F = (\frac{9}{5} \times 35) + 32.$

    $F = \frac{315}{5} + 32$

    $F = 63 + 32$

    $F = 95°$
20. **(C) 50°C.** We know from problem 20 that the formula to convert Centigrade to Fahrenheit is $F = \frac{9}{5}C + 32$. In this case, we know F, and wish to solve for C. The first step is to get "C" all by itself on one side of the equation.

    $F = \frac{9}{5}C + 32$

    $F - 32 = \frac{9}{5}C$

    $\frac{5}{9}(F - 32) = \frac{5}{9}(\frac{9}{5}C)$

    $\frac{5}{9}(F - 32) = C$

    $C = \frac{5}{9}(F - 32)$

    Therefore, the formula to convert Fahrenheit to Centigrade is $C = \frac{5}{9}(F - 32)$. Now, we simply plug in the number and do the math:

    $C = \frac{5}{9}(F - 32)$

    $C = \frac{5}{9}(122 - 32)$

    $C = \frac{5}{9} \times 90$

    $C = 50°C$
21. **(D) 7 hours 55 minutes.** Remember that a minute is a fraction $\left(\frac{1}{60}\right)$ of an hour. Converting the minutes to fractions, we arrive at $1\frac{30}{60} + 3\frac{40}{60} + 2\frac{45}{60}$. Because these fractions all share a common denominator, we can solve this two ways. The first way is to add the whole numbers together, and then add the fractions:

$1 + 3 + 2 = 6$

$\frac{30}{60} + \frac{40}{60} + \frac{45}{60} = \frac{105}{60}$

$6\frac{105}{60} = 7\frac{55}{60}$

The second method would be to convert the mixed numbers to fractions, then perform the addition:

$1\frac{30}{60} + 3\frac{40}{60} + 2\frac{45}{60}$

$\frac{90}{60} + \frac{220}{60} + \frac{165}{60} = \frac{475}{60}$

$\frac{475}{60} = 7\frac{55}{60}$

22. **(C) $\sqrt{41}$.** Graph the points and you'll find that the graph results in a right triangle with the line segment in the *x-y* plane representing the hypotenuse. We can solve this using the Pythagorean theorem.
    Vertical height of triangle = 5; horizontal side = 4; hypotenuse = $\sqrt{(25+16)}$ = $\sqrt{41}$
23. **(E) 144.** $n^4 = n^2 \times n^2 = 12 \times 12 = 144$.
24. **(D) 50.** The square root of a number is the number that, when multiplied by itself, results in the number. $50 \times 50 = 2{,}500$.
25. **(A) $\sqrt{5} + \sqrt{3} = \sqrt{(5+3)}$.** When adding square roots, you cannot combine unlike radicals.
26. **(E) 10.** The median is simply the middle number in a group.
27. **(C) 13.** Because there are two middle numbers in this group (12 and 14), the median is the average of the two.
28. **(B) 63.11.** To find the average of a group of numbers, first add the numbers together, then divide the sum by how many numbers are in the group.

    45.12
    55.00
    60.30
    92.00
    252.42

    252.42 ÷ 4 = 63.105 (rounded up to 63.11)
29. **(C) 2.035×10^3.** The problem is stated in scientific notation. *Scientific notation* is a method of writing or displaying numbers in terms of a decimal number between 1 and 10 multiplied by a power of 10. The scientific notation of 10,492, for example, is 1.0492×10^4.

    To multiply two numbers expressed in scientific notation, first multiply the non-exponential terms ($5.5 \times 3.7 = 20.35$). Next, add the exponents ($5 + -3 = 2$). Our result is 20.35×10^2. To express this in scientific notation, we must move the decimal point one place to the left and add one to the exponent, resulting in 2.035×10^3.
30. **(B) 2×10^{-3}.** To divide two numbers in scientific notation, we first divide the non-exponential terms ($4.2 \div 2.1 = 2$). Next we subtract the second exponent from the first ($-6 - -3 = -3$). Our result is 2×10^{-3}.

31. **(D) "per 100 parts."** Think of the word *century* (100 years). The root *cent* literally means 100. A percentage is a part of 100. Thus, $25\% = \frac{25}{100}$.
32. **(B) 70%.** To convert a decimal to a percentage, move the decimal point two places to the right, then add the percent sign (%).
33. **(C) 16%.** The fraction $\frac{4}{25}$ means $4 \div 25$ (.16). To change the decimal to a percentage, move the decimal point two places to the right (16%).
34. **(B) 4.9.** First, convert the % to a decimal (35% = .35). Next perform the multiplication ($14 \times .35 = 4.9$).
35. **(B) 275.** The formula to solve this problem is $\frac{12}{100} = \frac{33}{x}$.

$\frac{12}{100} = \frac{33}{x}$
$100 \times 33 = 12x$
$3{,}330 = 12x$
$3{,}330 \div 12 = x$
$x = 275$

36. **(E) increase to more than double.** The easiest way to solve this problem is to choose a number that satisfies the rules (x and y are both greater than zero). Substituting (for example) the number 25 for y:

$x = y - \left(\frac{50}{y}\right)$

$x = 25 - \left(\frac{50}{25}\right)$

$x = 23$

The value after doubling y would be $50 - \frac{50}{50} = 49$, which is more than double.

37. **(D) –1.**

$x = (\frac{1}{9} \times 45) - 6$

$x = \frac{45}{9} - 6$

$x = 5 - 6$

$x = -1$

38. **(C) $5\frac{5}{6}$.** To clear the denominators, multiply both sides by 5, then multiply both sides by 6. The result is

$x \times 6 = 7 \times 5$
$6x = 35$
$x = \frac{35}{6}$
$x = 5\frac{5}{6}$

39. **(D) 0.6.** The absolute value signs can make this problem tricky, because x can equal $4x - 3$, and also $-x$ can equal $4x - 3$.

Solving the two possible equations:

$x = 4x - 3$
$3 = 4x - x$
$3 = 3x$
$x = 1$ (not one of the answer choices)
$-x = 4x - 3$

$3 = 4x + x$
$3 = 5x$
$x = \frac{3}{5}$
$x = 0.6$ (which is answer (D).

40. **(D) 12, 15, and 18.** Pythagorean theorem states that $a^2 + b^2 = c^2$. 15^2 <u>is not</u> equal to 18^2.
41. **(B) 3.**

$4(2x - 1) = 20$	
$(2x - 1) = 5$	Divide each side of equation by 4
$2x - 1 = 5$	
$2x = 1 + 5$	Move constant –1 to the right
$2x = 6$	Combine constants.
$\frac{2x}{2} = \frac{6}{2}$	Next divide by 2, the coefficient of *x*.
$x = 3$	

42. **(A)** $\boldsymbol{6x^2y + 2xy}$.

$2x(3xy + y)$	
$2x(y + 3xy)$	Multiply the monomial term $2x$ by each term in the parentheses term, $(y + 3xy)$
$2xy + 6x^2y$	Sort terms in decreasing powers
$6x^2y + 2xy$	

43. **(A) 2.** First, solve the inequality as an equation. Any number with a value less than the answer would make the inequality true.
$3x - 14 = 3$
$3x = 3 + 14$
$3x = 17$
$x = 5\frac{2}{3}$
For the inequality to be true, *x* would have to be equal to or less than $5\frac{2}{3}$.
44. **(C) 6.** A reciprocal is the number by which a number can be multiplied to produce 1. So, the reciprocal of $\frac{1}{6}$ is 6 because $\frac{1}{6} \times 6 = 1$.
45. **(C)** $\boldsymbol{6a^2 + 43a + 36}$.
$(2a + 6 \times 2)(3a + 3) + a$
Multiply 6 * 2
$(2a + 12)(3a + 3) + a$
Reorder the terms:
$(12 + 2a)(3a + 3) + a.$
Reorder the terms:
$(12 + 2a)(3 + 3a) + a$
Multiply $(12 + 2a) \times (3 + 3a)$
$(12(3 + 3a) + 2a \times (3 + 3a)) + a$
$((3 \times 12 + 3a \times 12) + 2a \times (3 + 3a)) + a$
$((36 + 36a) + 2a \times (3 + 3a)) + a$
$(36 + 36a + (3 \times 2a + 3a * 2a)) + a$
$(36 + 36a + (6a + 6a^2)) + a$
Combine like terms: $36a + 6a = 42a$
$(36 + 42a + 6a^2) + a$

Reorder the terms:
$36 + 42a + a + 6a^2$
Combine like terms: $42a + a = 43a$
$36 + 43a + 6a^2$

46. **(A) $x = 7, -6$.** This is a quadratic equation. To solve a quadratic equation, we first factor it. Next, set each factor equal to zero.
$x^2 - x = 42$
$x^2 - x - 42 = 0$
$(x - 7)(x + 6) = 0$
$x - 7 = 0$
$x + 6 = 0$
$x = 7$
$x = -6$
47. **(E) $x = -1, y = 3$.**
$3x + 2y = 3$ and $x = 3y - 10$
We can see that the value of x is equal to $3y - 10$, so we replace x in the first equation with this value.
$3x + 2y = 3$, so $3(3y - 10) + 2y = 3$
$9y - 30 + 2y = 3$
$11y = 33$
$y = 3$
Now that we know the value of y, we can plug it into either equation and solve for x.
$x = 3(3) - 10$
$x = 9 - 10$
$x = -1$
48. **(C) $0, -\frac{1}{2}$.** To solve this type of problem, we can use the *Principle of Zero Products,* that states that if a and b are real numbers and ab is equal to zero, then either a, b, or both a and b are equal to zero.
$7x(4x + 2) = 0$
Set $7x$ and $4x + 2$ equal to zero:
$7x = 0$
$4x + 2 = 0.$
Solving for x, we arrive at $x = 0$, and $x = -\frac{1}{2}$
49. **(C) 6.** A cube is a solid with six faces (one top, one bottom, and four sides).
50. **(D) an angle less than 90 degrees.**
51. **(B) 3 or more.** A polygon is a shape with three or more lines.
52. **(E) 12.** Because this is a right triangle, we can use the Pythagorean theorem ($a^2 + b^2 = c^2$) to determine the length of the hypotenuse.
$3^2 + 4^2 = c^2$
$9 + 16 = c^2$
$25 = c^2$
$c = 5$
The length of the hypotenuse is 5, so the perimeter is 3 + 4 + 5, or 12.
53. **(C) 15 ft.** A pentagon has five sides. $3 \times 5 = 15$.
54. **(E) 30.28.** The rectangular portion has two long sides with a length of 10 ($10 \times 2 = 20$), and the bottom portion that measures 4 ($20 + 4 = 24$). The top

portion is one-half of a circle, with a radius of 2 (which means the circle would have a circumference of 4, if it was a complete circle). The circumference of a circle is *pi* times the diameter, but we only want one-half of this: $24 + \frac{1}{2}(4\pi)$.

$3.14 \times 4 = 12.56$

$12.56 \div 2 = 6.28$

$6.28 + 24 = 30.28$

55. **(B) 56.** We must first find the slant height using the Pythagorean theorem ($a^2 + b^2 = c^2$). $6^2 + 8^2 = 36 + 64 = 100$. The square root of 100 is 10, so the length of the missing side is 10. The perimeter is $(2 \times 18) + (2 \times 10)$, or 56.
56. **(B) 24 feet.** The perimeter of a square is the measurement of all four sides of the square. 4×6 feet = 24 feet.
57. **(E) 50.24.** To determine the circumference of a circle, we multiply *pi* (3.14) by the diameter of the circle. The diameter of a circle is twice the radius ($8 \times 2 = 16$), so $16 \times 3.14 = 50.24$.
58. **(C) 80 square feet.** To find the area of a rectangle, multiply the width times the length ($10 \times 8 = 80$).
59. **(D) 239.** This figure is really two shapes merged together. We can determine the area by computing the area of each shape. The top square has a width of 3 and a length of 3, for a total area of 9. The bottom shape has a width of 23 and a height of 10 (13 – 3), $23 \times 10 = 230$. $230 + 9 = 239$.
60. **(A) $78\frac{1}{2}$ square feet.** The formula to compute the area of a circle is $A = (\pi)r^2$.

    Since the radius of a circle is $\frac{1}{2}$ of the diameter, $A = 5^2\pi$.

    $A = 25 \times 3.14$

    $A = 78.5$ or $78\frac{1}{2}$
61. **(D) 324 cubic inches.** To determine the volume of a rectangular solid multiply the length of the solid times the width times the height ($9 \times 3 \times 12 = 324$).

Arithmetic Reasoning

Anyone that cannot cope with mathematics is not fully human. At best he is a tolerable subhuman who has learned to wear shoes, bathe and not make messes in the house.

—Lazarus Long (fictional character created by Robert A. Heinlein)

Commissioned officers are supposed to be pretty smart. The military services expect their commissioned officers to be problem-solvers. That means they must garner the ability to isolate the necessary elements of a problem from the extraneous data, and determine the best plan to arrive at a solution.

What better way to measure problem-solving ability (as well as mathematical knowledge) than word problems? All of the services test knowledge of arithmetic reasoning as part of their OCS/OCC/OTS selection process.

In the Air Force, arithmetic reasoning questions are used in the computation of the Navigator-Technical, Academic Aptitude, and Quantitative composite scores of the AFOQT. The subtest is comprised of 25 questions, with a 29-minute time limit.

For Navy, Coast Guard, and Marine Corps aviation candidates, arithmetic reasoning questions are included in the Math Skills subtest of the ASTB. There are 30 arithmetic reasoning and math knowledge questions on the subtest that must be answered in 25 minutes.

Arithmetic reasoning comprises a substantial percentage of the General Technical (GT) composite score used for Army OCS applicants and non-aviation applicants of the Marine Corps and Coast Guard. The arithmetic reasoning subtest of the ASVAB consists of 30 questions. Thirty-six minutes are allotted to complete this sub-test of the ASVAB. The 30 questions on the ASVAB are generally much easier than the questions found on the AFOQT or ASTB.

PROBLEM SOLVING

Understanding the Problem

The singular most important element of problem-solving is to determine what the problem is asking. Don't laugh. Many people forget this crucial step and begin searching the problem for data, without actually knowing what question is being asked.

For example, take the following question:

EXAMPLE

Pete, Will, and Bertha all work part-time at Burger King. Pete worked four shifts, and received $50.48, $40.28, $60.60, and $55.80, respectively. Will worked only two shifts, and received $30.80 for the first and $60 for the second. Bertha worked three shifts and earned $39.60, $55.40, and $34.80. Pete and Will decide to combine their money and buy a stereo that costs $350. How much money will they have to borrow from Bertha in order to make the purchase?

(A) $45.30
(B) $52.04
(C) $60.03
(D) $129.80
(E) $297.96

What is the question that's being asked? The problem that needs to be solved here is how much *additional* money do Pete and Will need after their wages are added together in order to afford the $350 stereo?

Know the Basics

You don't need to be Einstein to score well on the arithmetic reasoning sections of the tests used for officer qualification/selection. You're not going to be asked to compute an orbit to Mars. However, to do well, you need to know the basics of math. For example, to solve the problem above, you would need to know how to add and subtract decimals.

If you think you need a basic math review, see Chapter 7 (Mathematics Knowledge).

Examples of the "basics" you should know include:

- ✔ Adding, subtracting, multiplying, dividing whole numbers, decimals, percentages, and fractions
- ✔ Converting improper fractions to mixed numbers and vice versa
- ✔ Converting fractions to decimals (and vice versa), and decimals to percentages
- ✔ Basic algebra
- ✔ Squares and square roots
- ✔ Basic geometry, including calculating perimeters, and the area of squares, rectangles, boxes, triangles, trapezoids, and other geometrical shapes
- ✔ Simple conversions, such as inches to feet, quarts to gallons, square feet to acreage.

Finding the Relevant Factors

Many times questions will contain information that has absolutely nothing to do with solving the problem. Our sample question includes the wages earned by Bertha each day. This is misdirection—Bertha's total wages are irrelevant to determine how much extra money is needed by Pete and Will to buy the $350 stereo.

One of the best methods of picking the relevant factors out of the problem is to write an equation to solve the problem, then plugging in the data from the question.

For our sample problem, we could write:

$350 – (Wages of Pete + Wages of Will) = extra money needed

It then becomes much easier to pick the relevant factors out of the problem.

Eliminating Implausible Choices

On multiple–choice tests, it is sometimes possible to eliminate implausible or unlikely choices. The folks who write the tests will sometimes include choices from the obvious but incorrect ways to solve the problem, and if you know it's not the proper method, you can often eliminate that choice as a possible answer. Let's take another look at our example question again:

EXAMPLE

Pete, Will, and Bertha all work part-time at Burger King. Pete worked four shifts, and received $50.48, $40.28, $60.60, and $55.80, respectively. Will worked only two shifts, and received $30.80 for the first and $60 for the second. Bertha worked three shifts and earned $39.60, $55.40, and $34.80. Pete and Will decide to combine their money and buy a stereo that costs $350. How much money will they have to borrow from Bertha in order to make the purchase?

(A) $45.30
(B) $52.04
(C) $60.03
(D) $129.80
(E) $297.96

We know that Bertha's wages are not a factor in solving the problem. Therefore, the total of Bertha's wages ($129.80) is not correct. We can then eliminate choice (D) from our list of possible correct answers.

Using Pictures

Many times you can get a better sense of the relevant factors of a problem by sketching a simple picture on your scratch paper.

Take the following problem:

EXAMPLE

Chrissy wishes to buy a lot to build a new home. The lot she is most interested in has 200 feet of road frontage and is 500 feet deep. The broker tells her that the land is on sale for $9,000 per acre. How much will Chrissy have to spend to buy the lot?

(A) $20,700
(B) $25,000
(C) $27,500
(D) $30,000
(E) $32,500

Drawing a simple sketch may help us to visualize the entire problem:

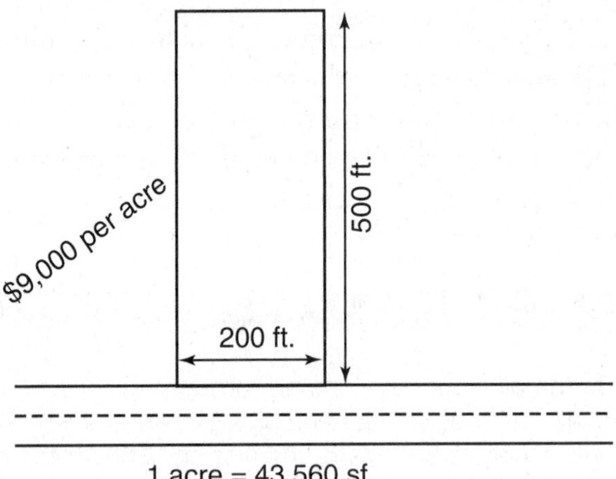

Our simple sketch includes all the information we need to solve the problem. We know (or should know) that we can obtain the area of the rectangle by multiplying its length times its width (200 ft × 500 ft = 100,000 sf). One acre equals 43,560 square feet, so dividing the total square feet by the number of square feet in one acre will result in the number of acres on this lot (100,000 sf ÷ 43,560 sf = 2.3 acres [rounded up]). 2.3 acres × $9,000 (cost per acre) = $20,700.

Solve the Complete Problem

Many word problems require you to perform several separate steps to arrive at the correct answer. Some people, especially under time pressure, may lose track of what they are actually trying to determine, and stop before they've completed all the necessary steps.

For example, the first step in solving our sample problem would be to add up the wages of Pete and Will. The sum of their wages is $297.96, which is one of the possible answers given (Choice (E)). However, the problem is not solved yet. We need to determine how much additional money will be required to purchase the $350 stereo, so we must subtract the sum ($297.96) from $350 to arrive at the correct answer (Choice (B) $52.04).

Answer Sheet for Practice Questions

1 Ⓐ Ⓑ Ⓒ Ⓓ Ⓔ	17 Ⓐ Ⓑ Ⓒ Ⓓ Ⓔ	33 Ⓐ Ⓑ Ⓒ Ⓓ Ⓔ	49 Ⓐ Ⓑ Ⓒ Ⓓ Ⓔ
2 Ⓐ Ⓑ Ⓒ Ⓓ Ⓔ	18 Ⓐ Ⓑ Ⓒ Ⓓ Ⓔ	34 Ⓐ Ⓑ Ⓒ Ⓓ Ⓔ	50 Ⓐ Ⓑ Ⓒ Ⓓ Ⓔ
3 Ⓐ Ⓑ Ⓒ Ⓓ Ⓔ	19 Ⓐ Ⓑ Ⓒ Ⓓ Ⓔ	35 Ⓐ Ⓑ Ⓒ Ⓓ Ⓔ	51 Ⓐ Ⓑ Ⓒ Ⓓ Ⓔ
4 Ⓐ Ⓑ Ⓒ Ⓓ Ⓔ	20 Ⓐ Ⓑ Ⓒ Ⓓ Ⓔ	36 Ⓐ Ⓑ Ⓒ Ⓓ Ⓔ	52 Ⓐ Ⓑ Ⓒ Ⓓ Ⓔ
5 Ⓐ Ⓑ Ⓒ Ⓓ Ⓔ	21 Ⓐ Ⓑ Ⓒ Ⓓ Ⓔ	37 Ⓐ Ⓑ Ⓒ Ⓓ Ⓔ	53 Ⓐ Ⓑ Ⓒ Ⓓ Ⓔ
6 Ⓐ Ⓑ Ⓒ Ⓓ Ⓔ	22 Ⓐ Ⓑ Ⓒ Ⓓ Ⓔ	38 Ⓐ Ⓑ Ⓒ Ⓓ Ⓔ	54 Ⓐ Ⓑ Ⓒ Ⓓ Ⓔ
7 Ⓐ Ⓑ Ⓒ Ⓓ Ⓔ	23 Ⓐ Ⓑ Ⓒ Ⓓ Ⓔ	39 Ⓐ Ⓑ Ⓒ Ⓓ Ⓔ	55 Ⓐ Ⓑ Ⓒ Ⓓ Ⓔ
8 Ⓐ Ⓑ Ⓒ Ⓓ Ⓔ	24 Ⓐ Ⓑ Ⓒ Ⓓ Ⓔ	40 Ⓐ Ⓑ Ⓒ Ⓓ Ⓔ	56 Ⓐ Ⓑ Ⓒ Ⓓ Ⓔ
9 Ⓐ Ⓑ Ⓒ Ⓓ Ⓔ	25 Ⓐ Ⓑ Ⓒ Ⓓ Ⓔ	41 Ⓐ Ⓑ Ⓒ Ⓓ Ⓔ	57 Ⓐ Ⓑ Ⓒ Ⓓ Ⓔ
10 Ⓐ Ⓑ Ⓒ Ⓓ Ⓔ	26 Ⓐ Ⓑ Ⓒ Ⓓ Ⓔ	42 Ⓐ Ⓑ Ⓒ Ⓓ Ⓔ	58 Ⓐ Ⓑ Ⓒ Ⓓ Ⓔ
11 Ⓐ Ⓑ Ⓒ Ⓓ Ⓔ	27 Ⓐ Ⓑ Ⓒ Ⓓ Ⓔ	43 Ⓐ Ⓑ Ⓒ Ⓓ Ⓔ	59 Ⓐ Ⓑ Ⓒ Ⓓ Ⓔ
12 Ⓐ Ⓑ Ⓒ Ⓓ Ⓔ	28 Ⓐ Ⓑ Ⓒ Ⓓ Ⓔ	44 Ⓐ Ⓑ Ⓒ Ⓓ Ⓔ	60 Ⓐ Ⓑ Ⓒ Ⓓ Ⓔ
13 Ⓐ Ⓑ Ⓒ Ⓓ Ⓔ	29 Ⓐ Ⓑ Ⓒ Ⓓ Ⓔ	45 Ⓐ Ⓑ Ⓒ Ⓓ Ⓔ	61 Ⓐ Ⓑ Ⓒ Ⓓ Ⓔ
14 Ⓐ Ⓑ Ⓒ Ⓓ Ⓔ	30 Ⓐ Ⓑ Ⓒ Ⓓ Ⓔ	46 Ⓐ Ⓑ Ⓒ Ⓓ Ⓔ	62 Ⓐ Ⓑ Ⓒ Ⓓ Ⓔ
15 Ⓐ Ⓑ Ⓒ Ⓓ Ⓔ	31 Ⓐ Ⓑ Ⓒ Ⓓ Ⓔ	47 Ⓐ Ⓑ Ⓒ Ⓓ Ⓔ	63 Ⓐ Ⓑ Ⓒ Ⓓ Ⓔ
16 Ⓐ Ⓑ Ⓒ Ⓓ Ⓔ	32 Ⓐ Ⓑ Ⓒ Ⓓ Ⓔ	48 Ⓐ Ⓑ Ⓒ Ⓓ Ⓔ	64 Ⓐ Ⓑ Ⓒ Ⓓ Ⓔ

Practice Questions

1. John wants to replace the trim on a small section of a wall. He takes measurements and decides that he will need 2 feet of trim. The trim is on sale for 10 cents per centimeter. There are 2.54 centimeters in one inch. How many centimeters of trim does John have to buy?

   (A) 60.96 centimeters
   (B) 60.16 centimeters
   (C) 63.58 centimeters
   (D) 58.3 centimeters
   (E) 59.6 centimeters

2. Thirty percent of the class read books over summer vacation. If 15 percent of those read *A Tale of Two Cities*, what percentage of the entire class read this book?

   (A) 25%
   (B) 10.5%
   (C) 7.3%
   (D) 4.5%
   (E) 6%

3. A farmer discovers that four percent of his apples spoil before arriving at the market. If he ships 1,000 apples, how many of them will arrive spoiled?

   (A) 16
   (B) 20
   (C) 34
   (D) 40
   (E) 45

4. 2,000 pounds of bolts are sent to Bob's Hardware in 50-pound containers. How many containers will the store receive?

   (A) 20
   (B) 30
   (C) 40
   (D) 50
   (E) 60

5. A ski-lift cable car has a sign that reads, "Maximum weight 400 pounds." Which of the following may ride on the cable car?

   (A) Three people, one weighing 180 pounds, another weighing 190 pounds, and one weighing 110 pounds
   (B) Two people, one weighing 140 pounds with a backpack weighing 60 pounds, the other weighing 150 pounds with a backpack weighing 40 pounds
   (C) Three people, one weighing 150 pounds, another weighing 150 pounds, and the third weighing 110 pounds
   (D) Two people, one weighing 160 pounds, and the other weighing 200 pounds with a backpack weighing 50 pounds
   (E) Four people, each weighing 150 pounds

6. Burt went prospecting for a week. On the first day, he found 7 pieces of gold. On the following days, he found 15, 14, 4, 8, 9, and 6 pieces of gold respectively. How many pieces of gold did Burt find on the average day?

   (A) 7
   (B) 8
   (C) 9
   (D) 10
   (E) 11

7. Bob and Alice both worked summer jobs at McDonalds. They each worked 20 hours per week for 8 weeks at $9.42 per hour. How much money did Bob and Alice earn together?

   (A) $3,014.40
   (B) $3,570.90
   (C) $4,020.63
   (D) $4,094.49
   (E) $4,120.30

8. Military regulations require that all military vehicles receive general maintenance every 15,000 miles. Vehicle #98B340 last had general maintenance performed when the odometer read 53,413 miles. The odometer now reads 57,213 miles. How many more miles can this vehicle travel before it will require general maintenance?

   (A) 10,500
   (B) 11,200
   (C) 12,100
   (D) 12,230
   (E) 13,433

9. Sixty pounds of weight are placed on a seesaw, eight feet away from the fulcrum. If 80 pounds of weight are added to the other side, how many feet from the fulcrum must the weight be placed in order to balance the seesaw?

   (A) 5 feet
   (B) 6 feet
   (C) 7 feet
   (D) 8 feet
   (E) 9 feet

10. John is the manager of an office supply store. He buys 200 reams of paper for $500. John wants to resell the paper in 100-sheet bundles and make a 20 percent profit. If one ream equals 500 sheets of paper, what will John have to charge for 100 sheets in order to ensure his profit?

    (A) $1.80
    (B) $.60
    (C) $2.80
    (D) $3.00
    (E) $3.15

11. You are given the task of storing 200 wooden crates in several rooms. Each crate must be placed on the floor and cannot be stacked upon each other. The crates measure 71 inches by 40 inches. If a room measures 25 feet by 30 feet, how many crates would be left to store if you stored the maximum possible number of crates in the first room?

    (A) 165
    (B) 164
    (C) 162
    (D) 155
    (E) 150

12. A farmer plants 100 rows of corn in an 8-hour day. His helper plants $1\frac{1}{2}$ that number of rows in half the time. How long will it take them to plant 200 rows of corn?

    (A) 4 hours
    (B) 5 hours
    (C) 6 hours
    (D) $7\frac{1}{2}$ hours
    (E) $8\frac{1}{2}$ hours

13. Betty had an annual income of $438,517. If she paid the state $613 in taxes, how much (to the nearest cent) does she pay in taxes for each $100 earned?

    (A) 9 cents
    (B) 10 cents
    (C) 11 cents
    (D) 13 cents
    (E) 14 cents

14. A squadron has 350 enlisted and 50 officers assigned. $\frac{3}{5}$ of the squadron graduated from a special training course this year, and $\frac{1}{4}$ of the squadron graduated last year. What fraction of the squadron has not yet graduated from the special training course?

   (A) $\frac{10}{13}$
   (B) $\frac{2}{3}$
   (C) $\frac{3}{20}$
   (D) $\frac{1}{4}$
   (E) $\frac{2}{5}$

15. Your new computer will depreciate 10 percent of its value the first year, 15 percent of its value the second year, and 20 percent of its value the third year. If you paid $2,500 for the computer, how much will it be worth after three years?

   (A) $1,110
   (B) $1,530
   (C) $1,610
   (D) $1,670
   (E) $1,710

16. A rectangle's bottom side is 5 times longer than the right side. If the right side is A, what is the area of the rectangle?

   (A) $2A^2$
   (B) $3A^2$
   (C) $4A^2$
   (D) $5A^2$
   (E) $5A$

17. The perimeter of a rectangle is 200 feet. The shortest two sides add up to 50 feet. What is the length of each of the longest two sides?

   (A) 65 feet
   (B) 75 feet
   (C) 85 feet
   (D) 95 feet
   (E) 105 feet

18. You need to fence in an area as shown below:

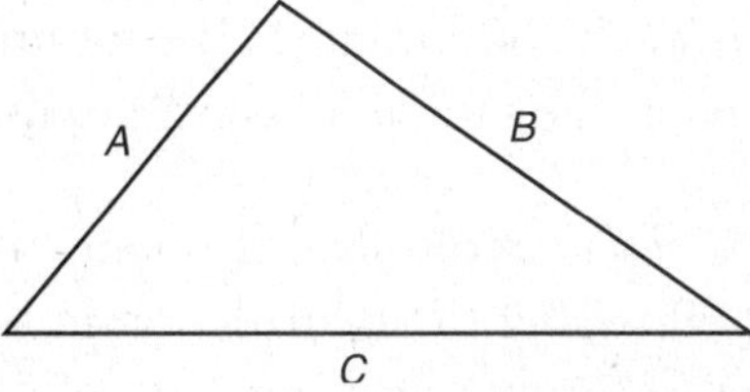

   If side A is 10 feet, and side B is two feet longer than side A, and side C is one foot longer than Side B, how many feet of fence will you have to purchase?

   (A) 25 feet
   (B) 30 feet
   (C) 35 feet
   (D) 90 feet
   (E) 105 feet

19. You are required to paint the floor of the building pictured below:

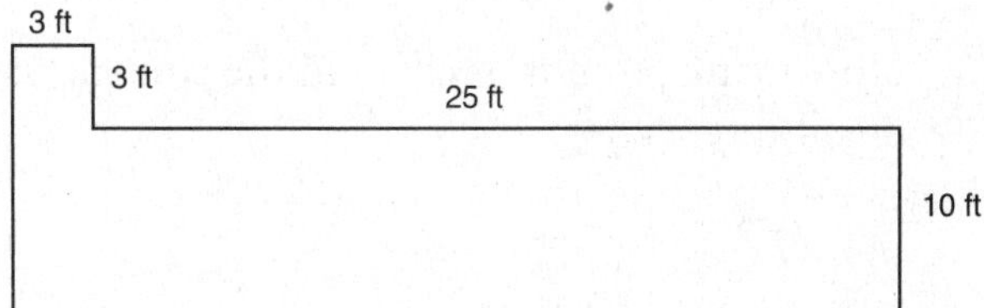

   You will need paint to cover how many square feet of floor?

   (A) 200 sq feet
   (B) 289 sq feet
   (C) 259 sq feet
   (D) 300 sq feet
   (E) 310 sq feet

20. Cell phone service costs $62.58 per month for 800 minutes. There is an initial fee of $25.00 to establish the service. For a one-year minimum contract, the customer can purchase a cell phone for $89.00. A $200 deposit is required, but it will be returned to the customer after one year if all bills are paid on time. The customer can also subscribe to monthly services such as Internet ($9.50 per month), interactive games ($3.00 per month), and text-messaging ($2.00 per month). Time used over the 800 minutes per month is charged at the rate of 50 cents per minute.

    A subscriber's monthly cell-phone bill totals $149.00. Using the information in the paragraph above, what percentage of the total bill was for basic cell phone service?

    (A) 35 percent
    (B) 42 percent
    (C) 58 percent
    (D) 63 percent
    (E) 78 percent

21. During a three-day period, an art student used $2\frac{1}{4}$ pounds of modeling clay the first day, $4\frac{5}{8}$ pounds of modeling clay the second day, and $\frac{1}{2}$ pound of modeling clay the third day. How many pounds of clay did the student use on all three days?

    (A) $7\frac{3}{8}$
    (B) $8\frac{1}{8}$
    (C) $8\frac{1}{4}$
    (D) $9\frac{1}{2}$
    (E) $9\frac{3}{4}$

22. Tim bought a new table for his living room. The table is round and divided into 4 equal sections by a large "X" inlaid on the table. The intersecting lines on the "X," therefore, form four identical triangles on the surface of the table. What is the angle of each of the points in the center of the table?

    (A) 60 degrees
    (B) 90 degrees
    (C) 110 degrees
    (D) 150 degrees
    (E) 180 degrees

23. Two drivers leave from the same place. The first driver heads north for 300 miles and the other driver heads east for 400 miles. If both roads were absolutely straight, how far away would the drivers be from each other (as the crow flies)?

    (A) 200 miles
    (B) 300 miles
    (C) 400 miles
    (D) 500 miles
    (E) 600 miles

24. Tom earns 2.8 times less money per hour than Becky makes. If Tom earns $5.50 per hour, how much per hour does Becky make?

    (A) $13.20
    (B) $14.50
    (C) $15.40
    (D) $16.30
    (E) $16.80

25. Twelve times $\frac{1}{2}$ of Shaun's age is 36. How old is Shaun?

    (A) 6
    (B) 7
    (C) 8
    (D) 18
    (E) 19

26. A theater finds that they can sell 300 admission tickets when they sell them for $9 each. However, if they sell tickets for $7 each, they can sell 450 tickets. How much more money in ticket sales does the theater make when they sell the tickets at a discount?

    (A) $350
    (B) $400
    (C) $450
    (D) $500
    (E) $550

27. A writer decides that she will complete $\frac{5}{8}$ of her manuscript before the end of the day. After working a few hours, she discovers that she has completed $\frac{3}{5}$ of the manuscript.

    How much more does she have to complete?

    (A) $\frac{1}{8}$
    (B) $\frac{3}{8}$
    (C) $\frac{1}{5}$
    (D) $\frac{1}{40}$
    (E) $\frac{3}{40}$

28. Bus A has some passengers aboard. Ten more passengers arrive and board the bus. More passengers arrive and board the bus until there is a total of four times as many passengers in the bus than there were when the first group of ten passengers arrived. Bus B has sixteen fewer passengers than twelve times as many passengers that were aboard Bus A before the first group of ten passengers arrived. If both busses now have the same number of passengers, how many passengers were originally on Bus A?

    (A) 7 passengers
    (B) 8 passengers
    (C) 9 passengers
    (D) 10 passengers
    (E) 11 passengers

29. A race car races around a track. On the first lap, the car is clocked at 120.5 mph. On the second lap, the car is clocked at 130.3 mph. On the third lap, the car is clocked at 150.8 mph. During the three laps, what was the average speed of the race car? (round your answer to the nearest tenth).

    (A) 401.8
    (B) 401.9
    (C) 422.6
    (D) 422.7
    (E) none of the above

30. The figure below consists of four equal-sized squares. Each square has an area equal to 25. What is the perimeter of this figure?

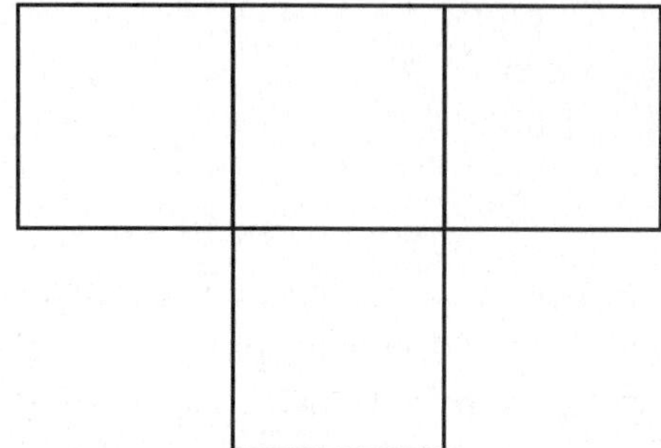

    (A) 30
    (B) 35
    (C) 40
    (D) 45
    (E) 50

31. A contractor charges 48 cents per square foot to lay carpet. How much would he charge to lay 20 square yards of carpet?

    (A) $73.80
    (B) $86.40
    (C) $94.60
    (D) $101.30
    (E) $130.20

32. Three workers each assemble 200 boxes per hour. At the end of an eight-hour shift, the foreman discovered that five percent of the boxes were incorrectly assembled. How many good boxes did these workers produce, total, at the end of the shift?

(A) 3,550
(B) 3,950
(C) 4,300
(D) 4, 450
(E) 4,560

33. In your pocket are 7 quarters, 3 dimes, 5 nickels, and 12 pennies. A burger, fries, and a cola cost $3.50. How much are you short?

(A) 94 cents
(B) 99 cents
(C) $1.05
(D) $1.08
(E) $1.19

34. Three people start a business. At the end of the year, they decide to split the profits based on the amount of time each spent working at the business. Josh receives $12,000. Christina put in 1.5 times the hours that Josh put into the business. Jeanie put in 3.5 times the hours that Christina put in. How much total profit did the business make during the year?

(A) $80,000
(B) $93,000
(C) $98,000
(D) $100,000
(E) $130,000

35. Four workers can re-roof a building in 42 days. However, on an upcoming project, the contractor knows that one of his workers can only work half-days. How many work-days should the contractor tell the customer the job will take?

(A) 45 days
(B) 47 days
(C) 48 days
(D) 49 days
(E) 50 days

36. One kilometer equals approximately $\frac{5}{8}$ of a mile. You drive 500 miles on a 1,000-kilometer trip. How many kilometers do you still have to travel?

(A) 200 kilometers
(B) 230 kilometers
(C) 250 kilometers
(D) 300 kilometers
(E) 330 kilometers

37. If you are in a car traveling 70 mph, how far will you travel in 45 minutes?

(A) $48\frac{3}{4}$ miles
(B) $52\frac{1}{2}$ miles
(C) 55 miles
(D) 60 miles
(E) $60\frac{1}{2}$ miles

38. If the average person eats 3.5 pounds of chocolate per year, how much would the average person consume in a decade?

(A) 3.5 pounds
(B) 35 pounds
(C) 350 pounds
(D) 3,500 pounds
(E) None of the above

39. An empty 25-gallon aquarium weighs 20 pounds. When completely filled with water, the aquarium weighs 228.7 pounds. Approximately how much is the weight of one gallon of water?

(A) 5.5
(B) 6.35
(C) 8.35
(D) 9.15
(E) 9.95

40. Carlos earns $12.50 per hour. If he works over 8 hours per day, he receives time and a half for any time worked over 8 hours. If Carlos worked 8.5 hours per day for a five-day work-week, how much did he earn?

(A) $425.88
(B) $475.88
(C) $546.88
(D) $596.88
(E) $600.88

41. A website has 1,850,000 "hits" per day. How many "hits" does the website have each year?

(A) 185,000,000
(B) 185,250,000
(C) 675,000,000
(D) 675,250,000
(E) none of the above

42. A homework assignment consisted of reading Chapter 4 of a history book. Chapter 4 is 45 pages long. Jimmy read 35 of the pages. What fraction of the chapter did Jimmy read?

(A) $\frac{7}{9}$
(B) $\frac{2}{3}$
(C) $\frac{3}{4}$
(D) $\frac{5}{8}$
(E) $\frac{4}{5}$

43. Tammy is planning to carpet the room shown below:

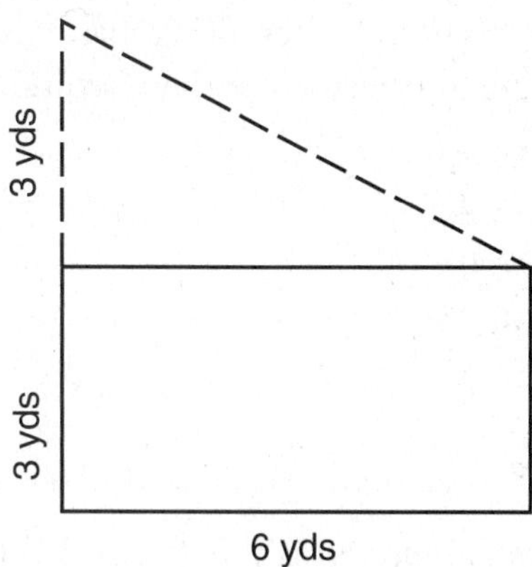

Her brother-in-law, Skip, tells her that he will carpet the area for $3.50 per square yard, plus $6.00 per hour labor. Assuming the job takes Skip four hours to complete, how much should he charge his sister-in-law?

(A) $118.50
(B) $150
(C) $165.50
(D) $170.33
(E) $175.75

44. It will take Bill 4 days to plant a garden with 17 rows. If Tammy can plant the same number of rows in 3 days, how long will it take to plant the garden if they work together?

(A) 1 day
(B) $1\frac{1}{2}$ days
(C) $1\frac{5}{7}$ days
(D) 2 days
(E) $2\frac{1}{4}$ days

45. A store sells Christmas decorations at a 25 percent discount the month after Christmas. If the store is selling a box of decorations for $4.20 seven days after Christmas, what was the original price before the discount?

    (A) $5.60
    (B) $5.88
    (C) $6.03
    (D) $6.23
    (E) $6.50

46. The formula used to convert Celsius to degrees Fahrenheit is $F = \frac{9}{5}C + 32$. If the outside temperature is zero degrees Celsius, what is the temperature in Fahrenheit?

    (A) 0
    (B) 32 degrees
    (C) 50 degrees
    (D) 100 degrees
    (E) 120 degrees

47. Number-6 washers cost $3 per pound. Number-8 washers cost $7 per pound. If the owner of a hardware store mixes together six pounds of number-6 washers and $1\frac{1}{2}$ pounds of number-8 washers, what is the cost per pound of the mixture?

    (A) $3.20
    (B) $3.80
    (C) $4.20
    (D) $4.80
    (E) $5.00

48. A driver travels 200 miles at an average speed of 50 mph. He then returns home, driving at an average speed of 60 mph. Approximately how long did it take him to complete the trip?

    (A) 5 hours, 20 minutes
    (B) 6 hours
    (C) 6 hours, 15 minutes
    (D) 7 hours, 20 minutes
    (E) 8 hours, 3 minutes

49. You are required to varnish the floor of the room pictured below:

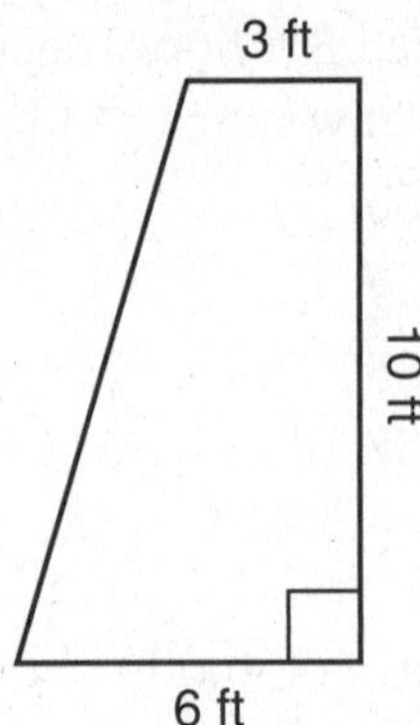

One gallon of varnish will coat 5 square feet of floor space. How much varnish will it take to coat the entire floor?

    (A) 5 gallons
    (B) 6 gallons
    (C) 7 gallons
    (D) 8 gallons
    (E) 9 gallons

50. Patty is saving for a car. The car she wants to buy costs $15,000, but she knows that there will be a 15 percent charge for tax and license fees. How much money does Patty need to save?

    (A) $15,650
    (B) $16,550
    (C) $17,250
    (D) $17,500
    (E) $18,000

51. Paul and George own a barbershop together, which they decide to sell for $200,000. The two decide to split the proceeds according to the ratio of money that each invested in the business. Paul put in the most money at a ratio of 5:3. How much money should Paul get from the sale?

    (A) $75,000
    (B) $100,000
    (C) $125,000
    (D) $150,000
    (E) $175,000

52. A plumber needs four sections of pipe, each 3 feet, 2 inches long to complete a project. Pipe is sold by the foot, for \$3.20 per foot. How much will the plumber have to pay for the pipe?

    (A) \$40.51
    (B) \$41.60
    (C) \$42.83
    (D) \$58. 91
    (E) \$59.30

53. A used car salesman earns 20 percent commission on the cars that he sells. On Monday, the salesman sold three cars, totaling \$45,000. For the remainder of the week, the salesman only sold two cars, with a total sales price of \$30,000. How much commission did the salesman make on the first day of sales?

    (A) \$6,000
    (B) \$7,000
    (C) \$9,000
    (D) \$12,000
    (E) \$15,000

54. A display selling apples at a supermarket contains 10 dozen apples when the display is full. The manager of the produce department is supposed to make sure the display is restocked when it is $\frac{1}{5}$ full. How many apples will be on display when it's time to restock?

    (A) 20
    (B) 24
    (C) 25
    (D) 30
    (E) 35

55. Jose is constructing a cardboard box. He begins with a 15 foot by 10 foot rectangle, and cuts 2 feet by 2 feet squares out of each corner to fold the box (see diagram below):

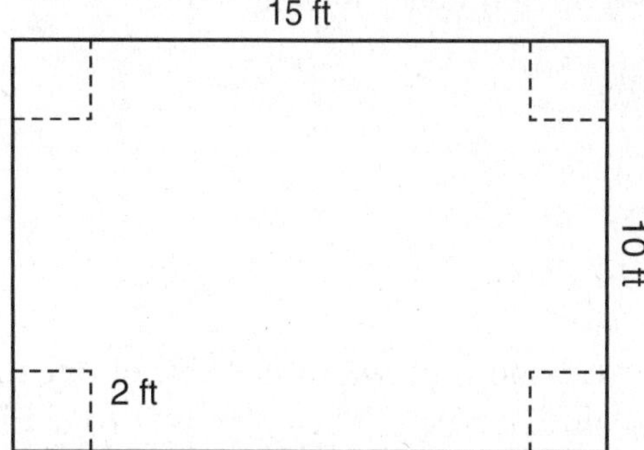

After Jose folds the box, what will be its volume?

    (A) 27 cubic feet
    (B) 50 cubic feet
    (C) 132 cubic feet
    (D) 150 cubic feet
    (E) 300 cubic feet

56. A rectangular room has ceilings that are 8 feet high. The length of the room is 10 feet, and the width of the room is 5 feet. Assuming that the room has no windows, and that you are to paint the doors as well, how much area would you have to cover with paint in order to cover the walls and floor of this room?

    (A) 290 square feet
    (B) 340 square feet
    (C) 500 square feet
    (D) 900 square feet
    (E) 1200 square feet

57. Cassandra saves $10\frac{1}{2}$ percent of her salary. If she makes \$550 per week, how much does she save each month?

    (A) \$105
    (B) \$200
    (C) \$231
    (D) \$252
    (E) \$276

58. The smoke detector in your house has a malfunction and beeps every 10 minutes. If it first beeps at 9:00 P.M., how many times will it beep by 3:00 A.M., when you finally give up and take a hammer to it?

    (A) 36
    (B) 37
    (C) 40
    (D) 45
    (E) 48

59. A roadmap is drawn to the scale of one inch equals five miles. When planning your trip, you notice that you will have to travel 10 inches (on the map) to the first turn, 7 inches to the second turn, and then 5 inches to your destination. Your custom van only gets 10 miles to the gallon of gas, and gas costs $1.65 per gallon. How much gas money will it cost you for the round trip?

    (A) $24.10
    (B) $18.15
    (C) $30.56
    (D) $36.30
    (E) $38.40

60. An office clerk buys a box of staples for 90 cents, a package of typing paper for $1.20, and a package of pens for $2.90. Assuming a 3.5% sales tax, how much change would he receive from a $10 bill?

    (A) $6.13
    (B) $5.75
    (C) $5.25
    (D) $4.99
    (E) $4.82

61. If it costs $7.90 per square foot to lay sodgrass, how much would it cost to sod a yard that is 9 by 20 feet?

    (A) $300
    (B) $450
    (C) $550
    (D) $1,422
    (E) $1,550

62. A farmer constructs a wooden bin (shown below) to store his grain. The bin is 6 feet long, 3 feet wide, and 3 feet deep. The bin rests on legs that are 3 feet tall to keep the grain away from the damp ground.

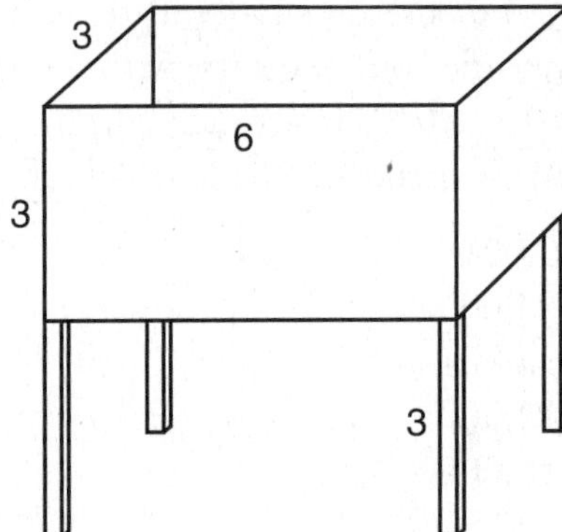

How many cubic feet of grain can the farmer store in this bin?

    (A) 25 cubic feet
    (B) 54 cubic feet
    (C) 60 cubic feet
    (D) 63 cubic feet
    (E) 70 cubic feet

63. A wholesale warehouse sells a square yard of material for $12.50. The exact same material can be purchased at a fabric discount store for $15.00 per square yard. What is the percent difference in the higher priced material?

    (A) The wholesale warehouse sells the material for 20 percent less than the fabric discount store.
    (B) The wholesale warehouse sells the material for 25 percent less than the fabric discount store.
    (C) The fabric discount store sells the material for 15 percent more than the wholesale warehouse.
    (D) The fabric discount store sells the material for 10 percent more than the wholesale warehouse.
    (E) There is not enough information available to correctly solve the problem.

64. On December 1st, the National Weather Service recorded 15.2 inches of snow in Grand Island, NE. On December 5th, the National Weather Service recorded 6.5 less inches of snow than fell on December 1st. On the 15th of December, 3 more inches fell than fell on December 5th. There was no additional snow during the remainder of the month. How many inches of snow fell in Grand Island, NE, during the month?

    (A) 22.5
    (B) 33.3
    (C) 35.6
    (D) 38.9
    (E) 40.0

Answer Key

1. A	14. C	27. D	40. C	53. C
2. D	15. B	28. A	41. D	54. B
3. D	16. D	29. E	42. A	55. C
4. C	17. B	30. E	43. A	56. A
5. B	18. C	31. B	44. C	57. C
6. C	19. B	32. E	45. A	58. B
7. A	20. B	33. D	46. B	59. D
8. B	21. A	34. B	47. B	60. E
9. B	22. B	35. C	48. D	61. D
10. B	23. D	36. A	49. E	62. B
11. B	24. C	37. B	50. C	63. A
12. A	25. A	38. B	51. C	64. C
13. E	26. C	39. C	52. B	

Answer Explanations

1. **(A) 60.96 centimeters.** There are 12 inches in one foot. Therefore, there are 24 inches in two feet (12 × 2). One inch equals 2.54 centimeters, so 24 inches is equal to 60.96 centimeters (2.54 × 24). The price (10 cents per centimeter) is misdirection and has nothing to do with solving the problem.
2. **(D) 4.5 percent.** To solve this problem, you simply multiply the percentages. The first step is to convert the two percentages (30% and 15%) to decimal by moving the decimals two places to the left (.30 and .15). Then, multiply the two decimal numbers (.3 × .15). The result is .045. Convert the result to percentage by moving the decimal two places to the right (4.5%).
3. **(D) 40.** First, convert the percentage to a decimal (4% equals .04). Next, multiply 1,000 by the converted percentage (1,000 × .04 = 40).
4. **(C) 40.** This is a division problem. Divide the total weight (2,000 lbs) by the weight of each container (50 lbs). (2,000 ÷ 50 = 40).
5. **(B) Two people, one weighing 140 pounds with a backpack weighing 60 pounds, the other weighing 150 pounds with a backpack weighing 40 pounds.** To obtain the correct answer, you have to add the total pounds in each possible answer to find the one that is equal to or less than the total weight authorized (400 pounds). 140 + 60 + 150 + 40 = 390.
6. **(C) 9.** To find an average, you add the numbers together, and then you divide the sum by the number of items added.

   $$7 + 15 + 14 + 4 + 8 + 9 + 6 = 63$$
   $$63 \div 7 = 9$$

7. **(A) $3,014.40.** You must first find the total hours worked by both Bob and Alice. Each worked 20 hours per week for 8 weeks. (20 × 8 = 160 hours each, or 320 hours total). Next, multiply the total hours worked by the hourly wage (320 × $9.42 = $3,014.40).
8. **(B) 11,200.** Subtract the previous mileage from the current mileage (57,213 – 53,413 = 3,800). The vehicle has traveled 3,800 miles since its last general maintenance. Now, subtract the result from 15,000 (15,000 – 3,800

= 11,200). The vehicle can travel another 11,200 miles before it reaches its maintenance limit.

9. **(B) 6 feet.** We solve this as an algebra equation:

$$60 \times 8 = 80y$$
$$80y = 480$$
$$y = (480 \text{ over } 80)$$
$$y = 6$$

10. **(B) $2.40.** The first step in solving this problem is to determine how much John is paying for 100 sheets of paper. Since one ream equals 500 sheets, 200 reams equals 100,000 sheets. So, John is paying $500 for 100,000 sheets of paper. We need to know how much John is paying for 100 sheets, so, we set up the equation:

$$100{,}000/100 = \$500/y$$
$$100{,}000y = 50{,}000$$
$$y = \$2.00$$

John is paying $2.00 for 100 sheets of paper. He wants to resell the paper at a 20 percent profit. Twenty percent of $2.00 equals 40 cents (2 × .20 = .40). Now, add the 40 cents to the $2.00 wholesale price that John paid for the paper. This results in a resale price of $2.40.

11. **(B) 164.** The first step in solving this problem is to convert the room size from feet to inches. You do this by multiplying the length and width by 12 (there are 12 inches in one foot). 25 × 12 = 300, and 30 × 12 = 360. The room is 300 inches by 360 inches.

The next step is to determine how many times the length of a crate will fit into the length of the room and how many times the width of a crate will fit into the width of a room. We do this by dividing the length of the room by the length of the crate and the width of the room by the width of a crate. 300 ÷ 40 = 7.5 and 360 ÷ 71 = 5.07. Therefore, 7 crates can be stored along the width, and 5 can be stored on the length. To discover how many can fit this way total, we multiply the whole numbers (7 × 5 = 35). Thirty-five crates would fit into this room when placed this way, meaning there would be 165 crates left to store.

We're not finished yet. Perhaps more crates could be stored if we placed them lengthwise in relation to the width of the room, instead of the length of the room. 300 ÷ 71 = 4.2; 360 ÷ 40 = 9. 4 × 9 = 36. Using this method, one additional crate could be stored in the room, leaving 164 crates left to store.

A mathematical alternative to solving the problem would be to determine the total storage area of the room and divide it by the total area of a crate. 300 × 360 = 108,000. 71 × 40 = 2,840. 108,000 ÷ 2,840 = 38.03; two more crates stored in the room than in answer (B). However, this method of calculation would be incorrect, because it doesn't take into account that the crate shapes are not flexible; they cannot be molded to fit into the shape of the room.

12. **(A) 4 hours.** The first step is to determine how fast the helper is planting corn. 1.5 × 100 = 150 rows of corn. .5 × 8 = 4. The helper plants 150 rows of corn in 4 hours. The next step is to determine how many rows of corn the farmer plants each hour, and how many rows of corn the helper plants each hour:

$100 \div 8 = 12.5$. The farmer plants $12\frac{1}{2}$ rows per hour.

$150 \div 4 = 37.5$. The helper plants $37\frac{1}{2}$ rows per hour.

Working together, they plant 50 rows of corn each hour (12.5 + 37.5). Finally, we determine how long it will take them to plant 200 rows of corn. We do this by dividing 200 by the number of rows planted each hour ($200 \div 50 = 50$). It would take 4 hours to plant 200 rows of corn.

13. **(E) 14 cents.** We can solve this using simple algebra. The first step is to determine how much tax Betty pays for each dollar earned:

$$\$438{,}517$$
$$x = \$613$$
$$x = 613/438{,}517$$
$$x = .0014 \text{ (rounded up)}$$

Now we determine how much tax Betty is paying for each \$100 earned ($.0014 \times 100 = .14$). Betty pays 14 cents in taxes for each \$100 earned.

14. **(C) $\frac{3}{20}$.** There are 400 people total in the squadron (350 + 50). $\frac{3}{5}$ of them graduated this year ($\frac{3}{5} \times 400 = 240$). $\frac{1}{4}$ of them graduated last year ($\frac{1}{4} \times 400 = 100$). 340 have graduated from the course (240 + 100), leaving 60 who have not yet been trained: $\frac{60}{400} = \frac{3}{20}$.

15. **(B) \$1,530.** Ten percent of \$2,500 ($.10 \times 2{,}500$) is \$250, so the computer is worth \$2,250 (2,500 – 250) after the first year. Fifteen percent of \$2,250 ($.15 \times 2{,}250$) is 337.50. After the second year, the computer is worth \$1,912.50 (2,250 – 337.50). Twenty percent of \$1,912.50 ($.20 \times 1{,}912.50$) is \$382.50. The computer is worth \$1,530 (1,912.50 – 382.50).

16. **(D) $5A^2$.** A rectangle's area is computed by multiplying the width of the rectangle by the length. In this case, the width is A, and the length is $5A$. We would set up the equation:

$$\text{Area} = A \times 5A$$
$$\text{Area} = 5A^2$$

17. **(B) 75 feet.** The perimeter is the measurement around the outside of the rectangle. Subtracting the total of the shortest two sides (50 feet) from the total perimeter gives us 150 ($200 - 50 = 150$). We divide the result by 2 to obtain the measurements of the two remaining sides ($150 \div 2 = 75$).

18. **(C) 35 feet.** The perimeter of a triangle is determined by adding the lengths of the three sides. Side A is 10 feet. Side B is two feet longer, or 12 feet. Side C is one foot longer than Side B, or 13 feet. $10 + 12 + 13 = 35$.

19. **(B) 205 sq feet.** The area of a square or rectangle is determined by multiplying the length times the width. In this problem, we have one square, measuring 3 feet by 3 feet. The area of that square is 9 square feet ($3 \times 3 = 9$). The bottom rectangle is 10 feet wide by 28 feet long (25 feet + 3 feet). Therefore, the area is 280 square feet (10×28). Add the two results together (280 + 9) and the sum is 289 square feet.

20. **(B) 42 percent.** This is a question with lots of extraneous information, designed to confuse. The only data necessary to solve the problem is the amount of basic cell phone service ($62.58) and the amount of the monthly bill ($149.00). To solve the problem, we divide $62.58 by $149 (62.58 ÷ 149 = .42). Move the decimal two places to the right to get our percentage (42%).

21. **(A) $7\frac{3}{8}$.** To solve this problem, we must add the three numbers $2\frac{1}{4}$, $4\frac{5}{8}$, and $\frac{1}{2}$. There are two ways to do this. For both methods, we must first find the common denominator, which is "8" in this case.

    Method 1: Convert the "$\frac{1}{4}$" in the number "$2\frac{1}{4}$" to "8ths." ($2\frac{1}{4} = 2\frac{2}{8}$)

    Next, convert the "$\frac{1}{2}$" to "8ths." ($\frac{1}{2} = \frac{4}{8}$)

    Our equation is now $2\frac{2}{8} + 4\frac{5}{8} + \frac{4}{8}$.

    Include the whole numbers into the fractions (convert to improper fractions). To do this, multiply the whole number by the denominator (bottom number of the fraction), then add the total to the numerator (top number in the fraction).

    $2\frac{2}{8} = \frac{18}{8}$ (2 × 8 + 2).

    $4\frac{5}{8} = \frac{37}{8}$ (4 × 8 + 5)

    Our equation now reads: $\frac{18}{8} + \frac{37}{8} + \frac{4}{8} = \frac{59}{8}$. $\frac{59}{8}$ can be reduced to $7\frac{3}{8}$.

    Method 2: Convert the $\frac{1}{4}$ and $\frac{1}{2}$ to "8ths" as shown above ($2\frac{2}{8}$, $\frac{4}{8}$).

    Add the fractions together ($\frac{2}{8} + \frac{5}{8} + \frac{4}{8} = \frac{11}{8} = 1\frac{3}{8}$).

    Now add the whole numbers together (2 + 4 + 1 = 7).

    Add the total of the whole numbers to the remaining fraction ($7 + \frac{3}{8} = 7\frac{3}{8}$).

22. **(B) 90 degrees.** When solving geometry problems, it is sometimes easier to draw the shape on your scratch paper to help visualize the problem.

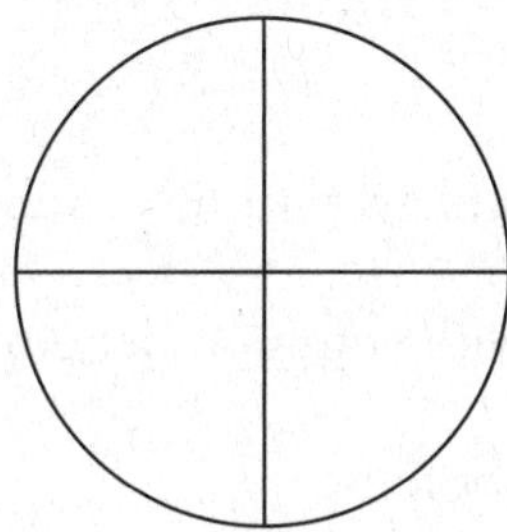

    The total number of degrees around the center is 360 degrees. The circle is divided into four equal angles, so to each angle can be determined by dividing 360 by 4 (360 ÷ 4 = 90).

23. **(D) 500 miles.** Again, it may help to draw the problem on your scratch paper to help visualize.

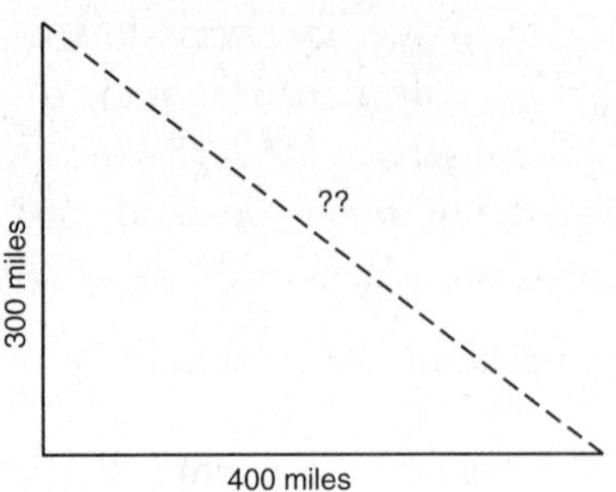

Since the two cars drove north and east, their paths form a 90-degree angle. When one of the angles of a triangle form a 90-degree angle, one can solve for the lengths of the sides of the triangle by making use of a common geometry formula: the Pythagorean theorem, $a^2 + b^2 = c^2$
To solve this problem:

$$300^2 + 400^2 = \text{distance}^2$$
$$90{,}000 + 160{,}000 = \text{distance}^2$$
$$250{,}000 = \text{distance}^2$$
$$\sqrt{250{,}000} = 500$$

24. **(C) $15.40.** This is a multiplication problem. To find the answer, multiply $5.50 by 2.8 (5.50 × 2.8 = 15.4).
25. **(A) 6.** We can best solve this as an algebra problem. Let the number we are trying to find be x.

$$12 \times \frac{1}{2}x = 36$$
$$6x = 36$$
$$x = 6$$

26. **(C) $450.** This problem can be solved using algebra. We wish to find the difference in the total sales, so let D = difference. So, D = total sales of the discounted option, minus the total sales of the first option.
x = total sales for the first option, and y = total sales for the discounted option. So, $x = 300 \times \$9$ and $y = 450 \times \$7$.

$$x = \$2{,}700, \text{ and } y = \$3{,}150$$
$$D = y - x, \text{ so } D = \$3{,}150 - \$2{,}700$$
$$D = \$450$$

27. **(D) $\frac{1}{40}$.** To solve this problem, you must subtract $\frac{3}{5}$ from $\frac{5}{8}$. First, convert the fractions to fractions with common denominators. In this case, $\frac{5}{8}$ would become $\frac{25}{40}$ and $\frac{3}{5}$ would become $\frac{24}{40}$.

$$\frac{25}{40} - \frac{24}{40} = \frac{1}{40}.$$

28. **(A) 7 passengers.** Let x = the number of passengers originally on Bus A. Ten more passengers arrive, which means there are now $x + 10$. More passengers arrive, until there are four times as many: $4(x + 10)$.
Bus B has 16 less than 12 times as many passengers on Bus A originally: $12x - 16$.

So, our final equation is $4(x + 10) = 12x - 16$

$$4x + 40 = 12x - 16$$
$$8x = 56$$
$$x = 7$$

29. **(E) none of the above.** To find the average, we add the speeds and then divide by the total number of laps:

$$120.5 + 130.3 + 150.8 = 401.6$$

$401.6 \div 3 = 133.86666666..... = 133.9$, which is not one of the listed answers.

30. **(E) 50.** Each square has an area of 25. Because area is equal to length times width, and because the lengths and widths are equal, that means the length and width of each square is 5.

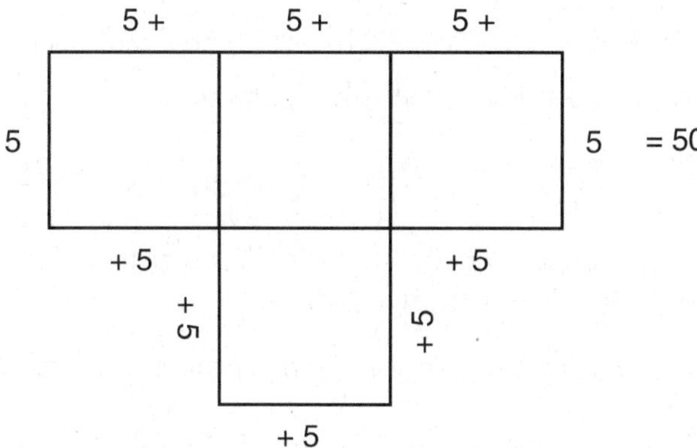

31. **(B) $86.40.** We're working with two separate measurements here (square feet and square yards), so the first step is to convert so that we're working with one measurement. If it costs 48 cents per square foot to lay carpet, then it would cost $\$.48 \times 9$ per square yard (1 square foot $= \frac{1}{9}$ of a square yard).

$$\$0.48 \times 9 = \$4.32 \text{ per square yard}$$
$$20 \times \$4.32 = \$86.40$$

32. **(E) 4,560.** Each worker assembled 200 boxes per hour. 600 boxes per hour were assembled total (3×200). At the end of the 8-hour shift, there were 4,800 boxes (8×600). Five percent of the boxes (240) were defective ($4,800 \times .05$). That leaves 4,560 boxes that were not defective ($4,800 - 240$).

33. **(D) $1.08.**
7 quarters = $1.75 ($7 \times .25$)
3 dimes = $.30 ($3 \times .10$)
5 nickels = $.25 ($5 \times .05$)
12 pennies = $.12 ($12 \times .01$)
$\$1.75 + \$.30 + \$.25 + \$.12 = \$2.42$
$\$3.50 - \$2.42 = \$1.08$

34. **(B) 93,000.** Josh received $12,000. Because Christina put in 1.5 times the amount of time Josh put in, she would receive $18,000 ($\$12,000 \times 1.5 = \$18,000$). Jeanie will receive 3.5 times the profit received by Christina ($\$18,000 \times 3.5 = \$63,000$)

$$\$12,000 + \$18,000 + \$63,000 = \$93,000$$

35. **(C) 48 days.** We solve this problem with algebra. y is the number of days required for $3\frac{1}{2}$ workers to complete the job. We know that 4 workers can complete the job in 42 days, so:

$$4 \times 42 = (3\tfrac{1}{2}) \times y.$$
$$168 = \frac{7}{2}y$$
$$168 \times \frac{2}{7} = y$$
$$\frac{336}{7} = y$$
$$y = 48$$

36. **(A) 200 kilometers.** To solve this problem, we must first convert the miles to kilometers. We do this by multiplying the mileage by $\frac{5}{8}$.

$$500 \div \frac{5}{8} = \frac{500}{1} \times \frac{8}{5} = \frac{100}{1} \times \frac{8}{1} = 100 \times 8 = 800 \text{ kilometers.}$$

You've driven 800 kilometers on a 1,000 kilometer trip. That means you have 200 kilometers left to drive (800 – 200).

37. **(B) $52\frac{1}{2}$ miles.** The first step in solving this problem is converting the minutes to hours. 45 minutes is $\frac{3}{4}$ of an hour, or .75. Distance equals rate *x* time, so:

$$D = 70 \times .75$$
$$D = 52.5 \text{ or } 52\tfrac{1}{2} \text{ miles.}$$

38. **(B) 35 pounds.** A decade is a period of 10 years. Therefore, to solve this problem, we multiply the average poundage consumed in one year (3.5) by 10.

(10 × 3.5 = 35).

39. **(C) 8.35.** The total weight of 25 gallons of water is 208.7 pounds (total weight, minus the weight of the empty aquarium, or 228.7 – 20 = 208.7).
   If 25 gallons of water weighs 208.7 pounds, then we can compute the weight of one gallon by dividing 208.7 by 25 (208.7 ÷ 25 = 8.348). Rounding up, the answer is 8.35.

40. **(C) $546.88.** Carlos worked a total of 40 hours during the week for regular pay (8 × 5 = 40). That means, he earned $500 in regular-time pay. He worked a total of $2\frac{1}{2}$ hours in overtime during the week ($\frac{1}{2} \times 5 = 2\frac{1}{2}$). Overtime pay is paid at the rate of $18.75 per hour (1.5 × $12.50). Therefore, Carlos earned $46.88 in overtime pay ($18.75 × 2.5 = $46.875, rounded up to $46.88). Carlos's total pay for the week is the total of regular pay and overtime pay ($500 + $46.88 = $546.88).

41. **(D) 675,250,000.** There are 365 days in a year. To solve the problem, we multiply the number of daily hits by 365 (1,850,000 × 365 = 675,250,000).

42. **(A) $\frac{7}{9}$.** Jimmy has read $\frac{35}{45}$ of the chapter. That fraction can be further reduced to $\frac{7}{9}$.

43. **(A) $118.50.** The first step is to determine the total area that needs to be carpeted. There are two shapes here, a rectangle and a triangle. To compute the area of a rectangle, we multiply the length of the rectangle by the width (3 yds × 6 yds = 18 sq yds). To compute the area of a triangle, we multiply the length of the two right angles and divide the number by 2. (3 × 6 = 18; 18 divided by 2 = 9).

    The total area to be carpeted is 27 square yards (18 + 9 = 27). Skip charges $3.50 per yard, so he should charge $94.50 ($3.50 × 27 = $94.50). Skip also charges $6.00 per hour, which—for four hours—would equal $24.00 ($6.00 × 4 = $24.00). Skip should charge his sister-in-law a total of $118.50 for the job ($94.50 + $24.00 = $118.50).

44. **(C) $1\frac{5}{7}$ days.** The number of rows is not relevant to solving the problem. We need to find out what fraction of the total garden each can plant in one day. Since Bill takes 4 days to complete the garden, he plants $\frac{1}{4}$ of the garden each day. Since Tammy takes only 3 days to plant the garden, she plants $\frac{1}{3}$ of the garden each day.

    To solve the problem, we use the equation: $\frac{1}{4} + \frac{1}{3} = \frac{1}{x}$

    If we multiply both sides of the equation by 12 (we got that number by multiplying the two denominators), we have:

$$12 = 3x + 4x$$
$$7x = 12$$
$$x = \frac{12}{7}$$
$$x = 1\frac{5}{7} \text{ days}$$

45. **(A) $5.60.** We know that $4.20 has been discounted 25 percent from the full price. Therefore, $4.20 equals 75 percent of the full price. The full price is $5.60 ($4.20 ÷ .75 = $5.60).

46. **(B) 32 degrees.** This is an example of a problem where the answer should be obvious after just a quick glance. $F = \frac{95}{C} + 32$. Since C = 0, then F = 32.

47. **(B) $3.80.** We can solve this problem using algebra. Let x = the cost per pound of the final mixture of washers. We know that the total cost of the mixture is equal to the total cost of the number-6 washers, plus the total cost of the number-8 washers. Therefore, we can say that $C = A + B$, with A equal to the total cost of number-6 washers, and B equal to the total cost of number-8 washers.

    In terms of x, C is the cost per pound times the number of total pounds in the mixture. Therefore, $C = 7.5x$.

Since we know the value of C, we can substitute the numbers:

$$7.5x = (3 \times 6) + (7 \times 1.5)$$
$$7.5x = 18 + 10.5$$
$$7.5x = 28.5$$
$$x = 28.5 \div 7.5$$
$$x = \$3.80$$

48. **(D) 7 hours, 20 minutes.** It takes the driver 4 hours to drive the first leg of the trip (200 ÷ 50 = 4). It takes him 3.33….. hours to drive back (200 ÷ 60 = 3.33…). .33 can be rounded to approximately 20 minutes.
49. **(E) 9 gallons.** The first step in solving this problem is to determine how much total area needs to be covered with varnish. Since the top and bottom of the figure are parallel, the room is in the shape of a trapezoid. To find the area of a trapezoid, we add the measurements of the top and bottom, multiply the sum by the height, and divide the result by 2; (Top + Bottom) × (Height) ÷ 2.

    Plugging in the dimensions, we have (3 + 6) × (10) ÷ 2 = 45 square feet.

    One gallon of varnish coats 5 square feet of floor, so it would take 9 gallons to finish the job (45 ÷ 5 = 9).
50. **(C) $17,250.** To solve the problem, we must first compute 15 percent of $15,000 ($15,000 × .15 = $2,250). We add that amount to the original car price ($15,000 + $2,250 = $17,250).
51. **(C) $125,000.** The first step in solving this problem is to convert the ratio (5:3) to fractions. Add both sides of the ratio together to determine the denominator of the fractions (5 + 3 = 8). Paul's investment can be expressed as $\frac{5}{8}$ of the total, while George's investment can be viewed as $\frac{3}{8}$ of the investment.

    To determine Paul's share, we can divide the total sale price ($200,000) by 8 to determine the amount of $\frac{1}{8}$ of the price ($200,000 ÷ 8 = $25,000). To find $\frac{5}{8}$, we multiply the result by 5 ($25,000 × 5 = $125,000).
52. **(B) $41. 60.** Each piece of pipe is 38 inches long (3 feet × 12 + 2 inches). The plumber will require a minimum of 152 inches of pipe to complete the project (38 inches × 4). 152 inches is 12.66 feet of pipe. Because pipe is only sold by the foot, the plumber will have to purchase 13 feet of pipe. 13 feet of pipe will cost $41.60 ($3.20 × 13).
53. **(C) $9,000.** The total of the cars sold on Monday was $45,000. Twenty percent of that number is $9,000 ($45,000 × .20 = $9,000). The amount sold during the rest of the week ($30,000) is not applicable to the problem.
54. **(B) 24.** We must first discover how many apples there are when the display is full. One dozen is equal to 12, so 10-dozen equals 120 (12 × 10). $\frac{1}{5}$ of 120 = 24 (120 ÷ 5 = 24).
55. **(C) 132 cubic feet.** Volume is determined by multiplying the width times length times height. When the two feet by two feet squares are cut out, the box will measure 11 feet (15 feet – 4) by 6 feet (10 feet – 4) by 2 feet. The volume of the box is 132 cubic feet (11 × 6 × 2 = 132).

56. **(A) 290 square feet.** Two of the walls in this room are 8 feet by 10 feet. The other two walls in this room are 8 feet by 5 feet. The floor is 10 feet by 5 feet. We are not painting the ceiling. We determine area of a rectangle by multiplying the width times the length:

    8 by 10 foot wall: ($8 \times 10 = 80$).

    There are two such walls, so $2 \times 80 = 160$.

    8 by 5 foot wall: ($8 \times 5 = 40$).

    There are two such walls, so $2 \times 40 = 80$.

    10 by 5 foot floor: ($5 \times 10 = 50$).

    Adding our results, ($160 + 80 + 50 = 290$), we determine that we must cover 290 square feet of wall/floor space.
57. **(C) $231.** Because the question is asking us to determine a percentage of Cassandra's salary each *month*, the first step is to determine her total pay for the month, assuming one month consists of four weeks. Cassandra earns $550 per week, so she earns $2,200 per month ($550 × 4 = $2,200). She saves $10\frac{1}{2}$ percent, or 10.5 percent of her monthly salary. Cassandra saves $231.00 per month ($2,200 × .105 = $231).
58. **(B) 37.** The time period between 9:00 P.M. and 3:00 A.M. is 6 hours, which you can convert to 360 minutes. The smoke detector beeps every 10 minutes, so you divide the total number of minutes by the time-period that the smoke detector beeped ($360 \div 10 = 36$). Now add one, because it beeps at the beginning of the period ($36 + 1 = 37$).
59. **(D) $36.30.** We have to solve this problem in multiple steps. First, determine the distance of the trip: 10 inches + 7 inches + 5 inches = 22 inches. On the map, 1 inch equals 5 miles. Therefore, 22 inches is equal to 110 miles ($22 \times 5 = 110$).

    For a round trip, we have to double that amount, so the length of the entire trip is 220 miles ($2 \times 110 = 220$).

    Since the van travels 10 miles on one gallon of gas, it will require 22 gallons to complete the trip ($220 \div 10 = 22$).

    Gas costs $1.65 per gallon, so you will have to purchase $36.30 worth of gas for the trip ($1.65 × 22 = $36.30).
60. **(E) $4.82.** The total of the purchase is $5.00 ($.90 + $1.20 + $2.90 = $5.00). 3.5% of that amount is 17.5 cents ($5 \times .035 = 17.5$). Round this up to 18 cents (because you can't charge $\frac{1}{2}$ of a cent). The total bill comes to $5.18. The office clerk should receive $4.82 in change ($10.00 – $5.18 = $4.82).
61. **(D) $1,422.** First, we determine the total area by multiplying the width of the yard by the length (9 feet × 20 feet = 180 square feet). The total cost to sod the yard can now be determined by multiplying the area of the yard (180 square feet) by the cost per square foot ($7.90 per square foot). 180 × $7.90 = $1,422 to sod the yard.
62. **(B) 54 cubic feet.** The formula to determine area is length × width × height. The bin is 6 feet long by 3 feet wide by 3 feet high. The area of the bin is 54 cubic feet ($6 \times 3 \times 3 = 54$). The lengths of the legs don't matter.

63. **(A) The wholesale warehouse sells the material for 20 percent less than the fabric discount store.** To determine the difference in price, we subtract the lower price from the more expensive price ($15.00 – $12.50 = $2.50). We can then divide the difference by the lower price to determine the percentage of difference ($2.50 ÷ $12.50 = 0.20, or 20 percent).
64. **(C) 35.6.** 15.2 inches fell on December 1. On December 5, 6.5 inches less snow fell, or 8.7 inches (15.2 – 6.5 = 8.7). On December 15, 3 more inches of snow fell than on December 5, or 11.7 inches (8.7 + 3 = 11.7).

    Add the total inches of snow for each of the three days (15.2 + 8.7 + 11.7 = 35.6 inches of snow).

General Science

CHAPTER 9

Science is best defined as a careful, disciplined, logical search for knowledge about any and all aspects of the universe, obtained by examination of the best available evidence and always subject to correction and improvement upon discovery of better evidence. What's left is magic. And it doesn't work.

—James Randi

Only one of the services tests officer candidates on their knowledge of general science. If you're applying to become an officer in the Army, Navy, Marine Corps, or Coast Guard, you can skip this chapter entirely. If your goal is a commission in the Air Force, on the other hand, the AFOQT contains 20 questions in the area of general science.

Unless you're already a science buff, it's almost impossible to study for a 20-question quiz about general science in a reasonable time period because the term is so broad. General science literally includes every field of scientific endeavor known to mankind. You will see questions that vary widely in scope. For example, one question may ask you how solar energy is transmitted in the universe, and the very next question may ask you what mineral element is part of hemoglobin.

The good news is that the Air Force does not expect you to be another Charles Darwin. The general science portion of the AFOQT is a very, very small percentage of the overall test (20 questions out of 480). The other good news is that the score of this subtest applies only to the *Navigator-Technical Score* of the AFOQT. If you have no desire to be a navigator in the Air Force, you may also want to skip this chapter and spend your study time in other, more significant areas.

It would be impossible to cover the entire field of general science in a book of this scope. All we can do is cover the major areas you are most likely to see on the test. On the bright side, questions you'll see on the test won't be too difficult—along the lines of something you may see in a general science trivia game.

ABOUT GENERAL SCIENCE

General science can be divided into three basic categories: life, physical, and earth sciences. Life science includes areas such as *biology*, which is the study of life, including human anatomy, nutrition, and medicine; *zoology* (the study of animals); and *botany* (the study of plants). *Physics* and *chemistry* are examples of the physical sciences. Physics involves the study of matter and energy, with a special emphasis on mechanical and electrical forces. Chemistry is the study of the composition, structure, and properties of matter. Earth science includes meteorology (study and prediction of weather), and environmental sciences.

Fields of Science

The following are some (not nearly all) of the major disciplines and branches of general science:

Agriculture: The science, art, and business of cultivating soil, producing crops, and raising livestock; farming.

Archeology: The systematic study of past human life and culture by the recovery and examination of remaining material evidence, such as graves, buildings, tools, and pottery.

Astronomy: The scientific study of matter in outer space, especially the positions, dimensions, distribution, motion, composition, energy, and evolution of celestial bodies and phenomena.

Biology: The science of life and of living organisms, including their structure, function, growth, origin, evolution, and distribution.

Biotechnology: The branch of molecular biology that studies the use of microorganisms to perform specific industrial processes.

Botany: The science or study of plants.

Chemistry: The science of the composition, structure, properties, and reactions of matter, especially of atomic and molecular systems.

Ecology: The science of the relationships between organisms and their environments.

Entomology: The scientific study of insects.

Forestry: The science and art of cultivating, maintaining, and developing forests.

Genealogy: The study or investigation of ancestry and family histories.

Genetics: The branch of biology that deals with heredity, especially the mechanisms of hereditary transmission and the variation of inherited characteristics among similar or related organisms.

Geology: The scientific study of the origin, history, and structure of the earth.

Hematology: The science encompassing the medical study of the blood and blood-producing organs.

Herpetology: The branch of zoology that deals with reptiles and amphibians.

Ichthyology: The branch of zoology that deals with the study of fish.

Meteorology: The science that deals with the phenomena of the atmosphere, especially weather and weather conditions.

Microbiology: The branch of biology that deals with microorganisms and their effects on other living organisms.

THE SCIENTIFIC METHOD

You probably recall this term from your high school or college science classes. Scientists solve problems by doing experiments and performing careful observations. The primary advantage to this disciplined approach is that the experiments and observations can be reproduced by any skeptic. It is from these ideas that the *scientific method* was developed. There are several steps to problem solving using the scientific method:

1. Observe some aspect of the universe.
2. Invent a tentative explanation, called a *hypothesis*, that is consistent with what you have observed.
3. Use the hypothesis to make predictions.
4. Test those predictions by performing experiments or further observations and modify the hypothesis in the light of your results.
5. Repeat steps 3 and 4 until there are no discrepancies between theory and experiment and/or observation.

When consistency is obtained, the hypothesis becomes a *theory* and provides a coherent set of propositions that explain a class of phenomena. To a scientist, a theory is a conceptual framework that explains existing observations and predicts new ones.

When a theory is proven consistently over time, it may become considered a *law* or *principle*.

Ockham's Razor

Also known as the *law of parsimony*, Ockham's Razor (also spelled Occam's Razor) is a rule in science and philosophy stating that entities should not be multiplied needlessly. This rule is interpreted to mean that the simplest of two or more competing theories is preferable and that an explanation for unknown phenomena should first be attempted in terms of what is already known. In other words, when two theories explain something, the simplest one is more likely to be true, or "Keep it simple, stupid."

SCIENTIFIC MEASUREMENTS

Most scientists use a system of measurements called the *metric system* for precise measurements and to ensure their data can be interpreted by scientists all around the world. The metric system is a standard of measurement based on the decimal system (multiples and fractions of 10).

Under the metric system, the unit of measurement for length is the *meter*. The standard unit of measurement for volume is the *liter*, and the *gram* is the unit of measurement for weight.

Metric Abbreviations

m = meter
mm = millimeter
cm = centimeter
km = kilometer
g = gram
mg = milligram
kg = kilogram
L = liter
mL = milliliter
m^2 = square meter
m^3 = cubic meter
km^2 = square kilometer
t = metric ton
ha = hectare

Metric Prefixes

0.1 = deci (example: *decimeter* or *deciliter*)
0.01 = centi
0.001 = milli
10 = deca
100 = hector
1000 = kilo
10,000 = mega

Conversion Factors

Multiply inches by 2.54 to get centimeters
Multiply feet by 0.305 to get meters
Multiply miles by 1.6 to get kilometers
Divide pounds by 2.2 to get kilograms
Multiply ounces by 28 to get grams
Multiply fluid ounces by 30 to get milliliters
Multiply gallons by 3.8 to get liters

Special Relationships

1 milliliter = 1 cubic centimeter
1 milliliter of water has a mass of approximately 1 gram
1 liter of water has a mass of approximately 1 kilogram
1 cubic meter of water has a mass of approximately 1 metric ton (1,000 kg)

Temperature

In science, temperature is measured using the *Celsius scale* (°C). On the *Fahrenheit scale*, common in everyday use in the United States, the freezing point of water is 32°F and the boiling point is 212°F. On the Celsius scale, water freezes at 0°C and boils at 100°C.

To convert Fahrenheit to Celsius, subtract 32°, divide the result by 9, then, multiply by 5.

To convert Celsius to Fahrenheit, multiply by 9, divide by 5, and add 32°.

LIFE SCIENCE

Classification

There are literally billions of different types of organisms on Earth. Most scientists estimate there are about 10 million different species of organisms living on Earth. In the mid-1700s, Swedish botanist Carolus Linnaeus (1707–1778) developed a method of identifying, classifying, and labeling organisms into a system of *scientific classification* that relies on relationships and similarities of different organisms. To date, about 2.1 million species have been classified.

The scientific classification system consists of seven levels: Kingdom, Phylum, Class, Order, Family, Genus, and Species. The *Kingdom* is the broadest (top) level and contains the most types of organisms. *Species* is the most specific level and contains the fewest types of organisms. In other words, relationships between organisms of the same species are very close.

All known organisms are given scientific names consisting of two words. The genus in which the organism belongs is the first word in the name, and the species is the second. For example, *Homo sapiens* (human beings) belong to the genus *Homo* and to the species *sapiens.* When writing the name of an organism, the genus (first word) is always capitalized, and the species (second word) is not. The entire term is always written in italics.

Cells

The *cell* is the basic structure of virtually all living things. The *Cell Theory* is one of the foundations of modern biology. Its major tenets are:

1. All living things are composed of one or more cells.
2. The chemical reactions of living cells take place within cells.
3. All cells originate from pre-existing cells.
4. Cells contain hereditary information that is passed from one generation to another.

Cell Components

Cell Membrane: The *cell membrane* is also called the cytomembrane, plasmalemma, or plasma membrane. It also acts as a selectively permeable barrier to allow certain chemicals, specifically water, to pass and others to not pass.

Cytoplasm: The protoplasm (living matter) outside the nucleus of a cell.

Organelles: Formed bodies within the cytoplasm that perform certain functions.

Nucleus: A round or oval body that is surrounded by the nuclear envelope and contains the genetic information necessary for control of cell structure and function.

Endoplasmic Reticulum: A membrane network within the cytoplasm of cells involved in the synthesis, modification, and transport of cellular materials.

Ribosome: The sites of protein synthesis. They are not membrane-bound and occur in all cells.

Golgi Body: A net-like structure in the cytoplasm of animal cells (especially in those cells that produce secretions).

Mitochondrion: A spherical or elongated organelle in the cytoplasm, containing genetic material and many enzymes important for cell metabolism, including those responsible for the conversion of food to usable energy.

Lysosome: A membrane-bound organelle in the cytoplasm of most cells containing various hydrolytic enzymes that function in intracellular digestion.

Differences Between Plant and Animal Cells

Animal cells differ from plant cells in three primary ways:

1. Plant cells have a firm cell wall that supports and protects the cell, while animal cells don't have such a structure.
2. Plant cells have larger storage areas than animal cells.
3. Many plant cells contain chloroplasts that contain chlorophyll, a chemical that helps the plant create energy from sunlight.

Cell Processes

Cells perform various functions that help the cell survive. These functions are known as *processes.* A few of the major processes of a cell are:

Metabolism: The chemical processes occurring within a living cell or organism that are necessary for the maintenance of life. In metabolism, some substances are broken down to yield energy for vital processes while other substances, necessary for life, are synthesized.

Osmosis: Movement of water through cell membranes.

Phagocytosis: The engulfing and ingestion of bacteria or other foreign bodies.

Photosynthesis: The process in green plants and certain other organisms by which carbohydrates are synthesized from carbon dioxide and water using light as an energy source. Most forms of photosynthesis release oxygen as a byproduct.

Respiration: Elimination of waste materials at the cellular level.

The Human Body

The human body can be broken down into major systems that cooperate with each other to help keep the body alive and functioning. The major systems of the human body are:

Skeletal: The *skeletal system* is the name given to our *skeleton.* The human skeletal system protects vital organs, gives the human body its shape, and helps us to move. When you are born you have about 350 bones. But, as you grow, some of the bones fuse together, so as an adult human you have 206 bones. The skeleton is broken down into two major parts: the *axial skeleton* and the *appendicular skeleton.* The axial skeleton includes the skull, the spine, the ribs, and the sternum (80 bones). The appendicular skeleton consists of the shoulders, pelvis, and the attached limb bones (126 bones). In addition to providing a frame to support our bodies, bones are important in that some bones create red blood cells from the bone marrow, while other bones create white blood cells that help us to fight infections.

Digestive: The *digestive system* works like an assembly line to break down food particles into smaller molecules that can then be used by the circulatory system. In its simplest terms, the digestive system is a tube that runs from the mouth to the anus. But, along the way, several processes take place. Digestion starts in the mouth, where our teeth chew food into smaller pieces, and our saliva lubricates the food to help us swallow; enzymes in the saliva also begin the chemical breakdown of the food. As the food moves through the system, different organs mix the food with an extraordinary amount of different chemicals that then act to break the food down into small particles that can be absorbed into the bloodstream and lymph systems. Some of the food is used for energy, some is used to repair and replace cells, and some of the food is stored for future use. Not everything we eat, however, can be digested, and this is disposed of as waste.

Muscular: Our muscles are attached to bones by tendons and other tissues. They work by converting chemical energy into tensile and contracting forces. The human body has more than 600 muscles. They are connected to the brain and spinal cord by millions of nerves. There are three types of muscles: cardiac, smooth, and skeletal. Cardiac muscles power the heart to pump blood through the body. Smooth muscles surround or are a part of the internal organs. Both cardiac muscles and smooth muscles are referred to as involuntary muscles because we can't control them consciously. We can consciously control our skeletal muscles, and we use them to command our bodies to move. Skeletal muscles make up about 40 percent of a male's body weight and about 23 percent of a female's.

Lymphatic: The *lymphatic system* helps our bodies fight infection and disease by producing certain white blood cells and antibodies. The system is connected to the cardiovascular system by a network of capillaries. The lymphatic system also supports the distribution of foods and nutrients throughout the body. The three principle functions of the system are: (1) to collect and return interstitial fluid, including plasma protein, to the blood, and thus help maintain fluid balance; (2) to defend the body against disease by producing lymphocytes; and (3) to absorb lipids from the intestines and transport them to the blood. Virtually every organ in the human body contains a small amount of lymphatic tissue.

Endocrine: The *endocrine system* consists of a collection of glands that produce *hormones* (chemical messengers). These hormones are released into the bloodstream and transported to organs and tissues throughout the body. Hormones regulate metabolism, growth, and sexual development.

Nervous: The *nervous system* gathers and stores information (both internal and external), and uses the information to control the other systems of the body. Our nervous system is not really one single system, but rather several interrelated systems. The *central nervous system* consists of the brain and the spinal cord. The *peripheral nervous system* controls functions that are not under conscious control, such as your heartbeat or digestive system. The nervous system works by generating electrical impulses along the length of cells. These impulses can travel up to 250 mph to transmit information to and from the cells.

Cardiovascular and Respiratory: The *cardiovascular system* consists of the heart and lungs, and the *respiratory system* includes those organs that are responsible for transporting oxygen to the blood stream. Generally, when we think of the respiratory system, our first thought is of the lungs, but every cell in the body is involved in the process. The lungs take in air, extract the oxygen, and expel carbon dioxide as a waste product. The acts of yawning, sneezing, coughing, speech, and smell are also operations of the respiratory system. The cardiovascular and respiratory systems are controlled automatically (without conscious control) by the brain.

Reproductive: The male and female *reproductive systems* use the process of combining two cells from different individuals to perpetuate the species. In humans, when a sperm cell from a male and an ovum cell from a female fuse together, the process is called *fertilization.* After fertilization, the new cell created by the fusion of the sperm and the ovum resides in the womb of the female for nine months, after which a new baby is born.

Urinary: The *urinary tract* includes the kidneys, two ureters, and the urethra. The ureters are tubes that connect the kidney to the bladder, and the urethra is a tube leading from the bladder to the outside of the body. The kidneys act as a filtering system for the blood by filtering fluids and reabsorbing about 99 percent of the fluids back into the blood stream (keeping essential nutrients such as glucose, salt, and minerals), and disposing of dangerous materials by passing them to the bladder in the form of urine. The expandable bladder stores the waste until it can be conveniently disposed. Interestingly, less than one-half of a kidney is capable of doing the work that two kidneys usually do.

Life Span: *Homo sapiens* (human beings) live to an average age of 80 years (for females) and 78 years (for males). Before 1900, the average life expectancy was 47 years, and very few people lived to the age of 70 years. In prehistoric times, the average life span was about 18 years.

EARTH SCIENCE

Earth is the third-closest planet to the Sun in our solar system. Of all the planets in the solar system, Earth is the only one capable of sustaining life as we know it.

The Seasons

The Earth travels through space at an average speed of 18.5 miles per second. Earth's orbit around the sun is slightly elliptical, which means Earth's distance from the sun changes as it orbits. Many people mistakenly believe that the Earth's distance from the sun determines how hot or how cold the temperature is, but that's not the case.

As the Earth travels through space, it is also rotating on its axis at a speed of about 1,070 miles per hour at the equator. The Earth is also tilted 23.5 degrees on its axis (a straight line through the Earth from the North Pole to the South Pole). As the Earth orbits the sun, the axis remains the same, which means at certain points during the orbit (one year) the northern hemisphere is tilted toward the sun, while the southern hemisphere is tilted away, and at the opposite point of the orbit, the southern hemisphere is tilted toward the sun while the northern hemisphere is tilted away. This causes the sun's light and energy to concentrate on different areas of the Earth, at varying angles, throughout the year.

In the United States, we actually experience "summer" when the Earth is at its farthest distance from the sun. It's at this point in its orbit that the North Pole is tilted most toward the sun. Scientists call this the *Summer Solstice* for the northern hemisphere, and it begins each year around June 21 or 22. At this point of the Earth's orbit, the sun's energy is concentrated more on the northern hemisphere, while the southern hemisphere is tilted away from the sun and receives energy at a sharper angle with less intensity. While the northern hemisphere is experiencing its summer, the southern hemisphere is experiencing its winter. While this is the Summer Solstice for the northern hemisphere, it's referred to as the *Winter Solstice* for the southern hemisphere.

When the Earth is closest to the sun (which happens on December 21 or 22 each year), the northern hemisphere is tilted away from the sun (bringing about the Winter Solstice in the northern hemisphere), and the South Pole is pointed toward the sun (resulting in the Summer Solstice in the southern hemisphere).

Spring and Fall occur when the Earth is midway through its journey from winter to summer and summer to winter, respectively. The Vernal equinox (March 20 or 21 of each year) marks the coming of spring in the northern hemisphere and fall in the southern hemisphere. Conversely, the Autumnal equinox (September 22 or 23) marks the commencement of spring in the south and fall in the north. At these times, the sun is directly over the equator and the length of day and night are roughly equal to each other over most of the entire planet.

Earth Facts

Relationship to the Sun: The Earth is the third planet from the Sun. Its average distance from the Sun is about 93.1 million miles. On closest approach, the Earth is about 91.4 million miles away from the Sun and 94.5 million miles at its farthest orbit point. The planet orbits the Sun at a speed of 18.5 miles per second (about 66,500 mph). It takes the Earth 365.2422 days to make one complete orbit around the Sun.

Size, Mass, and Distance: The Earth has a diameter of 7,928 miles at its equator, and 7,902 miles when measured around its poles. The circumference of the Earth is 24,907 miles. Our planet has a surface area of 197 million square miles. The highest point on Earth is Mount Everest, which is 29,028 feet above sea level. The lowest point (on land) is the Dead Sea, which is 1,320 feet below sea level. The deepest point is the Mariana Trench in the Pacific Ocean, which is 35,802 feet below sea level.

Temperature: The Earth has an average surface temperature of 61°F. The coldest average temperature occurs in Antarctica (–60°F), and the hottest average temperature (130°F) occurs in the Sahara Desert, Africa. The coldest temperature on record (–128.6°F) occurred on July 31, 1983, in Vostok, Antarctica, and the hottest recorded temperature (136°F) occurred on September 13, 1922 in El Azizia, Libya.

Chemical Composition: Oxygen: 46.6 percent; Silicon: 27.7 percent; Aluminum: 8.1 percent; Iron: 5 percent; Calcium: 3.6 percent; Sodium: 2.8 percent; Potassium: 2.6 percent; Magnesium: 2.1 percent; Other: 1.5 percent.

Water Supply: Seventy percent of the Earth is covered by water. Ninety-seven percent of the Earth's water is salt water, and only three percent is fresh. Only about .3 percent of the Earth's water supply is usable by humans. Earth's total water supply is about 326 million cubic miles, broken down as follows:

- Oceans: 317 million cubic miles
- Ice caps, glaciers: Seven (7) million cubic miles
- Ground water: Two (2) million cubic miles.
- Fresh water lakes: 30,000 cubic miles
- Inland seas: 25,000 cubic miles
- Soil moisture: 16,000 cubic miles
- Atmosphere: 3,100 cubic miles
- Rivers: 300 cubic miles

Air Supply: Earth's air is composed of 78 percent nitrogen, 21 percent oxygen, and 1 percent other materials. Ninety-three percent of the "other materials" is composed of argon, and a little over 3 percent is composed of carbon dioxide.

Layers of the Earth

The Earth is made up of four layers, comprising its surface, interior, and atmosphere. We'll discuss the atmosphere shortly. The other three layers are:

The Crust. The Earth's crust is primarily composed of calcium and sodium. The crust is rocky and brittle and comprises the thinnest layer of the Earth's surface and interior. The crust is about 0–51 miles thick and is at its thinnest point under the oceans (0 to 6 miles thick).

The Mantle. About 1,792 miles thick, this is the largest layer. The mantle is composed of iron, magnesium, aluminum, silicon, and oxygen silicate compounds. Unlike the crust, which is brittle, the mantle is relatively flexible.

The Core. The core consists of two layers: the inner layer, which is solid, and the outer layer, which is molten. The outer core is about 1,410 miles thick, while the inner core is about 756 miles thick. The outer core is very hot, estimated to be between 5,000°F and 9,000°F. The inner core is just as hot, but remains solid because it is under such extreme pressure.

Earth's Atmosphere

Like the surface and interior, the Earth's atmosphere is also a series of layers. Earth's atmosphere is composed mostly of nitrogen and oxygen, with dust particles, clouds (water vapor), and microbes (living organisms) floating throughout. The atmosphere consists of the following layers:

- Troposphere: Extends up from the surface to about five miles at the poles and about 10 miles at the equator.
- Stratosphere: Extends from the troposphere to about 30 miles above the surface.
- Mesosphere: Extends from the stratosphere to about 50 miles above the surface.
- Ionosphere: Extends from the mesosphere to about 70 miles above the surface.
- Thermosphere: Extends from the ionosphere to around 350 miles above the surface.

PHYSICAL SCIENCE

Physical sciences examine the nature and properties of nonliving matter. Two of the major disciplines in this field are astronomy and chemistry.

The Solar System

Our solar system is made up of nine planets and other bodies such as moons, asteroids, comets, and meteoroids. One moon orbits Earth about every 27 days and 8 hours. There are at least 91 other moons orbiting the other planets in our solar system. All planets in our solar system, with the exception of Mercury and Venus, have moons.

We divide the planets in our solar system into two groups: the inner planets and the outer planets. The inner planets (in order from distance to the Sun) are Mercury, Venus, Earth, and Mars. These planets are composed mostly of rock and metals. The outer planets are made up mostly of icy particles and gases, and consist of Jupiter, Saturn, Uranus, Neptune, and Pluto. (*Note:* In August 2006, Pluto was downgraded to the status of a "minor" or "dwarf" planet, so for the purpose of future exams it will not be considered a planet.)

Mercury

Mercury is the closest planet to the Sun, but it is not the hottest. Mercury is also the second smallest planet in the solar system, only slightly larger than the Earth's Moon. The surface of the planet is covered with craters, and the small planet has no moons or rings.

- Diameter: 4,878 km (3,030 miles)
- Minimum distance from Sun: 28.6 million miles
- Maximum distance from Sun: 43.4 million miles
- Minimum distance from Earth: 48.0 million miles
- Rotation period about axis: 58.65 days
- Revolution period about the Sun: 0.24 years
- Surface gravity: 0.38 × Earth's
- Temperature range on Mercury: (–300°F to 800°F)
- Satellites: 0

Venus

Venus is often called Earth's "sister planet," but it is actually very different. Venus is slightly smaller than Earth, but it has an average temperature higher than any other planet in the solar system.

- Diameter: 12,104 km (7,522 miles)
- Minimum distance from Sun: 67 million miles
- Maximum distance from Sun: 68 million miles
- Minimum distance from Earth: 25 million miles
- Rotation period about axis: 243 days (retrograde)
- Revolution period about the Sun: 0.62 years
- Surface gravity: .90 × Earth's
- Average temperature: 855°F
- Satellites: 0

Earth

This is our home planet. Earth is the largest of the inner planets, and the only one capable of sustaining life as we know it.

- Diameter: 12,753 km (7,926 miles)
- Minimum distance from the Sun: 91 million miles
- Maximum distance from the Sun: 94.5 million miles
- Rotational period about axis: 24 hours
- Revolution period about Sun: 365 days
- Surface gravity: 9.78 m/s^2
- Average temperature: 61°F
- Satellites: 1

Mars

Mars is the fourth planet from the Sun and is the most similar to Earth. Like Earth, Mars has polar caps, seasons, clouds, and fog. However, it is much colder than Earth and does not have an atmosphere capable of sustaining life as we know it.

- Diameter: 6,785 km (4,217 miles)
- Minimum distance from Sun: 128 million miles
- Maximum distance from Sun: 155 million miles
- Minimum distance from Earth: 35 million miles
- Rotation period about axis: 24.6 hrs
- Revolution period about the Sun: 1.88 years
- Surface gravity: 0.37 × Earth's
- Temperature range: –129°C to 0°C
- Satellites: 2

Jupiter

Jupiter is the largest planet in our solar system. The planet contains most of the solar system's mass (not counting the Sun).

- Diameter: 142,800 km (88,736 miles)
- Minimum distance from Sun: 460 million miles
- Maximum distance from Sun: 508 million miles
- Minimum distance from Earth: 365 million miles
- Rotation period about axis: 9.8 hours
- Revolution period about the Sun: 12 years
- Surface gravity: 2.64 × Earth's
- Average temperature (at the top of the clouds): –101°F
- Satellites: 60 known moons

Saturn

Saturn is the second-largest planet in our solar system. It is most famous for its fabulous rings that stretch over 600 miles from edge to edge.

- Diameter: 119,871 km (74,500 miles)
- Minimum distance from Sun: 840 million miles
- Maximum distance from Sun: 938 million miles
- Minimum distance from Earth: 746 million miles
- Rotation period about axis: 10.67 hrs
- Revolution period about the Sun: 29.5 years
- Surface gravity: .92 × Earth's
- Temperature (at cloud tops): –170°C (–274°F)
- Satellites: 31 known moons, many rings

Uranus

Uranus is the third-largest planet in the solar system. It's the only planet in the system that rotates on its side.

- Diameter: 51,488 km (32,000 miles)
- Minimum distance from Sun: 1.7 billion miles
- Maximum distance from Sun: 1.87 billion miles
- Minimum distance from Earth: 1.6 billion miles
- Rotation period about axis: 17.24 hrs
- Revolution period about the Sun: 84 years
- Surface gravity: 0.89 × Earth's
- Temperature (at cloud tops): –328°F
- Satellites: 27 known moons, faint rings

Neptune

Neptune is the fourth largest of the planets in the solar system. While we normally consider this the eighth planet, Pluto sometimes crosses inside of its orbit and becomes the "eighth planet," and Neptune then becomes the farthest planet from the Sun until Pluto crosses Neptune's orbit again.

- Diameter: 49,493 km (30,760 miles)
- Minimum distance from Sun: 2.77 billion miles
- Maximum distance from Sun: 2.82 billion miles
- Minimum distance from Earth: 2.68 billion miles
- Rotation period about axis: 17.24 hrs
- Revolution period about the Sun: 165 years
- Surface gravity: 1.12 × Earth's
- Temperature (at cloud tops): –346°F
- Satellites: 13 known moons, faint rings

Pluto

Pluto is classified as a dwarf planet. It's even smaller than Earth's moon. While an "outer planet," it's not a gas giant. Pluto is composed primarily of nitrogen-ice and rock.

- Diameter: 2,301 km (1,430 miles)
- Minimum distance from Sun: 2.7 billion miles
- Maximum distance from Sun: 4.6 billion miles
- Minimum distance from Earth: 2.7 billion miles
- Rotation period about axis: 6.4 days (retrograde)
- Revolution period about the Sun: 248 years
- Surface gravity: 0.06 × Earth's
- Average surface temperature: –380°F
- Satellites: 1 known

Basic Chemistry

Chemistry is the science of substances and their properties. The discipline is concerned most with how and why various elements combine or separate to form different substances. Chemists are primarily concerned with atoms, molecules, elements, and compounds.

Under certain conditions, such as the addition of heat and increasing or decreasing pressure, different materials will react with each other, creating new substances. Chemists study these reactions, and also predict new reactions.

Anything that has mass and occupies space is *matter.* All matter is made up of various atoms combined to form *elements.* The basic building block of an element is the *atom.* The atom is the smallest part of an element that retains the characteristics of that element.

Atoms consist of negatively-charged particles called electrons and positively-charged particles called protons. The electrons orbit around the center of the nucleus (the center of the atom). The nucleus is made up of uncharged neutrons. Protons float around the inside of the nucleus. The number of protons contained in the nucleus determines the element's *atomic weight.*

Each atom has electrons arranged in orbits, shells, or levels around its nucleus. There are certain rules to how these orbits are established:

In the first orbit, a maximum of two electrons are allowed.

A maximum of eight electrons are allowed in the second orbit. For example, lithium is element number 3, meaning it has three electrons and three protons. The atom has two electrons in the first orbit (the maximum allowed) and one electron in the second orbit. Neon (element #10) has two electrons in the first orbit and eight electrons in the second orbit.

The third orbit is "full" when it has eight electrons, but it could actually hold up to a maximum of 18 electrons.

Likewise, the fourth orbit is "full" when it has eight electrons, but it could have a maximum of 32 electrons.

The electrons must fill up the lower orbits before starting on a higher orbit. However, with the larger atoms, there are more complex rules on how orbits are filled.

All other things being equal, elements "want" their outer orbits to be either "full" or completely empty of electrons. For example, chlorine has three orbits or shells, with seven electrons in the outer orbit. It would "like" to have eight. Likewise, sodium has three orbits, with only one electron in its outer orbit. Sodium would like to get rid of that electron, so it would have eight in its outer (second) orbit. Therefore, chlorine combines easily with sodium.

The science of chemistry primarily relates to the outer orbits of the elements involved. Chemical activity is determined by the number of electrons contained in the outer orbits of the atoms. Chemical compounds are formed when elements can trade or share electrons in their outer orbits, so that the shells of each element either contain the maximum allowed or are completely empty.

A *molecule* is the chemical combination of two or more atoms. Molecules can be from the same element (such as oxygen, O_2), or be combined from different elements (such as water, H_2O).

The Periodic Table

All the elements occurring naturally on Earth have been named by scientists and given shorthand symbols (see chart). There are 92 elements that occur naturally. There are also several elements that have been created artificially, but these are unstable.

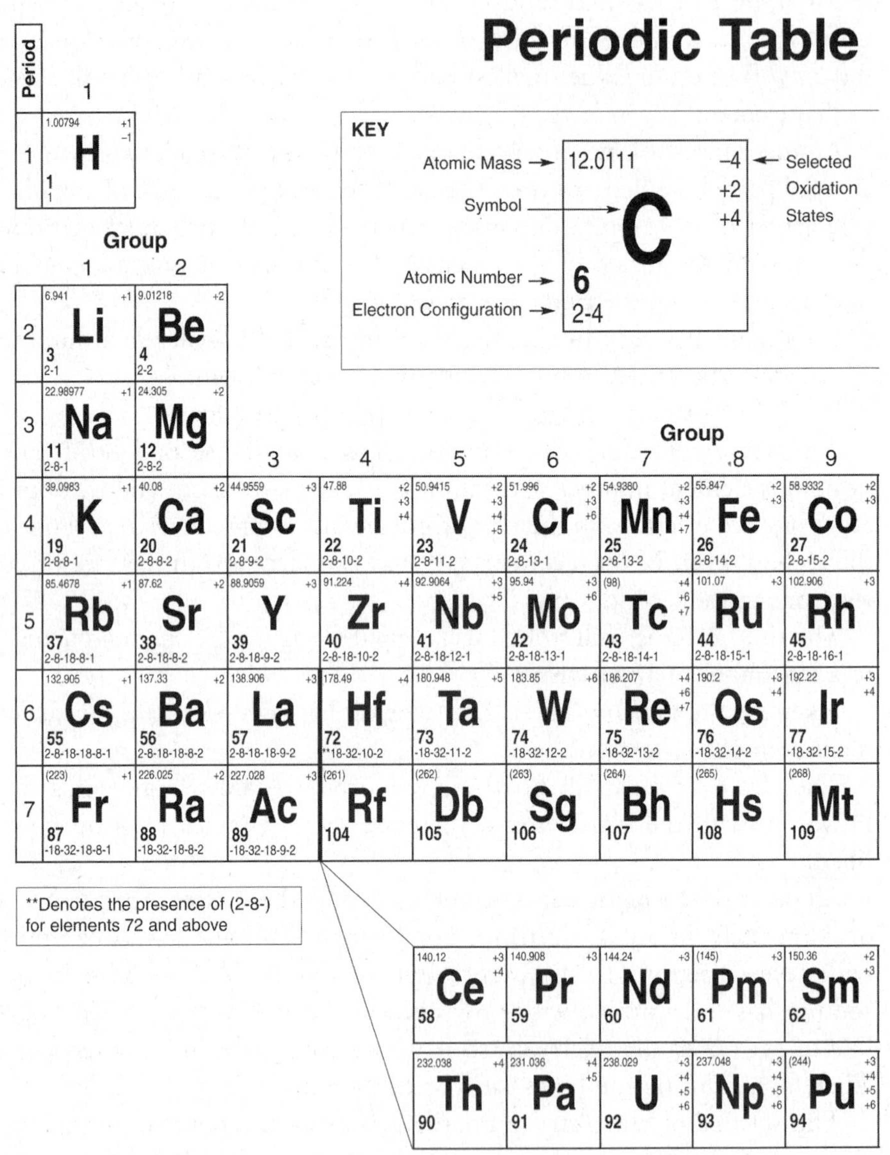

of the Elements

Relative atomic masses are based on $^{12}C = 12.000$

Note: Mass numbers in parentheses are mass numbers of the most stable or common isotope.

Group

10	11	12	13	14	15	16	17	18
								4.00260 0 **He** 2 2
			10.81 +3 **B** 5 2-3	12.0111 −4 +2 +4 **C** 6 2-4	14.0067 −3 −2 −1 +1 +2 +3 +4 +5 **N** 7 2-5	15.9994 −2 **O** 8 2-6	18.998403 −1 **F** 9 2-7	20.179 0 **Ne** 10 2-8
			26.98154 +3 **Al** 13 2-8-3	28.0855 −4 +2 +4 **Si** 14 2-8-4	30.97376 −3 +3 +5 **P** 15 2-8-5	32.06 −2 +4 +6 **S** 16 2-8-6	35.453 −1 +1 +3 +5 +7 **Cl** 17 2-8-7	39.948 0 **Ar** 18 2-8-8
58.69 +2 +3 **Ni** 28 2-8-16-2	63.546 +1 +2 **Cu** 29 2-8-18-1	65.39 +2 **Zn** 30 2-8-18-2	69.72 +3 **Ga** 31 2-8-18-3	72.59 −4 +2 +4 **Ge** 32 2-8-18-4	74.9216 −3 +3 +5 **As** 33 2-8-18-5	78.96 −2 +4 +6 **Se** 34 2-8-18-6	79.904 −1 +1 +5 **Br** 35 2-8-18-7	83.80 0 +2 **Kr** 36 2-8-18-8
106.42 +2 +4 **Pd** 46 2-8-18-18	107.868 +1 **Ag** 47 2-8-18-18-1	112.41 +2 **Cd** 48 2-8-18-18-2	114.82 +3 **In** 49 2-8-18-18-3	118.71 +2 +4 **Sn** 50 2-8-18-18-4	121.75 −3 +3 +5 **Sb** 51 2-8-18-18-5	127.60 −2 +4 +6 **Te** 52 2-8-18-18-6	126.905 −1 +1 +5 +7 **I** 53 2-8-18-18-7	131.29 0 +2 +4 +6 **Xe** 54 2-8-18-18-8
195.08 +2 +4 **Pt** 78 -18-32-17-1	196.967 +1 +3 **Au** 79 -18-32-18-1	200.59 +1 +2 **Hg** 80 -18-32-18-2	204.383 +1 +3 **Tl** 81 -18-32-18-3	207.2 +2 +4 **Pb** 82 -18-32-18-4	208.980 +3 +5 **Bi** 83 -18-32-18-5	(209) +2 +4 **Po** 84 -18-32-18-6	(210) **At** 85 -18-32-18-7	(222) 0 **Rn** 86 -18-32-18-8
(269) **Uun*** 110	(272) **Uuu** 111	(277) **Uub** 112		(285) **Uuq** 114				

*The systematic names and symbols for elements of atomic numbers above 109 will be used until the approval of trivial names by IUPAC.

151.96 +2 +3 **Eu** 63	157.25 +3 **Gd** 64	158.925 +3 **Tb** 65	162.50 +3 **Dy** 66	164.930 +3 **Ho** 67	167.26 +3 **Er** 68	168.934 +3 **Tm** 69	173.04 +2 +3 **Yb** 70	174.967 +3 **Lu** 71

(243) +3 +4 +5 +6 **Am** 95	(247) +3 **Cm** 96	(247) +3 +4 **Bk** 97	(251) +3 **Cf** 98	(252) +3 **Es** 99	(257) **Fm** 100	(258) **Md** 101	(259) **No** 102	(260) **Lr** 103

Answer Sheet for Practice Questions

1 Ⓐ Ⓑ Ⓒ Ⓓ Ⓔ	11 Ⓐ Ⓑ Ⓒ Ⓓ Ⓔ	21 Ⓐ Ⓑ Ⓒ Ⓓ Ⓔ	31 Ⓐ Ⓑ Ⓒ Ⓓ Ⓔ
2 Ⓐ Ⓑ Ⓒ Ⓓ Ⓔ	12 Ⓐ Ⓑ Ⓒ Ⓓ Ⓔ	22 Ⓐ Ⓑ Ⓒ Ⓓ Ⓔ	32 Ⓐ Ⓑ Ⓒ Ⓓ Ⓔ
3 Ⓐ Ⓑ Ⓒ Ⓓ Ⓔ	13 Ⓐ Ⓑ Ⓒ Ⓓ Ⓔ	23 Ⓐ Ⓑ Ⓒ Ⓓ Ⓔ	33 Ⓐ Ⓑ Ⓒ Ⓓ Ⓔ
4 Ⓐ Ⓑ Ⓒ Ⓓ Ⓔ	14 Ⓐ Ⓑ Ⓒ Ⓓ Ⓔ	24 Ⓐ Ⓑ Ⓒ Ⓓ Ⓔ	34 Ⓐ Ⓑ Ⓒ Ⓓ Ⓔ
5 Ⓐ Ⓑ Ⓒ Ⓓ Ⓔ	15 Ⓐ Ⓑ Ⓒ Ⓓ Ⓔ	25 Ⓐ Ⓑ Ⓒ Ⓓ Ⓔ	35 Ⓐ Ⓑ Ⓒ Ⓓ Ⓔ
6 Ⓐ Ⓑ Ⓒ Ⓓ Ⓔ	16 Ⓐ Ⓑ Ⓒ Ⓓ Ⓔ	26 Ⓐ Ⓑ Ⓒ Ⓓ Ⓔ	36 Ⓐ Ⓑ Ⓒ Ⓓ Ⓔ
7 Ⓐ Ⓑ Ⓒ Ⓓ Ⓔ	17 Ⓐ Ⓑ Ⓒ Ⓓ Ⓔ	27 Ⓐ Ⓑ Ⓒ Ⓓ Ⓔ	37 Ⓐ Ⓑ Ⓒ Ⓓ Ⓔ
8 Ⓐ Ⓑ Ⓒ Ⓓ Ⓔ	18 Ⓐ Ⓑ Ⓒ Ⓓ Ⓔ	28 Ⓐ Ⓑ Ⓒ Ⓓ Ⓔ	38 Ⓐ Ⓑ Ⓒ Ⓓ Ⓔ
9 Ⓐ Ⓑ Ⓒ Ⓓ Ⓔ	19 Ⓐ Ⓑ Ⓒ Ⓓ Ⓔ	29 Ⓐ Ⓑ Ⓒ Ⓓ Ⓔ	39 Ⓐ Ⓑ Ⓒ Ⓓ Ⓔ
10 Ⓐ Ⓑ Ⓒ Ⓓ Ⓔ	20 Ⓐ Ⓑ Ⓒ Ⓓ Ⓔ	30 Ⓐ Ⓑ Ⓒ Ⓓ Ⓔ	

Practice Questions

1. A scientist who studies animals would be called a __________ .

   (A) geologist
   (B) toxicologist
   (C) zoologist
   (D) biologist
   (E) geneticist

2. Which species does not belong in the following list?

   (A) barracuda
   (B) boa
   (C) tiger
   (D) elephant
   (E) monkey

3. A group of tissues in the human body that work together to perform a specific function is called a/an __________ .

   (A) cell
   (B) major system
   (C) organ
   (D) biological functionary
   (E) molecule

4. In which of the following orders of insects would you find beetles?

   (A) coleoptera
   (B) lepidoptera
   (C) neuroptera
   (D) thysanura
   (E) aphaniptera

5. A scientist who studies insects would be called a/an __________ .

   (A) ornithologist
   (B) entomologist
   (C) proctologist
   (D) horologist
   (E) psychiatrist

6. Animals that eat plants and other animals are called:

   (A) carnivores
   (B) herbivores
   (C) omnivores
   (D) predators
   (E) none of the above

7. Which planet in the solar system has the least surface gravity?

   (A) Earth
   (B) Mars
   (C) Mercury
   (D) Pluto
   (E) Uranus

8. How many legs does an arachnid have?

   (A) 4
   (B) 6
   (C) 8
   (D) 10
   (E) more than 10

9. A herpetologist would be primarily concerned with the study of __________ .

   (A) insects
   (B) mammals
   (C) reptiles
   (D) weather
   (E) birds

10. Excepting the three tiny bones in each ear, how many bones are there in a normal adult skeleton?

    (A) 100
    (B) 200
    (C) 300
    (D) 400
    (E) 500

11. An elephant cannot __________ .

(A) manipulate small objects
(B) jump
(C) swim
(D) procreate
(E) run

12. Blood is returned to the heart through tubes called __________ .

(A) arteries
(B) veins
(C) capillaries
(D) circulatory system
(E) kidneys

13. What kind of bird can build a nest that weighs more than a ton?

(A) ostrich
(B) bald eagle
(C) hawk
(D) minor
(E) transient

14. A paleontologist would be interested in the study of __________ .

(A) ancient civilizations
(B) birds
(C) farming
(D) dinosaurs
(E) blood types

15. Which planet in our solar system has the shortest "year?"

(A) Mercury
(B) Mars
(C) Earth
(D) Venus
(E) Pluto

16. Chloroplasts are found in which type of cells?

(A) perpendicular cells
(B) axis cells
(C) animal cells
(D) plant cells
(E) inverted cells

17. Your forearm contains two bones. One bone is called the ulna. What is the other bone called?

(A) tibia
(B) scapula
(C) radius
(D) humerus
(E) sacrum

18. Which planet in our solar system has the longest day?

(A) Earth
(B) Jupiter
(C) Venus
(D) Pluto
(E) Saturn

19. Which of Earth's *natural* elements has the highest atomic number?

(A) hydrogen
(B) lead
(C) sulfur
(D) lanthanum
(E) uranium

20. The lowest or most narrow level of the classification of organisms is called __________ .

(A) kingdom
(B) genus
(C) phylum
(D) class
(E) species

21. Water freezes at what temperature?

(A) 0°C
(B) 10°C
(C) 100°C
(D) –10°C
(E) –100°C

22. Under natural conditions, large quantities of organic matter decay after each year's plant growth has been completed. As a result of such conditions,
    (A) many animals are deprived of adequate food supplies.
    (B) soil erosion is accelerated.
    (C) soils maintain their fertility.
    (D) earthworms are added to the soil.
    (E) pollution increases.

23. Most scientists believe that the reason dinosaurs became extinct was because
    (A) they were killed by volcanoes.
    (B) they were killed by meteorites.
    (C) they exterminated each other.
    (D) they failed to adapt to a changing environment.
    (E) they were hunted to extinction by competing mammals.

24. Which of the following is a chemical reaction?
    (A) burning charcoal in your barbecue
    (B) melting ice
    (C) a magnet
    (D) boiling water
    (E) both (B) and (D)

25. The lightest natural element on Earth is called __________ .
    (A) helium
    (B) hydrogen
    (C) oxygen
    (D) boron
    (E) terbium

26. Which gas is the most plentiful in the air on Earth?
    (A) argon
    (B) oxygen
    (C) nitrogen
    (D) carbon dioxide
    (E) chlorine

27. Where are electrons found in an atom?
    (A) in the nucleus
    (B) attached to protons
    (C) in orbital layers around the nucleus
    (D) inside the core
    (E) only in the outer ring(s)

28. H_2O is the chemical formula for __________ .
    (A) water
    (B) ice
    (C) both (A) and (B)
    (D) oxygen
    (E) hydrogen

29. What percentage of all elements are metals?
    (A) 10 percent
    (B) 25 percent
    (C) 50 percent
    (D) 75 percent
    (E) 80 percent

30. How many meters are there in one kilometer?
    (A) 10
    (B) 100
    (C) 1,000
    (D) 10,000
    (E) 100,000

31. An oxide is formed when an element is chemically combined with which of the following type of specific element?
    (A) carbon
    (B) oxygen
    (C) helium
    (D) sodium
    (E) either (A) or (B)

32. A very strong acid would have a pH closer to __________ .
    (A) 1
    (B) 7
    (C) 14
    (D) 18
    (E) 20

33. Carbon has an atomic number of 6. How many protons would the element contain?

    (A) 3
    (B) 6
    (C) 12
    (D) between 3 and 6
    (E) none of the above

34. Elements with the same number of protons but different numbers of neutrons are called __________.

    (A) compounds
    (B) complex elements
    (C) isotopes
    (D) atoms
    (E) imbalanced

35. What percent of the world's population lives in the United States?

    (A) 1 percent
    (B) 3 percent
    (C) 6 percent
    (D) 8 percent
    (E) 10 percent

36. Which of the following is the deepest ocean?

    (A) Pacific Ocean
    (B) Atlantic Ocean
    (C) Baltic Sea
    (D) Arctic Ocean
    (E) Indian Ocean

37. Which of the planets in our solar system has the most known moons?

    (A) Saturn
    (B) Jupiter
    (C) Venus
    (D) Pluto
    (E) Mercury

38. What does the color of a star signify?

    (A) size
    (B) surface temperature
    (C) distance from view
    (D) orbital velocity
    (E) mass

39. What planet does the moon named *Io* orbit?

    (A) Earth
    (B) Mars
    (C) Venus
    (D) Jupiter
    (E) Saturn

Answer Key

1. C	9. C	17. C	25. B	33. B
2. A	10. B	18. C	26. C	34. C
3. C	11. B	19. E	27. C	35. C
4. A	12. B	20. E	28. C	36. A
5. B	13. B	21. A	29. D	37. B
6. C	14. D	22. C	30. C	38. B
7. C	15. A	23. D	31. B	39. D
8. C	16. D	24. A	32. A	

Answer Explanations

1. **(C) zoologist.** Zoology is the study of animals.
2. **(A) barracuda.** The barracuda is a fish, while the other choices are animals that live on land.
3. **(C) organ.** An organ is made up of tissues that operate cooperatively to perform a specific function.
4. **(A) coleoptera.** Coleoptera is the largest order of insects and is comprised of the beetles and weevils.
5. **(B) entomologist.** Entomology is the study of insects.
6. **(C) omnivores.** Carnivores eat only other animals and herbivores eat only plants. Omnivores eat both.
7. **(C) Mercury.** Mercury has only .3772 of the Earth's surface gravity. Pluto has less gravity (.06 of Earth's), but is no longer considered a planet.
8. **(C) 8.** An arachnid is an animal with eight legs in four pairs, such as a spider, tic, or scorpion.
9. **(C) reptiles.** Herpetology is the study of reptiles.
10. **(B) 200.** A normal human skeleton has 206 bones. Subtracting the six tiny bones in the ears gives us 200.
11. **(B) jump.** Elephants lack the capacity to have all four legs off the ground at the same time (except when lying down, of course).
12. **(B) veins.** Blood leaves the heart through arteries and returns to the heart through a system of veins.
13. **(B) bald eagle.** Bald eagles add to their nests each year, and over time, they can weigh more than a ton.
14. **(D) dinosaurs.** Paleontology is the study of dinosaurs.
15. **(A) Mercury.** Mercury is the closest planet to the sun. It also has the shortest year.
16. **(D) plant cells.** Chloroplasts help plant cells turn sunlight into energy for the plant.
17. **(C) radius.** The ulna and radius are the two bones that are contained in the human forearm.
18. **(C) Venus.** It takes Venus about 248 days to rotate once on its axis.
19. **(E) uranium**. Lanthanum has a higher atomic number than uranium, but it is not a natural element.
20. **(E) species.** This is the lowest level of the organism classification system.
21. **(A) 0°C.** On the Celsius scale, the freezing point of water is 0 degrees.

22. **(C) soils maintain their fertility.** When organic matter decays under natural conditions, the process restores needed nutrients to the soil.
23. **(D) they failed to adapt to a changing environment.** The extinction of all sizes and varieties of dinosaurs all over the world cannot be explained by local phenomena, nor on a one-by-one basis. The most reasonable conclusion is that the dinosaurs failed to adapt and were unable to survive as climatic conditions changed radically.
24. **(A) burning charcoal in your barbecue.** Combustion is a chemical reaction.
25. **(B) hydrogen.** Hydrogen has an atomic number (atomic weight) of 1.
26. **(C) nitrogen.** Nitrogen makes up about 78 percent of the gases found in Earth's atmosphere.
27. **(C) in orbital layers around the nucleus.** Electrons orbit around the nucleus (the center of the atom).
28. **(C) both (A) and (B).** Freezing water does not change its chemical makeup.
29. **(D) 75 percent.** Metals make up 3/4 of the known elements.
30. **(C) 1,000.** "Kilo" means "thousand," so there are 1,000 meters in a kilometer.
31. **(B) oxygen.** Remember the prefix "ox" in "oxide."
32. **(A) 1.** The pH scale runs from 1 to 14. A pH of 1 would be a very strong acid, a pH of 7 would be neutral, and a pH of 14 would be a strong base.
33. **(B) 6.** The atomic number is the same as the number of protons contained in the element.
34. **(C) isotopes.** An isotope is an element that has the same number of protons as another element, but a different number of neutrons.
35. **(C) 6 percent.** The U.S. contains six percent of the world's population.
36. **(A) Pacific Ocean.** The Pacific Ocean averages about 4,000 meters deep.
37. **(B) Jupiter.** Jupiter has 60 *known* moons.
38. **(B) surface temperature.** The temperature of the star determines its color. Blue stars are hotter than red stars.
39. **(D) Jupiter.** *Io* is one of the 60 known moons of Jupiter.

CHAPTER 10

Mechanical Comprehension

What the country needs are a few labor-making inventions.

—Arnold H. Glasow

Individuals applying for Navy OCS, as well as Marine Corps and Coast Guard aviation applicants, are tested on their knowledge of basic mechanical principles. The Air Force removed the mechanical comprehension subtest from the AFOQT during its last revision. The ASTB contains 30 multiple–choice mechanical comprehension questions.

Air Force and Army officer hopefuls and non-aviation Marine Corps and Coast Guard officer applicants can skip this chapter.

On the Mechanical Comprehension subtests, you'll primarily see questions concerning simple machines and have to provide explanations of how they work. You may also see questions that display a diagram or illustration and ask you to provide explanations on the operations of the machine or mechanical device shown.

To perform well on this subtest you should also brush up on your mathematical skills (see Chapter 7). You'll often see questions that require you to make calculations based on mathematical physics to explain certain mechanical principles.

UNDERSTANDING MECHANICS

Humans have used machines to help us make tasks easier ever since we climbed down out of the trees and invented the wheel. A "machine" can be as complex as the internal combustion engine that runs your Chevy, or as simple as the hinge on a door. Your Chevy's engine supplies force through a (relatively) complex process of chemical combustion that moves pistons through a cylinder, which—in turn—moves levers that cause a shaft to rotate. In the latter case, a hinge on a door is designed to decrease resistance, and allows us to move the door more easily.

Machines and mechanisms serve the primary purpose of allowing us to apply force more efficiently.

In physics, *force* is defined as *a vector quantity that tends to produce an acceleration of a body in the direction of its application.* Let's try that again, but this time in English: force is the power or strength that allows us to change the speed of an object. Force can be used to make an object start, stop, speed up, slow down, or change direction.

Sir Isaac Newton gave us a mathematical formula to define force in his second law of motion: $F = ma$, or force is equal to mass times acceleration.

This is why (all other things being equal) a heavyweight fighter can punch harder (produce more force) than a lightweight fighter. The heavyweight fighter has more mass. Of course, if the lightweight fighter hits faster (more acceleration) than the heavyweight, his faster punches may "balance out" the heavier mass of the heavyweight and result in punches with the same amount of force. $F = ma$ is also why a professional boxer can hit harder than an amateur. The professional has years of practice, which has increased his speed (more acceleration).

Mass

Many people make the mistake of confusing weight with mass. The mass of an object refers to the amount of matter that object contains. The weight of an object, on the other hand, refers to the force of gravity acting upon that object. Think of it this way: *Mass* means "how much stuff" there is in the object, and *weight* means how hard the gravity of Earth (or any other planetary body) is pulling that "stuff." Mass is measured in kg, and will remain the same whether that object is on Earth, in space, on Mars, or anywhere else. The mass of an object doesn't change because of location, gravitational forces, speed, or relationship to various forces.

Weight, on the other hand, will change according to the location of the object. An object on the moon weighs approximately 1/6 of what it would on Earth.

Types of Force

Forces can be classified into several types. Here are a few.

Applied Force: This is a force that is applied to an object by a person or another object. For example, if a person is pushing a heavy crate across the floor, then the person is applying a force that is acting upon the object.

Gravity Force: The force of gravity is the force by which the Earth, moon, or other massively large object attracts another object toward itself. On Earth, the force of gravity pulls objects "downward" toward the center of the earth. The force of gravity on Earth is always equal to the weight of the object; the surface gravity of the other planets is measured relative to Earth's gravity.

Normal Force: This is sometimes called *balanced forces.* When two or more forces act so that their combination cancels each other out, we have equilibrium, which is a condition where there is no net force and the velocity of an object doesn't change. For example, if a glass is resting upon a table, then the table is exerting an upward force upon the glass that counteracts the force of gravity. Sometimes, a normal force is exerted horizontally between two objects that are in contact with each other.

Friction Force: Friction force is the force exerted by a surface as an object moves across it or makes an effort to move across it. The friction force opposes the motion of the object. For example, if your car is traveling down the road at 35 mph and you place the car in neutral, the car will gradually slow down due to the friction from the roadway acting against the tires (air resistance also plays a part, and we'll discuss that shortly). If we wish to slow down even faster, we would apply the brakes, which would cause a disk or pad to press against the wheel cylinder, increasing friction and thereby slowing the car's motion.

Friction depends upon the nature of the two surfaces and upon the degree to which they are pressed together. It's much easier to push a heavy crate across a smooth floor than it is to push it across the lawn.

Friction can often be reduced by applying a lubricant. If you oil the hinges on a door, this reduces the amount of friction created by the surface of the hinges rubbing together, and makes the door easier to open.

Air Resistance Force: Air resistance is a special type of frictional force that acts upon objects as they move through the air. As with other frictional forces, the force of air resistance always opposes the directional motion of the object. Air resistance force is most notable with objects traveling at a high speed or for objects with a large surface area.

Spring Force: Spring force is the force exerted by a compressed or stretched spring upon any object that is attached to it. For most springs, the measurement of the force is directly proportional to the amount of stretch or compression of the spring.

Spring scales use the concept of spring force to measure all kinds of other forces. Spring scales are calibrated in force units—either force-pounds or *newtons* (*N*). It takes 4.45 newtons to equal one force-pound.

Tensional Force: When tension is transmitted through a string, rope, or wire pulled tight by forces acting from each end, the result is tensional force. The force is the amount of tension directed along the string, rope, or wire, and pulls equally on the objects on either end. For example, if we attach a spring scale to a rope, then attach one end to a brick wall and pull on the other end with a force equal to 30 *N* (Newtons), the scale would show us that the tension of the rope is 30 *N* (see diagram below).

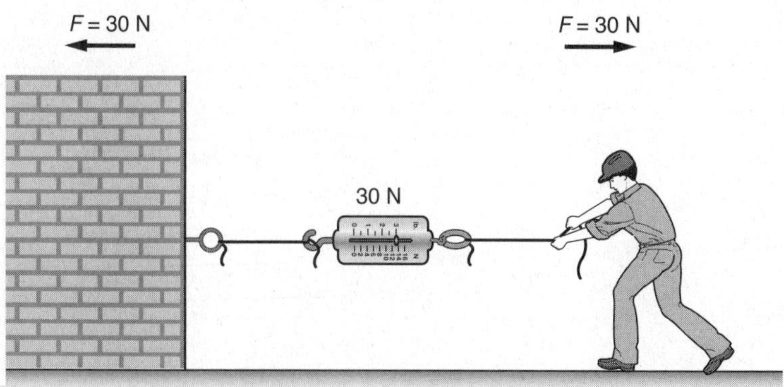

Elastic Recoil Force: Solid matter (as opposed to liquid or gases) has a specific shape. Solids resist changes in shape, and by doing so, exert a force in opposition to any applied force. For example, if we suspend a wooden board on two bricks and then push down in the middle of the board, the board will bend, but we can feel the force of the board trying to regain its original shape. The force we feel is called elastic recoil.

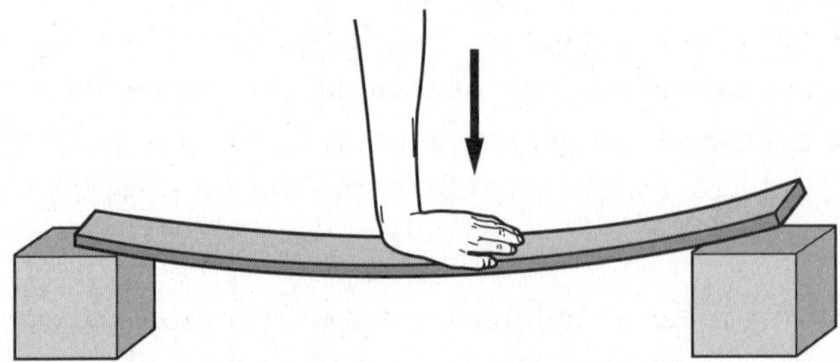

Buoyancy Force: Buoyancy force is a force that acts "upwards" on any object submerged in a gas or liquid. If you take an inflatable beach ball into the pool and try to submerge it under the water, you can feel the force of buoyancy trying to push the ball back to the top. On the other hand, if you drop a brick into the water, it will sink. That's because the weight of the brick is greater than the buoyancy of the water. A helium-filled balloon rises in the air because its weight is less than the buoyancy of the surrounding air.

Magnetic Force: We've all played with magnets as a kid (some of us still play with them). Magnets produce a force that strongly attracts ferromagnetic materials such as iron, nickel, and cobalt. Additionally, when two magnets or magnetic objects are close to each other, there is a force that attracts the opposite poles together. Conversely, when two magnetic objects have like poles facing each other, the magnetic force pushes them apart.

Static Electricity Force: Static electricity is a force of electrical charges built up on the surface of a material. We call it "static" because there is no current flowing as in AC or DC electricity. Static electricity is usually caused when certain materials are rubbed together. The result is that objects may be attracted to each other or may repel each other. Common examples of static electricity force are static cling and flyaway hair.

Newton's Three Laws of Motion

The measurements of forces against moving objects can be explained and described by physical principles discovered over 300 years ago by Sir Isaac Newton. Newton worked in many areas of mathematics and physics. He developed the theories of gravitation in 1666, when he was only 23 years old. Some 20 years later, in 1686, he presented his three laws of motion in the *Principia Mathematica Philosophiae Naturalis.* Newton's three laws of motion state:

1. **Every object persists in its state of rest or uniform motion in a straight line unless it is compelled to change that state by forces impressed on it.**

   Newton's first law is the definition of inertia. The key point here is that if there is no net force acting on an object (if all the external forces cancel each other out), then the object will maintain a constant velocity. If that velocity is zero, then the object remains at rest. If an external force is applied, the velocity will change because of the force.

2. **Force is equal to the change in momentum (mV) per change in time. (For a constant mass, force equals mass times acceleration.)**

   The second law explains how the velocity of an object changes when it is subjected to an external force. The law defines a *force* to be equal to change in *momentum* (mass times velocity) per change in time. For an object with a constant mass (m), the second law states that the force (F) is the product of an object's mass and its acceleration, or $F = ma$.

   For an externally applied force, the change in velocity depends on the mass of the object. A force will cause a change in velocity; likewise, a change in velocity will generate a force. The equation works both ways.

3. **For every action, there is an equal and opposite reaction.**

   The third law states that for every action (force) in nature there is an equal and opposite reaction. In other words, if object A exerts a force on object B, then object B also exerts an equal force on object A. Notice that the forces are exerted on different objects. The third law can be used to explain the generation of lift by a wing and the production of thrust by a jet engine.

Work

In physics, *work* is defined as "*a force acting upon an object to cause a displacement.*" In other words, work occurs when a force moving an object overcomes a resistance. In measuring units of work, the force is usually measured in pounds, while the distance is measured in feet. So, the measure for work is often called *foot-pounds.*

Another standard measurement for work is Joules (this is the metric version). One Joule is equivalent to one Newton of force causing a displacement of one meter. In mathematical terms, $1J = 1N*m$.

In order for a force to qualify as having done work on an object, there must be a displacement (the object must move) and the force must cause the movement. A horse pulling a wagon is an example of work. A weightlifter lifting a barbell over his head is performing work. So is the teacher who is writing a lesson on the blackboard.

Three factors must be known when computing the amount of work that has occurred. We must know the amount of force applied, the distance of displacement, and the angle theta (θ). The angle theta is the angle between the force and the displacement vector.

The mathematical formula is:

$W = F \times D \times \cos\theta$, or work is equal to force times the displacement times the cosine of the angle theta.

In the above equation, the angle theta is the most difficult concept to explain.

Remember, the angle theta is not just the angle of the displacement, but rather it is the angle between the displacement and the force applied.

If the force applied is in the exact same direction of the displacement, the angle theta is zero.

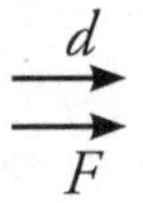

$$\overset{d}{\longrightarrow}$$
$$\underset{F}{\longrightarrow}$$

$$\theta = 0°$$

If the force applied is in the opposite direction of the displacement, then the angle theta is 180 degrees.

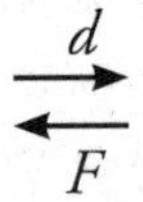

$$\overset{d}{\longrightarrow}$$
$$\underset{F}{\longleftarrow}$$

$$\theta = 180°$$

If the force applied is at a right angle to the displacement, the angle theta is 90 degrees.

$$\overset{d}{\longrightarrow} \quad \uparrow F$$

$$\theta = 90°$$

Let's try a tricky example. Imagine a waiter carrying a tray with one hand, walking across the floor. Would it surprise you to learn that the amount of *work* he is doing to the tray is equal to zero? It's true.

The waiter's hand is applying a force (straight up) to support the tray. But the tray is moving (displacing) in a direction that is at a right angle to the force being applied by the hand.

$$W = F^{*}D^{*}\cos\theta$$

The cosine of 90° is 0°, so we can see in the formula that the result for *W* will be zero.

It's true that the waiter performed "work" on the tray when he lifted it (applied force with his hand to move it to shoulder level). It can also be argued that he performed "work" on the tray with his hand to begin the forward motion. But, once the tray was moving horizontally, the tray will continue its horizontal movement at a constant speed without a forward force. A vertical force can never cause a horizontal displacement; thus, a vertical force does not do work on a horizontally displaced object!

Note the two examples below. A common mistake in computing work would be to use the angle of the incline in the formula. However, in both cases the angle of the displacement to the angle of the force applied is the same, 0°. So, in both of these cases, the angle theta would be zero.

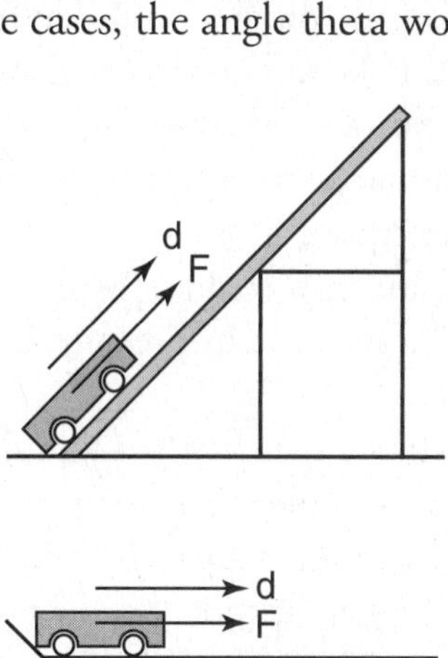

Mechanical Advantage

As mentioned previously, when we use machines to multiply the force we use, they help us perform tasks more easily. Machines and mechanisms give us a *mechanical advantage*. Mathematically, this can be expressed as

Mechanical Advantage = Resistance/effort.

Some machines and mechanisms give a large mechanical advantage, while others provide a mechanical advantage of only two or three (which means you can do two or three times the work with the same amount of effort).

Power

In physics, power is the amount of work done per unit of time. This can be expressed mathematically as

Power = Work/Time

The standard unit of measurement for power is the watt. One watt is equal to one Joule per second. Remember that one Joule is equivalent to one Newton of force causing a displacement of one meter.

When speaking about mechanics and mechanisms, power is often measured in units of *horsepower.* An average horse can do 33,000 foot-pounds of work in one minute. Therefore, one horsepower is equivalent to 33,000 foot-pounds per minute, or the power required to lift 550 pounds one foot in one second, which is equivalent to about 746 watts.

Pressure

When an object is immersed in a liquid, the fluid exerts pressure on the object. For a liquid in a state of rest, the difference in pressure between two points is dependent on the density of the liquid and the difference in depth between the two points. All swimmers have experienced this fact. The deeper a swimmer dives down into the water, the more pressure she can feel. Water weighs about 62.5 pounds per square inch, so for each foot the swimmer submerges further, she is subjected to an increase in pressure of 62.5 pounds per square foot.

Because a liquid is (almost) incompressible, there is no significant change in density with increasing depth. The increase in pressure is due solely to the increase in depth.

Because gases have a much lower density than liquids, the pressure variations of a gas are more complicated. For example, air pressure at sea level is about 15 pounds per square inch (psi). But, because air is a gas, it is more compressible than a liquid and its density decreases with higher altitude. So, air pressure is dependent upon the density of the air and changes in altitude. The average air pressure at 18,000 feet is about one-half of the air pressure at sea level.

The force of pressure is measured in pounds per square inch or psi. The mathematical formula is expressed as:

Pressure (psi) = Force (lbs)/Area (sq inch), or $P = F/A$

Leverage

Levers are simple machines that help us increase force. An everyday example of a lever is the seesaw on a playground.

Levers make work simpler by pivoting on a point of support called a fulcrum; they act to reduce resistance and multiply the effect of effort. The amount of effort needed to move the effort arm to overcome the resistance of the resistance arm depends on how long the effort arm is compared to the length of the resistance arm.

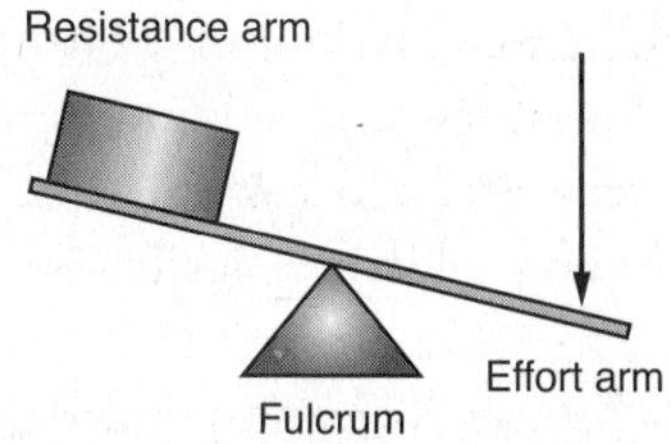

If the effort arm is longer than the resistance arm, less effort is required to overcome the resistance of the resistance arm than if the arms were the same length. If the effort arm is shorter than the resistance arm, more effort would be required to overcome the resistance than if both lengths were equal.

In mathematical terms, we can state

Mechanical Advantage = Effort Arm/Resistance Arm

For example, if the effort arm is six feet long and the resistance arm is two feet long, our mechanical advantage would be three.

In the figure below, a man is using the lever principle to move a heavy rock that he would otherwise not be able to move without mechanical assistance. Note that the effort arm on his lever is much longer than the resistance arm. This acts to greatly reduce the resistance to the movement of the rock.

CLASSES OF LEVERS

Levers are categorized into one of three classes, depending on the relative positions of the pivot, load, and effort. A pair of pliers is an example of a first-class lever. In this class, the pivot is positioned between the effort and the load. In a second-class lever, such as a nutcracker, the load is between the pivot and the effort. A pair of tongs is an example of a third-class lever. In this class, the effort is between the pivot and the load.

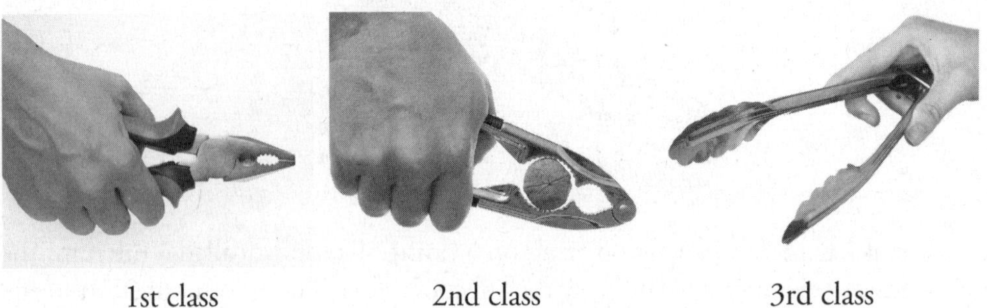

1st class 2nd class 3rd class

Pulleys

Anyone who's ever had to pull an engine out of a car knows the value of pulleys. A block and tackle (fancy term for pulleys) can allow an unassisted person to lift several thousand pounds. A pulley is a wheel that carries a flexible rope, cord, cable, chain, or belt on its rim and is used to lift a load vertically. But how does it work to reduce the amount of force necessary to move an object?

Take a look at the diagram below. We've suspended a heavy crate from the ceiling using two ropes.

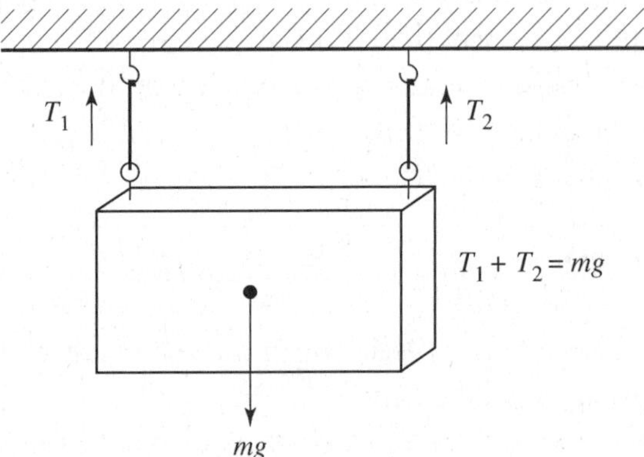

We use "T" to represent the upward tension in the ropes to hold the crate up. The sum of the tension on the two ropes is equal to the weight of the crate. In other words, each rope is supporting half of the weight of the crate.

In the next diagram we use a single rope, threaded through a wheel to accomplish the same purpose.

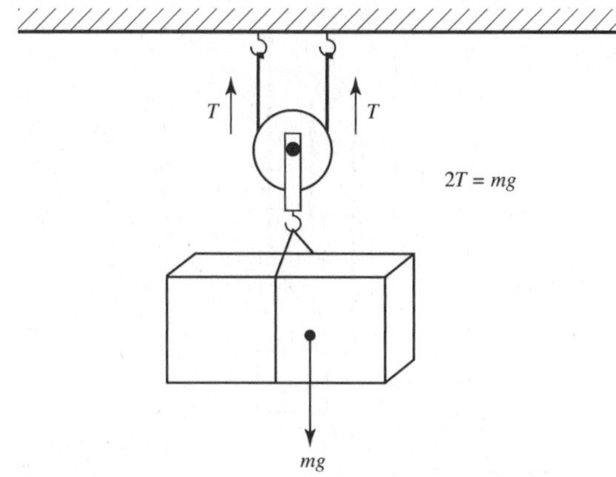

The tension on the rope is the same throughout, with the rope on each side of the wheel supporting half the weight of the crate. If the tension of the rope were different on either side of the wheel, the wheel would turn until the tension on both sides was equal.

Now we'll take the operation to the final step—grab one side of the rope (leaving the other side attached to the ceiling) and you can lift the crate by overcoming only 1/2 of its weight.

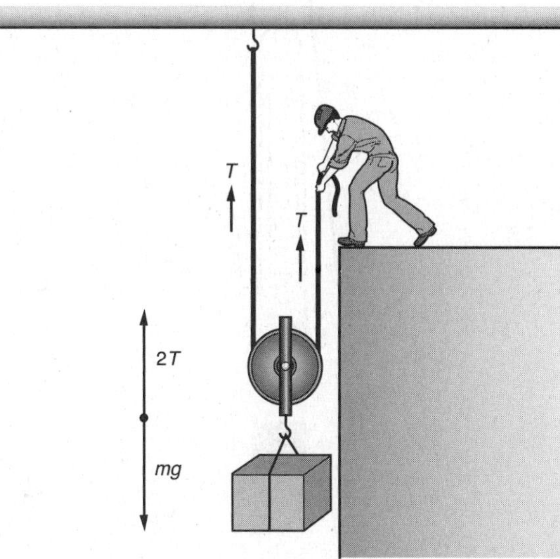

In physics, as in life, there is no such thing as a free lunch. In other words, you can't get something for nothing. By using the pulley, we can lift the object by applying one-half of the force required otherwise, but we have to pull the rope farther than if we were lifting the crate without a pulley. With the pulley, to raise the crate a distance of 10 feet, each side of the rope must shorten by 10 feet, which means we would have to pull 20 feet of rope through the wheel.

Pulleys can be combined to reduce effort even further. In the next diagram, there are three ropes supporting the weight of the crate.

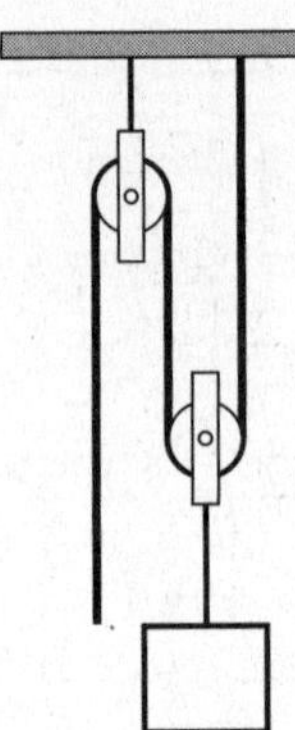

In order to lift the crate, we would only have to supply a force that is 1/3 of what we would need to lift it directly. However (remember the "no free lunch" principle), we would have to pull the rope three times as far.

In the following diagram, there are six sections of rope. So these pulleys would multiply the force by six times, but we would have to pull the rope six times as far.

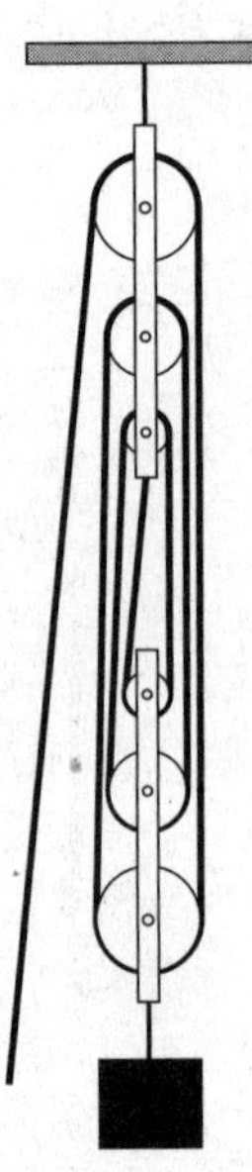

Inclined Planes

The *inclined plane* is a plane surface set at an angle (other than a right angle) against a horizontal surface. In short, it's a *loading ramp.* We can use an inclined plane to help us overcome a large resistance by applying a smaller amount of force over a longer distance.

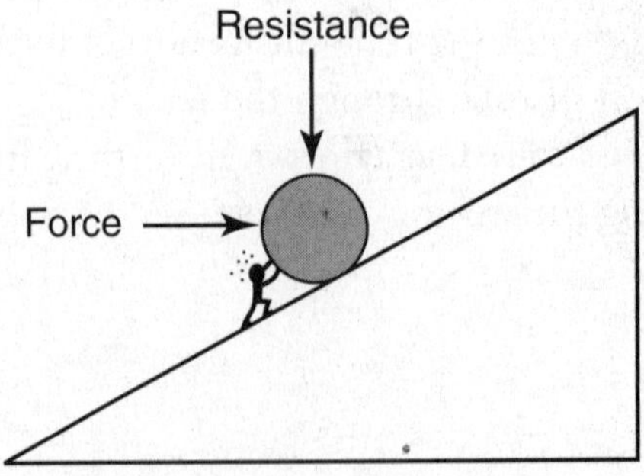

For example, let's say we needed to lift a 100-pound object into a truck bed four feet off the ground. It would require 100 pounds of force for four feet to move the object. However, if we used a ramp that was eight feet long, it would take one-half as much force. By doubling the distance we gain a mechanical advantage of two.

The mechanical advantage of an inclined plane can be stated as *rL*/*rH* = *oW*/*F*, where:

rL = ramp length
rH = ramp height
oW = object weight
F = force required to move the object

WEDGES

A wedge is a type of inclined plane, but it normally stands on its narrow end. Like an inclined plane, a wedge reduces the amount of force required to move an object (usually by cutting an object). The wedge moves through an object and separates the output force into these same two components, which varies directly with the length of the sloping side and inversely with the angle it makes with the object it's slicing through.

Wedges are used for splitting and cutting in such common tools as the fork, knife, saw blade, chisel, file, and axe. Many power tools, such as the lathe, miller, shaper, drill, and chain saw, also receive their mechanical advantage from the wedge.

Winches and Gears

Winches provide a mechanical advantage much in the same way that levers do. Take a look at the diagram below.

In the diagram, the man is applying effort to the crank, which has a much smaller radius than the shaft that the load-bearing rope is attached to. Because the crank and the shaft turn together, the torque of the handle is equal to the torque of the load (the tension of the chain). We can state the concept mathematically as

Mechanical Advantage = radius of shaft/radius of crank

Gears are used to transmit motion from one place to another. Gears are also used to increase or decrease force, torque, or speed, or change direction. Gears are measured by counting the number of teeth they have. Gears are designed to work with other gears. One gear turns another that turns another, and so on... (in order to do so, their teeth must mesh together properly to avoid slippage).

Take a look at the diagram below.

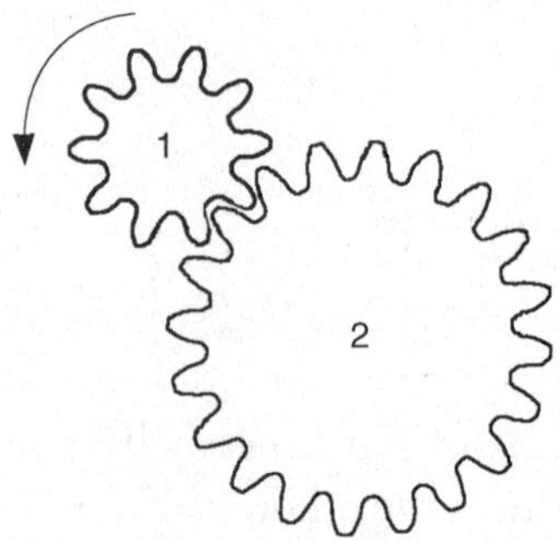

The smaller gear has 10 teeth while the larger gear has 20 teeth. This can be expressed as a ratio of 10:20 or 1:2. That means the smaller gear will have to complete two revolutions for each revolution of the larger gear.

Another principle to remember is gears that are next to each other rotate in opposite directions:

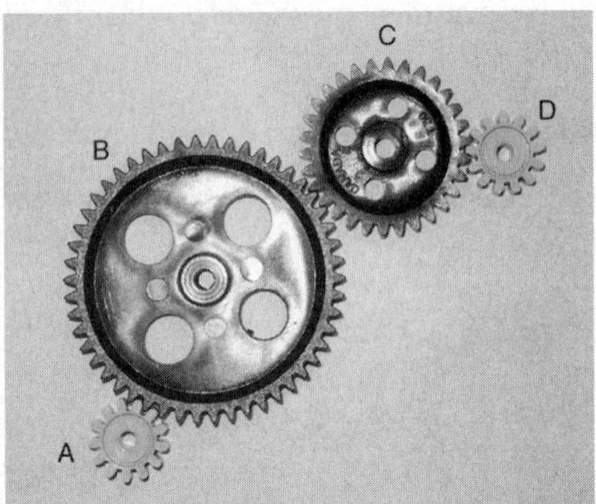

If we have an odd number of gears connected in a series, the first and last gear will rotate in the same direction. However, if we have an even number of gears connected, the first and last gears will rotate in opposite directions.

Hydraulic Jacks

Hydraulic systems use an incompressible fluid, such as oil or water, to transmit forces from one location to another within the fluid. Pascal's law states that when there is an increase in pressure at any point in a confined fluid, there is an equal increase at every other point in the container.

A hydraulic jack consists of two liquid-connected pistons in cylinders, one with a smaller diameter than the other. A force applied to the narrow piston applies a certain pressure (force per unit area) to the liquid, which is transmitted to the larger piston. Because the area of this piston is larger, the force exerted on it is larger. As a result, the force is magnified. However, the smaller piston must move a greater distance than the larger piston.

Answer Sheet for Practice Questions

1 Ⓐ Ⓑ Ⓒ Ⓓ	13 Ⓐ Ⓑ Ⓒ Ⓓ	24 Ⓐ Ⓑ Ⓒ Ⓓ	35 Ⓐ Ⓑ Ⓒ Ⓓ
2 Ⓐ Ⓑ Ⓒ Ⓓ	14 Ⓐ Ⓑ Ⓒ Ⓓ	25 Ⓐ Ⓑ Ⓒ Ⓓ	36 Ⓐ Ⓑ Ⓒ Ⓓ
3 Ⓐ Ⓑ Ⓒ Ⓓ	15 Ⓐ Ⓑ Ⓒ Ⓓ	26 Ⓐ Ⓑ Ⓒ Ⓓ	37 Ⓐ Ⓑ Ⓒ Ⓓ
4 Ⓐ Ⓑ Ⓒ Ⓓ	16 Ⓐ Ⓑ Ⓒ Ⓓ	27 Ⓐ Ⓑ Ⓒ Ⓓ	38 Ⓐ Ⓑ Ⓒ Ⓓ
5 Ⓐ Ⓑ Ⓒ Ⓓ	17 Ⓐ Ⓑ Ⓒ Ⓓ	28 Ⓐ Ⓑ Ⓒ Ⓓ	39 Ⓐ Ⓑ Ⓒ Ⓓ
6 Ⓐ Ⓑ Ⓒ Ⓓ	18 Ⓐ Ⓑ Ⓒ Ⓓ	29 Ⓐ Ⓑ Ⓒ Ⓓ	40 Ⓐ Ⓑ Ⓒ Ⓓ
7 Ⓐ Ⓑ Ⓒ Ⓓ	19 Ⓐ Ⓑ Ⓒ Ⓓ	30 Ⓐ Ⓑ Ⓒ Ⓓ	41 Ⓐ Ⓑ Ⓒ Ⓓ
8 Ⓐ Ⓑ Ⓒ Ⓓ	20 Ⓐ Ⓑ Ⓒ Ⓓ	31 Ⓐ Ⓑ Ⓒ Ⓓ	42 Ⓐ Ⓑ Ⓒ Ⓓ
9 Ⓐ Ⓑ Ⓒ Ⓓ	21 Ⓐ Ⓑ Ⓒ Ⓓ	32 Ⓐ Ⓑ Ⓒ Ⓓ	43 Ⓐ Ⓑ Ⓒ Ⓓ
10 Ⓐ Ⓑ Ⓒ Ⓓ	22 Ⓐ Ⓑ Ⓒ Ⓓ	33 Ⓐ Ⓑ Ⓒ Ⓓ	44 Ⓐ Ⓑ Ⓒ Ⓓ
11 Ⓐ Ⓑ Ⓒ Ⓓ	23 Ⓐ Ⓑ Ⓒ Ⓓ	34 Ⓐ Ⓑ Ⓒ Ⓓ	45 Ⓐ Ⓑ Ⓒ Ⓓ
12 Ⓐ Ⓑ Ⓒ Ⓓ			

Practice Questions

1. If gear B is the driving gear and is spinning counterclockwise at the point in time shown, gear A will

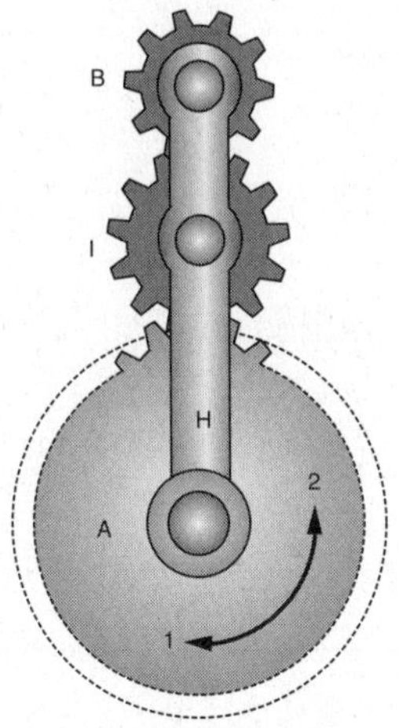

(A) not move.
(B) turn counterclockwise.
(C) turn clockwise.
(D) alternate directions.

2. Which water tower will provide the most water?

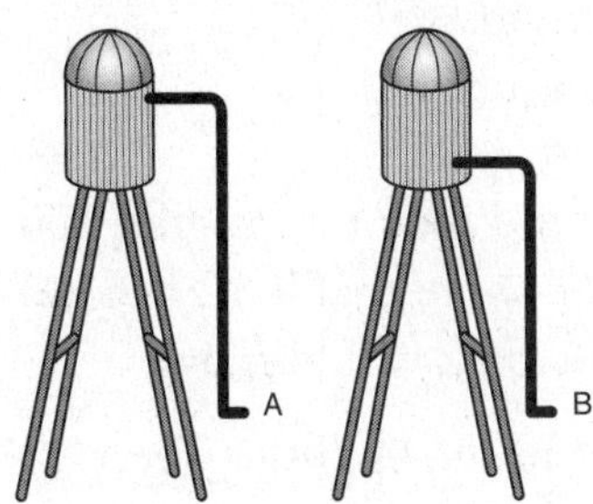

(A) Tower A
(B) Tower B
(C) They will both provide the same amount.
(D) It can't be determined from the information known.

3. Two 30-lb. blocks are attached to the ceiling using ropes, as shown below. Which of the following statements is true?

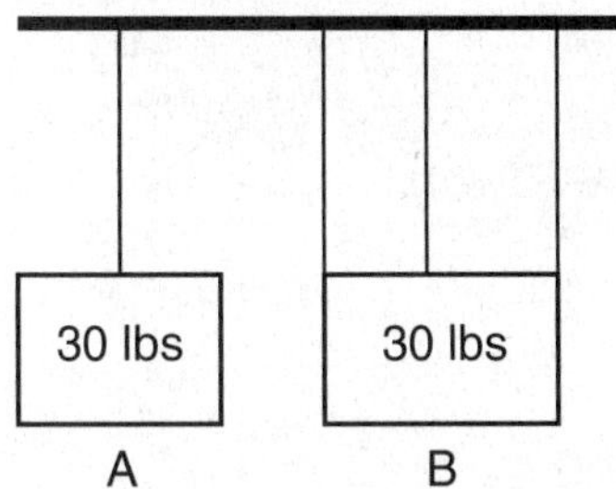

(A) All the ropes are under the same tension.
(B) The rope supporting block A is under $\frac{1}{3}$ of the tension of block B.
(C) The ropes supporting block B are under $\frac{1}{3}$ of the tension of block A.
(D) The rope in block A is supporting twice the weight of the ropes holding block B.

4. In the illustration below, a crank is rotating counterclockwise to drive a piston. At this point in time, the piston is halfway to fully compressed (where it moves to the lowest position). How far will the crank have rotated when the piston is uncompressed (uppermost position)?

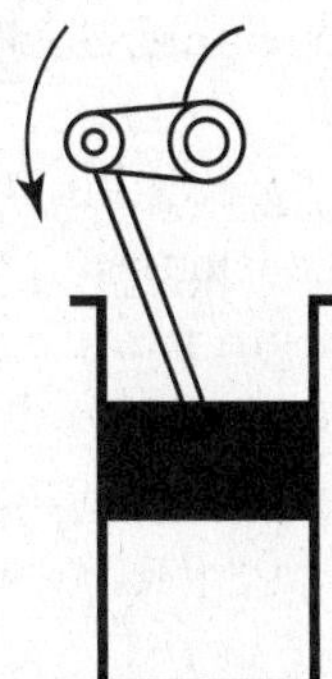

(A) $\frac{3}{4}$ of a revolution
(B) $\frac{1}{2}$ of a revolution
(C) $1\frac{1}{4}$ of a revolution
(D) $1\frac{1}{2}$ of a revolution

5. Gear A has 15 teeth and gear B has 10 teeth. If gear A makes 10 revolutions, how many revolutions will gear B make?

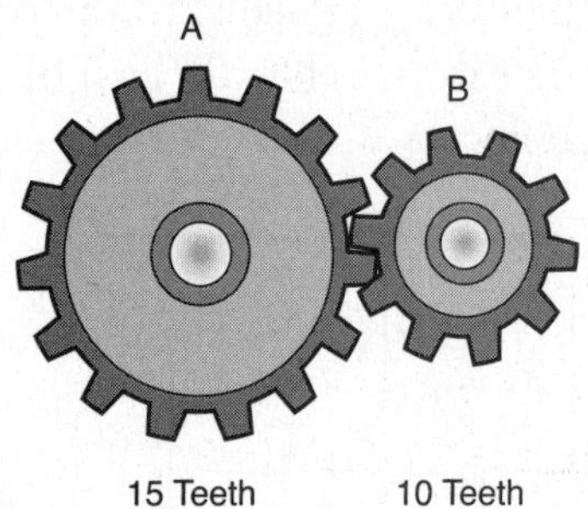

(A) 5
(B) 7
(C) 10
(D) 15

6. In the figure below, if gear A revolves at a rate of 10 times per second, then gear D

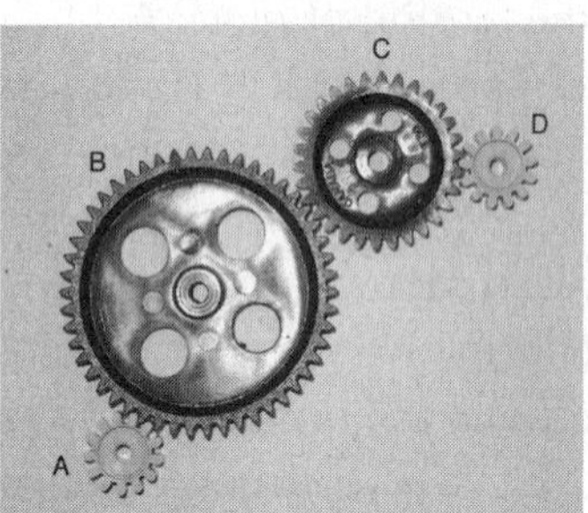

(A) will revolve at the same speed.
(B) will revolve at a slower speed.
(C) will revolve at a faster speed.
(D) will revolve counterclockwise.

7. A girl and a boy are sitting on a seesaw on a playground. The length of the entire seesaw is 12 feet. If the girl is sitting on the extreme right edge of the seesaw and weighs 50 pounds, how many feet from the edge will the 100-pound boy have to sit to balance the seesaw?

(A) 2 feet
(B) 3 feet
(C) 4 feet
(D) 5 feet

8. A 500-pound crate is to be moved to the bed of a truck that is three feet high. In order to reduce the amount of effort needed to move the box to $\frac{1}{3}$ of what would normally be required, we would need an inclined plane ______________ feet long.

(A) 5
(B) 9
(C) 12
(D) 15

9. The force required to balance the following lever would be ______________.

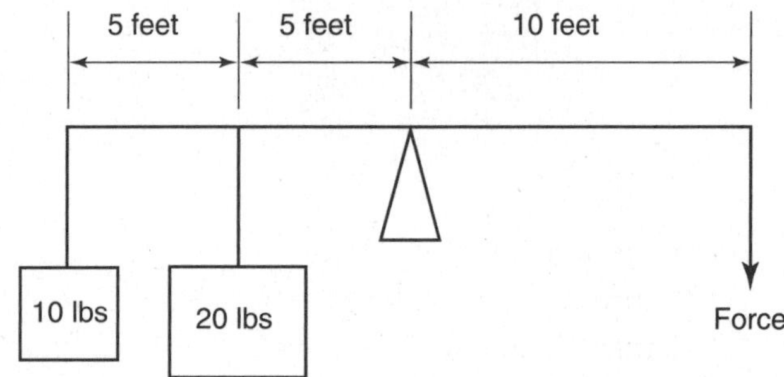

(A) 10 pounds
(B) 20 pounds
(C) 30 pounds
(D) 40 pounds

10. A 150-pound man jumps off a 600-pound boat to the shore that is 12 feet away. In theory, the boat would move

(A) 3 feet in the opposite direction.
(B) 5 feet in the opposite direction.
(C) 9 feet in the opposite direction.
(D) 10 feet in the opposite direction.

11. As the shaft in the diagram below spins faster, balls A and B will

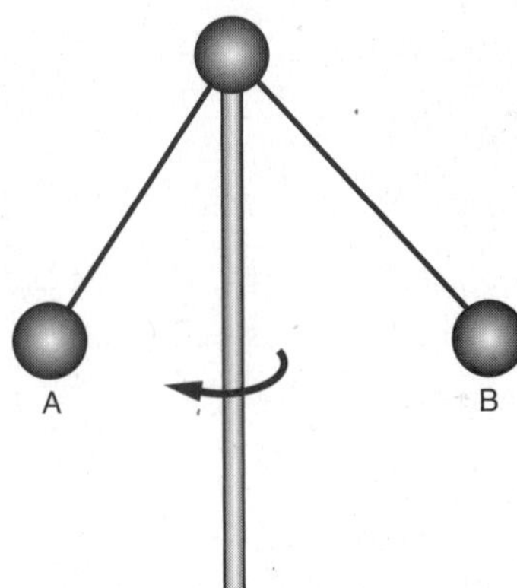

(A) move outward and downward.
(B) move outward and upward.
(C) move up.
(D) move down.

12. Water flows into a water tower at a rate of 120 gallons per hour and flows out at the rate of two gallons per minute. The level of the water in the tower will

(A) remain the same.
(B) rise.
(C) lower.
(D) rise initially, then lower.

13. The bicycle shown below has 20 teeth in the front gear and 10 teeth in the rear gear. How many times will the rear tire rotate each time the pedals go around?

(A) $\frac{1}{2}$
(B) 1
(C) 2
(D) 4

14. In the diagram below, we have a theoretical pulley that has no resistance. If a downward force is applied to weight A, what will be the result?

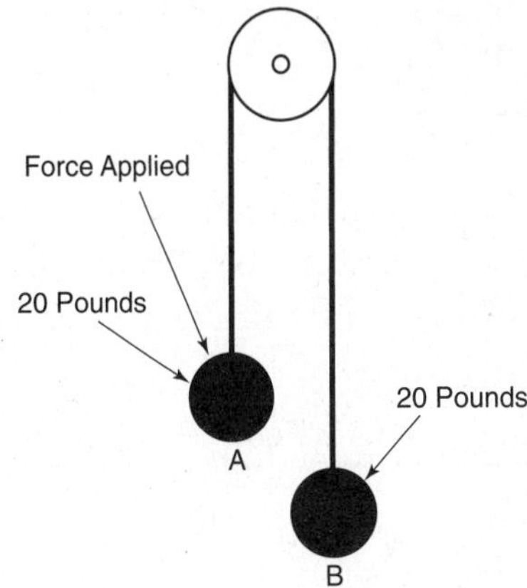

(A) Weight A will move downward until it is level with weight B.
(B) Weight A will move downward until it passes weight B, then move upward until it is level with weight B.
(C) Weight A will continue to move downward until it is stopped by weight B bumping into the pulley.
(D) Weight A will move until it has closed $\frac{1}{2}$ of the difference in height between itself and weight B.

15. Which pulley will revolve the fastest?

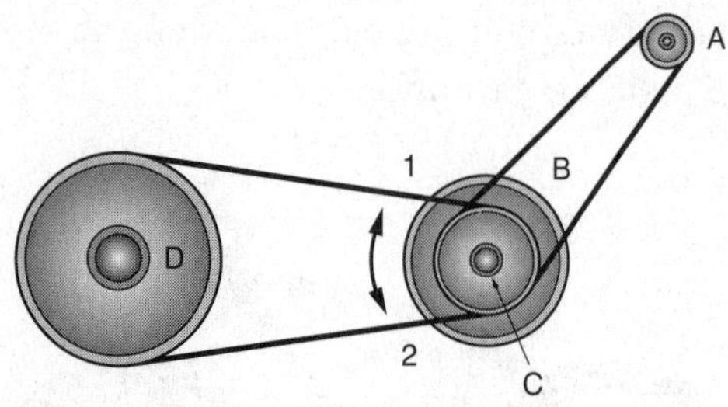

(A) A
(B) B
(C) C
(D) D

16. According to Einstein, if a 500-pound cart hits a brick wall at 10 mph, then a 400-pound cart would hit the wall with the same amount of force if traveling at a speed of ____________.

(A) 15 mph
(B) $12\frac{1}{25}$ mph
(C) $13\frac{1}{30}$ mph
(D) $15\frac{1}{2}$ mph

17. On average, air pressure at sea level is about 15 psi. What amount of pressure (force) would be exerted by air on the surface area below?

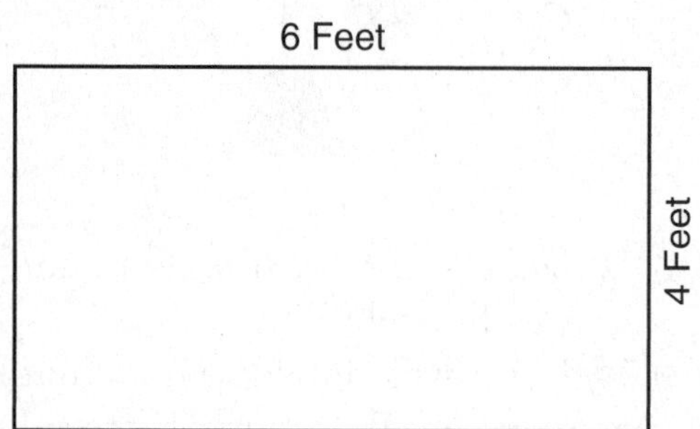

(A) 150 pounds
(B) 25 pounds
(C) 180 pounds
(D) 360 pounds

18. An axe is an example of what type of mechanical device?

(A) cutting
(B) inclined plane
(C) chopping
(D) gravitational

19. The force produced by a helium balloon rising high in the air is called ____________.

(A) gravity
(B) static electricity
(C) buoyancy
(D) recoil

20. In the following diagram, what is most likely to happen?

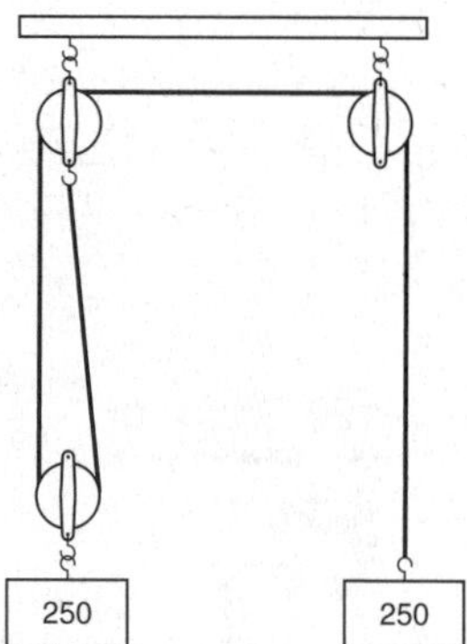

(A) The right-hand weight will travel downward.
(B) The left-hand weight will travel downward.
(C) The weights will not move.
(D) Cannot be determined from the information provided.

21. Brake systems use what kind of force(s) to bring a car to a stop?

(A) resistance
(B) hydraulic
(C) gravity
(D) both (A) and (B)

22. In the example below, the mechanical advantage would be ____________.

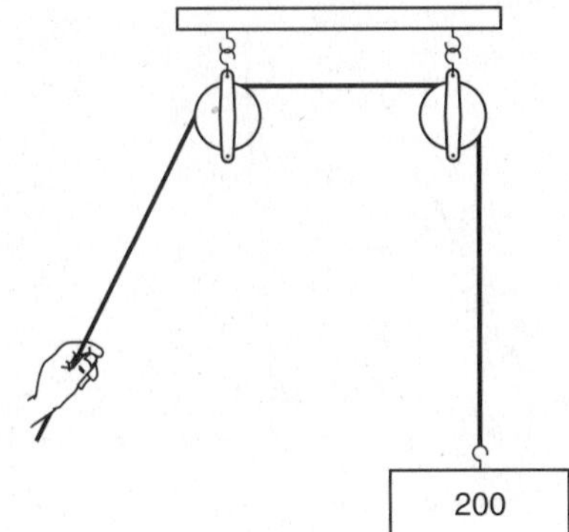

(A) 1
(B) 2
(C) 3
(D) 4

23. When the mechanism below is operating, how many of the gears will turn in a counterclockwise direction?

(A) 1
(B) 2
(C) 3
(D) Cannot be determined from the information provided.

24. Pascal's law is applied to ____________.

(A) gravitational forces
(B) inclined planes
(C) pressure applied to confined fluids
(D) magnetism

25. In order for the set screw to hit the contact point three times, cam A would have to complete ____________.

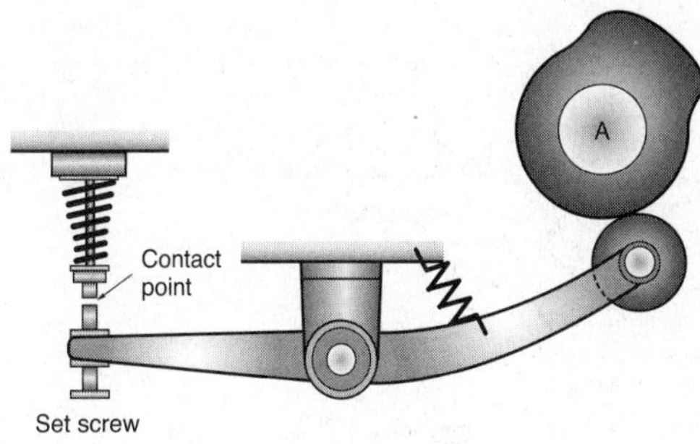

(A) one revolution
(B) two revolutions
(C) three revolutions
(D) one-half of a revolution

26. A water tank is 10 feet long, 6 feet wide, and 4 feet deep. When filled with water, what is the pressure exerted on the bottom of the tank?

(A) 2.7 psi
(B) 0.75 psi
(C) 2.92 psi
(D) 1.74 psi

27. Condensation usually occurs on pipes that

(A) contain cold water.
(B) contain hot water.
(C) are at high altitude.
(D) are insulated.

28. A book, a pair of metal pliers, a wooden table, and a wool jacket are all the same temperature. Which will feel the coldest?

(A) book
(B) pliers
(C) table
(D) jacket

29. If gear 1 is turning in the direction shown, which gears will turn clockwise?

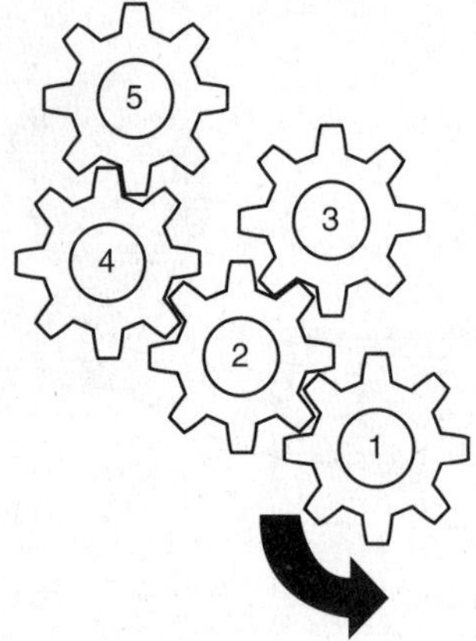

(A) 2 and 5
(B) 3, 4, and 5
(C) 4 and 3
(D) 2, 5, and 4

30. Which of the following right angles is braced most solidly?

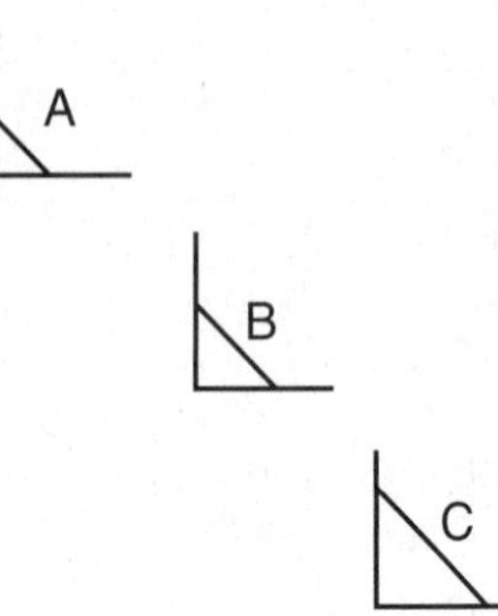

(A) A
(B) B
(C) C
(D) All are braced equally.

31. A parachutist's fall is affected primarily by what two types of forces?

(A) gravity and magnetism
(B) gravity and temperature
(C) gravity and air resistance
(D) gravity and buoyancy

32. To lift the block two feet, how many feet of rope would have to be pulled?

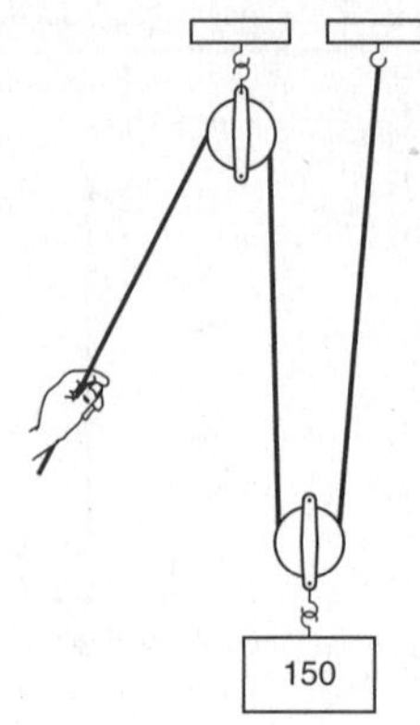

(A) 2 feet
(B) 4 feet
(C) 6 feet
(D) 8 feet

33. When two magnets have like poles facing each other

(A) the magnets will pull together.
(B) the magnets will push apart.
(C) the magnets will generate electricity.
(D) the magnets will spark.

34. Static electricity is

(A) alternating current (AC).
(B) direct current (DC).
(C) battery current.
(D) none of the above

35. In the example below, if the fulcrum is moved closer to the weight on the resistance arm, the result will be

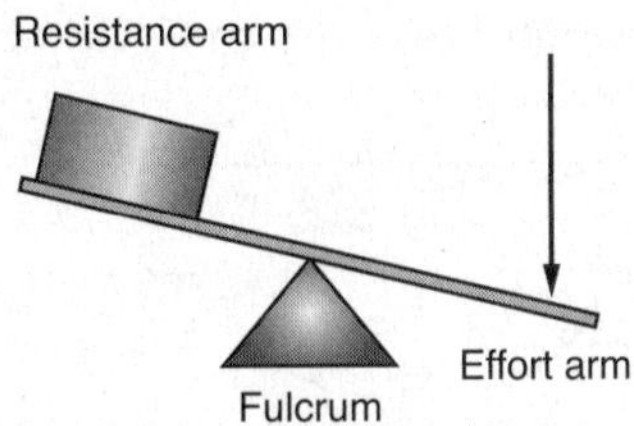

(A) the weight will be easier to lift and travel higher.
(B) the weight will be easier to lift and not travel as high.
(C) the weight will be harder to lift, and travel higher.
(D) the weight will be harder to lift and not travel as high.

36. What class of lever is the man below making use of?

(A) first class lever
(B) second class lever
(C) third class lever
(D) fourth class lever

37. In the water system below, assume the tank is empty and all the valves are closed. In order to ensure the tank fills and maintains approximately $\frac{1}{2}$ of its capacity, which valves would have to be open?

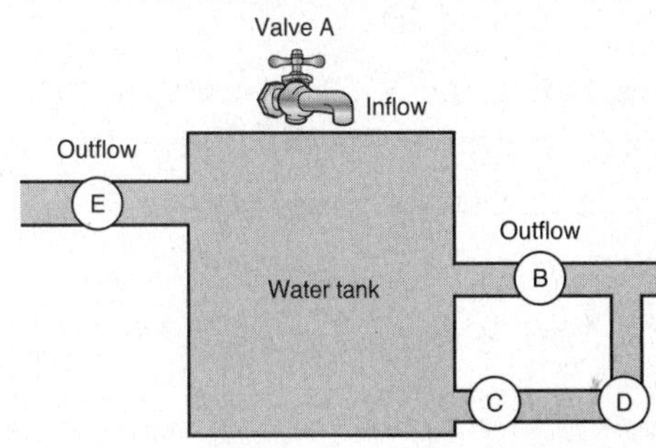

(A) A, B, and D
(B) A, B, and C
(C) A, E, and C
(D) A, E, C, and D

38. If pulley A is rotating in the direction indicated, then pulley C will

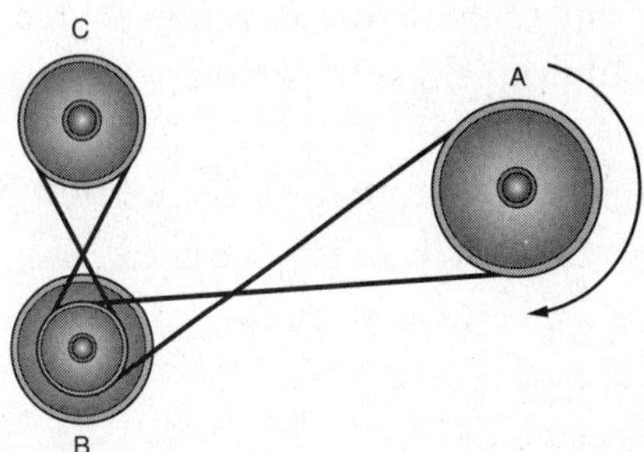

(A) rotate in the same direction as pulley A.
(B) rotate in the same direction as pulley B.
(C) rotate in the same direction as pulleys A and B.
(D) rotate in opposite directions of pulleys A and B.

39. In the pulley system depicted in question 38, which pulley will rotate the slowest?
    (A) pulley A
    (B) pulley B
    (C) pulley C
    (D) All will rotate at the same speed.

40. Disregarding the effects of weather, the average air pressure at 18,000 feet is ____________.
    (A) 15 psi
    (B) 7.5 psi
    (C) 10.5 psi
    (D) 15.5 psi

41. When you heat water in an enclosed container so the steam cannot escape, pressure builds up. As the pressure increases, what happens to the temperature of the water?
    (A) The temperature rises.
    (B) The temperature lowers.
    (C) The temperature remains the same.
    (D) The temperature rises one degree for each additional psi of pressure.

42. As the temperature rises, the motion of a pendulum tends to be ____________.
    (A) faster
    (B) slower
    (C) the same
    (D) It depends on the altitude.

43. What is the difference between mass and weight?
    (A) There is no difference.
    (B) Mass depends on the altitude of an object, while weight remains constant.
    (C) The mass of an object remains the same, but weight depends on gravitational forces.
    (D) Mass can be changed by buoyancy, but this force has no effect on weight.

44. Water is being pumped into the pipe depicted below at a rate of 200 gallons per minute. Note that the pipe is constricted at the point represented by the letter B. Which of the following statements is the most accurate?

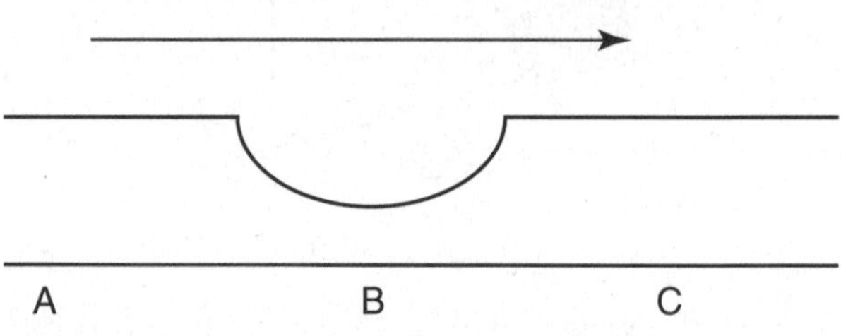

    (A) The velocity of the water at point B is the same as the velocity of the water at point A.
    (B) The volume of water flowing past point B per minute is the same as the volume of water flowing past point C per minute.
    (C) The velocity of the water at point C is greater than the velocity of the water at point A.
    (D) A greater volume of water per minute is flowing past point B than is flowing past point A.

45. When two or more forces act so that their combination cancels each other out, the condition is called ____________.
    (A) imperial
    (B) similar
    (C) equational
    (D) equilibrium

Answer Key

1. B	9. B	17. D	25. C	33. B	41. A
2. B	10. C	18. B	26. D	34. D	42. B
3. C	11. B	19. C	27. A	35. B	43. C
4. A	12. A	20. A	28. B	36. B	44. B
5. D	13. C	21. D	29. A	37. A	45. D
6. A	14. C	22. B	30. C	38. A	
7. B	15. A	23. C	31. C	39. A	
8. C	16. B	24. C	32. C	40. B	

Answer Explanations

1. **(B) turn counterclockwise**. When there is an odd number of gears connected in a series, the first gear and the last gear will turn in the same direction.
2. **(B) tower B.** The pipe on tower A is attached at the top of the tower and will stop providing water when the water level drops below the level where the pipe is attached.
3. **(C) the ropes supporting block B are under $\frac{1}{3}$ of the tension of block A.** Because there are three ropes supporting block B, each rope is supporting $\frac{1}{3}$ of the 30-pound weight.
4. **(A) $\frac{3}{4}$ of a revolution**. By the time the piston is fully compressed, the crank would have made $\frac{1}{4}$ of a turn. When $\frac{1}{2}$ uncompressed, it would have made $\frac{1}{2}$ of a revolution, and when fully uncompressed, it would have made $\frac{3}{4}$ of a revolution.
5. **(D) 15.** We can solve this as a simple algebra problem. Let x = the number of revolutions for gear B:
   $15 \times 10 = 10x$
   $10x = 15 \times 10$
   $10x = 150$
   $x = \frac{150}{10}$
   $x = 15$
6. **(A) They will revolve at the same speed**. When two gears in a series are the same size, they will revolve at the same speed, regardless of the size of the other gears in the series.
7. **(B) 3 feet.** Remember, a seesaw is nothing more than a lever. The mechanical advantage is determined by the length of each arm in relation to the fulcrum. In this case, there are six feet on each side of the fulcrum and the boy weighs twice as much as the girl. To overcome that distance, the boy would have to move half of the length (three feet) on his side of the fulcrum.
8. **(C) 12 feet long**. To reduce the effort of moving an object to a height of three feet by $\frac{1}{3}$, we would need an inclined plane (ramp) that is three times the distance of the height: $3 \times 3 = 9$.
9. **(B) 20 pounds.** To balance the lever the sum of the moments on each side of the fulcrum must be zero.

Our formula would be (10 feet × 10 pounds) + (5 feet × 20 pounds) = 10 feet × Force

200 (foot–pounds) = 10 feet × F

200/10 = F

F = 20 pounds

10. **(C) 9 feet in the opposite direction.** Newton's third law of motion states that for every action there is an equal and opposite reaction. We can set up the problem mathematically as follows:

$$x = \text{movement of the boat}$$
$$12 \times 150 = 600x$$
$$1800 = 600x$$
$$1800/600 = x$$
$$x = 9$$

11. **(B) move outward and upward.** Centrifugal force from the spin will cause the balls to move outward and tension on the strings will cause them to move upward.
12. **(A) remain the same.** The water is flowing in at a rate of 120 gallons per hour. If we convert that to minutes $\left(\frac{120}{60}\right)$, we find that the water is flowing in at the rate of two gallons per minute, the same as the outflow.
13. **(C) 2.** The ratio of the front gear to the rear gear is 20:10 or 2:1.
14. **(C) Weight A will continue to move downward until it is stopped by weight B bumping into the pulley.** Remember, this theoretical pulley has no resistance. Newton's first law of motion states that a body at rest will stay at rest unless acted on by a force. Conversely, a body in motion will stay in motion unless acted on by a force (inertia). Because this pulley has no resistance, weight A will continue in motion until some other force (weight B hitting the pulley) causes it to stop.
15. **(A) A.** The smallest pulley in a series will spin the fastest.
16. **(B) $12\frac{1}{25}$ mph.** Force is equal to mass times acceleration. We can set up our equation as:

$$500 \times 10 = F \times 400$$
$$5000 = 400F$$
$$\frac{5000}{400} = F$$
$$F = \frac{50}{4}$$
$$F = 12\frac{1}{25}$$

17. **(D) 360 pounds.** The surface area of a rectangle is found by multiplying the length times the width of the rectangle (6 × 4 = 24). Power equals force divided by the area in square inches ($P = F/A$). We can rearrange the formula as $F = A \times P$. When we substitute the known quantities, F = 15 × 24 = 360 pounds.
18. **(B) inclined plane.** An axe is classified as a wedge, which is a type of inclined plane.
19. **(C) buoyancy.** Buoyancy force is a force that acts "upwards" on any object submerged in a gas or a liquid.

20. **(A) The right-hand weight will travel downward.** The left-hand weight has two supporting sections of rope and the right-hand weight only has one. That means the left-hand weight will be exerting $\frac{1}{2}$ of the amount of force as the right-hand weight.
21. **(D) both (A) and (B).** Brake systems in automobiles use hydraulic force to move pads or disks against the wheel cylinder, which slows the vehicle with resistance.
22. **(B) 2.** Don't be confused by the number of pulleys. While there are two wheels (pulleys) pictured, there are still only two sections of rope supporting the weight, so the mechanical advantage is 2.
23. **(C) 3.** In a series of gears, every other gear revolves in the same direction. Since there are six gears in the mechanism, three will turn clockwise and three will turn counterclockwise.
24. **(C) pressure applied to confined fluids.** Pascal's law states that when there is an increase in pressure at any point in a confined fluid, there is an equal increase at every other point in the container.
25. **(C) three revolutions.** Cam A has only one lobe (high spot), so it will move the lever once for each revolution.
26. **(D) 1.74 psi.** The total force at the bottom of the tank is equal to the weight of the water. Since water weighs about 62.5 pounds per square foot and the tank holds 240 cubic feet of water, $240 \times 62.5 = 15{,}000$ pounds. The formula for pressure is $P = F/A$. Remember, however, that in using this formula, area must be in square inches. The area of the bottom of the tank would be $10 \times 6 \times 144$, because 144 square inches equals one square foot. Substituting the values:

    $$P = 15{,}000/(10 \times 6 \times 144) = 1.74 \text{ psi}$$
27. **(A) contain cold water.** Condensation normally happens when a container holds liquid that is colder than the ambient air temperature.
28. **(B) pliers.** Metal objects feel cooler to the touch than nonmetallic objects.
29. **(A) 2 and 5.** Gear 1 is turning counterclockwise, gear 2 is turning in the opposite direction (clockwise), gears 3 and 4 are turning counterclockwise, and gear 4 is causing gear 5 to turn clockwise.
30. **(C) C.** The brace on angle C covers more area than either of the other two angles.
31. **(C) gravity and air resistance.** The force of gravity works to pull the parachutist toward the center of the earth, while the force of air resistance slows her descent.
32. **(C) six feet.** There are three supporting ropes in this pulley system, giving a mechanical advantage of three, but requiring three times the amount of rope to be pulled. 3×2 feet = 6 feet.
33. **(B) the magnets will push apart.** When two magnetic objects have like poles facing each other, they repel each other.
34. **(D) none of the above.** Static electricity is neither a direct current nor an alternating current; hence its name, *static.*
35. **(B) the weight will be easier to lift and not travel as high.** The closer the fulcrum is to the end of the resistance arm, the less force is required to lift the weight, but the less distance the weight will travel.

36. **(B) second-class lever.** On a wheelbarrow, the load is in the middle with the effort at one end and the fulcrum at the other—the definition of a second-class lever.
37. **(A) A, B, and D.** Water inflows through valve A, and outflows when the tank is $\frac{1}{2}$ full through valve B. However, in order for the water to continue through the system, valve D would also have to be opened.
38. **(A) rotate in the same direction as pulley A.** Pulley A causes pulley B to rotate in the opposite direction, and pulley B causes pulley C to rotate in the opposite direction from B.
39. **(A) pulley A.** Just like gears, the larger the pulley in a system, the slower it revolves.
40. **(B) 7.5 psi.** Average air pressure at sea level is 15 psi. At 18,000 feet the air pressure is about $\frac{1}{2}$ of the average pressure at sea-level. 15 $\frac{\text{psi}}{2}$ = 7.5 psi.
41. **(A) the temperature rises.** Additional pressure causes the molecules to compress, which results in a release of heat.
42. **(B) slower.** Cold causes a pendulum to contract making it swing faster. Conversely, warmer temperatures cause a pendulum to expand, which slows it down.
43. **(C) the mass of an object remains the same, but weight depends on gravitational forces.** Remember that mass is the *stuff* contained in an object, but the weight of an object depends on gravity *acting* on that stuff.
44. **(B) The volume of water flowing past point B per minute is the same as the volume of water flowing past point C per minute.** The volume of water flowing per minute must be the same at all three points. The amount of mass coming in must equal the amount of mass going out. As there is no water added or removed after point A, there cannot be any change in volume.
45. **(D) equilibrium.** When two or more forces balance, the condition is such that they have reached equilibrium.

Flight Aptitude

CHAPTER 11

Any idiot can get an airplane off the ground, but an aviator earns his keep by bringing it back anytime, anywhere, under any circumstances that man and God can dream up.

—Walter Cunningham

Ever since the movie *Top Gun* was released, followed by popular military TV shows such as *Pensacola—Wings of Gold*, it seems that everybody and his brother (and sister) wants to become a military fighter pilot.

The problem is that there are thousands more candidates who want to become aviators than the military has jobs for. The military also spends big bucks on aviation training. So it needs a method to determine which officer candidates have the potential to learn how to fly before they spend those bucks—and they have such a way, included in the subtests of the Air Force Officer Qualifying Test and the Navy/Marine Corps Aviation Selection Test Battery.

Those who wish to become a pilot or navigator aboard military aircraft need to score high on these portions of the qualifying exams. The scores for aviation qualification are derived from sections of the Navy and Air Force tests, and can be divided into two broad areas: flying aptitude (flight principles, interpreting gages and instruments, aviation terminology, etc.), and spatial relationships (how solid objects relate to each other when they are rotated, put together, or turned over).

This chapter is not intended to turn you into a pilot. That takes months of hard study and practical experience. What this chapter will do is provide an overview of the information that you will find on the subtests, along with several example questions. Additionally, serious candidates can increase their chances of scoring well on these subtests and (ultimately) being selected as aviation candidates by taking advantage of the following tips:

- **Take Flying Lessons.** If you have the financial means, opportunity, and time, attending a certified flight school and obtaining a private pilot's license will not only help you on the flight aptitude portions of the tests, but in the selection process as well. The military loves candidates who already have a private pilot's license. Not only does it save them money in basic flight training costs, but it shows beyond any doubt that the individual has the aptitude to learn basic flying skills.
- **Practice with Flight Simulation Software Programs.** Many flight simulation software programs available for home computers these days are very realistic. In fact, many military aviation students use the most famous of these, *Microsoft® Flight Simulator,* while in military flight training to sharpen their basic skills. Practice with such programs can dramatically improve your understanding of basic flight principles, characteristics of flight, and basic flying rules.

- **Study Magazines and Books that Depict Spatial Relationship Puzzles.** This includes maze puzzles that are common in many puzzle magazines. Don't forget the Internet, as there are many puzzle pages on the web. Some examples are:
  http://www.strongmuseum.org/kids/tangram.html
  http://www.aimsedu.org/puzzle/Heart/heart2.html
  http://www.paperfolding.com/
  http://www.jigzone.com/
  http://www.crea-soft.com/online-jigsaw-puzzle/
  http://www.amazeingart.com/free-mazes.html

BASICS OF FLIGHT

As I said before, this chapter is not intended to turn you into a pilot. In the flight aptitude section we'll cover the very basics of flight. Much of the information in this section is courtesy of the Federal Aviation Administration (FAA), which is the U.S. Government agency that (among other things) regulates licensing requirements for pilots.

Aircraft Structure

Although airplanes are designed for a variety of purposes, most of them have the same major components. The overall characteristics are largely determined by the original design objectives. Most airplane structures include a fuselage, wings, an empennage, landing gear, and a power plant.

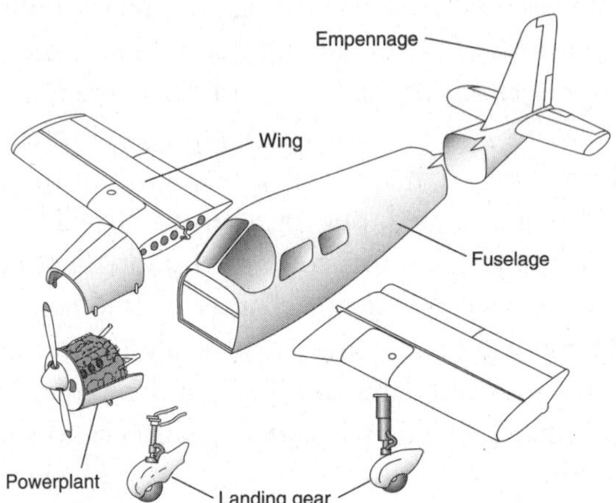

Fuselage

The fuselage includes the cabin and/or cockpit that contains seats for the occupants and the controls for the airplane. In addition, the fuselage may also provide room for cargo and attachment points for the other major airplane components.

On single-engine airplanes, the engine is usually attached to the front of the fuselage. There is a fireproof partition between the rear of the engine and the cockpit or cabin to protect the pilot and passengers from accidental engine fires. This partition is called a firewall and is usually made of stainless steel or other heat-resistant material.

Wings

The wings are airfoils attached to each side of the fuselage and are the main lifting surfaces that support the airplane in flight. There are numerous wing designs, sizes, and shapes used by the various manufacturers. Each fulfills a certain need with respect to the expected performance for the particular airplane. How the wing produces lift is explained later.

Wings may be attached at the top, middle, or lower portion of the fuselage. These designs are referred to as high-, mid-, and low-wing, respectively. The number of wings can also vary. Airplanes with a single set of wings are referred to as monoplanes, while those with two sets are called biplanes.

Attached to the rear, or trailing, edges of the wings are two types of control surfaces referred to as ailerons and flaps. Ailerons extend from about the midpoint of each wing outward toward the tip and move in opposite directions to create aerodynamic forces that cause the airplane to roll. Flaps extend outward from the fuselage to near the midpoint of each wing. The flaps are normally flush with the wing's surface during cruising flight. When extended, the flaps move simultaneously downward to increase the lifting force of the wing for takeoffs and landings.

Empennage

The correct name for the tail section of an airplane is *empennage.* The empennage includes the entire tail group, consisting of fixed surfaces such as the vertical stabilizer and the horizontal stabilizer. The movable surfaces include the rudder, the elevator, and one or more trim tabs.

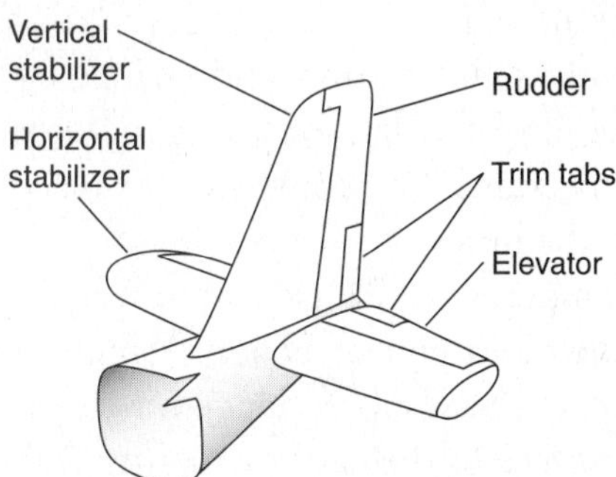

The rudder is attached to the back of the vertical stabilizer. During flight, it is used to move the airplane's nose left and right. The rudder is used in combination with the ailerons for turns during flight. The elevator, which is attached to the back of the horizontal stabilizer, is used to move the nose of the airplane up and down during flight.

Trim tabs are small, movable portions of the trailing edge of the control surface. These movable trim tabs, which are controlled from the cockpit, reduce control pressures. Trim tabs may be installed on the ailerons, rudder, and/or elevator.

Landing Gear

The landing gear is the principal support of the airplane when parked, taxiing, taking off, or landing. The most common type of landing gear consists of wheels, but airplanes can also be equipped with floats for water operations, or skis for landing on snow.

The landing gear consists of three wheels—two main wheels and a third wheel positioned either at the front or rear of the airplane. Landing gear employing a rear-mounted wheel is called conventional landing gear. Airplanes with conventional landing gear are sometimes referred to as tail-wheel airplanes. When the third wheel is located on the nose, it is called a nose-wheel, and the design is referred to as a tricycle gear. A steerable nose-wheel or tail-wheel permits the airplane to be controlled throughout all operations while on the ground.

Power Plant

The power plant usually includes both the engine and the propeller. The primary function of the engine is to provide the power to turn the propeller. It also generates electrical power, provides a vacuum source for some flight instruments, and in most single-engine airplanes, provides a source of heat for the pilot and passengers. The engine is covered by a cowling, or in the case of some airplanes, surrounded by a nacelle. The purpose of the cowling or nacelle is to streamline the flow of air around the engine and to help cool the engine by ducting air around the cylinders. The propeller, mounted on the front of the engine, translates the rotating force of the engine into a forward-acting force called thrust that helps move the airplane through the air.

The Atmosphere

The atmosphere in which flight is conducted is an envelope of air that surrounds Earth and rests upon its surface. It is as much a part of Earth as the seas or the land. However, air differs from land and water inasmuch as it is a mixture of gases. It has mass, weight, and indefinite shape.

Air, like any other fluid, is able to flow and change its shape when subjected to even minute pressures because of its lack of strong molecular cohesion. For example, gas will completely fill any container into which it is placed, expanding or contracting to adjust its shape to the limits of the container.

The atmosphere is composed of 78 percent nitrogen, 21 percent oxygen, and 1 percent other gases, such as argon or helium. Since some of these elements are heavier than others, there is a natural tendency for these heavier elements, such as oxygen, to settle to the surface of the earth, while the lighter elements are lifted up to the region of higher altitude. This explains why most of the oxygen is contained below 35,000 feet altitude.

Because air has mass and weight, it is a body, and as a body, it reacts to the scientific laws of bodies in the same manner as other gaseous bodies. This body of air resting upon the surface of the earth has weight and at sea level develops an average pressure of 14.7 pounds on each square inch of surface, or 29.92 inches of mercury—but as its thickness is limited, the higher the altitude, the less air there is above. For this reason, the weight of the atmosphere at 18,000 feet is only one-half what it is at sea level.

Atmospheric Pressure

Although there are various kinds of pressure, this discussion is mainly concerned with atmospheric pressure. It is one of the basic factors in weather changes, helps lift the airplane, and actuates some of the important flight instruments in the airplane.

These instruments are the altimeter, the airspeed indicator, the rate-of-climb indicator, and the manifold pressure gauge.

Although air is very light, it has mass and is affected by the attraction of gravity. Therefore, like any other substance, it has weight, and because of its weight, it has force. Since it is a fluid substance, this force is exerted equally in all directions, and its effect on bodies within the air is called pressure. Under standard conditions at sea level, the average pressure exerted on the human body by the weight of the atmosphere around it is approximately 14.7 pounds per inch. The density of air has significant effects on the airplane's capability. As air becomes less dense, it reduces (1) power because the engine takes in less air, (2) thrust because the propeller is less efficient in thin air, and (3) lift because the thin air exerts less force on the airfoils.

Since air is a gas, it can be compressed or expanded. When air is compressed, a greater amount of air can occupy a given volume. Conversely, when pressure on a given volume of air is decreased, the air expands and occupies a greater space. That is, the original column of air at a lower pressure contains a smaller mass of air. In other words, the density is decreased. In fact, density is directly proportional to pressure. If the pressure is doubled, the density is doubled, and if the pressure is lowered, so is the density. This is true, however, only at a constant temperature.

Temperature

The effect of increasing the temperature of a substance is to decrease its density. Conversely, decreasing the temperature has the effect of increasing the density. Thus, the density of air varies inversely as the absolute temperature varies. This is true only at constant pressure.

In the atmosphere, both temperature and pressure decrease with altitude, and have conflicting effects upon density. However, the fairly rapid drop in pressure as altitude is increased usually has the dominating effect. Hence, density can be expected to decrease with altitude.

Humidity

The preceding paragraphs have assumed that the air was perfectly dry. In reality, it is never completely dry. The small amount of water vapor suspended in the atmosphere may be almost negligible under certain conditions, but in other conditions humidity may become an important factor in the performance of an airplane. Water vapor is lighter than air; consequently, moist air is lighter than dry air. It is lightest or least dense when, in a given set of conditions, it contains the maximum amount of water vapor. The higher the temperature, the greater the amount of water vapor air can hold. When comparing two separate air masses, the first warm and moist (both qualities tending to lighten the air) and the second cold and dry (both qualities making it heavier), the first necessarily must be less dense than the second. Pressure, temperature, and humidity have a great influence on airplane performance, because of their effects upon density.

Newton's Laws

In the 17th century, philosopher and mathematician Sir Isaac Newton propounded three basic laws of motion. It is certain that he did not have the airplane in mind when he did so, but almost everything known about motion goes back to his three simple laws. These laws, named after Newton, are as follows:

First Law

Newton's first law states, "A body at rest tends to remain at rest, and a body in motion tends to remain moving at the same speed and in the same direction."

This simply means that, in nature, nothing starts or stops moving until some outside force causes it to do so. An airplane at rest on the ramp will remain at rest unless a force strong enough to overcome its inertia is applied. Once it is moving, however, its inertia keeps it moving, subject to the various other forces acting on it. These forces may add to its motion, slow it down, or change its direction.

Second Law

Newton's second law states, "When a body is acted upon by a constant force, its resulting acceleration is inversely proportional to the mass of the body and is directly proportional to the applied force."

What is being dealt with here are the factors involved in overcoming Newton's First Law of Inertia. It covers both changes in direction and speed, including starting up from rest (positive acceleration) and coming to a stop (negative acceleration, or deceleration).

Third Law

Newton's third law states, "Whenever one body exerts a force on another, the second body always exerts on the first a force that is equal in magnitude but opposite in direction."

The recoil of a gun as it is fired is a graphic example of Newton's third law. The champion swimmer who pushes against the side of the pool during the turnaround, or the infant learning to walk would both fail but for the phenomena expressed in this law. In an airplane, the propeller moves and pushes back the air; consequently, the air pushes the propeller (and thus the airplane) in the opposite direction—forward. In a jet airplane, the engine pushes a blast of hot gases backward; the force of equal and opposite reaction pushes against the engine and forces the airplane forward. The movement of all vehicles is a graphic illustration of Newton's third law.

Magnus Effect

The explanation of lift can best be explained by looking at a cylinder rotating in an air stream. The local velocity near the cylinder is composed of the air stream velocity and the cylinder's rotational velocity, which decreases with distance from the cylinder. On a cylinder that is rotating in such a way that the top surface area is rotating in the same direction as the airflow, the local velocity at the surface is high on top and low on the bottom.

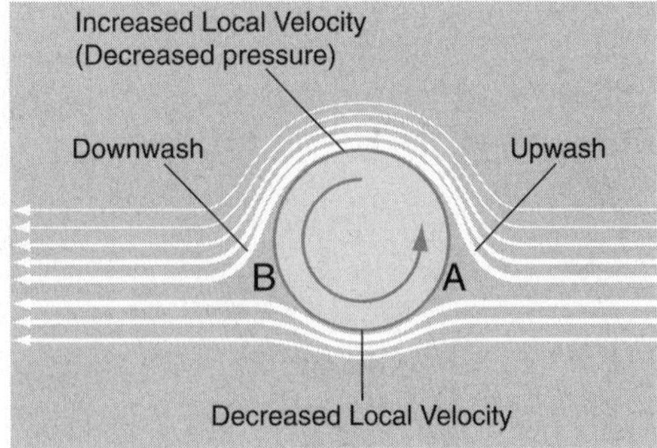

As shown in the below diagram, at point "A," a stagnation point exists where the airstream line that impinges on the surface splits; some air goes over and some air goes under. Another stagnation point exists at "B," where the two airstreams rejoin and resume at identical velocities. We now have upwash ahead of the rotating cylinder and downwash at the rear.

The difference in surface velocity accounts for a difference in pressure, with the pressure being lower on the top than the bottom. This low-pressure area produces an upward force known as the "Magnus Effect." This mechanically-induced circulation illustrates the relationship between circulation and lift.

As can be seen in the below diagram, an airfoil with a positive angle of attack develops air circulation as its sharp trailing edge forces the rear stagnation point to be aft of the trailing edge, while the front stagnation point is below the leading edge.

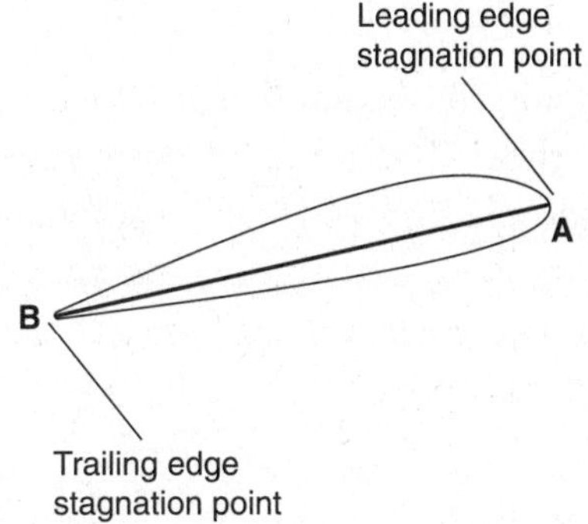

Axes of Flight

Whenever an airplane changes its flight attitude or position in flight, it rotates about one or more of three axes, which are imaginary lines that pass through the airplane's center of gravity. The axes of an airplane can be considered as imaginary axles around which the airplane turns, much like the axle around which a wheel rotates. At the point where all three axes intersect, each is at a 90° angle to the other two. The axis that extends lengthwise through the fuselage from the nose to the tail is the longitudinal axis. The axis that extends crosswise from wingtip to wingtip is the lateral axis. The axis that passes vertically through the center of gravity is the vertical axis.

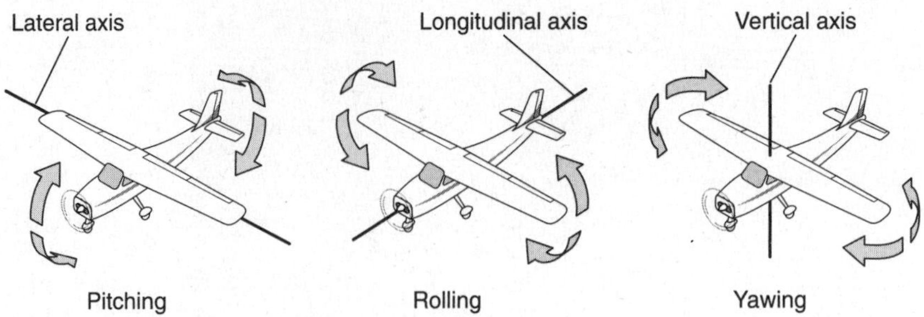

The airplane's motion about its longitudinal axis resembles the roll of a ship from side to side. In fact, the names used in describing the motion about an airplane's three axes were originally nautical terms. They have been adapted to aeronautical terminology because of the similarity of motion between an airplane and a seagoing ship.

In light of the adoption of nautical terms, the motion about the airplane's longitudinal axis is called "roll"; motion about its lateral axis is referred to as "pitch." Finally, an airplane moves about its vertical axis in a motion that is termed "yaw"—that is, a horizontal (left and right) movement of the airplane's nose. The three motions of the airplane (roll, pitch, and yaw) are controlled by three control surfaces. Roll is controlled by the ailerons, pitch is controlled by the elevators, and yaw is controlled by the rudder.

Flight Controls

Aircraft flight control systems are classified as primary and secondary. The primary control systems consist of those that are required to safely control an airplane during flight. These include the ailerons, elevator (or stabilator), and rudder. Secondary control systems improve the performance characteristics of the airplane or relieve the pilot of wrestling with excessive control forces. Examples of secondary control systems are wing flaps and trim systems.

Primary Flight Controls

Airplane control systems are carefully designed to provide a natural feel, and at the same time, allow adequate responsiveness to control inputs. At low airspeeds, the controls usually feel soft and sluggish, and the airplane responds slowly to control applications. At high speeds, the controls feel firm and the response is more rapid.

Movement of any of the three primary flight control surfaces changes the airflow and pressure distribution over and around the airfoil. These changes affect the lift and drag produced by the airfoil/control surface combination, which allows a pilot to control the airplane about its three axes of rotation.

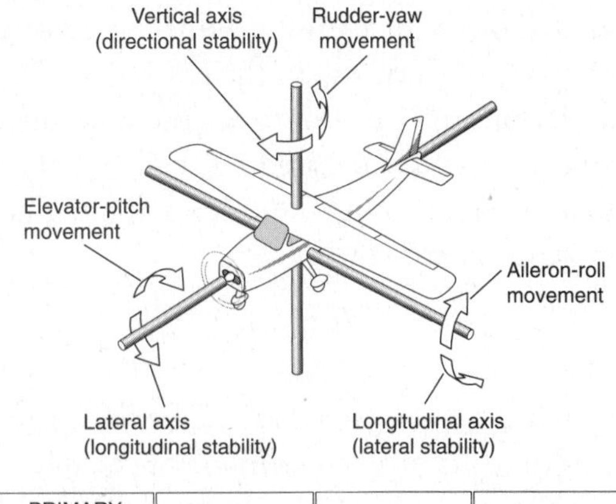

PRIMARY CONTROL SURFACE	AIRPLANE MOVEMENT	AXES OF ROTATION	TYPE OF STABILITY
Aileron	Roll	Longitudinal	Lateral
Elevator/ stability	Pitch	Lateral	Longitudinal
Rudder	Yaw	Vertical	Directional

AILERONS

Ailerons control roll about the longitudinal axis. The ailerons are attached to the outboard trailing edge of each wing and move in the opposite direction from each other. Ailerons are connected by cables, bell-cranks, pulleys, or push-pull tubes to each other and to the control wheel.

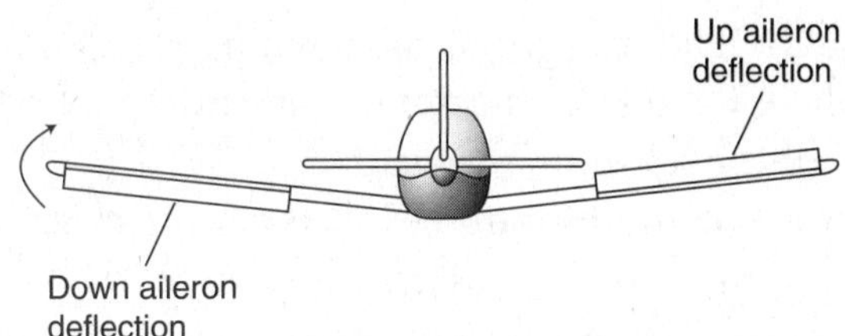

Moving the control wheel or joystick to the right causes the right aileron to deflect upward and the left aileron to deflect downward. The upward deflection of the right aileron decreases the wing's camber, resulting in decreased lift on the right wing. The corresponding downward deflection of the left aileron increases that wing's camber, resulting in increased lift on the left wing. Thus, the increased lift on the left wing and the decreased lift on the right wing cause the airplane to roll to the right.

ADVERSE YAW

Since the downward deflected aileron produces more lift, it also produces more drag. This added drag attempts to yaw the airplane's nose in the direction of the raised wing. This is called adverse yaw.

The rudder is used to counteract adverse yaw, and the amount of rudder control required is greatest at low airspeeds, high angles of attack, and with large aileron deflections. However, with lower airspeeds, the vertical stabilizer/rudder combination becomes less effective, and magnifies the control problems associated with adverse yaw.

All turns are coordinated by use of ailerons, rudder, and elevator. Applying aileron pressure is necessary to place the airplane in the desired angle of bank, while simultaneously applying rudder pressure to counteract the resultant adverse yaw. During a turn, the angle of attack must be increased by applying elevator pressure because more lift is required than when in straight-and-level flight. The steeper the turn, the more back elevator pressure is needed.

ELEVATOR

The elevator controls pitch about the lateral axis. Like the ailerons on small airplanes, the elevator is connected to the control column in the cockpit by a series of mechanical linkages. Aft movement of the control column deflects the trailing edge of the elevator surface up. This is usually referred to as "up elevator."

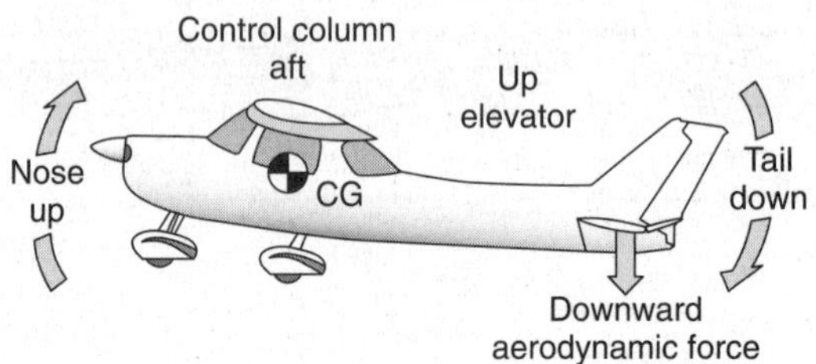

The up-elevator position decreases the camber of the horizontal tail surface and creates a downward aerodynamic force that is greater than the normal tail-down force that exists in straight-and-level flight. The overall effect causes the tail of the airplane to move down and the nose to pitch up. The pitching moment occurs about the center of gravity (CG). The strength of the pitching moment is determined by the distance between the CG and the horizontal tail surface, as well as by the aerodynamic effectiveness of the horizontal tail surface.

Moving the control column forward has the opposite effect. In this case, elevator camber increases, creating more lift (less tail-down force) on the horizontal stabilizer/elevator. This moves the tail upward and pitches the nose down. Again, the pitching moment occurs about the CG.

Rudder

The rudder controls movement of the airplane about its vertical axis. This motion is called yaw. Like the other primary control surfaces, the rudder is a movable surface hinged to a fixed surface, in this case, to the vertical stabilizer, or fin. Moving the left or right rudder pedal controls the rudder. When the rudder is deflected into the airflow, a horizontal force is exerted in the opposite direction.

By pushing the left pedal, the rudder moves left. This alters the airflow around the vertical stabilizer/rudder, and creates a sideward lift that moves the tail to the right and yaws the nose of the airplane to the left. Rudder effectiveness increases with speed, so large deflections at low speeds and small deflections at high speeds may be required to provide the desired reaction. In propeller-driven aircraft, any slipstream flowing over the rudder increases its effectiveness.

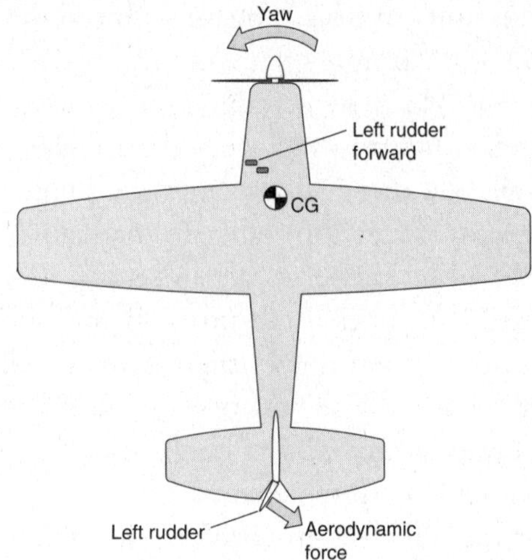

Secondary Flight Controls

Secondary flight control systems may consist of the flaps, leading edge devices, spoilers, and trim devices.

Flaps

Flaps are the most common high-lift devices used on practically all airplanes. These surfaces, which are attached to the trailing edge of the wing, increase both lift and induced drag for any given angle of attack. Flaps allow a compromise between high cruising speed and low landing speed, because they may be extended when needed, and retracted into the wing's structure when not needed.

Leading Edge Devices

High-lift devices can also be applied to the leading edge of the airfoil. The most common types are fixed slats, movable slats, and leading edge flaps.

Spoilers

On some airplanes, high-drag devices called spoilers are deployed from the wings to spoil the smooth airflow, reducing lift and increasing drag. Spoilers are used for roll control on some aircraft, one of the advantages being the elimination of adverse yaw. To turn right, for example, the spoiler on the right wing is raised, destroying some of the lift and creating more drag on the right. The right wing drops, and the airplane banks and yaws to the right. Deploying spoilers on both wings at the same time allows the aircraft to descend without gaining speed. Spoilers are also deployed to help shorten ground roll after landing. By destroying lift, they transfer weight to the wheels, improving braking effectiveness.

Trim Systems

Although the airplane can be operated throughout a wide range of attitudes, airspeeds, and power settings, it can only be designed to fly "hands off" within a very limited combination of these variables. Therefore, trim systems are used to relieve the pilot of the need to maintain constant pressure on the flight controls. Trim systems usually consist of cockpit controls and small hinged devices attached to the trailing edge of one or more of the primary flight control surfaces. They are designed to help minimize a pilot's workload by aerodynamically assisting movement and position of the flight control surface to which they are attached.

The most common installation on small airplanes is a single trim tab attached to the trailing edge of the elevator. Most trim tabs are manually operated by a small, vertically mounted control wheel. However, a trim crank may be found in some airplanes. The cockpit control includes a tab position indicator. Placing the trim control in the full nose-down position moves the tab to its full up position. With the tab up and into the air-stream, the airflow over the horizontal tail surface tends to force the trailing edge of the elevator down. This causes the tail of the airplane to move up, and results in a nose-down pitch change.

If you set the trim tab to the full nose-up position, the tab moves to its full-down position. In this case, the air flowing under the horizontal tail surface hits the tab and tends to force the trailing edge of the elevator up, reducing the elevator's angle of attack. This causes a tail-down movement of the airplane and a nose-up pitch change.

In spite of the opposite direction movement of the trim tab and the elevator, control of trim is natural to a pilot. If you have to exert constant back pressure on the control column, the need for nose-up trim is indicated. The normal trim procedure is to continue trimming until the airplane is balanced and the nose-heavy condition is no longer apparent. Pilots normally establish the desired power, pitch, attitude, and configuration first, and then trim the airplane to relieve control pressures that may exist for that flight condition. Any time power, pitch, attitude, or configuration are changed, re-trimming will normally be necessary to relieve the control pressures for the new flight condition.

Flight Instruments

Flight instruments enable an airplane to be operated with maximum performance and enhanced safety, especially when flying long distances.

Altimeter

The altimeter measures the height of the airplane above a given pressure level. Since it is the only instrument that gives altitude information, the altimeter is one of the most vital instruments in the airplane.

The pressure altimeter is an aneroid barometer that measures the pressure of the atmosphere at the level where the altimeter is located, and presents an altitude indication in feet. The altimeter uses static pressure as its source of operation. Air is denser at sea level than aloft, so as altitude increases, atmospheric pressure decreases. This difference in pressure at various levels causes the altimeter to indicate changes in altitude.

The presentation of altitude varies considerably between different types of altimeters. Some have one pointer while others have two or more. Only the multi-pointer type will be discussed in this chapter. The dial of a typical altimeter is graduated with numerals arranged clockwise from 0 to 9. Movement of the aneroid element is transmitted through gears to the three hands that indicate altitude. The shortest hand indicates altitude in tens of thousands of feet; the intermediate hand in thousands of feet; and the longest hand in hundreds of feet.

This indicated altitude is correct, however, only when the sea level barometric pressure is standard (29.92 inches of mercury), the sea level free air temperature is standard (+15°C or 59°F), and the pressure and temperature decrease at a standard rate with an increase in altitude. Adjustments for nonstandard conditions are accomplished by setting the corrected pressure into a barometric scale located on the face of the altimeter. Only after the altimeter is set does it indicate the correct altitude.

Knowing the airplane's altitude is vitally important to a pilot. The pilot must be sure that the airplane is flying high enough to clear the highest terrain or obstruction along the intended route. It is especially important to have accurate altitude information when visibility is restricted. To clear obstructions, the pilot must constantly be aware of the altitude of the airplane and the elevation of the surrounding terrain. To reduce the possibility of a midair collision, it is essential to maintain altitude in accordance with air traffic rules.

TYPES OF ALTITUDE

Altitude is vertical distance above some point or level used as a reference. There are as many kinds of altitude as there are reference levels from which altitude is measured, and each may be used for specific reasons. Pilots are mainly concerned with five types of altitudes:

1. **Indicated Altitude**—The altitude read directly from the altimeter (uncorrected) when it is set to the current altimeter setting.
2. **True Altitude**—The vertical distance of the airplane above sea level—the actual altitude. It is often expressed as feet above mean sea level (MSL). Airport, terrain, and obstacle elevations on aeronautical charts are true altitudes.
3. **Absolute Altitude**—The vertical distance of an airplane above the terrain, or above ground level (AGL).
4. **Pressure Altitude**—The altitude indicated when the altimeter setting window (barometric scale) is adjusted to 29.92. This is the altitude above the standard datum plane, which is a theoretical plane where air pressure (corrected to 15°C) equals 29.92 inches of mercury (Hg). Pressure altitude is used to compute density altitude, true altitude, true airspeed, and other performance data.

5. **Density Altitude**—This altitude is pressure altitude corrected for variations from standard temperature. When conditions are standard, pressure altitude and density altitude are the same. If the temperature is above standard, the density altitude is higher than pressure altitude. If the temperature is below standard, the density altitude is lower than pressure altitude. This is an important altitude because it is directly related to the airplane's performance.

As an example, consider an airport with a field elevation of 5,048 feet MSL where the standard temperature is 5°C. Under these conditions, pressure altitude and density altitude are the same—5,048 feet. If the temperature changes to 30°C, the density altitude increases to 7,855 feet. This means an airplane would perform on takeoff as though the field elevation were 7,855 feet at standard temperature. Conversely, a temperature of –25°C would result in a density altitude of 1,232 feet. An airplane would have much better performance under these conditions.

Vertical Speed Indicator

The vertical speed indicator (VSI), which is sometimes called a vertical velocity indicator (VVI), indicates whether the airplane is climbing, descending, or in level flight. The rate of climb or descent is indicated in feet per minute. If properly calibrated, the VSI indicates zero in level flight.

The vertical speed indicator is capable of displaying two different types of information:

1. Trend information shows an immediate indication of an increase or decrease in the airplane's rate of climb or descent.
2. Rate information shows a stabilized rate of change in altitude.

For example, if maintaining a steady 500 feet per minute (fpm) climb, and the nose is lowered slightly, the VSI immediately senses this change and indicates a decrease in the rate of climb. This first indication is called the trend. After a short time, the VSI needle stabilizes on the new rate of climb, which in this example is something less than 500 fpm. The time from the initial change in the rate of climb until the VSI displays an accurate indication of the new rate is called the "lag." Rough control technique and turbulence can extend the lag period and cause erratic and unstable rate indications. Some airplanes are equipped with an instantaneous vertical speed indicator (IVSI) that incorporates accelerometers to compensate for the lag in the typical VSI.

Airspeed Indicator

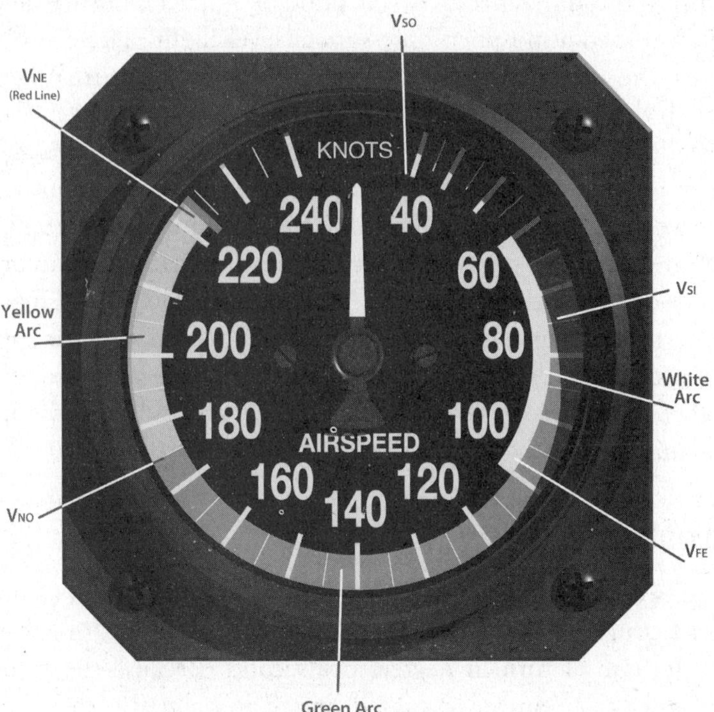

- **White arc**—This arc is commonly referred to as the flap operating range, since its lower limit represents the full flap stall speed and its upper limit provides the maximum flap speed. Approaches and landings are usually flown at speeds within the white arc.
- **Lower limit of white arc (V_{SO})**—The stalling speed or the minimum steady flight speed in the landing configuration. In small airplanes, this is the power-off stall speed at the maximum landing weight in the landing configuration (gear and flaps down).
- **Upper limit of the white arc (V_{FE})**—The maximum speed with the flaps extended.
- **Green arc**—This is the normal operating range of the airplane. Most flying occurs within this range.
- **Lower limit of green arc (V_{S1})**—The stalling speed or the minimum steady flight speed obtained in a specified configuration. For most airplanes, this is the power-off stall speed at the maximum takeoff weight in the clean configuration (gear up if retractable, and flaps up).
- **Upper limit of green arc (V_{NO})**—The maximum structural cruising speed. Do not exceed this speed except in smooth air.
- **Yellow arc**—Caution range. Fly within this range only in smooth air, and then only with caution.
- **Red line (V_{NE})**—Never-exceed speed. Operating above this speed is prohibited, since it may result in damage or structural failure.

Airspeed Indicator

The airspeed indicator is a sensitive differential pressure gauge that measures and shows promptly the difference between pitot or impact pressure, and static pressure, the undisturbed atmospheric pressure at level flight. These two pressures will be equal when the airplane is parked on the ground in calm air. When the airplane moves through the air, the pressure on the pitot line becomes greater than the pressure in the static lines. This difference in pressure is registered by the airspeed pointer on the face of the instrument, which is calibrated in miles per hour, knots, or both.

Airplanes weighing 12,500 pounds or less, manufactured after 1945, and certified by the FAA are required to have airspeed indicators marked in accordance with a standard color-coded marking system. This system of color-coded markings enables a pilot to determine at a glance certain airspeed limitations that are important to the safe operation of the airplane. For example, if during the execution of a maneuver, it is noted that the airspeed needle is in the yellow arc and rapidly approaching the red line, the immediate reaction should be to reduce airspeed.

Turn Indicators

Airplanes use two types of turn indicators—the turn-and-slip indicator and the turn coordinator. Because of the way the gyro is mounted, the turn-and-slip indicator only shows the rate of turn in degrees per second. Because the gyro on the turn coordinator is set at an angle, or canted, it can initially also show roll rate. Once the roll stabilizes, it indicates rate of turn. Both instruments indicate turn direction and quality (coordination), and also serve as a backup source of bank information in the event an attitude indicator fails. Coordination is achieved by referring to the inclinometer, which consists of a liquid-filled curved tube with a ball inside.

The inclinometer is used to depict airplane yaw, which is the side-to-side movement of the airplane's nose. During coordinated, straight-and-level flight, the force of gravity causes the ball to rest in the lowest part of the tube, centered between the reference lines. Coordinated flight is maintained by keeping the ball centered. If the ball is not centered, it can be centered by using the rudder. To do this, apply rudder pressure on the side where the ball is deflected. Use the simple rule, "step on the ball," to remember which rudder pedal to press.

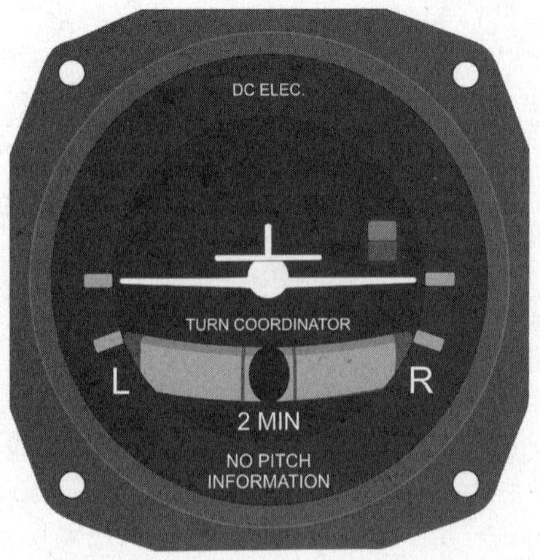

If aileron and rudder movements are coordinated during a turn, the ball remains centered in the tube. If aerodynamic forces are unbalanced, the ball moves away from the center of the tube.

Attitude Indicator

The attitude indicator, with its miniature airplane and horizon bar, displays a picture of the attitude of the airplane. The relationship of the miniature airplane to the horizon bar is the same as the relationship of the real airplane to the actual horizon. The instrument gives an instantaneous indication of even the slightest changes in attitude.

The gyro in the attitude indicator is mounted on a horizontal plane and depends upon rigidity in space for its operation. The horizon bar represents the true horizon. This bar is fixed to the gyro and remains in a horizontal plane as the airplane is pitched or banked about its lateral or longitudinal axis, indicating the attitude of the airplane relative to the true horizon.

An adjustment knob is provided with which the pilot may move the miniature airplane up or down to align the miniature airplane with the horizon bar to suit the pilot's line of vision. Normally, the miniature airplane is adjusted so that the wings overlap the horizon bar when the airplane is in straight-and-level cruising flight.

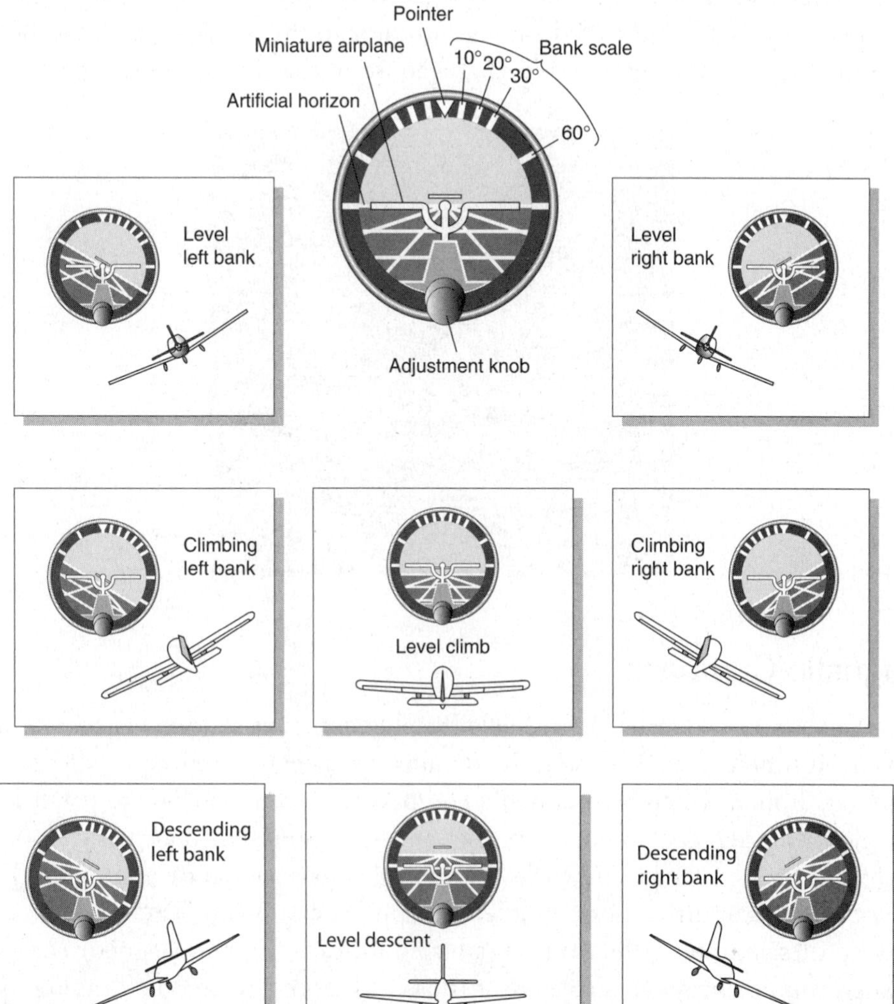

The pitch and bank limits depend upon the make and model of the instrument. Limits in the banking plane are usually from 100° to 110°, and the pitch limits are usually from 60° to 70°. If either limit is exceeded, the instrument will tumble or spill and will give incorrect indications until re-stabilized. A number of modern attitude indicators will not tumble.

The attitude indicator is reliable and the most realistic flight instrument on the instrument panel. Its indications are very close approximations of the actual attitude of the airplane.

Heading Indicator

The heading indicator (or directional gyro) is fundamentally a mechanical instrument designed to facilitate the use of the magnetic compass. Errors in the magnetic compass are numerous, making straight flight and precision turns to headings difficult to accomplish, particularly in turbulent air. A heading indicator, however, is not affected by the forces that make the magnetic compass difficult to interpret.

Some heading indicators receive a magnetic north reference from a magnetic slaving transmitter, and generally need no adjustment. Heading indicators that do not have this automatic north-seeking capability are called "free" gyros, and require periodic adjustment. It is important to check the indications frequently (approximately every 15 minutes) and reset the heading indicator to align it with the magnetic compass when required. Adjust the heading indicator to the magnetic compass heading when the airplane is straight and level at a constant speed to avoid compass errors.

Magnetic Compass

The magnetic compass, which is usually the only direction-seeking instrument in the airplane, is simple in construction. It contains two steel magnetized needles fastened to a float, around which is mounted a compass card. The needles are parallel, with their north-seeking ends pointing in the same direction. The compass card has letters for cardinal headings, and each 30° interval is represented by a number, the last zero of which is omitted. For example, 30° appears as a 3 and 300° appears as a 30. Between these numbers, the card is graduated for each 5°. The magnetic compass is required equipment on all airplanes. It is used to set the gyroscopic heading indicator, correct for precession, and as a backup in the event the heading indicator(s) fails.

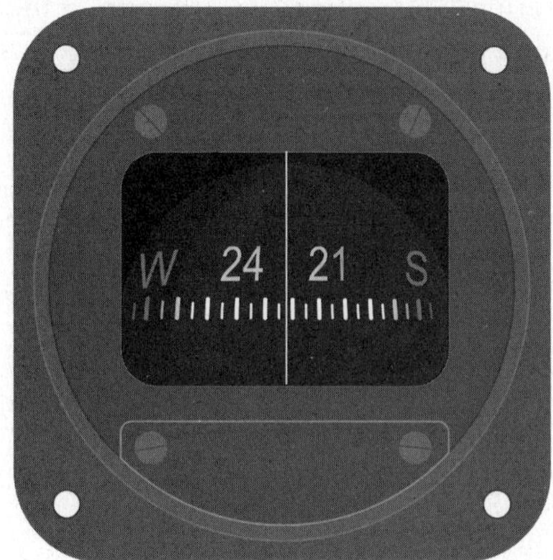

Although the magnetic field of the Earth lies roughly north and south, the Earth's magnetic poles do not coincide with its geographic poles that are used in the construction of aeronautical charts. Consequently, at most places on the Earth's surface, the direction-sensitive steel needles that seek the Earth's magnetic field will not point to true north, but to magnetic north. Furthermore, local magnetic fields from mineral deposits and other conditions may distort the Earth's magnetic field, and cause additional error in the position of the compass' north-seeking magnetized needles with reference to true north.

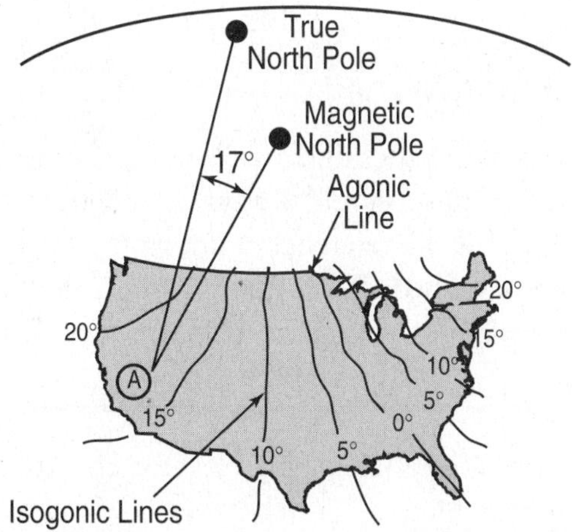

The angular difference between magnetic north—the reference for the magnetic compass—and true north is variation. Lines that connect points of equal variation are called isogonic lines. The line connecting points where the magnetic variation is zero is an agonic line. To convert from true courses or headings to magnetic, subtract easterly variation and add westerly variation. Reverse the process to convert from magnetic to true.

Vertical Card Compass

A newer design, the vertical card compass significantly reduces the inherent error of the older compass designs. It consists of an azimuth on a rotating vertical card, and resembles a heading indicator with a fixed miniature airplane to accurately present the heading of the airplane. The presentation is easy to read, and the pilot can see the complete 360° dial in relation to the airplane heading.

Basic Flight Maneuvers

There are four basic fundamental flight maneuvers upon which all flying tasks are based: straight-and-level flight, turns, climbs, and descents. All controlled flight consists of either one, or a combination of more than one, of these basic maneuvers. If a pilot is able to perform these maneuvers well, and the pilot's proficiency is based on accurate "feel" and control analysis rather than mechanical movements, the ability to perform any assigned maneuver will only be a matter of obtaining a clear visual and mental conception of it.

Affects of Flight Controls

Pilots must understand that the aircraft controls never change in the results produced in relation to the pilot. The pilot should always consider him/herself as the center of movement of the airplane, or the reference point from which the movements of the airplane are judged and described. With that in mind, the following will always be true, regardless of the airplane's attitude in relation to the Earth:

- When back pressure is applied to the elevator control, the airplane's nose rises in relation to the pilot.
- When forward pressure is applied to the elevator control, the airplane's nose lowers in relation to the pilot.
- When right pressure is applied to the aileron control, the airplane's right wing lowers in relation to the pilot.
- When left pressure is applied to the aileron control, the airplane's left wing lowers in relation to the pilot.
- When pressure is applied to the right rudder pedal, the airplane's nose moves (yaws) to the right in relation to the pilot.
- When pressure is applied to the left rudder pedal, the airplane's nose moves (yaws) to the left in relation to the pilot.

Attitude Flying

In contact flying (VFR, or Visual Flight Rules), *flying by attitude* means visually establishing the airplane's attitude with reference to the natural horizon. Attitude is the angular difference measured between an airplane's axis and the line of the Earth's horizon. Pitch attitude is the angle formed by the longitudinal axis, and bank attitude is the angle formed by the lateral axis. Rotation about the airplane's vertical axis (yaw) is termed an attitude relative to the airplane's flight path, but not relative to the natural horizon.

In attitude flying, airplane control is composed of four components: pitch control, bank control, power control, and trim.

- Pitch control is the control of the airplane about the lateral axis by using the elevator to raise and lower the nose in relation to the natural horizon.
- Bank control is control of the airplane about the longitudinal axis by use of the ailerons to attain a desired bank angle in relation to the natural horizon.
- Power control is used when the flight situation indicates a need for a change in thrust.
- Trim is used to relieve all possible control pressures held after a desired attitude has been attained.

The primary rule of attitude flying is:

ATTITUDE + POWER = PERFORMANCE

The basic elements of attitude flying are as follows:

- The pilot establishes and maintains the airplane's attitude by positioning the airplane in relation to the natural horizon. At least 90 percent of the pilot's attention should be devoted to this end, along with scanning for other airplanes. If, during a recheck of the pitch and/or bank, either or both are found to be other than desired, the pilot applies an immediate correction to return the aircraft to the proper attitude. Continuous checks and immediate correction allow little chance for the airplane to deviate from the desired heading, altitude, and flight path.
- The pilot confirms the airplane's attitude and monitors its performance by referring to flight instruments. If the airplane's performance, as indicated by flight instruments, needs correction, the pilot determines the amount of correction needed, and then applies it with reference to the natural horizon. The pilot then rechecks the aircraft's attitude and performance by referring to flight instruments. The pilot maintains the corrected attitude by reference to the natural horizon.
- The pilot should monitor the airplane's performance by making numerous quick glances at the flight instruments. However, the pilot should not spend more than 10 percent of his or her attention inside the cockpit. The pilot must develop the skill to instantly focus on the appropriate flight instrument, and then immediately return to outside reference to control the airplane's attitude.

Straight-and-Level Flight

It is impossible to emphasize too strongly the necessity for forming correct habits in flying straight and level. All other flight maneuvers are in essence a deviation from this fundamental flight maneuver.

Straight-and-level flight is flight in which a constant heading and altitude are maintained. It is accomplished by making immediate and measured corrections for deviations in direction and altitude from unintentional slight turns, descents, and climbs.

The *pitch attitude* for level flight (constant altitude) is usually obtained by selecting some portion of the airplane's nose as a reference point, and then keeping that point in a fixed position relative to the horizon.

Using the principles of attitude flying, the pilot should cross-check pitch attitude occasionally against the altimeter to determine whether or not the pitch attitude is correct. If altitude is being gained or lost, the pilot should readjust the pitch attitude in relation to the horizon and then recheck the altimeter to determine if altitude is now being maintained. The pilot applies application of forward or back-elevator pressure to control this attitude.

Straight flight (laterally level flight) is accomplished by visually checking the relationship of the airplane's wingtips with the horizon. Both wingtips should be equidistant above or below the horizon (depending on whether the airplane is a high-wing or low-wing type), and the pilot should apply any necessary adjustments with the ailerons, noting the relationship of control pressure and the airplane's attitude. Anytime the wings are banked, even ever so slightly, the airplane will turn. The pilot should make occasional reference to the heading indicator to note any changes in direction.

Common errors in the performance of straight-and-level flight are as follows:

- Attempting to use improper reference points on the airplane to establish attitude.
- Forgetting the location of pre-selected reference points on subsequent flights.
- Attempting to establish or correct airplane attitude using flight instruments rather than outside visual reference.
- Attempting to maintain direction using only rudder control.
- Habitually flying with one wing low.
- "Chasing" the flight instruments rather than adhering to the principles of attitude flying.
- Too tight a grip on the flight controls, resulting in over-control and lack of feel.
- Pushing or pulling on the flight controls rather than exerting pressure against the airstream.
- Improper scanning and/or devoting insufficient time to outside visual reference (head in the cockpit).
- Fixation on the nose (pitch attitude) reference point.
- Unnecessary or inappropriate control inputs.
- Failure to make timely and measured control inputs when deviations from straight-and-level flight are detected.
- Inadequate attention to sensory inputs in developing a feel for the airplane.

Level Turns

An aircraft turns by banking the wings in the direction of the desired turn. The pilot selects a specific angle of bank and applies control pressure to achieve the desired bank angle. Once the bank angle is established, the pilot continues to exert the pressure to maintain the desired bank angle.

All four primary controls are used in close coordination when making turns. Their functions are as follows:

- The ailerons bank the wings and so determine the rate of turn at any given airspeed.
- The elevator moves the nose of the airplane up or down in relation to the pilot, and perpendicular to the wings. Doing that, it both sets the pitch attitude in the turn and "pulls" the nose of the airplane around the turn.
- The throttle provides thrust that may be used for airspeed to tighten the turn.
- The rudder offsets any yaw effects developed by the other controls. The rudder does not turn the airplane as many people believe.

For purposes of this discussion, we'll divide turns into three classes: shallow turns, medium turns, and steep turns.

- **Shallow turns** are those in which the bank (less than approximately 20°) is so shallow that the inherent lateral stability of the airplane is acting to level the wings unless some aileron is applied to maintain the bank.
- **Medium turns** are those resulting from a degree of bank (approximately 20° to 45°) at which the airplane remains at a constant bank.
- **Steep turns** are those resulting from a degree of bank (45° or more) at which the "over-banking tendency" of an airplane overcomes stability, and the bank increases unless aileron is applied to prevent it.

Changing the direction of the wing's lift toward one side or the other causes the airplane to be pulled in that direction. The pilot does this by applying coordinated aileron and rudder to bank the airplane in the direction of the desired turn.

When an airplane is flying straight and level, the total lift is acting perpendicular to the wings and to the Earth. As the airplane is banked into a turn, the lift then becomes the resultant of two components.

1. The vertical lift component, continues to act perpendicular to the Earth and opposes gravity.
2. The horizontal lift component (centripetal) acts parallel to the Earth's surface and opposes inertia (apparent centrifugal force). These two lift components act at right angles to each other, causing the resultant total lifting force to act perpendicular to the banked wing of the airplane. It is the horizontal lift component that actually turns the airplane—not the rudder.

The pilot applies aileron to bank the airplane, the lowered aileron (on the rising wing) produces a greater drag than the raised aileron (on the lowering wing). This increased aileron yaws the airplane toward the rising wing, or opposite to the direction of turn. To counteract this adverse yawing moment, the pilot must apply rudder pressure simultaneously with aileron in the desired direction of turn. This action is required to produce a coordinated turn.

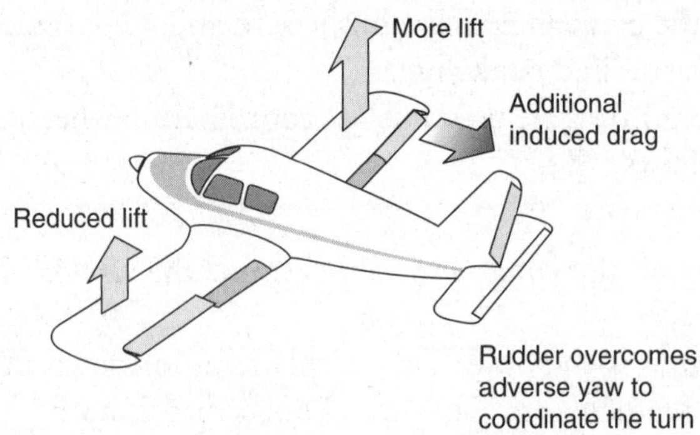

After the bank has been established in a medium banked turn, all pressure applied to the aileron may be relaxed. The airplane will remain at the selected bank with no further tendency to yaw since there is no longer a deflection of the ailerons. As a result, the pilot may also relax pressure on the rudder pedals and allow the rudder to streamline itself with the direction of the slipstream. Maintaining rudder pressure after the turn is established will cause the airplane to skid to the outside of the turn. If a definite effort is made to center the rudder rather than let it streamline itself to the turn, it is probable that some opposite rudder pressure will be exerted inadvertently. This will force the airplane to yaw opposite its turning path, causing the airplane to slip to the inside of the turn. The ball in the turn-and slip indicator will be displaced off-center whenever the airplane is skidding or slipping sideways (see section on Flight Instruments starting on page 236). In proper coordinated flight, there is no skidding or slipping.

In all constant altitude, constant airspeed turns, the pilot must increase the angle of attack of the wing when rolling into the turn by applying up elevator. This is required because part of the vertical lift has been diverted to horizontal lift. Thus, the total lift must be increased to compensate for this loss.

When changing from a shallow bank to a medium bank, the airspeed of the wing on the outside of the turn increases in relation to the inside wing as the radius of turn decreases. The additional lift developed because of this increase in speed of the wing balances the inherent lateral stability of the airplane. At any given airspeed, aileron pressure is not required to maintain the bank. If the bank is allowed to increase from a medium to a steep bank, the radius of turn decreases further. The lift of the outside wing causes the bank to become steeper, and opposite aileron is necessary to keep the bank constant.

As the radius of the turn becomes smaller, a significant difference develops between the speed of the inside wing and the speed of the outside wing. The wing on the outside of the turn travels a longer circuit than the inside wing, yet both complete their respective circuits in the same length of time. Therefore, the outside wing travels faster than the inside wing, and as a result, it develops more lift. This creates an overbanking tendency that the pilot must control by the use of the ailerons.

Because the outboard wing is developing more lift, it also has more induced drag. This causes a slight slip during steep turns that the pilot must correct by use of the rudder.

The rollout from a turn is similar to the roll-in except the pilot applies the flight controls in the opposite direction. Aileron and rudder are applied in the direction of the rollout or toward the high wing. As the angle of bank decreases, the pilot relaxes elevator pressure as necessary to maintain altitude.

OVERBANKING TENDENCY

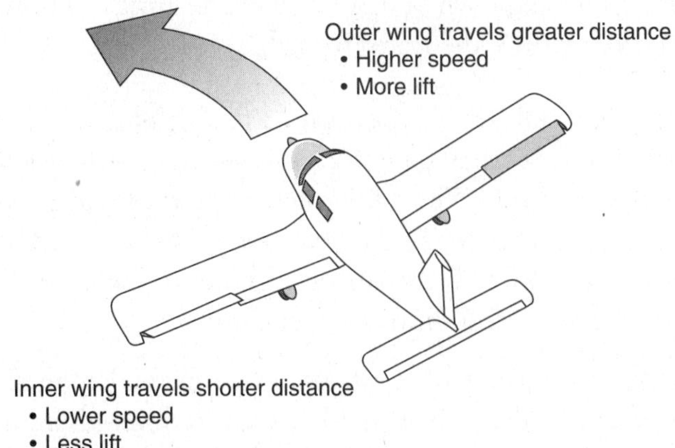

Since the airplane will continue turning as long as there is any bank, the rollout must be started before reaching the desired heading. The amount of lead required to roll out on the desired heading will depend on the degree of bank used in the turn. Normally, the lead is one-half of the degrees of bank. For example, if the bank is 30°, lead the rollout by 15°. As the wings become level, the pilot should smoothly relax control pressures so that the controls are neutralized as the airplane returns to straight-and-level flight. As the rollout is being completed, the pilot should give attention to outside visual references, as well as the attitude and heading indicators to determine that the wings are being leveled and the turn stopped.

Common errors in the performance of level turns are as follows:

- Failure to adequately clear the area before beginning the turn.
- Attempting to execute the turn solely by instrument reference.
- Attempting to sit up straight, in relation to the ground, during a turn, rather than riding with the airplane.
- Insufficient feel for the airplane as evidenced by the inability to detect slips/ skids without reference to flight instruments.
- Attempting to maintain a constant bank angle by referencing the "cant" of the airplane's nose.
- Fixating on the nose reference while excluding wingtip reference.
- "Ground shyness"—making "flat turns" (skidding) while operating at low altitudes in a conscious or subconscious effort to avoid banking close to the ground.
- Holding rudder in the turn.
- Gaining proficiency in turns in only one direction (usually the left).
- Failure to coordinate the use of throttle with other controls.
- Altitude gain/loss during the turn.

Climbs and Climbing Turns

When an airplane enters a climb, it changes its flight path from level flight to an inclined plane or climb attitude. In a climb, weight no longer acts in a direction perpendicular to the flight path. It acts in a rearward direction. This causes an increase in total drag requiring an increase in thrust (power) to balance the forces. An airplane can only sustain a climb angle when there is sufficient thrust to offset increased drag; therefore, climb is limited by the thrust available.

- **Normal climb**—Normal climb is performed at an airspeed recommended by the airplane manufacturer. Normal climb speed is generally somewhat higher than the airplane's best rate of climb. The additional airspeed provides better engine cooling, easier control, and better visibility over the nose. Normal climb is sometimes referred to as "cruise climb." Complex or high performance airplanes may have a specified cruise climb in addition to normal climb.
- **Best rate of climb**—Best rate of climb (V_Y) is performed at an airspeed where the most excess power is available over that required for level flight. This condition of climb will produce the most gain in altitude in the least amount of time (maximum rate of climb in feet per minute). The best rate of climb made at full allowable power is a maximum climb.
- **Best angle of climb**—Best angle of climb (V_X) is performed at an airspeed that will produce the most altitude gain in a given distance. Best angle-of-climb airspeed (V_X) is considerably lower than best rate of climb (V_Y) and is the airspeed where the most excess thrust is available over that required for level flight. The best angle of climb will result in a steeper climb path, although the airplane will take longer to reach the same altitude than it would at best rate of climb. The best angle of climb, therefore, is used in clearing obstacles after takeoff.

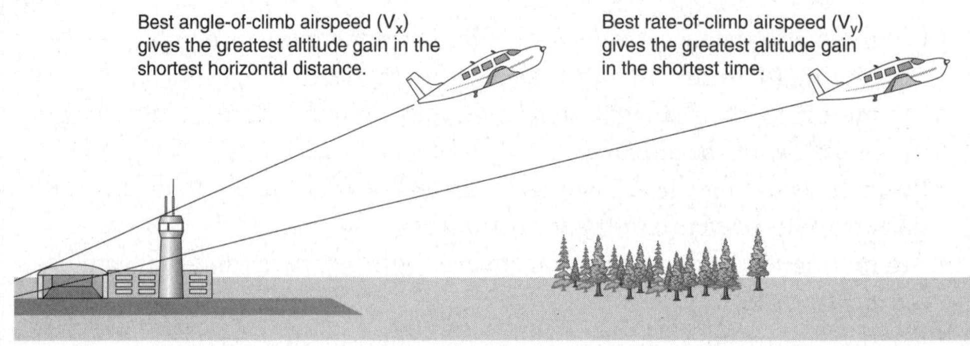

A straight climb is entered by gently increasing pitch attitude to a predetermined level using back-elevator pressure, and simultaneously increasing engine power to the climb power setting. Due to an increase in downwash over the horizontal stabilizer as power is applied, the airplane's nose will tend to immediately begin to rise of its own accord to an attitude higher than that at which it would stabilize. The pilot must be prepared for this.

To enter the climb, simultaneously advance the throttle and apply back-elevator pressure to raise the nose of the airplane to the proper position in relation to the horizon. As power is increased, the airplane's nose will rise due to increased download on the stabilizer. This is caused by increased slipstream. As the pitch attitude increases and the airspeed decreases, progressively more right rudder must be applied to compensate for propeller effects and to hold a constant heading.

After the climb is established, the pilot must maintain back-elevator pressure to keep the pitch attitude constant. As the airspeed decreases, the elevators will try to return to their neutral or streamlined position, and the airplane's nose will tend to lower. Throughout the climb, since the power is fixed at the climb power setting, the airspeed is controlled by the use of elevator.

To return to straight-and-level flight from a climb, the pilot should initiate the level-off at approximately 10 percent of the rate of climb. For example, if the airplane is climbing at 500 fpm, leveling off should start 50 feet below the desired altitude. The pilot must lower the nose gradually because a loss of altitude will result if the pitch attitude is changed to the level flight position without allowing the airspeed to increase proportionately.

After the airplane is established in level flight at a constant altitude, climb power should be retained temporarily so that the airplane will accelerate to the cruise airspeed more rapidly. When the speed reaches the desired cruise speed, the pilot should set the throttle setting and the propeller control (if equipped) to the cruise power setting.

In the performance of climbing turns, pilots should consider the following:

- With a constant power setting, the same pitch attitude and airspeed cannot be maintained in a bank as in a straight climb due to the increase in the total lift required.
- The degree of bank should not be too steep. A steep bank significantly decreases the rate of climb. The bank should always remain constant.
- It is necessary to maintain a constant airspeed and constant rate of turn in both right and left turns. The coordination of all flight controls is a primary factor.
- At a constant power setting, the airplane will climb at a slightly shallower climb angle because some of the lift is being used to turn the airplane.

There are two ways to establish a climbing turn. Either establish a straight climb and then turn, or enter the climb and turn simultaneously.

During climbing turns, as in any turn, the loss of vertical lift and induced drag due to increased angle of attack becomes greater as the angle of bank is increased, so shallow turns should be used to maintain an efficient rate of climb. If a medium or steep banked turn is used, climb performance will be degraded.

Common errors in the performance of climbs and climbing turns are as follows:

- Attempting to establish climb pitch attitude by referencing the airspeed indicator, resulting in "chasing" the airspeed.
- Applying elevator pressure too aggressively, resulting in an excessive climb angle.
- Applying elevator pressure too aggressively during level-off, resulting in negative "G" forces.
- Inadequate or inappropriate rudder pressure during climbing turns.
- Allowing the airplane to yaw in straight climbs, usually due to inadequate right rudder pressure.
- Fixation on the nose during straight climbs, resulting in climbing with one wing low.
- Failure to initiate a climbing turn properly with use of rudder and elevators, resulting in little turn, but rather a climb with one wing low.
- Improper coordination resulting in a slip that counteracts the effect of the climb, resulting in little or no altitude gain.
- Inability to keep pitch and bank attitude constant during climbing turns.
- Attempting to exceed the airplane's climb capability.

Descents

When an airplane enters a descent, it changes its flight path from level to an inclined plane.

- **Partial Power Descent**—The normal method of losing altitude is to descend with partial power. This is often termed "cruise" or "enroute" descent. The airspeed and power setting recommended by the airplane manufacturer for prolonged descent should be used. The target descent rate should be 400–500 fpm. The airspeed may vary from cruise airspeed to that used on the downwind leg of the landing pattern. The pilot should select the desired airspeed, pitch attitude, and power combination and keep them constant throughout the descent.

- **Descent at Minimum Safe Airspeed**—A minimum safe airspeed descent is a nose-high, power assisted descent condition principally used for clearing obstacles during a landing approach to a short runway. The airspeed used for this descent condition is recommended by the airplane manufacturer and normally is no greater than 1.3 VSO. Some characteristics of the minimum safe airspeed descent are a steeper than normal descent angle, and the excessive power that may be required to produce acceleration at low airspeed should "mushing" and/or an excessive rate of descent be allowed to develop.

- **Glides**—A glide is a basic maneuver in which the airplane loses altitude in a controlled descent with little or no engine power; forward motion is maintained by gravity pulling the airplane along an inclined path, and the descent rate is controlled by the pilot balancing the forces of gravity and lift.

Under various flight conditions, the drag factor may change through the operation of the landing gear and/or flaps. When the landing gear or the flaps are extended, drag increases and the airspeed will decrease unless the pitch attitude is lowered. As the pitch is lowered, the glidepath becomes steeper and reduces the distance traveled. With the power off, a windmilling propeller also creates considerable drag, thereby retarding the airplane's forward movement.

The level-off from a descent must be started before reaching the desired altitude because of the airplane's downward inertia. The amount of lead depends on the rate of descent and the pilot's control technique. With too little lead, there will be a tendency to descend below the selected altitude. For example, assuming a 500-foot per minute rate of descent, the altitude must be led by 100–150 feet to level off at an airspeed higher than the glide speed. At the lead point, the pilot should increase power to the appropriate level flight cruise setting so the desired airspeed will be attained at the desired altitude. The nose tends to rise as both airspeed and downwash on the tail section increase. The pilot must be prepared for this and smoothly control the pitch attitude to attain level flight attitude so that the level-off is completed at the desired altitude.

Common errors in the performance of descents are as follows:

- Failure to adequately clear the area.
- Inadequate back-elevator control during glide entry, resulting in too steep a glide.
- Failure to slow the airplane to approximate glide speed prior to lowering pitch attitude.
- Attempting to establish/maintain a normal glide solely by reference to flight instruments.
- Inability to sense changes in airspeed through sound and feel.
- Inability to stabilize the glide (chasing the airspeed indicator).
- Attempting to "stretch" the glide by applying back-elevator pressure.
- Skidding or slipping during gliding turns due to inadequate appreciation of the difference in rudder action as opposed to turns with power.
- Failure to lower pitch attitude during gliding turn entry resulting in a decrease in airspeed.
- Excessive rudder pressure during recovery from gliding turns.
- Inadequate pitch control during recovery from straight glides.
- "Ground shyness"—resulting in cross-controlling during gliding turns near the ground.
- Failure to maintain constant bank angle during gliding turns.

Pitch and Power

No discussion of climbs and descents would be complete without touching on the question of what controls altitude and what controls airspeed. The pilot must understand the effects of both power and elevator control, working together during different conditions of flight. The closest one can come to a formula for determining airspeed/altitude control that is valid under all circumstances is a basic principle of attitude flying that states:

"At any pitch attitude, the amount of power used will determine whether the airplane will climb, descend, or remain level at that attitude."

Through a wide range of nose-low attitudes, a descent is the only possible condition of flight. The addition of power at these attitudes will only result in a greater rate of descent at a faster airspeed.

Through a range of attitudes from very slightly nose-low to about 30° nose-up, a typical light airplane can be made to climb, descend, or maintain altitude depending on the power used. In about the lower third of this range, the airplane will descend at idle power without stalling. As pitch attitude is increased, however, engine power will be required to prevent a stall. Even more power will be required to maintain altitude, and even more for a climb. In a small plane, at a pitch attitude approaching 30° nose-up, all available power will provide only enough thrust to maintain altitude. A slight increase in the steepness of climb or a slight decrease in power will produce a descent. From that point, the least inducement will result in a stall.

Nautical Information

In addition to basic flying questions, Navy OCS applicants and Marine Corps/Coast Guard aviation OCS applicants must demonstrate knowledge of basic nautical information and terminology. This sort of makes sense when you remember that Navy and Marine Corps aviators are often required to land, take-off, and taxi aircraft on aircraft carriers. If the controller requests you to "taxi to starboard," it would be good to know that "starboard" means the right-hand side of the ship.

NAUTICAL TERMS AND PHRASES

Acknowledge: When a message is received over I.C. system, it must be acknowledged at once, i.e., "Foc's'le aye, aye."

All Hands Up Anchor or All Hands Bring Ship to Anchor: All hands to quarters. Divisions (whose duty it is) stand by ground tackle. Used in peace time, or in ceremonies.

All Hands to General Quarters: All hands man battle stations on the double.

All Hands to Quarters: All men assemble in their assigned parades for muster, or Captain's inspection.

Anchors Aweigh: The anchor has broken ground.

Before the Mast: Literally, the position of the crew whose living quarters on board were in the forecastle (the section of a ship forward of the foremast). The term is also used more generally to describe seamen as compared with officers, in phrases such as "he sailed before the mast."

Belay: To make fast to a pin or cleat.

Belay That, or Belay the Last Word: Pay no attention to the command or order given, or cease action if the order has been placed partially into action.

Binnacle List: A ship's sick-list. A binnacle was the stand on which the ship's compass was mounted. In the eighteenth century and probably before, a list was given to the officer or mate of the watch containing the names of men unable to report for duty. The list was kept at the binnacle.

Boot camp: During the Spanish-American War, Sailors wore leggings called boots, which came to mean a Navy (or Marine) recruit. These recruits trained in "boot" camps.

Bow: Front of the ship.

Bravo Zulu: This is a naval signal, conveyed by flaghoist or voice radio, meaning "well done"; it has also passed into the spoken and written vocabulary. It can be combined with the "negative" signal, spoken or written NEGAT, to say "NEGAT Bravo Zulu," or "not well done." There are some "myths and legends" attached to this signal. The one most frequently heard has Admiral Halsey sending it to ships of Task Force 38 during World War II. He could not have done this, since the signal did not exist at that time.

Brightwork: Brightwork originally referred to polished metal objects, and bright woodwork to wood that was kept scraped and scrubbed, especially topside. Bright it should be and work it is.

Bull Ensign (also Boot or George Ensign): The Bull Ensign is the senior ensign of a Navy command (ship, squadron, or shore activity). In addition to normal duties, the Bull Ensign assumes various additional responsibilities such as teaching less-experienced ensigns about life at sea, planning and coordinating wardroom social activities, making sure that the officers' mess runs smoothly, and serving as an officer (such as treasurer) for Navy-related social organizations. The Bull Ensign is responsible for preventing junior ensigns in his command from embarrassing themselves and the Navy. Though the position often has little formal authority, the Bull Ensign serves as the focal point for the unit's expression of spirit and pride.

Carrying [ ] Degrees Rudder, Sir: Report by helmsman to relief or conning officer giving average number of degrees right (left) rudder required to keep ship on course due to wind, tide, etc.

Cast Off All Lines: Let go all lines.

Charlie Noble: Charlie Noble is an "it," not a "he." A British merchant service captain, Charles Noble, is said to be responsible for the origin, about 1850, of this nickname for the galley smokestack. It seems that Captain Noble, discovering that the stack of his ship's galley was made of copper, ordered that it be kept bright. The ship's crew then started referring to the stack as the "Charley Noble."

Clean Bill of Health: This widely-used term has its origins in the document issued to a ship showing that the port it sailed from suffered from no epidemic or infection at the time of departure.

Come Right to Course: Make a slight change in course; usually a change of less than fifteen degrees.

Coxswain: A coxswain or cockswain was at first the swain (boy servant) in charge of the small cock or cockboat that was kept aboard for the ship's captain and was used to row him to and from the ship. The term has been in use in England dating back to at least 1463. With the passing of time, the coxswain became the helmsman of any boat, regardless of size.

Deck: Floor.

Dogwatch: A dogwatch at sea is the period between 4 and 6 P.M., the first dogwatch, or the period between 6 and 8 P.M., the second dogwatch. The watches aboard ships are as follows:

Noon to 4:00 P.M.:	Afternoon watch
4:00 P.M. to 6:00 P.M.	First dogwatch
6:00 P.M. to 8:00 P.M.	Second dogwatch
8:00 P.M. to midnight	1st night watch
Midnight to 4:00 A.M.	Middle watch or mid watch
4:00 to 8:00 A.M.	Morning watch
8:00 A.M. to noon	Forenoon watch

The dogwatches are only two hours each, so the same Sailors aren't always on duty at the same time each afternoon. Some experts say dogwatch is a corruption of dodge watch and others associate dogwatch with the fitful sleep of Sailors called dog sleep, because it is a stressful watch. But no one really knows the origin of this term, which dates back to 1700.

Down the hatch: Here's a drinking expression that seems to have its origins in sea freight, where cargoes are lowered into the hatch. First used by seamen, it has only been traced back to the turn of the century.

Duffle: A name given to a Sailor's personal effects. Also spelled duffel, it referred to his principal clothing as well as to the sea-bag in which it was carried and stowed. The term comes from the Flemish town of Duffel near Antwerp, and refers to a rough woolen cloth made there.

Dungarees: The modern Sailor's work clothes. The term is not modern, however, but dates back to the 18th century and comes from the Hindi word *dungri*, which is a type of Indian cotton cloth.

Ease the Rudder: Decrease the present rudder angle; given when the ship is turning too rapidly or is coming to the heading required, for example, "Ease to 10."

Fathom: Although a fathom is now a nautical unit of length equal to six feet, it was once defined by an act of Parliament as "the length of a man's arms around the object of his affections." The word derives from the Old English *Faethm*, which means "embracing arms."

Flying Dutchman: One superstition has it that any mariner who sees the ghost ship called the Flying Dutchman will die within the day. The tale of the Flying Dutchman trying to round the Cape of Good Hope against strong winds and never succeeding, then trying to make Cape Horn and failing there, too, has been the most famous of maritime ghost stories for more than 300 years. The cursed spectral ship sailing back and forth on its endless voyage, its ancient white-haired crew crying for help while hauling at her sail, inspired Samuel Taylor Coleridge to write his classic, "*The Rime of the Ancient Mariner*," to name but one famous literary work. The real Flying Dutchman is supposed to have set sail in 1660.

Fouled anchor: The fouled (rope- or chain-entwined) anchor so prevalent in our Navy's designs and insignia is a symbol at least 500 years old that has it origins in the British traditions adopted by our naval service.

Frocking: An early use of "frock" (15th century) referred to the long habit characteristically worn by monks. Through the centuries, frock came to describe various loose garments of some length. The "frock coat," which was a long-skirted garment coming almost to the knees, became a popular fashion for men in the early 19th century and was quickly adopted for military uniforms. It is possible that the frock coat was so called because the length was reminiscent of earlier clothing articles.

Regarding the practice of frocking itself, there are various instances in Navy Regulations at least as early as 1802 of personnel assuming the uniform of the next higher rank, not necessarily with higher pay, when appointed by proper authority to assume the duties and responsibilities of that rank prior to actual promotion. These appointments were sometimes temporary, as when it was necessary to rapidly swell the ranks during war time, especially in the Civil War. Other instances concerned a commander's need to fill an unforeseen vacancy for which there was no one of equal rank. In this case, a junior who was qualified for promotion would assume the uniform and duties pending approval by the Navy Department.

General Drills: Emergency drills for all hands, such as general quarters, abandon ship, fire, and collision.

General Quarters: All hands man battle stations on the double.

Give Her More Rudder: Increase the rudder angle already on, to make the ship turn more rapidly.

Handsomely: Slowly and carefully, with the emphasis on carefully, as in, "Walk back handsomely."

Hatch: Doorway.

Head (ship's toilet): The use of the term "head" to refer to a ship's toilet dates to at least as early as 1708, when Woodes Rogers (English privateer and Governor of the Bahamas) used the word in his book, *A Cruising Voyage Around the World.* Another early usage is in Tobias Smollett's novel of travel and adventure, *Roderick Random,* published in 1748. "Head" in a nautical sense referring to the bow or fore part of a ship dates to 1485. The ship's toilet was typically placed at the head of the ship near the base of the bowsprit, where splashing water served to naturally clean the toilet area.

Holystone: Soft sandstone often used to scrub the decks of ships. Sailors had to kneel as if in prayer when scrubbing the decks. Holystone was also called so because it is full of holes.

Keelhauling: A naval punishment on board ships said to have originated with the Dutch but adopted by other navies during the 15th and 16th centuries. A rope was rigged from yardarm to yardarm, passing under the bottom of the ship, and the unfortunate delinquent secured to it, sometimes with lead or iron weights attached to his legs. He was hoisted up to one yardarm and then dropped suddenly into the sea, hauled underneath the ship, and hoisted up to the opposite yardarm, the punishment being repeated after he had time to recover his breath. The U.S. Navy never practiced keelhauling.

Keep Her So: Given when the steersman reports the ship's heading and it is desired to steady her.

Knot: A unit of speed, one nautical mile per hour, approximately 1.85 kilometers (1.15 statute miles) per hour.

Make a Hole: Get out of the way.

Man Overboard: Man the boat or boats and pick up the man as soon as possible. Special conditions are set for wartime.

Man Your Boat: Put on life preservers, or not according to standing orders and take station in your boat.

Mayday: The distress call for voice radio for vessels and people in serious trouble at sea. The term was made official by an international telecommunications conference in 1948 and is an anglicizing of the French *m'aidez* (help me).

Nautical Mile: A unit of length used in sea and air navigation based on the length of one minute of arc of a great circle, especially an international and U.S. unit equal to 1,852 meters (about 6,076 feet). Also called *sea mile.*

Now Hear This: A phrase that calls attention to an order or command about to follow.

On the Double: On the run, quickly. Double time.

Pipe Down, Set the Watch, 1st Section: At Pipe Down just after getting underway, men fall out from quarters and continue ship's work.

Piping: Boatswains have been in charge of the deck force since the days of sail. Setting sails, heaving lines, and hoisting anchors required coordinated team effort and boatswains used whistle signals to order these coordinated actions. When visitors were hoisted aboard or over the side, the pipe was used to order "Hoist Away" or "Avast heaving." In time, piping became a naval honor on shore as well as at sea.

Port and starboard: Port and starboard are shipboard terms for left and right, respectively. Confusing those two could cause a shipwreck. In Old England, the starboard was the steering paddle or rudder, and ships were always steered from the right side on the back of the vessel. Larboard referred to the left side, the side on which the ship was loaded. So how did larboard become port? Shouted over the noise of the wind and the waves, larboard and starboard sounded too much alike. The word port means the opening in the "left" side of the ship from which cargo was unloaded. Sailors eventually started using the term to refer to that side of the ship. Use of the term "port" was officially adopted by the U.S. Navy by General Order, 18 February 1846.

Radar: An acronym standing for "radio detecting and ranging."

Right (Left) (10) Degrees Rudder: Indicates a turn of the rudder a designated number of degrees to the right or to the left of amidships.

Right (Left) Full Rudder: Give all of the left or right rudder that can be obtained without danger of jamming the rudder against ship.

Right (Left) Handsomely: To change the rudder angle with care, as in coming alongside a dock.

Right (Left) Standard Rudder: Indicates a turn of the rudder to the right or left of amidships that number of degrees necessary to make a turn with standard tactical diameter.

Rudder Amidships: Place the rudder in line with the keel of the ship.

Scuba: An acronym standing for "Self-Contained Underwater Breathing Apparatus."

Scuttlebutt: The cask of drinking water on ships was called a scuttlebutt. Since Sailors exchanged gossip when they gathered at the scuttlebutt for a drink of water, scuttlebutt became U.S. Navy slang for gossip or rumors. A butt was a wooden cask that held water or other liquids. To scuttle is to drill a hole, as in tapping a cask.

Side Boys: Tending the side with side boys, as we know it in modern practice, originated a long time ago. It was customary in the days of sail to hold conferences on the flagships both when at sea and in open roadstead. Also, officers were invited to dinner on other ships while at sea, weather permitting. Sometimes the sea was such that visitors were hoisted aboard in boatswain's chairs. Members of the crew did the hoisting, and it is from the aid they rendered in tending the side that the custom originated of having a certain number of men always in attendance. Some have reported the higher the rank, the heavier the individual; therefore, more side boys.

Smoking Lamp: The exact date and origin of the smoking lamp has been lost. However, it probably came into use during the 16th century when seamen began smoking on board vessels. The smoking lamp was a safety measure. It was devised mainly to keep the fire hazard away from highly combustible woodwork and gunpowder. Most navies established regulations restricting smoking to certain areas. Usually, the lamp was located in the forecastle or the area directly surrounding the galley indicating that smoking was permitted in this area. Even after the invention of matches in the 1830s, the lamp was an item of convenience to the smoker. When particularly hazardous operations or work required that smoking be curtailed, the unlighted lamp relayed the message. "The smoking lamp is lighted" or "the smoking lamp is out' were the expressions indicating that smoking was permitted or forbidden.

The smoking lamp has survived only as a figure of speech. When the officer of the deck says "the smoking lamp is out" before drills, refueling or taking ammunition, that is the Navy's way of saying "cease smoking."

Sonar: Sound Navigation Ranging. An acronym for underwater echo-ranging equipment, originally for detecting submarines by small warships.

Stand Easy: Allows the men at station to relax at their stations.

Steady As You Go: Maintain the course the vessel is on at the instant of command.

Stern: Rear of the ship.

Striking the Flag: Striking the ensign was and is the universally-recognized indication of surrender.

Suit: Nautical term, dating from at least the early 1600s, meaning the outfit of sails used by a ship. The term was revived after World War II, when a Navy ship's complement of electronics could be referred to as its electronics suit, and its total armament might be called its weapons suit. The word is sometimes incorrectly spelled "suite."

Swab Down (Deck): Wash down the deck.

Take Cover: Gun crews and others proceed to gun crew shelter on the double. Given when angle of elevation is such as to permit shell fragments falling on the deck or to avoid a spray gas attack.

Tar, Jack Tar: Tar, a slang term for a Sailor, has been in use since at least 1676. The term "Jack Tar" was used by the 1780s. Early Sailors wore overalls and broad-brimmed hats made of tar-impregnated fabric called tarpaulin cloth. The hats, and the Sailors who wore them, were called tarpaulins, which may have been shortened to tars.

Toe the line: The space between each pair of deck planks in a wooden ship was filled with a packing material called "oakum" and then sealed with a mixture of pitch and tar. The result, from afar, was a series of parallel lines a half-foot or so apart, running the length of the deck. Once a week, as a rule, usually on Sunday, a warship's crew was ordered to fall in at quarters—that is, each group of men into which the crew was divided would line up in formation in a given area of the deck. To insure a neat alignment of each row, the Sailors were directed to stand with their toes just touching a particular seam. Another use for these seams was punitive. The youngsters in a ship, be they ship's boys or student officers, might be required to stand with their toes just touching a designated seam for a length of time as punishment for some minor infraction of discipline, such as talking or fidgeting at the wrong time. A tough captain might require the miscreant to stand there, not talking to anyone, in fair weather or foul, for hours at a time. Hopefully, he would learn it was easier and more pleasant to conduct himself in the required manner rather than suffer the punishment. From these two uses of deck seams comes our cautionary word to obstreperous youngsters to "toe the line."

Turn To: Commence ship's work.

Uncover: Remove headwear.

Very Well: An officer's response indicating that the situation is understood, for example, given to the steersman after his report. "All right" should not be used, since it might be construed to mean "right rudder."

What's Your Heading: A request to the steersman to report the course he is on.

Aircraft Carriers

Aircraft carriers provide a wide range of possible response for the U.S. Navy and Marine Corps.

The carrier mission is to (1) provide a credible, sustainable, independent forward presence and conventional deterrence in peacetime; (2) operate as the cornerstone of joint/allied maritime expeditionary forces in times of crisis; and (3) operate and support aircraft attacks on enemies, protect friendly forces, and engage in sustained independent operations in war.

The aircraft carrier continues to be the centerpiece of the forces necessary for forward presence. Whenever there has been a crisis, the first question has been, "Where are the carriers?" Carriers support and operate aircraft that engage in attacks on airborne, afloat, and ashore targets that threaten free use of the sea, and engage in sustained operations in support of other forces.

Aircraft carriers are deployed worldwide in support of U.S. interests and commitments. They can respond to global crises in ways ranging from peacetime presence to full-scale war. Together with their on-board air wings, the carriers have vital roles across the full spectrum of conflict.

An aircraft carrier is a large city and airport all contained on a massive ship. There are several important operational parts of an aircraft carrier that all prospective Navy and Marine Corps aviation candidates should know.

Arresting cables: Each carrier-based aircraft has a tailhook, a hook bolted to an eight-foot bar extending from the after part of the aircraft. It is with the tailhook that the pilot catches one of the four steel cables stretched across the deck, bringing the plane, traveling at 150 miles per hour, to a complete stop in about 320 feet. The cables are set to stop each aircraft at the same place on the deck, regardless of the size or weight of the plane.

The Bridge: This is the primary control position for every ship when the ship is underway, and the place where all orders and commands affecting the ship, her movements, and routine originate.

An Officer of the Deck (OOD) is always on the bridge when the ship is underway. Each OOD stands a four-hour watch and is the officer designated by the Commanding Officer (CO) to be in charge of the ship. The OOD is responsible for the safety and operation of the ship, including navigation, ship handling, communications, routine tests and inspections, reports, supervision of the watch team, and carrying out the Plan of the Day.

Also on the bridge are the **helmsman** who steers the ship, and the **lee helmsman** who operates the engine order control, telling the engine room how much speed to make. There are also **lookouts**, and the **Boatswain's Mate of the Watch** (BMOW) who supervises the helmsman, lee helmsman, and lookouts.

The Quartermaster of the Watch assists the OOD in navigation, reports all changes in weather, temperature, and barometer readings, and keeps the ship's log.

Catapults: The four steam-powered catapults thrust a 48,000-pound aircraft 300 feet, from zero to 165 miles per hour, in two seconds. On each plane's nose gear is a T-bar that locks into the catapult's shuttle that pulls the plane down the catapult. The flight deck crew can launch two aircraft and land one every 37 seconds in daylight, and one per minute at night.

Elevators: Each of the four deck-edge elevators can lift two aircraft from the cavernous hangar deck to the 4.5-acre flight deck in seconds.

Meatball: This series of lights aids the pilot in lining up for the landing. In the center are amber and red lights with Fresnel lenses. Although the lights are always on, the Fresnel lens only makes one light at a time seem to glow, as the angle at which the pilot looks at the lights changes. If the lights appear above the green horizontal bar, the pilot is too high. If it is below, the pilot is too low, and if the lights are red, the pilot is very low. If the red lights on either side of the amber vertical bar are flashing, it is a wave-off.

Pri-Fly. Primary Flight Control ("Pri-Fly") is the control tower for the flight operations on the carrier. Here, the "Air Boss" controls the takeoffs, landings, those aircraft in the air near the ship, and the movement of planes on the flight deck, which itself resembles a well-choreographed ballet.

Comprehending Spatial Relationships

Aviators perform in a 3D environment, and so the services have developed a series of subtests that measure a candidate's ability to perceive relationships among 3D objects. The AFOQT contains three subtests designed to measure an applicant's ability to comprehend spatial relationships: hidden figures, block-counting, and rotated blocks.

Additionally, while the Air Force retained the rotated blocks and hidden figures subtests, they are no longer used in computing the pilot and navigator composite scores (they may be re-implemented in the future, however, so they are included here).

The AFOQT also contains a subtest called instrument comprehension that the Air Force does not officially consider a spatial relationship test, but is very similar to the spatial relationship questions on the Navy's ASTB (see practice questions).

The ASTB has just one subtest that is designed to test a candidate's ability to perceive the attitude of an aircraft in relation to an aircraft carrier.

Hidden Figures

On the Hidden Figures subtest of the AFOQT the objective is to discover which of five figures are hidden in a complex drawing. The correct shape will always be the exact same size and in the same rotational position as the shapes shown above the drawing.

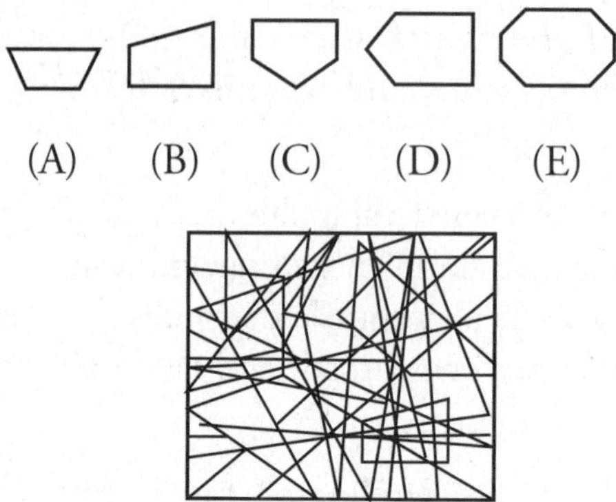

In this case, the correct answer would be (B).

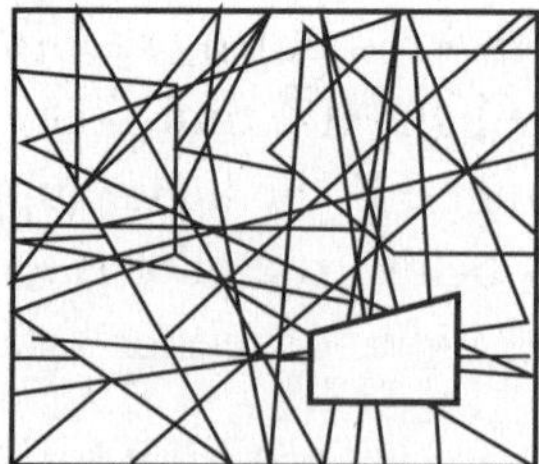

On the AFOQT subtest, there will be 15 problems of this type that must be solved in 8 minutes.

Block Counting

Block counting is a spatial relationship subtest found on the AFOQT that measures your ability to perceive and deduce what you cannot actually see. Your goal is to determine how many blocks are touched by designated numbered blocks that are stacked. Every block in the stack may be assumed to be the same size and shape of the other blocks in the stack. A block is considered to touch the numbered block if any part, even a corner or an edge, touches.

Take a look at the following example:

EXAMPLE

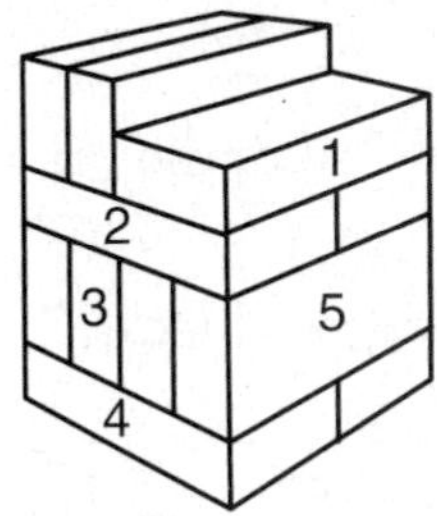

In the example above, block 1 touches three blocks. It touches the two blocks below it and the block behind it.

Block 2 touches eight blocks. It touches the block beside it, the three blocks above it, and the four blocks below it.

Block 3 touches the two blocks above it, the two blocks below it, and one block on each side of it, for a total of six blocks.

Block 4 also touches five blocks. It touches the block beside it and the four blocks above it.

Block 5 touches the block behind it, the two blocks below it, and the two blocks above it, totaling five blocks.

The AFOQT contains 20 block-counting problems that must be solved in 3 minutes.

Rotated Blocks

This spatial apperception subtest of the AFOQT measures your ability to visualize objects as they are rotated along a 3D axis. You will be shown a graphic of a block-shaped object, followed by five graphical choices. In only one of the choices is the object the same as the first graphic, only rotated into a different position.

Take a look at the two blocks below:

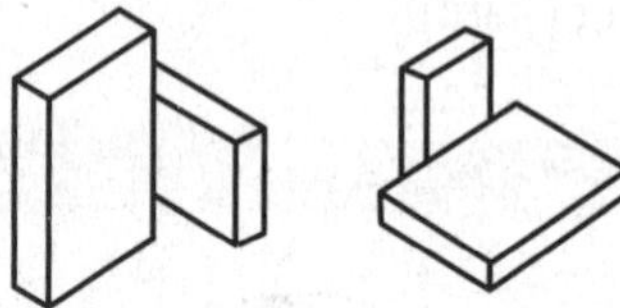

These blocks are the same, but the second block has been rotated into a different position.

Now take a look at the following two blocks:

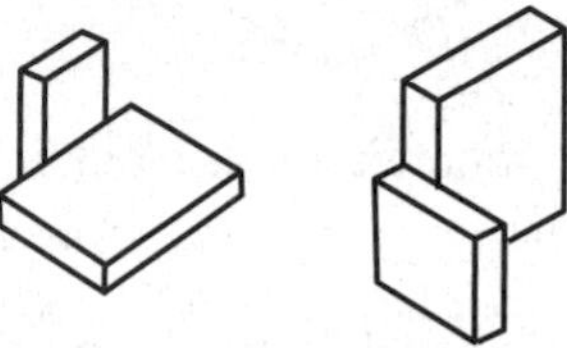

These blocks are not the same, nor can they ever be identical, no matter how they are rotated.

Try the example below:

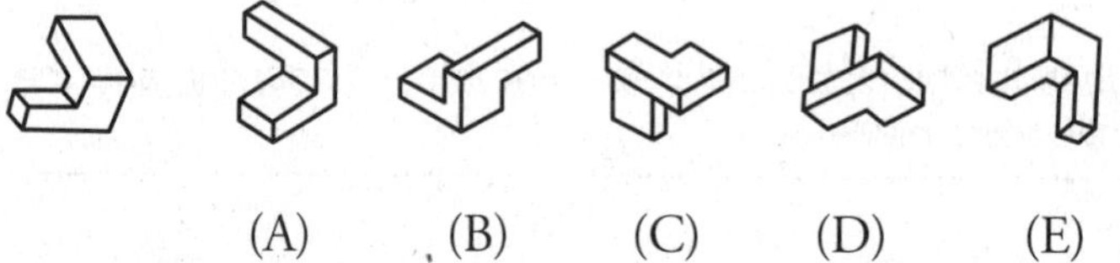

The correct answer would be block E. The other blocks are similar, but do not quite match the block shown at the beginning of the series. On the AFOQT there are 15 rotated block problems that must be solved in 13 minutes.

Navy Spatial Apperception

The test for Navy OCS applicants and Marine Corps/Coast Guard aviation candidates has only one type of spatial relationship problem. The test measures your ability to determine the position of an aircraft in relation to the outside environment.

The subtest depicts a view of what a pilot is seeing from the cockpit of an aircraft. This view is followed by a series of graphics that show aircraft at various angles and positions. The objective is to choose the aircraft that most closely relates to the view from the cockpit. In order to accomplish this, one must note whether the aircraft is climbing, descending, or banking in a turn. One must also note the direction the aircraft is flying in relation to the land mass and sea.

Take a look at the following example:

EXAMPLE

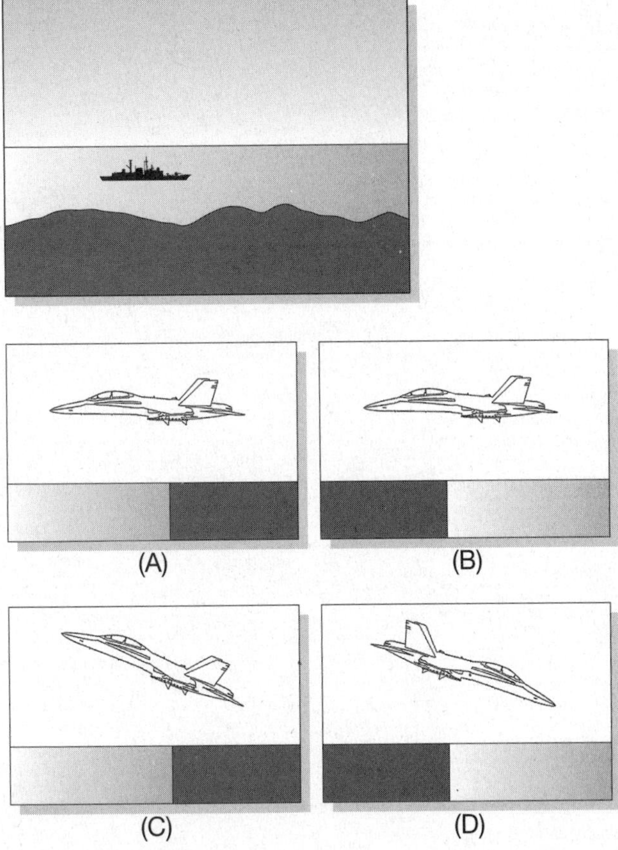

In this case, the correct answer would be (A). The first graphic depicts a view from an aircraft that is in level flight (no climb, descent, or bank) and is flying away from the land, heading out to sea. Choice (B) shows an aircraft that is in level flight, but is flying away from the sea, toward the land. Choice (C) shows an aircraft flying away from the land, toward the sea, but climbing. Choice (D) shows an aircraft flying away from the land, but descending. Choice (A) is the only choice that depicts an aircraft in level flight, heading away from the land, toward the sea.

On the ASTB, there are 25 problems of this type that must be answered in 10 minutes.

Answer Sheet for Practice Questions

1 Ⓐ Ⓑ Ⓒ Ⓓ Ⓔ
2 Ⓐ Ⓑ Ⓒ Ⓓ Ⓔ
3 Ⓐ Ⓑ Ⓒ Ⓓ Ⓔ
4 Ⓐ Ⓑ Ⓒ Ⓓ Ⓔ
5 Ⓐ Ⓑ Ⓒ Ⓓ Ⓔ
6 Ⓐ Ⓑ Ⓒ Ⓓ Ⓔ
7 Ⓐ Ⓑ Ⓒ Ⓓ Ⓔ
8 Ⓐ Ⓑ Ⓒ Ⓓ Ⓔ
9 Ⓐ Ⓑ Ⓒ Ⓓ Ⓔ
10 Ⓐ Ⓑ Ⓒ Ⓓ Ⓔ
11 Ⓐ Ⓑ Ⓒ Ⓓ Ⓔ
12 Ⓐ Ⓑ Ⓒ Ⓓ Ⓔ
13 Ⓐ Ⓑ Ⓒ Ⓓ Ⓔ
14 Ⓐ Ⓑ Ⓒ Ⓓ Ⓔ
15 Ⓐ Ⓑ Ⓒ Ⓓ Ⓔ
16 Ⓐ Ⓑ Ⓒ Ⓓ Ⓔ
17 Ⓐ Ⓑ Ⓒ Ⓓ Ⓔ
18 Ⓐ Ⓑ Ⓒ Ⓓ Ⓔ
19 Ⓐ Ⓑ Ⓒ Ⓓ Ⓔ
20 Ⓐ Ⓑ Ⓒ Ⓓ Ⓔ
21 Ⓐ Ⓑ Ⓒ Ⓓ Ⓔ
22 Ⓐ Ⓑ Ⓒ Ⓓ Ⓔ
23 Ⓐ Ⓑ Ⓒ Ⓓ Ⓔ
24 Ⓐ Ⓑ Ⓒ Ⓓ Ⓔ
25 Ⓐ Ⓑ Ⓒ Ⓓ Ⓔ
26 Ⓐ Ⓑ Ⓒ Ⓓ Ⓔ
27 Ⓐ Ⓑ Ⓒ Ⓓ Ⓔ
28 Ⓐ Ⓑ Ⓒ Ⓓ Ⓔ
29 Ⓐ Ⓑ Ⓒ Ⓓ Ⓔ
30 Ⓐ Ⓑ Ⓒ Ⓓ Ⓔ
31 Ⓐ Ⓑ Ⓒ Ⓓ Ⓔ
32 Ⓐ Ⓑ Ⓒ Ⓓ Ⓔ
33 Ⓐ Ⓑ Ⓒ Ⓓ Ⓔ
34 Ⓐ Ⓑ Ⓒ Ⓓ Ⓔ
35 Ⓐ Ⓑ Ⓒ Ⓓ Ⓔ
36 Ⓐ Ⓑ Ⓒ Ⓓ Ⓔ
37 Ⓐ Ⓑ Ⓒ Ⓓ Ⓔ
38 Ⓐ Ⓑ Ⓒ Ⓓ Ⓔ
39 Ⓐ Ⓑ Ⓒ Ⓓ Ⓔ
40 Ⓐ Ⓑ Ⓒ Ⓓ Ⓔ
41 Ⓐ Ⓑ Ⓒ Ⓓ Ⓔ
42 Ⓐ Ⓑ Ⓒ Ⓓ Ⓔ
43 Ⓐ Ⓑ Ⓒ Ⓓ Ⓔ
44 Ⓐ Ⓑ Ⓒ Ⓓ Ⓔ
45 Ⓐ Ⓑ Ⓒ Ⓓ Ⓔ
46 Ⓐ Ⓑ Ⓒ Ⓓ
47 Ⓐ Ⓑ Ⓒ Ⓓ
48 Ⓐ Ⓑ Ⓒ Ⓓ
49 Ⓐ Ⓑ Ⓒ Ⓓ
50 Ⓐ Ⓑ Ⓒ Ⓓ
51 Ⓐ Ⓑ Ⓒ Ⓓ
52 Ⓐ Ⓑ Ⓒ Ⓓ
53 Ⓐ Ⓑ Ⓒ Ⓓ
54 Ⓐ Ⓑ Ⓒ Ⓓ
55 Ⓐ Ⓑ Ⓒ Ⓓ

Practice Questions

1. Which of the following is not considered a major component of an aircraft structure?

   (A) cabin
   (B) fuselage
   (C) empennage
   (D) wings
   (E) power plant

2. Moving the control wheel or stick to the right will cause the right aileron to __________.

   (A) retract
   (B) extend
   (C) rotate upward
   (D) rotate downward
   (E) none of the above

3. If the control wheel or stick is moved forward, then:

   (A) airspeed will increase.
   (B) airspeed will decrease.
   (C) aircraft pitch will change.
   (D) both (A) and (C).
   (E) both (B) and (C).

4. In military aviation, *Zulu time* is

   (A) flight time.
   (B) time until takeoff.
   (C) time in Greenwich, England.
   (D) Pacific Standard Time.
   (E) Eastern Standard Time.

5. If the left rudder is pressed, then the aircraft will __________.

   (A) turn
   (B) bank
   (C) yaw
   (D) descend
   (E) climb

6. In military aviation, the word *Mach* refers to __________.

   (A) angle of attack
   (B) speed of sound
   (C) altitude
   (D) pitch
   (E) gear position

7. As the radius of a turn decreases, then:

   (A) positive G-forces are increased.
   (B) positive G-forces are decreased.
   (C) negative G-forces are increased.
   (D) inverse G-forces are increased.
   (E) G-forces remain the same.

8. As altitude increases, in order to maintain the same amount of lift, an aircraft must

   (A) increase drag forces.
   (B) decrease drag forces.
   (C) fly slower.
   (D) fly faster.
   (E) decrease pitch.

9. If a pilot is instructed to land on Runway 27 using a straight-in approach, the aircraft heading should be __________.

   (A) 27 degrees
   (B) East
   (C) 2700 degrees
   (D) 270 degrees
   (E) 2.7 degrees

10. When flaps are extended

   (A) drag increases.
   (B) lift increases.
   (C) airspeed increases.
   (D) drag and lift increase.
   (E) drag, lift, and airspeed increase.

11. The below gage indicates that the pilot should

(A) increase bank.
(B) decrease bank.
(C) depress the right rudder pedal.
(D) depress the left rudder pedal.
(E) increase airspeed.

12. Assuming no increase in thrust, which of the following will eventually result in a stall?

(A) increase in pitch
(B) decrease in pitch
(C) extending flaps
(D) retracting flaps
(E) both (C) and (B)

13. Which two flight controls are used to control the rate of a turn?

(A) flaps and rudder
(B) rudder and ailerons
(C) flaps and ailerons
(D) elevator and flaps
(E) elevator and ailerons

14. An aircraft on a heading of 325 is flying ___________.

(A) Northeast
(B) Southeast
(C) Northwest
(D) East
(E) Southwest

15. Under normal VFR conditions, how much of a pilot's attention should be focused on the cockpit instruments?

(A) 5 percent
(B) 10 percent
(C) 15 percent
(D) 20 percent
(E) 25 percent

16. Large yellow X's painted on the end of a runway indicates

(A) touch-down zone.
(B) touch-and-go zones.
(C) the runway is closed.
(D) approach zone.
(E) departure zone.

17. The axis that extends lengthwise through the fuselage from the nose to the tail is known as

(A) the vertical axis.
(B) the longitudinal axis.
(C) the horizontal axis.
(D) the lateral axis.
(E) the cross axis.

18. The transponder code that indicates an in-flight emergency is ___________.

(A) 7700
(B) 7777
(C) 7911
(D) 7500
(E) 7555

19. The control system that is used to relieve the pilot from having to maintain constant pressure on the flight controls is the

(A) pitch system.
(B) the gyroscopic system.
(C) the trim system.
(D) the parasitic system.
(E) the pitot static system.

20. The attitude indicated below depicts an aircraft that is

(A) climbing right-hand turn.
(B) descending right-hand turn.
(C) level right-hand turn.
(D) level left-hand turn.
(E) descending left-hand turn.

Questions 21–30 apply to Navy OCS candidates and Marine Corps/Coast Guard aviation candidates only.

21. The walls (vertical partitions) on a ship are called ___________.

(A) hulls
(B) bulkheads
(C) decks
(D) walls
(E) frames

22. In ship navigation using the 24-hour clock, 4:25 P.M. would be written as ___________.

(A) 0425
(B) 1425
(C) 1625
(D) 14.25
(E) 16.25

23. A *fathom* is equal to ___________.

(A) six miles
(B) six feet
(C) six yards
(D) six meters
(E) six centimeters

24. On an aircraft carrier, "grapes" are ___________.

(A) pilots
(B) navigators
(C) aircraft refuelers
(D) enlisted sailors
(E) commissioned officers

25. An "okay trap" is when a carrier pilot lands safely and hooks onto

(A) the number one wire.
(B) the number two wire.
(C) the number three wire.
(D) the number four wire.
(E) the number five wire.

26. On an aircraft carrier, the length of a standard watch for the Officer of the Deck is ___________.

(A) 2 hours
(B) 4 hours
(C) 6 hours
(D) 8 hours
(E) 10 hours

27. If the lights of the "meatball" appear to be above the green horizon bar, that means

(A) the pilot is flying too high.
(B) the pilot is flying too low.
(C) the pilot is on the flight path.
(D) the pilot is flying too far to the right.
(E) the pilot is flying too far to the left.

28. The rear of a ship is referred to as the ___________.

(A) bow
(B) port
(C) starboard
(D) keel
(E) stern

29. "Make a hole" means
    (A) open a hatch.
    (B) step aside.
    (C) paint a deck.
    (D) climb a ladder.
    (E) fire a ship's weapon.

30. On U.S. aircraft carriers, the catapult is operated by __________.
    (A) nuclear power
    (B) electrical power
    (C) hydraulic presses
    (D) steam
    (E) springs

Questions 31–35 apply to Air Force OTS applicants only.

Directions: Questions 31–35 are hidden mazes. Each drawing contains one of the figures shown above the drawing. Find the figure that is hidden in the drawing below it. The correct figure in each drawing will always be of the same size and in the same position as it appears at the top.

31.

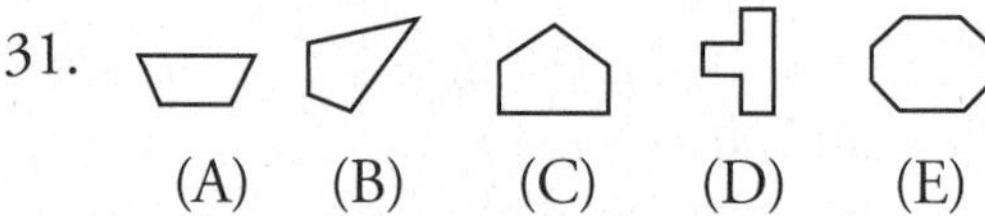

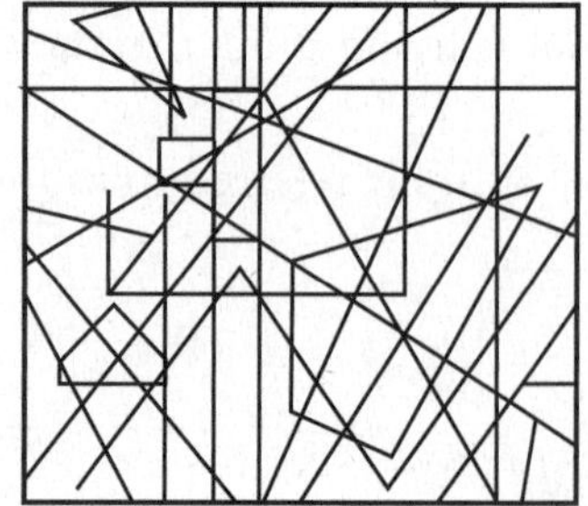

32.

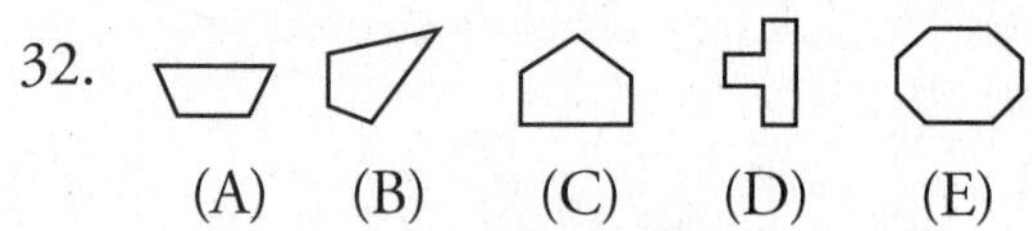

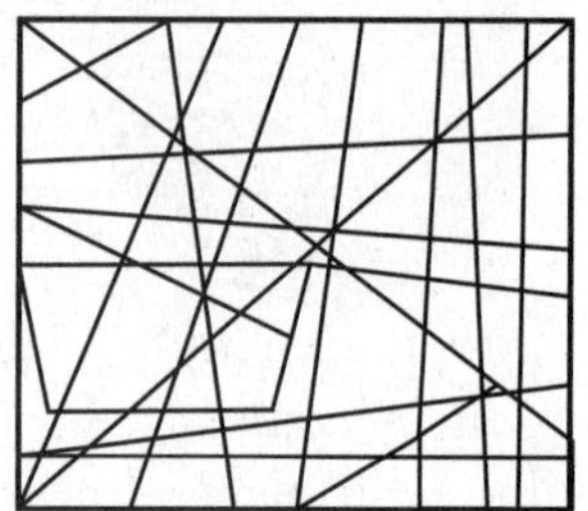

33.

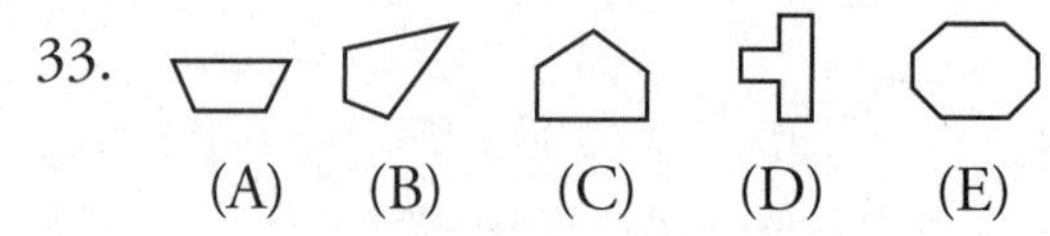

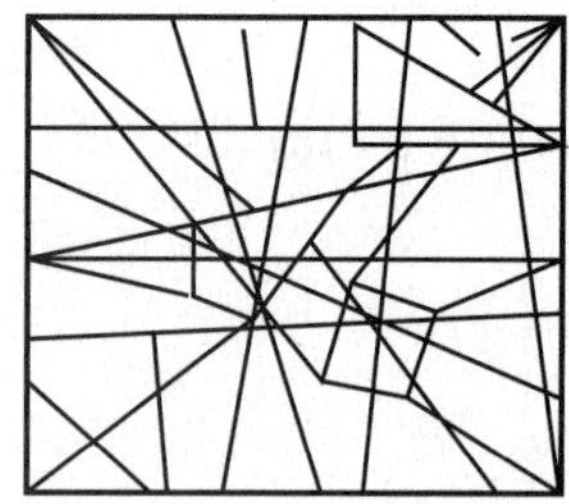

34.

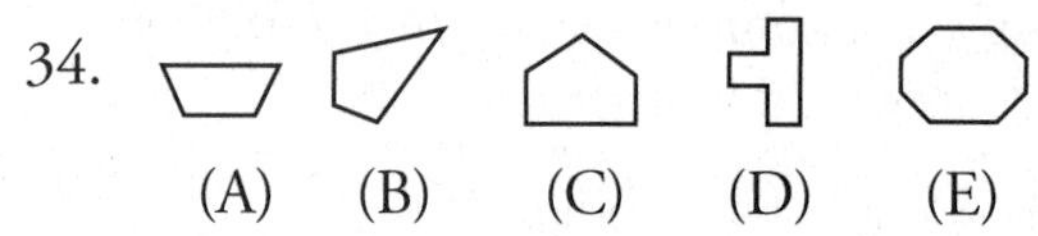

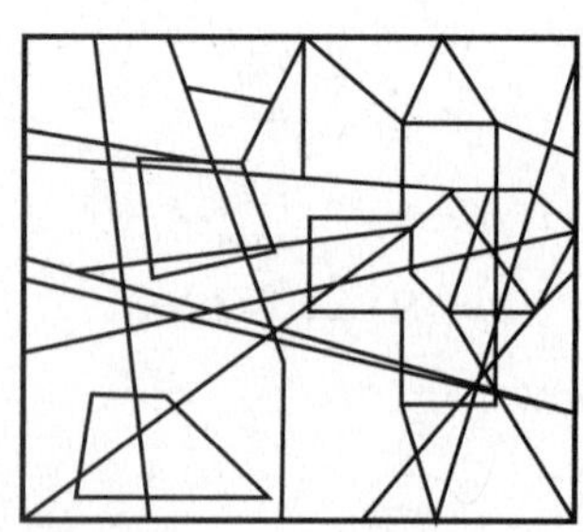

35.

(A) (B) (C) (D) (E)

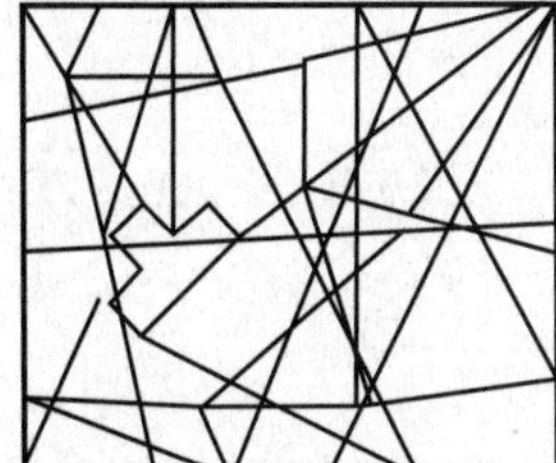

Questions 36–40 apply to Air Force OTS candidates only.

Directions: Questions 36–40 pertain to the block pictured below.

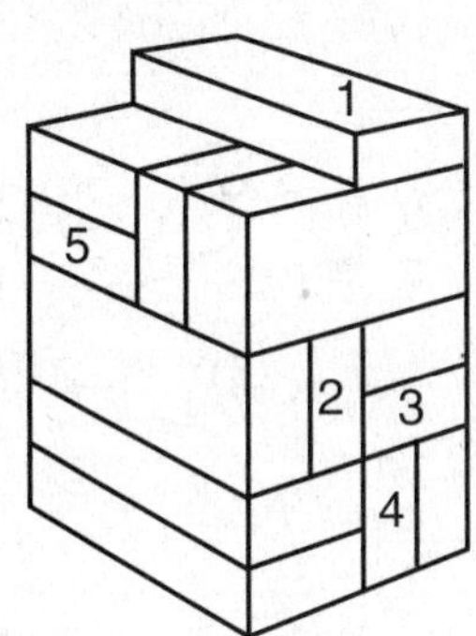

36. Block 1 touches _________ blocks.
   (A) one
   (B) two
   (C) three
   (D) four
   (E) five

37. Block 2 touches _________ blocks.
   (A) four
   (B) five
   (C) six
   (D) eight
   (E) nine

38. Block 3 touches _________ blocks.
   (A) four
   (B) five
   (C) six
   (D) seven
   (E) eight

39. Block 4 touches _________ blocks.
   (A) three
   (B) four
   (C) five
   (D) six
   (E) seven

40. Block 5 touches _________ blocks.
   (A) two
   (B) three
   (C) four
   (D) five
   (E) six

Questions 41–45 apply to Air Force OTS candidates only.

Directions: Questions 41–45 are rotating blocks. Find the block that most closely resembles the block shown in the first graphic of the series.

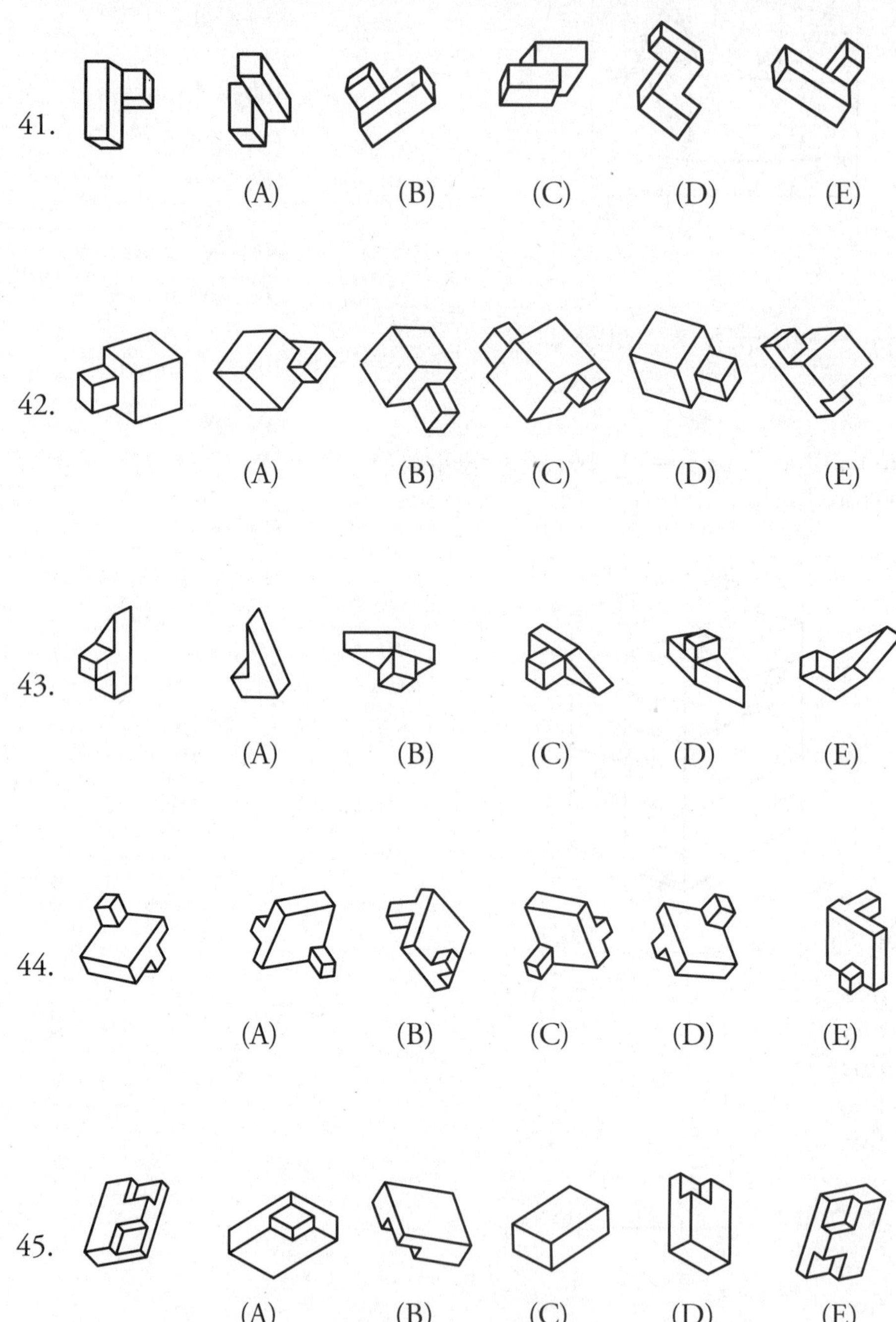

Questions 46–50 are for Air Force OTS candidates only.

Directions: Questions 46–50 measure your ability to judge the heading and position of an aircraft based on two standard cockpit instruments—the artificial horizon (attitude indicator) and the compass. In the pictorial displays, if the aircraft is heading directly away from the viewer, it is heading north. If it is heading directly toward the viewer, it is heading south. If it is heading to the viewer's left, it is heading west, and to the viewer's right, the aircraft is heading east.

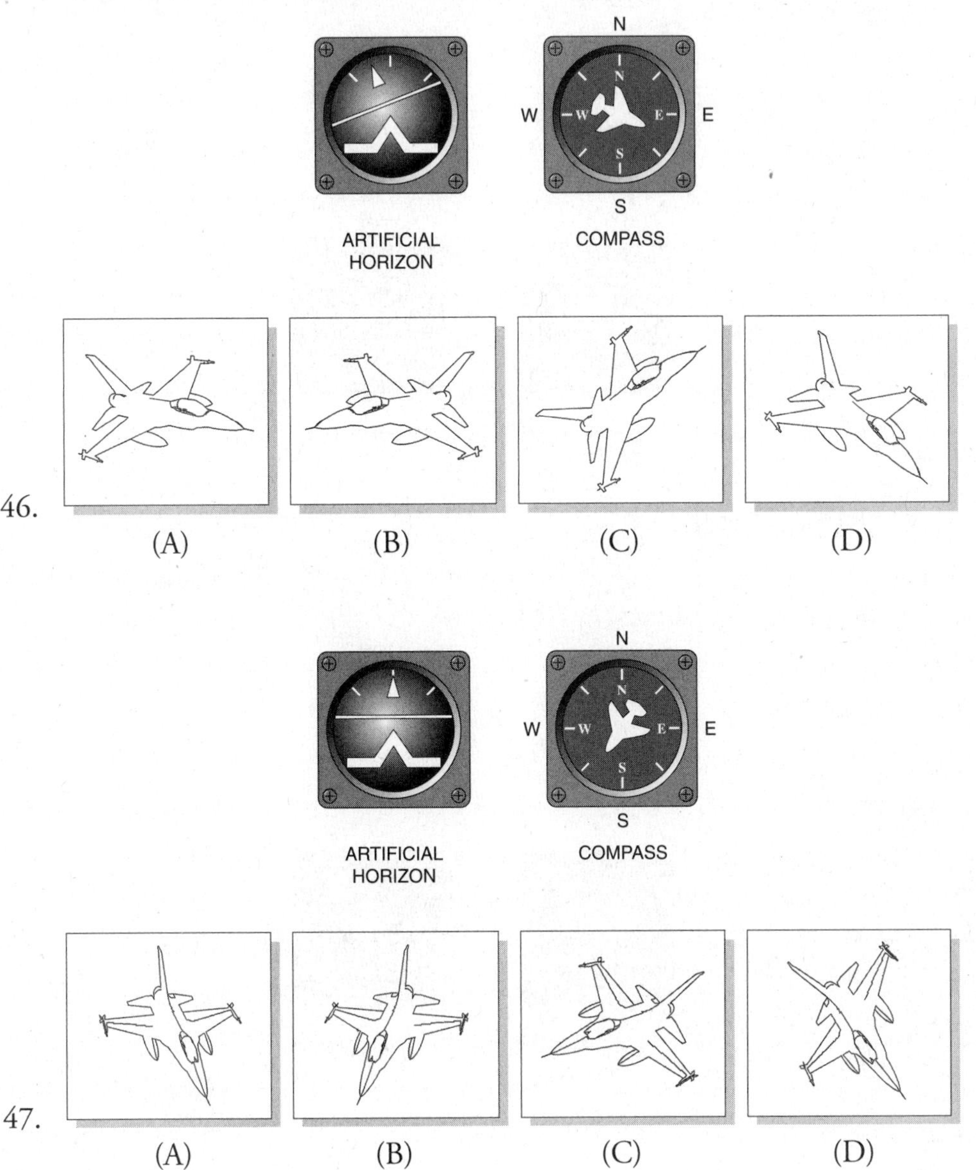

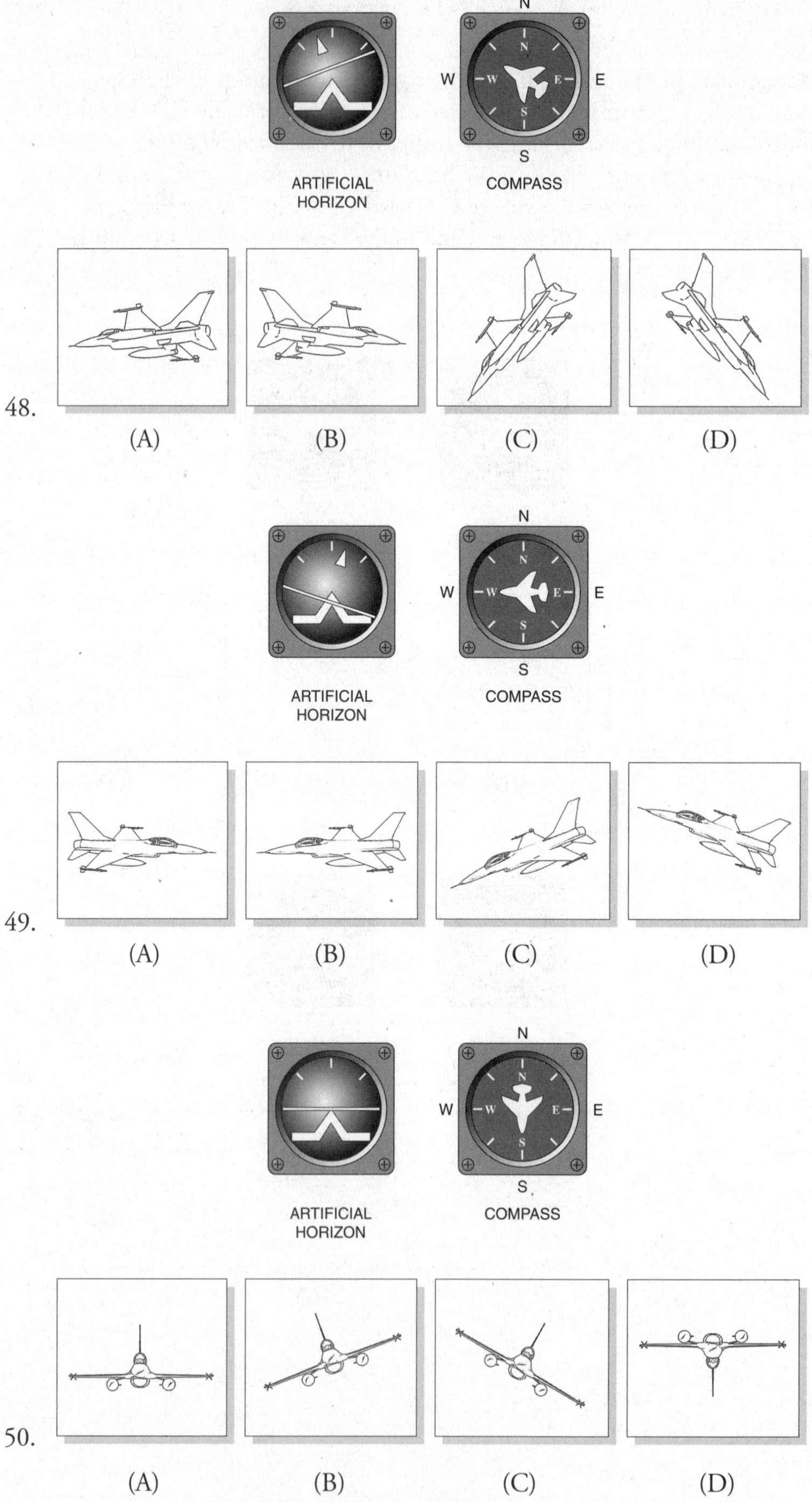
N
W
E
S
ARTIFICIAL HORIZON
COMPASS
48.
(A)
(B)
(C)
(D)
N
W
E
S
ARTIFICIAL HORIZON
COMPASS
49.
(A)
(B)
(C)
(D)
N
W
E
S
ARTIFICIAL HORIZON
COMPASS
50.
(A)
(B)
(C)
(D)

Questions 51–55 are for Navy OCS candidates and Marine Corps/Coast Guard aviation applicants only.

Directions: Questions 51–55 are Navy spatial apperception questions. In the first graphic, you'll see a pictorial of the view a pilot is seeing outside of the cockpit. Your objective is to choose the aircraft that most closely represents the view from the cockpit in relation to axis rotation and direction.

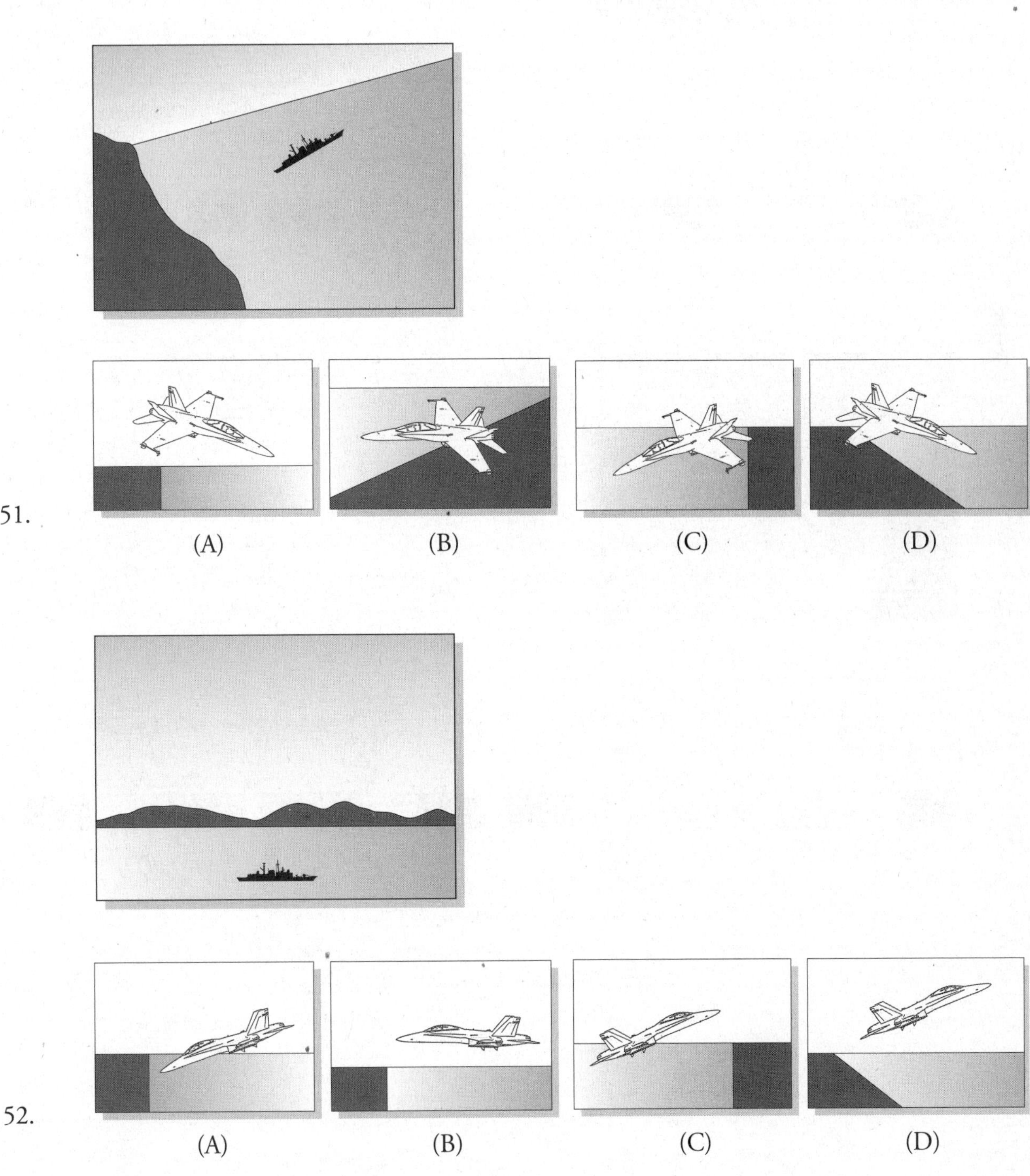

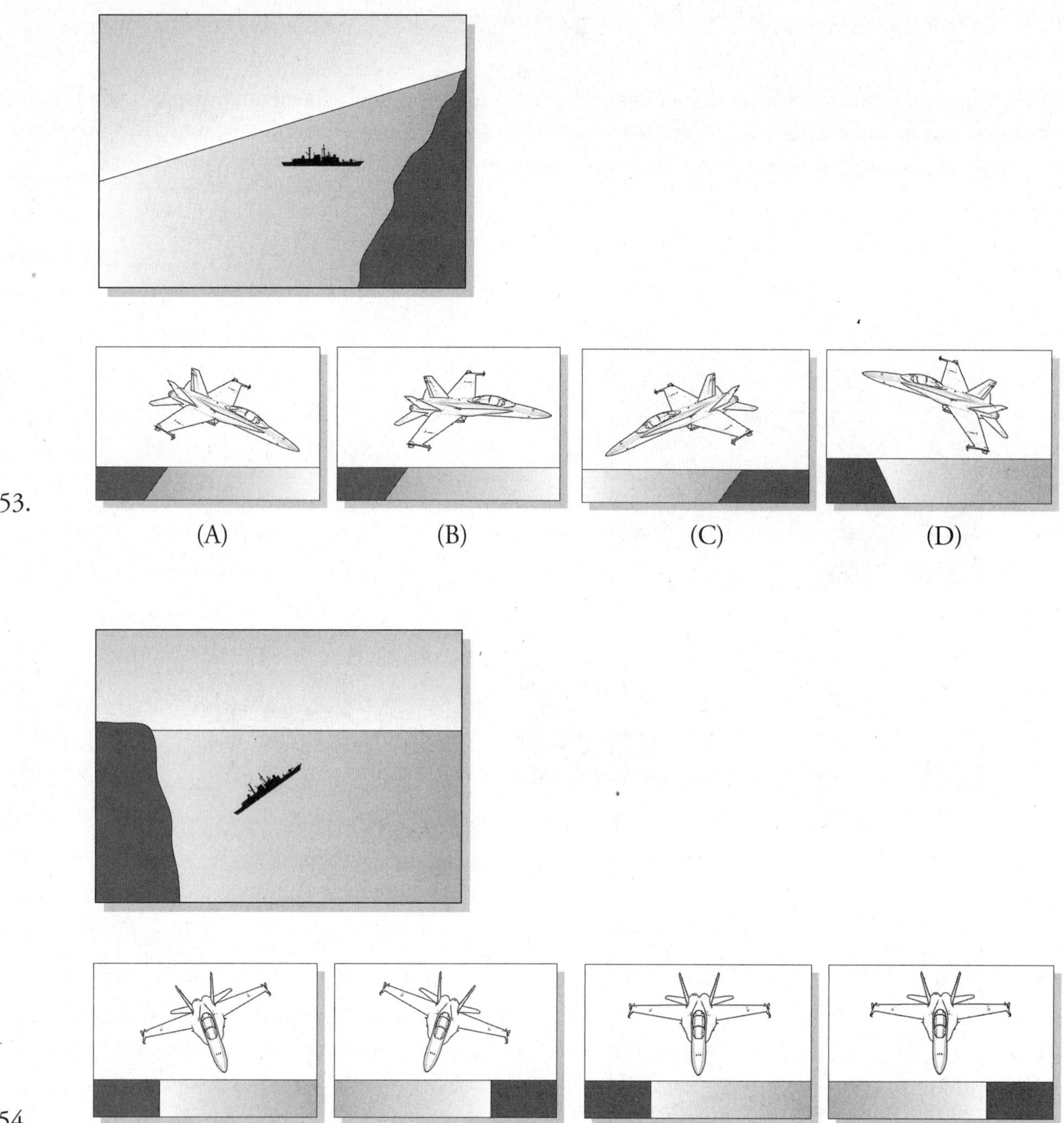
53.
(A)
(B)
(C)
(D)
54.
(A)
(B)
(C)
(D)

55.

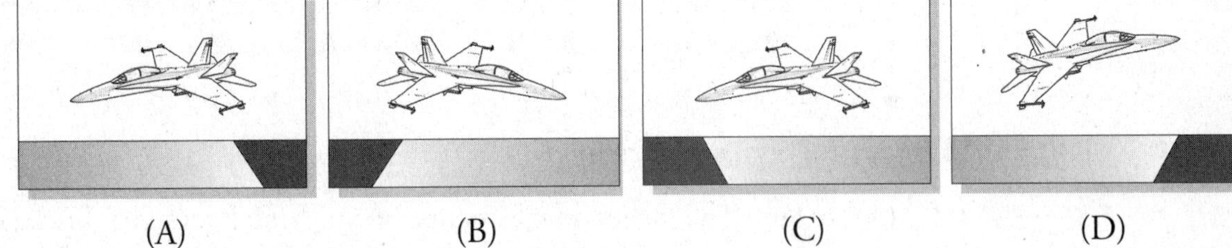

Answer Key

1. A	12. A	23. B	34. E	45. E
2. C	13. E	24. C	35. A	46. A
3. D	14. C	25. C	36. C	47. B
4. C	15. B	26. B	37. D	48. C
5. C	16. C	27. A	38. B	49. D
6. B	17. B	28. E	39. C	50. A
7. A	18. A	29. B	40. D	51. D
8. D	19. C	30. D	41. B	52. C
9. D	20. C	31. D	42. D	53. A
10. D	21. B	32. C	43. C	54. D
11. D	22. C	33. B	44. A	55. B

Answer Explanations

1. **(A) cabin.** The major components of an aircraft are the fuselage, wings, empennage, landing gear, and a power plant (the cabin is part of the fuselage).
2. **(C) rotate upward.** Rotating the control wheel or stick to the right causes the right aileron to rotate upwards and the left aileron to rotate downwards, which results in the aircraft banking to the right.
3. **(D) both (A) and (C).** If the control wheel or stick is moved forward, the aircraft pitch will decrease, resulting in an increase in airspeed.
4. **(C) time in Greenwich, England.** Zulu time refers to Greenwich Mean Time, which is the time in Greenwich, England. Greenwich Mean Time is widely used in both military and civil aviation. In the military, it's referred to as *Zulu Time.*
5. **(C) yaw.** Depressing the rudder pedal causes the aircraft to yaw.
6. **(B) speed of sound.** One *Mach* equals the speed of sound. An aircraft flying at twice the speed of sound is flying at Mach 2.
7. **(A) positive G-forces are increased.** As a turn tightens (the circle of the turn becomes smaller), more positive G-forces are induced on the pilot and aircraft.
8. **(D) fly faster.** As altitude increases, air becomes less dense, so a greater airspeed is required to generate the same amount of lift.
9. **(D) 270 degrees.** Runway 27 refers to a runway with a heading of 270 degrees. Runway 33 would refer to a runway positioned with an approach heading of 330 degrees, etc.
10. **(D) drag and lift increase.** Extending the flaps increases aircraft lift, and increases the drag forces on the aircraft, which decreases the aircraft speed.
11. **(D) depress the left rudder pedal.** To keep the ball on the inclinometer center, to prevent skidding and sliding turns, remember the rule, "step on the ball."
12. **(A) increase in pitch.** As the pitch angle increases, airspeed decreases. With no additional thrust, as pitch increases, airspeed will eventually decrease to a point where the aircraft will enter a stall (not enough lift).
13. **(E) elevator and ailerons.** Ailerons are used to place the aircraft in a bank, then the elevator is used to move the nose "upward" or "downward" (in relation to the pilot).

14. **(C) Northwest.** Straight or due North is 360 degrees, due East is 90 degrees, due South is 180 degrees, and due West is 270 degrees.
15. **(B) 10 percent.** Under normal VFR conditions, 90 percent of a pilot's attention should be focused on the view outside of the cockpit.
16. **(C) the runway is closed.** Large yellow X's are painted on runways that are either permanently closed or closed for a long period of time for repair/renovation.
17. **(B) the longitudinal axis.** The other two axes are the lateral axis and the vertical axis.
18. **(A) 7700.** This transponder code is the international code for in-flight emergency.
19. **(C) the trim system.** Trim controls are designed to help minimize a pilot's workload by aerodynamically assisting movement and position of the flight control surface to which they are attached.
20. **(C) level right-hand turn**. The instrument depicts an aircraft that is turning to the right in level flight.
21. **(B) bulkheads.** This term is used to describe all vertical partitions on a ship.
22. **(C) 1625.** Military time (24-hour clock) uses four numerals. Midnight is 0000, 1:00 A.M. is 0100, 12:00 noon is 1200, 1:00 P.M. is 1300, 2:00 P.M. is 1400, and so on.
23. **(B) six feet.** A fathom is a nautical measurement of six feet.
24. **(C) aircraft refuelers.** They are nicknamed "grapes" because they wear purple jerseys on the flight deck.
25. **(C) the number three wire.** By tradition, carrier pilots try to hook onto the third arresting cable wire. Catching wire #1 or #2 indicates the pilot touched down too early. Catching wire #4 indicates the pilot overshot the correct landing zone.
26. **(B) 4 hours.** Each OOD stands a four-hour watch and is the officer designated by the Commanding Officer (CO) to be in charge of the ship.
27. **(A) the pilot is flying too high.** If the lights appear above the green horizontal bar, the pilot is too high. If it is below, the pilot is too low, and if the lights are red, the pilot is very low.
28. **(E) stern.** The bow is the front of the ship, and the rear is the stern.
29. **(B) step aside.** On Navy ships, when one hears "make a hole" it means to get out of the way because the sailor needs to get past.
30. **(D) steam.** The catapults used to launch aircraft are powered by steam.
31. **(D)**

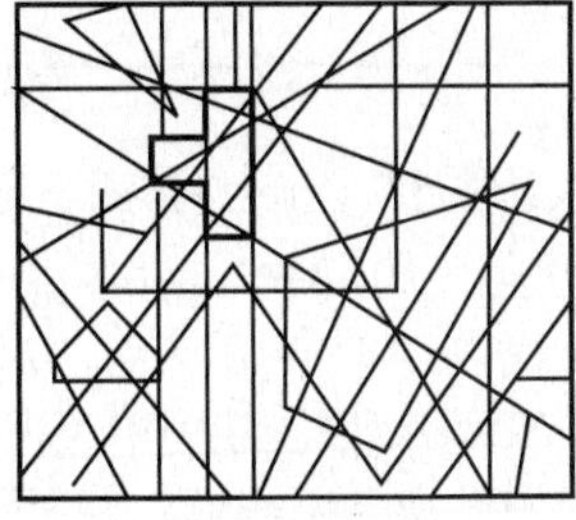

32. **(C)**

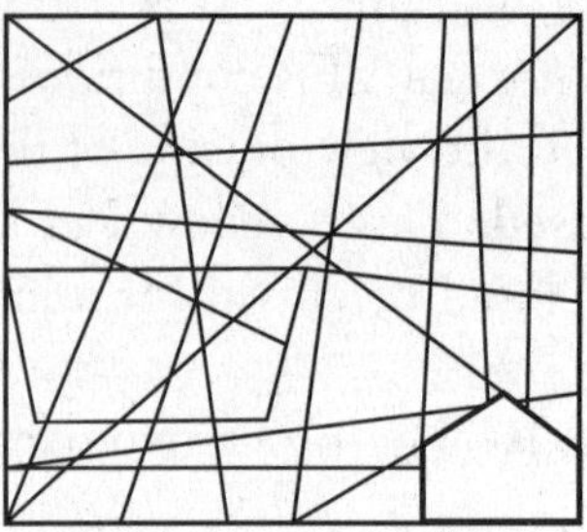

33. **(B)**

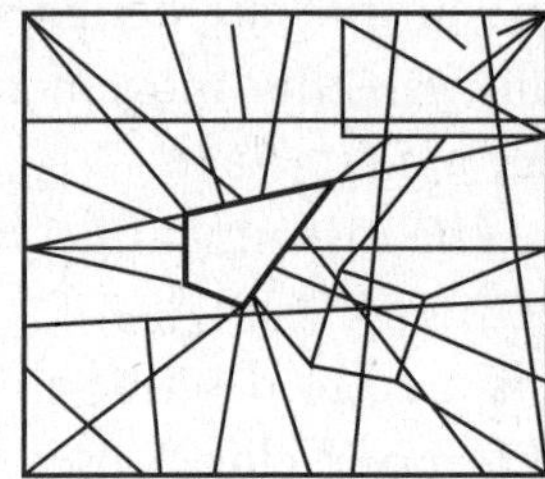

34. **(E)**

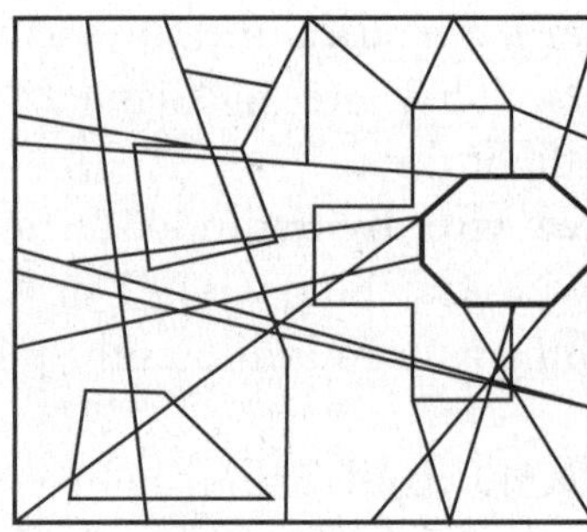

35. **(A)**

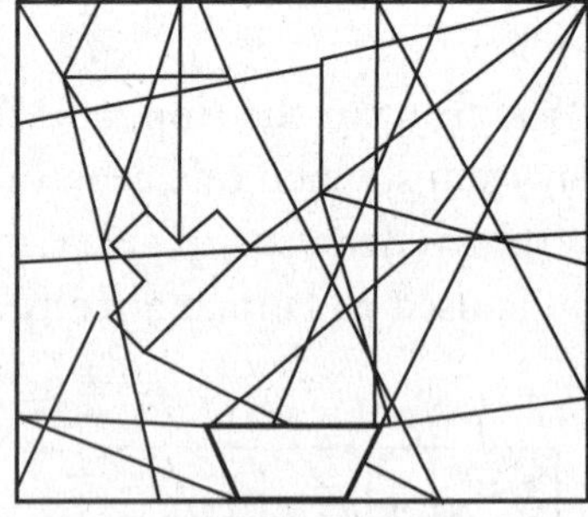

36. **(C) three.** Block one touches the three blocks under it.
37. **(D) eight.** Block two touches the two blocks on the left, one block on the right, one block on the lower corner (block 4), one block on the left, two blocks on top, and one block on the top rear (block 5).
38. **(B) five.** Block 3 touches the block above it, the two blocks below it, block #2, and the corner of the block next to block #4.
39. **(C) five.** Block 4 touches the two blocks on the left, the block on the right, the block above it, and the corner of block #2.

40. **(D) five.** Block 5 touches the block above it, the blocks beside it, and three blocks below it.
41. **(B)**
42. **(D)**
43. **(C)**
44. **(A)**
45. **(E)**
46. **(A)** The aircraft is pointed to the right and slightly toward the viewer (East-South-East) and is in a slight right-bank.
47. **(B)** The aircraft is pointed to the left and toward the viewer (West-South-West) and is in a dive with wings level.
48. **(C)** The aircraft is pointed to the left and heading slightly away from the viewer (West-North-West) in a steep descent and a slight turn to the right.
49. **(D)** The aircraft is facing to the left (West)and performing a climbing left turn.
50. **(A)** The aircraft is heading straight toward the viewer (South) and is flying straight and level.
51. **(D)** The cockpit view depicts an aircraft that is in a descending right turn, flying along the coast (slightly toward the sea).
52. **(C)** The cockpit view depicts an aircraft in a level climb, heading toward land.
53. **(A)** The cockpit view depicts an aircraft in a descending right turn, heading out to sea.
54. **(D)** The cockpit view depicts an aircraft in a straight descent, flying along the coast, with the coast on the left side of the aircraft.
55. **(B)** The cockpit view depicts an aircraft heading away from land, in a slight right-hand, descending turn.

Self-Description Inventory

CHAPTER 12

If you have anything really valuable to contribute to the world it will come through the expression of your own personality, that single spark of divinity that sets you off and makes you different from every other living creature.

—Bruce Barton

The Air Force added a completely new subtest when they recently revised the AFOQT. The bad news is this new subtest has 220 questions. The good news is that these questions have no right or wrong answers, and your responses are not used to generate any of the AFOQT composite scores, nor are they used in the OTS or flight school selection process.

The ASTB used to have a similar subtest called a "Biographical Inventory," or "BI," but the Navy removed this subtest in 2001. The BI considered extracurricular background experiences relevant to success in the fast-paced and demanding aviation program. Although the BI was initially a powerful predictor of attrition, its ability to predict which students will complete aviation training has essentially declined to zero over a period of years.

The Air Force stores this information in a computer database. Years in the future, the Air Force hopes to compile enough personality indicator information to determine which personality types do best in Air Force Officer Training School and various officer job programs.

In other words, you don't have to worry about these questions. You can be completely honest and spontaneous, and it won't have any bearing on whether or not you are selected for OTS or any specific Air Force officer program, such as pilot or navigator.

Because this is not something you can study for (there are no right or wrong answers), and because the responses aren't used to generate AFOQT composite scores or used in the selection process, we're not going to include this subtest in the AFOQT practice tests in chapters 13 and 14. However, to give you a general idea of what to expect, we've included a few sample questions below.

PERSONALITY TRAITS

The Self-Description Inventory measures personal traits and attitudes. The inventory consists of a list of statements. Your task is to read each statement carefully and decide how well each one describes you, using the following answer key:

A	B	C	D	E
Strongly Disagree	Moderately Disagree	Neither Agree nor Disagree	Moderately Agree	Strongly Agree

You should work quickly but reply to all statements. Give your first impression about how well each statement describes you by comparing yourself to people in your same sex and age group. Don't spend a long time deciding what your answer should be. There is no right or wrong answer to each statement. Answer all statements, even if you're not sure of your answer.

1. I always try to finish what I start.
2. I generally get along well with most people.
3. I get nervous if I have to speak in public.
4. People often get upset with me for not showing up on time.
5. I like to listen to many different kinds of music.
6. Usually I let my work goals take priority over my personal interests.
7. I am not comfortable supervising others.
8. I am pleased when friends drop in to see me.
9. I don't like to be involved in group activities.
10. I have higher work standards than do most people.
11. I am talkative.
12. I can be unsympathetic.
13. I am more controlled than random.
14. I don't mind being the center of attention.
15. I love large parties.
16. I use difficult words.
17. I am outgoing.
18. I do not think about decisions.
19. I am easily hurt.
20. I seek out the patterns of the universe.
21. I do things according to a plan.
22. I do things at my own pace.
23. I am reserved.
24. I would rather please myself than others.
25. I dislike routine.
26. I am always worried about something.
27. I do things at the last minute.
28. I get upset easily.
29. I like order.
30. I am highly theoretical.
31. I am more interested in intellectual pursuits than anything else.
32. I am not sympathetic to the feelings of everyone.
33. I am attracted to solving complex problems.
34. I am disorganized.
35. I say little.
36. I get stressed out easily.
37. I am unfazed by setbacks in life.
38. I keep my emotions under control.
39. I detach to analyze factors from multiple perspectives.
40. I have many fears.
41. I am more relaxed than stressed.
42. I do the opposite of what is asked.
43. I am usually prepared.
44. I keep in the background.
45. I prefer very structured environments.
46. I tend to be the life of the party.
47. I am unplanned.
48. I put the needs of everyone ahead of my own.
49. I am messy.
50. I will do anything for others.
51. I find theoretical physics interesting.
52. My own happiness and success are more important than the happiness and success of others.
53. I am scientific.
54. I am often late.
55. My thoughtfulness and charitable nature are my foundation.

Practice Test for Air Force OTS Applicants

CHAPTER 13

The Air Force Officer Qualifying Test (AFOQT) 1

The AFOQT is required for all applicants for Air Force Officer Training School (OTS). The AFOQT consists of 12 timed subtests, with a total of 480 questions. However, on this practice test we have not included the 220-question self-description inventory subtest (see Chapter 12). The self-description inventory subtest has no right or wrong answers and is not used in calculating any of the AFOQT composite scores, nor is it used in the OTS selection process.

This practice test consists of 11 subtests with a total of 250 questions. Subtest scores are combined to generate one or more of the five composite scores used to help predict success in certain types of Air Force commissioned officer training programs.

Answer Sheet for Practice Test 1

Subtest 1–Verbal Analogies

1 Ⓐ Ⓑ Ⓒ Ⓓ Ⓔ	8 Ⓐ Ⓑ Ⓒ Ⓓ Ⓔ	14 Ⓐ Ⓑ Ⓒ Ⓓ Ⓔ	20 Ⓐ Ⓑ Ⓒ Ⓓ Ⓔ
2 Ⓐ Ⓑ Ⓒ Ⓓ Ⓔ	9 Ⓐ Ⓑ Ⓒ Ⓓ Ⓔ	15 Ⓐ Ⓑ Ⓒ Ⓓ Ⓔ	21 Ⓐ Ⓑ Ⓒ Ⓓ Ⓔ
3 Ⓐ Ⓑ Ⓒ Ⓓ Ⓔ	10 Ⓐ Ⓑ Ⓒ Ⓓ Ⓔ	16 Ⓐ Ⓑ Ⓒ Ⓓ Ⓔ	22 Ⓐ Ⓑ Ⓒ Ⓓ Ⓔ
4 Ⓐ Ⓑ Ⓒ Ⓓ Ⓔ	11 Ⓐ Ⓑ Ⓒ Ⓓ Ⓔ	17 Ⓐ Ⓑ Ⓒ Ⓓ Ⓔ	23 Ⓐ Ⓑ Ⓒ Ⓓ Ⓔ
5 Ⓐ Ⓑ Ⓒ Ⓓ Ⓔ	12 Ⓐ Ⓑ Ⓒ Ⓓ Ⓔ	18 Ⓐ Ⓑ Ⓒ Ⓓ Ⓔ	24 Ⓐ Ⓑ Ⓒ Ⓓ Ⓔ
6 Ⓐ Ⓑ Ⓒ Ⓓ Ⓔ	13 Ⓐ Ⓑ Ⓒ Ⓓ Ⓔ	19 Ⓐ Ⓑ Ⓒ Ⓓ Ⓔ	25 Ⓐ Ⓑ Ⓒ Ⓓ Ⓔ
7 Ⓐ Ⓑ Ⓒ Ⓓ Ⓔ			

Subtest 2–Arithmetic Reasoning

1 Ⓐ Ⓑ Ⓒ Ⓓ Ⓔ	8 Ⓐ Ⓑ Ⓒ Ⓓ Ⓔ	14 Ⓐ Ⓑ Ⓒ Ⓓ Ⓔ	20 Ⓐ Ⓑ Ⓒ Ⓓ Ⓔ
2 Ⓐ Ⓑ Ⓒ Ⓓ Ⓔ	9 Ⓐ Ⓑ Ⓒ Ⓓ Ⓔ	15 Ⓐ Ⓑ Ⓒ Ⓓ Ⓔ	21 Ⓐ Ⓑ Ⓒ Ⓓ Ⓔ
3 Ⓐ Ⓑ Ⓒ Ⓓ Ⓔ	10 Ⓐ Ⓑ Ⓒ Ⓓ Ⓔ	16 Ⓐ Ⓑ Ⓒ Ⓓ Ⓔ	22 Ⓐ Ⓑ Ⓒ Ⓓ Ⓔ
4 Ⓐ Ⓑ Ⓒ Ⓓ Ⓔ	11 Ⓐ Ⓑ Ⓒ Ⓓ Ⓔ	17 Ⓐ Ⓑ Ⓒ Ⓓ Ⓔ	23 Ⓐ Ⓑ Ⓒ Ⓓ Ⓔ
5 Ⓐ Ⓑ Ⓒ Ⓓ Ⓔ	12 Ⓐ Ⓑ Ⓒ Ⓓ Ⓔ	18 Ⓐ Ⓑ Ⓒ Ⓓ Ⓔ	24 Ⓐ Ⓑ Ⓒ Ⓓ Ⓔ
6 Ⓐ Ⓑ Ⓒ Ⓓ Ⓔ	13 Ⓐ Ⓑ Ⓒ Ⓓ Ⓔ	19 Ⓐ Ⓑ Ⓒ Ⓓ Ⓔ	25 Ⓐ Ⓑ Ⓒ Ⓓ Ⓔ
7 Ⓐ Ⓑ Ⓒ Ⓓ Ⓔ			

Subtest 3–Word Knowledge

1 Ⓐ Ⓑ Ⓒ Ⓓ Ⓔ	8 Ⓐ Ⓑ Ⓒ Ⓓ Ⓔ	14 Ⓐ Ⓑ Ⓒ Ⓓ Ⓔ	20 Ⓐ Ⓑ Ⓒ Ⓓ Ⓔ
2 Ⓐ Ⓑ Ⓒ Ⓓ Ⓔ	9 Ⓐ Ⓑ Ⓒ Ⓓ Ⓔ	15 Ⓐ Ⓑ Ⓒ Ⓓ Ⓔ	21 Ⓐ Ⓑ Ⓒ Ⓓ Ⓔ
3 Ⓐ Ⓑ Ⓒ Ⓓ Ⓔ	10 Ⓐ Ⓑ Ⓒ Ⓓ Ⓔ	16 Ⓐ Ⓑ Ⓒ Ⓓ Ⓔ	22 Ⓐ Ⓑ Ⓒ Ⓓ Ⓔ
4 Ⓐ Ⓑ Ⓒ Ⓓ Ⓔ	11 Ⓐ Ⓑ Ⓒ Ⓓ Ⓔ	17 Ⓐ Ⓑ Ⓒ Ⓓ Ⓔ	23 Ⓐ Ⓑ Ⓒ Ⓓ Ⓔ
5 Ⓐ Ⓑ Ⓒ Ⓓ Ⓔ	12 Ⓐ Ⓑ Ⓒ Ⓓ Ⓔ	18 Ⓐ Ⓑ Ⓒ Ⓓ Ⓔ	24 Ⓐ Ⓑ Ⓒ Ⓓ Ⓔ
6 Ⓐ Ⓑ Ⓒ Ⓓ Ⓔ	13 Ⓐ Ⓑ Ⓒ Ⓓ Ⓔ	19 Ⓐ Ⓑ Ⓒ Ⓓ Ⓔ	25 Ⓐ Ⓑ Ⓒ Ⓓ Ⓔ
7 Ⓐ Ⓑ Ⓒ Ⓓ Ⓔ			

Subtest 4—Mathematics Knowledge

1 Ⓐ Ⓑ Ⓒ Ⓓ Ⓔ
2 Ⓐ Ⓑ Ⓒ Ⓓ Ⓔ
3 Ⓐ Ⓑ Ⓒ Ⓓ Ⓔ
4 Ⓐ Ⓑ Ⓒ Ⓓ Ⓔ
5 Ⓐ Ⓑ Ⓒ Ⓓ Ⓔ
6 Ⓐ Ⓑ Ⓒ Ⓓ Ⓔ
7 Ⓐ Ⓑ Ⓒ Ⓓ Ⓔ
8 Ⓐ Ⓑ Ⓒ Ⓓ Ⓔ
9 Ⓐ Ⓑ Ⓒ Ⓓ Ⓔ
10 Ⓐ Ⓑ Ⓒ Ⓓ Ⓔ
11 Ⓐ Ⓑ Ⓒ Ⓓ Ⓔ
12 Ⓐ Ⓑ Ⓒ Ⓓ Ⓔ
13 Ⓐ Ⓑ Ⓒ Ⓓ Ⓔ
14 Ⓐ Ⓑ Ⓒ Ⓓ Ⓔ
15 Ⓐ Ⓑ Ⓒ Ⓓ Ⓔ
16 Ⓐ Ⓑ Ⓒ Ⓓ Ⓔ
17 Ⓐ Ⓑ Ⓒ Ⓓ Ⓔ
18 Ⓐ Ⓑ Ⓒ Ⓓ Ⓔ
19 Ⓐ Ⓑ Ⓒ Ⓓ Ⓔ
20 Ⓐ Ⓑ Ⓒ Ⓓ Ⓔ
21 Ⓐ Ⓑ Ⓒ Ⓓ Ⓔ
22 Ⓐ Ⓑ Ⓒ Ⓓ Ⓔ
23 Ⓐ Ⓑ Ⓒ Ⓓ Ⓔ
24 Ⓐ Ⓑ Ⓒ Ⓓ Ⓔ
25 Ⓐ Ⓑ Ⓒ Ⓓ Ⓔ

Subtest 5—Instrument Comprehension

1 Ⓐ Ⓑ Ⓒ Ⓓ
2 Ⓐ Ⓑ Ⓒ Ⓓ
3 Ⓐ Ⓑ Ⓒ Ⓓ
4 Ⓐ Ⓑ Ⓒ Ⓓ
5 Ⓐ Ⓑ Ⓒ Ⓓ
6 Ⓐ Ⓑ Ⓒ Ⓓ
7 Ⓐ Ⓑ Ⓒ Ⓓ
8 Ⓐ Ⓑ Ⓒ Ⓓ
9 Ⓐ Ⓑ Ⓒ Ⓓ
10 Ⓐ Ⓑ Ⓒ Ⓓ
11 Ⓐ Ⓑ Ⓒ Ⓓ
12 Ⓐ Ⓑ Ⓒ Ⓓ
13 Ⓐ Ⓑ Ⓒ Ⓓ
14 Ⓐ Ⓑ Ⓒ Ⓓ
15 Ⓐ Ⓑ Ⓒ Ⓓ
16 Ⓐ Ⓑ Ⓒ Ⓓ
17 Ⓐ Ⓑ Ⓒ Ⓓ
18 Ⓐ Ⓑ Ⓒ Ⓓ
19 Ⓐ Ⓑ Ⓒ Ⓓ
20 Ⓐ Ⓑ Ⓒ Ⓓ

Subtest 6—Block Counting

1 Ⓐ Ⓑ Ⓒ Ⓓ Ⓔ
2 Ⓐ Ⓑ Ⓒ Ⓓ Ⓔ
3 Ⓐ Ⓑ Ⓒ Ⓓ Ⓔ
4 Ⓐ Ⓑ Ⓒ Ⓓ Ⓔ
5 Ⓐ Ⓑ Ⓒ Ⓓ Ⓔ
6 Ⓐ Ⓑ Ⓒ Ⓓ Ⓔ
7 Ⓐ Ⓑ Ⓒ Ⓓ Ⓔ
8 Ⓐ Ⓑ Ⓒ Ⓓ Ⓔ
9 Ⓐ Ⓑ Ⓒ Ⓓ Ⓔ
10 Ⓐ Ⓑ Ⓒ Ⓓ Ⓔ
11 Ⓐ Ⓑ Ⓒ Ⓓ Ⓔ
12 Ⓐ Ⓑ Ⓒ Ⓓ Ⓔ
13 Ⓐ Ⓑ Ⓒ Ⓓ Ⓔ
14 Ⓐ Ⓑ Ⓒ Ⓓ Ⓔ
15 Ⓐ Ⓑ Ⓒ Ⓓ Ⓔ
16 Ⓐ Ⓑ Ⓒ Ⓓ Ⓔ
17 Ⓐ Ⓑ Ⓒ Ⓓ Ⓔ
18 Ⓐ Ⓑ Ⓒ Ⓓ Ⓔ
19 Ⓐ Ⓑ Ⓒ Ⓓ Ⓔ
20 Ⓐ Ⓑ Ⓒ Ⓓ Ⓔ

Subtest 7–Table Reading

1 Ⓐ Ⓑ Ⓒ Ⓓ Ⓔ
2 Ⓐ Ⓑ Ⓒ Ⓓ Ⓔ
3 Ⓐ Ⓑ Ⓒ Ⓓ Ⓔ
4 Ⓐ Ⓑ Ⓒ Ⓓ Ⓔ
5 Ⓐ Ⓑ Ⓒ Ⓓ Ⓔ
6 Ⓐ Ⓑ Ⓒ Ⓓ Ⓔ
7 Ⓐ Ⓑ Ⓒ Ⓓ Ⓔ
8 Ⓐ Ⓑ Ⓒ Ⓓ Ⓔ
9 Ⓐ Ⓑ Ⓒ Ⓓ Ⓔ
10 Ⓐ Ⓑ Ⓒ Ⓓ Ⓔ
11 Ⓐ Ⓑ Ⓒ Ⓓ Ⓔ
12 Ⓐ Ⓑ Ⓒ Ⓓ Ⓔ
13 Ⓐ Ⓑ Ⓒ Ⓓ Ⓔ
14 Ⓐ Ⓑ Ⓒ Ⓓ Ⓔ
15 Ⓐ Ⓑ Ⓒ Ⓓ Ⓔ
16 Ⓐ Ⓑ Ⓒ Ⓓ Ⓔ
17 Ⓐ Ⓑ Ⓒ Ⓓ Ⓔ
18 Ⓐ Ⓑ Ⓒ Ⓓ Ⓔ
19 Ⓐ Ⓑ Ⓒ Ⓓ Ⓔ
20 Ⓐ Ⓑ Ⓒ Ⓓ Ⓔ
21 Ⓐ Ⓑ Ⓒ Ⓓ Ⓔ
22 Ⓐ Ⓑ Ⓒ Ⓓ Ⓔ
23 Ⓐ Ⓑ Ⓒ Ⓓ Ⓔ
24 Ⓐ Ⓑ Ⓒ Ⓓ Ⓔ
25 Ⓐ Ⓑ Ⓒ Ⓓ Ⓔ
26 Ⓐ Ⓑ Ⓒ Ⓓ Ⓔ
27 Ⓐ Ⓑ Ⓒ Ⓓ Ⓔ
28 Ⓐ Ⓑ Ⓒ Ⓓ Ⓔ
29 Ⓐ Ⓑ Ⓒ Ⓓ Ⓔ
30 Ⓐ Ⓑ Ⓒ Ⓓ Ⓔ
31 Ⓐ Ⓑ Ⓒ Ⓓ Ⓔ
32 Ⓐ Ⓑ Ⓒ Ⓓ Ⓔ
33 Ⓐ Ⓑ Ⓒ Ⓓ Ⓔ
34 Ⓐ Ⓑ Ⓒ Ⓓ Ⓔ
35 Ⓐ Ⓑ Ⓒ Ⓓ Ⓔ
36 Ⓐ Ⓑ Ⓒ Ⓓ Ⓔ
37 Ⓐ Ⓑ Ⓒ Ⓓ Ⓔ
38 Ⓐ Ⓑ Ⓒ Ⓓ Ⓔ
39 Ⓐ Ⓑ Ⓒ Ⓓ Ⓔ
40 Ⓐ Ⓑ Ⓒ Ⓓ Ⓔ

Subtest 8–Aviation Information

1 Ⓐ Ⓑ Ⓒ Ⓓ Ⓔ
2 Ⓐ Ⓑ Ⓒ Ⓓ Ⓔ
3 Ⓐ Ⓑ Ⓒ Ⓓ Ⓔ
4 Ⓐ Ⓑ Ⓒ Ⓓ Ⓔ
5 Ⓐ Ⓑ Ⓒ Ⓓ Ⓔ
6 Ⓐ Ⓑ Ⓒ Ⓓ Ⓔ
7 Ⓐ Ⓑ Ⓒ Ⓓ Ⓔ
8 Ⓐ Ⓑ Ⓒ Ⓓ Ⓔ
9 Ⓐ Ⓑ Ⓒ Ⓓ Ⓔ
10 Ⓐ Ⓑ Ⓒ Ⓓ Ⓔ
11 Ⓐ Ⓑ Ⓒ Ⓓ Ⓔ
12 Ⓐ Ⓑ Ⓒ Ⓓ Ⓔ
13 Ⓐ Ⓑ Ⓒ Ⓓ Ⓔ
14 Ⓐ Ⓑ Ⓒ Ⓓ Ⓔ
15 Ⓐ Ⓑ Ⓒ Ⓓ Ⓔ
16 Ⓐ Ⓑ Ⓒ Ⓓ Ⓔ
17 Ⓐ Ⓑ Ⓒ Ⓓ Ⓔ
18 Ⓐ Ⓑ Ⓒ Ⓓ Ⓔ
19 Ⓐ Ⓑ Ⓒ Ⓓ Ⓔ
20 Ⓐ Ⓑ Ⓒ Ⓓ Ⓔ

Subtest 9–Rotated Blocks

1 Ⓐ Ⓑ Ⓒ Ⓓ Ⓔ
2 Ⓐ Ⓑ Ⓒ Ⓓ Ⓔ
3 Ⓐ Ⓑ Ⓒ Ⓓ Ⓔ
4 Ⓐ Ⓑ Ⓒ Ⓓ Ⓔ
5 Ⓐ Ⓑ Ⓒ Ⓓ Ⓔ
6 Ⓐ Ⓑ Ⓒ Ⓓ Ⓔ
7 Ⓐ Ⓑ Ⓒ Ⓓ Ⓔ
8 Ⓐ Ⓑ Ⓒ Ⓓ Ⓔ
9 Ⓐ Ⓑ Ⓒ Ⓓ Ⓔ
10 Ⓐ Ⓑ Ⓒ Ⓓ Ⓔ
11 Ⓐ Ⓑ Ⓒ Ⓓ Ⓔ
12 Ⓐ Ⓑ Ⓒ Ⓓ Ⓔ
13 Ⓐ Ⓑ Ⓒ Ⓓ Ⓔ
14 Ⓐ Ⓑ Ⓒ Ⓓ Ⓔ
15 Ⓐ Ⓑ Ⓒ Ⓓ Ⓔ

Subtest 10–General Science

1 Ⓐ Ⓑ Ⓒ Ⓓ Ⓔ	6 Ⓐ Ⓑ Ⓒ Ⓓ Ⓔ	11 Ⓐ Ⓑ Ⓒ Ⓓ Ⓔ	16 Ⓐ Ⓑ Ⓒ Ⓓ Ⓔ
2 Ⓐ Ⓑ Ⓒ Ⓓ Ⓔ	7 Ⓐ Ⓑ Ⓒ Ⓓ Ⓔ	12 Ⓐ Ⓑ Ⓒ Ⓓ Ⓔ	17 Ⓐ Ⓑ Ⓒ Ⓓ Ⓔ
3 Ⓐ Ⓑ Ⓒ Ⓓ Ⓔ	8 Ⓐ Ⓑ Ⓒ Ⓓ Ⓔ	13 Ⓐ Ⓑ Ⓒ Ⓓ Ⓔ	18 Ⓐ Ⓑ Ⓒ Ⓓ Ⓔ
4 Ⓐ Ⓑ Ⓒ Ⓓ Ⓔ	9 Ⓐ Ⓑ Ⓒ Ⓓ Ⓔ	14 Ⓐ Ⓑ Ⓒ Ⓓ Ⓔ	19 Ⓐ Ⓑ Ⓒ Ⓓ Ⓔ
5 Ⓐ Ⓑ Ⓒ Ⓓ Ⓔ	10 Ⓐ Ⓑ Ⓒ Ⓓ Ⓔ	15 Ⓐ Ⓑ Ⓒ Ⓓ Ⓔ	20 Ⓐ Ⓑ Ⓒ Ⓓ Ⓔ

Subtest 11–Hidden Figures

1 Ⓐ Ⓑ Ⓒ Ⓓ Ⓔ	5 Ⓐ Ⓑ Ⓒ Ⓓ Ⓔ	9 Ⓐ Ⓑ Ⓒ Ⓓ Ⓔ	13 Ⓐ Ⓑ Ⓒ Ⓓ Ⓔ
2 Ⓐ Ⓑ Ⓒ Ⓓ Ⓔ	6 Ⓐ Ⓑ Ⓒ Ⓓ Ⓔ	10 Ⓐ Ⓑ Ⓒ Ⓓ Ⓔ	14 Ⓐ Ⓑ Ⓒ Ⓓ Ⓔ
3 Ⓐ Ⓑ Ⓒ Ⓓ Ⓔ	7 Ⓐ Ⓑ Ⓒ Ⓓ Ⓔ	11 Ⓐ Ⓑ Ⓒ Ⓓ Ⓔ	15 Ⓐ Ⓑ Ⓒ Ⓓ Ⓔ
4 Ⓐ Ⓑ Ⓒ Ⓓ Ⓔ	8 Ⓐ Ⓑ Ⓒ Ⓓ Ⓔ	12 Ⓐ Ⓑ Ⓒ Ⓓ Ⓔ	

Subtest 1—Verbal Analogies

Directions: This subtest measures ability to reason and see relationships between words. The subtest is comprised of 25 questions that must be answered in 8 minutes. Choose the answer that best completes the analogy given at the beginning of the question.

1. BOOK is to CHAPTER as BUILDING is to
   (A) elevator
   (B) lobby
   (C) roof
   (D) story
   (E) wing

2. RAILS are to TRAIN as HIGHWAY is to
   (A) shoulder
   (B) road
   (C) automobile
   (D) tires
   (E) tree

3. CARROT is to VEGETABLE as
   (A) dogwood is to oak
   (B) foot is to paw
   (C) pepper is to spice
   (D) sheep is to lamb
   (E) veal is to beef

4. FACT is to BIOGRAPHY as FICTION is to
   (A) book
   (B) lie
   (C) manuscript
   (D) novel
   (E) DVD

5. CONCAVE is to CONVEX as
   (A) cavity is to mound
   (B) hill is to hole
   (C) oval is to oblong
   (D) round is to pointed
   (E) square is to round

6. STILLNESS is to SOUND as DARKNESS is to
   (A) night
   (B) light
   (C) quiet
   (D) pink
   (E) car

7. GOWN is to GARMENT as GASOLINE is to
   (A) coolant
   (B) fuel
   (C) grease
   (D) lubricant
   (E) oil

8. BIRD is to NEST as
   (A) dog is to doghouse
   (B) squirrel is to tree
   (C) beaver is to dam
   (D) cat is to litter box
   (E) book is to library

9. DOCTOR is to HOSPITAL as PROFESSOR is to
   (A) jail
   (B) high school
   (C) store
   (D) farm
   (E) college

10. CUB is to BEAR as
    (A) piano is to orchestra
    (B) puppy is to dog
    (C) cat is to kitten
    (D) eagle is to bird
    (E) fork is to spoon

11. HYPER is to HYPO as
    (A) actual is to theoretical
    (B) diastolic is to systolic
    (C) over is to under
    (D) small is to large
    (E) stale is to fresh

12. EXCERPT is to NOVEL as

(A) critique is to play
(B) review is to manuscript
(C) swatch is to cloth
(D) foreword is to preface
(E) recital is to performance

13. IMMIGRATION is to EMIGRATION as

(A) arrival is to departure
(B) flight is to voyage
(C) legal is to illegal
(D) migration is to travel
(E) passport is to visa

14. PERSPICACIOUS is to INSIGHT as CHURLISH is to

(A) enmity
(B) ardent
(C) rapacious
(D) magnanimity
(E) wealthy

15. OCTAGON is to SQUARE as HEXAGON is to

(A) cube
(B) polygon
(C) pyramid
(D) rectangle
(E) triangle

16. SNAKE is to VERTEBRATE as PENGUIN is to

(A) dolphin
(B) bird
(C) backbone
(D) eagle
(E) fish

17. PERJURE is to STATE as

(A) abandon is to desert
(B) concentrate is to focus
(C) marvel is to wonder
(D) rob is to steal
(E) trespass is to enter

18. ACTORS are to TROUPE as PLOTTERS are to

(A) government
(B) cast
(C) directors
(D) cabal
(E) professors

19. TELL is to TOLD as

(A) ride is to rode
(B) slay is to slew
(C) sink is to sank
(D) weave is to wove
(E) weep is to wept

20. LION is to CARNIVORE as

(A) man is to vegetarian
(B) ape is to monkey
(C) lizard is to mammal
(D) buffalo is to omnivore
(E) shark is to scavenger

21. PRATTLE is to SPEAK as PROMENADE is to

(A) accept
(B) stop
(C) walk
(D) shout
(E) reject

22. SHEEP is to LAMB as HORSE is to

(A) colt
(B) doe
(C) fawn
(D) mare
(E) ram

23. CURTSY is to RESPECT as

(A) Assume is to disguise
(B) bestir is to deferment
(C) fret is to contentment
(D) forgo is to diversion
(E) fidget is to uneasiness

24. IGNORE is to OVERLOOK as
    - (A) agree is to consent
    - (B) attach is to separate
    - (C) climb is to walk
    - (D) dull is to sharpen
    - (E) learn is to remember

25. FREQUENTLY is to SELDOM as
    - (A) always is to never
    - (B) everybody is to everyone
    - (C) generally is to usually
    - (D) occasionally is to constantly
    - (E) sorrow is to sympathy

Subtest 2—Arithmetic Reasoning

Directions: This subtest measures general mathematical reasoning. The questions are designed to determine one's ability to arrive at solutions to math word problems. The subtest consists of 25 questions that must be answered in 29 minutes.

1. Susan can paint a room in 6 hours, while Tom can paint the same room in 5 hours. Working together, how long will it take them to paint the room?
    - (A) 2.73 hours
    - (B) 2.90 hours
    - (C) 3.43 hours
    - (D) 3.54 hours
    - (E) 4.01 hours

2. An athlete jogs 15 laps around a circular track. If the total distance jogged is 3 kilometers, what is the distance around the track?
    - (A) 0.2 meters
    - (B) 2 meters
    - (C) 20 meters
    - (D) 200 meters
    - (E) 2000 meters

3. Yolanda invested $500 in an investment account and received $650 after three years. How much was her annual interest rate?
    - (A) 6%
    - (B) 8%
    - (C) 10%
    - (D) 12%
    - (E) 14%

4. A crate containing a tool weighs 12 pounds. If the tool weighs 9 pounds, 9 ounces, how much does the crate weigh?
    - (A) 2 pounds, 7 ounces
    - (B) 2 pounds, 9 ounces
    - (C) 3 pounds, 3 ounces
    - (D) 3 pounds, 7 ounces
    - (E) 3 pounds, 9 ounces

5. A refrigerator costs $400 to purchase outright, or it can be rented for a non-refundable deposit of $50 and monthly payments of $25. After how many months would the cost of rental equal the purchase cost?
    - (A) 10 months
    - (B) 12 months
    - (C) 14 months
    - (D) 16 months
    - (E) 18 months

6. In order to check on a shipment of 500 articles, a sampling of 50 articles was carefully inspected. Of the sample, 4 articles were found to be defective. On this basis, what is the probable percentage of defective articles in the original shipment?
    - (A) 8%
    - (B) 4%
    - (C) 0.8%
    - (D) 0.4%
    - (E) .04%

7. Gravel is mixed with cement at a ratio of 5 parts of cement to 1 part of gravel. How many pounds of cement are there in 48 pounds of this mixture?

   (A) 20 pounds
   (B) 30 pounds
   (C) 40 pounds
   (D) 50 pounds
   (E) 60 pounds

8. Assume that it takes an average of three man-hours to stack one ton of a particular item. In order to stack 36 tons in 6 hours, the number of persons required is ___________.

   (A) 9
   (B) 12
   (C) 13
   (D) 18
   (E) 21

9. A gas station sets its gas price by raising the wholesale cost by 40 percent and adding $0.20. What must the wholesale price of gas be if the station is selling the gas for $3.00 per gallon?

   (A) $1.50 per gallon
   (B) $2.00 per gallon
   (C) $1.75 per gallon
   (D) $2.75 per gallon
   (E) $2.85 per gallon

10. A room measuring 15 feet wide, 25 feet long, and 12 feet high is scheduled to be painted. If there are two windows in the room, each 7 feet by 5 feet, and a glass door, 6 feet by 4 feet, then the area of wall space to be painted measures ___________.

    (A) 842 square feet
    (B) 866 square feet
    (C) 901 square feet
    (D) 925 square feet
    (E) 4,406 square feet

11. Captain Taggarty scored an average of 54 points per flight on the bombing range in his first 5 flights. Lieutenant Thompson scored an average of 59 points per flight on the bombing range during her first 6 flights. What is the average of points scored in all 11 flights?

    (A) 54.3
    (B) 55.4
    (C) 56.7
    (D) 57.3
    (E) 58.4

12. The price of a $100 item after successive discounts of 10 percent and 15percent is ___________.

    (A) $75.00
    (B) $75.50
    (C) $76.00
    (D) $76.50
    (E) $77.00

13. In 2001, the death rate from heart attacks in the U.S. was 174.4 per 100,000. This was a $31\frac{3}{4}$ percent decrease from 1998. What was the death rate per 100,000 in 1998?

    (A) 150.3
    (B) 200.45
    (C) 255.53
    (D) 300.4
    (E) 310.8

14. On a scaled drawing of an office building floor, $\frac{1}{2}$ inch represents three feet of actual floor dimension. A floor that is actually 75 feet wide and 132 feet long would have which of the following dimensions on the scaled drawing?

    (A) 12.5 inches wide and 22 inches long
    (B) 17 inches wide and 32 inches long
    (C) 25 inches wide and 44 inches long
    (D) 29.5 inches wide and 52 inches long
    (E) none of these

15. The radius of a circle is increased by 5 inches. This increases its area by 155π square inches. What is the original radius of the circle?

    (A) 13 inches
    (B) 15 inches
    (C) 17 inches
    (D) 19 inches
    (E) 20 inches

16. If there are red, green, and yellow marbles in a jar and 20 percent of these marbles are either red or green, what are the chances of blindly picking a yellow marble out of the jar?

    (A) 1 out of 3
    (B) 1 out of 5
    (C) 2 out of 3
    (D) 2 out of 5
    (E) 4 out of 5

17. The sum of two numbers is 10. Three times the smaller number plus 5 times the larger number equals 42. What is the larger number?

    (A) 4
    (B) 5
    (C) 6
    (D) 7
    (E) 9

18. A passenger plane can carry two tons of cargo. A freight plane can carry six tons of cargo. If an equal number of both kinds of planes are used to ship 160 tons of cargo and each plane carries its maximum cargo load, how many tons of cargo are shipped on the passenger planes?

    (A) 40 tons
    (B) 60 tons
    (C) 80 tons
    (D) 100 tons
    (E) 120 tons

19. For the first five years, the loan value of a Porsche is determined by the formula $V = -\$4{,}000a + \$50{,}000$, where V is the value and a is the age of the car in years. What is the loan value for a Porsche that is 5 years old?

    (A) \$25,000
    (B) \$30,000
    (C) \$35,000
    (D) \$40,000
    (E) \$45,000

20. Two angles are supplementary. If the first angle measures 60°, what is the measurement of the second angle?

    (A) 30 degrees
    (B) 90 degrees
    (C) 120 degrees
    (D) 360 degrees
    (E) 180 degrees

21. 800 people attended the opening show at the circus. An advanced ticket cost \$14.50 and admission at the door was \$22.00. If \$16,640 was taken in total attendance, how many paid attendance at the door?

    (A) 550
    (B) 672
    (C) 705
    (D) 725
    (E) 735

22. Mack drove his truck to Omaha at the rate of 40 mph. He made the return trip driving at a rate of 45 mph. If it took 30 minutes longer to drive to Omaha than it did to drive home, how long did it take him to drive home?

    (A) 3 hours
    (B) 3 hours and 30 minutes
    (C) 4 hours
    (D) 4 hours and 30 minutes
    (E) 4 hours and 45 minutes

23. A bricklayer charges $8.00 per square foot to lay a patio. How much would it cost for the bricklayer to lay a 12-foot by 16-foot patio?

 (A) $960
 (B) $192
 (C) $224
 (D) $1,536
 (E) $1,392

24. Lizzie must get at least $120,000 for her house in order to break even with the original mortgage. If the real estate agent gets 6 percent of the selling price, then what is the minimum amount that Lizzie should accept for the house in order to pay off the mortgage?

 (A) $115,000
 (B) $125,000
 (C) $130,000
 (D) $135,000
 (E) $140,000

25. A personal trainer earns a 65 percent commission on her training sales. If she sells $530.00 worth of training, how much commission does she make?

 (A) $874.50
 (B) $34.45
 (C) $344.50
 (D) $185.50
 (E) $207.30

Subtest 3—Word Knowledge

Directions: This subtest measures verbal comprehension involving the ability to understand written language. The questions are designed to measure vocabulary ability. The subtest consists of 25 questions that must be answered in 5 minutes. Choose the answer that MOST NEARLY means the same as the capitalized word in the question stem.

1. ADAMANT

 (A) belligerent
 (B) cowardly
 (C) inflexible
 (D) justified
 (E) petty

2. PROPRIETOR

 (A) steady
 (B) owner
 (C) disliked
 (D) renowned
 (E) technician

3. ASSENT

 (A) acquire
 (B) climb
 (C) consent
 (D) emphasize
 (E) participate

4. SUPERFICIAL

 (A) truthful
 (B) managerial
 (C) shallow
 (D) support
 (E) nylon

5. AUTHENTIC
   (A) detailed
   (B) genuine
   (C) literary
   (D) practical
   (E) precious

6. TYPICAL
   (A) exhaustive
   (B) plentiful
   (C) relaxing
   (D) characteristic
   (E) reliant

7. COUNTERACT
   (A) criticize
   (B) conserve
   (C) erode
   (D) neutralize
   (E) retreat

8. PERPENDICULAR
   (A) unskilled
   (B) relaxed
   (C) upright
   (D) mocking
   (E) tempting

9. DILATED
   (A) cleared
   (B) clouded
   (C) decreased
   (D) enlarged
   (E) tightened

10. ATHLETIC
   (A) lazy
   (B) vigorous
   (C) macho
   (D) frail
   (E) revolve

11. FORTNIGHT
   (A) two days
   (B) one week
   (C) two weeks
   (D) one month
   (E) two months

12. FOREMAN
   (A) boss
   (B) owner
   (C) proprietor
   (D) first
   (E) doctor

13. INCIDENTAL
   (A) casual
   (B) eventful
   (C) infrequent
   (D) unexpected
   (E) unnecessary

14. HINDER
   (A) river
   (B) moisten
   (C) prevent
   (D) walk
   (E) prepare

15. NOTORIOUS
   (A) annoying
   (B) condemned
   (C) ill-mannered
   (D) official
   (E) well-known

16. NONPAREIL
   (A) resourceful
   (B) excellent
   (C) trivial
   (D) makeshift
   (E) low

17. MEDIATE
    (A) maverick
    (B) plan
    (C) require
    (D) intercede
    (E) forecast

18. RANKLE
    (A) forbear
    (B) irritate
    (C) chains
    (D) matriculate
    (E) security

19. EAGER
    (A) tedium
    (B) façade
    (C) panicked
    (D) enthusiastic
    (E) argue

20. CONFLAGRATION
    (A) mutilate
    (B) titillate
    (C) fire
    (D) makeshift
    (E) retire

21. SUCCINCT
    (A) concise
    (B) helpful
    (C) important
    (D) misleading
    (E) sweet

22. SYMPTOM
    (A) cure
    (B) disease
    (C) mistake
    (D) sign
    (E) test

23. PANORAMA
    (A) play
    (B) corruption
    (C) digital
    (D) scene
    (E) investment

24. CHRONOMETER
    (A) clock
    (B) pressure gage
    (C) altimeter
    (D) computer
    (E) page

25. PERCOLATE
    (A) brew
    (B) filter
    (C) mix
    (D) prepare
    (E) oxygenate

Subtest 4—Mathematics Knowledge

Directions: This subtest measures functional ability in using learned mathematical relationships. The subtest consists of 25 questions that must be answered in 25 minutes. Choose the answer that best answers the question.

1. Which of the following integers is not a prime number?
    (A) 3
    (B) 5
    (C) 7
    (D) 9
    (E) 11

2. $2x(3xy + y)$ is equivalent to ___________.

(A) $6xy + 2xy$
(B) $6x^2y + 2xy$
(C) $3xy + 2xy$
(D) $3x^2y + xy$
(E) $2x^2y + xy$

3. If $5x + 3y = 29$ and $x - y = 1$, then $x =$ ___________.

(A) 1
(B) 2
(C) 3
(D) 4
(E) 5

4. $(5.37 \times 10^2) \times (2.54 \times 10^5) =$ ___________.

(A) 13.6398×10
(B) 13.6398×10^{10}
(C) 13.6398×10^3
(D) 13.6398×10^7
(E) 13.6398×10^5

5. If x is an odd integer, which one of the following is an even integer?

(A) $2x + 1$
(B) $2x - 1$
(C) $x^2 + x$
(D) $x^2 + x - 1$
(E) none of the above

6. $\frac{1}{2}x - \frac{1}{10} = \frac{1}{5}x + \frac{1}{2}$. $x =$

(A) 2
(B) 4
(C) 6
(D) 8
(E) 10

7. 10^x divided by 10^y equals ___________.

(A) $10\frac{x}{y}$
(B) 10^{xy}
(C) 10^{x+y}
(D) 10^{x-y}
(E) none of the above

8. $(9i + 6)(3i - 7) =$

(A) $27i^2 - 7i$
(B) $-45i - 69$
(C) $18i - 4$
(D) $18i + 4$
(E) none of the above

9. One million may be represented as ___________.

(A) 10^4
(B) 10^5
(C) 10^6
(D) 10^7
(E) 10^8

10. Convert 6.39×10^5 to regular notation.

(A) $(6.39)^5 \times 10$
(B) 639,000
(C) 639.10
(D) 0.000639
(E) none of the above

11. $\left(\frac{2}{5}\right)^2$ equals ___________.

(A) $\frac{1}{2}$
(B) $\frac{4}{5}$
(C) $\frac{2}{25}$
(D) $\frac{3}{25}$
(E) $\frac{4}{25}$

12. $x^2y + xy^2 + 6x + 4 - (4x^2y + 3xy^2 - 2x + 5) =$ ___________.

(A) $2x^2 - 3xy - 5$
(B) $6xy + 4x^2 + 1$
(C) $-3x^2 - 2xy^2 + 8x - 1$
(D) $-2xy + 4xy^2 + 7$
(E) none of the above

13. If $3^n = 9$, what is the value of 4^{n+1}?

(A) 25
(B) 30
(C) 35
(D) 47
(E) 64

14. $-x^2 - x + 30 = 0$

(A) 6, 5
(B) –6, 5
(C) –6, –5
(D) 6, –5
(E) none of the above

15. 10^{-2} is equal to ___________.

(A) 0.001
(B) 0.01
(C) 0.1
(D) 1.0
(E) 100.

16. What does the angle 480° equal in radian measure?

(A) $8\pi/3$
(B) $16\pi/4$
(C) $2\pi/3$
(D) $5\pi/2$
(E) none of the above

17. The expression $\sqrt{28} - \sqrt{7}$ reduces to which of the following?

(A) $\sqrt{4}$
(B) $\sqrt{7}$
(C) $3\sqrt{7}$
(D) $\sqrt{21}$
(E) $-\sqrt{35}$

18. Solve for r: $\pi(r + 5)(r + 5) = 155\pi + \pi r^2$

(A) 8
(B) 10
(C) 13
(D) 15
(E) 18

19. The sum of the angle measures of a pentagon is ___________.

(A) 360°
(B) 540°
(C) 720°
(D) 900°
(E) 1180°

20. Solve for x: $3x + 5(10 - x) = 42$

(A) 2
(B) 3
(C) 4
(D) 5
(E) 6

21. If the ratio of $3x$ to $5y$ is 1:2, what is the ratio of x to y?

(A) $\frac{1}{2}$
(B) $\frac{2}{3}$
(C) $\frac{3}{4}$
(D) $\frac{4}{5}$
(E) $\frac{5}{6}$

22. The distance between two points on a graph whose rectangular coordinates are (2,4) and (5,8) is most nearly ___________.

(A) 4.7
(B) 4.8
(C) 4.9
(D) 5.0
(E) 5.1

23. Which of the following lengths of a side of an equilateral triangle has a perimeter divisible by both 3 and 5?

(A) 3
(B) 4
(C) 5
(D) 6
(E) 7

24. The cube root of 729 is equal to the square of ___________.

(A) 11
(B) 9
(C) 7
(D) 5
(E) 3

25. What is the appropriate number that would follow the last number in the following series of numbers arranged in a logical order?

2 4 12 48 __

(A) 96
(B) 144
(C) 192
(D) 204
(E) 240

Subtest 5—Instrument Comprehension

Directions: This subtest has 20 questions that must be answered in 6 minutes. The questions are designed to measure your ability to determine the position of an airplane in flight from reading instruments showing its compass heading, its amount of climb or dive, and its degree of bank to right or left.

In each item, the left-hand dial is labeled **ARTIFICIAL HORIZON**. On the face of this dial the small aircraft silhouette remains stationary, while the positions of the heavy black line and the black pointer vary with changes in the position of the airplane in which the instrument is located.

How to Read the Artificial Horizon Dial

The heavy black line represents the **HORIZON LINE**. The black pointer shows the degree of **BANK** to the right or left.

Dial 1 shows an airplane neither climbing nor diving, with no bank.

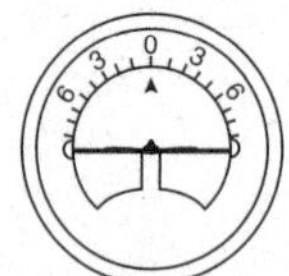

Artificial Horizon

If the airplane is neither climbing nor diving, the horizon line is directly on the silhouette's fuselage. If the airplane has no bank, the black pointer is seen to point to zero.

Dial 2 shows an airplane climbing and banking 45 degrees to the pilot's right.

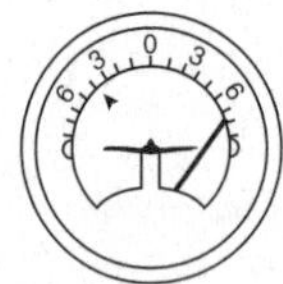

Artificial Horizon

If the airplane is climbing, the fuselage silhouette is seen between the horizon line and the pointer. The greater the amount of climb, the greater the distance between the horizon line and the fuselage silhouette. If the airplane is banked to the pilot's right, the pointer is seen to the left of zero.

Dial 3 shows an airplane diving and banked 45 degrees to the pilot's left.

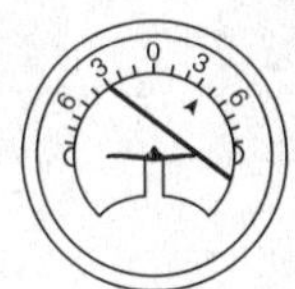

Artificial Horizon

If the airplane is diving, the horizon line is seen between the fuselage silhouette and the pointer. The greater the amount of dive, the greater the distance between the horizon line and the fuselage silhouette. If the airplane is banked to the pilot's left, the pointer is seen to the right of zero.

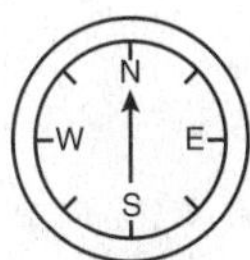

Compass
Dial 4

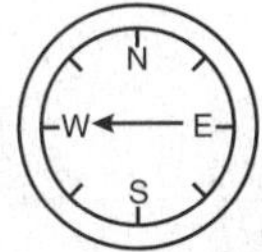

Compass
Dial 5

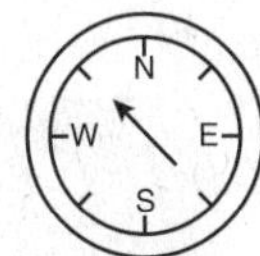

Compass
Dial 6

On each item, the right-hand dial is labeled **COMPASS**. On this dial, the arrow shows the compass direction in which the airplane is headed at the moment.

Dial 4 shows it headed north; dial 5 shows it headed west; and dial 6 shows it headed northwest.

Each item in this test consists of two dials and four silhouettes of airplanes in flight. Your task is to determine which one of the four airplanes is **MOST NEARLY** in the position indicated by the two dials. **YOU ARE ALWAYS LOOKING NORTH AT THE SAME ALTITUDE AS EACH OF THE PLANES. EAST IS ALWAYS TO YOUR RIGHT AS YOU LOOK AT THE PAGE.**

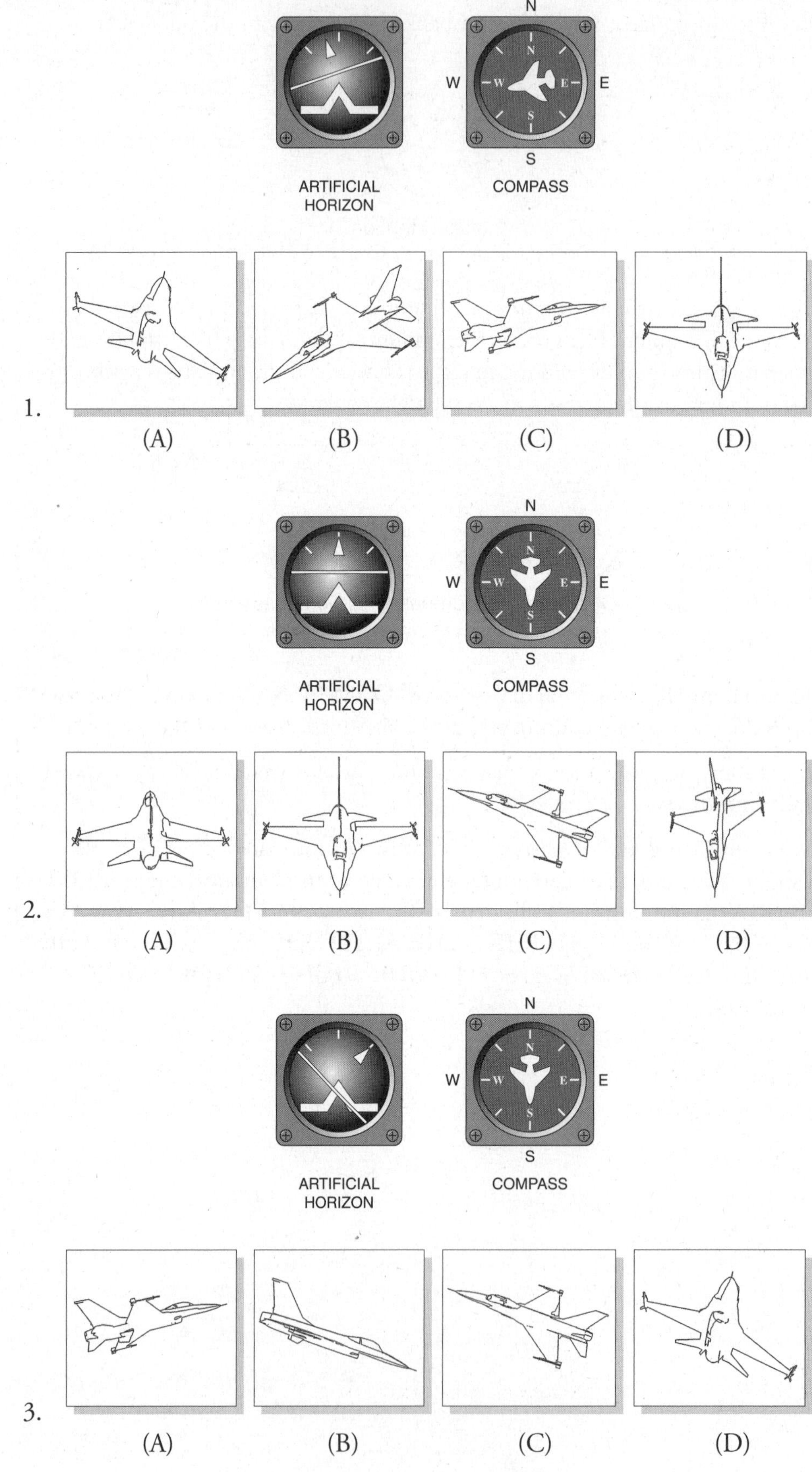
N
W
E
S
ARTIFICIAL HORIZON
COMPASS
1.
(A)
(B)
(C)
(D)
N
W
E
S
ARTIFICIAL HORIZON
COMPASS
2.
(A)
(B)
(C)
(D)
N
W
E
S
ARTIFICIAL HORIZON
COMPASS
3.
(A)
(B)
(C)
(D)

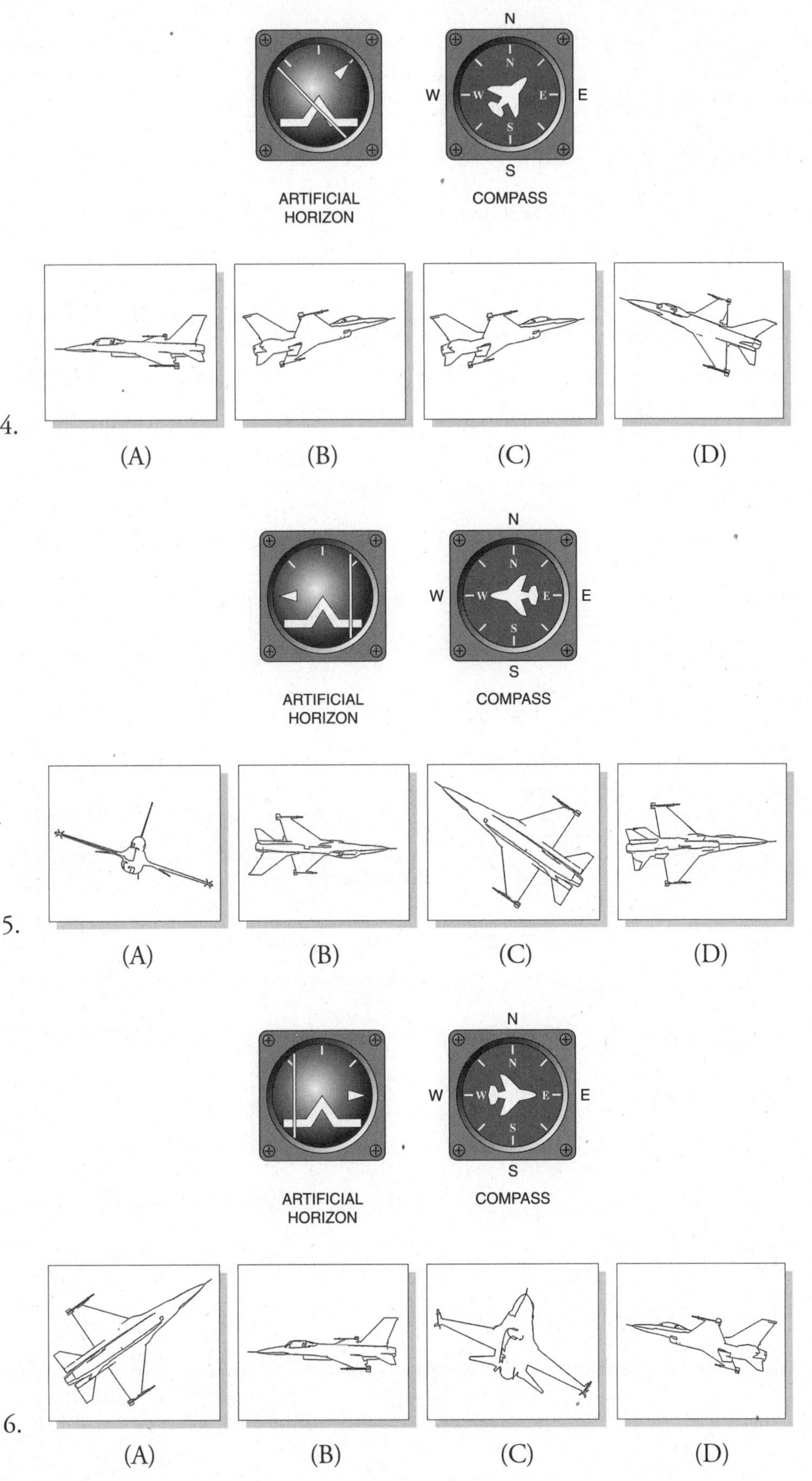
N
W
E
S
ARTIFICIAL HORIZON
COMPASS
4.
(A)
(B)
(C)
(D)
N
W
E
S
ARTIFICIAL HORIZON
COMPASS
5.
(A)
(B)
(C)
(D)
N
W
E
S
ARTIFICIAL HORIZON
COMPASS
6.
(A)
(B)
(C)
(D)

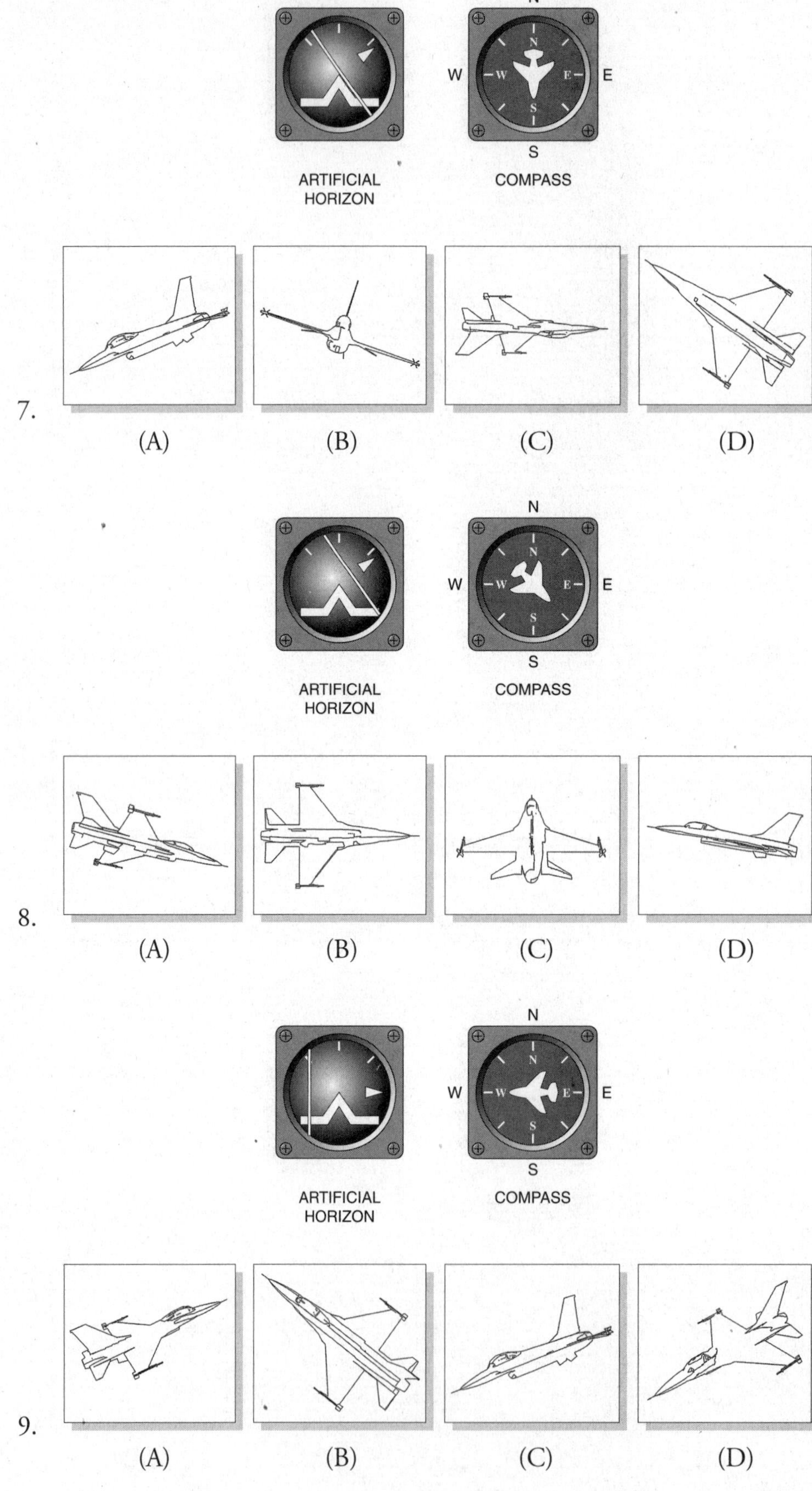
N
W
E
S
ARTIFICIAL HORIZON
COMPASS
7.
(A)
(B)
(C)
(D)
N
W
E
S
ARTIFICIAL HORIZON
COMPASS
8.
(A)
(B)
(C)
(D)
N
W
E
S
ARTIFICIAL HORIZON
COMPASS
9.
(A)
(B)
(C)
(D)

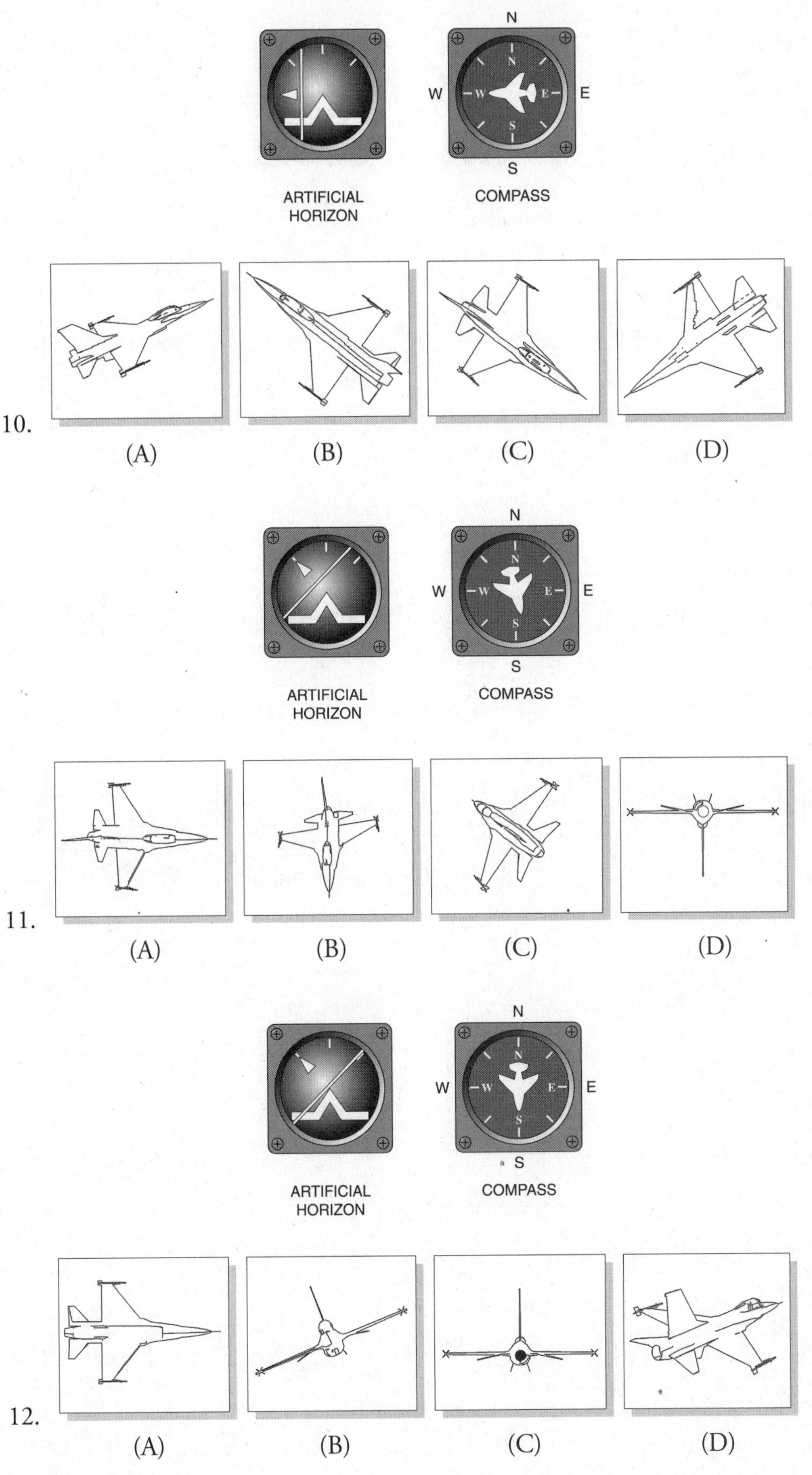
N
W
E
S
ARTIFICIAL HORIZON
COMPASS
10.
(A)
(B)
(C)
(D)
N
W
E
S
ARTIFICIAL HORIZON
COMPASS
11.
(A)
(B)
(C)
(D)
N
W
E
S
ARTIFICIAL HORIZON
COMPASS
12.
(A)
(B)
(C)
(D)

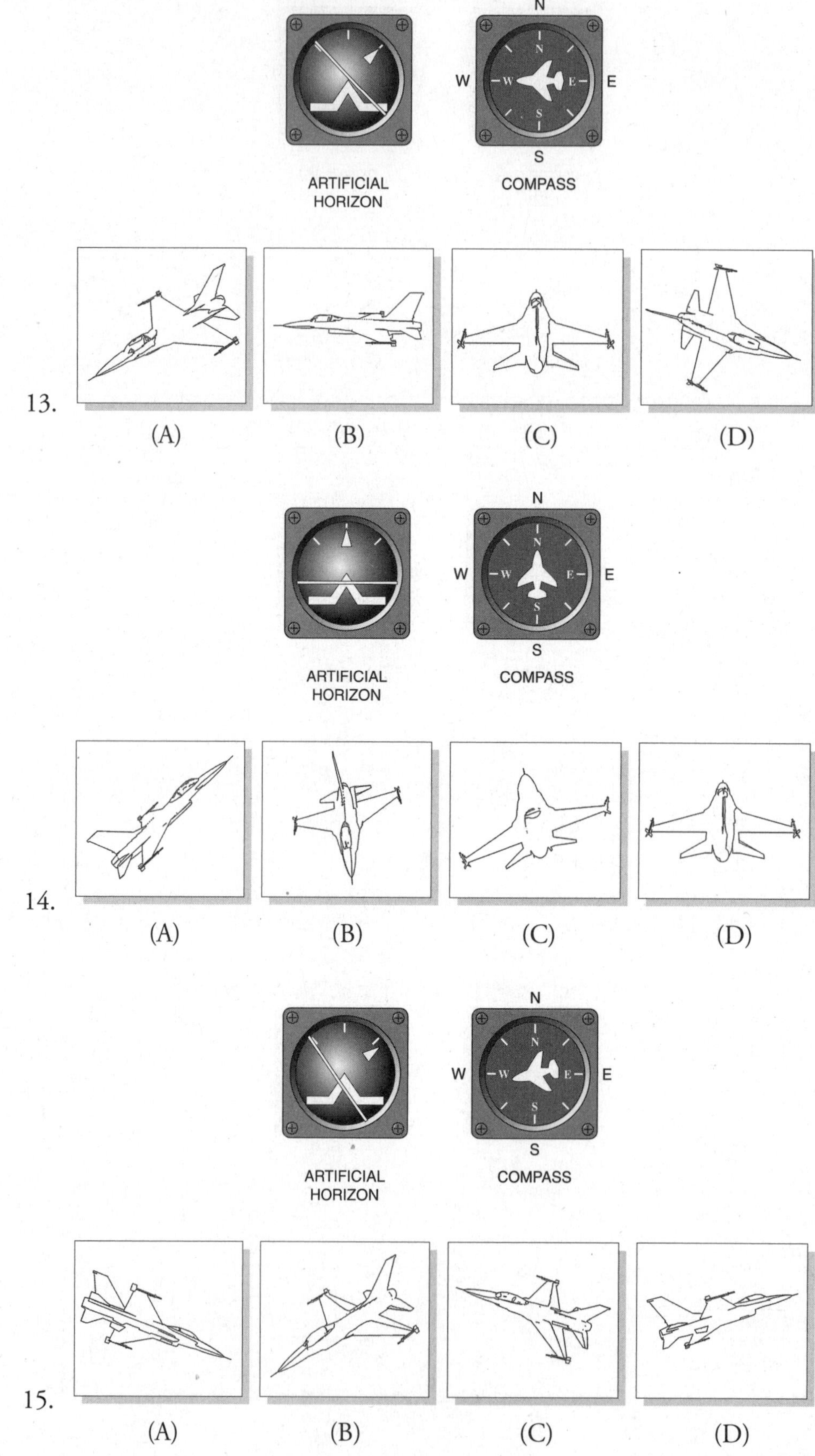
N
W
E
S
ARTIFICIAL HORIZON
COMPASS
13.
(A)
(B)
(C)
(D)
N
W
E
S
ARTIFICIAL HORIZON
COMPASS
14.
(A)
(B)
(C)
(D)
N
W
E
S
ARTIFICIAL HORIZON
COMPASS
15.
(A)
(B)
(C)
(D)

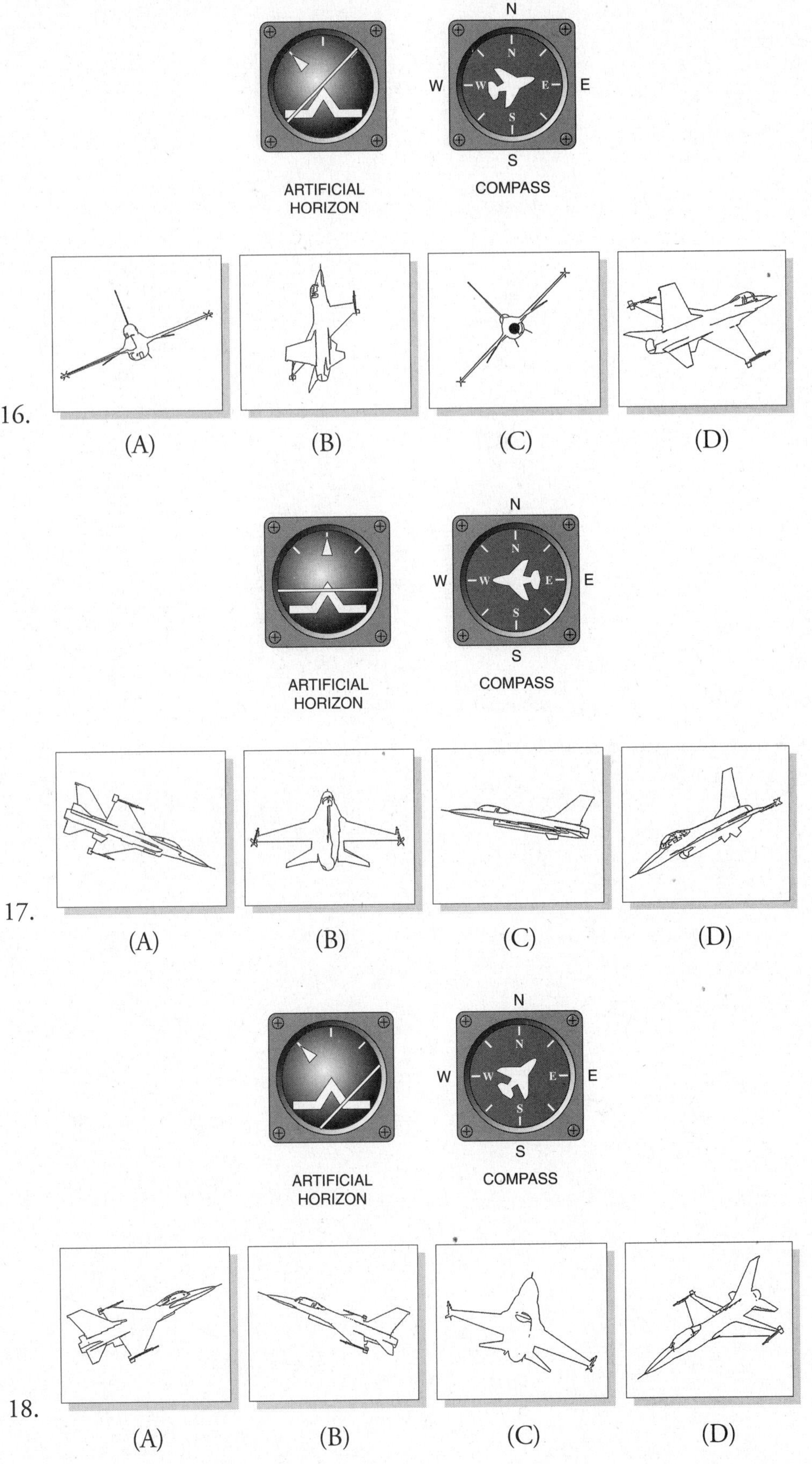
N
W
E
S
N
W
E
S
ARTIFICIAL HORIZON
COMPASS
16.
(A)
(B)
(C)
(D)
N
W
E
S
N
W
E
S
ARTIFICIAL HORIZON
COMPASS
17.
(A)
(B)
(C)
(D)
N
W
E
S
N
W
E
S
ARTIFICIAL HORIZON
COMPASS
18.
(A)
(B)
(C)
(D)

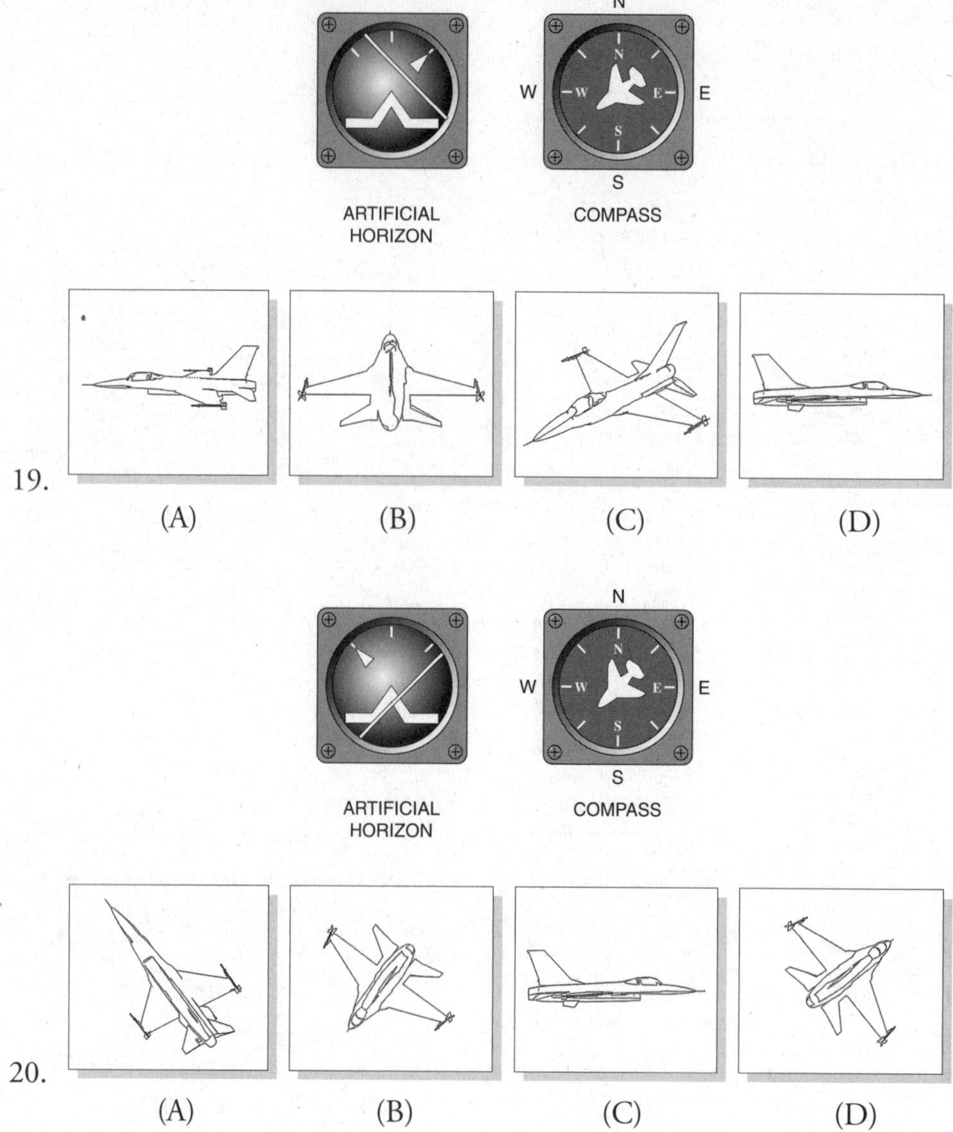
N
W
E
S
ARTIFICIAL HORIZON
COMPASS
19.
(A)
(B)
(C)
(D)
N
W
E
S
ARTIFICIAL HORIZON
COMPASS
20.
(A)
(B)
(C)
(D)

Subtest 6—Block Counting

Directions: This subtest consists of 20 questions that must be answered in 3 minutes. The questions are designed to measure your ability to visualize a three-dimensional pile of blocks and determine how many pieces are touched by certain numbered blocks. All of the blocks in each pile are the same size and shape. A block is considered to touch the numbered block if any part, even a corner or an edge, touches.

Questions 1 through 5 are to be answered based on the figure below.

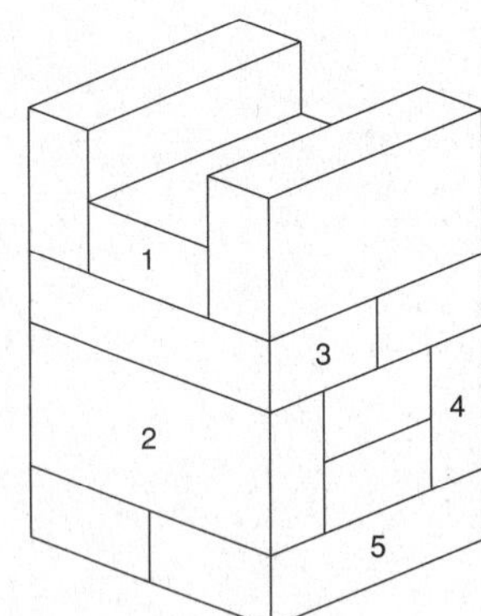

1. Block 1 touches ___________ blocks.

    (A) three
    (B) four
    (C) five
    (D) six
    (E) seven

2. Block 2 touches ___________ blocks.

    (A) three
    (B) four
    (C) five
    (D) six
    (E) seven

3. Block 3 touches ___________ blocks.

    (A) three
    (B) four
    (C) five
    (D) six
    (E) seven

4. Block 4 touches ___________ blocks.

    (A) three
    (B) four
    (C) five
    (D) six
    (E) seven

5. Block 5 touches ___________ blocks.

    (A) three
    (B) four
    (C) five
    (D) six
    (E) seven

Questions 6 through 10 are to be answered based on the figure below.

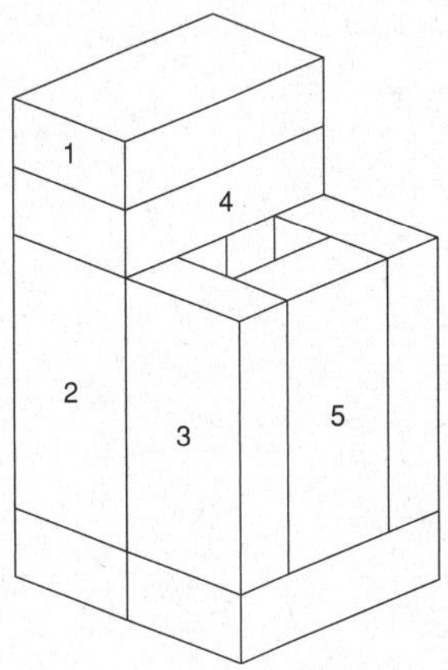

6. Block 1 touches ___________ blocks.

    (A) one
    (B) two
    (C) three
    (D) four
    (E) five

7. Block 2 touches __________ blocks.

   (A) one
   (B) two
   (C) three
   (D) four
   (E) five

8. Block 3 touches __________ blocks.

   (A) three
   (B) four
   (C) five
   (D) six
   (E) seven

9. Block 4 touches __________ blocks.

   (A) three
   (B) four
   (C) five
   (D) six
   (E) seven

10. Block 5 touches __________ blocks.

   (A) three
   (B) four
   (C) five
   (D) six
   (E) seven

Questions 11 through 15 are to be answered based on the figure below.

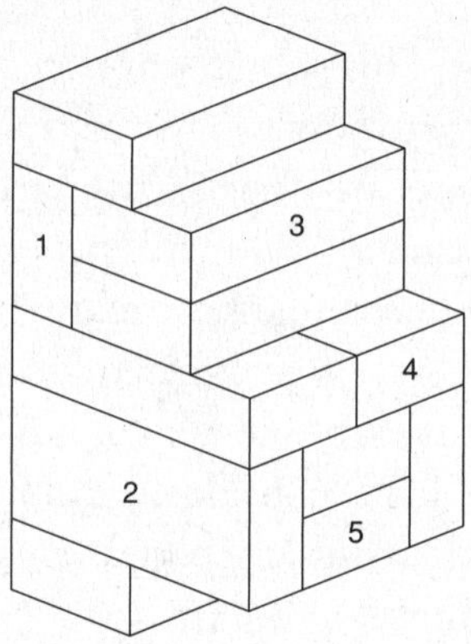

11. Block 1 touches __________ blocks.

   (A) three
   (B) four
   (C) five
   (D) six
   (E) seven

12. Block 2 touches __________ blocks.

   (A) three
   (B) four
   (C) five
   (D) six
   (E) seven

13. Block 3 touches __________ blocks.

   (A) three
   (B) four
   (C) five
   (D) six
   (E) seven

14. Block 4 touches __________ blocks.

    (A) three
    (B) four
    (C) five
    (D) six
    (E) seven

15. Block 5 touches __________ blocks.

    (A) three
    (B) four
    (C) five
    (D) six
    (E) seven

Questions 16 through 20 are to be answered based on the figure below.

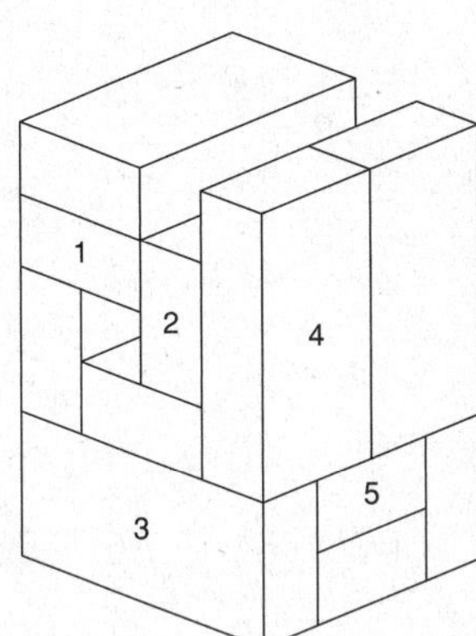

16. Block 1 touches __________ blocks.

    (A) three
    (B) four
    (C) five
    (D) six
    (E) seven

17. Block 2 touches __________ blocks.

    (A) three
    (B) four
    (C) five
    (D) six
    (E) seven

18. Block 3 touches __________ blocks.

    (A) three
    (B) four
    (C) five
    (D) six
    (E) seven

19. Block 4 touches __________ blocks.

    (A) three
    (B) four
    (C) five
    (D) six
    (E) seven

20. Block 5 touches __________ blocks.

    (A) three
    (B) four
    (C) five
    (D) six
    (E) seven

Subtest 7—Table Reading

Directions: This subtest measures ability to read tables quickly and accurately. The subtest consists of 40 questions that must be answered in 7 minutes.

Questions 1 through 10 are based on the table below. Note that the X values are shown at the top of the table and the Y values are shown on the left of the table. Find the entry that occurs at the intersection of the row and the column corresponding to the values given.

X Value

		4	3	2	1	0	–1	–2	–3	–4	–5
	–4	20	22	24	25	26	27	29	31	32	33
	–3	42	44	49	50	51	52	53	54	55	57
	–2	4	5	6	7	8	9	11	13	15	17
	–1	25	26	27	28	29	31	32	33	34	35
Y Value	0	32	34	35	36	37	39	40	41	51	52
	1	12	13	14	16	18	19	20	22	23	24
	2	45	43	40	39	38	37	36	34	30	29
	3	67	66	64	63	62	62	61	55	56	57
	4	49	47	46	45	44	43	42	41	40	39
	5	21	22	55	56	67	68	69	70	69	67

1. X; 0, Y; 4
   (A) 38
   (B) 29
   (C) 44
   (D) 55
   (E) 69

2. X; 4, Y; 3
   (A) 67
   (B) 44
   (C) 38
   (D) 21
   (E) 65

3. X; 3, Y; –3
   (A) 38
   (B) 19
   (C) 22
   (D) 36
   (E) 44

4. X; –2, Y; –2
   (A) 18
   (B) 11
   (C) 27
   (D) 41
   (E) 62

5. X; 3, Y; –1
   (A) 44
   (B) 29
   (C) 26
   (D) 18
   (E) 24

6. X; –4, Y; –4
   (A) 32
   (B) 29
   (C) 67
   (D) 41
   (E) 23

7. X; 2, Y; 4
   (A) 21
   (B) 31
   (C) 52
   (D) 55
   (E) 46

8. X; 2, Y; –3
   (A) 18
   (B) 49
   (C) 29
   (D) 41
   (E) 57

9. X; –1, Y; 2
   (A) 18
   (B) 19
   (C) 7
   (D) 37
   (E) 9

10. X; 4, Y; 0
   (A) 4
   (B) 21
   (C) 38
   (D) 32
   (E) 61

Questions 11 through 20 are to be answered based on the following table:

Air Force Weight Chart for Initial Accessions

Height	Maximum Weight	Minimum Weight
58	131	91
59	136	94
60	141	97
61	145	100
62	150	104
63	155	107
64	160	110
65	165	114
66	170	117
67	175	121
68	180	125
69	186	128
70	191	132
71	197	136
72	202	140
73	208	144
74	214	148
75	220	152
76	225	156
77	231	160
78	237	164
79	244	168
80	250	173

11. The maximum weight for an individual 69 inches tall is __________.

    (A) 170 pounds
    (B) 175 pounds
    (C) 186 pounds
    (D) 188 pounds
    (E) 190 pounds

12. The maximum weight for an individual 62 inches tall is __________.

    (A) 147 pounds
    (B) 150 pounds
    (C) 152 pounds
    (D) 154 pounds
    (E) 155 pounds

13. The minimum weight for an individual 65 inches tall is __________.

    (A) 110 pounds
    (B) 112 pounds
    (C) 113 pounds
    (D) 114 pounds
    (E) 115 pounds

14. The maximum weight for an individual 58 inches tall is __________.

    (A) 131 pounds
    (B) 132 pounds
    (C) 135 pounds
    (D) 137 pounds
    (E) 139 pounds

15. The maximum weight for an individual 75 inches tall is __________.

    (A) 208 pounds
    (B) 210 pounds
    (C) 214 pounds
    (D) 218 pounds
    (E) 220 pounds

16. The minimum weight for an individual 69 inches tall is __________.

    (A) 120 pounds
    (B) 122 pounds
    (C) 126 pounds
    (D) 128 pounds
    (E) 130 pounds

17. The minimum weight for an individual 78 inches tall is __________.

    (A) 162 pounds
    (B) 164 pounds
    (C) 168 pounds
    (D) 170 pounds
    (E) 172 pounds

18. The minimum weight for an individual 66 inches tall is __________.

    (A) 110 pounds
    (B) 112 pounds
    (C) 113 pounds
    (D) 115 pounds
    (E) 117 pounds

19. The maximum weight for an individual 70 inches tall is __________.

    (A) 189 pounds
    (B) 191 pounds
    (C) 193 pounds
    (D) 194 pounds
    (E) 197 pounds

20. The minimum weight for an individual 64 inches tall is __________.

    (A) 108 pounds
    (B) 109 pounds
    (C) 110 pounds
    (D) 112 pounds
    (E) 114 pounds

Questions 21 through 30 are to be answered based on the following chart:

Portland Bus Schedule

Departure Location	Dep Time	St # 1	St # 2	St # 3	St # 4	St # 5
River Place	5:15A	==	==	6:07A	6:24A	6:41A
Portland State	5:20A	==	==	6:14A	6:31A	6:48A
10th & Yamhill	5:26A	==	==	6:19A	6:36A	6:53A
16th & Northrup	5:30A	5:45A	6:05A	6:31A	6:48A	7:05A
23rd & Marshall	5:34A	5:49A	6:09A	6:36A	6:53A	7:10A
River Place	6:58A	7:15A	7:32A	7:49A	8:06A	8:20A
Portland State	7:05A	7:22A	7:39A	7:56A	8:13A	8:27A
10th & Yamhill	7:10A	7:27A	7:44A	8:01A	8:18A	8:32A
16th & Northrup	7:22A	7:39A	7:56A	8:13A	8:30A	8:44A
23rd & Marshall	7:27A	7:44A	8:01A	8:18A	8:35A	8:49A
River Place	8:34A	8:48A	9:02A	9:16A	9:30A	9:43A
Portland State	8:41A	8:55A	9:09A	9:23A	9:37A	9:50A
10th & Yamhill	8:46A	9:00A	9:14A	9:28A	9:42A	9:55A
16th & Northrup	8:58A	9:12A	9:26A	9:40A	9:54A	10:07A
23rd & Marshall	9:03A	9:17A	9:31A	9:45A	9:59A	10:12A
River Place	9:56A	10:09A	10:22A	10:35A	10:48A	11:01A
Portland State	10:03A	10:16A	10:29A	10:42A	10:55A	11:08A
10th & Yamhill	10:08A	10:21A	10:34A	10:47A	11:00A	11:13A
16th & Northrup	10:20A	10:33A	10:46A	10:59A	11:12A	11:25A
23rd & Marshall	10:25A	10:38A	10:51A	11:04A	11:17A	11:30A
River Place	11:14A	11:27A	11:40A	11:53A	12:06P	12:19P
Portland State	11:21A	11:34A	11:47A	12:00P	12:13P	12:26P
10th & Yamhill	11:26A	11:39A	11:52A	12:05P	12:18P	12:31P
16th & Northrup	11:38A	11:51A	12:04P	12:17P	12:30P	12:43P
23rd & Marshall	11:43A	11:56A	12:09P	12:22P	12:35P	12:48P
River Place	12:32P	12:45P	12:58P	1:11P	1:24P	1:37P
Portland State	12:39P	12:52P	1:05P	1:18P	1:31P	1:44P
10th & Yamhill	12:44P	12:57P	1:10P	1:23P	1:36P	1:49P
16th & Northrup	12:56P	1:09P	1:22P	1:35P	1:48P	2:01P
23rd & Marshall	1:01P	1:14P	1:27P	1:40P	1:53P	2:06P

21. The bus departing 16th and Northrup at 10:20 A.M. will arrive at Stop #4 at ___________.

    (A) 11:14 A.M.
    (B) 11:47 A.M.
    (C) 11:12 A.M.
    (D) 11:27 A.M.
    (E) 11:26 A.M.

22. The bus departing 10th and Yamhill at 7:10 A.M. will arrive at Stop #3 at ___________.

    (A) 8:18 A.M.
    (B) 8:01 A.M.
    (C) 8:13 A.M.
    (D) 7:56 A.M.
    (E) 7:49 A.M.

23. The bus departing 23rd and Marshall at 7:27 A.M. will arrive at Stop #1 at ___________.

    (A) 8:34 A.M.
    (B) 8:55 A.M.
    (C) 7:39 A.M.
    (D) 9:02 A.M.
    (E) 7:44 A.M.

24. The bus that departs Portland State at 10:03 A.M. will arrive at Stop #5 at ___________.

    (A) 11:01 A.M.
    (B) 11:13 A.M.
    (C) 10:48 A.M.
    (D) 11:08 A.M.
    (E) 10:55 A.M.

25. The bus that departs River Place at 8:34 A.M. will arrive at Stop #3 at ___________.

    (A) 9:23 A.M.
    (B) 9:16 A.M.
    (C) 9:09 A.M.
    (D) 9:30 A.M.
    (E) 9:27 A.M.

26. The bus that departs Portland State at 5:20 A.M. will arrive at Stop #2 at ___________.

    (A) 6:14 A.M.
    (B) 6:07 A.M.
    (C) 6:19 A.M.
    (D) 6:05 A.M.
    (E) none of the above

27. The bus that departs 10th and Yamhill at 10:08 A.M. will arrive at Stop #3 at ___________.

    (A) 10:47 A.M.
    (B) 10:34 A.M.
    (C) 10:59 A.M.
    (D) 10:42 A.M.
    (E) 11:00 A.M.

28. The bus that departs 23rd and Marshall at 1:01 P.M. will arrive at Stop #3 at ___________.

    (A) 1:27 P.M.
    (B) 1:35 P.M.
    (C) 1:53 P.M.
    (D) 1:40 P.M.
    (E) 1:48 P.M.

29. The bus that departs 16th and Northrup at 5:30 A.M. will arrive at Stop #4 at ___________.

    (A) 6:31 A.M.
    (B) 6:48 A.M.
    (C) 6:53 A.M.
    (D) 6:36 A.M.
    (E) 7:05 A.M.

30. The bus that departs Portland State at 8:41 A.M. will arrive at Stop #2 at ___________.

    (A) 9:09 A.M.
    (B) 9:14 A.M.
    (C) 9:16 A.M.
    (D) 9:02 A.M.
    (E) 8:55 AM

Questions 31 through 40 are based on the table below. Note that the X values are shown at the top of the table and the Y values are shown on the left of the table. Find the entry that occurs at the intersection of the row and the column corresponding to the values given.

X Value

Y Value		–4	–3	–2	–1	0	1	2	3	4
	–4	JFU	DHF	URJ	DUE	FIR	HDY	KDH	YDK	SBC
	–3	DJV	CNF	NSY	JDH	DIE	JDR	AHS	GEH	BCF
	–2	XFD	LKG	NDU	JDR	SVC	UMN	ASG	XXX	JDN
	–1	SHG	BCF	DYT	BSH	IND	UDJ	STD	HSR	JDH
Y Value	0	SBG	BDR	SCD	SHY	JDH	SBG	STY	SVF	YDH
	1	ASV	BCG	TSF	SLF	BHF	DYF	JDB	CHG	SCG
	2	ASI	VHF	DCG	EYR	XVC	DKI	DHW	SVC	AXG
	3	BNG	WSB	AVD	FGI	KSV	DHY	SVG	JDY	ASB
	4	DHO	PDN	DGY	DUU	DGT	DJH	DUH	AQG	DHY

31. X; –3, Y; 4
    (A) DHO
    (B) PDN
    (C) DGY
    (D) WSB
    (E) ASI

32. X; 0, Y; –2
    (A) TSF
    (B) FGI
    (C) DYF
    (D) IND
    (E) SVC

33. X; –2, Y; 2
    (A) KNL
    (B) DCG
    (C) JFI
    (D) FGT
    (E) DWE

34. X; 2, Y; –3
    (A) AHS
    (B) DKI
    (C) GER
    (D) KIU
    (E) SDF

35. X; 3, Y; 3
    (A) JUH
    (B) DSH
    (C) HYU
    (D) JDY
    (E) JTI

36. X; –4, Y; 4
    (A) DJH
    (B) GYU
    (C) DHO
    (D) YTR
    (E) RHJ

37. X; 4, Y; 0
    (A) JID
    (B) YDH
    (C) HKI
    (D) SER
    (E) FNJ

38. X; –3, Y; 0
    (A) JDU
    (B) DHY
    (C) BDR
    (D) SSR
    (E) GFR

39. X; 2, Y; 3
    (A) FUY
    (B) DSK
    (C) ERT
    (D) SVG
    (E) NHG

40. X; 0, Y; –1
    (A) IND
    (B) IYG
    (C) SDH
    (D) DEW
    (E) DGR

Subtest 8—Aviation Information

Directions: This subtest measures knowledge of general aeronautical concepts and terminology (past and current). The test consists of 20 questions that must be answered in 8 minutes.

1. An aircraft instructed to land on runway 23L would establish an approach heading of

   (A) 023 degrees
   (B) 230 degrees
   (C) 23 feet AGL
   (D) 230 feet AGL
   (E) 23 feet level flight

2. The four aerodynamic forces acting on an airplane are

   (A) drag, gravity, power, and velocity.
   (B) drag, friction, power, and velocity.
   (C) drag, lift, thrust, and weight.
   (D) friction, power, velocity, and weight.
   (E) gravity, lift, thrust, and weight.

3. Moving the control stick to the right or left affects which aircraft controls?

   (A) flaps
   (B) ailerons
   (C) elevator
   (D) vertical stabilizer
   (E) trim tabs

4. The operation of modern airplanes is dependent upon the use of instruments. These instrument dials, displayed in the airplane's cockpit, are referred to as "flight instruments" or "engine instruments." Which one of the following is not a flight instrument?

   (A) airspeed indicator
   (B) altimeter
   (C) attitude indicator
   (D) tachometer
   (E) vertical velocity indicator

5. Flaps are generally used

   (A) during takeoff.
   (B) during landings.
   (C) at high altitudes.
   (D) during coordinated turns.
   (E) both (A) and (B)

6. A flashing green air traffic control signal directed to an aircraft on the surface is a signal that the pilot

   (A) is cleared to taxi.
   (B) is cleared for takeoff.
   (C) should exercise extreme caution.
   (D) should taxi clear of the runway in use.
   (E) should stop taxiing.

7. In creating lift, the relationship between the speed of the wind moving underneath the wing compared to the speed of the wind moving over the wing can best be described as

   (A) the air moving over the wing moves faster than the air moving under the wing.
   (B) the air moving under the wing moves faster than the air moving over the wing.
   (C) the air moving under the wing moves at the same speed as the air moving over it.
   (D) the airflow moving over the wing stops.
   (E) the airflow moving under the wing stops.

8. The propeller blades are curved on one side and flat on the other side to

    (A) increase their strength.
    (B) produce thrust.
    (C) provide proper balance.
    (D) reduce air friction.
    (E) reduce drag.

9. On the ground, an aircraft is steered by

    (A) moving the stick or turning the yoke.
    (B) engine thrust.
    (C) pushing on the rudder peddles.
    (D) applying turning trim.
    (E) moving the ailerons.

10. Depressing the left rudder pedal would move the tail of the aircraft ___________.

    (A) right
    (B) left
    (C) up
    (D) down
    (E) none of the above

11. An aircraft on a heading of 300 degrees is heading ___________.

    (A) northeast
    (B) southeast
    (C) east
    (D) west
    (E) northwest

12. An aircraft is flying straight and level at 15,000 feet, at a constant airspeed of 180 knots, with a 3-degree nose up attitude. If the pilot applies thrust to bring the airspeed up to 200 knots, but applies no pressure to the stick, the aircraft will ___________.

    (A) climb
    (B) descend
    (C) remain at a constant altitude
    (D) bank
    (E) stall

13 "Zulu Time" refers to ___________.

    (A) Pacific Standard Time (PST)
    (B) Eastern Standard Time (EST)
    (C) Daylight Savings Time
    (D) the time in Greenwich, England
    (E) the time on the Equator

14. Supersonic means

    (A) faster than the speed of light.
    (B) faster than 200 mph.
    (C) faster than the speed of sound.
    (D) cruise speed.
    (E) really loud.

15. For weight and balance computations, what is the standard weight that has been established for gasoline used in aircraft?

    (A) 5 lbs/gal
    (B) 12 lbs/gal
    (C) 3 lbs/gal
    (D) 7.6 lbs/gal
    (E) 6 lbs/gal

16. The pilot of an airplane can best detect the approach of a stall by the

    (A) increase in speed of the engine.
    (B) increase in pitch and intensity of the sound of the air moving past the plane.
    (C) increase in effectiveness of the rudder.
    (D) ineffectiveness of the ailerons and elevator.
    (E) decrease in pitch and intensity of the sound of the air moving past the plane.

17. What makes an airplane turn?

    (A) centrifugal force
    (B) horizontal component of lift
    (C) rudder and aileron
    (D) rudder, aileron, and elevator
    (E) vertical component of lift

18. At the airport depicted below, larger aircraft should request to land on which runways?

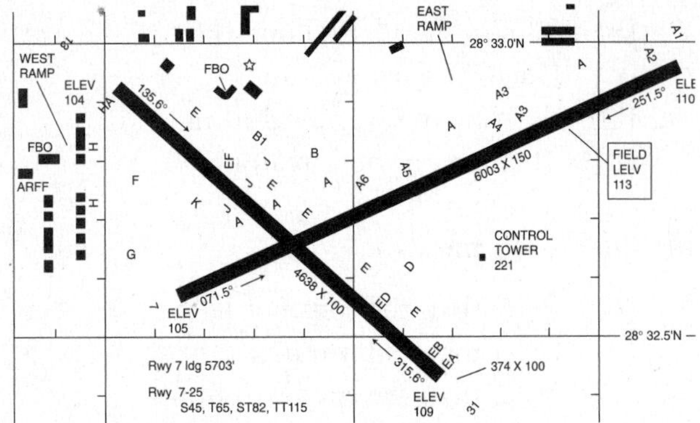

(A) 13 or 25
(B) 13 or 7
(C) 7 or 25
(D) 31 or 7
(E) 13 or 31

19. In the diagram depicted above (question 18), the short runway is aligned in which direction?

(A) North-South direction
(B) East-West direction
(C) NW-SE direction
(D) NE-SW direction
(E) none of the above

20. In the below diagram, the pilot has banked the aircraft

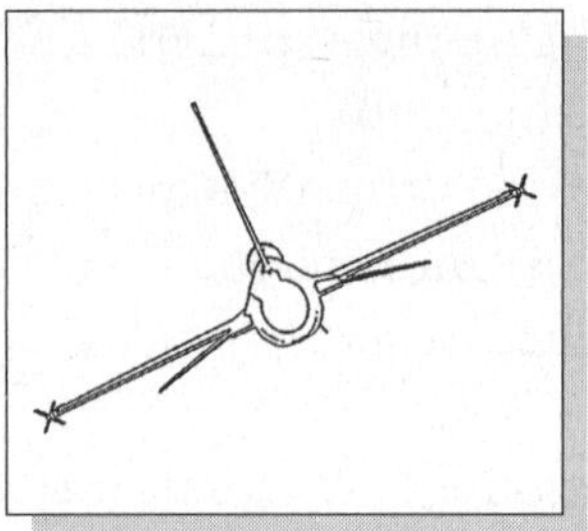

(A) 30 degrees to the left
(B) 45 degrees to the left
(C) 60 degrees to the left
(D) 30 degrees to the right
(E) 45 degrees to the right

Subtest 9—Rotated Blocks

Directions: This subtest has 15 questions that must be answered in 13 minutes. The questions are designed to measure your ability to visualize and manipulate objects in space. In each item, you are shown a picture of a block. You must find a second block that is just like the first.

Look at the two blocks below. Although viewed from different points, the blocks are the same.

Look at the two blocks below. They are not alike. They can never be turned so that they will be alike.

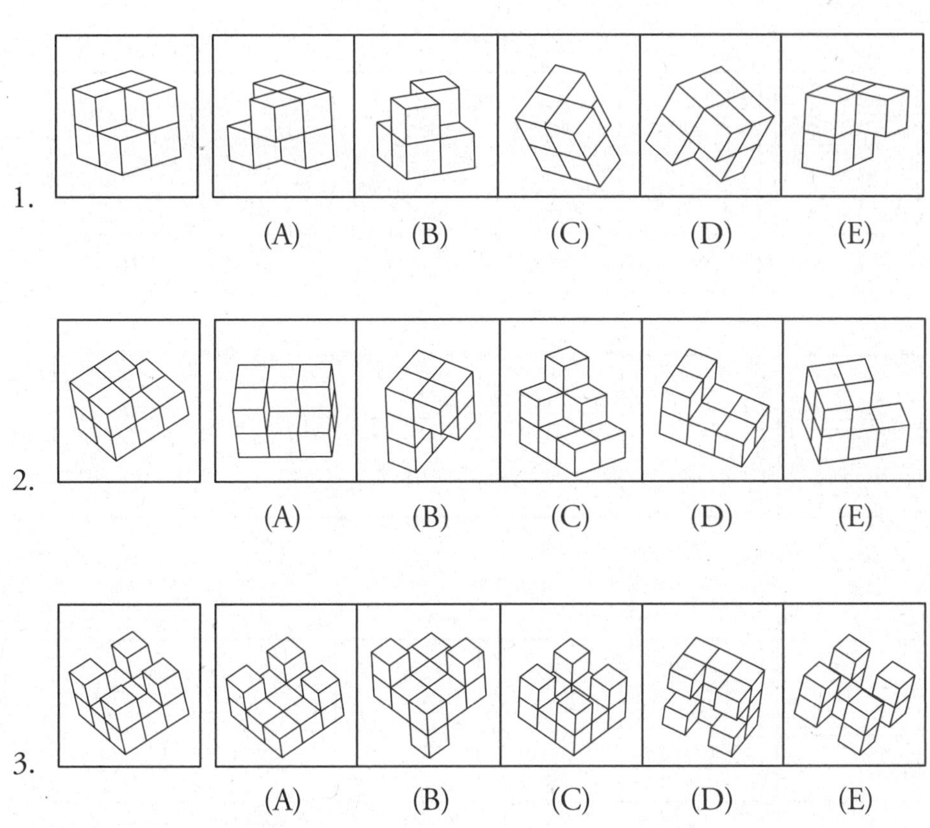

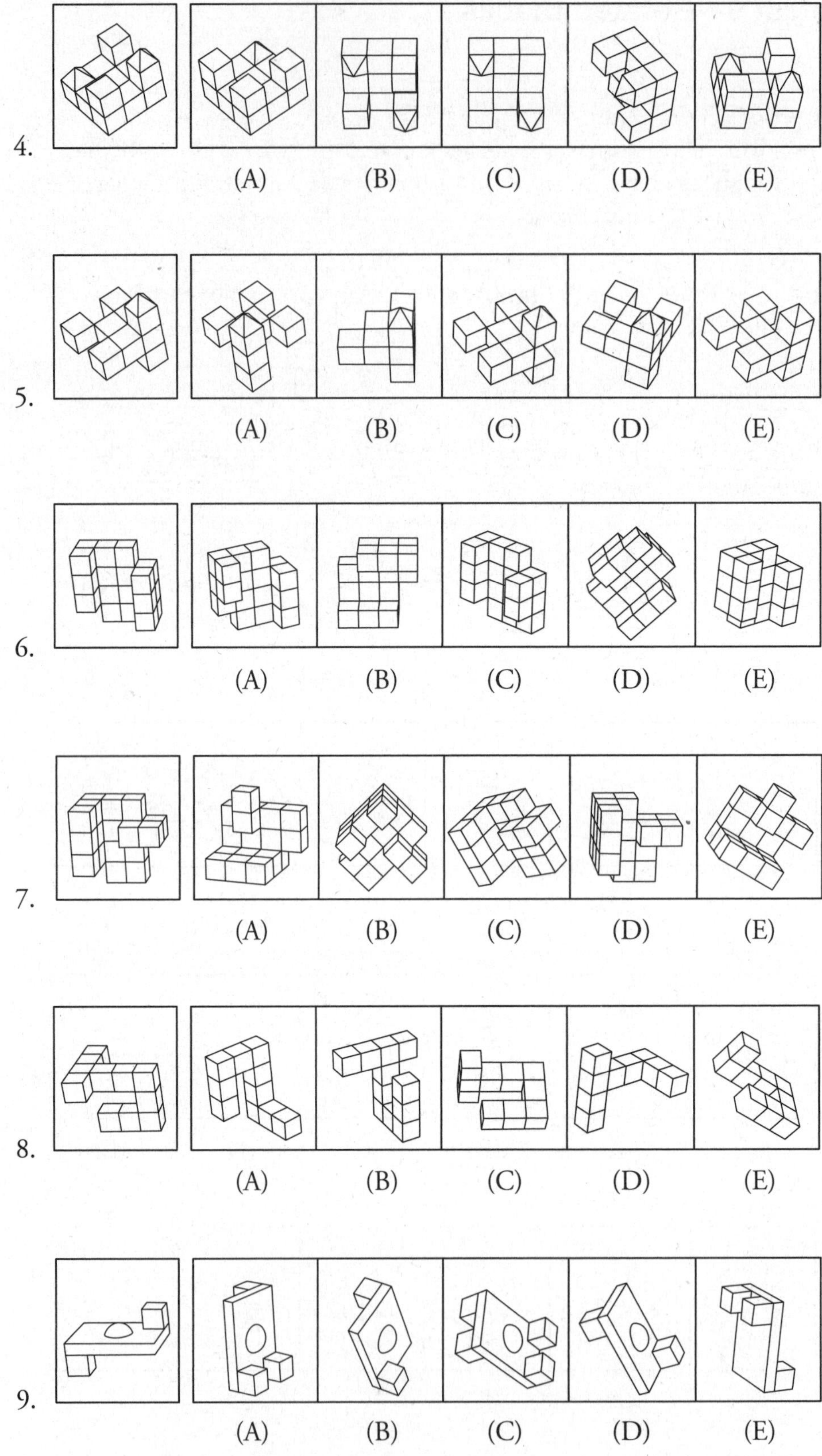
4.
(A) (B) (C) (D) (E)
5.
(A) (B) (C) (D) (E)
6.
(A) (B) (C) (D) (E)
7.
(A) (B) (C) (D) (E)
8.
(A) (B) (C) (D) (E)
9.
(A) (B) (C) (D) (E)

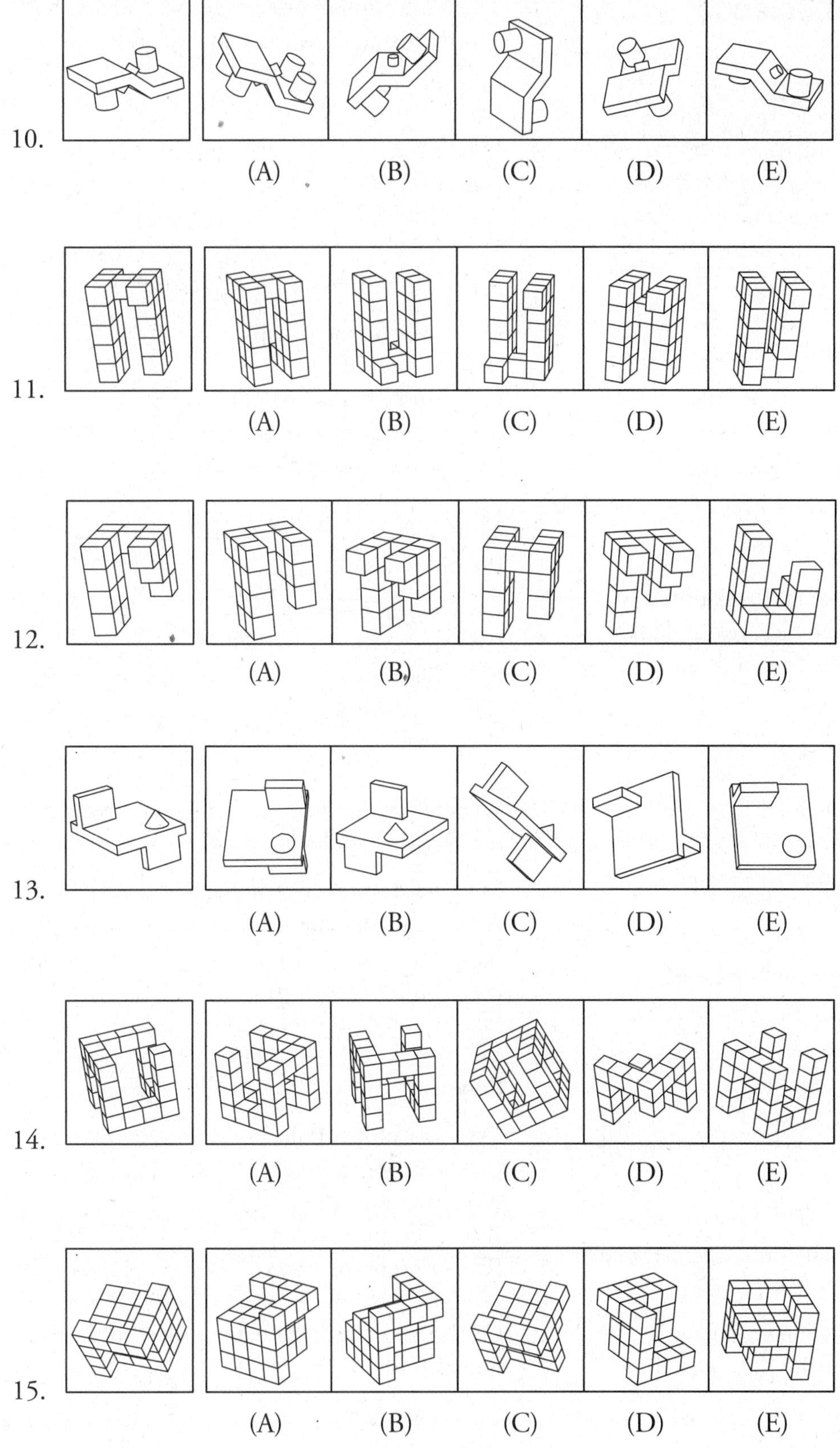

10.
(A)
(B)
(C)
(D)
(E)
11.
(A)
(B)
(C)
(D)
(E)
12.
(A)
(B)
(C)
(D)
(E)
13.
(A)
(B)
(C)
(D)
(E)
14.
(A)
(B)
(C)
(D)
(E)
15.
(A)
(B)
(C)
(D)
(E)

Subtest 10—General Science

Directions: This subtest measures verbal comprehension in the area of science. It consists of 20 questions that must be answered in 10 minutes. Read the question and choose the selection that best answers the question.

1. In chemistry, what are alpha particles?
   (A) oxygen nuclei
   (B) plutonium nuclei
   (C) barium nuclei
   (D) helium nuclei
   (E) carbon nuclei

2. Under natural conditions, large quantities of organic matter decay after each year's plant growth has been completed. As a result of such conditions
   (A) many animals are deprived of adequate food supplies.
   (B) soil erosion is accelerated.
   (C) soils maintain their fertility.
   (D) earthworms are added to the soil.
   (E) pollution increases.

3. A "dalton" is a unit of measurement for measuring __________.
   (A) mass
   (B) gravity
   (C) electricity
   (D) atoms
   (E) specific gravity

4. The most likely reason why dinosaurs became extinct was that they
   (A) were killed by erupting volcanoes.
   (B) were eaten as adults by the advancing mammalian groups.
   (C) failed to adapt to a changing environment.
   (D) killed each other in combat.
   (E) were destroyed by meteorites.

5. The adult human of average age and size has approximately how many quarts of blood?
   (A) 4
   (B) 6
   (C) 8
   (D) 10
   (E) 12

6. A person with high blood pressure should
   (A) take frequent naps.
   (B) avoid salt.
   (C) eat only iodized salt.
   (D) exercise vigorously.
   (E) avoid proteins.

7. The smallest of the FORMED elements of the blood are the __________.
   (A) white cells
   (B) red cells
   (C) platelets
   (D) erythrocytes
   (E) none of the above

8. Spiders can be distinguished from insects by the fact that spiders have
   (A) hard outer coverings.
   (B) large abdomens.
   (C) four pairs of legs.
   (D) biting mouth parts.
   (E) jointed appendages.

9. Polaris is
   (A) the North Pole.
   (B) the South Pole.
   (C) the North Star.
   (D) The sun.
   (E) a moon of Venus.

10. Of the following, the lightest element known on earth is __________.
    (A) hydrogen
    (B) oxygen
    (C) helium
    (D) air
    (E) nitrogen

11. A fish breathes with ___________.

    (A) lungs
    (B) gills
    (C) sockets
    (D) scales
    (E) none of the above

12. The time it takes for light from the sun to reach Earth is approximately

    (A) four years.
    (B) eight minutes.
    (C) four months.
    (D) eight years.
    (E) one week.

13. The type of element an atom is is determined by

    (A) the number of electrons.
    (B) the number of protons.
    (C) the number of neutrons.
    (D) the specific gravity.
    (E) none of the above

14. A new drug for treatment of tuberculosis was being tested in a hospital. Patients in Group A actually received doses of the new drug; those in Group B were given only sugar pills. Group B represents a(n) ___________.

    (A) scientific experiment
    (B) scientific method
    (C) experimental error
    (D) experimental control
    (E) hypothesis

15. Seasons are caused primarily by

    (A) Earth's distance from the Sun.
    (B) the thickness of the ozone layer.
    (C) Earth's tilting on its axis.
    (D) the jet stream.
    (E) none of the above

16. Radium is stored in lead containers because

    (A) the lead absorbs the harmful radiation.
    (B) radium is a heavy substance.
    (C) lead prevents the disintegration of the radium.
    (D) lead is cheap.
    (E) lead is brittle.

17. Planets in our solar system rotate

    (A) clockwise.
    (B) counterclockwise.
    (C) clockwise and counterclockwise.
    (D) at the same rotational speeds.
    (E) none of the above

18. Limes were eaten by British sailors in order to prevent ___________.

    (A) anemia
    (B) beriberi
    (C) night blindness
    (D) rickets
    (E) scurvy

19. A common name for sodium chloride (NaCl) is ___________.

    (A) sugar
    (B) baking soda
    (C) baking powder
    (D) salt
    (E) none of the above

20. Of the following planets, the one that has the shortest revolutionary period around the sun is ___________.

    (A) Mercury
    (B) Jupiter
    (C) Earth
    (D) Venus
    (E) Mars

Subtest 11—Hidden Figures

Directions: This subtest consists of 15 questions that must be answered in 8 minutes. The questions are designed to measure your ability to see a simple figure in a complex drawing. For each section of five questions there are five figures, lettered A, B, C, D, and E. Below these are five numbered drawings. You are to determine which lettered figure is contained in each of the numbered drawings.

Each numbered drawing contains only one of the lettered figures. The correct figure in each drawing will always be in the same position as it appears in the lettered figures above the question. Therefore, do not rotate the page in order to find it. Look at each numbered drawing and decide which one of the five lettered figures is contained in it.

Questions 1–5 are to be answered based on the shapes below.

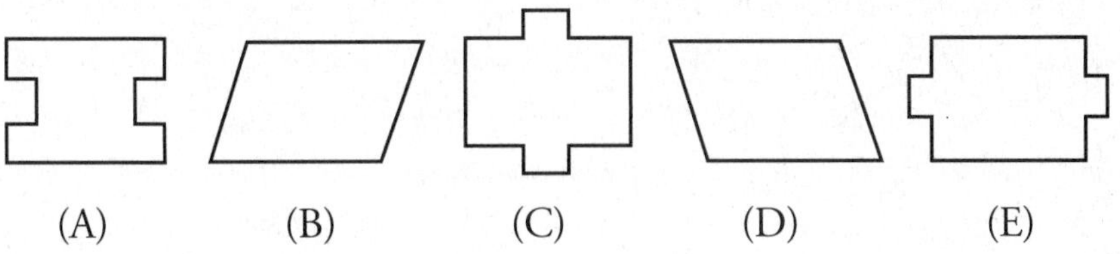

1. 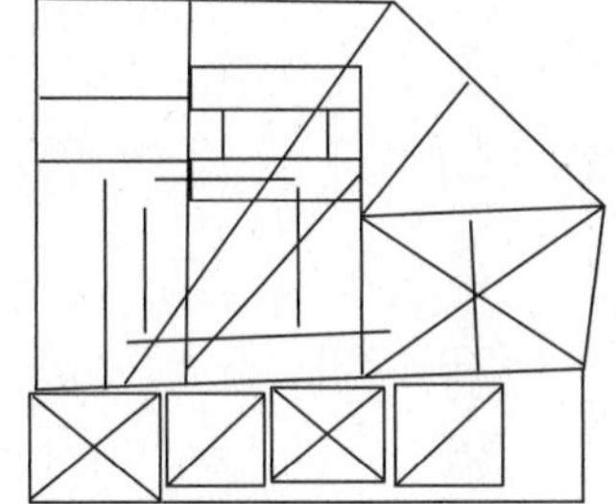

(A) figure A
(B) figure B
(C) figure C
(D) figure D
(E) figure E

2. 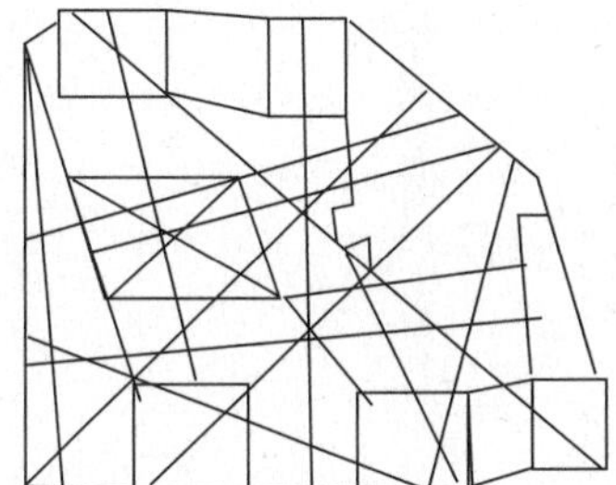

(A) figure A
(B) figure B
(C) figure C
(D) figure D
(E) figure E

3. 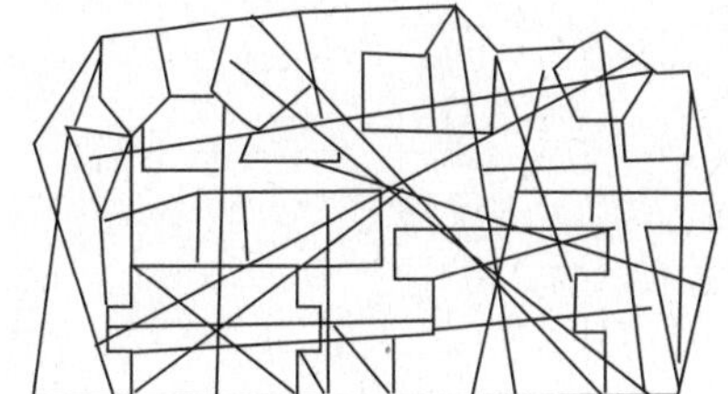

(A) figure A
(B) figure B
(C) figure C
(D) figure D
(E) figure E

4. 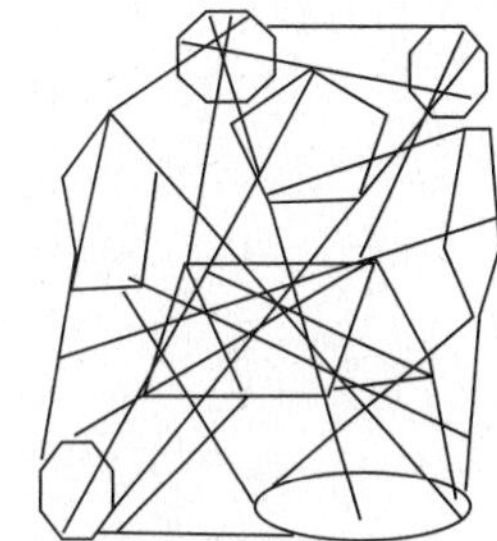

(A) figure A
(B) figure B
(C) figure C
(D) figure D
(E) figure E

5. 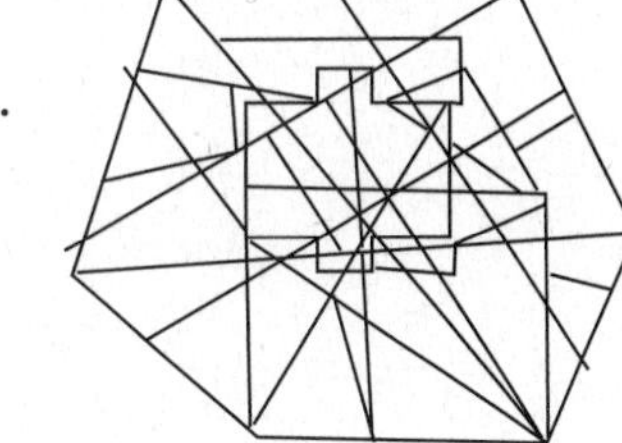

(A) figure A
(B) figure B
(C) figure C
(D) figure D
(E) figure E

Questions 6 through 10 are to be answered using the symbols below:

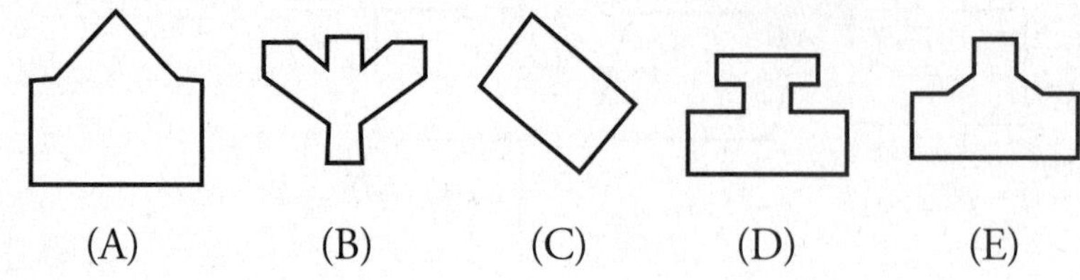

6.

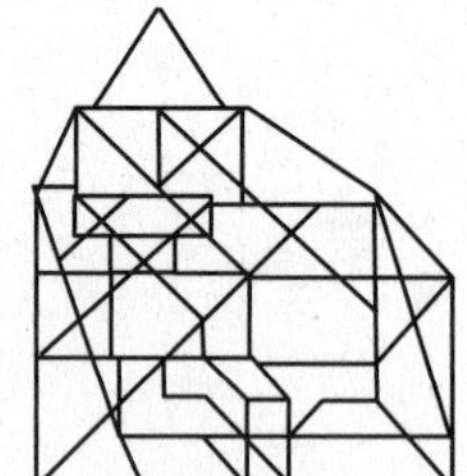

(A) figure A
(B) figure B
(C) figure C
(D) figure D
(E) figure E

7.

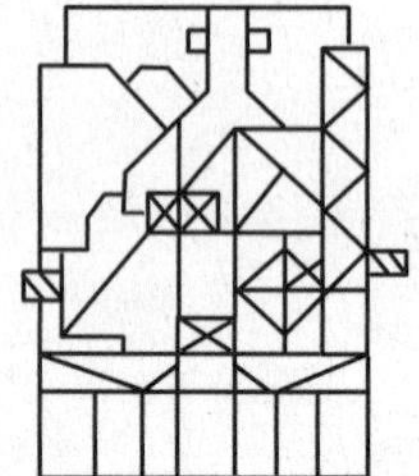

(A) figure A
(B) figure B
(C) figure C
(D) figure D
(E) figure E

8.

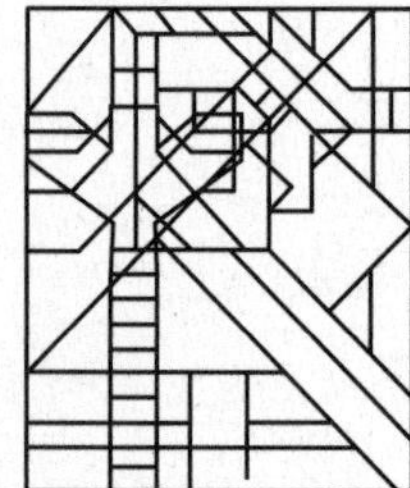

(A) figure A
(B) figure B
(C) figure C
(D) figure D
(E) figure E

9.

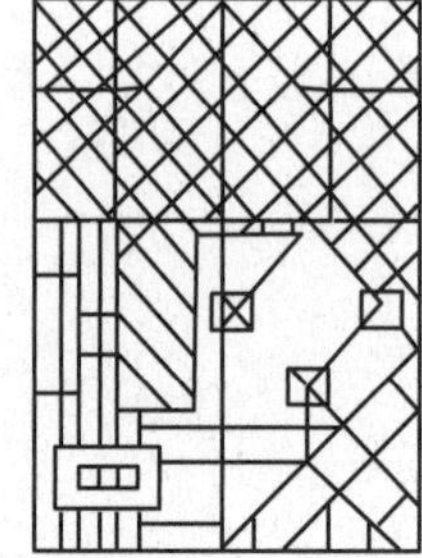

(A) figure A
(B) figure B
(C) figure C
(D) figure D
(E) figure E

10.

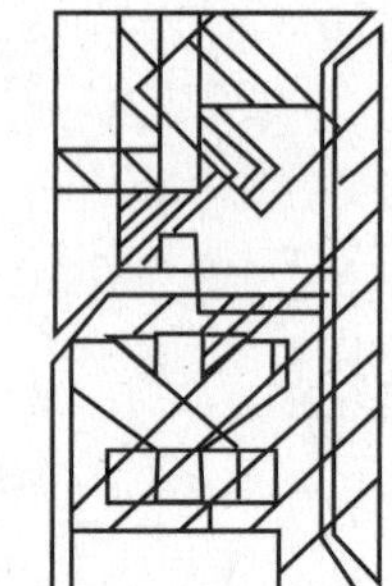

(A) figure A
(B) figure B
(C) figure C
(D) figure D
(E) figure E

Questions 11 through 15 are to be answered using the symbols below:

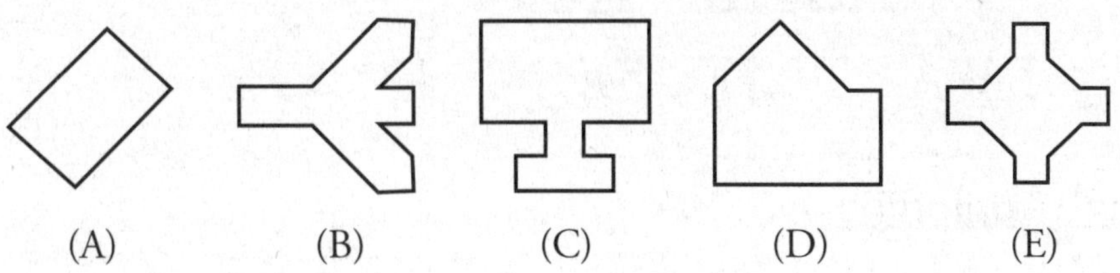

11.

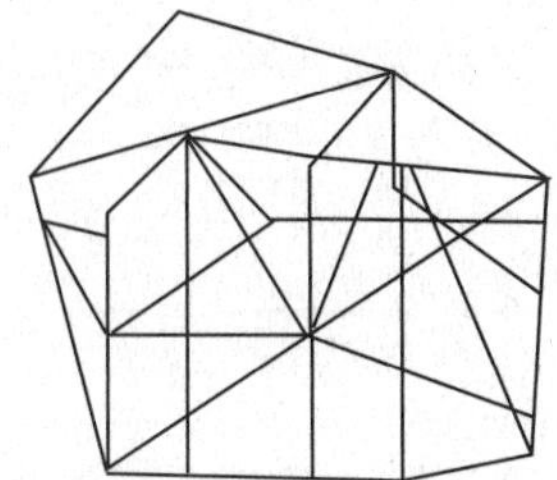

(A) figure A
(B) figure B
(C) figure C
(D) figure D
(E) figure E

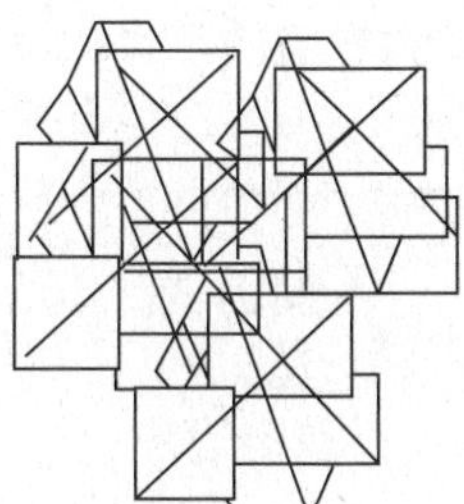

12.

(A) figure A
(B) figure B
(C) figure C
(D) figure D
(E) figure E

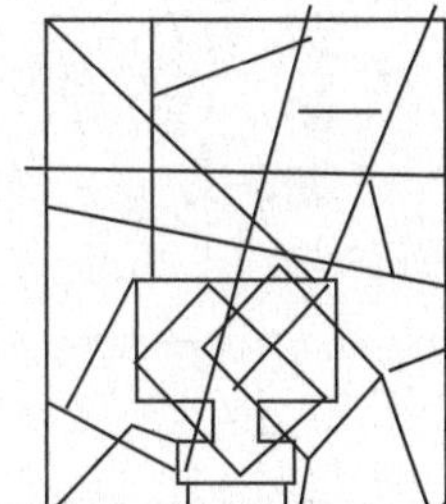

13.

(A) figure A
(B) figure B
(C) figure C
(D) figure D
(E) figure E

14.

(A) figure A
(B) figure B
(C) figure C
(D) figure D
(E) figure E

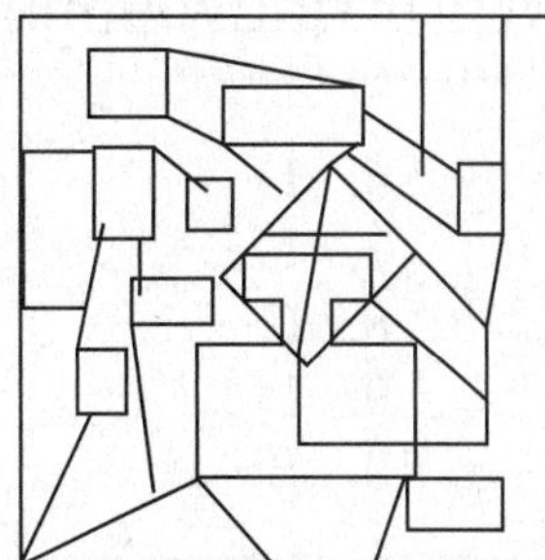

15.

(A) figure A
(B) figure B
(C) figure C
(D) figure D
(E) figure E

Answer Key

PRACTICE TEST 1

Subtest 1—Verbal Analogies

1. D
2. C
3. C
4. D
5. A
6. B
7. B
8. C
9. E
10. B
11. C
12. C
13. A
14. A
15. E
16. B
17. E
18. D
19. E
20. E
21. C
22. A
23. E
24. A
25. A

Subtest 2—Arithmetic Reasoning

1. A
2. D
3. C
4. A
5. C
6. A
7. C
8. D
9. B
10. B
11. C
12. D
13. C
14. A
15. A
16. E
17. C
18. A
19. B
20. C
21. B
22. D
23. D
24. B
25. C

Subtest 3—Word Knowledge

1. C
2. B
3. C
4. C
5. B
6. D
7. D
8. C
9. D
10. B
11. C
12. A
13. A
14. C
15. E
16. B
17. D
18. B
19. D
20. C
21. A
22. D
23. D
24. A
25. B

Subtest 4—Mathematics Knowledge

1. D
2. B
3. D
4. D
5. C
6. A
7. D
8. B
9. C
10. B
11. E
12. C
13. E
14. B
15. B
16. A
17. B
18. C
19. B
20. C
21. E
22. D
23. C
24. E
25. E

Subtest 5—Instrument Comprehension

1. B
2. B
3. D
4. B
5. C
6. A
7. B
8. A
9. B
10. D
11. B
12. B
13. B
14. D
15. C
16. D
17. C
18. A
19. C
20. A

Subtest 6—Block Counting

1. B	5. B	9. E	13. A	17. C
2. C	6. A	10. A	14. C	18. C
3. D	7. E	11. C	15. B	19. C
4. C	8. D	12. B	16. A	20. D

Subtest 7—Table Reading

1. C	9. D	17. B	25. B	33. B
2. A	10. D	18. E	26. E	34. A
3. E	11. C	19. B	27. A	35. D
4. B	12. B	20. C	28. D	36. C
5. C	13. D	21. C	29. B	37. B
6. A	14. A	22. B	30. A	38. C
7. E	15. E	23. E	31. B	39. D
8. B	16. D	24. D	32. E	40. A

Subtest 8—Aviation Information

1. B	5. E	9. C	13. D	17. B
2. C	6. A	10. A	14. C	18. C
3. B	7. A	11. E	15. E	19. C
4. D	8. B	12. A	16. D	20. D

Subtest 9—Rotated Blocks

1. D	4. E	7. A	10. D	13. C
2. B	5. D	8. B	11. B	14. B
3. D	6. E	9. D	12. E	15. A

Subtest 10—General Science

1. D	5. B	9. C	13. B	17. C
2. C	6. B	10. A	14. D	18. E
3. A	7. C	11. B	15. C	19. D
4. C	8. C	12. B	16. A	20. A

Subtest 11—Hidden Figures

1. A	4. B	7. E	10. B	13. C
2. D	5. C	8. B	11. D	14. C
3. E	6. D	9. A	12. D	15. A

Answer Explanations to AFOQT 1 Practice Test

SUBTEST 1—VERBAL ANALOGIES

1. **(D) story.** A chapter is a numbered division of a book; a story is a numbered floor of a building.
2. **(C) automobile.** Trains travel on rails; automobiles travel on highways.
3. **(C) pepper is to spice.** A carrot is a type of vegetable; pepper is a type of spice.
4. **(D) novel.** A biography is a book consisting of facts about an individual; a novel is a book with fictional characters.
5. **(A) cavity is to mound.** Concave means hollow and curved like a cavity; something convex is bulging and curved like a mound.
6. **(B) light**. Stillness and sound are antonyms; darkness and light are antonyms.
7. **(B) fuel.** Gown is a type of garment; gasoline is a type of fuel.
8. **(C) beaver is to dam.** Birds build nests, beavers build dams. While (A) and (B) could have been correct answers, since they are places the animals can live, there is no way to choose the "best" answer using this interpretation, so the correct answer would be using a definition of what the animals build.
9. **(E) college.** A doctor works in a hospital; a professor works in a college ((E) is a better answer than(B). While some high schools have "professors," most have "teachers").
10. **(B) puppy is to dog.** A cub is a baby bear; a puppy is a baby dog.
11. **(C) over is to under**. Hyper is a prefix meaning over; hypo is a prefix meaning under.
12. **(C) swatch is to cloth.** An excerpt is an extract from (piece of) a novel; a swatch is a piece of a cloth.
13. **(A) arrival is to departure.** Immigration is the act of arriving in a new country. Emigration is the act of leaving or departing one country to settle in another.
14. **(A) enmity.** Perspicacious and insight are synonyms, meaning sharp or keen of mind; churlish and enmity are synonyms, both meaning dislike or rudeness.
15. **(E) triangle.** An octagon is an eight-sided polygon; a square is a four-sided one. A hexagon is a six-sided polygon; a triangle is a three-sided one.
16. **(B) bird.** A snake is a type of vertebrate; a penguin is a type of bird.
17. **(E) trespass is to enter.** To perjure is to willfully make a false statement under oath; to trespass is to wrongfully enter the property of another. Both are illegal actions.
18. **(D) cabal.** A troupe is a group of actors; a cabal is a group of plotters or conspirators.
19. **(E) weep is to wept.** Told is the past and past participle form of tell; wept is the past and past participle form of weep.
20. **(E) shark is to scavenger.** A defining characteristic of a lion is that it is carnivorous; a defining characteristic of a shark is that it is a scavenger.
21. **(C) walk.** Prattle means to speak in an idle, casual manner; promenade means to walk in a casual manner.
22. **(A) colt.** A lamb is a young sheep; a colt is a young horse.
23. **(E) fidget is to uneasiness.** A curtsy (bow) is a sign of respect; fidgeting is a sign of uneasiness.

24. **(A) agree is to consent.** Ignore and overlook have the same or a similar meaning; agree and consent are synonyms.
25. **(A) always is to never.** Frequently and seldom have opposite meanings; always and never are antonyms.

SUBTEST 2—ARITHMETIC REASONING

1. **(A) 2.73 hours.** Let x = the number of hours to paint the room together. In one hour Susan can do $\frac{1}{6}$ of the job, while Tom can do $\frac{1}{5}$ of the job.

$$\frac{1}{6}x + \frac{1}{5}x = 1 \text{ (where 1 represents 100\% of the job)}$$
$$(\frac{1}{6} + \frac{1}{5})x = 1$$
$$(\frac{5}{30} + \frac{6}{30})x = 1$$
$$\frac{11}{30}x = 1$$
$$x = \frac{30}{11}$$
$$x = 2.73 \text{ hours}$$

2. **(D) 200 meters.** 3 kilometers = 3000 meters; $\frac{3000}{15}$ = 200 meters.
3. **(C) 10%.** Simple interest can be computed with the formula $I = Prt$, where I is the interest, P is the principle invested, r is the interest rate, and t is equal to time.

$$I = Prt$$
$$150 = (500)r(3)$$
$$150 = 1500r$$
$$150/1500 = r$$
$$r = .10$$
$$r = 10\%$$

4. **(A) 2 pounds, 7 ounces.** 12 pounds = 11 pounds, 16 ounces; weight of tool = 9 pounds, 9 ounces. 11 pounds, 16 ounces minus 9 pounds, 9 ounces = 2 pounds, 7 ounces.
5. **(C) 14 months.** Let x = number of rental months needed to make the costs equal. This occurs when the purchase price (P) equals the rental cost (R), or $P = R$. We know that P = \$400, and $R = 50 + 25x$.

$$R = 50 + 25x$$
$$400 = 50 + 25x$$
$$25x = 350$$
$$x = 14 \text{ months}$$

6. **(A) 8%.** Sample size is 50. Number of defects found in sample = 4. $\frac{4}{50}$ = 8%.

If 8% defects were found in the sample, it is probable that the percentage of defective articles in the original shipment is also 8%.

7. **(C) 40 pounds.** Let x = number of pounds of cement. As a ratio, the problem can be stated as 5 parts is to 6 parts, as x pounds is to 48 pounds:

$$\frac{5}{6} = \frac{x}{48}$$
$$5 \times 48 = 6x$$
$$x = \frac{240}{6}$$
$$x = 40$$

8. **(D) 18.** 36 tons × 3 man-hours = 108 man-hours to stack 36 tons.

$$\frac{108}{6} = 18 \text{ persons.}$$

9. **(B) $2.00 per gallon.**
Let x = the wholesale price. Therefore, 40% of the wholesale price is $0.40x$. The retail price of the gas is the wholesale price plus 40% of the wholesale price plus $0.20.

$$x + 0.40x + 0.20 = 3.00$$
$$1x + 0.40x + 0.20 = 3.00$$
$$1.4x + 0.2 = 3.00$$
$$1.4x = 2.80$$
$$x = \frac{2.80}{1.40}$$
$$x = 2.$$

10. **(B) 866 square feet.** 25 × 12 = 300 sq. ft. = area of long wall; 300 × 2 = 600 sq. ft. 15 × 12 = 180 sq. ft. = area of short wall; 180 × 2 = 360 sq. ft. 600 + 360 = 960 sq. ft. = total wall area. 7 × 5 = 35 sq. ft. = area of window; 35 × 2 = 70 sq. ft. = area of windows. 6 × 4 = 24 sq. ft. = area of glass door. 70 + 24 = 94 sq. ft. = total glass area. 960 – 94 = 866 sq. ft. of wall space to be painted.
11. **(C) 56.7 points.** Captain Taggarty's total score is 270 points (5 × 54). Lieutenant Thompson's total score is 354 points (6 × 59).

$$\frac{(270+354)}{11} = 56.7 \text{ points.}$$

12. **(D) $76.50.** $100 × .10 = $10.00; $100 – $10 = $90. $90 × .15 = $13.50; $90.00 – 13.50 = $76.50.
13. **(C) 255.53.**
Let x = death rate in 1998.

$$x - 31\tfrac{3}{4}\% = 174.4$$
$$x - 0.3175x = 174.4$$
$$x(1 - 0.3175) = 174.4$$
$$0.6825x = 174.4$$
$$x = \frac{174.4}{0.6825}$$
$$x = 255.53$$

14. **(A) 12.5 inches wide and 22 inches long.** $\frac{1}{2}$ inch on a scaled drawing = 3 feet of actual floor dimension. $\frac{75}{3} = 25\frac{1}{2}$ inches = 12.5 inches; $\frac{132}{3} = 44\frac{1}{2}$ inches = 22 inches.

15. **(A) 13 inches.**
Let r = original radius. $R + 5$ equals the new radius. The formula $A = \pi r^2$ represents the original area. We know that the new area is 155π square inches larger than the original area, so $155\pi + A = \pi(r + 5)^2 = 155\pi + \pi r^2$.

$$\pi(r + 5)(r + 5) = 155\pi + \pi r^2$$
$$\pi(r^2 + 10r + 25) = 155\pi + \pi r^2$$
$$\pi r^2 + 10r\pi + 25\pi = 155\pi + \pi r^2$$
$$10r\pi + 25\pi = 155\pi$$
$$10r\pi = 130\pi$$
$$r = \frac{130\pi}{10\pi}$$
$$r = 13$$

16. **(E) 4 out of 5.** If 20% are either red or green, 80% are yellow. The chance of blindly picking a yellow marble is 4 out of 5 (80%).
17. **(C) 6.** Let x = the smaller number. As the sum of the two numbers is 10, then the larger number is represented by $10 - x$.

$$3x + 5(10 - x) = 42$$
$$3x + 50 - 5x = 42$$
$$-2x + 50 = 42$$
$$-2x = -8$$
$$x = \frac{-8}{-2}$$
$$x = 4$$

As the smaller number (x) is equal to 4, the larger number ($10 - x$) is equal to 6.
18. **(A) 40 tons.** 2 tons + 6 tons = 8 tons carried by 1 passenger and 1 freight plane. $\frac{160}{8}$ = 20 pairs of passenger and freight planes needed. 20 passenger planes carrying 2 tons each = 40 tons of cargo.
19. **(B) $30,000**

$$V = -\$4000a + \$50{,}000$$
$$a = 5$$
$$V = (-\$4000 \times 5) + \$50{,}000$$
$$V = -\$20{,}000 + \$50{,}000$$
$$V = \$30{,}000$$

20. **(C) 120 degrees.**
The sum of two supplementary angles is 180°

Let a = second angle
$$a + 60 = 180$$
$$a = 120$$

21. **(B) 672.**
Let x = number of advanced tickets
Let y = number paid at the door
Given: $14.5x$ = amount advanced tickets made
Given $22y$ = amount made at the door
$14x5x + 22y = 16640$
$x + y = 800$ // total number of people attending
$y = 800 - x$ // subtract x from both sides to get the value of y
$14.5x + 22(800 - x) = 16640$. // substitute known value for y into the formula

$14.5x + 17600 - 22x = 16640$ // clear the parentheses
$-7.5x = 16640 - 17600$ // combine like terms
$-7.5x = -960$
$x = 128$ // number of tickets sold in advance
$800 - 128 = 672$ (number who paid at the door)

22. **(D) 4 hours and 30 minutes.**
Rate × Time = Distance
Let Rh = Rate Going Home
Let Th = Time Going Home
Given: $Rh = 45$ mph
Given: $Rh \times Th = 45Th$ // Distance from Omaha to home
Let Ro = Rate to Omaha
Let To = Time to Omaha
Given: $Ro = 40$ mph
Given: $To = Th + 0.5$ // It took 0.5 hours longer to drive home
$Ro{*}To = 40(Th + 0.5)$ // Distance from home to Omaha
23. **(D) $1,536.**
The total square footage of the patio is 192 square feet (12 feet × 16 feet = 192 square feet). The cost per square foot is $8.00, so $8.00 × 192 square feet = $1,536.
24. **(B) $125,000.**
Let x = selling price
Given: Lizzie's share = x – 0.06x$ (selling price minus the real estate agent's commission)
x – 0.06x \geq$ $120,000 (Lizzie's share must be greater or equal to the amount needed to break even with the mortgage)
$x - .06x \geq 120{,}000$
$.96x \geq 120{,}000$
$x \geq 12{,}000/.96$
$x \geq \$125{,}000$
25. **(C) $344.50.**
Multiply her total sales by her percent commission: $530.00 × 0.65 = $344.50.

SUBTEST 3—WORD KNOWLEDGE

1. **(C) inflexible.** Used as an adjective, *adamant* means impervious to pleas, appeals, or reason; stubbornly unyielding.
2. **(B) owner.** A *proprietor* is one who owns or owns and manages a business or other such establishment.
3. **(C) consent.** Used as a noun, *assent* means agreement or concurrence.
4. **(C) shallow**. Used as an adjective, *superficial* means apparent rather than actual or substantial.
5. **(B) genuine.** Used as an adjective, *authentic* means conforming to fact and therefore worthy of trust, reliance, or belief.
6. **(D) characteristic.** *Typical* means exhibiting the qualities, traits, or characteristics that identify a kind, class, group, or category.
7. **(D) neutralize.** Used as a verb, *counteract* means to oppose and mitigate the effects of something by contrary action.

8. **(C) upright.** Used as an adjective, *perpendicular* means being at right angles to the horizontal; vertical.
9. **(D) enlarged.** Used as an adjective, *dilated* means having been widened; expanded.
10. **(B) vigorous.** Used as an adjective, *athletic* means involving physical activity or exertion.
11. **(C) two weeks.** Used as a noun, *fortnight* means a period of 14 days; two weeks.
12. **(A) boss.** Used as a noun, *foreman* means a man/woman who serves as the leader of a work crew, as in a factory.
13. **(A) casual.** Used as an adjective, *incidental* means of a minor, casual, or subordinate nature.
14. **(C) prevent.** Used as a verb, *hinder* means to interfere with action or progress.
15. **(E) well-known.** Used as an adjective, *notorious* means known widely and usually unfavorably, or infamous.
16. **(B) excellent.** Used as an adjective, *nonpareil* means having no equal; peerless.
17. **(D) intercede.** Used as a verb, *mediate* means to resolve or settle by working with conflicting parties.
18. **(B) irritate.** Used as a verb, *rankle* means to cause persistent irritation or annoyance.
19. **(D) enthusiastic.** Used as a noun, *melodrama* means a play or film characterized by exaggerated emotions.
20. **(C) fire.** Used as a noun, *conflagration* means a large, destructive fire.
21. **(A) concise.** Used as an adjective, *succinct* means characterized by clear, precise expression in few words; concise and terse.
22. **(D) sign.** Used as a noun, *symptom* means a characteristic sign or indication of the existence of something else.
23. **(D) scene.** Used as a noun, *panorama* means an unbroken view of a surrounding area.
24 **(A) clock.** Used as a noun, *chronometer* means an exceptionally precise timepiece.
25. **(B) filter.** Used as a verb, *percolate* means to cause to pass through a porous substance or to filter.

SUBTEST 4—MATHEMATICS KNOWLEDGE

1. **(D) 9.** A natural number that has no other factors except 1 and itself is a prime number. The number 9 is divisible by 1, 3, and 9.
2. **(B) $6x^2y + 2xy$.** $2x(3xy + y) = 2x(3xy) + 2x(y) = 6x^2y + 2xy$.
3. **(D) 4.**

$$\begin{aligned} 5x + 3(x - 1) &= 29 \\ 5x + 3x - 3 &= 29 \\ 8x &= 32 \\ x &= 4 \end{aligned}$$

4. **(D) 13.6398×10^7.** To multiply scientific notation, first multiply the base of both numbers ($5.37 \times 2.54 = 13.6398$). Next, add the exponents ($2 + 5 = 7$).

5. **(C) $x^2 + x$.** Squaring an odd integer results in an odd integer. Adding an odd integer to it results in an even integer. Options (A), (B), and (D) remain odd.
6. **(A) 2.**

$$\frac{1}{2}x - \frac{1}{10} = \frac{1}{5}x + \frac{1}{2}$$
$$10\left(\frac{1}{2}x - \frac{1}{10}\right) = 10\left(\frac{1}{5}x + \frac{1}{2}\right)$$
$$\frac{10}{2}x - \frac{10}{10} = \frac{10}{5}x + \frac{10}{2}$$
$$5x - 1 = 2x + 5$$
$$3x = 6$$
$$x = 2$$

7. **(D) 10^{x-y}.** To divide powers of the same base, subtract the exponent of the denominator from the exponent of the numerator.
8. **(B) $-45i - 69$.**

$$(9i + 6)(3i - 7)$$
$$27i^2 - 63i + 18i - 42$$
$$27(-1) - 63i + 18i - 42$$
$$-27 - 63i + 18i - 42$$
$$-69 - 45i$$
$$-45i - 69$$

9. **(C) 10^6.** $1{,}000{,}000 = 10^6$.
10. **(B) 639,000.** To convert scientific notation to regulation notation, move the decimal place to the right (for a positive exponent), the same number of spaces as the exponent (in this case, 5).
11. **(E) $\frac{4}{25}$.** $\left(\frac{2}{5}\right)^2 = \frac{2}{5} \times \frac{2}{5} = \frac{4}{25}$.
12. **(C) $-3x^2 - 2xy^2 + 8x - 1$.**

$$x^2y + xy^2 + 6x + 4 - (4x^2y + 3xy^2 - 2x + 5) =$$
$$x^2y + xy^2 + 6x + 4 - 4x^2y - 3xy^2 + 2x - 5 =$$
$$x^2y - 4x^2y + xy^2 - 3xy^2 + 6x + 2x + 4 - 5 =$$
$$(1-4)x^2y + (1-3)xy^2 + (6 + 2)x - 1 =$$
$$-3x^2y - 2xy^2 + 8x - 1$$

13. **(E) 64.** $3^n = 9$; $n = 2$. $4^{n+1} = 4^{2+1} = 4^3 = 64$.
14. **(B) $-6, 5$.**

$$-x^2 - x + 30 = 0$$
$$-(-x^2 - x + 30) = -0$$
$$x^2 + x - 30 = 0$$
$$(x + 6)(x - 5) = 0$$
$$x + 6 = 0 \text{ and } x - 5 = 0$$
$$x = -6, \text{ and } x = 5$$

15. **(B) 0.01.** $10^{-2} = \left(\frac{1}{10}\right)^2 = \frac{1}{100} = 0.01$.

16. **(A) $\frac{8\pi}{3}$.** π radians = 180°. To convert an angle to degrees, you multiply the angle by $\frac{\pi}{180}$.

$480 \times \frac{\pi}{180} =$

$\frac{480\pi}{180} = \frac{8\pi}{3}$

17. **(B) $\sqrt{7}$.**

$\sqrt{28} - \sqrt{7} = \sqrt{7 \times 4} - \sqrt{7} = 2\sqrt{7} - \sqrt{7} = \sqrt{7}.$

18. **(C) 13.**

$$\begin{aligned}
\pi(r+5)(r+5) &= 155\pi + \pi r^2 \\
\pi(r^2 + 10r + 25) &= 155\pi + \pi r^2 \\
\pi r^2 + 10r\pi + 25\pi &= 155\pi + \pi r^2 \\
10r\pi + 25\pi &= 155\pi \\
10r\pi &= 130\pi \\
r &= 130\pi/10\pi \\
r &= 13
\end{aligned}$$

19. **(B) 540°.** A pentagon has 5 sides. (Number of sides – 2) × 180 = sum of angles.

$$3 \times 180 = 540°.$$

20. **(C) 4.**

$$\begin{aligned}
3x + 5(10 - x) &= 42 \\
3x + 50 - 5x &= 42 \\
-2x + 50 &= 42 \\
-2x &= \frac{-8}{-2} \\
x &= \frac{-8}{-2} \\
x &= 4
\end{aligned}$$

21. **(E) $\frac{5}{6}$.** $\frac{3x}{5y} = \frac{1}{2}$; $6x = 5y$; $\frac{6x}{y} = 5$; $\frac{x}{y} = \frac{5}{6}$.

22. **(D) 5.0.**
The coordinates form a right triangle with a horizontal leg of 3 and a vertical leg of 4. The distance between the two points is the hypotenuse of the right triangle.
Hypotenuse^2 = $3^2 + 4^2 = 25$
Hypotenuse = $\sqrt{25} = 5$.

23. **(C) 5.** 5 × 3 = 15 which is divisible by both 3 and 5; 9, 12, 18, and 21 are not divisible by 5.

24. **(E) 3.** The cube root of 729 is 9 (9 × 9 × 9). 9 is the square of 3 (3 × 3).

25. **(E) 240.** The pattern for the arrangement is shown below:
2 4 12 48 ___
×2 ×3 ×4 ×5
Multiplying 48 by 5, we find the correct answer to be 240.

SUBTEST 5—INSTRUMENT COMPREHENSION

Question	Answer	Direction	Pitch	Bank
1.	B	West-southwest	Nose Down	Left
2.	B	South	Nose Down	Zero
3.	D	South	Nose Up	Left
4.	B	Northeast	Nose Up	Left
5.	C	West	Nose Up	Right
6.	A	East	Nose Up	Left
7.	B	South	Zero	Left
8.	A	Southeast	Nose Down	Left
9.	B	West	Nose Up	Left
10.	D	West	Nose Down	Right
11.	B	South	Nose Down	Right
12.	B	South	Zero	Right
13.	B	Left	Zero	Left
14.	D	North	Nose Up	Zero
15.	C	West-southwest	Nose Up	Left
16.	D	East-northeast	Zero	Right
17.	C	West	Nose Up	Zero
18.	A	Northeast	Nose Up	Right
19.	C	Southwest	Nose Down	Left
20.	A	Southwest	Nose Up	Right

SUBTEST 6—BLOCK COUNTING

1. **(B) four.** Block 1 touches two blocks below and one block on either side.
2. **(C) five.** Block 2 touches two blocks on the right, and two blocks below.
3. **(D) six.** Block 3 touches one flock on the right, two blocks below, and three blocks above.
4. **(C) five.** Block 4 touches one block above, two blocks below, and two blocks on the left.
5. **(B) four.** Block 5 touches one block on the left and three blocks above.
6. **(A) one.** Block 1 touches one block below.
7. **(E) five.** Block 2 touches two blocks below, one block on the front-right, one block on the rear-right, and one block above.
8. **(D) six.** Block 3 touches two blocks behind, one block above, two blocks below, and one block on the right.
9. **(E) seven.** Block 4 touches six blocks below and one block above.

10. **(A) three.** Block 5 touches one block below and one block on either side.
11. **(C) five.** Block 1 touches one block on top, two blocks on the right-front, and two blocks below.
12. **(B) four.** Block 2 touches one block above, one block below, and two blocks on the right.
13. **(A) three.** Block 3 touches one block below, one block behind, and one block above.
14. **(C) five.** Block 4 touches two blocks above, one block on the left, and two blocks below.
15. **(B) four.** Block 5 touches one block above, one below, and one block on either side.
16. **(A) three.** Block 1 touches one block above, one block on the right, and one block below.
17. **(C) five.** Block 2 touches one block behind, one block above, one block below, and two blocks in front-right.
18. **(C) five.** Block 3 touches three blocks above and two blocks on the right.
19. **(C) five.** Block 4 touches two blocks behind, one block on the right, and two blocks below.
20. **(D) six.** Block 5 touches three blocks above, one block below, and one block on either side.

SUBTEST 7—TABLE READING

1. **(C) 44.**
2. **(A) 67.**
3. **(E) 44.**
4. **(B) 11.**
5. **(C) 26.**
6. **(A) 32.**
7. **(E) 46.**
8. **(B) 49.**
9. **(D) 37.**
10. **(D) 32.**
11. **(C) 186 pounds.**
12. **(B) 150 pounds.**
13. **(D) 114 pounds.**
14. **(A) 131 pounds.**
15. **(E) 220 pounds.**
16. **(D) 128 pounds.**
17. **(B) 164 pounds.**
18. **(E) 117 pounds.**
19. **(B) 191 pounds.**
20. **(C) 110 pounds.**
21. **(C) 11:12 A.M.**
22. **(B) 8:01 A.M.**
23. **(E) 7:44 A.M.**
24. **(D) 11:08 A.M.**
25. **(B) 9:16 A.M.**
26. **(E) none of the above.**
27. **(A) 10:47 A.M.**
28. **(D) 1:40 P.M.**
29. **(B) 6:48 A.M.**
30. **(A) 9:09 A.M.**
31. **(B) PDN.**
32. **(E) SVC.**
33. **(B) DCG.**
34. **(A) AHS.**
35. **(D) JDY.**
36. **(C) DHO.**
37. **(B) YDH.**
38. **(C) BDR.**
39. **(D) SVG.**
40. **(A) IND.**

SUBTEST 8—AVIATION INFORMATION

1. **(B) 230 degrees.** Runway numbers are associated with the compass direction that the runway is aligned with. 23L means a heading of 230 degrees (the "L" stands for the left-hand runway at airports with two runways aligned in the same direction). Runway 18 would indicate an approach heading of 180, runway 02, an approach heading of 020, etc.
2. **(C) drag, lift, thrust, and weight.** While the airplane is propelled through the air and sufficient lift is developed to sustain it in flight, there are four forces acting on the airplane. These are: thrust or forward force; lift or upward force; drag or rearward acting force; and weight or downward force.
3. **(B) ailerons.** Moving the control stick to the left or right causes the ailerons to raise and lower, which results in the aircraft rotating on its horizontal axis (banking).
4. **(D) tachometer.** The tachometer is an instrument for indicating the speed at which the engine crankshaft is rotating. The other options are all flight instruments.
5. **(E) both (A) and (B).** Flaps are secondary flight controls that increase lift and drag. They are primarily used to increase lift during slower airspeeds for takeoffs and landings.
6. **(A) is cleared to taxi.** A flashing green signal directed to an aircraft on the ground signals that the pilot is cleared to taxi.
7. **(A) the air moving over the wing moves faster than the air moving under the wing.** This increased speed results in a lower air pressure over the wing, compared to the air pressure under the wing, and creates lift.
8. **(B) produce thrust.** The propeller blades, just like a wing, are curved on one side and straight on the other side. As the engine rotates the propeller, forces similar to those on the wing provide "lift" in a forward direction and produce thrust.
9. **(C) pushing on the rudder peddles.** When nose gear steering is engaged, pressing the rudder peddles causes the nose wheel to turn (assuming the aircraft is moving on the ground).
10. **(A) right.** Depressing the left rudder peddle would yaw the aircraft to the left. In other words, the tail would displace to the right, while the nose of the aircraft would displace to the left.
11. **(E) northwest.** 360 degrees is north, 090 degrees is east, 180 degrees is south, and 270 degrees is west. A heading of 300 falls between 270 and 360, so a heading of 300 would indicate a direction of north and west.
12. **(A) climb.** The aircraft has a slight nose-up attitude, which is sufficient for level flight at 180 knots, and increase in airspeed will increase lift, causing the aircraft to climb.
13. **(D) The time in Greenwich England**. Its official name is Coordinated Universal Time or UTC. This time zone had previously been called Greenwich Mean Time (GMT) but was replaced with UTC in 1972 as the official world time standard changed.
14. **(C) faster than the speed of sound.** An aircraft is said to be going "supersonic" when it exceeds the speed of sound.
15. **(E) 6 lbs/gal.** The standard weight for gasoline for aircraft weight and balance computations is 6 pounds for every gallon of gasoline.

16. **(D) ineffectiveness of the ailerons and elevator.** The feeling of control pressures is very important in recognizing the approach of a stall. As speed is reduced, the "live" resistance to pressures on the controls becomes progressively less. Pressures exerted on the controls tend to become movements of the control surfaces, and the lag between those movements and the response of the airplane becomes greater until, in a complete stall, all controls can be moved with almost no resistance and with little immediate effect on the airplane.
17. **(B) horizontal component of lift.** The lift acting upward and opposing weight is called the vertical lift component. The lift acting horizontally and opposing inertia or centrifugal force is called the horizontal lift component. The horizontal lift component is the sideward force that forces the airplane from straight flight and causes it to turn.
18. **(C) 7 or 25.** Runways 7 and 25 are 6003 feet long. Runways 13 and 31 are only 4638 feet long.
19. **(C) NW–SE direction.** Runway 31 (compass heading 310) points to the North-West, and runway 13 (compass heading 130) is pointing to the South-East.
20. **(D) 30 degrees to the right.** Note the angle of the wings. The pilot has banked the aircraft 30 degrees to the right.

SUBTEST 9—ROTATED BLOCKS

1. **(D)**	4. **(E)**	7. **(A)**	10. **(D)**	13. **(C)**
2. **(B)**	5. **(D)**	8. **(B)**	11. **(B)**	14. **(B)**
3. **(D)**	6. **(E)**	9. **(D)**	12. **(E)**	15. **(A)**

SUBTEST 10—GENERAL SCIENCE

1. **(D) helium nuclei.** Alpha particles contain two protons and two neutrons. The fact that alpha particles passing through a thin metal film ricocheted was the first experimental evidence of the atomic nucleus.
2. **(C) soils maintain their fertility.** When organic matter decays, it decomposes into its constituent elements. These elements are returned to the soil, thus increasing its fertility.
3. **(A) mass.** A dalton is a unit of mass, defined as $\frac{1}{12}$ the mass of a carbon-12 nucleus. It's also called the atomic mass unit.
4. **(C) failed to adapt to a changing environment.** The extinction of all sizes and varieties of dinosaurs all over the world cannot be explained by local phenomena, nor on a one-by-one basis. The most reasonable conclusion is that the dinosaurs failed to adapt and were unable to survive as climatic conditions changed radically.
5. **(B) 6.** An adult human of average age and size has about 6 quarts of blood.
6. **(B) avoid salt.** Salt contributes to high blood pressure. The critical element in the action of salt upon the blood pressure is sodium. Iodine or the lack of it plays no role in raising blood pressure.
7. **(C) platelets.** Platelets are the smallest formed elements of blood.
8. **(C) four pairs of legs.** All spiders have four pairs of legs. True insects have three pairs of legs.

9. **(C) the North Star.** The North Star, or Polaris, is the brightest star in the constellation Ursa Minor, the little bear (also known as the Little Dipper).
10. **(A) hydrogen.** The atomic weight of hydrogen is 1.0080, that of helium is 4.003, and of oxygen is 16.00. Air is a mixture of gases, not an element. The atomic weight of nitrogen is 14.0067.
11. **(B) gills.** Fish have gills that transfer oxygen dissolved in the water into their blood.
12. **(B) eight minutes.** Light travels at the rate of 186,292 miles a second. The sun is about 92,900,000 miles from the Earth, so its light arrives here in just over 8 minutes.
13. **(B) the number of protons.** The number of protons determines which element an atom is: 1 proton is hydrogen, and oxygen has 8 protons. Neutrons have mass, but don't change what element an atom is.
14. **(D) an experimental control.** Group B served as the control group. If the condition of patients in Group A were to improve significantly more than that of patients in Group B, scientists might have reason to believe in the effectiveness of the drug.
15. **(C) the Earth's tilting on its axis.** Seasons happen because the Earth is tilted on its axis. As the Earth orbits the sun, the angle of the sun in the sky changes, since the Earth is tilted. The part of the Earth tilted toward the sun sees the sun go higher for longer, and experiences summer. The part tilted away from the sun gets less light each day, the sun looks lower, and winter is cold.
16. **(A) the lead absorbs the harmful radiation.** Radiation cannot pass through lead.
17. **(C) some rotate clockwise; others rotate counterclockwise.** All of the planets in our solar system rotate counterclockwise except for Venus and Uranus. Venus rotates clockwise, and Uranus rotates vertically, compared to its orbit around the Sun.
18. **(E) scurvy.** Scurvy is a disease caused by a vitamin C deficiency. Limes are rich in vitamin C.
19. **(D) salt.** Table salt is mostly sodium chloride. Non-iodized salt is pure sodium chloride.
20. **(A) Mercury.** Mercury is the closest planet to the Sun. Therefore, it has the shortest revolutionary period around the sun.

SUBTEST 11—HIDDEN FIGURES

1. **(A) figure A.**

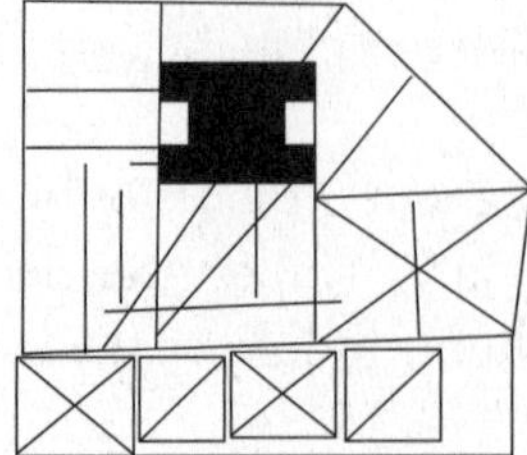

2. **(D) figure D.**

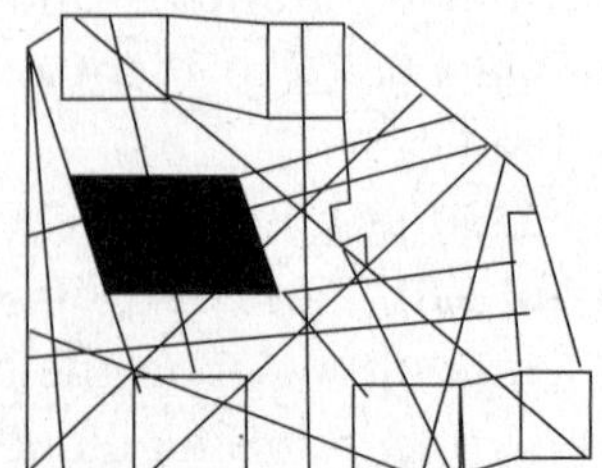

3. **(E) figure E.**

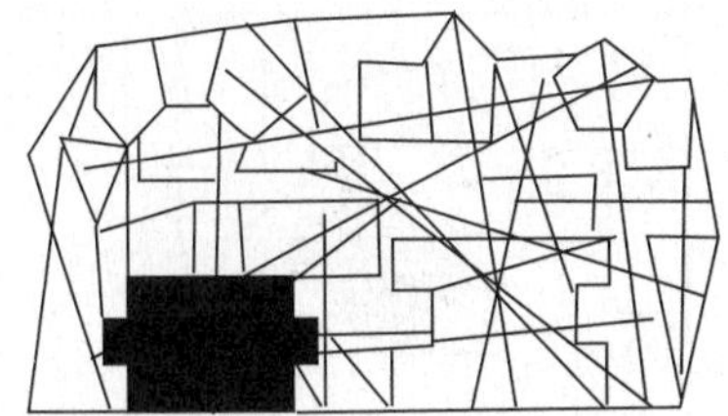

4. **(B) figure B.**

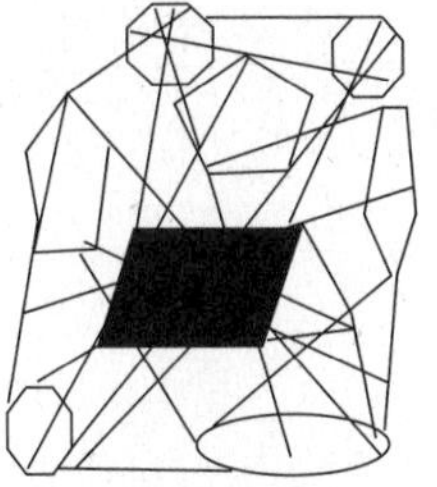

5. **(C) figure C.**

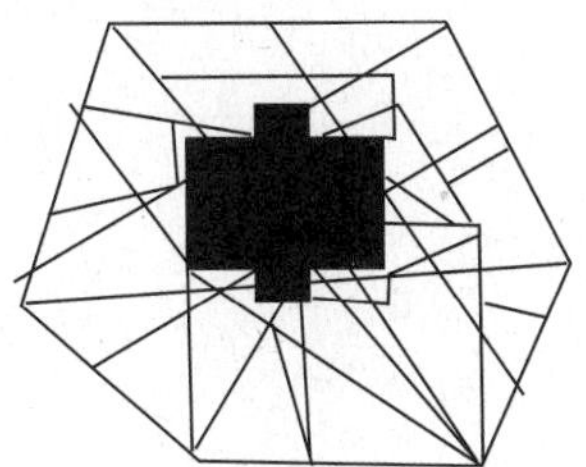

6. **(D) figure D.**

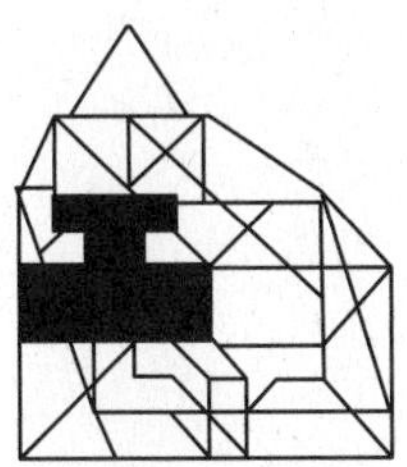

7. **(E) figure E.**

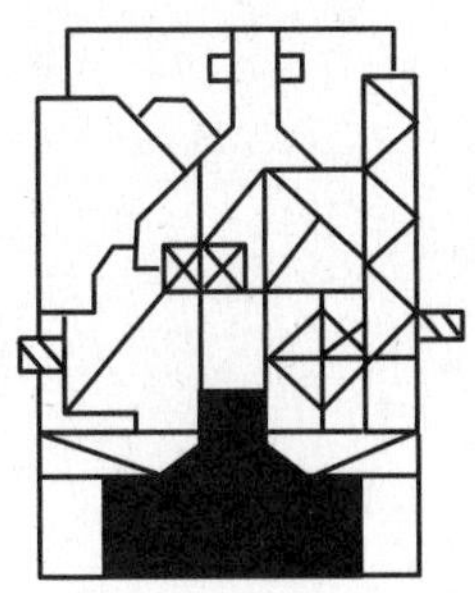

8. **(B) figure B.**

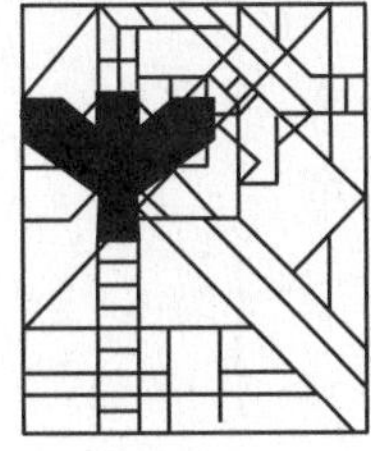

9. **(A) figure A.**

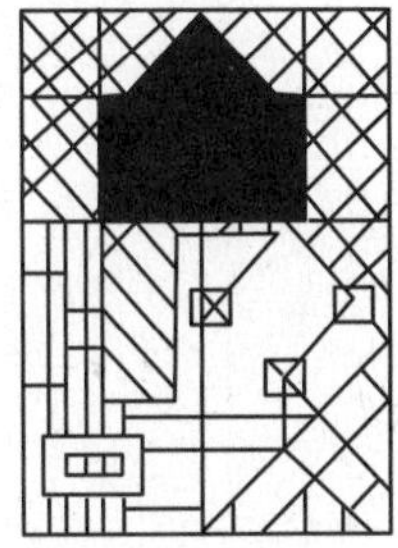

10. **(B) figure B.**

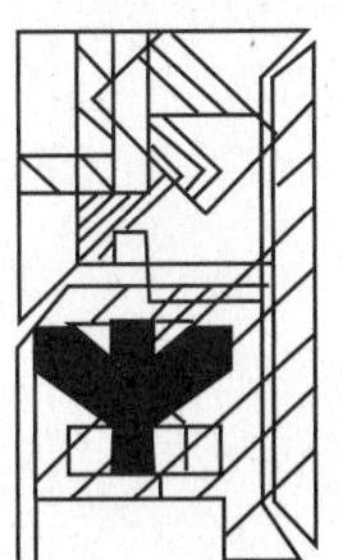

11. **(D) figure D.**

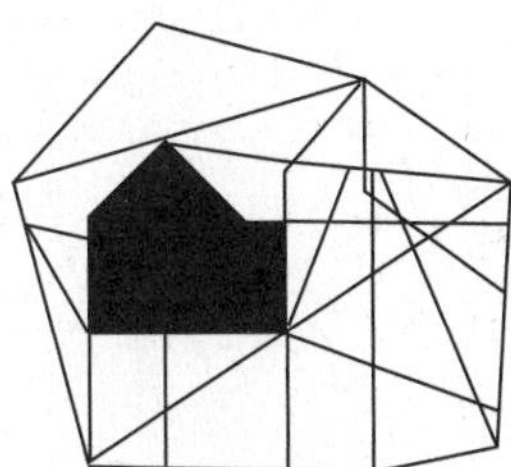

12. **(D) figure D.**

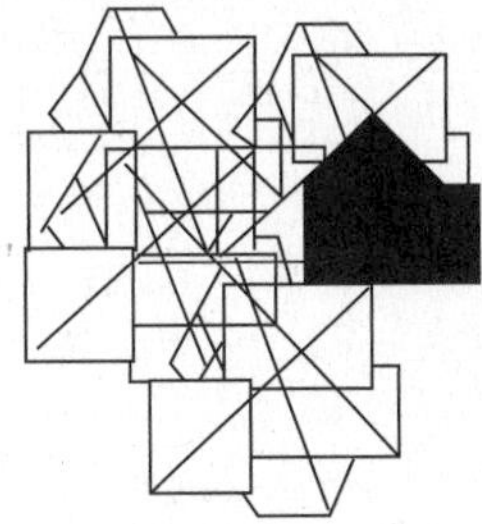

13. **(C) figure C.**

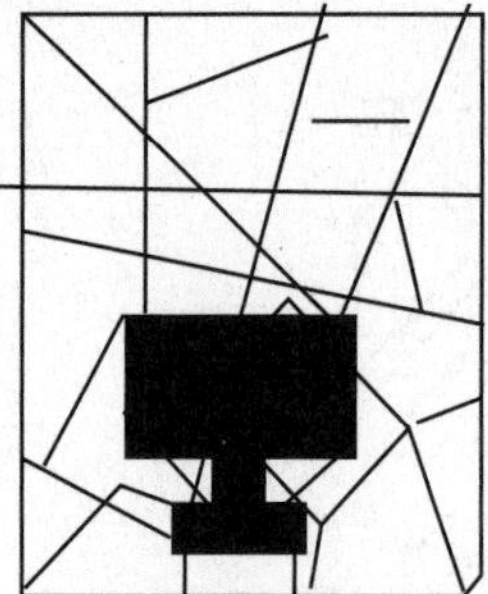

14. **(C) figure C.**

15. **(A) figure A.**

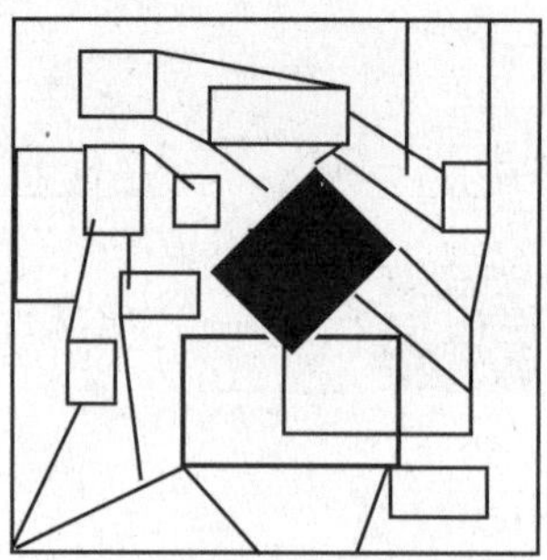

CHAPTER 14

Practice Test for Air Force OTS Applicants

The Air Force Officer Qualifying Test (AFOQT) 2

The AFOQT is required for all applicants for Air Force Officer Training School (OTS). The AFOQT consists of 12 timed subtests, with a total of 480 questions. However, on this practice test we have not included the 220-question self-description inventory subtest (see Chapter 12). The self-description inventory subtest has no right or wrong answers and is not used in calculating any of the AFOQT composite scores, nor is it used in the OTS selection process.

This practice test consists of 11 subtests, comprised of 250 questions. Subtest scores are combined to generate one or more of the five composite scores used to help predict success in certain types of Air Force commissioned officer training programs.

Answer Sheet for Practice Test 2

Subtest 1—Verbal Analogies

1 Ⓐ Ⓑ Ⓒ Ⓓ Ⓔ	8 Ⓐ Ⓑ Ⓒ Ⓓ Ⓔ	14 Ⓐ Ⓑ Ⓒ Ⓓ Ⓔ	20 Ⓐ Ⓑ Ⓒ Ⓓ Ⓔ
2 Ⓐ Ⓑ Ⓒ Ⓓ Ⓔ	9 Ⓐ Ⓑ Ⓒ Ⓓ Ⓔ	15 Ⓐ Ⓑ Ⓒ Ⓓ Ⓔ	21 Ⓐ Ⓑ Ⓒ Ⓓ Ⓔ
3 Ⓐ Ⓑ Ⓒ Ⓓ Ⓔ	10 Ⓐ Ⓑ Ⓒ Ⓓ Ⓔ	16 Ⓐ Ⓑ Ⓒ Ⓓ Ⓔ	22 Ⓐ Ⓑ Ⓒ Ⓓ Ⓔ
4 Ⓐ Ⓑ Ⓒ Ⓓ Ⓔ	11 Ⓐ Ⓑ Ⓒ Ⓓ Ⓔ	17 Ⓐ Ⓑ Ⓒ Ⓓ Ⓔ	23 Ⓐ Ⓑ Ⓒ Ⓓ Ⓔ
5 Ⓐ Ⓑ Ⓒ Ⓓ Ⓔ	12 Ⓐ Ⓑ Ⓒ Ⓓ Ⓔ	18 Ⓐ Ⓑ Ⓒ Ⓓ Ⓔ	24 Ⓐ Ⓑ Ⓒ Ⓓ Ⓔ
6 Ⓐ Ⓑ Ⓒ Ⓓ Ⓔ	13 Ⓐ Ⓑ Ⓒ Ⓓ Ⓔ	19 Ⓐ Ⓑ Ⓒ Ⓓ Ⓔ	25 Ⓐ Ⓑ Ⓒ Ⓓ Ⓔ
7 Ⓐ Ⓑ Ⓒ Ⓓ Ⓔ			

Subtest 2—Arithmetic Reasoning

1 Ⓐ Ⓑ Ⓒ Ⓓ Ⓔ	8 Ⓐ Ⓑ Ⓒ Ⓓ Ⓔ	14 Ⓐ Ⓑ Ⓒ Ⓓ Ⓔ	20 Ⓐ Ⓑ Ⓒ Ⓓ Ⓔ
2 Ⓐ Ⓑ Ⓒ Ⓓ Ⓔ	9 Ⓐ Ⓑ Ⓒ Ⓓ Ⓔ	15 Ⓐ Ⓑ Ⓒ Ⓓ Ⓔ	21 Ⓐ Ⓑ Ⓒ Ⓓ Ⓔ
3 Ⓐ Ⓑ Ⓒ Ⓓ Ⓔ	10 Ⓐ Ⓑ Ⓒ Ⓓ Ⓔ	16 Ⓐ Ⓑ Ⓒ Ⓓ Ⓔ	22 Ⓐ Ⓑ Ⓒ Ⓓ Ⓔ
4 Ⓐ Ⓑ Ⓒ Ⓓ Ⓔ	11 Ⓐ Ⓑ Ⓒ Ⓓ Ⓔ	17 Ⓐ Ⓑ Ⓒ Ⓓ Ⓔ	23 Ⓐ Ⓑ Ⓒ Ⓓ Ⓔ
5 Ⓐ Ⓑ Ⓒ Ⓓ Ⓔ	12 Ⓐ Ⓑ Ⓒ Ⓓ Ⓔ	18 Ⓐ Ⓑ Ⓒ Ⓓ Ⓔ	24 Ⓐ Ⓑ Ⓒ Ⓓ Ⓔ
6 Ⓐ Ⓑ Ⓒ Ⓓ Ⓔ	13 Ⓐ Ⓑ Ⓒ Ⓓ Ⓔ	19 Ⓐ Ⓑ Ⓒ Ⓓ Ⓔ	25 Ⓐ Ⓑ Ⓒ Ⓓ Ⓔ
7 Ⓐ Ⓑ Ⓒ Ⓓ Ⓔ			

Subtest 3—Word Knowledge

1 Ⓐ Ⓑ Ⓒ Ⓓ Ⓔ	8 Ⓐ Ⓑ Ⓒ Ⓓ Ⓔ	14 Ⓐ Ⓑ Ⓒ Ⓓ Ⓔ	20 Ⓐ Ⓑ Ⓒ Ⓓ Ⓔ
2 Ⓐ Ⓑ Ⓒ Ⓓ Ⓔ	9 Ⓐ Ⓑ Ⓒ Ⓓ Ⓔ	15 Ⓐ Ⓑ Ⓒ Ⓓ Ⓔ	21 Ⓐ Ⓑ Ⓒ Ⓓ Ⓔ
3 Ⓐ Ⓑ Ⓒ Ⓓ Ⓔ	10 Ⓐ Ⓑ Ⓒ Ⓓ Ⓔ	16 Ⓐ Ⓑ Ⓒ Ⓓ Ⓔ	22 Ⓐ Ⓑ Ⓒ Ⓓ Ⓔ
4 Ⓐ Ⓑ Ⓒ Ⓓ Ⓔ	11 Ⓐ Ⓑ Ⓒ Ⓓ Ⓔ	17 Ⓐ Ⓑ Ⓒ Ⓓ Ⓔ	23 Ⓐ Ⓑ Ⓒ Ⓓ Ⓔ
5 Ⓐ Ⓑ Ⓒ Ⓓ Ⓔ	12 Ⓐ Ⓑ Ⓒ Ⓓ Ⓔ	18 Ⓐ Ⓑ Ⓒ Ⓓ Ⓔ	24 Ⓐ Ⓑ Ⓒ Ⓓ Ⓔ
6 Ⓐ Ⓑ Ⓒ Ⓓ Ⓔ	13 Ⓐ Ⓑ Ⓒ Ⓓ Ⓔ	19 Ⓐ Ⓑ Ⓒ Ⓓ Ⓔ	25 Ⓐ Ⓑ Ⓒ Ⓓ Ⓔ
7 Ⓐ Ⓑ Ⓒ Ⓓ Ⓔ			

Subtest 4–Mathematics Knowledge

1 Ⓐ Ⓑ Ⓒ Ⓓ Ⓔ
2 Ⓐ Ⓑ Ⓒ Ⓓ Ⓔ
3 Ⓐ Ⓑ Ⓒ Ⓓ Ⓔ
4 Ⓐ Ⓑ Ⓒ Ⓓ Ⓔ
5 Ⓐ Ⓑ Ⓒ Ⓓ Ⓔ
6 Ⓐ Ⓑ Ⓒ Ⓓ Ⓔ
7 Ⓐ Ⓑ Ⓒ Ⓓ Ⓔ
8 Ⓐ Ⓑ Ⓒ Ⓓ Ⓔ
9 Ⓐ Ⓑ Ⓒ Ⓓ Ⓔ
10 Ⓐ Ⓑ Ⓒ Ⓓ Ⓔ
11 Ⓐ Ⓑ Ⓒ Ⓓ Ⓔ
12 Ⓐ Ⓑ Ⓒ Ⓓ Ⓔ
13 Ⓐ Ⓑ Ⓒ Ⓓ Ⓔ
14 Ⓐ Ⓑ Ⓒ Ⓓ Ⓔ
15 Ⓐ Ⓑ Ⓒ Ⓓ Ⓔ
16 Ⓐ Ⓑ Ⓒ Ⓓ Ⓔ
17 Ⓐ Ⓑ Ⓒ Ⓓ Ⓔ
18 Ⓐ Ⓑ Ⓒ Ⓓ Ⓔ
19 Ⓐ Ⓑ Ⓒ Ⓓ Ⓔ
20 Ⓐ Ⓑ Ⓒ Ⓓ Ⓔ
21 Ⓐ Ⓑ Ⓒ Ⓓ Ⓔ
22 Ⓐ Ⓑ Ⓒ Ⓓ Ⓔ
23 Ⓐ Ⓑ Ⓒ Ⓓ Ⓔ
24 Ⓐ Ⓑ Ⓒ Ⓓ Ⓔ
25 Ⓐ Ⓑ Ⓒ Ⓓ Ⓔ

Subtest 5–Instrument Comprehension

1 Ⓐ Ⓑ Ⓒ Ⓓ
2 Ⓐ Ⓑ Ⓒ Ⓓ
3 Ⓐ Ⓑ Ⓒ Ⓓ
4 Ⓐ Ⓑ Ⓒ Ⓓ
5 Ⓐ Ⓑ Ⓒ Ⓓ
6 Ⓐ Ⓑ Ⓒ Ⓓ
7 Ⓐ Ⓑ Ⓒ Ⓓ
8 Ⓐ Ⓑ Ⓒ Ⓓ
9 Ⓐ Ⓑ Ⓒ Ⓓ
10 Ⓐ Ⓑ Ⓒ Ⓓ
11 Ⓐ Ⓑ Ⓒ Ⓓ
12 Ⓐ Ⓑ Ⓒ Ⓓ
13 Ⓐ Ⓑ Ⓒ Ⓓ
14 Ⓐ Ⓑ Ⓒ Ⓓ
15 Ⓐ Ⓑ Ⓒ Ⓓ
16 Ⓐ Ⓑ Ⓒ Ⓓ
17 Ⓐ Ⓑ Ⓒ Ⓓ
18 Ⓐ Ⓑ Ⓒ Ⓓ
19 Ⓐ Ⓑ Ⓒ Ⓓ
20 Ⓐ Ⓑ Ⓒ Ⓓ

Subtest 6–Block Counting

1 Ⓐ Ⓑ Ⓒ Ⓓ Ⓔ
2 Ⓐ Ⓑ Ⓒ Ⓓ Ⓔ
3 Ⓐ Ⓑ Ⓒ Ⓓ Ⓔ
4 Ⓐ Ⓑ Ⓒ Ⓓ Ⓔ
5 Ⓐ Ⓑ Ⓒ Ⓓ Ⓔ
6 Ⓐ Ⓑ Ⓒ Ⓓ Ⓔ
7 Ⓐ Ⓑ Ⓒ Ⓓ Ⓔ
8 Ⓐ Ⓑ Ⓒ Ⓓ Ⓔ
9 Ⓐ Ⓑ Ⓒ Ⓓ Ⓔ
10 Ⓐ Ⓑ Ⓒ Ⓓ Ⓔ
11 Ⓐ Ⓑ Ⓒ Ⓓ Ⓔ
12 Ⓐ Ⓑ Ⓒ Ⓓ Ⓔ
13 Ⓐ Ⓑ Ⓒ Ⓓ Ⓔ
14 Ⓐ Ⓑ Ⓒ Ⓓ Ⓔ
15 Ⓐ Ⓑ Ⓒ Ⓓ Ⓔ
16 Ⓐ Ⓑ Ⓒ Ⓓ Ⓔ
17 Ⓐ Ⓑ Ⓒ Ⓓ Ⓔ
18 Ⓐ Ⓑ Ⓒ Ⓓ Ⓔ
19 Ⓐ Ⓑ Ⓒ Ⓓ Ⓔ
20 Ⓐ Ⓑ Ⓒ Ⓓ Ⓔ

Subtest 7–Table Reading

1 Ⓐ Ⓑ Ⓒ Ⓓ Ⓔ	11 Ⓐ Ⓑ Ⓒ Ⓓ Ⓔ	21 Ⓐ Ⓑ Ⓒ Ⓓ Ⓔ	31 Ⓐ Ⓑ Ⓒ Ⓓ Ⓔ
2 Ⓐ Ⓑ Ⓒ Ⓓ Ⓔ	12 Ⓐ Ⓑ Ⓒ Ⓓ Ⓔ	22 Ⓐ Ⓑ Ⓒ Ⓓ Ⓔ	32 Ⓐ Ⓑ Ⓒ Ⓓ Ⓔ
3 Ⓐ Ⓑ Ⓒ Ⓓ Ⓔ	13 Ⓐ Ⓑ Ⓒ Ⓓ Ⓔ	23 Ⓐ Ⓑ Ⓒ Ⓓ Ⓔ	33 Ⓐ Ⓑ Ⓒ Ⓓ Ⓔ
4 Ⓐ Ⓑ Ⓒ Ⓓ Ⓔ	14 Ⓐ Ⓑ Ⓒ Ⓓ Ⓔ	24 Ⓐ Ⓑ Ⓒ Ⓓ Ⓔ	34 Ⓐ Ⓑ Ⓒ Ⓓ Ⓔ
5 Ⓐ Ⓑ Ⓒ Ⓓ Ⓔ	15 Ⓐ Ⓑ Ⓒ Ⓓ Ⓔ	25 Ⓐ Ⓑ Ⓒ Ⓓ Ⓔ	35 Ⓐ Ⓑ Ⓒ Ⓓ Ⓔ
6 Ⓐ Ⓑ Ⓒ Ⓓ Ⓔ	16 Ⓐ Ⓑ Ⓒ Ⓓ Ⓔ	26 Ⓐ Ⓑ Ⓒ Ⓓ Ⓔ	36 Ⓐ Ⓑ Ⓒ Ⓓ Ⓔ
7 Ⓐ Ⓑ Ⓒ Ⓓ Ⓔ	17 Ⓐ Ⓑ Ⓒ Ⓓ Ⓔ	27 Ⓐ Ⓑ Ⓒ Ⓓ Ⓔ	37 Ⓐ Ⓑ Ⓒ Ⓓ Ⓔ
8 Ⓐ Ⓑ Ⓒ Ⓓ Ⓔ	18 Ⓐ Ⓑ Ⓒ Ⓓ Ⓔ	28 Ⓐ Ⓑ Ⓒ Ⓓ Ⓔ	38 Ⓐ Ⓑ Ⓒ Ⓓ Ⓔ
9 Ⓐ Ⓑ Ⓒ Ⓓ Ⓔ	19 Ⓐ Ⓑ Ⓒ Ⓓ Ⓔ	29 Ⓐ Ⓑ Ⓒ Ⓓ Ⓔ	39 Ⓐ Ⓑ Ⓒ Ⓓ Ⓔ
10 Ⓐ Ⓑ Ⓒ Ⓓ Ⓔ	20 Ⓐ Ⓑ Ⓒ Ⓓ Ⓔ	30 Ⓐ Ⓑ Ⓒ Ⓓ Ⓔ	40 Ⓐ Ⓑ Ⓒ Ⓓ Ⓔ

Subtest 8–Aviation Information

1 Ⓐ Ⓑ Ⓒ Ⓓ Ⓔ	6 Ⓐ Ⓑ Ⓒ Ⓓ Ⓔ	11 Ⓐ Ⓑ Ⓒ Ⓓ Ⓔ	16 Ⓐ Ⓑ Ⓒ Ⓓ Ⓔ
2 Ⓐ Ⓑ Ⓒ Ⓓ Ⓔ	7 Ⓐ Ⓑ Ⓒ Ⓓ Ⓔ	12 Ⓐ Ⓑ Ⓒ Ⓓ Ⓔ	17 Ⓐ Ⓑ Ⓒ Ⓓ Ⓔ
3 Ⓐ Ⓑ Ⓒ Ⓓ Ⓔ	8 Ⓐ Ⓑ Ⓒ Ⓓ Ⓔ	13 Ⓐ Ⓑ Ⓒ Ⓓ Ⓔ	18 Ⓐ Ⓑ Ⓒ Ⓓ Ⓔ
4 Ⓐ Ⓑ Ⓒ Ⓓ Ⓔ	9 Ⓐ Ⓑ Ⓒ Ⓓ Ⓔ	14 Ⓐ Ⓑ Ⓒ Ⓓ Ⓔ	19 Ⓐ Ⓑ Ⓒ Ⓓ Ⓔ
5 Ⓐ Ⓑ Ⓒ Ⓓ Ⓔ	10 Ⓐ Ⓑ Ⓒ Ⓓ Ⓔ	15 Ⓐ Ⓑ Ⓒ Ⓓ Ⓔ	20 Ⓐ Ⓑ Ⓒ Ⓓ Ⓔ

Subtest 9–Rotated Blocks

1 Ⓐ Ⓑ Ⓒ Ⓓ Ⓔ	5 Ⓐ Ⓑ Ⓒ Ⓓ Ⓔ	9 Ⓐ Ⓑ Ⓒ Ⓓ Ⓔ	13 Ⓐ Ⓑ Ⓒ Ⓓ Ⓔ
2 Ⓐ Ⓑ Ⓒ Ⓓ Ⓔ	6 Ⓐ Ⓑ Ⓒ Ⓓ Ⓔ	10 Ⓐ Ⓑ Ⓒ Ⓓ Ⓔ	14 Ⓐ Ⓑ Ⓒ Ⓓ Ⓔ
3 Ⓐ Ⓑ Ⓒ Ⓓ Ⓔ	7 Ⓐ Ⓑ Ⓒ Ⓓ Ⓔ	11 Ⓐ Ⓑ Ⓒ Ⓓ Ⓔ	15 Ⓐ Ⓑ Ⓒ Ⓓ Ⓔ
4 Ⓐ Ⓑ Ⓒ Ⓓ Ⓔ	8 Ⓐ Ⓑ Ⓒ Ⓓ Ⓔ	12 Ⓐ Ⓑ Ⓒ Ⓓ Ⓔ	

Subtest 10–General Science

1 Ⓐ Ⓑ Ⓒ Ⓓ Ⓔ	6 Ⓐ Ⓑ Ⓒ Ⓓ Ⓔ	11 Ⓐ Ⓑ Ⓒ Ⓓ Ⓔ	16 Ⓐ Ⓑ Ⓒ Ⓓ Ⓔ
2 Ⓐ Ⓑ Ⓒ Ⓓ Ⓔ	7 Ⓐ Ⓑ Ⓒ Ⓓ Ⓔ	12 Ⓐ Ⓑ Ⓒ Ⓓ Ⓔ	17 Ⓐ Ⓑ Ⓒ Ⓓ Ⓔ
3 Ⓐ Ⓑ Ⓒ Ⓓ Ⓔ	8 Ⓐ Ⓑ Ⓒ Ⓓ Ⓔ	13 Ⓐ Ⓑ Ⓒ Ⓓ Ⓔ	18 Ⓐ Ⓑ Ⓒ Ⓓ Ⓔ
4 Ⓐ Ⓑ Ⓒ Ⓓ Ⓔ	9 Ⓐ Ⓑ Ⓒ Ⓓ Ⓔ	14 Ⓐ Ⓑ Ⓒ Ⓓ Ⓔ	19 Ⓐ Ⓑ Ⓒ Ⓓ Ⓔ
5 Ⓐ Ⓑ Ⓒ Ⓓ Ⓔ	10 Ⓐ Ⓑ Ⓒ Ⓓ Ⓔ	15 Ⓐ Ⓑ Ⓒ Ⓓ Ⓔ	20 Ⓐ Ⓑ Ⓒ Ⓓ Ⓔ

Subtest 11–Hidden Figures

1 Ⓐ Ⓑ Ⓒ Ⓓ Ⓔ	5 Ⓐ Ⓑ Ⓒ Ⓓ Ⓔ	9 Ⓐ Ⓑ Ⓒ Ⓓ Ⓔ	13 Ⓐ Ⓑ Ⓒ Ⓓ Ⓔ
2 Ⓐ Ⓑ Ⓒ Ⓓ Ⓔ	6 Ⓐ Ⓑ Ⓒ Ⓓ Ⓔ	10 Ⓐ Ⓑ Ⓒ Ⓓ Ⓔ	14 Ⓐ Ⓑ Ⓒ Ⓓ Ⓔ
3 Ⓐ Ⓑ Ⓒ Ⓓ Ⓔ	7 Ⓐ Ⓑ Ⓒ Ⓓ Ⓔ	11 Ⓐ Ⓑ Ⓒ Ⓓ Ⓔ	15 Ⓐ Ⓑ Ⓒ Ⓓ Ⓔ
4 Ⓐ Ⓑ Ⓒ Ⓓ Ⓔ	8 Ⓐ Ⓑ Ⓒ Ⓓ Ⓔ	12 Ⓐ Ⓑ Ⓒ Ⓓ Ⓔ	

Subtest 1—Verbal Analogies

Directions: This subtest measures ability to reason and see relationships between words. The subtest is comprised of 25 questions that must be answered in eight minutes. Choose the answer that best completes the analogy given at the beginning of the question.

1. ALPHA is to OMEGA as
   (A) appendix is to preface
   (B) beginning is to end
   (C) head is to body
   (D) intermission is to finale
   (E) prelude is to intermission

2. LOOM is to WEAVER as EASEL is to
   (A) carpenter
   (B) artist
   (C) error
   (D) training
   (E) machinist

3. MICROMETER is to MACHINIST as TROWEL is to
   (A) blacksmith
   (B) electrician
   (C) mason
   (D) pressman
   (E) welder

4. SHIPS are to FLEET as
   (A) banana is to orange
   (B) sandal is to foot
   (C) religion is to church
   (D) manic is to depressed
   (E) persons is to crowd

5. DOZEN is to SCORE as
   (A) VII is to XII
   (B) IIX is to XX
   (C) IIX is to XL
   (D) XII is to XX
   (E) XII is to XL

6. CARELESSNESS is to REPRIMAND as EFFICIENCY is to
   (A) practice
   (B) experience
   (C) reward
   (D) mistake
   (E) temperature

7. EMERALD is to GREEN as
   (A) canary is to yellow
   (B) cocoa is to brown
   (C) navy is to blue
   (D) royal is to purple
   (E) ruby is to red

8. DALMATIAN is to DOG as
   (A) oriole is to bird
   (B) horse is to pony
   (C) shark is to great white
   (D) ant is to insect
   (E) stock is to savings

9. TENET is to THEOLOGIAN as
   (A) predecessor is to heir
   (B) hypothesis is to biologist
   (C) recluse is to rivalry
   (D) arrogance is to persecution
   (E) guitarist is to rock band

10. FLY is to FLOWN as FALL is to
    (A) fallen
    (B) fell
    (C) fall
    (D) failed
    (E) faked

11. HORIZONTAL is to VERTICAL as WARP is to
    (A) count
    (B) pile
    (C) selvage
    (D) weave
    (E) woof

12. EXORCISM is to DEMON as
    (A) matriculation is to induction
    (B) banishment is to member
    (C) qualm is to angel
    (D) heuristic is to method
    (E) manifesto is to spirit

13. KILOMETER is to METER as
    (A) century is to decade
    (B) century is to year
    (C) decade is to month
    (D) millennium is to century
    (E) millennium is to year

14. UNPRECEDENTED is to PREVIOUS OCCURRENCE as
    (A) naïve is to harmony
    (B) incomparable is to equal
    (C) improper is to vacillation
    (D) eccentric is to intensity
    (E) random is to recidivism

15. ORDINATION is to PRIEST as
    (A) election is to official
    (B) inauguration is to president
    (C) matriculation is to student
    (D) nomination is to officer
    (E) retirement is to minister

16. INTEREST is to OBSESSION as DECIMATION is to
    (A) insouciance
    (B) assiduity
    (C) caprice
    (D) annihilation
    (E) procrastination

17. ORDINANCE is to REGULATION as ORDNANCE is to
    (A) law
    (B) military
    (C) ammunition
    (D) numerical
    (E) statute

18. COFFER is to VALUABLES as SANCTUARY is to
    (A) refuge
    (B) sea
    (C) mountain
    (D) avalanche
    (E) book

19. UNIT is to DOZEN as
    (A) day is to week
    (B) hour is to day
    (C) minute is to hour
    (D) month is to year
    (E) week is to month

20. DISHEARTENED is to HOPE as
    (A) enervated is to ennui
    (B) buoyant is to effervescence
    (C) amoral is to ethics
    (D) munificent is to altruism
    (E) nefarious is to turpitude

21. MNEMONIC is to MEMORY as PACEMAKER is to

(A) lungs
(B) rhythm
(C) blood
(D) pulse
(E) heartbeat

22. ZENITH is to NADIR as

(A) best is to worst
(B) heaviest is to lightest
(C) highest is to lowest
(D) most is to least
(E) widest is to narrowest

23. DIDACTIC is to TEACH as

(A) specious is to revile
(B) cunning is to steal
(C) forensic is to debate
(D) troubled is to broach
(E) puissant is to injure

24. SQUARE is to CIRCLE as PERIMETER is to

(A) arc
(B) circumference
(C) diameter
(D) radius
(E) sector

25. VEHICLE is to BUS as

(A) football is to handball
(B) game is to baseball
(C) hunting is to fishing
(D) play is to sport
(E) sport is to recreation

Subtest 2—Arithmetic Reasoning

Directions: This subtest measures general mathematical reasoning. The questions are designed to determine your ability to arrive at solutions to math word problems. The subtest consists of 25 questions that must be answered in 29 minutes.

1. If each brick is 3 inches wide and 5 inches long, how many bricks would you need to build a wall that will measure 10 feet by 16 feet?

(A) 940
(B) 980
(C) 1,302
(D) 1,536
(E) 1,623

2. The floor area in an Air Force warehouse measures 200 feet by 200 feet. What is the maximum safe floor load if the maximum weight the floor area can hold is 4,000 tons?

(A) 100 pounds per square foot
(B) 120 pounds per square foot
(C) 140 pounds per square foot
(D) 160 pounds per square foot
(E) 200 pounds per square foot

3. How much carpet would be necessary to cover a room that is 8 feet long and 6 feet wide?

(A) 14 square feet
(B) 20 square feet
(C) 48 square feet
(D) 60 square feet
(E) 80 square feet

4. Assume that the United States Mint produces one million nickels a month. The total value of the nickels produced during a year is __________.

(A) $50,000
(B) $60,000
(C) $250,000
(D) $500,000
(E) $600,000

5. A bakery specializes in peach and apple pies. Out of a batch of 26 pies, 4 are peach. What percent of the pies are peach?

(A) 10.3 percent
(B) 15.4 percent
(C) 20.5 percent
(D) 25.6 percent
(E) 27.3 percent

6. There are 20 cigarettes in one pack and 10 packs of cigarettes in a carton. A certain brand of cigarette contains 12 mg of tar per cigarette. How many grams of tar are contained in one carton of these cigarettes? (1 gram = 1000 milligrams)

(A) .024 grams
(B) 0.24 grams
(C) 2.4 grams
(D) 24 grams
(E) 240 grams

7. The Hair Palace gives a $5\frac{1}{2}$ percent discount to senior citizens. If Pam is 67 years old, and her hair restyling costs $75, what is the amount of her bill once the discount is applied?

(A) $55.88
(B) $57.88
(C) $66.88
(D) $70.88
(E) $73.88

8. Two office workers have been assigned to address 750 envelopes. One addresses twice as many envelopes per hour as the other. If it takes five hours for them to complete the job, what was the rate of the slower worker?

(A) 50 envelopes per hour
(B) 75 envelopes per hour
(C) 100 envelopes per hour
(D) 125 envelopes per hour
(E) 150 envelopes per hour

9. A new computer purchased for $2,800 depreciates at a rate of 22 percent per year. How much is the computer worth after 30 months?

(A) $1,505
(B) $1, 603
(C) $1,691
(D) $1,703
(E) $1,758

10. A pound of margarine contains four equal sticks of margarine. The wrapper of each stick has markings that indicate how to divide the stick into eight sections, each section measuring one tablespoon. If a recipe calls for four tablespoons of margarine, the amount to use is

(A) $\frac{1}{16}$ lb.
(B) $\frac{1}{8}$ lb.
(C) $\frac{1}{4}$ lb.
(D) $\frac{1}{2}$ lb.
(E) $\frac{3}{4}$ lb.

11. The daily charge for a rental car is $18.00, plus 35 cents per mile driven. If the day's bill was $39.00, how far was the car driven?

(A) 40 miles
(B) 50 miles
(C) 60 miles
(D) 70 miles
(E) 80 miles

12. A certain governmental agency had a budget last year of $1,100,500. Its budget this year was 7% higher than that of last year. The budget for next year is 8% higher than this year's budget. Which one of the following is the agency's budget for next year?

    (A) $1,117,600
    (B) $1,161,600
    (C) $1,261,700
    (D) $1,265,600
    (E) $1,271,700

13. Tom and Kyle live 5 miles apart. If Tom leaves his house on a bicycle, heading for Kyle's house, traveling at 8 mph, and Kyle leaves his house, jogging at a rate of 7 mph, heading for Tom's house, how long will it take for them to meet?

    (A) 10 minutes
    (B) 15 minutes
    (C) 20 minutes
    (D) 25 minutes.
    (E) 30 minutes

14. If the weight of water is 62.4 pounds per cubic foot, the weight of the water that fills a rectangular container 6 inches by 6 inches by 1 foot is __________.

    (A) 3.9 pounds
    (B) 7.8 pounds
    (C) 15.6 pounds
    (D) 31.2 pounds
    (E) 62.4 pounds

15. A rectangle is one inch longer than it is wide. If the diameter of the rectangle is five inches, what are the dimensions of the rectangle?

    (A) 4 inches × 5 inches
    (B) 3 inches × 4 inches
    (C) 1 inch × 2 inches
    (D) 5 inches × 6 inches
    (E) 6 inches × 7 inches

16. An Air Force recruiting station enlisted 560 people. Of these, 25 percent were under 20 years old and 35 percent were 20 to 22 years old. How many of the recruits were over 22 years old?

    (A) 196
    (B) 224
    (C) 244
    (D) 280
    (E) 336

17. The final test in a course counts as one-fourth of the course grade. The average of four quizzes counts as the remaining three-fourths of the final grade. If a student's quiz scores are 61, 63, 65, and 83, what does she need to make on the final test to raise her average to 70?

    (A) 75
    (B) 76
    (C) 78
    (D) 79
    (E) 80

18. The area of a square is 36 square inches. If the side of this square is doubled, the area of the new square will be

    (A) 72 square inches
    (B) 108 square inches
    (C) 216 square inches
    (D) 244 square inches
    (E) none of the above

19. Martha and John are planning their wedding reception. The caterer has given them two options: under Plan A, the caterer will charge a set fee of $25 per person. Under Plan B, the caterer would charge $1,300 plus $20 for each guest in excess of the first 25 who attend. Assuming that more than 25 guests will attend, how many people must attend before Plan B becomes the cheaper plan?

    (A) 150
    (B) 193
    (C) 261
    (D) 283
    (E) 290

20. A purse has 25 coins worth $4.90. If the purse contains only dimes and quarters, how many quarters are in the purse?

(A) 10
(B) 14
(C) 16
(D) 18
(E) 20

21. The length of a rectangular patio is 1 foot less than 3 times its width. If the perimeter of the patio is 46 feet, what are the dimensions of the patio?

(A) 5 × 15 feet
(B) 7 × 14 feet
(C) 8 × 10 feet
(D) 6 × 17 feet
(E) 5 × 7 feet

22. Two integers have a total of 65. Four times the smaller integer is equal to the larger integer. Find the larger integer.

(A) 48
(B) 52
(C) 58
(D) 62
(E) 63

23. Samantha worked 30 hours last week. She earned $418. If she was paid $432, how many hours did she work?

(A) 31
(B) 32
(C) 33
(D) 34
(E) 36

24. A collection of coins has a value of $7.30. There are two more nickels than dimes and 3 times as many quarters as dimes. How many dimes are there?

(A) 8
(B) 10
(C) 12
(D) 14
(E) 16

25. Two men agree to divide the profit on a business venture in the ratio of 4 to 7. If the total profit on the venture was $6,196, what is the share of the second man (the one with the larger share)?

(A) $3942.91
(B) $4003.23
(C) $4129.40
(D) $4232.39
(E) $4439.22

Subtest 3—Word Knowledge

Directions: This subtest measures verbal comprehension involving the ability to understand written language. The questions are designed to measure vocabulary ability. The subtest consists of 25 questions that must be answered in 5 minutes. Choose the answer that MOST NEARLY means the same as the capitalized word in the question stem.

1. ALTERCATION

(A) controversy
(B) defeat
(C) irritation
(D) substitution
(E) vexation

2. ILLUSTRATE

(A) demonstrate
(B) value
(C) agree
(D) help
(E) perpetuate

3. ATTRITION

(A) act of expanding
(B) act of giving up
(C) act of purifying
(D) act of solving
(E) act of wearing down

4. INSIGHTFUL
   (A) perceptive
   (B) voluntary
   (C) infamous
   (D) religious
   (E) temporary

5. CONDUCIVE
   (A) confusing
   (B) cooperative
   (C) energetic
   (D) helpful
   (E) respectful

6. ILLUSORY
   (A) deceptive
   (B) genuine
   (C) insightful
   (D) silly
   (E) trademark

7. DELETERIOUS
   (A) delightful
   (B) frail
   (C) harmful
   (D) late
   (E) tasteful

8. COMMANDING
   (A) exciting
   (B) zealous
   (C) authoritative
   (D) unusual
   (E) racist

9. FLEXIBLE
   (A) flammable
   (B) fragile
   (C) pliable
   (D) rigid
   (E) separable

10. OPPORTUNITY
    (A) placement
    (B) refined
    (C) tiresome
    (D) chance
    (E) knowledge

11. IMPARTIAL
    (A) complete
    (B) fair
    (C) incomplete
    (D) sincere
    (E) watchful

12. ACCOUNTANT
    (A) bookkeeper
    (B) banker
    (C) lawyer
    (D) police officer
    (E) taxidermist

13. INDOLENT
    (A) hopeless
    (B) lazy
    (C) lenient
    (D) rude
    (E) selfish

14. REBUFF
    (A) forget
    (B) ignore
    (C) recover
    (D) polish
    (E) snub

15. SPURIOUS
    (A) false
    (B) maddening
    (C) obvious
    (D) odd
    (E) stimulating

16. INAPT
    (A) incompetent
    (B) adequate
    (C) problematic
    (D) animated
    (E) liberate

17. HUMANITARIAN
    (A) relief
    (B) canopy
    (C) pragmatic
    (D) Samaritan
    (E) customer

18. MARITIME
    (A) travel
    (B) stratosphere
    (C) aquatic
    (D) underground
    (E) return

19. LITIGIOUS
    (A) argumentative
    (B) lawyer
    (C) program
    (D) performance
    (E) jail

20. HARANGUE
    (A) speech
    (B) irritate
    (C) temporal
    (D) commendation
    (E) antisocial

21. SULLEN
    (A) angrily silent
    (B) grayish yellow
    (C) mildly nauseated
    (D) soaking wet
    (E) very dirty

22. TEDIOUS
    (A) demanding
    (B) dull
    (C) hard
    (D) simple
    (E) surprising

23. RECREANT
    (A) lazy
    (B) coward
    (C) priest
    (D) fireman
    (E) ocean-going

24. GLUTINOUS
    (A) sticky
    (B) overeater
    (C) open
    (D) separated
    (E) divorce

25. DISSONANCE
    (A) rely
    (B) performance
    (C) sound
    (D) truthful
    (E) argue

Subtest 4—Mathematics Knowledge

Directions: This subtest measures functional ability in using learned mathematical relationships. The subtest consists of 25 questions that must be answered in 25 minutes. Choose the answer that best answers the question.

1. The distance in miles around a circular course with a radius of 35 miles is ________.

   (use $pi = \frac{22}{7}$)

   (A) 110 miles
   (B) 156 miles
   (C) 220 miles
   (D) 440 miles
   (E) 880 miles

2. Find the area of the shaded portion of the figure below.

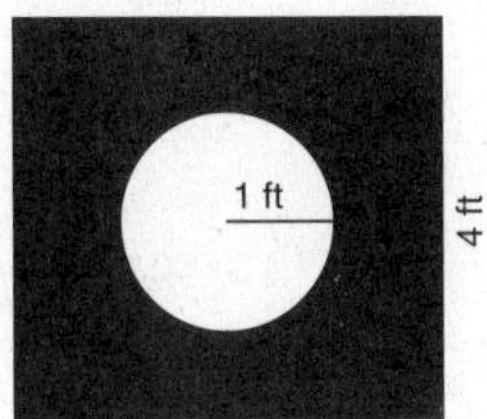

   (A) 10.57 square feet
   (B) 11.17 square feet
   (C) 12.86 square feet
   (D) 13.44 square feet
   (E) 14 square feet

3. Solve for x: $\frac{2x}{7} = 2x^2$

   (A) $\frac{1}{7}$
   (B) $\frac{2}{7}$
   (C) 2
   (D) 7
   (E) 14

4. Apply the Distributive Property and simplify the following: $-7(4x + 5) - 8$

   (A) $-28x + 43$
   (B) $28x - 43$
   (C) $-28x - 43$
   (D) $28x + 43$
   (E) none of the above

5. $\frac{x-2}{x^2-6x+8}$ can be reduced to

   (A) $\frac{1}{x-4}$
   (B) $\frac{1}{x-2}$
   (C) $\frac{x-2}{x+2}$
   (D) $\frac{1}{x+2}$
   (E) $\frac{1}{x+4}$

6. What is the area of the shape below?

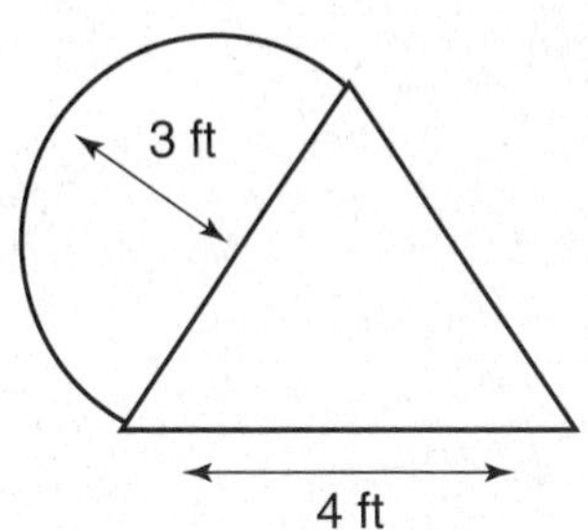

   (A) $4\pi + 12$ square feet
   (B) $6(\pi - 4)$ square feet
   (C) $\frac{9\pi}{2} + 12$ square feet
   (D) $6\pi - 24$ square feet
   (E) none of the above

7. $(-3)^3 =$

   (A) 9
   (B) −9
   (C) 27
   (D) −27
   (E) none of the above

Practice Test 2

8. How much carpet would be necessary to cover a room that is 8 feet long and 6 feet wide?

(A) 14 square feet
(B) 20 square feet
(C) 48 square feet
(D) 60 square feet
(E) 65 square feet

9. Ten thousand may be represented as __________.

(A) 10^4
(B) 10^5
(C) 10^6
(D) 10^7
(E) 10^8

10. Convert 6.39×10^{-4} to regular notation.

(A) $(6.39)^5 \times 10$
(B) 639,000
(C) 639.10
(D) 0.000639
(E) none of the above

11. $\left(\frac{3}{4}\right)^3 =$

(A) $\frac{9}{16}$
(B) $\frac{27}{16}$
(C) $\frac{9}{4}$
(D) $\frac{64}{27}$
(E) $\frac{27}{64}$

12. $5x + 7 = 6(x - 2) - 4(2x - 3)$

(A) 0
(B) –1
(C) 1
(D) 2
(E) –2

13. If $3^n = 9$, what is the value of $4x - n$?

(A) 25
(B) 30
(C) 35
(D) 47
(E) none of the above

14. The graph of $x^2 - y^2 - 3x + 4y - 5$ is which of the following?

(A) circle
(B) semicircle
(C) ellipse
(D) hyperbola
(E) square

15. 4^{-2} is equal to

(A) 0.001
(B) 0.01
(C) 16
(D) $\frac{1}{16}$
(E) $\frac{-1}{16}$

16. Solve for x: $x - 31\frac{3}{4}\% = 174.4$

(A) 255.5
(B) 207.3
(C) 135.4
(D) 300.3
(E) 40.5

17. The hypotenuse of a right triangle whose legs are 5″ and 12″ is __________.

(A) 7″
(B) 13″
(C) 14″
(D) 17″
(E) none of the above

18. The diagonal formula for a rectangle is $D^2 = L^2 + W^2$. If $D = 5$ and $L = W + 1$, solve for W.

    (A) 3
    (B) 4
    (C) 5
    (D) 6
    (E) 7

19. The sum of the angle measures of a hexagon is __________.

    (A) 360°
    (B) 540°
    (C) 720°
    (D) 900°
    (E) 1180°

20. Solve for x: $\frac{3}{4}(68) + \frac{1}{4}(x) = 70$

    (A) 50
    (B) 56
    (C) 65
    (D) 73
    (E) 76

21. A scale of $\frac{1}{24{,}000}$ is the same as a scale of __________.

    (A) $\frac{1}{32}$ inch = 1 yard
    (B) 1 inch = 2,000 feet
    (C) 1 foot = $\frac{1}{2}$ mile
    (D) 1 yard = 2 miles
    (E) none of the above

22. The volume of a cylinder with a radius of r and a height of h is __________.

    (A) πrh
    (B) $2\pi rh$
    (C) $2\pi r^2 h$
    (D) $4\pi r^2 h$
    (E) none of the above

23. The numerical value of $\frac{4!}{3!}$ is __________.

    (A) .75
    (B) 1
    (C) 1.25
    (D) 1.33
    (E) 4

24. If the log of x is 2.5464, the number of digits in x to the left of the decimal point is __________.

    (A) 0
    (B) 1
    (C) 2
    (D) 3
    (E) 4

25. What is the appropriate option for the next two letters in the following series of letters that follow some definite pattern?

    A R C S E T G __ __

    (A) UH
    (B) HI
    (C) UI
    (D) IU
    (E) IH

Subtest 5—Instrument Comprehension

Directions: This subtest has 20 questions that must be answered in 6 minutes. The questions are designed to measure your ability to determine the position of an airplane in flight from reading instruments showing its compass heading, its amount of climb or dive, and its degree of bank to right or left.

In each item, the left-hand dial is labeled **ARTIFICIAL HORIZON**. On the face of this dial the small aircraft silhouette remains stationary, while the positions of the heavy black line and the black pointer vary with changes in the position of the airplane in which the instrument is located.

How to Read the Artificial Horizon Dial

The heavy black line represents the **HORIZON LINE**. The black pointer shows the degree of **BANK** to the right or left.

Dial 1 shows an airplane neither climbing nor diving, with no bank.

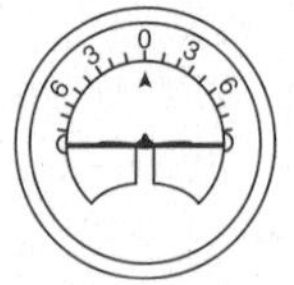

Artificial Horizon

If the airplane is neither climbing nor diving, the horizon line is directly on the silhouette's fuselage. If the airplane has no bank, the black pointer is seen to point to zero.

Dial 2 shows an airplane climbing and banking 45 degrees to the pilot's right.

Artificial Horizon

If the airplane is climbing, the fuselage silhouette is seen between the horizon line and the pointer. The greater the amount of climb, the greater the distance between the horizon line and the fuselage silhouette. If the airplane is banked to the pilot's right, the pointer is seen to the left of zero.

Dial 3 shows an airplane diving and banked 45 degrees to the pilot's left.

Artificial Horizon

If the airplane is diving, the horizon line is seen between the fuselage silhouette and the pointer. The greater the amount of dive, the greater the distance between the horizon line and the fuselage silhouette. If the airplane is banked to the pilot's left, the pointer is seen to the right of zero.

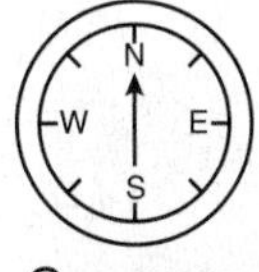

Compass Dial 4

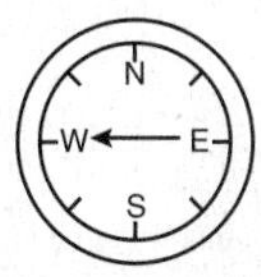

Compass Dial 5

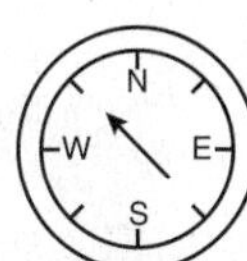

Compass Dial 6

On each item, the right-hand dial is labeled **COMPASS**. On this dial, the arrow shows the compass direction in which the airplane is headed at the moment.

Dial 4 shows it headed north; dial 5 shows it headed west; and dial 6 shows it headed northwest.

Each item in this test consists of two dials and four silhouettes of airplanes in flight. Your task is to determine which one of the four airplanes is **MOST NEARLY** in the position indicated by the two dials. **YOU ARE ALWAYS LOOKING NORTH AT THE SAME ALTITUDE AS EACH OF THE PLANES. EAST IS ALWAYS TO YOUR RIGHT AS YOU LOOK AT THE PAGE.**

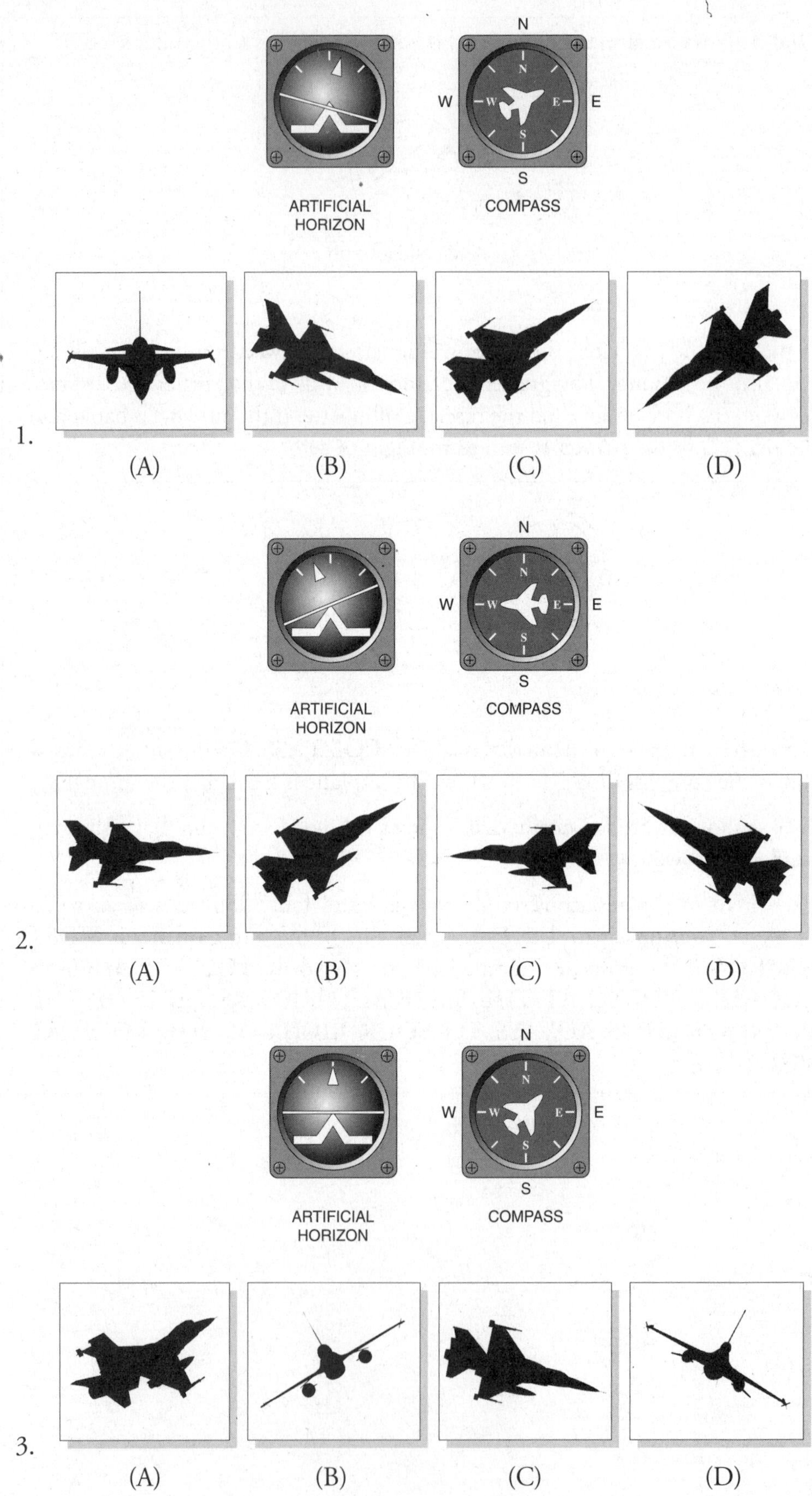
N
W
E
S
ARTIFICIAL HORIZON
COMPASS
1.
(A)
(B)
(C)
(D)
N
W
E
S
ARTIFICIAL HORIZON
COMPASS
2.
(A)
(B)
(C)
(D)
N
W
E
S
ARTIFICIAL HORIZON
COMPASS
3.
(A)
(B)
(C)
(D)

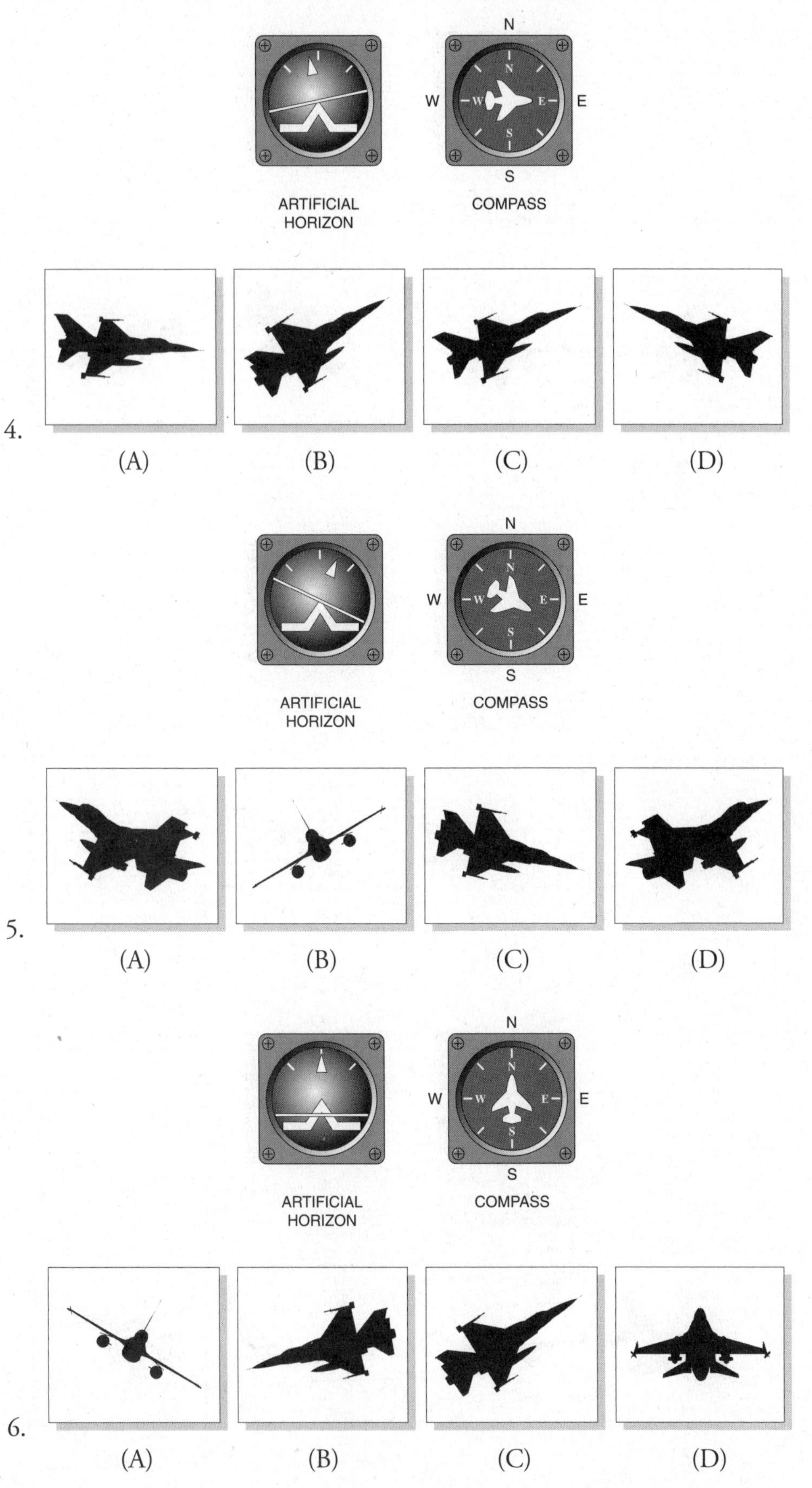
N
W
E
S
ARTIFICIAL HORIZON
COMPASS
4.
(A)
(B)
(C)
(D)
N
W
E
S
ARTIFICIAL HORIZON
COMPASS
5.
(A)
(B)
(C)
(D)
N
W
E
S
ARTIFICIAL HORIZON
COMPASS
6.
(A)
(B)
(C)
(D)

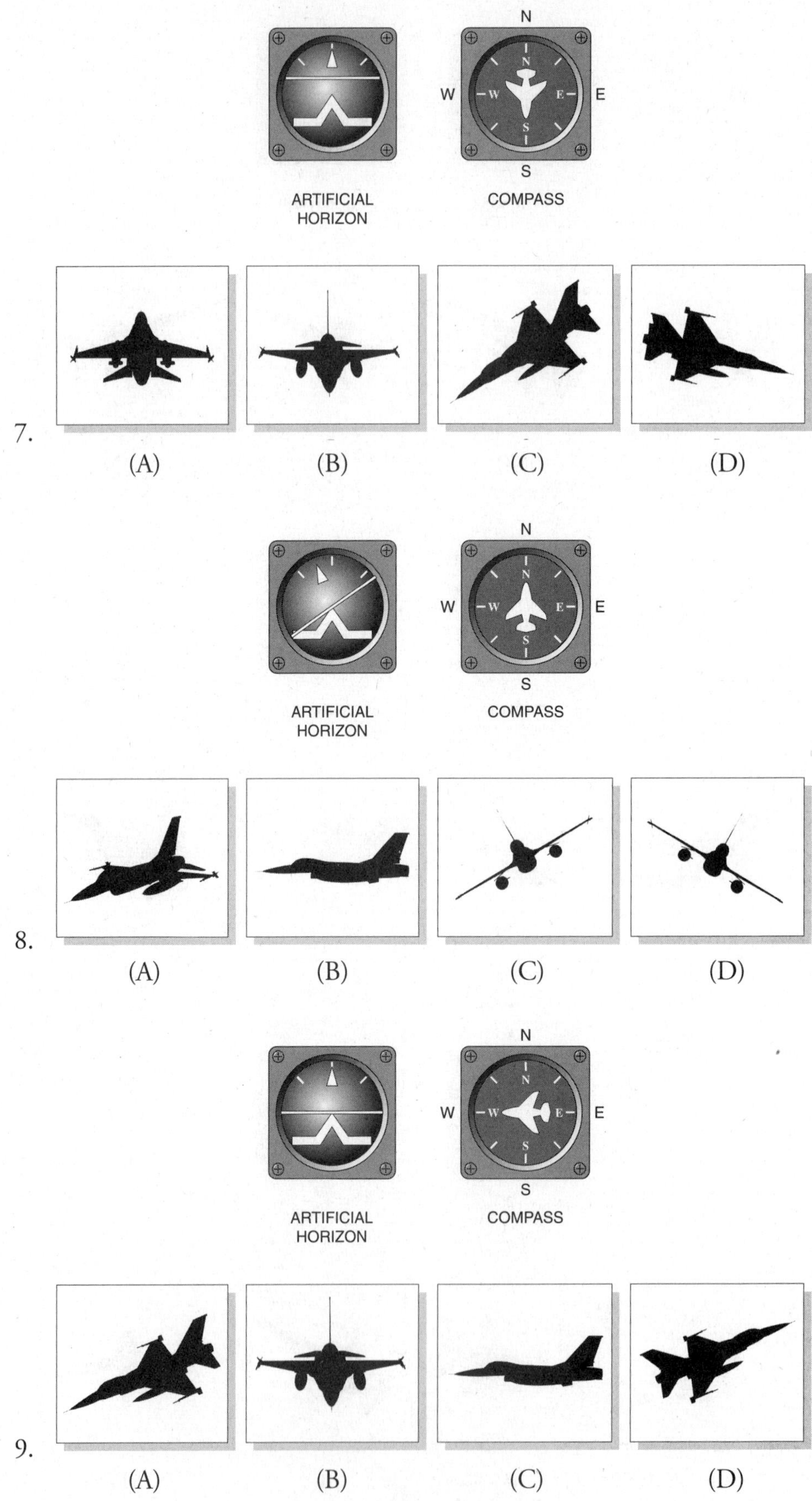
N
W
E
S
ARTIFICIAL HORIZON
COMPASS
7.
(A)
(B)
(C)
(D)
N
W
E
S
ARTIFICIAL HORIZON
COMPASS
8.
(A)
(B)
(C)
(D)
N
W
E
S
ARTIFICIAL HORIZON
COMPASS
9.
(A)
(B)
(C)
(D)

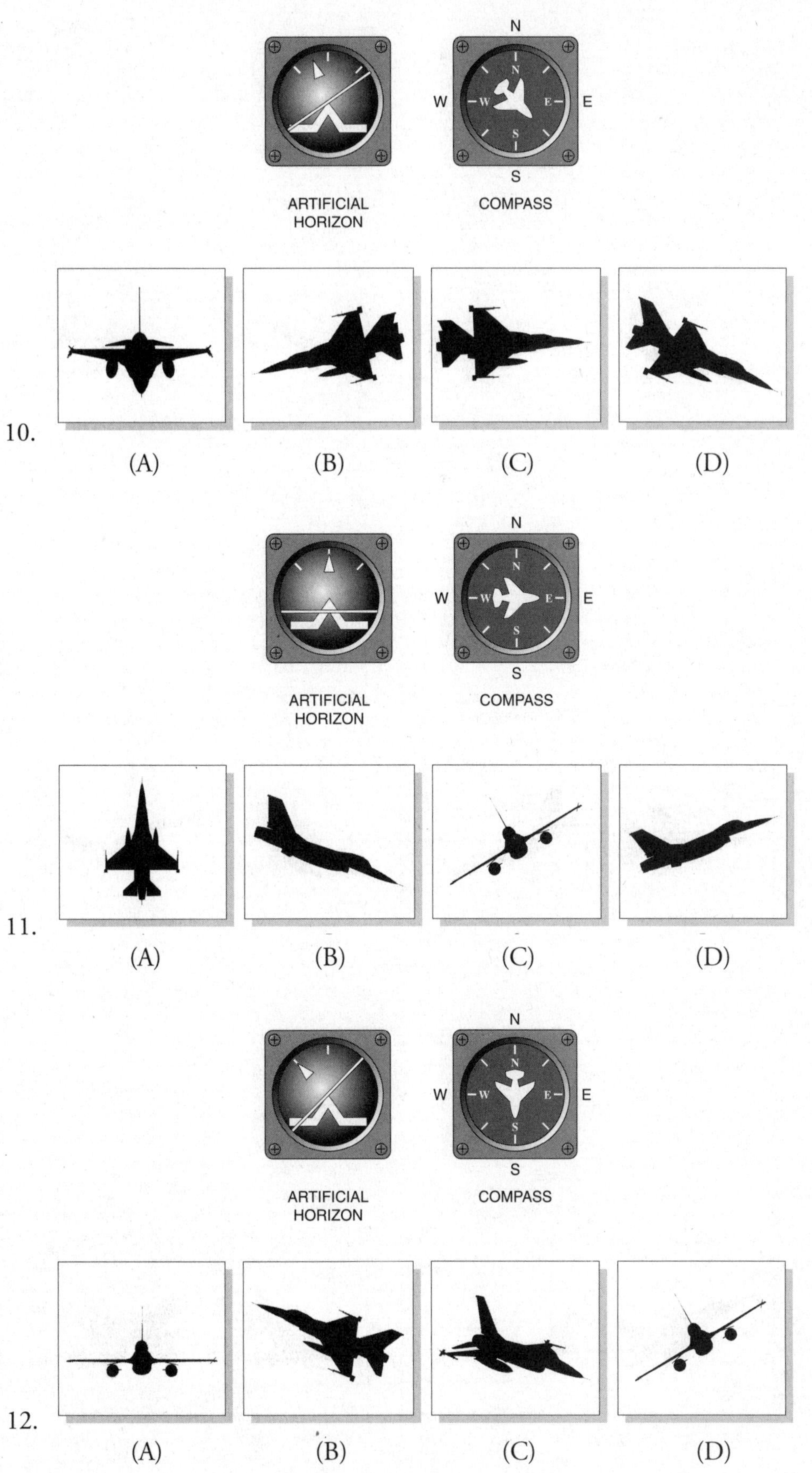
N
W
E
S
ARTIFICIAL HORIZON
COMPASS
10.
(A)
(B)
(C)
(D)
N
W
E
S
ARTIFICIAL HORIZON
COMPASS
11.
(A)
(B)
(C)
(D)
N
W
E
S
ARTIFICIAL HORIZON
COMPASS
12.
(A)
(B)
(C)
(D)

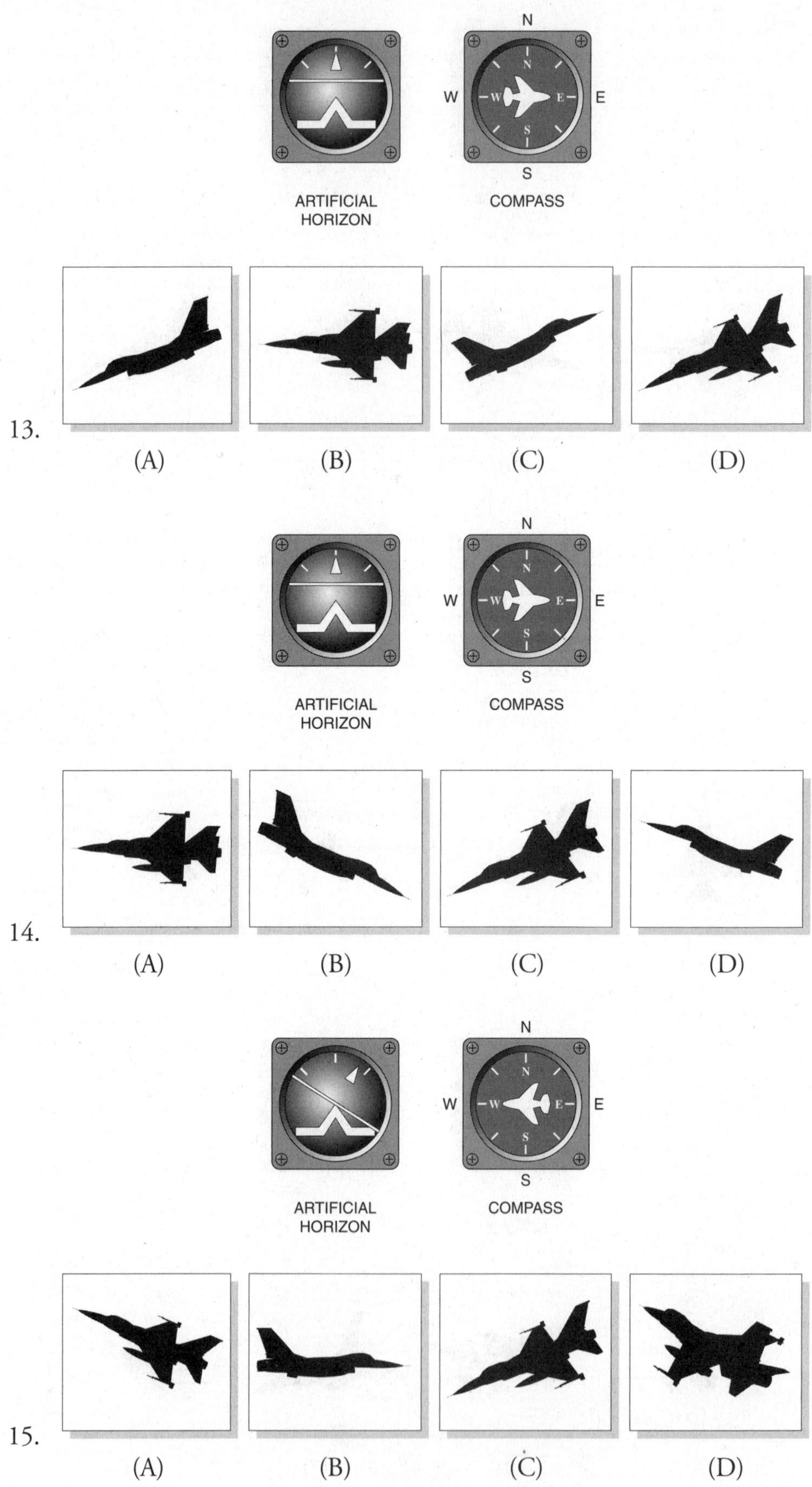
N
W
E
S
ARTIFICIAL HORIZON
COMPASS
13.
(A)
(B)
(C)
(D)
N
W
E
S
ARTIFICIAL HORIZON
COMPASS
14.
(A)
(B)
(C)
(D)
N
W
E
S
ARTIFICIAL HORIZON
COMPASS
15.
(A)
(B)
(C)
(D)

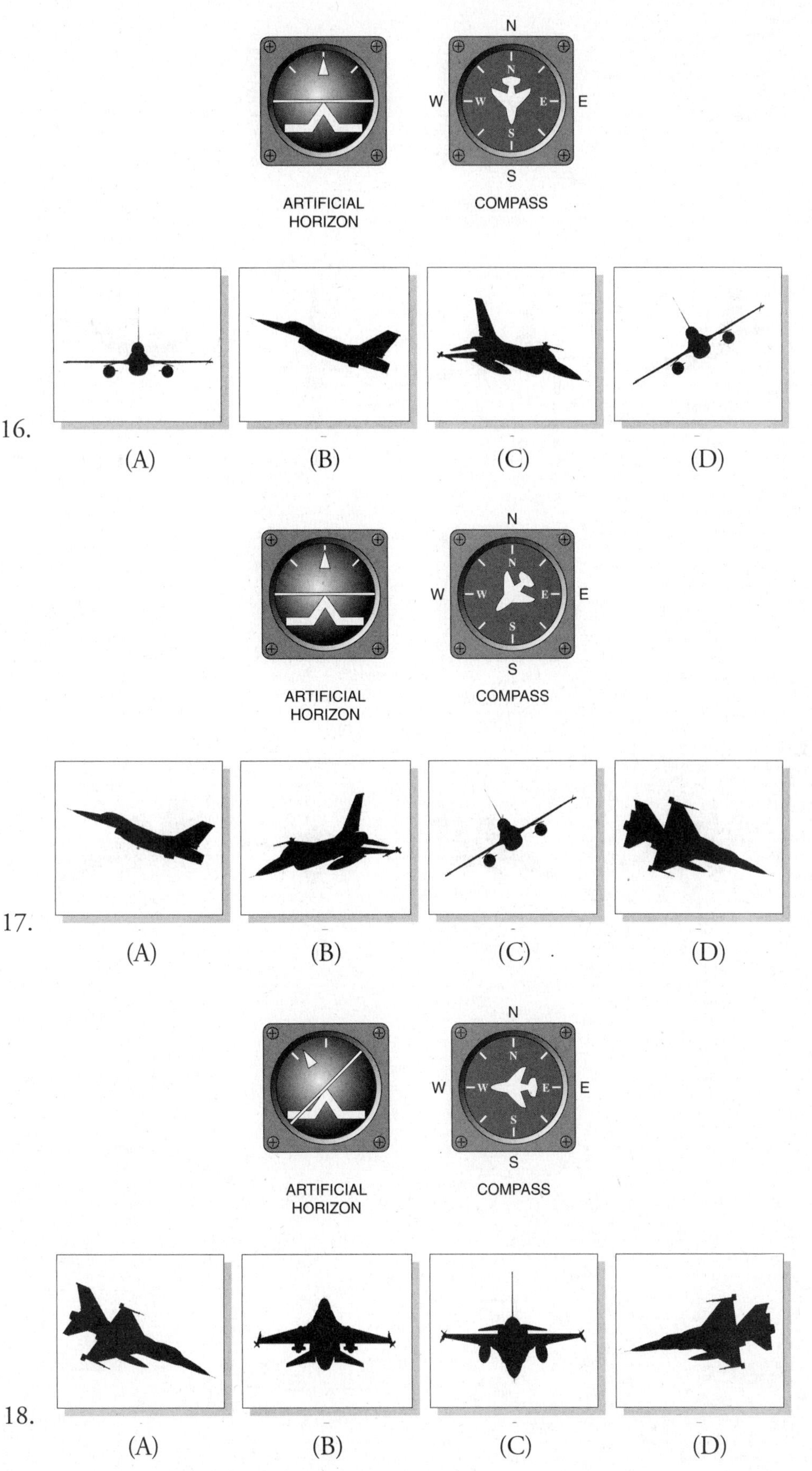

N
W
E
S
ARTIFICIAL HORIZON
COMPASS
16.
(A)
(B)
(C)
(D)
N
W
E
S
ARTIFICIAL HORIZON
COMPASS
17.
(A)
(B)
(C)
(D)
N
W
E
S
ARTIFICIAL HORIZON
COMPASS
18.
(A)
(B)
(C)
(D)

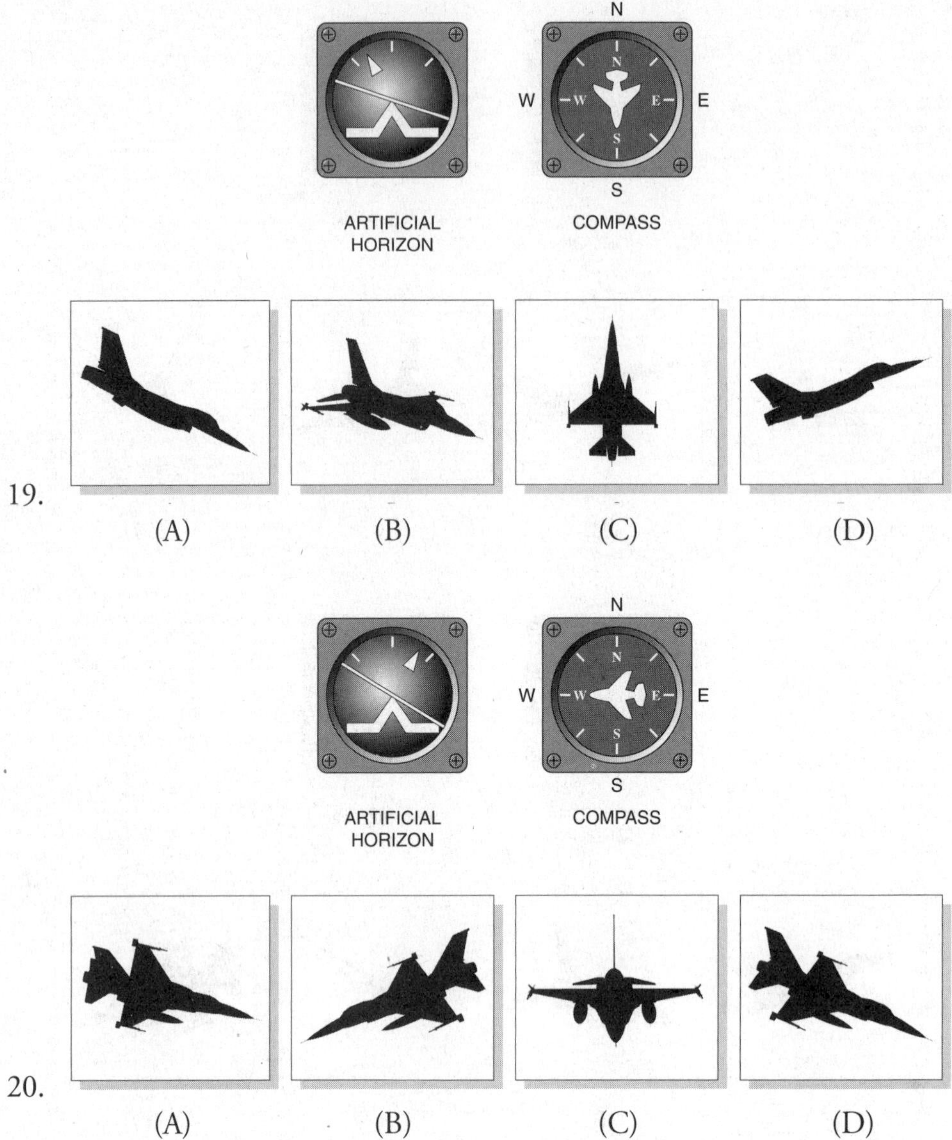
ARTIFICIAL HORIZON
N
W
E
S
COMPASS
19.
(A)
(B)
(C)
(D)
ARTIFICIAL HORIZON
N
W
E
S
COMPASS
20.
(A)
(B)
(C)
(D)

Subtest 6—Block Counting

Directions: This subtest consists of 20 questions that must be answered in 3 minutes. The questions are designed to measure your ability to visualize a three-dimensional pile of blocks and determine how many pieces are touched by certain numbered blocks. *All of the blocks in each pile are the same size and shape.* A block is considered to touch the numbered block if any part, even a corner or an edge, touches.

Questions 1 through 5 are to be answered based on the figure below.

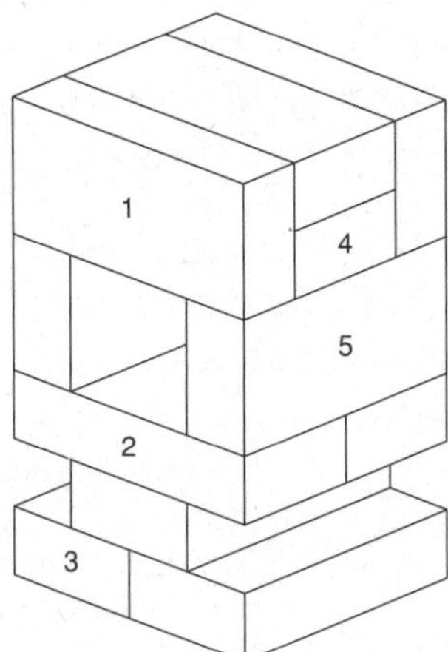

1. Block 1 touches __________ blocks.
   (A) three
   (B) four
   (C) five
   (D) six
   (E) seven

2. Block 2 touches __________ blocks.
   (A) three
   (B) four
   (C) five
   (D) six
   (E) seven

3. Block 3 touches __________ blocks.
   (A) one
   (B) two
   (C) three
   (D) four
   (E) five

4. Block 4 touches __________ blocks.
   (A) three
   (B) four
   (C) five
   (D) six
   (E) seven

5. Block 5 touches __________ blocks.
   (A) three
   (B) four
   (C) five
   (D) six
   (E) seven

Questions 6 through 10 are to be answered based on the figure below.

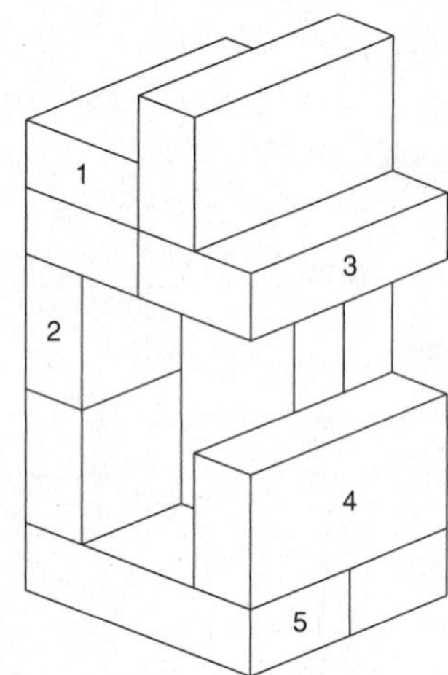

6. Block 1 touches __________ blocks.

   (A) three
   (B) four
   (C) five
   (D) six
   (E) seven

7. Block 2 touches __________ blocks.

   (A) three
   (B) four
   (C) five
   (D) six
   (E) seven

8. Block 3 touches __________ blocks.

   (A) three
   (B) four
   (C) five
   (D) six
   (E) seven

9. Block 4 touches __________ blocks.

   (A) three
   (B) four
   (C) five
   (D) six
   (E) seven

10. Block 5 touches __________ blocks.

    (A) three
    (B) four
    (C) five
    (D) six
    (E) seven

Questions 11 through 15 are to be answered based on the figure below.

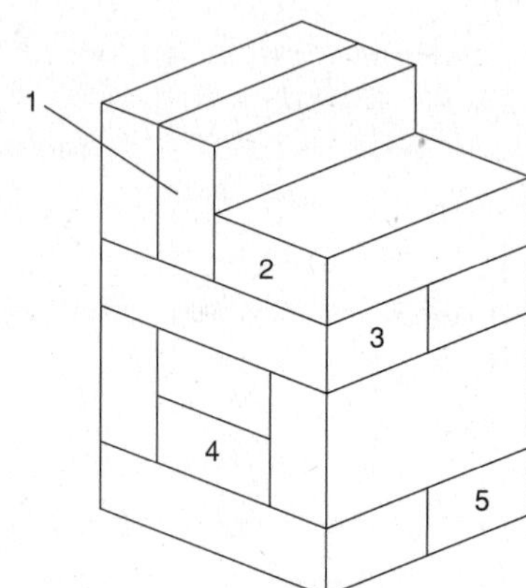

11. Block 1 touches __________ blocks.

    (A) three
    (B) four
    (C) five
    (D) six
    (E) seven

12. Block 2 touches __________ blocks.

    (A) three
    (B) four
    (C) five
    (D) six
    (E) seven

13. Block 3 touches __________ blocks.

    (A) three
    (B) four
    (C) five
    (D) six
    (E) seven

Practice Test 2

14. Block 4 touches __________ blocks.

    (A) three
    (B) four
    (C) five
    (D) six
    (E) seven

15. Block 5 touches __________ blocks.

    (A) three
    (B) four
    (C) five
    (D) six
    (E) seven

Questions 16 through 20 are to be answered based on the figure below.

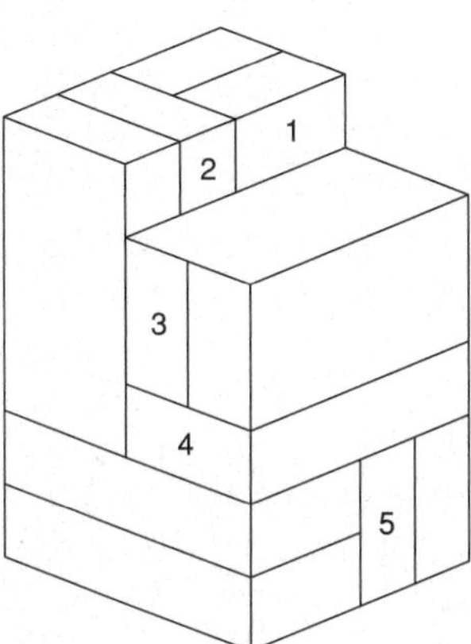

16. Block 1 touches __________ blocks.

    (A) four
    (B) five
    (C) six
    (D) seven
    (E) eight

17. Block 2 touches __________ blocks.

    (A) four
    (B) five
    (C) six
    (D) seven
    (E) eight

18. Block 3 touches __________ blocks.

    (A) four
    (B) five
    (C) six
    (D) seven
    (E) eight

19. Block 4 touches __________ blocks.

    (A) four
    (B) five
    (C) six
    (D) seven
    (E) eight

20. Block 5 touches __________ blocks.

    (A) four
    (B) five
    (C) six
    (D) seven
    (E) eight

Subtest 7 – Table Reading

Directions: This subtest measures ability to read tables quickly and accurately. The subtest consists of 40 questions that must be answered in 7 minutes. See Chapter 6 for more information and practice questions.

Questions 1 through 10 are based on the table below. Note that the X values are shown at the top of the table and the Y values are shown on the left of the table. Find the entry that occurs at the intersection of the row and the column corresponding to the values given.

X Value

Y Value		**4**	**3**	**2**	**1**	**0**	**–1**	**–2**	**–3**	**–4**	**–5**
	–4	4	5	8	0	8	6	–4	3	0	8
	–3	9	6	4	9	7	–5	2	8	6	8
	–2	4	7	9	–4	3	8	8	9	–6	7
	–1	4	–7	9	7	–6	5	7	–3	9	7
Y Value	**0**	–4	7	9	8	7	5	–4	5	6	–7
	1	3	4	5	–6	2	7	–8	6	4	3
	2	–4	6	9	8	6	–4	5	2	9	7
	3	4	–6	8	–4	7	8	3	9	–7	6
	4	5	7	0	7	3	8	0	4	6	3
	5	–8	6	8	5	–8	4	8	–4	6	–5

1. X; –5, Y 3
   - (A) 0
   - (B) 6
   - (C) 9
   - (D) 3
   - (E) 4

2. X; 3, Y; 1
   - (A) 4
   - (B) 3
   - (C) 8
   - (D) 6
   - (E) 0

3. X; 1, Y; –2
   - (A) 6
   - (B) –6
   - (C) –4
   - (D) 3
   - (E) –8

4. X; 3, Y; 0
   - (A) –1
   - (B) –3
   - (C) 7
   - (D) –2
   - (E) –4

5. X; 2, Y; 2
   - (A) 7
   - (B) 9
   - (C) –3
   - (D) –8
   - (E) 4

6. X; –4, Y; 1
   - (A) –1
   - (B) –7
   - (C) 5
   - (D) 8
   - (E) 4

7. X; –5, Y; –2
   - (A) 4
   - (B) 7
   - (C) –3
   - (D) 2
   - (E) 0

8. X; 0, Y; 3
   - (A) 7
   - (B) 6
   - (C) 2
   - (D) –4
   - (E) –1

9. X; 0, Y, –2
   - (A) 3
   - (B) 4
   - (C) –9
   - (D) –7
   - (E) 0

10. X; 2, Y; –2
    - (A) 1
    - (B) 9
    - (C) –1
    - (D) 4
    - (E) 5

Questions 11 through 15 are to be answered based on the following table:

Commissioned Officer Basic Pay, Based on Rank and Years of Service

Rank	14	16	18	20	22	24	26
O-10				12,818.70	12,818.70	12,818.70	12,818.70
O-9				11,689.50	11,857.50	12,101.10	12,525.60
O-8	9,916.20	10,222.80	10,666.20	11,075.40	11,348.70	11,348.70	11,348.70
O-7	8,607.90	9,371.10	10,015.80	10,015.80	10,015.80	10,015.80	10,066.50
O-6	6,633.30	7,263.90	7,634.10	8,004.00	8,214.60	8,427.60	8,841.30
O-5	6,236.10	6,630.60	6,818.10	7,003.80	7,214.40	7,214.40	7,214.40
O-4	5,945.40	6,054.30	6,117.60	6,117.60	6,117.60	6,117.60	6,117.60
O-3	5,240.70	5,240.70	5,240.70	5,240.70	5,240.70	5,240.70	5,240.70
O-2	3,852.00	3,852.00	3,852.00	3,852.00	3,852.00	3,852.00	3,852.00
O-1	3,039.60	3,039.60	3,039.60	3,039.60	3,039.60	3,039.60	3,039.60

11. An O-7 with 22 years of service makes ___________.

(A) 6,117.60
(B) 11,348.70
(C) 10,015.80
(D) 8,214.60
(E) 11,075.40

12. An O-3 with 18 years of service makes ___________.

(A) 6,818.10
(B) 6,117.60
(C) 3,852.00
(D) 5,240.70
(E) 6,054.30

13. An O-2 with 14 years of service makes ___________.

(A) 3,852.00
(B) 5,240.70
(C) 6,054.30
(D) 7,003.80
(E) 3,039.60

14. An O-6 with 20 years of service makes ___________.

(A) 10,015.80
(B) 8,004.00
(C) 7,634.10
(D) 8,214.60
(E) 7,003.80

15. An O-10 with 22 years of service makes ___________.

(A) 12,101.10
(B) 12,525.60
(C) 11,857.50
(D) 12,818.70
(E) 10,015.80

Questions 16 through 20 are to be answered based on the following table:

Commissioned Officer Basic Pay, Based on Rank and Years of Service

Rank	<2	2	3	4	6	8	10	12
O-8	8,271.00	8,541.90	8,721.60	8,772.00	8,996.10	9,371.10	9,458.10	9,814.20
O-7	6,872.70	7,191.90	7,339.80	7,457.10	7,669.80	7,879.50	8,122.50	8,364.90
O-6	5,094.00	5,596.20	5,963.40	5,963.40	5,985.90	6,242.70	6,276.60	6,276.60
O-5	4,246.50	4,783.68	5,115.00	5,117.10	5,383.50	5,507.40	5,779.20	5,978.70
O-4	3,663.90	4,241.40	4,524.30	4,587.60	4,850.10	5,131.80	5,482.20	5,755.80
O-3	3,221.40	3,651.90	3,941.70	4,297.50	4,503.00	4,728.90	4,875.30	5,115.90
O-2	2,783.10	3,170.10	3,651.00	3,774.30	3,852.00	3,852.00	3,852.00	3,852.00
O-1	2,416.20	2,514.60	3,039.60	3,039.60	3,039.60	3,039.60	3,039.60	3,039.60

16. An O-3 with 8 years of service makes ___________.

    (A) 3,852.00
    (B) 4,875.30
    (C) 4,503.00
    (D) 5,115.90
    (E) 4,728.90

17. An O-5 with 6 years of service makes ___________.

    (A) 5,117.10
    (B) 5,383.50
    (C) 5,507.40
    (D) 5,985.90
    (E) 4,850.10

18. An O-7 with 3 years of service makes ___________.

    (A) 7,339.80
    (B) 7,191.90
    (C) 7,457.10
    (D) 5,963.40
    (E) 8,721.60

19. An O-3 with less than 2 years of service makes ___________.

    (A) 2,783.10
    (B) 3,663.90
    (C) 3,651.90
    (D) 3,221.40
    (E) 3,170.10

20. An O-4 with 6 years of service makes ___________.

    (A) 5,383.50
    (B) 4,503.00
    (C) 4,850.10
    (D) 4,587.60
    (E) 5,131.80

Questions 21 through 25 are to be answered based on the following table:

Military Desertion Rates

Fiscal Year	Number of Deserters	Rate Per 1,000
	Army	
1997	2,218	4.58
1998	2,520	5.20
1999	2,966	6.13
2000	3,949	8.16
2001	4,597	9.50
2002	4,483	9.26
2003	3,678	7.60
2004	2,376	4.91
	Air Force	
1997	26	0.07
1998	27	0.07
1999	45	0.12
2000	46	0.12
2001	62	0.17
2002	88	0.24
2003	56	0.15
2004	50	0.14
	Navy	
1997	1,858	4.86
1998	2,038	5.33
1999	2,485	6.50
2000	3,255	8.51
2001	1,619	4.23
2003	Not Available	
2004	Not Available	

Fiscal Year	Number of Deserters	Rate Per 1,000
	Marine Corps	
1997	1,375	7.94
1998	1,460	8.43
1999	1,689	9.75
2000	2,019	11.66
2001	1,310	7.57
2002	1,136	6.56
2003	1,236	7.14
2004	1,297	7.49

21. The number of deserters in the Air Force in FY 2003 was __________.

    (A) 56
    (B) 57
    (C) 58
    (D) 59
    (E) 60

22. The rate-per-1,000 desertion rate for the Marine Corps in FY 2000 was __________.

    (A) 7.57
    (B) 7.14
    (C) 11.66
    (D) 9.75
    (E) 7.49

23. The number of Army deserters in FY 2001 was __________.

    (A) 2,966
    (B) 3,949
    (C) 4,483
    (D) 4,597
    (E) 2,520

24. The rate-per-1,000 desertion rate for the Navy in FY 1997 was __________.

    (A) 4.86
    (B) 5.33
    (C) 6.50
    (D) 8.51
    (E) 4.23

25. The number of deserters in the Navy in FY 2003 was __________.

    (A) 1,858
    (B) 2,038
    (C) 2,485
    (D) 1,619
    (E) not available

Questions 26 through 30 are to be answered based on the following chart:

Monthly Housing Allowance for Commissioned Officers with Dependents (California)

Location	O-1	O-2	O-3	O-4	O-5	O-6	O-7
OAKLAND, CA	1,505	1,721	2,076	2,698	3,135	3,161	3,198
SAN FRANCISCO, CA	2,731	2,773	2,879	3,182	3,396	3,424	3,464
CHINA LAKE NAVWEPCEN, CA	966	1,132	1,284	1,432	1,535	1,548	1,566
FRESNO, CA	1,170	1,215	1,510	1,678	1,793	1,808	1,829
LEMOORE NAS, CA	966	1,092	1,488	1,555	1,598	1,611	1,630
CAMP PENDLETON, CA	1,400	1,578	2,011	2,115	2,184	2,202	2,228
VENTURA, CA	1,622	1,970	2,166	2,464	2,674	2,696	2,727
VANDENBERG AFB, CA	1,370	1,579	1,860	1,925	1,968	1,984	2,007
MARIN/SONOMA, CA	1,625	1,718	2,173	2,541	2,796	2,819	2,852
BARSTOW/FORT IRWIN, CA	1,177	1,270	1,377	1,509	1,602	1,615	1,634
EDWARDS AFB, CA	1,214	1,349	1,570	1,699	1,787	1,802	1,823
SAN BERNADINO, CA	1,307	1,536	1,639	1,698	1,739	1,753	1,774
TWENTY NINE PALMS MCB, CA	1,003	1,130	1,379	1,514	1,607	1,620	1,639
BEALE AFB, CA	1,092	1,308	1,648	1,763	1,840	1,855	1,877
SACRAMENTO, CA	1,349	1,629	1,662	1,793	1,886	1,902	1,924
STOCKTON, CA	1,164	1,316	1,439	1,560	1,644	1,658	1,677
VALLEJO/TRAVIS AFB, CA	1,485	1,600	1,892	1,979	2,038	2,055	2,079
LOS ANGELES, CA	1,788	1,987	2,203	2,456	2,633	2,655	2,686
SAN DIEGO, CA	1,677	1,894	2,050	2,259	2,406	2,426	2,454
MONTEREY, CA	1,534	1,805	2,200	2,327	2,412	2,432	2,460
BAKERSFIELD, CA	1,077	1,153	1,509	1,626	1,705	1,719	1,739
RIVERSIDE, CA	1,520	1,773	1,925	1,972	2,003	2,020	2,043
HUMBOLDT COUNTY, CA	1,092	1,419	1,465	1,601	1,696	1,710	1,730
SANTA CLARA COUNTY, CA	1,683	1,871	2,098	2,411	2,631	2,653	2,684
SAN LUIS OBISPO, CA	1,506	1,768	1,846	2,009	2,124	2,142	2,166
BRIDGEPORT, CA	1,242	1,508	1,697	1,825	1,914	1,930	1,952
EL CENTRO, CA	1,078	1,271	1,491	1,526	1,548	1,561	1,579
FORT BRAGG, CA	1,140	1,270	1,588	1,613	1,626	1,639	1,659
PALMDALE, CA	1,410	1,533	1,830	2,056	2,213	2,231	2,257

26. An O-4 stationed in San Diego, CA, receives a monthly housing allowance of

__________.

(A) $2,050
(B) $2,406
(C) $1,805
(D) $2,259
(E) $2,412

27. An O-6 stationed in Bridgeport, CA, receives a monthly housing allowance of

__________.

(A) $1,561
(B) $1,952
(C) $1,914
(D) $1,548
(E) $1,930

28. An O-3 stationed in Ventura, CA, receives a monthly housing allowance of

__________.

(A) $1,970
(B) $2,166
(C) $2,464
(D) $1,860
(E) $2,011

29. An O-7 stationed in Stockton, CA, receives a monthly housing allowance of

__________.

(A) $1,658
(B) $1,924
(C) $1,677
(D) $2,079
(E) $2,055

30. An O-2 stationed in Fresno, CA, receives a monthly housing allowance of

__________.

(A) $1,215
(B) $1,170
(C) $1,132
(D) $2,011
(E) $1,678

Questions 31 through 40 are are based on the table below. Note that the X values are shown at the top of the table and the Y values are shown on the left of the table. Find the entry that occurs at the intersection of the row and the column corresponding to the values given.

X Value

Y Value	–4	–3	–2	–1	0	1	2	3	4
–4	JFI	DIR	JGF	FHD	KGI	OFH	DTS	JDK	NVJ
–3	DGR	CNF	NSY	JDH	JYT	JDR	AHS	GEH	BCF
–2	DFI	LKG	NDU	JDR	SVC	UMN	ASG	GTR	JDN
–1	KIO	BCF	YJH	BSH	YUJ	UDJ	STD	HSR	JDH
0	HJY	BDR	SCD	HYG	JDH	IOL	YTH	SVF	YDH
1	RTY	BCG	TSF	SLF	BHF	DYF	JDB	CHG	SCG
2	UIK	VHF	JUY	GTY	TYJ	DKI	TJK	SVC	AXG
3	DFY	WSB	AVD	FGI	KSV	DHY	SVG	GTU	ASB
4	YKJ	PDN	DGY	DUU	DGT	DJH	DUH	AQG	DHY

31. X; –1, Y; 4
    (A) DHO
    (B) DUU
    (C) DGY
    (D) WSB
    (E) ASI

32. X;1, Y;–2
    (A) TSF
    (B) FGI
    (C) UMN
    (D) IND
    (E) SVC

33. X; –2, Y; 4
    (A) KNL
    (B) DCG
    (C) JFI
    (D) FGT
    (E) DWE

34. X; 2, Y; –3
    (A) AHS
    (B) DKI
    (C) GER
    (D) DGY
    (E) SDF

35. X; 3, Y; –3
    (A) JUH
    (B) GEH
    (C) HYU
    (D) JDY
    (E) JTI

36. X; –4, Y; –4
    (A) DJH
    (B) GYU
    (C) DHO
    (D) YTR
    (E) JFI

37. X; 0, Y; 0
    (A) JID
    (B) YDH
    (C) HKI
    (D) SER
    (E) JDH

38. X; –2, Y; 0
    (A) JDU
    (B) DHY
    (C) BDR
    (D) SCD
    (E) GFR

39. X; 2, Y; –3
    (A) AHS
    (B) DSK
    (C) ERT
    (D) SVG
    (E) NHG

40. X; 3, Y; –1
    (A) HSR
    (B) IYG
    (C) SDH
    (D) DEW
    (E) DGR

Subtest 8—Aviation Information

Directions: This subtest measures knowledge of general aeronautical concepts and terminology (past and current). The test consists of 20 questions that must be answered in 8 minutes.

1. When entering a climb from level flight, the weight of the aircraft
   (A) results in increased drag.
   (B) results in decreased drag.
   (C) is directly perpendicular to the flight path.
   (D) results in increased angle of attack.
   (E) results in decreased angle of attack.

2. An airplane wing is designed to produce lift resulting from relatively
   (A) positive air pressure below and above the wing's surface.
   (B) negative air pressure below the wing's surface and positive air pressure above the wing's surface.
   (C) positive air pressure below the wing's surface and negative air pressure above the wing's surface.
   (D) negative air pressure below and above the wing's surface.
   (E) neutral air pressure below and above the wing's surface.

3. Turbulence is caused by
   (A) convective air currents.
   (B) obstructions to wind flow.
   (C) wind shear.
   (D) none of the above
   (E) all of the above

4. Which statement is true regarding the forces acting on an aircraft in a steady flight condition (no change in speed or flight path)?
   (A) Lift equals weight and thrust equals drag.
   (B) Lift equals thrust and weight equals drag.
   (C) Lift equals drag and thrust equals weight.
   (D) Lift is greater than weight and thrust is less than drag.
   (E) Lift is less than weight and thrust is greater than drag.

5. The force indicated by the arrow in the below graphic represents ____________.

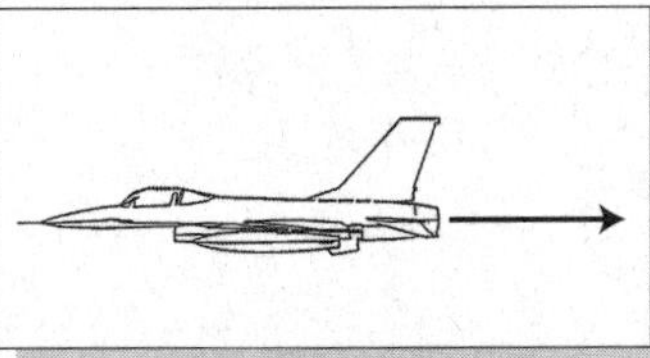

   (A) lift
   (B) drag
   (C) weight
   (D) thrust
   (E) none of the above

6. What is the difference between a steady red and a flashing red light signal from the tower to an aircraft approaching to land?
   (A) Both light signals mean the same except the flashing red light requires a more urgent reaction.
   (B) Both light signals mean the same except the steady red light requires a more urgent reaction.
   (C) A steady red light signals to continue circling and a flashing red light signals that the airport is unsafe for landing.
   (D) A steady red light signals to continue circling and a flashing red light signals to continue, but exercise extreme caution.
   (E) A steady red light signals that the airport is unsafe and a flashing red light signals to use a different runway.

Practice Test 2

7. A minimally safe airspeed descent is principally used
   (A) for low level flight patterns.
   (B) for normal landing approaches.
   (C) when flaps are inoperative.
   (D) on runways above sea-level.
   (E) when clearing obstacles during landing.

8. When in the down (extended) position, wing-flaps provide
   (A) decreased wing camber (curvature).
   (B) less lift and less drag.
   (C) less lift but more drag.
   (D) greater lift but less drag.
   (E) greater lift and more drag.

9. Relative to its speed over the ground, to maintain the same amount of lift, an aircraft must generally travel ____________ at 10,000 feet than it does at 1,000 feet.
   (A) slower
   (B) faster
   (C) the same speed
   (D) either (A) or (C)
   (E) either (B) or (C)

10. What are the four forces that act on an aircraft in flight?
    (A) lift, bank, inertia, and gravity
    (B) bank, weight, inertia, and drag
    (C) lift, resistance, gravity, and drag
    (D) acceleration, drag, weight, and gravity
    (E) lift, thrust, weight, and drag

11. Which of the following is <u>not</u> a primary flight control?
    (A) aileron
    (B) rudder
    (C) elevator
    (D) flaps
    (E) none of the above

12. In aircraft communications, when a flight is identified as "heavy," such as "Foxtrot 29er heavy, you are cleared to land on runway 28L," the word "heavy" means
    (A) more than $\frac{1}{2}$ full on fuel.
    (B) fully fueled.
    (C) more than 250,000 pounds of gross weight.
    (D) passengers on board.
    (E) unexpended munitions on board.

13. What does the term "yaw" mean?
    (A) directional turning from the tail section
    (B) rate of descent
    (C) rate of climb
    (D) airspeed
    (E) bank

14. The "IFF" on a military aircraft
    (A) indicates free flow of fuel.
    (B) indicates free flow of air into the jet engine compressor.
    (C) indicates rate of indicated free fall of a power-off glide.
    (D) indicates whether an aircraft is an enemy or an ally.
    (E) determines the flap positions.

15. The line placed on an airspeed indicator to warn that operating above the indicated level is dangerous is colored ____________.
    (A) yellow
    (B) green
    (C) red
    (D) black
    (E) blue

16. What is one advantage of an airplane said to be inherently stable?

    (A) The airplane will not spin.
    (B) The airplane will be difficult to stall.
    (C) The airplane will require less fuel.
    (D) The airplane will require less effort to control.
    (E) The airplane will not over-bank during steep turns.

17. The pilot always advances the throttle during a ____________.

    (A) nose dive
    (B) landing
    (C) turn
    (D) spin
    (E) climb

18. When taking off into a headwind, the result will be

    (A) shorter takeoff distance and increased climb angle.
    (B) shorter takeoff distance and decreased climb angle.
    (C) longer takeoff distance and increased climb angle.
    (D) longer takeoff distance and decreased climb angle.
    (E) have no effect on aircraft performance.

19. If the elevator tabs on a plane are lowered, the plane will tend to

    (A) nose up.
    (B) nose down.
    (C) pitch fore and aft.
    (D) go into a slow roll.
    (E) wing over.

20. If one end of a runway is numbered 27, what number would designate the other end of the same runway?

    (A) 27
    (B) 33
    (C) 09
    (D) 45
    (E) 18

Subtest 9 — Rotated Blocks

Directions: This subtest has 15 questions that must be answered in 13 minutes. The questions are designed to measure your ability to visualize and manipulate objects in space. In each item, you are shown a picture of a block. You must find a second block that is just like the first.

Look at the two blocks below. Although viewed from different points, the blocks are the same.

Look at the two blocks below. They are not alike. They can never be turned so that they will be alike.

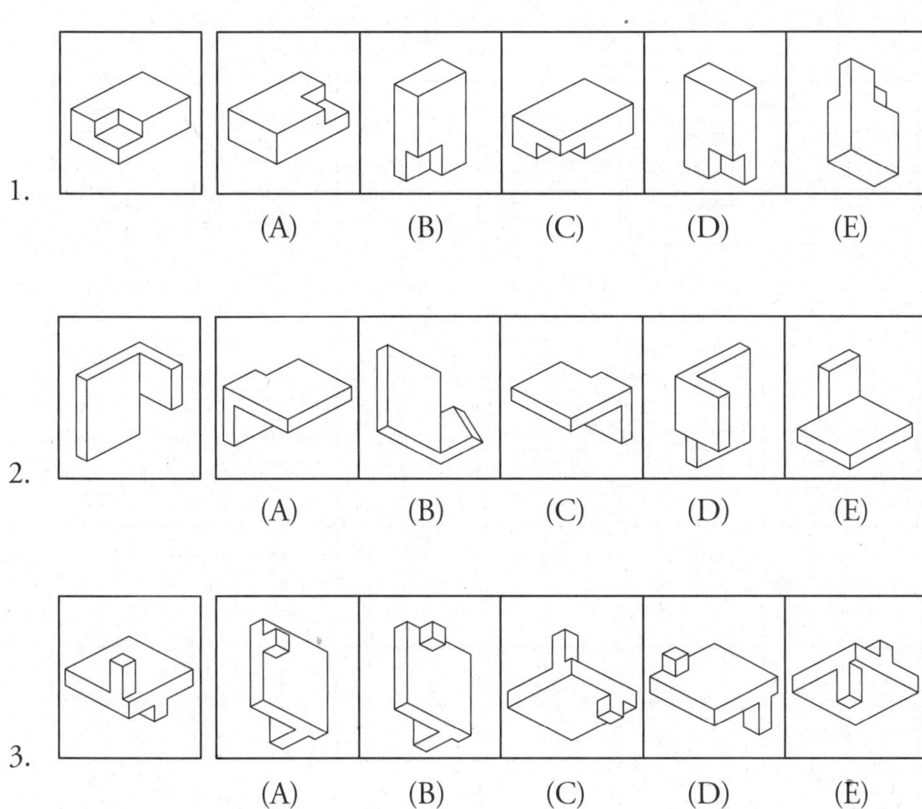

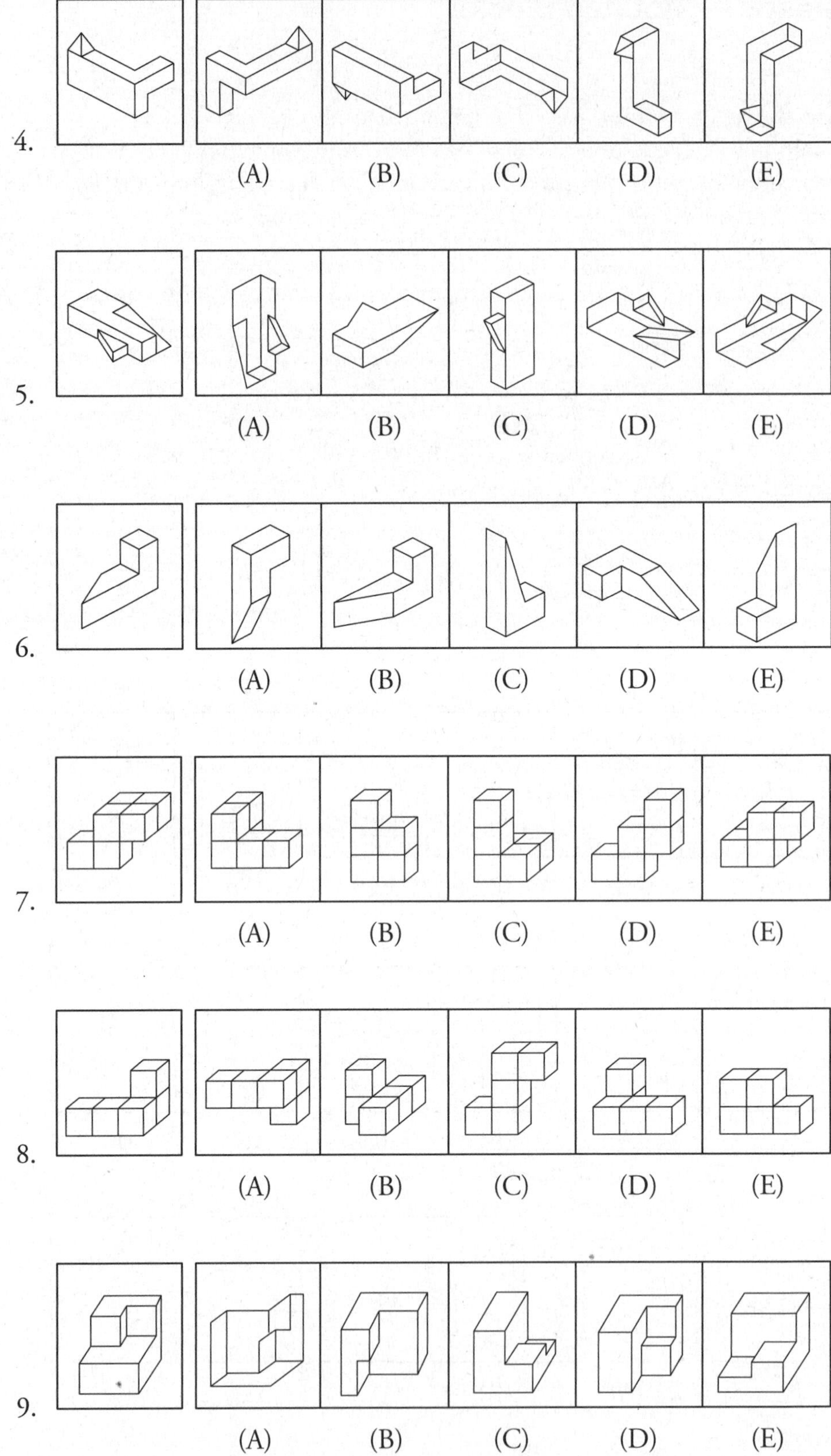
4.
(A) (B) (C) (D) (E)
5.
(A) (B) (C) (D) (E)
6.
(A) (B) (C) (D) (E)
7.
(A) (B) (C) (D) (E)
8.
(A) (B) (C) (D) (E)
9.
(A) (B) (C) (D) (E)

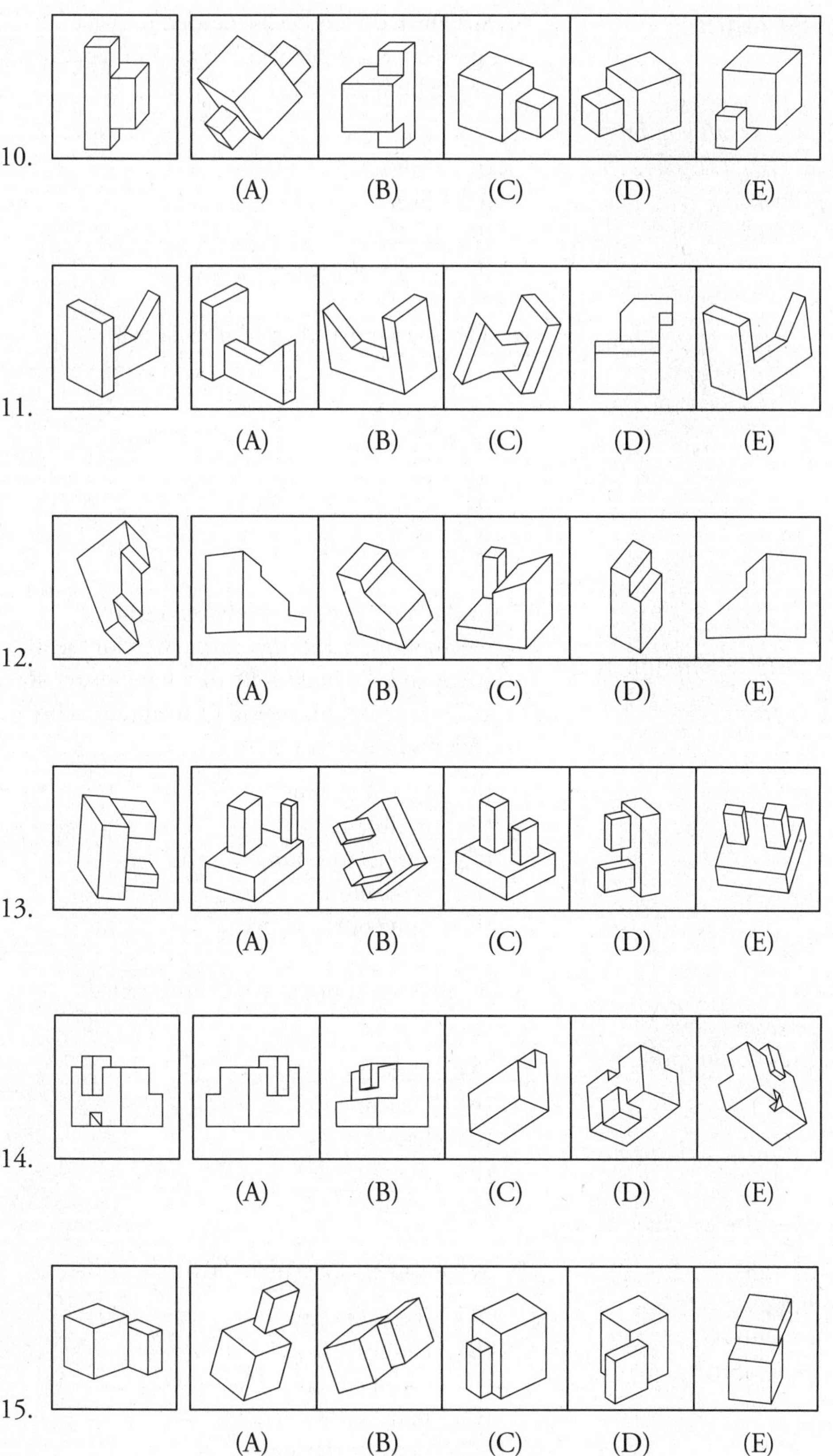
10.
(A)
(B)
(C)
(D)
(E)
11.
(A)
(B)
(C)
(D)
(E)
12.
(A)
(B)
(C)
(D)
(E)
13.
(A)
(B)
(C)
(D)
(E)
14.
(A)
(B)
(C)
(D)
(E)
15.
(A)
(B)
(C)
(D)
(E)

Subtest 10—General Science

Directions: This subtest measures your comprehension in the area of science. It consists of 20 questions that must be answered in 10 minutes. Read the question and choose the selection that best answers the question.

1. The Baumé scale is used to measure ____________.
   (A) electricity
   (B) specific gravity
   (C) acceleration
   (D) mass
   (E) weight

2. The thin, clear layer that forms the front part of the eyeball is called the ____________.
   (A) pupil
   (B) iris
   (C) lens
   (D) retina
   (E) cornea

3. The *Antoine equation* is used to
   (A) measure atomic mass.
   (B) measure distances between planets.
   (C) estimate the vapor pressures of pure liquids or solids.
   (D) calculate buoyancy.
   (E) measure work-force.

4. Which of the following is a chemical change?
   (A) magnetizing a rod of iron
   (B) burning one pound of coal
   (C) mixing flake graphite with oil
   (D) vaporizing one gram of mercury in a vacuum
   (E) melting ice

5. Surplus red blood cells, needed to meet an emergency, are MAINLY stored in what organ of the human body?
   (A) pancreas
   (B) spleen
   (C) liver
   (D) kidneys
   (E) none of the above

6. The chief nutrient in lean meat is ____________.
   (A) starch
   (B) protein
   (C) fat
   (D) carbohydrates
   (E) Vitamin B

7. In the human brain, body temperature, metabolism, heart rate, sexual development, sleep, and the body's use of fat and water are influenced by this region of the brain. This region of the brain is the ____________.
   (A) hypothalamus
   (B) midbrain
   (C) corpus callosum
   (D) cerebellum
   (E) none of the above

8. An important ore of uranium is called ____________.
   (A) hematite
   (B) chalcopyrite
   (C) bauxite
   (D) pitchblende
   (E) feldspar

9. What causes the stars to "twinkle?"
   (A) the ozone layer
   (B) clouds
   (C) turbulent air
   (D) temperature variants
   (E) none of the above

10. Of the following gases in the air, the most plentiful is ____________.
    (A) argon
    (B) oxygen
    (C) nitrogen
    (D) carbon dioxide
    (E) hydrogen

11. Electrons that move through an electric circuit as current have a
    (A) positive charge.
    (B) negative charge.
    (C) neutral charge.
    (D) positive charge alternating with a negative charge.
    (E) no charge at all.

12. Of the following types of clouds, the ones that occur at the greatest height are called ____________.
    (A) cirrus
    (B) nimbus
    (C) cumulus
    (D) stratus
    (E) altostratus

13. Fire is a form of ____________.
    (A) solid
    (B) liquid
    (C) gas
    (D) matter
    (E) energy

14. After adding salt to water, the freezing point of the water is ____________.
    (A) variable
    (B) inverted
    (C) the same
    (D) raised
    (E) lowered

15. Rust is caused by a chemical reaction known as ____________.
    (A) precipitation
    (B) osmosis
    (C) oxidation
    (D) combination
    (E) none of the above

16. The type of joint that attaches the arm to the shoulder blade is known as a(n) ____________.
    (A) hinge
    (B) pivot
    (C) immovable
    (D) gliding
    (E) ball and socket

17. When heat is transferred through a solid, the process is called ____________.
    (A) convection
    (B) conduction
    (C) heat-transfer
    (D) condensation
    (E) none of the above

18. The time that it takes for Earth to rotate 45° is ____________.
    (A) two hours
    (B) four hours
    (C) one hour
    (D) three hours
    (E) five hours

19. At higher altitudes, water boils
    (A) at a higher temperature.
    (B) at a lower temperature.
    (C) at the same temperature.
    (D) will not boil at all above 20,000 feet.
    (E) none of the above

20. What is the name of the negative particle that circles the nucleus of the atom?
    (A) neutron
    (B) meson
    (C) proton
    (D) electron
    (E) isotope

Subtest 11—Hidden Figures

Directions: This subtest consists of 15 questions that must be answered in 8 minutes. The questions are designed to measure your ability to see a simple figure in a complex drawing. For each section of five questions there are five figures, lettered A, B, C, D, and E. Below these are five numbered drawings. You are to determine which lettered figure is contained in each of the numbered drawings.

Each numbered drawing contains only one of the lettered figures. The correct figure in each drawing will always be in the same position as it appears in the lettered figures above the question. Therefore, do not rotate the page in order to find it. Look at each numbered drawing and decide which one of the five lettered figures is contained in it.

Questions 1 through 6 are to be answered using the below symbols:

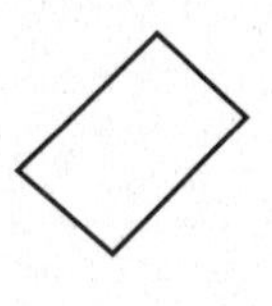
(A)

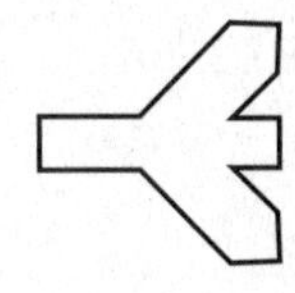
(B)

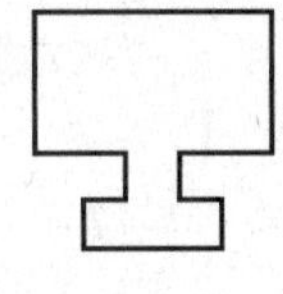
(C)

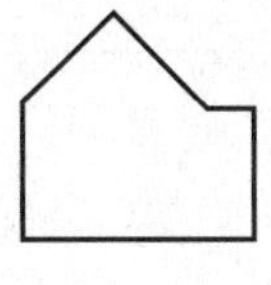
(D)

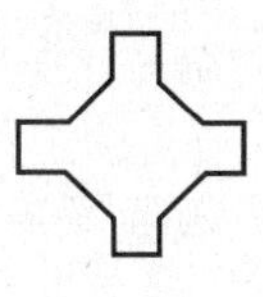
(E)

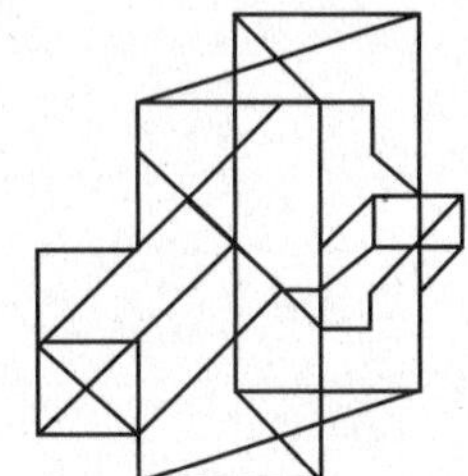

1.
(A) figure A
(B) figure B
(C) figure C
(D) figure D
(E) figure E

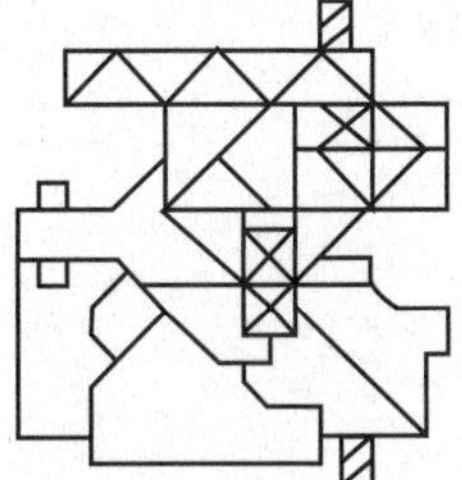

2.
(A) figure A
(B) figure B
(C) figure C
(D) figure D
(E) figure E

3.
(A) figure A
(B) figure B
(C) figure C
(D) figure D
(E) figure E

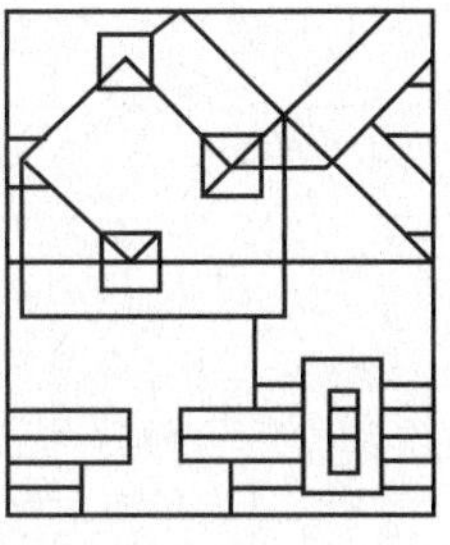

4.
(A) figure A
(B) figure B
(C) figure C
(D) figure D
(E) figure E

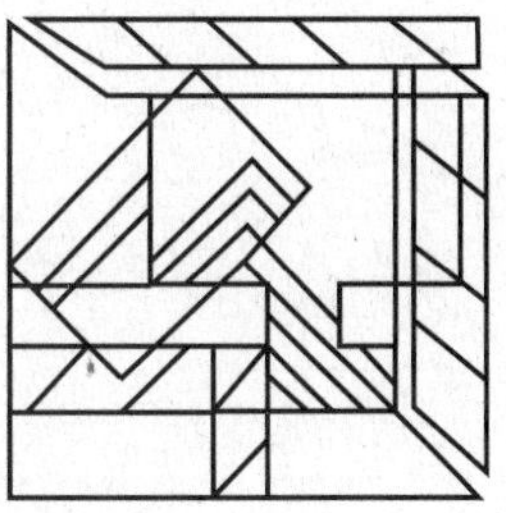

5.
(A) figure A
(B) figure B
(C) figure C
(D) figure D
(E) figure E

Questions 6 through 10 are to be answered based on the shapes below.

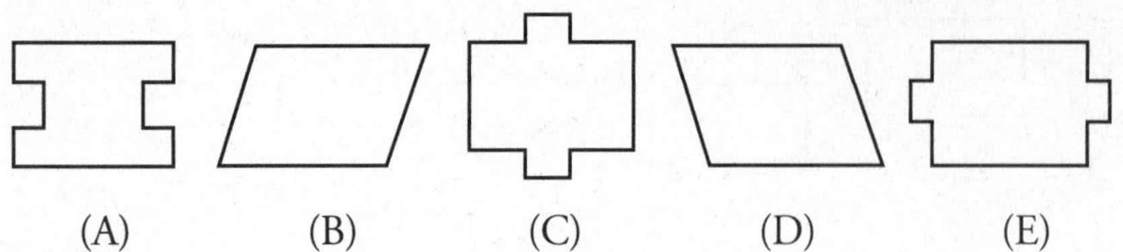

6. 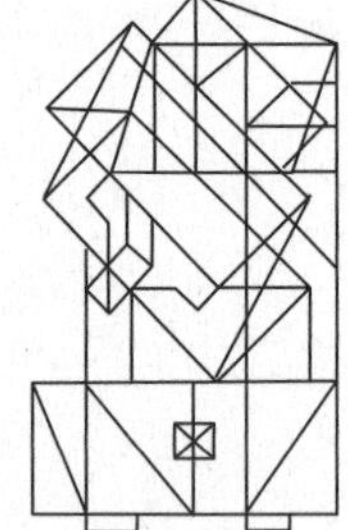

(A) figure A
(B) figure B
(C) figure C
(D) figure D
(E) figure E

7. 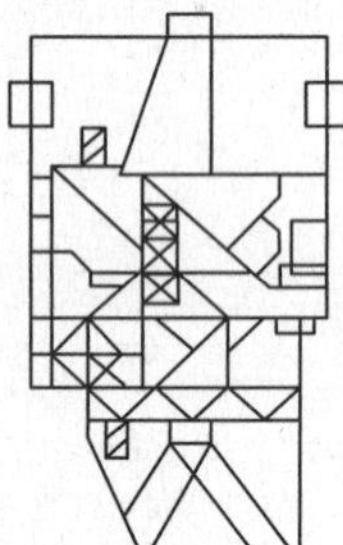

(A) figure A
(B) figure B
(C) figure C
(D) figure D
(E) figure E

8. 

(A) figure A
(B) figure B
(C) figure C
(D) figure D
(E) figure E

9. 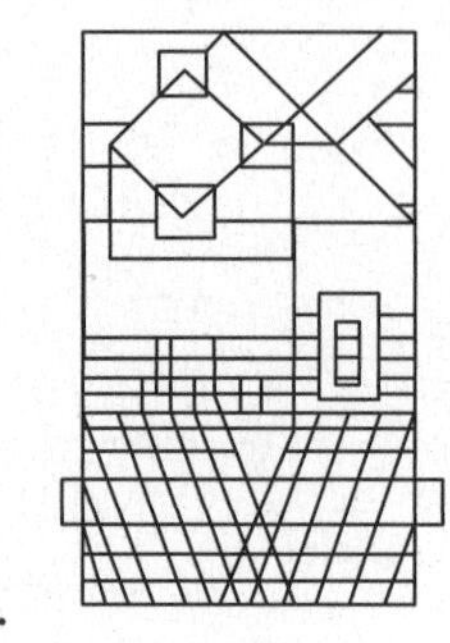

(A) figure A
(B) figure B
(C) figure C
(D) figure D
(E) figure E

10. 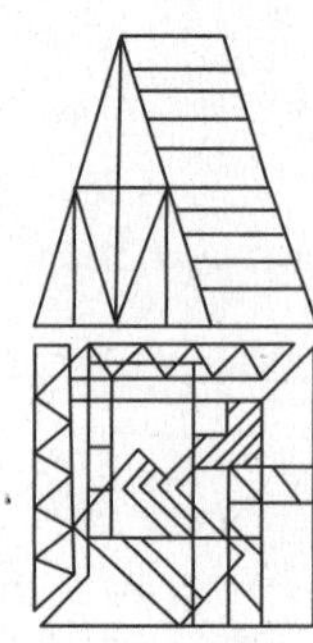

(A) figure A
(B) figure B
(C) figure C
(D) figure D
(E) figure E

Questions 11 through 15 are to be answered based on the shapes below.

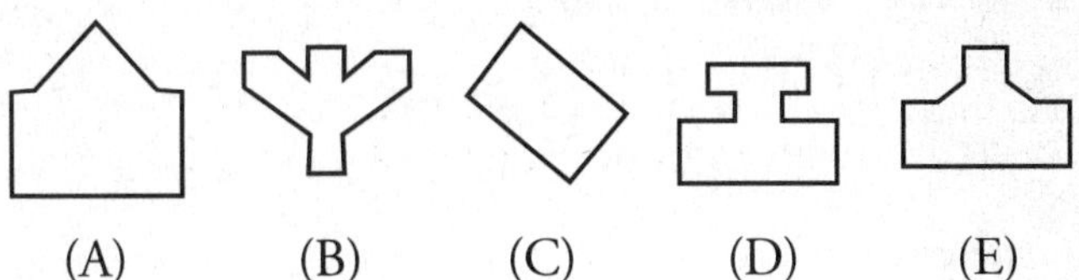

11.

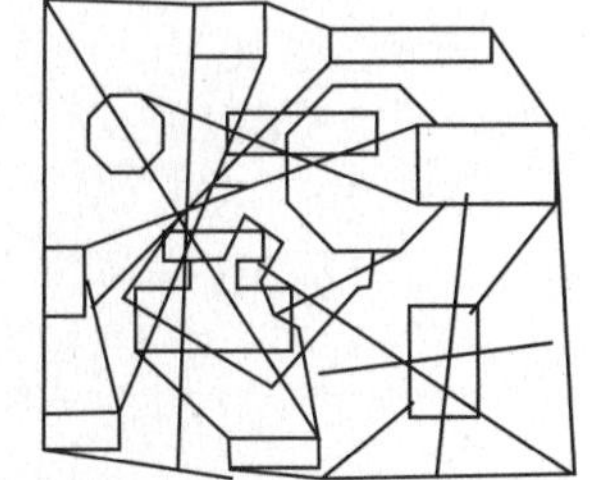

(A) figure A
(B) figure B
(C) figure C
(D) figure D
(E) figure E

12.

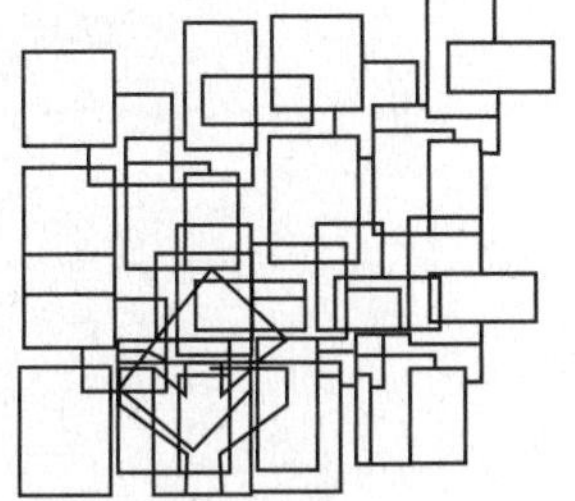

(A) figure A
(B) figure B
(C) figure C
(D) figure D
(E) figure E

13.

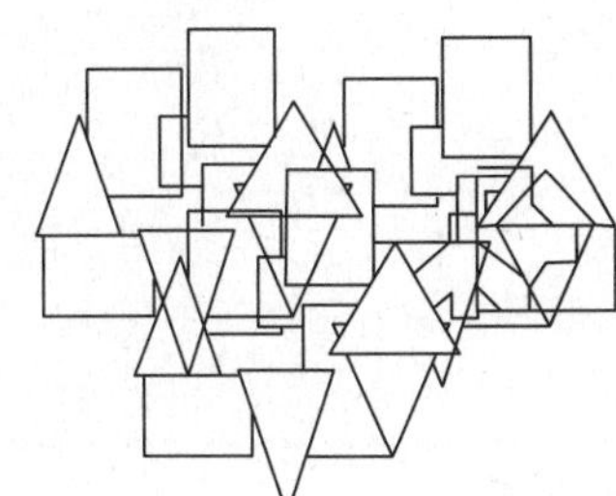

(A) figure A
(B) figure B
(C) figure C
(D) figure D
(E) figure E

14.

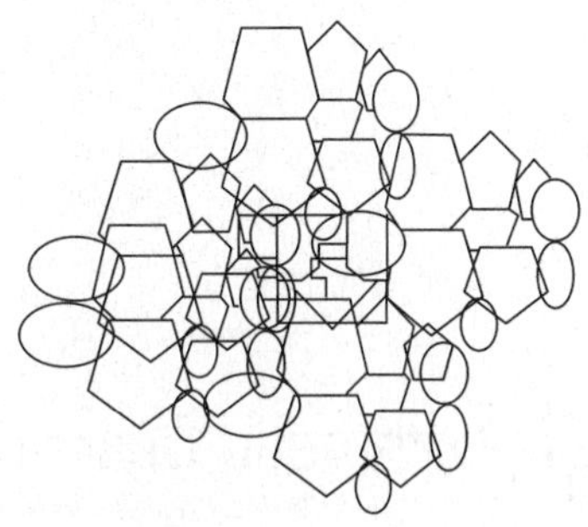

(A) figure A
(B) figure B
(C) figure C
(D) figure D
(E) figure E

15.

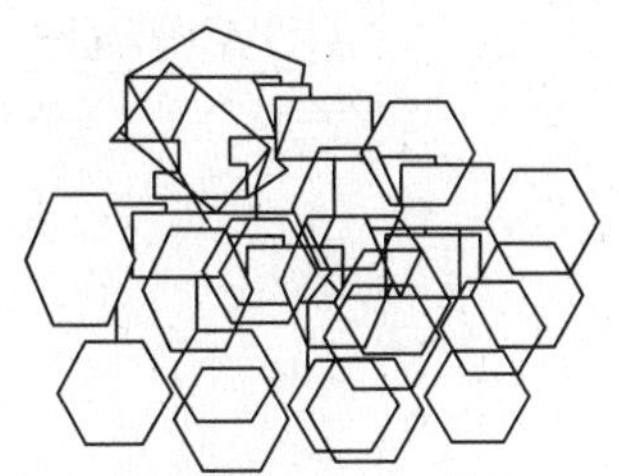

(A) figure A
(B) figure B
(C) figure C
(D) figure D
(E) figure E

Answer Key

PRACTICE TEST 2

Subtest 1—Verbal Analogies

1. B	6. C	11. E	16. D	21. E
2. B	7. E	12. B	17. C	22. C
3. C	8. A	13. E	18. A	23. C
4. E	9. B	14. B	19. D	24. B
5. D	10. A	15. B	20. C	25. B

Subtest 2—Arithmetic Reasoning

1. D	6. C	11. C	16. B	21. D
2. E	7. D	12. E	17. B	22. B
3. C	8. A	13. C	18. E	23. A
4. E	9. A	14. C	19. C	24. A
5. B	10. B	15. B	20. C	25. A

Subtest 3—Word Knowledge

1. A	6. A	11. B	16. A	21. A
2. A	7. C	12. A	17. D	22. B
3. E	8. C	13. B	18. C	23. B
4. A	9. C	14. E	19. A	24. A
5. D	10. D	15. A	20. A	25. C

Subtest 4—Mathematics Knowledge

1. C	6. C	11. E	16. A	21. B
2. C	7. D	12. B	17. B	22. E
3. A	8. C	13. E	18. A	23. E
4. C	9. A	14. D	19. C	24. D
5. A	10. D	15. D	20. E	25. C

Subtest 5—Instrument Comprehension

1. C	5. C	9. C	13. C	17. B
2. D	6. D	10. D	14. B	18. D
3. A	7. B	11. D	15. A	19. C
4. A	8. D	12. D	16. A	20. B

Subtest 6—Block Counting

1. B	5. C	9. B	13. E	17. D
2. B	6. A	10. B	14. C	18. B
3. B	7. B	11. B	15. C	19. E
4. C	8. C	12. A	16. C	20. D

Subtest 7—Table Reading

1. B	9. A	17. B	25. E	33. B
2. A	10. B	18. A	26. D	34. D
3. C	11. C	19. D	27. E	35. B
4. C	12. D	20. C	28. B	36. E
5. B	13. A	21. A	29. C	37. E
6. E	14. B	22. C	30. A	38. D
7. B	15. D	23. D	31. B	39. A
8. A	16. E	24. A	32. C	40. A

Subtest 8—Aviation Information

1. A	5. B	9. B	13. A	17. E
2. C	6. C	10. E	14. D	18. A
3. E	7. E	11. D	15. C	19. A
4. A	8. E	12. C	16. D	20. C

Subtest 9—Rotated Blocks

1. D	4. D	7. E	10. B	13. C
2. C	5. B	8. B	11. A	14. E
3. C	6. A	9. E	12. A	15. D

Subtest 10—General Science

1. B	5. B	9. C	13. E	17. B
2. E	6. B	10. C	14. E	18. D
3. C	7. A	11. B	15. C	19. B
4. B	8. D	12. A	16. E	20. D

Subtest 11—Hidden Figures

1. A	4. D	7. A	10. D	13. A
2. A	5. C	8. E	11. D	14. E
3. E	6. B	9. C	12. B	15. C

Answer Explanations to AFOQT 2

SUBTEST 1—VERBAL ANALOGIES

1. **(B) beginning is to end.** Alpha is the first letter or the beginning of the Greek alphabet; omega is the last letter or end of the Greek alphabet.
2. **(B) artist.** A loom is a tool used by a weaver; an easel is a tool used by an artist.
3. **(C) mason.** A micrometer is a tool used by a machinist. A trowel is a tool used by a mason.
4. **(E) persons is to crowd**. Several ships constitute a fleet; several persons constitute a crowd.
5. **(D) XII is to XX.** Dozen or 12 is represented by Roman numeral XII. Score or 20 is represented by Roman numeral XX.
6. **(C) reward.** Carelessness generally leads to a reprimand, while efficiency leads to praise or reward.
7. **(E) ruby is to red.** An emerald is a green gem; a ruby is a red gem.
8. **(A) oriole is to bird.** A Dalmatian is a species of dog; an oriole is a species of bird.
9. **(B) hypothesis is to biologist.** A tenet is a belief and is studied by theologians, who study religion; a hypothesis is a belief that is studied by scientists (in this case, a biologist).
10. **(A) fallen.** Flown is the past participle to the infinitive, *to fly*; fallen is the past participle to the infinitive to fall.
11. **(E) woof.** Horizontal is at right angle to the vertical. In yarns, the warp is at a right angle to the woof.
12. **(B) banishment is to member.** Exorcism is a process to chase away a spirit; banishment is the process to chase away a member.
13. **(E) millennium is to year.** A kilometer is equal to 1,000 meters. A millennium is equal to a period of 1,000 years.
14. **(B) incomparable is to equal**. Unprecedented and previous occurrence are antonyms, as are incomparable and equal.
15. **(B) inauguration is to president**. A priest is inducted into office by a formal ceremony called an ordination. A president is inducted into office by a formal ceremony called an inauguration.
16. **(D) annihilation.** Obsession is extreme, unending interest, annihilation is the extreme of decimation.
17. **(C) ammunition.** An ordinance is a rule or regulation; ordnance is ammunition.
18. **(A) refuge.** A coffer is a container to store valuables; a sanctuary is a place of refuge.
19. **(D) month is to year.** A dozen contains 12 units; a year consists of 12 months.
20. **(C) amoral is to ethics.** Disheartened means without hope; amoral means without ethics.
21. **(E) heartbeat.** A mnemonic functions to aid memory; a pacemaker aids in the regulation of one's heartbeat.
22. **(C) highest is to lowest.** Zenith is the highest point; nadir is the lowest point.

23. **(C) forensic is to debate.** Didactic refers to the teaching process; forensic refers to the debating process.
24. **(B) circumference.** The outer boundary of a square is its perimeter. The outer boundary of a circle is its circumference.
25. **(B) game is to baseball**. A bus is a type of vehicle; baseball is a type of game.

SUBTEST 2—ARITHMETIC REASONING

1. **(D) 1,536.** To find the area of the brick wall, use the formula $A = lw$ (10 ft × 16 ft = 160 sq ft). Because the bricks are measured in inches, we convert 160 sq ft to sq in. There are 144 sq in a sq ft (160 × 144 = 23,040 sq in). Next determine the area of one brick (3 × 5 = 15 sq in). Divide that number into the area of the wall (23,040 ÷ 15 = 1,536 bricks).
2. **(E) 200 pounds per square foot.** 200 feet × 200 feet = 40,000 square feet of floor area; There are 2000 pounds in a ton; 4000 tons × 2000 = 8,000,000 pounds; $\frac{8{,}000{,}000}{40{,}000} = 200$ pounds.
3. **(C) 48 square feet.** To determine the area of a rectangle, use the formula $A = lw$ (8 × 6 = 48).
4. **(E) $600,000.** One million × 12 = 12 million = 12,000,000 (nickels per year); 12,000,000 × .05 = $600,000.00.
5. **(B) 15.4 percent.** The equation is $\frac{x}{100} = \frac{4}{26}$.

$$\frac{x}{100} = \frac{4}{26}$$
$$26x = 4 \times 100$$
$$26x = 400$$
$$x = \frac{400}{26}$$
$$x = 15.4$$

6. **(C) 2.4 grams.** There are 200 cigarettes in a carton (20 × 10 = 200). 12 mg × 200 = 2400 mg of tar in 200 cigarettes. 2400 mg = 2.4 grams.
7. **(D) $70.88.** First, change the percentage (5.5%) to a decimal (.055). Multiply by the amount of the original cost .055 × 75 = 4.12. This is the amount of the discount. Finally, subtract this amount from the original price: $75.00 – 4.12 = $70.88.
8. **(A) 50 envelopes per hour.** Let x = number of envelopes addressed in 1 hour by slower worker. $2x$ = number of envelopes addressed in 1 hour by faster worker. $3x \times 5 = 750$; $15x = 750$; $x = 50$ envelopes per hour for slower worker.
9. **(A) $1,505.** The formula to compute value after depreciation is $V = O(1 - P)^T$, where V equals the value, O equals the original cost, P equals the percentage of depreciation, and T = the time (in years).

$$V = O(1 - P)^T$$
$$V = 2{,}800(1 - 0.22)^{2.5}$$
$$V = 2{,}800(0.78)^{2.5}$$
$$V = 1{,}505$$

10. **(B) $\frac{1}{8}$ lb.** Each stick of margarine = $\frac{1}{4}$ lb. Each stick consists of eight sections or tablespoons. Four sections or tablespoons = $\frac{1}{2}$ of $\frac{1}{4}$ lb = $\frac{1}{8}$ lb.

11. **(C) 60 miles.**
Let x = number of miles driven.

$$39 = 18 + 0.35x$$
$$21 = 0.35x$$
$$\frac{21}{0.35} = x$$
$$x = 60$$

12. **(E) $1,271,700.** $1,100,500 × .07 = $77,035; $1,100,500 + $77,035 = $1,177,535 = this year's budget. $1,177,535 × .08 = $94,203; $1,177,535 + $94,203 = $1,271,738 which is closest to option (E).

13. **(C) 20 minutes.**
The combined rates of Tom and Kyle are 15 mph (8 + 7 = 15). Let x = the number of hours until they meet.

$$15x = 5 \text{ hours}$$
$$x = \frac{5}{15}$$
$$x = \frac{1}{3} \text{ hours, or 20 minutes.}$$

14. **(C) 15.6 pounds.** $\frac{1}{2} \times \frac{1}{2} \times 1 = \frac{1}{4}$ cu. ft.; $\frac{1}{4}$ of 62.4 = 15.6 pounds.

15. **(B) 3 inches × 4 inches.** The diagonal formula for a rectangle is $D^2 = L^2 + W^2$. We know that $D = 5$ and $L = W + 1$.
$D^2 = L^2 + W^2$.
$5^2 = (W + 1)^2 + W^2$
$25 = (W + 1)(W + 1) + W^2$
$25 = W^2 + 2W + 1 + W^2$
$25 = 2W^2 + 2W + 1$
$0 = 2W^2 + 2W - 24$
$\frac{1}{2}(0) = \frac{1}{2}(2W^2 + 2W - 24)$
$0 = W^2 + W - 12$
$0 = (W - 3)(W + 4)$
$W - 3 = 0$ and $W + 4 = 0$
$W = 3$ and $W = -4$ (-4 is not a possible solution)
$W = 3$, so the length $(W + 1) = 4$.

16. **(B) 224.** 25% + 35% = 60%. 60% were 22 years old or under 22 years of age. 40% were over 22 years old. 560 × .40 = 224.

17. **(B) 76.** Let x = final exam grade. The quiz average is 68.
$[\frac{(61 + 63 + 65 + 83)}{4} = 68]$.

$\frac{3}{4}$ of the quiz average (68) plus $\frac{1}{4}$ of the final exam (x) must equal 70.

$$\frac{3}{4}(68) + \frac{1}{4}(x) = 70$$
$$51 + \frac{x}{4} = 70$$
$$\frac{x}{4} = 19$$
$$x = 4 \times 19$$
$$x = 76$$

18. **(E) none of the above.** The square root of 36 = 6. Each side of the square = 6″. 6″ × 2 = 12″. 12″ × 12″ = 144 square inches.
19. **(C) 261.**
    Let x = number of people attending.
    Given: Plan A = $25x$ ($25 for each attending)
    Given: Plan B = $1300 + 20x$ ($1,300 plus $20 for each person attending)
    $1300 + 20x$ (Plan B) < $25x$ (Plan A)
    $1300 + 20x < 25x$
    $1300 < 5x$ // subtract $20x$ from each side
    $260 < x$
20. **(C) 16.**
    Let D = DIMES
    Let Q = QUARTERS
    Given $D + Q = 25$
    Given $4.9 = 0.1D + 0.25Q$
    $4.9 = 0.1(25–Q) + 0.25Q$
    Comment: Substitute $25–Q$ for D in $4.9 = 0.1D + 0.25Q$
    $4.9 = 2.5 – 0.1Q + 0.25Q$
    $0 = –2.4 – 0.1Q + 0.25Q$
    $Q = 16$
21. **(D) 6 × 17 feet.**
    Let P = PERIMETER
    Let L = LENGTH
    Let W = WIDTH
    Given $L = 3W – 1$
    Given $P = 46$
    Given $P = 2L + 2W$
    $46 = 2L + 2W$ // Substitute 46 for P in $P = 2L + 2W$
    $46 = 2(3W – 1) + 2W$ // Substitute $3W – 1$ for L in $46 = 2L + 2W$
    $46 = 6W – 2 + 2W$
    $0 = 8W – 48$
    $W = 6$
    $L = 17$ // Substitute $W = 6$ into $L = 3W–1$
22. **(B) 52.**
    Let L = LARGER
    Let S = SMALLER
    Given $S + L = 65$
    Given $4S = L$
    $4(65 – L) = L$ // Substitute $65 – L$ for S in $4S = L$
    $L=52$
23. **(A) 31.**
    Let D = DOLLARS
    Let H = HOURS
    Let d = dollars
    Let h = hours
    Given $D = 418$
    Given $H = 30$
    Given $d = 432$

Formula $\frac{D}{H} = \frac{d}{h}$
$Dh = Hd$ // Expand parentheses
$418h = 30(432)$ // Simplify
$418h = 12960$
$h = 31.0048$

24. **(A) 8.**
Let N = NICKELS
Let D = DIMES
Let Q = QUARTERS
Given $7.3 = 0.05N + 0.1D + 0.25Q$
Given $N = D+2$
Given $Q = 3D$
$7.3 = 0.05N + 0.1D + 0.25(3D)$ // Substitute $3D$ for N in $7.3 = 0.05N + 0.1D + 0.25Q$
$7.3 = 0.05(D + 2) + 0.1D + 0.25(3D)$ // $D + 2$ for Q in $7.3 = 0.05N + 0.1D + 0.25(3D)$
$7.3 = 0.05D + 0.1 + 0.1D + 0.75D$
$0 = 0.9D - 7.2$
$D = 8$

25. **(A) $3942.91.**
Let F = FIRSTMAN
Let S = SECONDMAN
Given $\frac{F}{S} = \frac{4}{7}$
Given $F + S = 6196$
$7F = 4S$ // Expand parentheses
$F = 6196 - S$ // Simplify
$4S = 7(6196 - S)$ // Simplify
$4S = 43372 - 7S$ // Simplify
Solution $S = 3942.91$

SUBTEST 3—WORD KNOWLEDGE

1. **(A) controversy.** Used as a noun, *altercation* means a vehement quarrel.
2. **(A) demonstrate.** *Illustrate*, used as a verb, means to clarify by giving an example.
3. **(E) act of wearing down.** Used as a noun, *attrition* means a rubbing away or wearing down by friction.
4. **(A) perceptive.** Used as an adjective, *insightful* means showing or having insight.
5. **(D) helpful.** Used as an adjective, *conducive* means tending to cause or bring about; contributive.
6. **(A) deceptive.** Used as an adjective, *illusory* means produced by, based on, or having the nature of an illusion; deceptive.
7. **(C) harmful.** Used as an adjective, *deleterious* means having a harmful effect; injurious.
8. **(C) authoritative.** Used as a verb, *commanding* means to direct with authority; give orders to.

9. **(C) pliable.** Used as an adjective, *flexible* means capable of being bent or flexed; pliable.
10. **(D) chance.** Used as a noun, *opportunity* means a chance for progress or advancement.
11. **(B) fair.** Used as an adjective, *impartial* means not biased; unprejudiced.
12. **(A) bookkeeper.** Used as a noun, *accountant* means one who keeps, audits, and inspects the financial records of individuals or business concerns and prepares financial and tax reports.
13. **(B) lazy.** Used as an adjective, *indolent* means disinclined to exert oneself; habitually lazy.
14. **(E) snub.** Used as a noun, *rebuff* means a blunt or abrupt repulse or refusal.
15. **(A) false.** Used as an adjective, *spurious* means lacking authenticity or validity in essence or origin.
16. **(A) incompetent.** Used as an adjective, *inapt* means awkward or clumsy.
17. **(D) Samaritan.** Used as a noun, *humanitarian* means one who is caring and giving.
18. **(C) aquatic.** Used as an adjective, *maritime* means of, relating to, or near the sea.
19. **(A) argumentative.** Used as an adjective, *litigious* means to show a trait to argue or disagree, even to the point of lawsuits.
20. **(A) speech.** Used as a noun, *harangue* means a long, pompous speech.
21. **(A) angrily silent.** Used as an adjective, *sullen* means showing a brooding ill humor or silent resentment.
22. **(B) dull.** Used as an adjective, *tedious* means tiresome by reason of length, slowness, or dullness.
23. **(B) coward.** Used as a noun, *recreant* means craven or cowardly.
24. **(A) sticky.** Used as an adjective, *glutinous* means adhesive.
25. **(C) sound.** Used as a noun, *dissonance* means a harsh, disagreeable combination of sounds.

SUBTEST 4—MATHEMATICS KNOWLEDGE

1. **(C) 220 miles.** Circumference = pi $\times$ diameter; circumference = 22.6 $\times$ 69 = 220 miles.
2. **(C) 12.86 square feet.** The area of the shaded portion is the area of the square minus the area of the circle. The area of the square is 16 square feet (4^2 or 4×4). The area of the circle is $\pi(r^2)$ or $\pi(1^2) = 3.14 \times 1$ or 3.14. The area of the shaded portion is 16 – 3.14 = 12.86.
3. **(A) $\frac{1}{7}$.**

$$\frac{2}{7} = 2x^2$$

$$\frac{2x}{14} = x^2$$

$$\frac{2}{14} = \frac{x^2}{x}$$

$$x = \frac{1}{7}.$$

4. **(C) $-28x - 43$.**
$-7(4x) -7(5) - 8$
$-28x - 35 - 8$
$-28x - 43$

5. **(A)** $\frac{\mathbf{1}}{\mathbf{x-4}} \cdot \frac{x-2}{x^2-6x+8} = \frac{x-2}{(x-2)(x-4)} = \frac{1}{x-4}$

6. **(C) $\frac{9\pi}{2}$ + 12 square feet.**
The radius of the half-circle is 3 feet. That means that the length of the base of the triangle is 6 feet (twice the radius of the circle). The area of the triangle is $\frac{1}{2}bh$ or $\frac{1}{2}(6 \times 4) = 12$. The area of the circle is $\pi * r^2$, which is equal to 9π. But we need $\frac{1}{2}$ of that, so it's $\frac{9\pi}{2}$. Adding the two together, we get $\frac{9\pi}{2} + 12$.

7. **(D) –27.** The odd integer power of a negative number is negative; the even integer power of a negative number is positive.

8. **(C) 48 square feet.** To determine the area of a rectangle, use the formula $A = lw$ $(8 \times 6 = 48)$.

9. **(A) 10^4.** $10{,}000 = 10^4$.

10. **(D) 0.000639.** To convert scientific notation to regulation notation, move the decimal place to the left (for a negative exponent), the same number of spaces as the exponent (in this case, 4).

11. **(E) $\frac{27}{64}$.** $\left(\frac{3}{4}\right)^3 = \frac{3}{4} \times \frac{3}{4} \times \frac{3}{4} = \frac{27}{64}$.

12. **(B) –1.**

$$\begin{aligned} 5x + 7 &= 6(x-2) - 4(2x-3) \\ 5x + 7 &= 6x - 12 - 8x + 12 \\ 5x + 7 &= -2x \\ 7x + 7 &= 0 \\ 7x &= -7 \\ x &= -1 \end{aligned}$$

13. **(E) none of the above.** With the information provided, x cannot be determined. $3^n = 9$; $n = 2$. $4x - n = 4x - 2$.

14. **(D) hyperbola.** As the x^2 and y^2 variables have different signs, the graph is a hyperbola.

15. **(D) $\frac{1}{16}$.** $4^{-2} = \frac{1}{4}^2 = \frac{1}{16}$.

16. **(A) 255.5.**

$$\begin{aligned} x - 31\tfrac{3}{4}\% &= 174.4 \\ x - 0.3175x &= 174.4 \\ x(1 - 0.3175) &= 174.4 \\ 0.6825x &= 174.4 \\ x &= \frac{174.4}{0.6825} \\ x &= 255.53 \end{aligned}$$

17. **(B) 13″.**
$H2 = 52 + 122$
$H2 = 25 + 144$
$H2 = 169$
$H = \sqrt{169}$
$H = 13.11$
18. **(A) 3.** We know that $D = 5$ and $L = W + 1$.
$D^2 = L^2 + W^2$.
$5^2 = (W + 1)^2 + W^2$
$25 = (W + 1)(W + 1) + W^2$
$25 = W^2 + 2W + 1 + W^2$
$25 = 2W^2 + 2W + 1$
$0 = 2W^2 + 2W - 24$
$\frac{1}{2}(0) = \frac{1}{2}(2W^2 + 2W - 24)$
$0 = W^2 + W - 12$
$0 = (W - 3)(W + 4)$
$W - 3 = 0$ and $W + 4 = 0$
$W = 3$ and $W = -4$ (-4 is not a possible solution)
19. **(C) 720°.** A hexagon has 6 sides. (Number of sides – 2) × 180 = sum of angles. 4 × 180 = 720°.
20. **(E) 76.**

$$\frac{3}{4}(68) + \frac{1}{4}(x) = 70$$
$$51 + \frac{x}{4} = 70$$
$$\frac{x}{4} = 19$$
$$x = 4 \times 19$$
$$x = 76$$

21. **(B) 1 inch = 2,000 feet.** 1 inch = 2,000 feet; 1 inch = 2,000 × 12 inches = 24,000 inches. No other option, converted into common terms, shows a scale of $\frac{1}{24{,}000}$.
22. **(E) none of the above.** The base of the cylinder, πr^2, times the height, h = volume of the cylinder. πr^2h is not one of the answers listed in the first four options.
23. **(E) 4.** $\frac{4!}{3!} = \frac{4\times3\times2\times1}{3\times2\times1} = 4$.
24. **(D) 3.** The logarithm, 2.5464, consists of two parts. The 2 is called the characteristic; the 5464 is called the mantissa. A character of 2 indicates three digits to the left of the decimal. For example, the logarithm of 100.00 is 102.00.
25. **(C) UI.** The first and each subsequent odd letter in the series are in regular alphabetical order skipping one letter each time: A C E G . . . The second and each subsequent even letter in the series are in straight alphabetical order: R S T . . . Accordingly, the next two letters in the series are U I.

SUBTEST 5—INSTRUMENT COMPREHENSION

Question	Answer	Direction	Pitch	Bank
1	C	Northeast	Nose Up	Right
2	D	West	Nose Up	Right
3	A	Northeast	Zero	Zero
4	A	East	Zero	Right
5	C	Southeast	Nose Down	Left
6	D	North	Nose Up	Zero
7	B	South	Nose Down	Zero
8	D	North	Nose Down	Right
9	C	West	Zero	Zero
10	D	Southeast	Nose Down	Right
11	D	East	Nose Up	Zero
12	D	South	Zero	Right
13	C	Northeast	Nose Up	Right
14	B	East	Nose Down	Zero
15	A	West	Nose Up	Left
16	A	South	Zero	Zero
17	B	Southwest	Zero	Zero
18	D	West	Nose Down	Left
19	C	South	Nose Up	Left
20	B	West	Nose Down	Left

SUBTEST 6—BLOCK COUNTING

1. **(B) four.** Block 1 touches two blocks below, and two blocks on the right.
2. **(B) four.** Block 2 touches two blocks above, one block on the right, and one block below.
3. **(B) two.** Block 3 touches one block above and one block on the right.
4. **(C) five.** Block 4 touches one block above, two blocks below, and one block on either side.
5. **(C) five.** Block 5 touches three blocks above and two blocks below.
6. **(A) three.** Block 1 touches two blocks below and one block on the right.
7. **(B) four.** Block 2 touches one block above, one block below, and two blocks on the front right.
8. **(C) five.** Block 3 touches two blocks behind, one block above, and two blocks below.

9. **(B) four.** Block 4 touches two blocks behind and two blocks below.
10. **(B) four.** Block 5 touches three blocks above and one block on the right.
11. **(B) four.** Block 1 touches one block behind, two blocks below, and one block to the right.
12. **(A) three**. Block 2 touches two blocks below and one block behind.
13. **(E) seven.** Block 3 touches three blocks on top, one block on the right, and three blocks below.
14. **(C) five.** Block 4 touches one block on top, two blocks below, and one on each side.
15. **(C) five.** Block 5 touches three blocks on top and one to the left.
16. **(C) six.** Block 1 touches one block behind, one block on the left, one block on the right-front, and three blocks below.
17. **(D) seven.** Block 2 touches two blocks on the right, one block on the left, one block on the front, and three blocks below.
18. **(B) five.** Block 3 touches three blocks behind, one block below, and one block to the right-front.
19. **(E) eight.** Block 4 touches three blocks behind, two blocks above, and three blocks below.
20. **(D) seven.** Block 5 touches one block on the right, two blocks on left, and four blocks above.

SUBTEST 7—TABLE READING

1. **(B) 6.**
2. **(A) 4.**
3. **(C) –4.**
4. **(C) 7.**
5. **(B) 9.**
6. **(E) 4.**
7. **(B) 7.**
8. **(A) 7.**
9. **(A) 3.**
10. **(B) 9.**
11. **(C) $10,015.80.**
12. **(D) $5,240.70.**
13. **(A) $3,852.00.**
14. **(B) $8,004.00.**
15. **(D) $12,818.70.**
16. **(E) $4,728.90.**
17. **(B) $5,383.50.**
18. **(A) $7,339.80.**
19. **(D) $3,221.40.**
20. **(C) $4,850.10.**
21. **(A) $56.**
22. **(C) $11.66.**
23. **(D) $4,597.**
24. **(A) $4.86.**
25. **(E) not available.**
26. **(D) $2,259.**
27. **(E) $1,930.**
28. **(B) $2,166.**
29. **(C) $1,677.**
30. **(A) $1,215.**
31. **(B) DUU.**
32. **(C) UMN.**
33. **(B) DCG.**
34. **(D) DGY.**
35. **(B) GEH.**
36. **(E) JFI.**
37. **(E) JDH.**
38. **(D) SCD.**
39. **(A) AHS.**
40. **(A) HSR.**

SUBTEST 8—AVIATION INFORMATION

1. **(A) results in increased drag.** When an airplane enters a climb, it changes its flight path from level flight to an inclined plane or climb attitude. In a climb, weight no longer acts in a direction perpendicular to the flight path. It acts in a rearward direction. This causes an increase in total drag.
2. **(C) positive air pressure below the wing's surface and negative air pressure above the wing's surface.** The top of the wing is curved while the bottom is relatively flat. The air flowing over the top travels a little farther than the air flowing along the flat bottom. This means that the air on top must go faster. Hence, the pressure decreases, resulting in a lower pressure on top of the wing and a higher pressure below. The higher pressure then pushes (lifts) the wing up toward the lower-pressure area.
3. **(E) all of the above.** Convective air currents, obstructions to wind flow, and wind shear are all major causes of flight turbulence.
4. **(A) lift equals weight and thrust equals drag.** In a steady flight condition, the always present forces that oppose each other are also equal to each other. That is, lift equals weight and thrust equals drag.
5. **(B) drag.** Drag is the force that resists forward motion of the aircraft.
6. **(C) A steady red light signals to continue circling and a flashing red light signals that the airport is unsafe for landing.** A steady red light from the tower to an aircraft in flight signals to continue circling; a flashing red light signals that the airport is unsafe for landing.
7. **(E) when clearing obstacles during landing.** A minimum safe airspeed descent is a nose-high, power-assisted descent condition principally used for clearing obstacles during a landing approach to a short runway.
8. **(E) greater lift and more drag.** When in the downward (extended) position, the wing-flaps pivot downward from the hinged points. This in effect increases the wing camber and angle of attack, thereby providing greater lift and more drag so that the airplane can descend or climb at a steeper angle or a slower airspeed.
9. **(B) faster.** Air is less dense at higher altitudes, so the higher an aircraft flies, the faster it must travel (in relation to the ground) in order to produce the same amount of lift.
10. **(E) lift, thrust, weight, and drag.** These are the four primary forces that affect an aircraft in flight.
11. **(D) flaps.** Aircraft flaps are categorized as secondary flight controls.
12. **(C) more than 250,000 pounds of gross weight.** The term applies to very large cargo and passenger aircraft.
13. **(A) directional turning from the tail.** When an aircraft is "yawed," the nose displaces (turns) to the right or left in relation to the direction of flight.
14. **(D) indicates whether an aircraft is an enemy or an ally.** IFF stands for "Identification Friend or Foe." It's a component that electronically communicates with other aircraft in the area to determine whether or not they are friendly forces.
15. **(C) red.** The radical line indicating dangerous operating ranges on the airspeed indicator is colored red.
16. **(D) the airplane will require less effort to control.** Stability is the inherent ability of a body, after its equilibrium is disturbed, to develop forces or

moments that tend to return the body to its original position. The ability of the airplane to return, of its own accord, to its original condition of flight after it has been disturbed by some outside force (such as turbulent air) makes the airplane easier to fly and requires less effort to control.

17. **(E) climb.** The thrust required to maintain straight and level flight at a given airspeed is not sufficient to maintain the same airspeed in a climb. Climbing flight takes more power than straight and level flight. Consequently, the engine power control must be advanced to a higher power setting.
18. **(A) shorter takeoff distance and increased climb angle.** A tailwind, on the other hand, would have the opposite effect, resulting in a longer takeoff distance and a decreased angle of climb.
19. **(A) nose up.** The elevator trim tab is a small auxiliary control surface hinged at the trailing edge of the elevators. The elevator trim tab acts on the elevators, which in turn act upon the entire airplane. A downward deflection of the trim tab will force the elevator upward, which will force the tail down and the nose up.
20. **(C) 09.** Runways are assigned numbers based on the magnetic compass direction of the runway. Runway 27 is a runway placed along the heading of 270 (west). The opposite direction would be heading 090 (east), and the runway would be numbered 09.

SUBTEST 9—ROTATED BLOCKS

1. **(D)**	4. **(D)**	7. **(E)**	10. **(B)**	13. **(C)**
2. **(C)**	5. **(B)**	8. **(B)**	11. **(A)**	14. **(E)**
3. **(C)**	6. **(A)**	9. **(E)**	12. **(A)**	15. **(D)**

SUBTEST 10—GENERAL SCIENCE

1. **(B) specific gravity.** The French chemist Antoine Baumé devised the scale for marking hydrometers.
2. **(E) cornea.** The cornea, a thin clear layer, forms the front part of the eyeball.
3. **(C) estimate the vapor pressures of pure liquids or solids.** The *Antoine equation* is a simple 3-parameter fit to experimental vapor pressures measured over a restricted temperature range.
4. **(B) burning one pound of coal.** Combustion is a chemical process.
5. **(B) spleen.** Surplus red blood cells are stored in the spleen until the body needs them for an emergency.
6. **(B) protein.** Protein is the chief nutrient in lean meat.
7. **(A) hypothalamus.** The hypothalamus controls body temperature, metabolism, heart rate, sexual development, sleep, and the body's use of fat and water.
8. **(D) pitchblende.** Uranium is found in pitchblende and other rare metals. Hematite is a source of iron; chalcopyrite is an ore of copper; bauxite is a source of aluminum; feldspar is a source of silicates.
9. **(C) turbulent air**. The scientific name for the twinkling of stars is stellar scintillation (or astronomical scintillation). Stars twinkle when we see them from Earth's surface because we are viewing them through thick layers of turbulent (moving) air in Earth's atmosphere.

10. **(C) nitrogen.** Nitrogen constitutes about four-fifths of the atmosphere by volume. Oxygen is the most plentiful gas on Earth, but not in the air.
11. **(B) negative charge.** Electric current is imagined to flow from positive to negative, but the electrons that move through wire are negative.
12. **(A) cirrus.** Cirrus clouds occur at 20,000 to 40,000 feet and are made up of ice crystals. Nimbus clouds are gray rain clouds; cumulus clouds are fluffy white clouds; stratus clouds are long, low clouds, generally at altitudes of 2,000 to 7,000 feet; altostratus clouds are at intermediate heights.
13. **(E) energy.** The 3 main kinds of matter are solid, liquid and gas. When there is a fire, solids turn into gases. But the fire itself isn't a gas—fire is a lot of light and heat. Light and heat are kinds of energy.
14. **(E) lowered.** The freezing point of a solution is generally lower than that of the pure solvent. In extreme cold weather, salt is placed on icy sidewalks to help melt the ice.
15. **(C) oxidation.** Rust is iron that was burned. Iron and steel are actually burning very slowly when they rust. Scientists call fire an oxidation reaction, when something combines with oxygen in the air to form a new substance.
16. **(E) ball and socket.** Ball and socket joints permit movement in almost all directions. The shoulder joint is a ball and socket joint.
17. **(B) conduction.** When heat is transferred through a solid, the process is called conduction. When heat is transferred through a liquid, the process is called convection.
18. **(D) three hours.** Earth rotates 360° in 24 hours; therefore it rotates 45° in three hours.
19. **(B) at a lower temperature**. At higher altitudes, it's easier to boil water because of the lower air pressure, so it boils at a lower temperature. Lower temperatures mean cooking takes longer, which is why there are high altitude instructions in recipes.
20. **(D) electron.** An electron is a negative particle. A proton is positively charged; a neutron is neutral and without charge: a meson has both positive and negative charges. An isotope is an atom of the same element but with a different number of neutrons.

SUBTEST 11—HIDDEN FIGURES

1. **(A) figure A.**

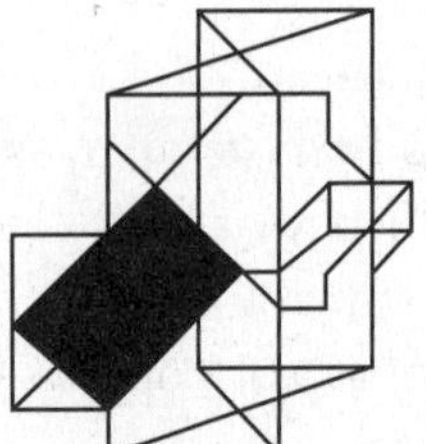

2. **(A) figure A.**

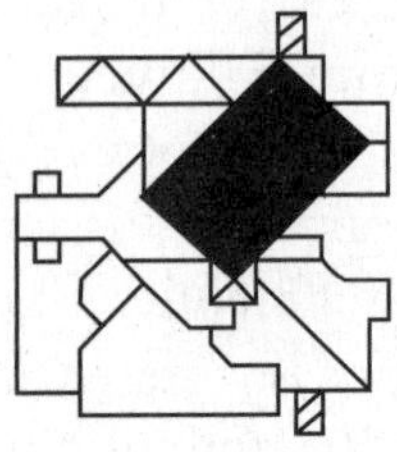

3. **(E) figure E.**

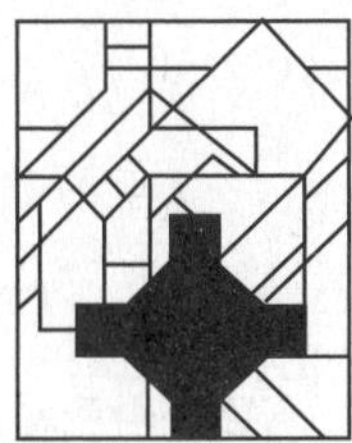

4. **(D) figure D.**

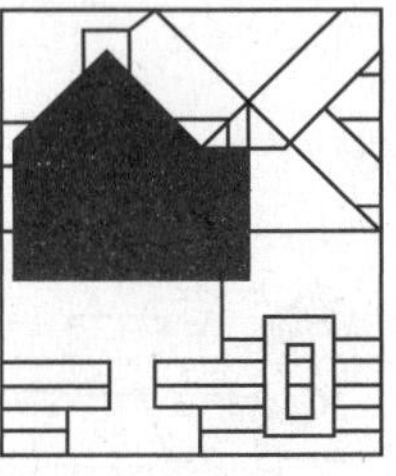

5. **(C) figure C.**

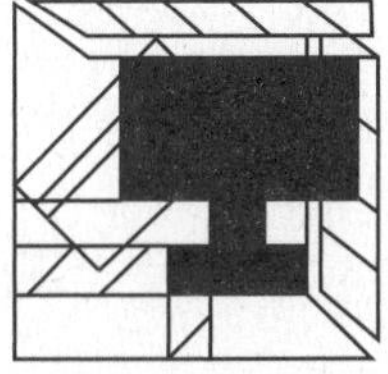

6. **(B) figure B.**

7. **(A) figure A.**

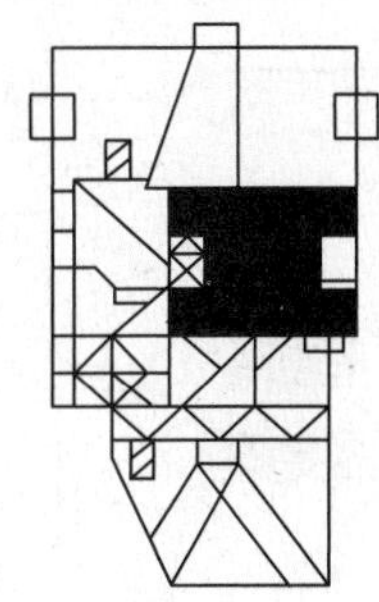

8. **(E) Figure E.**

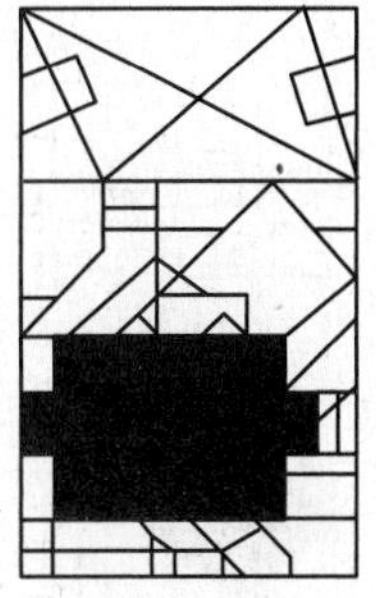

9. **(C) figure C.**

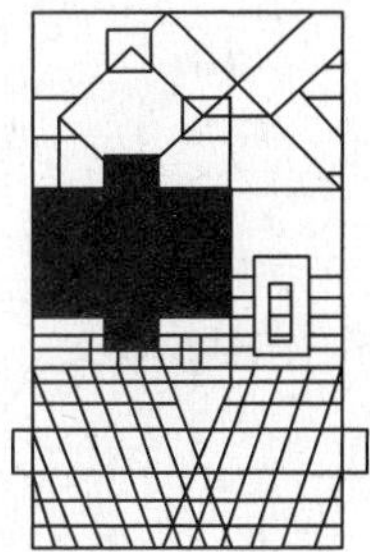

10. **(D) figure D.**

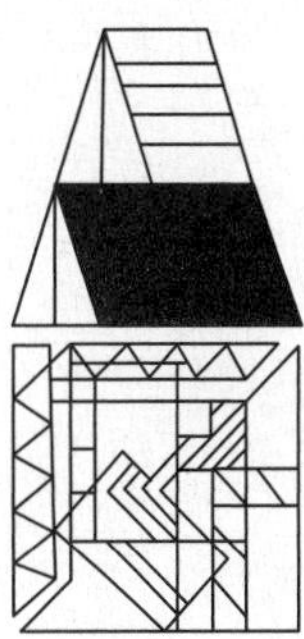

11. **(D) figure D.**

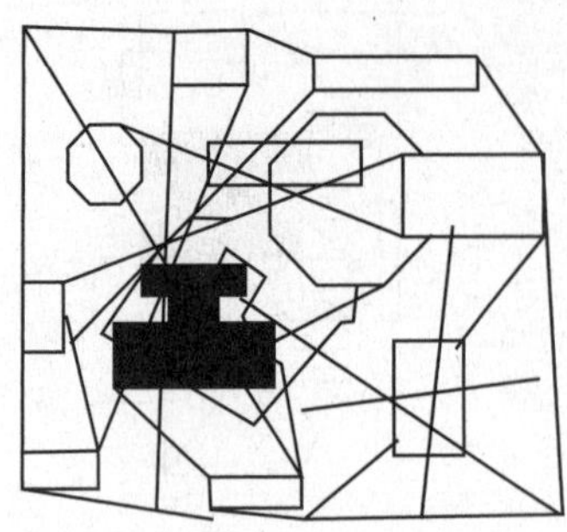

12. **(B) figure B.**

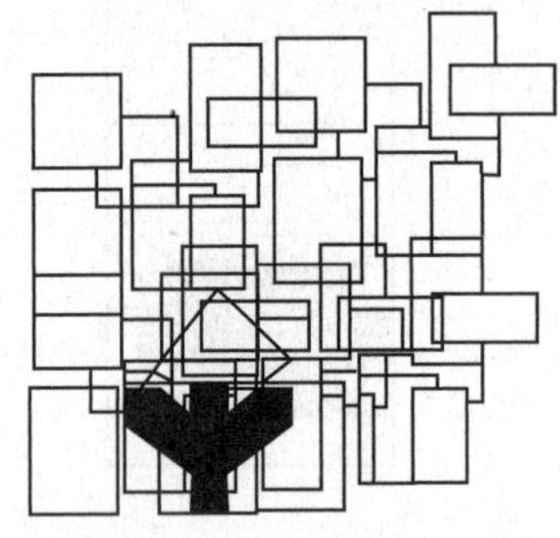

13. **(A) figure A.**

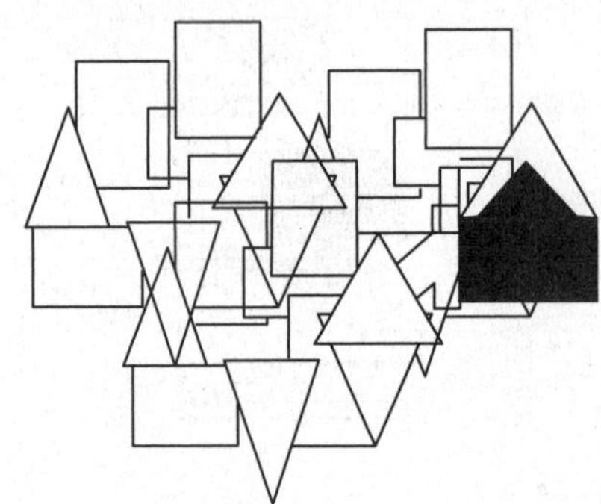

14. **(E) figure E.**

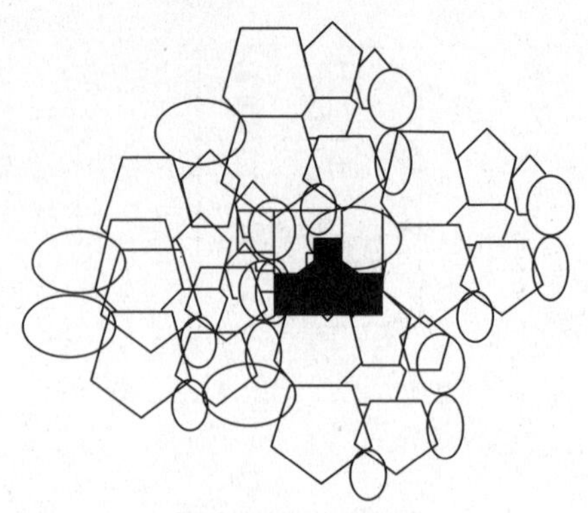

15. **(C) figure C.**

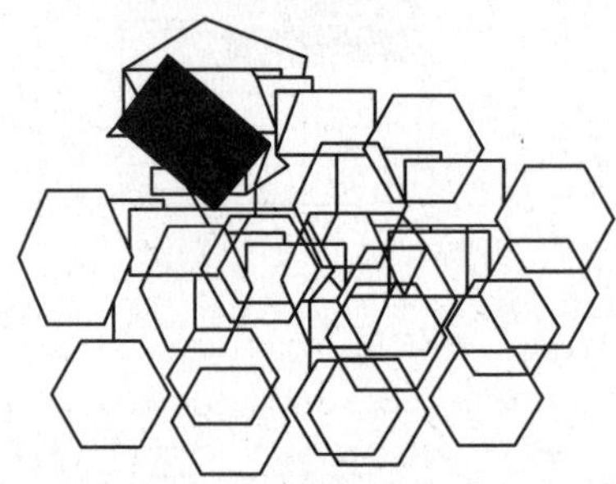

CHAPTER 15

Practice Test for Army and Non-Aviation Marine Corps/Coast Guard Applicants 1

The General Technical (GT) composite score from the ASVAB is used to determine qualification for Army and non-aviation Marine Corps and Coast Guard OCS/OCC candidates. Marine Corps candidates may also qualify by using SAT or ACT scores (see Chapter 3). Marine Corps and Coast Guard aviation candidates should take the Navy and Marine Corps Aviation Selection Test Battery practice test (see Chapters 18 and 19).

The GT composite score is determined from three subtests of the ASVAB: Paragraph Comprehension, Word Knowledge, and Arithmetic Reasoning. These three subtests comprise a total of 80 questions that must be answered in 60 minutes. If you take the computerized version of the ASVAB (CAT-ASVAB), these three subtests would be comprised of 43 total questions with a time limit of 69 minutes. For the purpose of the practice exam in this chapter, we will reproduce the number of questions contained in the paper version of the test.

Answer Sheet for Practice Test 3

Subtest 1–Paragraph Comprehension

1 Ⓐ Ⓑ Ⓒ Ⓓ
2 Ⓐ Ⓑ Ⓒ Ⓓ
3 Ⓐ Ⓑ Ⓒ Ⓓ
4 Ⓐ Ⓑ Ⓒ Ⓓ
5 Ⓐ Ⓑ Ⓒ Ⓓ
6 Ⓐ Ⓑ Ⓒ Ⓓ
7 Ⓐ Ⓑ Ⓒ Ⓓ
8 Ⓐ Ⓑ Ⓒ Ⓓ
9 Ⓐ Ⓑ Ⓒ Ⓓ
10 Ⓐ Ⓑ Ⓒ Ⓓ
11 Ⓐ Ⓑ Ⓒ Ⓓ
12 Ⓐ Ⓑ Ⓒ Ⓓ
13 Ⓐ Ⓑ Ⓒ Ⓓ
14 Ⓐ Ⓑ Ⓒ Ⓓ
15 Ⓐ Ⓑ Ⓒ Ⓓ

Subtest 2–Word Knowledge

1 Ⓐ Ⓑ Ⓒ Ⓓ
2 Ⓐ Ⓑ Ⓒ Ⓓ
3 Ⓐ Ⓑ Ⓒ Ⓓ
4 Ⓐ Ⓑ Ⓒ Ⓓ
5 Ⓐ Ⓑ Ⓒ Ⓓ
6 Ⓐ Ⓑ Ⓒ Ⓓ
7 Ⓐ Ⓑ Ⓒ Ⓓ
8 Ⓐ Ⓑ Ⓒ Ⓓ
9 Ⓐ Ⓑ Ⓒ Ⓓ
10 Ⓐ Ⓑ Ⓒ Ⓓ
11 Ⓐ Ⓑ Ⓒ Ⓓ
12 Ⓐ Ⓑ Ⓒ Ⓓ
13 Ⓐ Ⓑ Ⓒ Ⓓ
14 Ⓐ Ⓑ Ⓒ Ⓓ
15 Ⓐ Ⓑ Ⓒ Ⓓ
16 Ⓐ Ⓑ Ⓒ Ⓓ
17 Ⓐ Ⓑ Ⓒ Ⓓ
18 Ⓐ Ⓑ Ⓒ Ⓓ
19 Ⓐ Ⓑ Ⓒ Ⓓ
20 Ⓐ Ⓑ Ⓒ Ⓓ
21 Ⓐ Ⓑ Ⓒ Ⓓ
22 Ⓐ Ⓑ Ⓒ Ⓓ
23 Ⓐ Ⓑ Ⓒ Ⓓ
24 Ⓐ Ⓑ Ⓒ Ⓓ
25 Ⓐ Ⓑ Ⓒ Ⓓ
26 Ⓐ Ⓑ Ⓒ Ⓓ
27 Ⓐ Ⓑ Ⓒ Ⓓ
28 Ⓐ Ⓑ Ⓒ Ⓓ
29 Ⓐ Ⓑ Ⓒ Ⓓ
30 Ⓐ Ⓑ Ⓒ Ⓓ
31 Ⓐ Ⓑ Ⓒ Ⓓ
32 Ⓐ Ⓑ Ⓒ Ⓓ
33 Ⓐ Ⓑ Ⓒ Ⓓ
34 Ⓐ Ⓑ Ⓒ Ⓓ
35 Ⓐ Ⓑ Ⓒ Ⓓ

Subtest 3–Arithmetic Reasoning

1 Ⓐ Ⓑ Ⓒ Ⓓ
2 Ⓐ Ⓑ Ⓒ Ⓓ
3 Ⓐ Ⓑ Ⓒ Ⓓ
4 Ⓐ Ⓑ Ⓒ Ⓓ
5 Ⓐ Ⓑ Ⓒ Ⓓ
6 Ⓐ Ⓑ Ⓒ Ⓓ
7 Ⓐ Ⓑ Ⓒ Ⓓ
8 Ⓐ Ⓑ Ⓒ Ⓓ
9 Ⓐ Ⓑ Ⓒ Ⓓ
10 Ⓐ Ⓑ Ⓒ Ⓓ
11 Ⓐ Ⓑ Ⓒ Ⓓ
12 Ⓐ Ⓑ Ⓒ Ⓓ
13 Ⓐ Ⓑ Ⓒ Ⓓ
14 Ⓐ Ⓑ Ⓒ Ⓓ
15 Ⓐ Ⓑ Ⓒ Ⓓ
16 Ⓐ Ⓑ Ⓒ Ⓓ
17 Ⓐ Ⓑ Ⓒ Ⓓ
18 Ⓐ Ⓑ Ⓒ Ⓓ
19 Ⓐ Ⓑ Ⓒ Ⓓ
20 Ⓐ Ⓑ Ⓒ Ⓓ
21 Ⓐ Ⓑ Ⓒ Ⓓ
22 Ⓐ Ⓑ Ⓒ Ⓓ
23 Ⓐ Ⓑ Ⓒ Ⓓ
24 Ⓐ Ⓑ Ⓒ Ⓓ
25 Ⓐ Ⓑ Ⓒ Ⓓ
26 Ⓐ Ⓑ Ⓒ Ⓓ
27 Ⓐ Ⓑ Ⓒ Ⓓ
28 Ⓐ Ⓑ Ⓒ Ⓓ
29 Ⓐ Ⓑ Ⓒ Ⓓ
30 Ⓐ Ⓑ Ⓒ Ⓓ

Subtest 1—Paragraph Comprehension

Directions: This subtest consists of 15 questions that must be answered in 13 minutes. The subtest measures your ability to discern information in written paragraphs (see Chapter 6 for complete information).

Read each paragraph then select the answer that *best* completes the statement or answers the question.

Questions 1–3 are based on the following paragraph:

"Alan took possession of the house on January 1, and paid for it in full by means of an e-gold transfer. He had to do a fair bit of hand-holding with the realtor to get her set up and running on e-gold, but he loved to do that sort of thing, loved to sit at the elbow of a novitiate and guide her through the clicks and taps and forms. He loved to break off for impromptu lectures on the underlying principles of the transaction, and so he treated the poor realtor lady to a dozen addresses on the nature of international currency markets, the value of precious metal as a kind of financial *lingua franca* to which any currency could be converted, the poetry of vault shelves in a hundred banks around the world piled with the heaviest of metals, glinting dully in the fluorescent tube lighting, tended by gnomish bankers who spoke a hundred languages but communicated with one another by means of this universal tongue of weights and measures and purity."

1. The main character in this paragraph likes to lecture about ___________.

   (A) real estate
   (B) finances
   (C) politics
   (D) fluorescent lighting

2. In the above paragraph, the word *impromptu* means ___________.

   (A) irritating
   (B) organized
   (C) accidental
   (D) spontaneous

3. The main character considers shelves in a bank vault to be ___________.

   (A) a thing of beauty
   (B) highly secure
   (C) accessible
   (D) gnomish

"Shelldrake was a man of more pretence than real cultivation, as I afterwards discovered. He was in good circumstances, and always glad to receive us at his house, as this made him virtually the chief of our tribe, and the outlay for refreshments involved only the apples from his own orchard, and water from his well...."

4. The character described in the above paragraph

    (A) disliked houseguests.
    (B) liked houseguests.
    (C) grew oranges.
    (D) lived in the city.

Questions 5 and 6 are based on the following paragraph:

"Father Higgins had ventured to treat himself to a spectacle. He had attended, for the first time in his life, an exhibition of legerdemain; this one being given by that celebrated master of the black art, Professor Heller. He had seen the professor change turnips into gold watches, draw a dozen live pigeons in succession out of an empty box, send rings into ladies' handkerchiefs at the other end of the hall, catch a bullet out of an exploded pistol in his hand, and perform other marvels equally irrational and disturbing. From this raree-show Father Higgins had gone home feeling that he had witnessed something about as unearthly as he was likely to be confronted with in the next world."

5. In the above paragraph, the word *legerdemain* means ___________.

    (A) carnival
    (B) priest
    (C) sleight of hand
    (D) religion

6. What reaction did Father Higgins experience from the effects of the performance?

    (A) he was disturbed.
    (B) he was excited.
    (C) he was saddened.
    (D) he was bored.

Questions 7–10 are based on the following paragraph:

"Afghanistan's recent history is a story of war and civil unrest. The Soviet Union invaded in 1979, but was forced to withdraw 10 years later by anti-Communist mujaheddin forces. The Communist regime in Kabul collapsed in 1992. Fighting that subsequently erupted among the various mujaheddin factions eventually helped to spawn the Taliban, a hardline Pakistani-sponsored movement that fought to end the warlordism and civil war that gripped the country. The Taliban seized Kabul in 1996 and were able to capture most of the country, outside of Northern Alliance strongholds primarily in the north-east. Following the 11 September 2001 terrorist attacks, a U.S., Allied, and Northern Alliance military action toppled the Taliban for sheltering Osama bin Laden. In late 2001, a conference in Bonn, Germany, established a process for political reconstruction that ultimately resulted in the adoption of a new constitution and presidential election in 2004. On 9 October 2004, Hamid Karzai became the first democratically elected president of Afghanistan. The new Afghan government's next task is to hold National Assembly elections, tentatively scheduled for April 2005."

7. According to the passage, the political situation of Afghanistan can best be described as ___________.

   (A) organized
   (B) chaotic
   (C) diligent
   (D) practical

8. According to the passage, the prime purpose of establishing the Taliban movement was to

   (A) convert to democracy.
   (B) qualify for membership in the U.N.
   (C) re-establish the central religion.
   (D) end civil war.

9. According to the passage, which of the following statements is <u>not</u> true?

   (A) Afghanistan has never had a democratically-elected leader.
   (B) The Soviet occupation of Afghanistan was unsuccessful.
   (C) U.S. and Allied Forces attacked the Taliban in 2001.
   (D) The Northern Alliance strongholds were mostly in the northeast of the country.

10. According to the passage, the communist regime in Kabul collapsed ___________ years after the Soviet invasion began?

   (A) 10 years
   (B) 13 years
   (C) 15 years
   (D) 18 years

Questions 11 and 12 are based on the below paragraph:

"She was Garvington's sister, and the wife of Sir Hubert Pine, the millionaire, who was absent from the house party on this occasion. As a rule, she spoke little, and constantly wore a sad expression on her pale and beautiful face. And Agnes Pine really was beautiful, being one of those tall, slim willowy-looking women who always look well and act charmingly. And, indeed, her undeniable charm of manner probably had more to do with her reputation as a handsome woman than her actual physical grace. With her dark hair and dark eyes, her Greek features and ivory skin faintly tinted with a tea-rose hue, she looked very lovely and very sad. Why she should be, was a puzzle to many women, as being the wife of a superlatively rich man, she had all the joys that money could bring her. Still it was hinted on good authority–but no one ever heard the name of the authority–that Garvington being poor had forced her into marrying Sir Hubert, for whom she did not care in the least. People said that her cousin Noel Lambert was the husband of her choice, but that she had sacrificed herself, or rather had been compelled to do so, in order that Garvington might be set on his legs."

11. The character described in the above paragraph is described as __________.

(A) happily married
(B) unhappily married
(C) single
(D) divorced

12. According to the above passage, most women

(A) understood the main character's unhappiness.
(B) did not understand why she was unhappy.
(C) envied the main character.
(D) disliked the main character.

Questions 13 and 14 are based on the below paragraph:

"The occurrence of Alzheimer's disease (AD) is not a normal development in the aging process. Alzheimer's disease is characterized by a gradual loss of memory, decline in the ability to perform routine tasks, disorientation, difficulty in learning, loss of language skills, impaired judgment and ability to plan, and personality changes. Over time, these changes become so severe that they interfere with an individual's daily functioning, resulting eventually in death. While the disease can last from 3 to 20 years after the onset of symptoms, the average duration is 8 years."

13. In the above paragraph, the word disorientation means __________.

(A) joyous
(B) religious
(C) confused
(D) reliant

14. Which of the following statements is <u>not</u> true?

(A) On average, AD lasts about 8 years.
(B) AD can result in death.
(C) The symptoms of AD gradually get more severe as time passes.
(D) AD is a normal part of the aging process.

"Poultry waste has a traditional financial value. It's sold for \$3 to \$10 per ton as fertilizer. But when amended soils become too saturated with manure, nitrogen and phosphorus in the waste can leach into nearby rivers, streams, and groundwater supplies. Excess phosphorus in marine environments can stoke extensive algal blooms. These growth explosions and their subsequent breakdown steal valuable oxygen away from fish and other aquatic organisms, causing them to die off."

15. The main point of the above passage is

(A) Poultry waste can be made into fertilizer.
(B) Poultry waste is inexpensive.
(C) Fertilizer from manure is not the best choice for the environment.
(D) none of the above.

Subtest 2—Word Knowledge

Directions: This subtest measures the extent of your vocabulary. In each question, one word is underlined. Your task is to select the answer that means the same, or most nearly the same, as the underlined word. The subtest consists of 35 questions that must be answered in 11 minutes.

1. Proprietor most nearly means ___________.
   (A) steady
   (B) owner
   (C) disliked
   (D) renowned

2. Illustrate most nearly means ___________.
   (A) demonstrate
   (B) value
   (C) agree
   (D) help

3. Superficial most nearly means ___________.
   (A) truthful
   (B) managerial
   (C) false
   (D) support

4. Insightful most nearly means ___________.
   (A) perceptive
   (B) voluntary
   (C) infamous
   (D) religious

5. Typical most nearly means ___________.
   (A) exhaustive
   (B) plentiful
   (C) relaxing
   (D) characteristic

6. Illusory most nearly means ___________.
   (A) deceptive
   (B) genuine
   (C) insightful
   (D) silly

7. Perpendicular most nearly means ___________.
   (A) unskilled
   (B) relaxed
   (C) upright
   (D) mocking

8. Commanding most nearly means ___________.
   (A) exciting
   (B) zealous
   (C) authoritative
   (D) unusual

9. Athletic most nearly means ___________.
   (A) lazy
   (B) vigorous
   (C) macho
   (D) frail

10. Opportunity most nearly means ___________.
    (A) placement
    (B) refined
    (C) tiresome
    (D) chance

11. Foreman most nearly means ___________.
    (A) boss
    (B) owner
    (C) proprietor
    (D) first

12. Accountant most nearly means ___________.
    (A) bookkeeper
    (B) banker
    (C) lawyer
    (D) police officer

13. <u>Hinder</u> most nearly means ___________.

(A) river
(B) moisten
(C) prevent
(D) walk

14. <u>Pliable</u> most nearly means ___________.

(A) firm
(B) river
(C) texture
(D) malleable

15. <u>Operate</u> most nearly means ___________.

(A) meaningful
(B) represent
(C) rely
(D) function

16. <u>Obsolete</u> most nearly means ___________.

(A) new
(B) outmoded
(C) old
(D) progressive

17. <u>Annoying</u> most nearly means ___________.

(A) peculiar
(B) lawyer
(C) abrasive
(D) corrective

18. <u>Unexcelled</u> most nearly means ___________.

(A) excellent
(B) average
(C) beneficial
(D) progressive

19. The boys <u>debated</u> their proposed direction of travel.

(A) discussed
(B) explained
(C) mitigated
(D) managed

20. The magician asked the spectator to pull a <u>random</u> card out of the deck.

(A) specific
(B) red
(C) unplanned
(D) face

21. The doctor called the patient into the office to explain her <u>diagnosis</u>.

(A) decision
(B) identification
(C) intention
(D) plan

22. The client <u>refuted</u> the amount of the bill.

(A) referred
(B) opposed
(C) mitigated
(D) changed

23. He divulged the extent of his dating <u>promiscuity</u> in front of everyone.

(A) purpose
(B) purity
(C) high standards
(D) assortment

24. The silence in the room was <u>tangible</u>.

(A) invisible
(B) relaxing
(C) annoying
(D) appreciable

25. She certainly came to court <u>prepared</u>.

(A) absent–minded
(B) late
(C) early
(D) ready

26. The crowd was <u>enthusiastic</u> to see the clown enter.

(A) titillated
(B) bored
(C) apathetic
(D) lethargic

27. The darkness of the room amplified our fears.
    (A) minimized
    (B) analyzed
    (C) inflated
    (D) ended

28. Bette had an unusual vocation.
    (A) profession
    (B) religion
    (C) test
    (D) voice

29. Attendance at the ceremony is mandatory.
    (A) suggested
    (B) optional
    (C) required
    (D) expected

30. The judge decided to hold the defendant harmless for all damages.
    (A) irresponsible
    (B) responsible
    (C) exempt
    (D) liable

31. The effort he put into the job was insufficient to justify payment.
    (A) ample
    (B) inadequate
    (C) enough
    (D) required

32. The city council elected to construct a new daycare center.
    (A) design
    (B) erect
    (C) repair
    (D) evaluate

33. The rudiments of his plan are simplistic.
    (A) elements
    (B) requirements
    (C) spelling
    (D) firmness

34. The boys enjoyed a camaraderie not seen in many clubs.
    (A) party
    (B) conversation
    (C) interest
    (D) friendship

35. John's incessant bragging gets on my nerves.
    (A) irritating
    (B) loud
    (C) occasional
    (D) constant

Subtest 3—Arithmetic Reasoning

Directions: This subtest consists of 30 questions that must be answered in 36 minutes. The subtest measures your ability to use arithmetic to solve everyday problems—in short, algebra and geometry word problems.

1. A rectangle 20 meters longer than it is wide has an area of 125 square meters. What are the length and width?
   (A) length = 25, width = 5
   (B) length = 20, width = 6
   (C) length = 15, width = 10
   (D) length = 10, width = 5

2. William's father is 30 years older than William. In 10 years, the sum of their ages will be 90. How old is William?
   (A) 15
   (B) 20
   (C) 25
   (D) 30

3. Mack drove his truck to Omaha at the rate of 40 mph. He made the return trip driving at a rate of 45 mph. If it took 30 minutes longer to drive to Omaha than it did to drive home, how long did it take him to drive home?

   (A) 3 hours
   (B) 3 hours and 30 minutes
   (C) 4 hours
   (D) 4 hours and 30 minutes

4. Timmy worked 40 hours last week, earning $480 dollars. If he earns $432 this week, how many hours will he have worked?

   (A) 30
   (B) 32
   (C) 34
   (D) 36

5. Nicky has some nickels, dimes, and quarters worth $6.75. There are four times as many nickels as dimes, and five more quarters than dimes. How many dimes does she have?

   (A) 10
   (B) 12
   (C) 14
   (D) 15

6. Patty received an inheritance of $60,000. She invested part at 8 percent and placed the remainder in tax-free bonds at 7 percent. Her total annual income from the investment was $4,700. How much was invested at 8 percent?

   (A) $20,000
   (B) $30,000
   (C) $40,000
   (D) $50,000

7. Find the hypotenuse of a right triangle if the measures of its sides are 3 and 4.

   (A) 5
   (B) 6
   (C) 7
   (D) 8

8. Two integers have a total of 65. Four times the smaller integer is equal to the larger integer. Find the larger integer.

   (A) 48
   (B) 52
   (C) 58
   (D) 62

9. For the first five years, the loan value of a Porsche is determined by the formula $V = -\$4{,}000a + \$50{,}000$, where V is the value and a is the age of the car in years. What is the loan value for a Porsche that is 5 years old?

   (A) $25,000
   (B) $30,000
   (C) $35,000
   (D) $40,000

10. Three consecutive even numbers have a sum of 108. What is the first number (lowest) in the series?

    (A) 44
    (B) 54
    (C) 34
    (D) 24

11. The length of a rectangular patio is 1 foot less than 3 times its width. If the perimeter of the patio is 46 feet, what are the dimensions of the patio?

    (A) 5 feet × 15 feet
    (B) 7 feet × 14 feet
    (C) 8 feet × 10 feet
    (D) 6 feet × 17 feet

12. A computer system depreciates at the rate of $1,500 per year. If the original price of the system was $15,000, what is the salvage value after six years?

    (A) $5,000
    (B) $6,000
    (C) $8,000
    (D) $10,000

13. Three consecutive odd numbers have the sum of 75. Find the last (largest) number in the series.

 (A) 25
 (B) 27
 (C) 29
 (D) 31

14. Two numbers are in the ratio of 2 to 3, and their difference is 30. Find the smaller number.

 (A) 60
 (B) 65
 (C) 70
 (D) 75

15. The sides of a triangle are 13, 12, and 5. Find the perimeter.

 (A) 25
 (B) 30
 (C) 35
 (D) 40

16. A circle has a radius of 4 inches. What is the area of a sector of that circle if the arc of the sector has a measurement of 120 degrees?

 (A) 15.25
 (B) 16.75
 (C) 17.50
 (D) 18.25

17. Jerry has 4 more nickels than dimes, and the total value of his money is $1.25. How many nickels does he have?

 (A) 11
 (B) 15
 (C) 18
 (D) 20

18. Determine the circumference of a circle whose radius is 4.

 (A) 20.18
 (B) 22.31
 (C) 25.12
 (D) 26.28

19. A carpenter needs to cut a 14–foot board into 3 pieces so that the second piece is twice as long as the first, and the third is twice as long as the second. How long is the third piece?

 (A) 12 feet
 (B) 10 feet
 (C) 9 feet
 (D) 8 feet

20. The formula $h = 50t - 5t^2$ can be used to find the height in meters of an object shot upward at an initial velocity of 50 meters per second after t seconds. How long will it take for an object launched at 50 meters per second to arrive at a height of 120 meters?

 (A) 6 seconds
 (B) 8 seconds
 (C) 10 seconds
 (D) 12 seconds

21. A map of the world is scaled so that 2 inches represents 250 miles. How many miles is it between Moscow and Paris if the distance on the map is 15 inches?

 (A) 1625
 (B) 1875
 (C) 1955
 (D) 2022

22. 33 less than a number is 18. What is the number?

 (A) 35
 (B) 39
 (C) 42
 (D) 51

23. Two angles are supplementary. If the first angle measures 60°, what is the measurement of the second angle?

 (A) 30 degrees
 (B) 90 degrees
 (C) 120 degrees
 (D) 360 degrees

24. The length of a rectangle is 3 inches less than twice the width. If each dimension is increased by 4 inches, the area is increased by 88 square inches. Find the width of the original rectangle.

    (A) 5
    (B) 7
    (C) 9
    (D) 11

25. A purse has 25 coins worth $4.90. If the purse contains only dimes and quarters, how many quarters are in the purse?

    (A) 10
    (B) 14
    (C) 16
    (D) 18

26. Martha and John are planning their wedding reception. The caterer has given them two options: under Plan A, the caterer will charge a set fee of $25 per person. Under Plan B, the caterer would charge $1,300 plus $20 for each guest in excess of the first 25 who attend. Assuming that more than 25 guests will attend, how many people must attend before Plan B becomes the cheaper plan?

    (A) 150
    (B) 193
    (C) 261
    (D) 283

27. One side of an equilateral triangle is 8 feet. Find the perimeter.

    (A) 18
    (B) 20
    (C) 24
    (D) 28

28. The ratio of the length to the width of an object is 9 to 4. If the length is 36 feet, find the width.

    (A) 8
    (B) 12
    (C) 14
    (D) 16

29. 800 people attended the opening show at the circus. An advance ticket cost $14.50 and admission at the door was $22.00. If $16,640 was taken in total attendance, how many paid attendance at the door?

    (A) 550
    (B) 672
    (C) 705
    (D) 725

30. The width of a rectangle is 8 inches and the diagonal of the rectangle is 2 inches greater than its length. Find the length of the rectangle.

    (A) 5
    (B) 10
    (C) 15
    (D) 20

Answer Key

PRACTICE TEST 3

Subtest 1—Paragraph Comprehension

1. B
2. D
3. A
4. B
5. C
6. A
7. B
8. D
9. A
10. B
11. B
12. B
13. C
14. D
15. C

Subtest 2—Word Knowledge

1. B
2. A
3. C
4. A
5. D
6. A
7. C
8. C
9. B
10. D
11. A
12. A
13. C
14. D
15. D
16. B
17. C
18. A
19. A
20. C
21. B
22. B
23. D
24. D
25. D
26. A
27. C
28. A
29. C
30. C
31. B
32. B
33. A
34. D
35. D

Subtest 3—Arithmetic Reasoning

1. A
2. B
3. D
4. D
5. A
6. D
7. A
8. B
9. B
10. C
11. D
12. B
13. B
14. A
15. B
16. B
17. A
18. C
19. D
20. D
21. B
22. D
23. C
24. B
25. C
26. C
27. C
28. D
29. B
30. C

Answer Explanations to Practice Test

SUBTEST 1—PARAGRAPH COMPREHENSION

1. **(B) finances.** Alan loved to give lectures on the nature of international currency markets, the value of precious metals, etc.
2. **(D) spontaneous.** Alan would spontaneously (without prior planning) give lectures about the nature of finances.
3. **(A) a thing of beauty.** Alan speaks of the "poetry" of vault shelves.
4. **(B) liked houseguests.** Shelldrake was always glad to receive people at his house.
5. **(C) sleight of hand.** Father Higgins witnessed a performance of a magician.
6. **(A) he was disturbed.** The show left Father Higgins feeling that he had witnessed something "unearthly."
7. **(B) chaotic.** Chaotic means disorganized and disruptive, which describes the state of Afghanistan's recent political history.
8. **(D) end civil war.** The Taliban movement was sponsored by Pakistan to fight to end warlordism and civil war within the country.
9. **(A) Afghanistan has never had a democratically-elected leader.** The people of Afghanistan elected their first democratically–elected president in 2004.
10. **(B) 13 years.** The soviet invasion began in 1979 and the communist regime collapsed in 1992.
11. **(B) unhappily married.** Most believed that Garvington forced her to marry her husband.
12. **(B) did not understand why she was unhappy.** Most women were puzzled over her unhappiness, as she was married to a wealthy man.
13. **(C) confused.** One of the symptoms of AD is the confusion or disorientation of the individual.
14. **(D) AD is a normal part of the aging process.** This statement is not true. The first sentence in the paragraph states that AD is a disease that is not a normal development in the aging process.
15. **(C) Fertilizer from manure is not the best choice for the environment.** The main point made by the above passage is that fertilizers made from manure can have harmful effects on the water supplies.

SUBTEST 2—WORD KNOWLEDGE

1. **(B) owner.** A *proprietor* is one who owns or owns and manages a business or other such establishment.
2. **(A) demonstrate.** *Illustrate,* used as a verb, means to clarify by giving an example.
3. **(C) false.** Used as an adjective, *superficial* means apparent rather than actual or substantial.
4. **(A) perceptive.** Used as an adjective, *insightful* means showing or having insight; perceptive.
5. **(D) characteristic.** Used as an adjective, *typical* means exhibiting the qualities, traits, or characteristics that identify a kind, class, group, or category.
6. **(A) deceptive.** Used as an adjective, *illusory* means produced by, based on, or having the nature of an illusion; deceptive.

7. **(C) upright.** Used as an adjective, *perpendicular* means being at right angles to the horizontal; vertical.
8. **(C) authoritative.** Used as a verb, *commanding* means to direct with authority; give orders to.
9. **(B) vigorous.** Used as an adjective, *athletic* means involving physical activity or exertion.
10. **(D) chance.** Used as a noun, *opportunity* means a chance for progress or advancement.
11. **(A) boss.** Used as a noun, *foreman* means a man/woman who serves as the leader of a work crew, as in a factory.
12. **(A) bookkeeper.** Used as a noun, *accountant* means one who keeps, audits, and inspects the financial records of individuals or business concerns and prepares financial and tax reports.
13. **(C) prevent.** Used as a verb, hinder means to interfere with action or progress.
14. **(D) malleable**. Used as an *adjective*, pliable means easily bent or shaped.
15. **(D) function.** Used as a verb, *operate* means to perform a function; work.
16. **(B) outmoded.** Used as an adjective, *obsolete* means outmoded in design, style, or construction (Note: because something is old, does not necessarily mean it's obsolete – an object can be old, but still useful).
17. **(C) abrasive.** Used as an adjective, *annoying* means causing vexation or irritation.
18. **(A) excellent.** Used as an adjective, *unexcelled* means not capable of being improved.
19. **(A) discussed.** In the context of this sentence, *debate* means to engage in a formal discussion or argument.
20. **(C) unplanned.** In the context of this sentence, *random* means having no specific pattern, purpose, or objective.
21. **(B) identification.** In the context of this sentence, *diagnosis* means identification of the medical problem.
22. **(B) opposed.** In the context of this sentence, *refute* means to disagree with.
23. **(D) assortment.** In the context of this sentence, *promiscuity* means a history of being indiscriminate in the choice of dating partners.
24. **(D) appreciable.** In the context of this sentence, *tangible* means able to be noticed.
25. **(D) ready.** In the context of this sentence, *prepared* means to make ready beforehand for a specific purpose.
26. **(A) titillated.** In the context of this sentence, *enthusiastic* means excited, happy, or animated.
27. **(C) inflated.** In the context of this sentence, *amplified* means to make larger or more powerful.
28. **(A) profession.** In the context of this sentence, *vocation* means occupation or career.
29. **(C) required.** In the context of this sentence, *mandatory* means compulsory or required.
30. **(C) exempt.** In the context of this sentence, *harmless* means not responsible, or exempt.

31. **(B) inadequate.** In the context of this sentence, *insufficient* means inadequate or lacking.
32. **(B) erect.** In the context of this sentence, *construct* means to build.
33. **(A) elements.** In the context of this sentence, *rudiments* mean structure, parts, or elements.
34. **(D) friendship.** In the context of this sentence, *camaraderie* means close friendship.
35. **(D) constant.** In the context of this sentence, *incessant* means continuous or non-stopping.

SUBTEST 3—ARITHMETIC REASONING

1. **(A) length = 25, width = 5.**
   Let A = AREA
   Let L = LENGTH
   Let W = WIDTH
   Given $L = W+20$
   Given $A = 125$
   Given $A = LW$
   $A = LW$ // Area formula
   $125 = (W + 20)W$ // Substitute: $L = W + 20$
   $W^2 + 20W - 125 = 0$ // Simplify
   $W = (5, -25)$ // Solve for W
   $W = 5$ // Reject negative Width
   $L = 25$ // Calculate L using $L = W + 20$
2. **(B) 20.**
   Let F = FATHER
   Let W = WILLIAM
   Given $F = W + 30$
   Given $90 = F + 10 + W + 10$
   $90 = (W + 30) + 10 + W + 10$ // Substitute $W+30$ for F
   $W = 20$
3. **(D) 4 hours**
   Rate × Time = Distance
   Let Rh = Rate Going Home
   Let Th = Time Going Home
   Given: $Rh = 45$ mph
   Given: $Rh \times Th = 45Th$ // Distance from Omaha to home
   Let Ro = Rate to Omaha
   Let To = Time to Omaha
   Given: $Ro = 40$ mph
   Given: $To = Th + 0.5$ // It took 0.5 hours longer to drive home
   $Ro{*}To = 40(Th + 0.5)$ // Distance from home to Omaha
   Rates and times must equal the same distance, so we set them equal to each other:
   $40(Th + 0.5) = 45Th$
   $40Th + 20 = 45Th$
   $20 = 5Th$
   $Th = 4$ hours // Time from Omaha to home.

4. **(D) 36.**
   Let D = DOLLARS
   Let H = HOURS
   Let d = dollars
   Let h = hours
   Given $D = 480$
   Given $H = 40$
   Given $d = 432$
   Formula $D/H = d/h$
   $Dh = Hd$ // Substitute known values
   $480h = 40(432)$ // Simplify
   $480h = 17280$
   $h = 36$
5. **(A) 10.**
   Let N = NICKELS
   Let D = DIMES
   Let Q = QUARTERS
   Given $6.75 = 0.05N + 0.1D + 0.25Q$
   Given $N = 4D$
   Given $Q = D+5$
   $6.75 = 0.05N + 0.1D + 0.25(D + 5)$ // Substitute $D+5$ for N
   $6.75 = 0.05(4D) + 0.1D + 0.25(D + 5)$ // Substitute $4D$ for Q
   $6.75 = 0.2D + 0.1D + 0.25D + 1.25$
   $0 = 0.55D - 5.5$
   $.55D = 5.5$
   $D = 10$
6. **(D) $50,000.**
   Let x = the amount invested at 8%
   Let y = the amount invested at 7%
   Given: $y = \$60{,}000 - x$
   Given: $0.08x$ = interest received at 8%
   Given $0.07y$ = interest received at 8%
   $0.08x + 0.07y = \$4{,}700$
   $0.08x + 0.07(\$60{,}000 - x) = \$4{,}700$ // substitute known value for y.
   $0.08x + \$4{,}200 - 0.07x = \$4{,}700$
   $0.01x + \$4{,}200 = \$4{,}700$
   $0.01x = \$500$
   $x = \$50{,}000$
7. **(A) 5.**
   Let F = FIRST
   Let S = SECOND
   Let H = HYPOTENUSE
   Given $F = 3$
   Given $S = 4$
   Given $F^2 + S^2 = H^2$
   $3^2 + 4^2 = H^2$
   $25 = H^2$
   $H = 5$

8. **(B) 52.**
   Let L = LARGER
   Let S = SMALLER
   Given $S + L = 65$
   Given $4S = L$
   $4(65 - L) = L$ // Substitute $65–L$ for S
   $L = 52$
9. **(B) $30,000.**
   $V = -\$4{,}000a + \$50{,}000$
   $a = 5$
   $V = (-\$4{,}000 \times 5) + \$50{,}000$
   $V = -\$20{,}000 + \$50{,}000$
   $V = \$30{,}000$
10. **(C) 34.**
   Let F = FIRST
   Let S = SECOND
   Let T = THIRD
   Given $S = F + 2$
   Given $T = F + 4$
   Given $F + S + T = 108$
   $F + S + (F + 4) = 108$ // Substitute $F + 4$ for S
   $F + (F + 2) + (F + 4) = 108$ // Substitute $F + 2$ for T
   $3F + 6 = 108$
   $3F = 102$
   $F = 34$
11. **(D) 6 × 17 feet.**
   Let P = PERIMETER
   Let L = LENGTH
   Let W = WIDTH
   Given $L = 3W - 1$
   Given $P = 46$
   Given $P = 2L + 2W$
   $46 = 2L + 2W$ // Substitute 46 for P
   $46 = 2(3W - 1) + 2W$ // Substitute $3W - 1$ for L
   $46 = 6W - 2 + 2W$
   $0 = 8W - 48$
   $8W = 48$
   $W = 6$
   $L = 17$ // Substitute $W = 6$ into $L = 3W - 1$
12. **(B) $6,000.**
   Let x = salvage value
   Let y = amount depreciated
   Formula $x = \$15{,}000 - y$
   Given $y = 6 \times \$1{,}500$
   $x = \$15{,}000 - (6 \times \$1{,}500)$
   $x = \$15{,}000 - \$9{,}000$
   $x = \$6{,}000$

Answers–Practice Test 3

13. **(B) 27.**
Let F = FIRST
Let S = SECOND
Let T = THIRD
Given $S = F + 2$
Given $T = F + 4$
Given $F + S + T = 75$
$F + S + (F + 4) = 75$ // Substitute $F + 4$ for S
$F + (F + 2) + (F + 4) = 75$ // Substitute $F + 2$ for T
$F = 23$
$S = 25$ // $F = 23$ into $S = F + 2$
$T = 27$ // $F = 23$ into $T = F + 4$

14. **(A) 60.**
Let L = LARGER
Let S = SMALLER
Given $L/S = 3/2$
Given $L = S + 30$
$2L = 3S$ // Expand parentheses
$2(S + 30) = 3S$ // Substitute $S + 30$ for L
$2S + 60 = 3S$
$-S + 60 = 0$
$S = 60$

15. **(B) 30.** Add the length of the sides together. $13 + 12 + 5 = 30$.

16. **(B) 16.75.**
Formula: Area = pi times radius^2
$a = \pi r^2$
Full circle = 360°
Arc = $\frac{120°}{360°}$ or $\frac{1}{3}$ // we need to find the area for $\frac{1}{3}$ of the circle
$a = \left(\frac{1}{3}\right)\pi r^2$
$a = \left(\frac{1}{3}\right) * (3.14)4^2$ // substitute known values
$a = 16.75$

17. **(A) 11.**
Let N = NICKELS
Let D = DIMES
Let V = VALUE
Given $N = D + 4$
Given $1.25 = 0.05N + 0.1D$
$1.25 = 0.05(D + 4) + 0.1D$ // Substitute $D + 4$ for N
$1.25 = 0.05D + 0.2 + 0.1D$
$0 = 0.15D - 1.05$
$D = 7$
$N = 11$ // Substitute $D = 7$ into $N = D + 4$

18. **(C) 25.12**
Let C = CIRCUMFERENCE
Let R = RADIUS
Given $R = 4$

Formula $C = 2\pi R$
$C = 2\pi R$ // Circumference Formula
$C = 2*4\pi$ // Substitute 4 for Radius
$C = 8\pi$
$C = 8*3.14$ // Value of pi
$C = 25.12$

19. **(D) 8 feet.**
Let F = FIRST
Let S = SECOND
Let T = THIRD
Given $F + S + T = 14$
Given $S = 2F$
Given $T = 2S$
$T = 2(2F)$ // Substitute $2F$ for S
$T = 4F$
$F + (2F) + T = 14$ // Substitute $2F$ for S
$F + 2F + (4F) = 14$ // Substitute $4F$ for S in $F + 2F + T = 14$
$F = 2$
$S = 4$ // Substitute $F = 2$ into $S = 2F$
$T = 8$ // Substitute $F = 2$ into $T = 4F$

20. **(D) 12 seconds.**
Formula: $h = 50t - 5t^2$
Given: $h = 120$ meters
$120 = 50t - 5t^2$ // substitute known values
$-5t^2 + 50t - 120 = 0$ //rewrite into standard quadratic equation form and set equal to zero.
$t^2 - 10t + 24 = 0$ // divide both sides by -5
$(t - 12)(t + 2) =$ zero // factor
$t - 12 = 0, t + 2 = 0$
$t = 12, -2$ //discard -2 as negative value for this problem is not meaningful
$t = 12$ seconds

21. **(B) 1875.**
Let I = SCALE INCHES
Let M = SCALE MILES
Let I = inches distance
Let m = miles
Given $I/M = i/m$
Given $M = 250$
Given $I = 2$
Given $I = 15$
$\frac{2}{250} = \frac{15}{m}$ // Expand parentheses
$2m = 250*15$ // Simplify
$m = 1875$

22. **(D) 51.**
Let N = NUMBER
Given $N - 33 = 18$
$N = 51$

23. **(C) 120 degrees.**
The sum of two supplementary angles is 180°
Let a = second angle
$a + 60 = 180$
$a = 120$
24. **(B) 7.**
Let A = AREA
Let L = LENGTH
Let W = WIDTH
Given $L = 2W - 3$
Given $(L + 4)(W + 4) = LW + 88$
$LW + 4L + 4W + 16 = LW + 88$ // Expand parentheses
$4L + 4W + 16 = 88$
$4(2W - 3) + 4W + 16 = 88$ // Substitute $2W - 3$ for L
$8W - 12 + 4W + 16 = 88$
$12W - 12 = 72$
$W = 7$
25. **(C) 16.**
Let D = DIMES
Let Q = QUARTERS
Given $D + Q = 25$
Given $4.9 = 0.1D + 0.25Q$
$4.9 = 0.1(25 - Q) + 0.25Q$ // Substitute $25 - Q$ for D
$4.9 = 2.5 - 0.1Q + 0.25Q$
$0 = -2.4 -0.1Q +0.25Q$
$Q = 16$
26. **(C) 261.**
Let x = number of people attending.
Given: Plan A = $25x$ ($25 for each attending)
Given: Plan B = $1300 + 20x$ ($1,300 plus $20 for each person attending)
$1300 + 20x$ (Plan B) $< 25x$ (Plan A)
$1300 + 20x < 25x$
$1300 < 5x$ // subtract $20x$ from each side
$260 < x$
261 or more people attending will make Plan B less expensive.
27. **(C) 24.** An equilateral triangle has sides of equal length. $3 \times 8 = 24$.
28. **(D) 16.**
Let L = LENGTH
Let W = WIDTH
Given $\frac{L}{W} = \frac{9}{4}$
Given $L = 36$
$4L = 9W$
$144 = 9W$ // Substitute 36 for L
$W = 16$
29. **(B) 672.**
Let x = number of advance tickets
Let y = number paid at the door

Given: $14.5x$ = amount advance tickets made
Given $22y$ = amount made at the door
$14x5x + 22y = 16640$
$x + y = 800$ // total number of people attending
$y = 800 - x$ // subtract x from both sides to get the value of y
$14.5x + 22(800 - x) = 16640$. // substitute known value for y into the formula
$14.5x + 17600 - 22x = 16640$ // clear the parentheses
$-7.5x = 16640 - 17600$ // combine like terms
$-7.5x = -960$
$x = 128$ // number of tickets sold in advance
$800 - 128 = 672$ (number who paid at the door)

30. **(C) 15.**
Find LENGTH
Let D = DIAGONAL
Let L = LENGTH
Let W = WIDTH
Given $W = 8$
Given $D = L + 2$
Given $D^2 = L^2 + W^2$
$D^2 = L^2 + 64$ // Substitute 8 for W
$(L + 2)^2 = L^2 + 64$ // Substitute $L + 2$ for D
$L = 15$

CHAPTER 16

Practice Test for Army and Non-Aviation Marine Corps/Coast Guard Applicants 2

The General Technical (GT) composite score from the ASVAB is used to determine qualification for Army and non-aviation Marine Corps and Coast Guard OCS/OCC candidates. Marine Corps candidates may also qualify by using SAT or ACT scores (see Chapter 3). Marine Corps and Coast Guard aviation candidates should take the Navy and Marine Corps Aviation Selection Test Battery practice test (see Chapters 18 and 19).

The GT composite score is determined from three subtests of the ASVAB: Paragraph Comprehension, Word Knowledge, and Arithmetic Reasoning. These three subtests comprise a total of 80 questions that must be answered in 60 minutes. If you take the computerized version of the ASVAB (CAT-ASVAB), these three subtests would be comprised of 43 total questions with a time limit of 69 minutes. For the purpose of the practice exam in this chapter, we will reproduce the number of questions contained in the paper version of the test.

Answer Sheet for Practice Test 4

Subtest 1—Paragraph Comprehension

1 Ⓐ Ⓑ Ⓒ Ⓓ
2 Ⓐ Ⓑ Ⓒ Ⓓ
3 Ⓐ Ⓑ Ⓒ Ⓓ
4 Ⓐ Ⓑ Ⓒ Ⓓ
5 Ⓐ Ⓑ Ⓒ Ⓓ
6 Ⓐ Ⓑ Ⓒ Ⓓ
7 Ⓐ Ⓑ Ⓒ Ⓓ
8 Ⓐ Ⓑ Ⓒ Ⓓ
9 Ⓐ Ⓑ Ⓒ Ⓓ
10 Ⓐ Ⓑ Ⓒ Ⓓ
11 Ⓐ Ⓑ Ⓒ Ⓓ
12 Ⓐ Ⓑ Ⓒ Ⓓ
13 Ⓐ Ⓑ Ⓒ Ⓓ
14 Ⓐ Ⓑ Ⓒ Ⓓ
15 Ⓐ Ⓑ Ⓒ Ⓓ

Subtest 2—Word Knowledge

1 Ⓐ Ⓑ Ⓒ Ⓓ
2 Ⓐ Ⓑ Ⓒ Ⓓ
3 Ⓐ Ⓑ Ⓒ Ⓓ
4 Ⓐ Ⓑ Ⓒ Ⓓ
5 Ⓐ Ⓑ Ⓒ Ⓓ
6 Ⓐ Ⓑ Ⓒ Ⓓ
7 Ⓐ Ⓑ Ⓒ Ⓓ
8 Ⓐ Ⓑ Ⓒ Ⓓ
9 Ⓐ Ⓑ Ⓒ Ⓓ
10 Ⓐ Ⓑ Ⓒ Ⓓ
11 Ⓐ Ⓑ Ⓒ Ⓓ
12 Ⓐ Ⓑ Ⓒ Ⓓ
13 Ⓐ Ⓑ Ⓒ Ⓓ
14 Ⓐ Ⓑ Ⓒ Ⓓ
15 Ⓐ Ⓑ Ⓒ Ⓓ
16 Ⓐ Ⓑ Ⓒ Ⓓ
17 Ⓐ Ⓑ Ⓒ Ⓓ
18 Ⓐ Ⓑ Ⓒ Ⓓ
19 Ⓐ Ⓑ Ⓒ Ⓓ
20 Ⓐ Ⓑ Ⓒ Ⓓ
21 Ⓐ Ⓑ Ⓒ Ⓓ
22 Ⓐ Ⓑ Ⓒ Ⓓ
23 Ⓐ Ⓑ Ⓒ Ⓓ
24 Ⓐ Ⓑ Ⓒ Ⓓ
25 Ⓐ Ⓑ Ⓒ Ⓓ
26 Ⓐ Ⓑ Ⓒ Ⓓ
27 Ⓐ Ⓑ Ⓒ Ⓓ
28 Ⓐ Ⓑ Ⓒ Ⓓ
29 Ⓐ Ⓑ Ⓒ Ⓓ
30 Ⓐ Ⓑ Ⓒ Ⓓ
31 Ⓐ Ⓑ Ⓒ Ⓓ
32 Ⓐ Ⓑ Ⓒ Ⓓ
33 Ⓐ Ⓑ Ⓒ Ⓓ
34 Ⓐ Ⓑ Ⓒ Ⓓ
35 Ⓐ Ⓑ Ⓒ Ⓓ

Subtest 3—Arithmetic Reasoning

1 Ⓐ Ⓑ Ⓒ Ⓓ
2 Ⓐ Ⓑ Ⓒ Ⓓ
3 Ⓐ Ⓑ Ⓒ Ⓓ
4 Ⓐ Ⓑ Ⓒ Ⓓ
5 Ⓐ Ⓑ Ⓒ Ⓓ
6 Ⓐ Ⓑ Ⓒ Ⓓ
7 Ⓐ Ⓑ Ⓒ Ⓓ
8 Ⓐ Ⓑ Ⓒ Ⓓ
9 Ⓐ Ⓑ Ⓒ Ⓓ
10 Ⓐ Ⓑ Ⓒ Ⓓ
11 Ⓐ Ⓑ Ⓒ Ⓓ
12 Ⓐ Ⓑ Ⓒ Ⓓ
13 Ⓐ Ⓑ Ⓒ Ⓓ
14 Ⓐ Ⓑ Ⓒ Ⓓ
15 Ⓐ Ⓑ Ⓒ Ⓓ
16 Ⓐ Ⓑ Ⓒ Ⓓ
17 Ⓐ Ⓑ Ⓒ Ⓓ
18 Ⓐ Ⓑ Ⓒ Ⓓ
19 Ⓐ Ⓑ Ⓒ Ⓓ
20 Ⓐ Ⓑ Ⓒ Ⓓ
21 Ⓐ Ⓑ Ⓒ Ⓓ
22 Ⓐ Ⓑ Ⓒ Ⓓ
23 Ⓐ Ⓑ Ⓒ Ⓓ
24 Ⓐ Ⓑ Ⓒ Ⓓ
25 Ⓐ Ⓑ Ⓒ Ⓓ
26 Ⓐ Ⓑ Ⓒ Ⓓ
27 Ⓐ Ⓑ Ⓒ Ⓓ
28 Ⓐ Ⓑ Ⓒ Ⓓ
29 Ⓐ Ⓑ Ⓒ Ⓓ
30 Ⓐ Ⓑ Ⓒ Ⓓ

Subtest 1 — Paragraph Comprehension

Directions: This subtest consists of 15 questions that must be answered in 13 minutes. The subtest measures your ability to discern information in written paragraphs (see Chapter 6 for complete information).

Read each paragraph then select the answer that best completes the statement or answers the question.

"Mr. Bennet was so odd a mixture of quick parts, sarcastic humour, reserve, and caprice, that the experience of three-and-twenty years had been insufficient to make his wife understand his character. *Her* mind was less difficult to develop. She was a woman of mean understanding, little information, and uncertain temper. When she was discontented, she fancied herself nervous. The business of her life was to get her daughters married; its solace was visiting and news."

1. The character with the most complex personality is ___________.

   (A) Mrs. Bennet
   (B) Mr. Bennet
   (C) the daughter
   (D) Bill

Questions 2–5 are based on the following paragraph.

"Few of the great works of ancient Greek literature are easy reading. They nearly all need study and comment, and at times help from a good teacher, before they yield up their secret. And the *Poetics* cannot be accounted an exception. For one thing the treatise is fragmentary. It originally consisted of two books, one dealing with Tragedy and Epic, the other with Comedy and other subjects. We possess only the first. For another, even the book we have seems to be unrevised and unfinished. The style, though luminous, vivid, and in its broader division systematic, is not that of a book intended for publication. Like most of Aristotle's extant writing, it suggests the MS. of an experienced lecturer, full of jottings and adscripts, with occasional phrases written carefully out, but never revised as a whole for the general reader."

2. A good title for the above passage would be

   (A) "Ancient Greek Literature for Relaxing Reading."
   (B) "The Complete Works of Aristotle."
   (C) "Complexities of Ancient Greek Literature."
   (D) "A Comedy of Errors."

3. *Poetics* can best be described as

   (A) an unfinished manuscript.
   (B) a complete work of fiction.
   (C) a systematic observation of ancient Greek life.
   (D) a trilogy.

4. A subject not mentioned as included in *Poetics* is ____________.

   (A) tragedy
   (B) epic
   (C) love
   (D) humor

5. In the above passage, the word fragmentary means ____________.

   (A) gigantic
   (B) microscopic
   (C) continuous
   (D) disjointed

Questions 6 is based on the following paragraph.

> "In ancient times, and about two hundred years before the overthrow of Britain, the Welsh were instructed and confirmed in the faith by Faganus and Damianus, sent into the island at the request of King Lucius by Pope Eleutherius, and from that period when Germanus of Auxerre, and Lupus of Troyes, came over on account of the corruption which had crept into the island by the invasion of the Saxons, but particularly with a view of expelling the Pelagian heresy, nothing heretical or contrary to the true faith was to be found amongst the natives."

6. Germanus and Lupus traveled to Wales in order to

   (A) invade with the Saxons.
   (B) put an end to unorthodoxy and dishonesty.
   (C) rebuild the empire.
   (D) comply with a request from King Lucius and Pope Eleutherius.

Questions 7–9 are based on the following paragraph.

"The Portuguese began to trade with the island of Timor in the early 16th century and colonized it in mid-century. Skirmishing with the Dutch in the region eventually resulted in an 1859 treaty in which Portugal ceded the western portion of the island. Imperial Japan occupied East Timor from 1942 to 1945, but Portugal resumed colonial authority after the Japanese defeat in World War II. East Timor declared itself independent from Portugal on 28 November 1975 and was invaded and occupied by Indonesian forces nine days later. It was incorporated into Indonesia in July 1976 as the province of East Timor. An unsuccessful campaign of pacification followed over the next two decades, during which an estimated 100,000 to 250,000 individuals lost their lives. On 20 September 1999 the Australian-led peacekeeping troops of the International Force for East Timor (INTERFET) deployed to the country and brought the violence to an end. On 20 May 2002, East Timor was internationally recognized as an independent state."

7. An estimated 100,000 to 250,000 people lost their lives in East Timor during a period that lasted approximately ____________.

   (A) 10 years
   (B) 20 years
   (C) 30 years
   (D) 40 years

8. In the 17th century, Portugal ceded the western portion of the island to ____________.

   (A) Australia
   (B) Britain
   (C) the Netherlands
   (D) Indonesia

9. Indonesia invaded and occupied East Timor in 1975 on ____________.

   (A) November 28
   (B) November 30
   (C) December 4
   (D) December 7

Questions 10 is based on the following paragraph.

"Air carriers had until Nov. 1987 to comply with a new regulation that required the installation of new fire-blocking layers on aircraft seat cushions. This marked the end of a three-year compliance schedule. Air carriers replaced 650,000 foam seat cushions on the U.S. fleet. FAA research found that the new material did a better job retarding burning and provided 40 to 60 seconds of additional time for aircraft evacuation. All existing seats in the U.S. fleet meet the improved standards."

10. Which of the following statements is <u>not</u> true?

    (A) U.S. aircraft are now safer due to the new regulation.
    (B) More than half a million seat covers were replaced.
    (C) Air carriers were given four years to comply with the regulation.
    (D) The new cushions provide for faster evacuations in times of emergency.

Questions 11 is based on the following paragraph.

"There are upwards of 200,000 words in the recent editions of the large dictionaries, but the one-hundredth part of this number will suffice for all your wants. Of course you may think not, and you may not be content to call things by their common names; you may be ambitious to show superiority over others and display your learning or, rather, your pedantry and lack of learning. For instance, you may not want to call a spade a spade. You may prefer to call it a spatulous device for abrading the surface of the soil. Better, however, to stick to the old familiar, simple name that your grandfather called it. It has stood the test of time, and old friends are always good friends."

11. A good title for the above passage would be

    (A) "The Importance of an Extensive Vocabulary."
    (B) "Keep it Simple, Stupid."
    (C) "Memorizing the Dictionary."
    (D) "Maximizing Effective Communication Processes."

Questions 12 is based on the following paragraph.

"Throughout history all literature was in the public domain, but, in the United States, 'intellectual property' is traded as if it were some sort of tangible commodity. This is especially shameful when one considers that the public domain is precisely what drives the advancement of society. As the technology to promulgate and store information increases, so too does the ability to use that information as a framework for future advances. It is unfortunate that as the physical obstacles are overcome, legal ones are created to replace them."

12. The author believes that

    (A) copyright laws impede the advancement of our society.
    (B) technology is advancing too fast.
    (C) public libraries should be abolished.
    (D) the history of information technology should be explored.

Questions 13–15 are based on the following paragraph.

"Ozone (O_3) is a gas composed of three oxygen atoms. It is not usually emitted directly into the air, but at ground level is created by a chemical reaction between oxides of nitrogen (NO_x) and volatile organic compounds (VOC) in the presence of sunlight. Ozone has the same chemical structure whether it occurs miles above the earth or at ground level and can be 'good' or 'bad,' depending on its location in the atmosphere. 'Good' ozone occurs naturally in the stratosphere approximately 10 to 30 miles above Earth's surface and forms a layer that protects life on earth from the sun's harmful rays. In Earth's lower atmosphere, ground-level ozone is considered 'bad.'"

13. Whether or not ozone is beneficial or harmful depends primarily on

    (A) the temperature.
    (B) the type of ozone.
    (C) the weather.
    (D) the altitude.

14. "Good" ozone protects us from

    (A) meteors.
    (B) the sun's rays.
    (C) exhaust emissions.
    (D) ground erosion.

15. One factor that must be present for the creation of ground ozone is ______________.

    (A) carbon
    (B) water
    (C) sunlight
    (D) high pressure

Subtest 2 — Word Knowledge

Directions: This subtest measures the extent of your vocabulary. In each question, one word is underlined. Your task is to select the answer that means the same, or most nearly the same, as the underlined word. The subtest consists of 35 questions that must be answered in 11 minutes.

1. Conciliatory most nearly means ________.
   (A) exiting
   (B) aggressive
   (C) appeasing
   (D) hard–working

2. Meticulous most nearly means ________.
   (A) precise
   (B) inaccurate
   (C) calm
   (D) reckless

3. Discernible most nearly means ________.
   (A) dubious
   (B) manageable
   (C) obvious
   (D) palatable

4. Dogmatic most nearly means ________.
   (A) falsehood
   (B) opinionated
   (C) lazy
   (D) trustworthy

5. Reticent most nearly means ________.
   (A) secretive
   (B) apologetic
   (C) aggressive
   (D) problematic

6. Aesthetic most nearly means ________.
   (A) periodic
   (B) perishable
   (C) tangible
   (D) beautiful

7. Eccentric most nearly means ________.
   (A) rich
   (B) eclectic
   (C) oddball
   (D) personality

8. Capricious most nearly means ________.
   (A) resolvable
   (B) light-hearted
   (C) changeable
   (D) reliant

9. Plausible most nearly means ________.
   (A) reasonable
   (B) unlikely
   (C) possible
   (D) remark

10. Remonstrate most nearly means ________.
    (A) argue
    (B) manage
    (C) propose
    (D) relax

11. Scrutinize most nearly means ________.
    (A) examine
    (B) predict
    (C) position
    (D) glance

12. Candid most nearly means ________.
    (A) talkative
    (B) hidden
    (C) photo
    (D) honest

13. Resolute most nearly means __________.
    (A) paralyzed
    (B) determined
    (C) animated
    (D) ill

14. Homogeneous most nearly means __________.
    (A) mixture
    (B) separated
    (C) consistent
    (D) erratic

15. Wanton most nearly means __________.
    (A) practical
    (B) relentless
    (C) immoral
    (D) righteous

16. Kinetic most nearly means __________.
    (A) slow
    (B) masterful
    (C) applied
    (D) energetic

17. Futile most nearly means __________.
    (A) hopeless
    (B) resourceful
    (C) panic
    (D) possible

18. He forgot to kindle the fire.
    (A) extinguish
    (B) stimulate
    (C) target
    (D) focus

19. Betty's sedentary life will kill her one day.
    (A) rough
    (B) purposeless
    (C) practical
    (D) inactive

20. Becker's monetary loss was a result of blatant chicanery.
    (A) gambling
    (B) robbery
    (C) drinking
    (D) deception

21. He was a novice, so we gave him a break.
    (A) beginner
    (B) expert
    (C) parson
    (D) marvel

22. His remarks were rife with hackneyed phrases.
    (A) boring
    (B) inaccurate
    (C) overused
    (D) detailed

23. Lazarus didn't realize the extent of the ramifications his actions would have.
    (A) travel
    (B) consequences
    (C) falsehoods
    (D) pragmatics

24. On the advice of his doctor, Paul entered into a rigorous routine of exercise.
    (A) relaxing
    (B) perplexing
    (C) arduous
    (D) steady

25. We decided on a detailed plan to break Samantha out of her lethargy.
    (A) attitude
    (B) lassitude
    (C) petulance
    (D) appeasement

26. Tanya's behavior caused us to <u>relegate</u> her to the bedroom.

    (A) send
    (B) exile
    (C) push
    (D) move

27. He arrived at the hotel room <u>incognito</u>.

    (A) in disguise
    (B) in secret
    (C) recognized
    (D) incapacitated

28. There was no way we could tell that she would be so <u>vindictive</u> over the matter.

    (A) joyous
    (B) petty
    (C) angry
    (D) revengeful

29. After the accident, Mark was <u>delirious</u> for about ten minutes.

    (A) unconscious
    (B) confused
    (C) animated
    (D) pragmatic

30. The assembly lasted forever, accommodating <u>loquacious</u> bores who each talked for hours.

    (A) boring
    (B) time-consuming
    (C) chatty
    (D) interesting

31. That's the last time I will attend a performance of that <u>mundane</u> actor!

    (A) rude
    (B) magnetic
    (C) irritating
    (D) humdrum

32. How he aced the test without studying at all is still something of an <u>enigma</u>.

    (A) miracle
    (B) mystery
    (C) ambiguity
    (D) perspicuity

33. I'm afraid I don't quite get your <u>abstract</u> meaning.

    (A) complex
    (B) confused
    (C) practical
    (D) perplexed

34. While walking to my dorm room, I suddenly had an <u>epiphany</u> about your problem.

    (A) insight
    (B) proposal
    (C) tantamount
    (D) paradox

35. Perhaps I should go ahead and <u>relinquish</u> the rights to my new song.

    (A) retain
    (B) cherish
    (C) give up
    (D) assert

Subtest 3—Arithmetic Reasoning

Directions: This subtest consists of 30 questions that must be answered in 36 minutes. The subtest measures your ability to use arithmetic to solve everyday problems—in short, algebra and geometry word problems.

1. Mike likes the number 400, but hates the number 300. He also likes the number 100, but hates the number 99. Mike likes the number 3,600, but hates the number 3,700. Which of the following numbers would Mike like?

   (A) 40
   (B) 9
   (C) 110
   (D) 50

2. What is the radius of a circle whose area is 9π?

   (A) 1
   (B) 2
   (C) 3
   (D) 4.5

3. Timothy opened his piggy bank and found he had 24 coins, all of which were quarters or half–dollars. If he had twice as many quarters and half as many half–dollars, he would have $4 less. How much money does he have?

   (A) $8.50
   (B) $9.25
   (C) $11.00
   (D) $11.75

4. At a certain time of day, a building 250 feet tall casts a shadow of 225 feet, whereas a second building casts a shadow of 90 feet. How tall is the second building?

   (A) 100 feet
   (B) 125 feet
   (C) 130 feet
   (D) 135 feet

5. One hour after Barbie started walking from X to Y, a distance of 42 miles, David started walking along the same road from Y to X. If Barbie's walking rate was 3 miles per hour and David's was 4 miles per hour, how many miles had David walked when they met?

   (A) 24
   (B) 23
   (C) 22
   (D) 21

6. A mother is now 24 years older than her daughter. In 4 years, the mother will be three times as old as the daughter. How old is the daughter?

   (A) 4
   (B) 16
   (C) 12
   (D) 8

7. Katie works as a bartender and makes $5.60 per hour. She worked $22\frac{1}{2}$ hours and received $42.25 in tips. What was her total salary?

   (A) $150
   (B) $158.90
   (C) $163.40
   (D) $168.25

8. Two numbers are in the ratio of 2 to 3, and their difference is 30. Find the smaller number.

(A) 75
(B) 80
(C) 60
(D) 40

9. Barbara worked 40 hours last week. She earned $720. At that rate of pay, how much would she earn if she had worked only 35 hours?

(A) $625
(B) $630
(C) $635
(D) $640

10. If the hypotenuse of a right triangle is 13 feet and one side is 5, find the length of the other side.

(A) 12
(B) 14
(C) 15
(D) 16

11. Two consecutive integers have a total of 29. Find the largest integer.

(A) 9
(B) 11
(C) 15
(D) 17

12. The cost to manufacture and distribute x batches of toy dolls is given by this linear function: $C(x) = 10x + 25$, where $C(x)$ is measured in units of thousands of dollars. How much would it cost to manufacture and distribute 20 batches of toy dolls?

(A) $150,000
(B) $200,000
(C) $225,000
(D) $250,000

13. A store advertises 15 square yards of carpet installed for $275. At this price what will 33 square yards of carpet cost?

(A) $550
(B) $575
(C) $605
(D) $635

14. Betty prepares a mixture of nuts that has hazelnuts and walnuts in the ratio of 4 to 3. How many pounds of walnuts will she need to make 84 pounds of mixture?

(A) 28
(B) 30
(C) 32
(D) 36

15. Separate 71 into two parts such that one part exceeds the other by 7. What is the largest part?

(A) 35
(B) 37
(C) 39
(D) 41

16. Lizzie must get at least $120,000 for her house in order to break even with the original mortgage. If the real estate agent gets 6% of the selling price, what is the minimum amount that Lizzie should accept for the house in order to pay off the mortgage?

(A) $115,000
(B) $125,000
(C) $130,000
(D) $135,000

17. The sum of three consecutive odd integers is 135. What is the first integer?

(A) 25
(B) 31
(C) 43
(D) 52

18. Two men agree to divide the profit on a business venture in the ratio of 4 to 7. If the total profit on the venture was $6,196, what was the share of the second man (the one with the larger share)?

    (A) $3942.91
    (B) $4003.23
    (C) $4129.40
    (D) $4232.39

19. A collection of coins has a value of $7.30. There are 2 more nickels than dimes and 3 times as many quarters as dimes. How many dimes are there?

    (A) 8
    (B) 10
    (C) 12
    (D) 14

20. Steve is one year less than twice as old as James. If James is 13 years younger than Steve, how old is James?

    (A) 10
    (B) 12
    (C) 14
    (D) 16

21. 980 students attend a high school. 35% of the male students and 40% of the female students attended the homecoming dance. The total number of students at the dance was 369. How many female students attended the dance?

    (A) 480
    (B) 500
    (C) 510
    (D) 520

22. A number decreased by 372 gives the result 421. Find the number.

    (A) 740
    (B) 751
    (C) 764
    (D) 793

23. If the hypotenuse of a right triangle is 5 feet and first side is 4, find the length of the second side.

    (A) 3
    (B) 4
    (C) 5
    (D) 6

24. Find three consecutive odd integers such that if 4 times the second is added to 3 times the third, the result will be 27 times the first.

    (A) 1, 3, 5
    (B) 3, 5, 7
    (C) 5, 7, 9
    (D) 7, 9, 11

25. Ten years ago A was 5 times as old as B. At present, A is 3 times as old as B. Find the present age of B.

    (A) 10
    (B) 20
    (C) 25
    (D) 30

26. A rocket is fired straight up into the air with an initial velocity of 80 feet per second. The altitude (in feet) of the rocket at any given time during the acceleration phase can be determined by the polynomial $80x - 16x^2$, where x is equal to the number of seconds from lift-off. Assuming the rocket is still accelerating, find the altitude of the rocket 4 seconds after launch.

    (A) 15 feet
    (B) 33 feet
    (C) 52 feet
    (D) 64 feet

27. Mark has 10 more nickels than dimes, and the total value is $2.60. How many nickels does he have?

    (A) 20
    (B) 22
    (C) 24
    (D) 26

28. The perimeter of a rectangle is 210 inches. The length and width of the rectangle are in the ratio of 3 to 4. Find the length and width of the rectangle.

    (A) 40 × 60
    (B) 45 × 60
    (C) 50 × 70
    (D) 55 × 70

29. Find the circumference if the radius of a circle is 27 feet.

    (A) 140.3 feet
    (B) 145.72 feet
    (C) 153.91 feet
    (D) 169.56 feet

30. Samantha worked 30 hours last week, earning $418. If she was paid $432 next week, how many hours will she have worked?

    (A) 31
    (B) 32
    (C) 33
    (D) 34

Answer Key

PRACTICE TEST 4

Subtest 1—Paragraph Comprehension

1. B
2. C
3. A
4. C
5. D
6. B
7. B
8. C
9. D
10. C
11. B
12. A
13. D
14. B
15. C

Subtest 2—Word Knowledge

1. C
2. A
3. C
4. B
5. A
6. D
7. C
8. C
9. A
10. A
11. A
12. D
13. B
14. C
15. C
16. D
17. A
18. B
19. D
20. D
21. A
22. C
23. B
24. C
25. B
26. B
27. A
28. D
29. B
30. C
31. D
32. B
33. A
34. A
35. C

Subtest 3—Arithmetic Reasoning

1. B
2. C
3. C
4. A
5. A
6. D
7. D
8. C
9. C
10. A
11. C
12. C
13. C
14. D
15. C
16. B
17. C
18. A
19. A
20. C
21. D
22. D
23. A
24. A
25. B
26. D
27. C
28. B
29. D
30. A

Answer Explanations to Practice Test

SUBTEST 1—PARAGRAPH COMPREHENSION

1. **(B) Mr. Bennet.** The first sentence in the passage examines his complexity.
2. **(C) Complexities of Ancient Greek Literature.** The first two sentences in the passage refer to the difficulties of reading ancient Greed literature.
3. **(A) an unfinished manuscript.** *Poetics* is described as unrevised and unfinished.
4. **(C) love.** The three subjects mentioned in the passage that are included in Aristotle's work are tragedy, epic, and humor.
5. **(D) disjointed.** In the passage the word "fragmentary" is used to illustrate that the writing was incomplete and not well–organized.
6. **(B) put an end to unorthodoxy and dishonesty.** They came over on "....account of the corruption..." and "...with a view of expelling the Pelagian heresy,..."
7. **(B) 20 years.** The unsuccessful campaign of pacification lasted about two decades–20 years.
8. **(C) the Netherlands.** The treaty of 1859 ceded the western portion of the island to the Dutch.
9. **(D) December 7.** East Timor declared independence on November 28 and were invaded by Indonesia nine days later.
10. **(C) Air carriers were given four years to comply with the regulation.** Air carriers were given only three years to comply.
11. **(B) Keep it Simple, Stupid**. The passage describes the desirability of using simple, time-tested words, rather than more complicated, rarely-used words.
12. **(A) copyright laws impede the advancement of our society.** The main point of the passage is that laws that restrict the free access of literature impede our ability to use that information.
13. **(D) the altitude.** "Good" ozone occurs in the stratosphere and "bad" ozone is located in the lower atmosphere.
14. **(B) the sun's rays.** "Good" ozone forms a layer in the stratosphere which protects life on Earth from the sun's harmful rays.
15. **(C) sunlight.** Ground ozone is created by a chemical reaction between the oxides of nitrogen and organic compounds in the presence of sunlight.

SUBTEST 2—WORD KNOWLEDGE

1. **(C) appeasing.** Used as an adjective, *conciliatory* means to overcome the distrust or animosity of; appease.
2. **(A) precise.** Used as an adjective, *meticulous* means extremely careful and precise.
3. **(C) obvious.** Used as an adjective, *discernable* means perceptible, or able to be noticed.
4. **(B) opinionated.** Used as an adjective, *dogmatic* means authoritative, arrogant assertion of unproved principles.
5. **(A) secretive.** Used as an adjective, *reticent* means to keep one's thoughts, feelings, and personal affairs to oneself.

6. **(D) beautiful.** Used as an adjective, *aesthetic* means the appreciation of beauty or good taste.
7. **(C) oddball.** Used as a noun, *eccentric* means one who deviates markedly from an established norm.
8. **(C) changeable.** Used as an adjective, *capricious* means subject to whim; impulsive and unpredictable.
9. **(A) reasonable.** Used as an adjective, *plausible* means seemingly or apparently valid, likely, or acceptable.
10. **(A) argue.** Used as a verb, *remonstrate* means to plead in protest, objection, or reproof.
11. **(A) examine.** Used as a verb, *scrutinize* means to examine or look at closely.
12. **(D) honest.** Used as an adjective, *candid* means aboveboard, honest, or truthful.
13. **(B) determined.** Used as an adjective, *resolute* means firm, determined, or unwavering.
14. **(C) consistent**. Used as an adjective, *homogeneous* means uniform in structure or composition throughout.
15. **(C) immoral.** Used as an adjective, *wanton* means immoral, unchaste, or lewd.
16. **(D) energetic.** Used as an adjective, *kinetic* means motion.
17. **(A) hopeless.** Used as an adjective, *futile* means having no useful result.
18. **(B) stimulate.** In the context of the sentence, *kindle* means to stir up or stimulate.
19. **(D) inactive**. In the context of this sentence, *sedentary* means motionless or inactive.
20. **(D) deception.** In the context of this sentence, *chicanery* means deception by trickery.
21. **(A) beginner.** In the context of this sentence, *novice* means one who is inexperienced or a beginner.
22. **(C) overused.** In the context of this sentence, *hackneyed* means repeated too often; made trite through overuse.
23. **(B) consequences.** In the context of this sentence, *ramifications* mean consequences or negative results.
24. **(C) arduous.** In the context of this sentence, *rigorous* means hard, taxing, or arduous.
25. **(B) lassitude.** In the context of this sentence, *lethargy* means unmotivated, sluggish, or disinterested.
26. **(B) exile.** In the context of this sentence, *relegate* means to banish or place in exile.
27. **(A) in disguise.** In the context of this sentence, *incognito* means one who is disguised or concealed.
28. **(D) revengeful.** In the context of this sentence, *vindictive* means the act of seeking revenge.
29. **(B) confused.** In the context of this sentence, *delirious* means disorganized or confused.
30. **(C) chatty.** In the context of this sentence, *loquacious* means to talk too much; chatty.
31. **(D) humdrum.** In the context of this sentence, *mundane* means boring, everyday, unexciting.

32. **(B) mystery.** In the context of this sentence, *enigma* means an unexplained mystery.
33. **(A) complex.** In the context of this sentence, *abstract* means deep or complex thoughts or ideas.
34. **(A) insight.** In the context of this sentence, *epiphany* means a perception of reality by means of a sudden intuitive realization.
35. **(C) give up.** In the context of this sentence, *relinquish* means to abandon, forgo, or to give up.

SUBTEST 3—ARITHMETIC REASONING

1. **(B) 9.**
   The one factor in common with the numbers that Mike likes is that they are all perfect squares: $400 = 20^2$, $100 = 10^2$, and $3600 = 60^2$. 300, 99, and 3700 (the numbers Mike hates) are not perfect squares.
2. **(C) 3.**
   Let A = AREA
   Let R = RADIUS
   Given $A = 9\pi$
   Formula $A = \pi R^2$
   $A = \pi R^2$ // Circle Area Formula
   $9\pi = \pi R^2$ // Substitute 9 for A
   $R = 3$
3. **(C) $11.00.**
   Let Q = QUARTERS
   Let H = HALF-DOLLARS
   Let M = MONEY
   Given $Q + H = 24$
   Given $2Q(0.25) + 0.5H(0.5) = 0.25Q + 0.5H - 4$
   Given $M = 0.25Q + 0.5H$
   $0.5Q + 0.25H = 0.25Q + 0.5H - 4$ // Expand parentheses
   $0.25Q - 0.25H = -4$
   $0.25(24 - H) - 0.25H = -4$ // Substitute $24-H$ for Q
   $6 - 0.25H - 0.25H = -4$
   $-0.25H - 0.25H = -10$
   $H = 20$
   $Q = 4$ // Substitute $H=20$ into $Q = 24 - H$
   $M = 0.25Q + 10$ //Substitute $H = 20$ into $M = 0.25Q + 0.5H$
   $M = 11$ // Substitute $Q = 4$ into $M = 0.25Q + 10$
4. **(A) 100 feet.**
   Let S = SHADOW (FIRST BUILDING)
   Let T = TALL (FIRST BUILDING)
   Let s = shadow (second building)
   Let t = tall (second building)
   Given $S/T = S/t$
   Given $T = 250$
   Given $S = 225$
   Given $s = 90$

$225/250 = 90/t$ // Expand parentheses
$225t = 250*90$
$t = 100$

5. **(A) 24.**
Formula: distance equals rate times time
$d = rt$
$t = d/r$
$t = 42/(3 + 4)$ // substitute known values
$t = 6$ // time until they met
$6 \times 4 = 24$ miles // distance that David walked
6. **(D) 8.**
Let M = MOTHER
Let D = DAUGHTER
Given $M = D + 24$
Given $M + 4 = 3(D + 4)$
$M + 4 = 3D + 12$
$M = 3D + 8$
$3D + 8 = D + 24$ // Substitute $3D + 8$ for M
$D = 8$
7. **(D) \$168.25.**
Let S = Salary
Formula: $S = (\$5.60 \times 22.5) + \$42.25$ // hours worked times hourly wage, plus tips
$S = (5.6 \times 22.5) + 42.25$
$S = 126 + 42.25$
$S = 168.25$
8. **(C) 60.**
Let L = LARGER
Let S = SMALLER
Given $\frac{L}{S} = \frac{3}{2}$
Given $L = S + 30$
$2L = 3S$ // Expand parentheses
$2(S + 30) = 3S$ // Substitute $S + 30$ for L
$2S + 60 = 3S$
$-S + 60 = 0$
$S = 60$
9. **(C) \$635.**
Let H = HOURS WORKED
Let D = DOLLARS EARNED
Let h = hours (what if)
Let d = dollars (what if)
Given $H = 40$
Given $D = 720$
Given $h = 35$
Formula $\frac{H}{D} = \frac{h}{d}$
$Hd = Dh$ // Expand parentheses

$40d = 720(35)$
$40d = 25200$
$d = 630$

10. **(A) 12.**
Let H = HYPOTENUSE
Let F = FIRST
Let S = SECOND
Given $H = 13$
Given $F = 5$
Given $F^2 + S^2 = H^2$
$5^2 + S^2 = 13^2$ // Expand parentheses
$S = 12$

11. **(C) 15.**
Let S = SMALLER
Let L = LARGER
Given $S + L = 29$
Given $L - S = 1$
$L - (29 - L) = 1$ // Substitute $29 - L$ for S
$L = 15$

12. **(C) $225,000.**
Formula: $C(x) = 10x + 25$
$C(20) = 10*20 + 25$ // substitute known values
$C(20) = 225$
$C(20) = \$225,000$ // cost is in units of thousands of dollars

13. **(C) $605.**
Let Y = YARDS (FIRST EXAMPLE)
Let D = DOLLARS (FIRST EXAMPLE)
Let y = yards (second example)
Let d = dollars (second example)
Given $\frac{Y}{D} = \frac{y}{d}$
Given $D = 275$
Given $Y = 15$
Given $y = 33$
$15/275 = 33/d$ // Expand parentheses
$15d = 275*33$
$d = 605$

14. **(D) 36.**
Let H = HAZELNUTS
Let W = WALNUTS
Given $\frac{4}{3} = \frac{H}{W}$
Given $H + W = 84$
$4W = 3H$ // Expand parentheses
$H = 84 - W$
$4W = 3(84 - W)$
$4W = 252 - 3W$
$7W = 252$
$W = 36$

15. **(C) 39.**
Let F = FIRST
Let O = OTHER
Given $F + O = 71$
Given $F = O + 7$
$O + 7 + O = 71$ // Substitute $O + 7$ for F
$O = 32$
$F = 39$ // Substitute $O = 32$ into $F = O + 7$
16. **(B) $125,000.**
Let x = selling price
Given: Lizzie's share = $x - \$0.06x$ // minus the real estate agent's commission
$x - \$0.06x \geq \$12000$ // Lizzie's share must be greater or equal to the mortgage
$x - .06s \geq 12000$
$.96x \geq 12000$
$x \geq 1200/.96$
$x \geq \$125,000$
17. **(C) 43.**
Let F = FIRST
Let S = SECOND
Let T = THIRD
Given $F + S + T = 135$
Given $S = F + 2$
Given $T = F + 4$
$F + F + 2 + F + 4 = 135$ // Expand parentheses
$F + F + 2 + F + 4 = 135$ //Substitute $F + 4$ for S
$F + F + 2 + F + 4 = 135$ // Substitute $F + 2$ for T
$F = 43$
18. **(A) $3942.91.**
Let F = FIRSTMAN
Let S = SECONDMAN
Given $\frac{F}{S} = \frac{4}{7}$
Given $F + S = 6196$
$7F = 4S$ // Expand parentheses
$F = 6196 - S$
$4S = 7(6196 - S)$
$4S = 43372 - 7S$
$11S = 43372$
$S = 3942.91$
19. **(A) 8.**
Let N = NICKELS
Let D = DIMES
Let Q = QUARTERS
Given $7.3 = 0.05N + 0.1D + 0.25Q$
Given $N = D+2$
Given $Q = 3D$
$7.3 = 0.05N + 0.1D + 0.25(3D)$ // Substitute $3D$ for N
$7.3 = 0.05(D + 2) + 0.1D + 0.25(3D)$ // Substitute $D + 2$ for Q
$7.3 = 0.05D + 0.1 + 0.1D + 0.75D$

$0 = 0.9D - 7.2$
$D = 8$

20. **(C) 14.**
Let J = JAMES
Let S = STEVE
Given $S = 2J - 1$
Given $J = S - 13$
$S = 2(S - 13) - 1$ // Substitute S–13 for J
$S = 2S - 26 - 1$
$-S = -26 - 1$
$S = 27$
$J = 14$ // $S = 27$ into $J = S - 13$

21. **(D) 520.**
Let F = number of female students
Let M = number of male students
Formula: $0.35M + 0.4F = 369$ // convert percentages to decimals
Given: $M + F = 980$ // total number of students
$M = 980 - F$
$0.35(980 - F) + 0.4F = 369$ // substitute known value of M into the formula
$343 - 0.35F + .04F = 369$ // combine like terms
$0.05F = 26$
$F = 520$

22. **(D) 793.**
Let N = NUMBER
Given $N - 372 = 421$
$N = 793$

23. **(A) 3.**
Let H = HYPOTENUSE
Let F = FIRST
Let S = SECOND
Given $H = 5$
Given $F = 4$
Given $F^2 + S^2 = H^2$
$4^2 + S^2 = 5^2$ // Expand parentheses
$S = 3$

24. **(A) 1, 3, 5.**
Let S = SECOND
Let F = FIRST
Let T = THIRD
Given $S = F + 2$
Given $T = F + 4$
Given $4S + 3T = 27F$
$4S + 3(F + 4) = 27F$ // Substitute $F + 4$ for S
$4(F + 2) + 3(F + 4) = 27F$ // Substitute $F + 2$ for T
$4F + 8 + 3F + 12 = 27F$
$-20F + 8 + 12 = 0$
$F = 1$
$S = 3$ // $F = 1$ into $S = F + 2$
$T = 5$ // $F = 1$ into $T = F + 4$

25. **(B) 20.**
    Let $B = B$
    Let $A = A$
    Given $A - 10 = 5(B - 10)$
    Given $A = 3B$
    $A - 10 = 5B - 50$
    $A = 5B - 40$
    $5B - 40 = 3B$ // Substitute $5B - 40$ for A
    $B = 20$
26. **(D) 64 feet.**
    Let a = altitude of the rocket
    Formula: $a = 80x - 16^2$
    Given $x = 4$
    $a = (80*4) - 16*4^2$
    $a = 320 - 16*16$
    $a = 64$
27. **(C) 24.**
    Let N = NICKELS
    Let D = DIMES
    Let V = VALUE
    Given $N = D + 10$
    Given $2.6 = 0.05N + 0.1D$
    $2.6 = 0.05(D + 10) + 0.1D$ // Substitute $D + 10$ for N
    $2.6 = 0.05D + 0.5 + 0.1D$
    $0 = 0.15D - 2.1$
    $D = 14$
    $N = 24$ // Substitute $D = 14$ into $N = D + 10$
28. **(B) 45 × 60.**
    Let P = PERIMETER
    Let L = LENGTH
    Let W = WIDTH
    Given $P = 210$
    Given $L/W = 3/4$
    Given $P = 2L + 2W$
    $210 = 2L + 2W$ // Substitute 210 for P
    $4(-W + 105) = 3W$ // $-W + 105$ for L in $4L = 3W$
    $-4W + 420 = 3W$
    $-7W + 420 = 0$
    $W = 60$
    $L = 45$ // Substitute $W = 60$ into $L = -W + 105$
29. **(D) 159.56.**
    Let C = CIRCUMFERENCE
    Let R = RADIUS
    Given $R = 27$
    Formula $C = 2\pi R$
    $C = 2\pi R$ // Circumference Formula
    $C = 2*27\pi$ // Substitute 27 for Radius

$C = 54\pi$
$C = 54*3.14$
$C = 169.56$

30. **(A) 31.**
Let D = DOLLARS
Let H = HOURS
Let d = dollars
Let h = hours
Given $D = 418$
Given $H = 30$
Given $d = 432$
Formula $\frac{D}{H} = \frac{d}{h}$
$Dh = Hd$ // Expand parentheses
$418h = 30(432)$
$418h = 12960$
$h = 31.0048$

CHAPTER 17

Practice Test for Army and Non-Aviation Marine Corps/Coast Guard Applicants 3

The General Technical (GT) composite score from the ASVAB is used to determine qualification for Army and non-aviation Marine Corps and Coast Guard OCS/OCC candidates. Marine Corps candidates may also qualify by using SAT or ACT scores (see Chapter 3). Marine Corps and Coast Guard aviation candidates should take the Navy and Marine Corps Aviation Selection Test Battery practice test (see Chapters 18 and 19).

The GT composite score is determined from three subtests of the ASVAB: Paragraph Comprehension, Word Knowledge, and Arithmetic Reasoning. These three subtests comprise a total of 80 questions that must be answered in 60 minutes. If you take the computerized version of the ASVAB (CAT-ASVAB), these three subtests would be comprised of 43 total questions with a time-limit of 69 minutes. For the purpose of the practice exam in this chapter, we will reproduce the number of questions contained in the paper version of the test.

Answer Sheet for Practice Test 5

Subtest 1–Paragraph Comprehension

1 Ⓐ Ⓑ Ⓒ Ⓓ	5 Ⓐ Ⓑ Ⓒ Ⓓ	9 Ⓐ Ⓑ Ⓒ Ⓓ	13 Ⓐ Ⓑ Ⓒ Ⓓ
2 Ⓐ Ⓑ Ⓒ Ⓓ	6 Ⓐ Ⓑ Ⓒ Ⓓ	10 Ⓐ Ⓑ Ⓒ Ⓓ	14 Ⓐ Ⓑ Ⓒ Ⓓ
3 Ⓐ Ⓑ Ⓒ Ⓓ	7 Ⓐ Ⓑ Ⓒ Ⓓ	11 Ⓐ Ⓑ Ⓒ Ⓓ	15 Ⓐ Ⓑ Ⓒ Ⓓ
4 Ⓐ Ⓑ Ⓒ Ⓓ	8 Ⓐ Ⓑ Ⓒ Ⓓ	12 Ⓐ Ⓑ Ⓒ Ⓓ	

Subtest 2–Word Knowledge

1 Ⓐ Ⓑ Ⓒ Ⓓ	10 Ⓐ Ⓑ Ⓒ Ⓓ	19 Ⓐ Ⓑ Ⓒ Ⓓ	28 Ⓐ Ⓑ Ⓒ Ⓓ
2 Ⓐ Ⓑ Ⓒ Ⓓ	11 Ⓐ Ⓑ Ⓒ Ⓓ	20 Ⓐ Ⓑ Ⓒ Ⓓ	29 Ⓐ Ⓑ Ⓒ Ⓓ
3 Ⓐ Ⓑ Ⓒ Ⓓ	12 Ⓐ Ⓑ Ⓒ Ⓓ	21 Ⓐ Ⓑ Ⓒ Ⓓ	30 Ⓐ Ⓑ Ⓒ Ⓓ
4 Ⓐ Ⓑ Ⓒ Ⓓ	13 Ⓐ Ⓑ Ⓒ Ⓓ	22 Ⓐ Ⓑ Ⓒ Ⓓ	31 Ⓐ Ⓑ Ⓒ Ⓓ
5 Ⓐ Ⓑ Ⓒ Ⓓ	14 Ⓐ Ⓑ Ⓒ Ⓓ	23 Ⓐ Ⓑ Ⓒ Ⓓ	32 Ⓐ Ⓑ Ⓒ Ⓓ
6 Ⓐ Ⓑ Ⓒ Ⓓ	15 Ⓐ Ⓑ Ⓒ Ⓓ	24 Ⓐ Ⓑ Ⓒ Ⓓ	33 Ⓐ Ⓑ Ⓒ Ⓓ
7 Ⓐ Ⓑ Ⓒ Ⓓ	16 Ⓐ Ⓑ Ⓒ Ⓓ	25 Ⓐ Ⓑ Ⓒ Ⓓ	34 Ⓐ Ⓑ Ⓒ Ⓓ
8 Ⓐ Ⓑ Ⓒ Ⓓ	17 Ⓐ Ⓑ Ⓒ Ⓓ	26 Ⓐ Ⓑ Ⓒ Ⓓ	35 Ⓐ Ⓑ Ⓒ Ⓓ
9 Ⓐ Ⓑ Ⓒ Ⓓ	18 Ⓐ Ⓑ Ⓒ Ⓓ	27 Ⓐ Ⓑ Ⓒ Ⓓ	

Subtest 3–Arithmetic Reasoning

1 Ⓐ Ⓑ Ⓒ Ⓓ	9 Ⓐ Ⓑ Ⓒ Ⓓ	17 Ⓐ Ⓑ Ⓒ Ⓓ	24 Ⓐ Ⓑ Ⓒ Ⓓ
2 Ⓐ Ⓑ Ⓒ Ⓓ	10 Ⓐ Ⓑ Ⓒ Ⓓ	18 Ⓐ Ⓑ Ⓒ Ⓓ	25 Ⓐ Ⓑ Ⓒ Ⓓ
3 Ⓐ Ⓑ Ⓒ Ⓓ	11 Ⓐ Ⓑ Ⓒ Ⓓ	19 Ⓐ Ⓑ Ⓒ Ⓓ	26 Ⓐ Ⓑ Ⓒ Ⓓ
4 Ⓐ Ⓑ Ⓒ Ⓓ	12 Ⓐ Ⓑ Ⓒ Ⓓ	20 Ⓐ Ⓑ Ⓒ Ⓓ	27 Ⓐ Ⓑ Ⓒ Ⓓ
5 Ⓐ Ⓑ Ⓒ Ⓓ	13 Ⓐ Ⓑ Ⓒ Ⓓ	21 Ⓐ Ⓑ Ⓒ Ⓓ	28 Ⓐ Ⓑ Ⓒ Ⓓ
6 Ⓐ Ⓑ Ⓒ Ⓓ	14 Ⓐ Ⓑ Ⓒ Ⓓ	22 Ⓐ Ⓑ Ⓒ Ⓓ	29 Ⓐ Ⓑ Ⓒ Ⓓ
7 Ⓐ Ⓑ Ⓒ Ⓓ	15 Ⓐ Ⓑ Ⓒ Ⓓ	23 Ⓐ Ⓑ Ⓒ Ⓓ	30 Ⓐ Ⓑ Ⓒ Ⓓ
8 Ⓐ Ⓑ Ⓒ Ⓓ	16 Ⓐ Ⓑ Ⓒ Ⓓ		

Subtest 1—Paragraph Comprehension

Directions: This subtest consists of 15 questions that must be answered in 13 minutes. The subtest measures your ability to discern information in written paragraphs.

Read each paragraph, then select the answer that <u>*best*</u> completes the statement or answers the question.

Question 1 is based on the following paragraph.

““The great events in history are those where, upon special occasions, a man or a people have made a stand against tyranny, and have preserved or advanced freedom for the people. Sometimes tyranny has taken the form of the oppression of the many by the few in the same nation, and sometimes it has been the oppression of a weak nation by a stronger one. The successful revolt against tyranny, the terrible conflict resulting in the emancipation of a people, has always been the favorite theme of the historian, marking as it does a step in the progress of mankind from a savage to a civilized state.”

1. The author of this passage advocates
   (A) authoritative governments.
   (B) democratic freedoms.
   (C) religious expression.
   (D) documenting historical events.

Questions 2–4 are based on the following paragraph.

“In 1516 Spain and Austria were united under the Emperor Charles V, grandson of Ferdinand and Isabella; and, during his reign, the united kingdoms arose to a height of power almost equal to that of the empire of Charlemagne. The dominion of Charles extended from the Atlantic to the steppes of Poland, and from the Mediterranean to the Baltic. It included all of Western Continental Europe, except France and southern Italy. In 1556 Charles abdicated his throne, and divided his empire, giving Austria and Germany to his brother Ferdinand, and Spain and the Low Countries of Holland and Belgium to his son Philip II.”

2. Charles V was
   (A) a king.
   (B) killed in battle.
   (C) an emperor.
   (D) a president.

3. Which of the following countries did not count itself under Charles V's rule?

   (A) Poland
   (B) Spain
   (C) Austria
   (D) France

4. In the above paragraph, the word dominion means ____________.

   (A) territory
   (B) politics
   (C) tyranny
   (D) religion

Questions 5–6 are based on the following paragraph.

"Enormous open windows with heavy iron bars made the high and barren room the roosting place of hundreds of pigeons. The wind blew through the iron bars and the air was filled with a weird and pleasing music. It was the noise of the town below, but a noise which had been purified and cleansed by the distance. The rumbling of heavy carts and the clinking of horses' hoofs, the winding of cranes and pulleys, the hissing sound of the patient steam which had been set to do the work of man in a thousand different ways—they had all been blended into a softly rustling whisper which provided a beautiful background for the trembling cooing of the pigeons."

5. What lived in the room described above?

   (A) bats
   (B) horses
   (C) rats
   (D) birds

6. Which of the following statements is true?

   (A) The noisy room irritated the narrator.
   (B) The narrator found the sounds blending in the room to be pleasant.
   (C) The narrator worked daily with steam engines.
   (D) Enormous closed windows kept the rain out of the room.

Question 7 is based on the following paragraph.

"The 20th century has been a time of amazing change for women. When the century began, women in the United States did not have even the fundamental human right to vote and were largely absent, save in stereotyped roles, from the American workplace, including the Federal workplace. Today, women represent 42.8 percent of the permanent Federal workforce, compared to 46.4 percent in the Civilian Labor Force (CLF). The most important single factor in attracting and retaining women is direct, conscientious involvement by managers. Managers can identify where targeted recruiting efforts will best succeed and stimulate interest in public service careers. And at every phase of careers in public service, managers must mentor and lead their employees to obtain optimal results."

7. Men comprise about ________ percent of the civilian labor force.

   (A) 46 percent
   (B) 54 percent
   (C) 50 percent
   (D) 65 percent

Question 8 is based on the following paragraph.

"Arizona law prohibits anyone younger than age 21 from purchasing or consuming alcoholic beverages. Liquor is not sold between 1 A.M. and 6 A.M. Monday–Saturday and between 1 A.M. and 10 A.M. on Sundays. It is against the law to drink in a motor vehicle or from the original container in public places."

8. How many hours per week is it illegal to sell liquor in the state of Arizona?

   (A) 20
   (B) 29
   (C) 30
   (D) 39

Question 9 is based on the following paragraph.

"If they are to function effectively, organizations, like other systems, must achieve a natural harmony or coherence among their component parts. The structural and situational elements of an effective organization form themselves into a tightly knit, highly cohesive package. An organization whose parts are mismatched, however, cannot carry out its missions."

9. According to the passage, if managers are to design effective organizations, they need to

   (A) simplify organizational structures.
   (B) encourage greater specialization of labor.
   (C) emphasize the fit of organizational parts.
   (D) introduce more technological innovations.

Question 10 is based on the following paragraph.

"First, Clostridium botulinum, the bacterium that produces the poison, must be present. These bacteria are widespread in the environment and are considered by some to be everywhere. Second, the bacterium that produces the deadly toxin must be treated to an atmosphere that's free of oxygen and to temperatures that are just warm enough but not too warm. Those conditions have to be held long enough for the toxin to develop. Acid will prevent the growth of the organism and the production of toxin."

10. Which of the following conditions is necessary for botulism to develop?

    (A) presence of oxygen
    (B) a brief period of time
    (C) presence of acid
    (D) warm temperatures

Question 11 is based on the following paragraph.

"Leaders prepare for challenges through their career-long study and application of the art of leadership. Successful leaders generally exhibit common character traits and embrace experimental leadership principles. Leaders must strive to develop and hone their skills, build on expertise in their specialties, learn from others' experiences, and observe their environment."

11. Which word in the above paragraph is incorrectly used?

    (A) hone
    (B) career-long
    (C) experimental
    (D) environment

Question 12 is based on the following paragraph.

"*Mustela nigripes*, the rarely seen black-footed ferret, is often confused with *Mustela putorius*, the common European polecat. It is true that these two mammals resemble each other in some ways. However, they are two distinct and separate species with differences in color, body form, and other attributes."

12. Indeed, it is possible that many sightings of the black-footed ferret

    (A) were the result of seeing the European polecat running loose.
    (B) were of species other than the common European polecat.
    (C) were made of a related species of the same form and color.
    (D) were instead sightings of the *Mustela nigripes.*

Question 13 is based on the following paragraph.

"The protection of life and property against antisocial individuals within the country and enemies from without is generally recognized to be the most fundamental activity of government."

13. Of the following, the one that is not an aspect of the fundamental function of government as described above is

(A) sending a delegation to a foreign country to participate in a disarmament conference.
(B) prosecuting a drug peddler who has been selling dope to schoolchildren.
(C) fining a motorist who failed to stop at a traffic light.
(D) providing postal service.

Question 14 is based on the following paragraph.

"How do we evaluate the overall efficiency of an office, the efficiency of each section or unit, and that of the individual worker? Work measurement is essential for effective office management. We can have measurement without work standards, but we cannot have work standards without measurement. Usually, from two-thirds to three-fourths of all work can be measured. However, less than two-thirds of all work is actually measured, because measurement difficulties are encountered when office work is non-repetitive or when it is primarily mental rather than manual. These obstacles are used as excuses for non-measurement far more frequently than is justified."

14. The type of office work most difficult to measure would be

(A) answering letters of inquiry.
(B) answering telephone calls.
(C) checking requisitions.
(D) developing a new procedure for issuing supplies.

Question 15 is based on the following paragraph.

"The function of business is to increase the wealth of the country and the value and happiness of life. It does this by supplying the material needs of men and women. When the nation's business is successfully carried on, it renders public service of the highest value."

15. The passage best supports the statement that

(A) all businesses that render public service are successful.
(B) business is the only field of endeavor that increases happiness.
(C) human happiness is enhanced only by increasing material wants.
(D) the material needs of men and women are supplied by well-conducted businesses.

Subtest 2—Word Knowledge

Directions: This subtest measures the extent of your vocabulary. In each question, one word is underlined. Your task is to select the answer that means the same, or most nearly the same as the underlined word. The subtest consists of 35 questions that must be answered in 11 minutes.

1. Nonpareil most nearly means __________.
   (A) resourceful
   (B) excellent
   (C) trivial
   (D) makeshift

2. Inapt most nearly means __________.
   (A) incompetent
   (B) adequate
   (C) problematic
   (D) animated

3. Mediate most nearly means __________.
   (A) maverick
   (B) plan
   (C) require
   (D) intercede

4. Humanitarian most nearly means __________.
   (A) relief
   (B) canopy
   (C) pragmatic
   (D) Samaritan

5. Rankle most nearly means __________.
   (A) forbear
   (B) irritate
   (C) chains
   (D) matriculate

6. Maritime most nearly means __________.
   (A) travel
   (B) stratosphere
   (C) aquatic
   (D) underground

7. Melodrama most nearly means __________.
   (A) tedium
   (B) façade
   (C) panicked
   (D) enthusiastic

8. Litigious most nearly means __________.
   (A) argumentative
   (B) lawyer
   (C) program
   (D) performance

9. Conflagration most nearly means __________.
   (A) mutilate
   (B) titillate
   (C) fire
   (D) makeshift

10. Harangue most nearly means __________.
   (A) speech
   (B) irritate
   (C) temporal
   (D) commendation

11. Panorama most nearly means __________.
   (A) play
   (B) corruption
   (C) digital
   (D) scene

12. Recreant most nearly means __________.
   (A) lazy
   (B) coward
   (C) priest
   (D) fireman

13. Chronometer most nearly means __________.

    (A) clock
    (B) pressure gage
    (C) altimeter
    (D) computer

14. Glutinous most nearly means __________.

    (A) sticky
    (B) overeater
    (C) open
    (D) separated

15. Percolate most nearly means __________.

    (A) brew
    (B) filter
    (C) mix
    (D) prepare

16. Dissonance most nearly means __________.

    (A) rely
    (B) performance
    (C) sound
    (D) truthful

17. Kernel most nearly means __________.

    (A) portion
    (B) trial
    (C) necessary
    (D) seed

18. Illuminate most nearly means __________.

    (A) brighten
    (B) misalign
    (C) prepare
    (D) copy

19. I could see no discernible reason why Paul should be so late.

    (A) plausible
    (B) apparent
    (C) possible
    (D) reliable

20. Mr. Perkins was summoned to court in order to prove or disprove paternity.

    (A) fatherhood
    (B) motherhood
    (C) relationship
    (D) DNA

21. He most certainly has a formidable array of classes in his schedule.

    (A) boring
    (B) challenging
    (C) numerous
    (D) perplexing

22. Tom's incompetence scuttled any chance of getting the contract.

    (A) ruined
    (B) facilitated
    (C) enhanced
    (D) delayed

23. The boss' tirade sure upset a lot of employees last week.

    (A) antics
    (B) speech
    (C) conduct
    (D) lateness

24. The comedian's offensive jokes tended to alienate the audience.

    (A) excite
    (B) bore
    (C) relax
    (D) insult

25. Tammy's benign smile is her best feature.

    (A) pleasant
    (B) wide
    (C) expressive
    (D) unusual

26. I wish Father wouldn't be so forthright all of the time.

(A) lazy
(B) candid
(C) intoxicated
(D) deceitful

27. He seems to be impervious to any sort of insult.

(A) vulnerable
(B) immune
(C) permeable
(D) heedful

28. Jan bought one of the most beautiful kimonos that I've ever seen.

(A) flowers
(B) dishes
(C) cars
(D) gowns

29. No one on TV has yet matched the diversity of Johnny Carson's monologue.

(A) personality
(B) stage
(C) hair
(D) speech

30. Her estranged ex-husband was planning to take her to court once again.

(A) alienated
(B) threatened
(C) mild
(D) befriended

31. WARNING! This ride may cause grievous bodily injury.

(A) painful
(B) mild
(C) medical
(D) terminal

32. I hate to encroach on our friendship, but I need to borrow 20 dollars.

(A) borrow
(B) withdraw
(C) impinge
(D) rely

33. I can't see how that is germane to this conversation.

(A) necessary
(B) applicable
(C) irreverent
(D) infelicitous

34. The ominous black clouds caused us to head for the basement.

(A) auspicious
(B) menacing
(C) large
(D) high

35. The curtains undulated in the stiff breeze.

(A) waved
(B) blew off
(C) discolored
(D) deflated

Subtest 3—Arithmetic Reasoning

Directions: This subtest consists of 30 questions that must be answered in 36 minutes. The subtest measures your ability to use arithmetic to solve everyday problems—in short, algebra and geometry word problems.

1. What is the radius of a circle whose circumference is 6π?

   (A) 2
   (B) 3
   (C) 4
   (D) 5

2. One-fifth of a number added to the number itself has the sum of 42. Find the number.

   (A) 25
   (B) 30
   (C) 35
   (D) 40

3. A 12-foot-tall lamp post casts an 8–foot shadow at the same time that a nearby tree casts a 28-foot shadow. How tall is the tree?

   (A) 38 feet
   (B) 40 feet
   (C) 42 feet
   (D) 48 feet

4. Mr. Perkins left one-fourth of his estate to his wife, two-fifths to his son, one-eighth to his daughter and the remainder ($32,000) to charity. What was the total value of the estate?

   (A) $152,942
   (B) $170,028
   (C) $142,222
   (D) $138,720

5. The perimeter of a square is 8. Find the length of the side.

   (A) 2
   (B) 4
   (C) 6
   (D) 8

6. Rod bought a new vehicle for $12,590. If Rod's purchase price was 20% off the MSR price, what was the MSR price?

   (A) $15,737.50
   (B) $13, 932.25
   (C) $14,532.75
   (D) $14,539.50

7. The perimeter of a rectangle is 198 inches. The length and width of the rectangle are in the ratio of 5 to 4. Find the width of the rectangle.

   (A) 32
   (B) 38
   (C) 40
   (D) 44

8. The radius of a circle is 9. Find the diameter.

   (A) 6
   (B) 12
   (C) 18
   (D) 26

9. The area of a triangle is 37 square feet and the height is 10 feet. Find the base.

   (A) 6.9 feet
   (B) 7.4 feet
   (C) 8.1 feet
   (D) 8.9 feet

10. Find the area of a circle whose radius is 47 inches.

    (A) 5,432.3
    (B) 6,936.26
    (C) 7,212.14
    (D) 7,525.73

11. The area of a triangle is 36 square feet, and the base is 8. Find the height.

    (A) 3
    (B) 6
    (C) 9
    (D) 12

12. A round paper plate measures 10 inches from edge to edge. What is the area of the plate?

    (A) 46.3
    (B) 67.8
    (C) 78.5
    (D) 81.2

13. The area of a square is 36 square feet. Find the length of each side.

    (A) 6 feet
    (B) 3 feet
    (C) 36 feet
    (D) 9 feet

14. Seismologists measured the effects of an earthquake over a circular area of 1,808.64 square miles. What is the radius of the area measured?

    (A) 24 miles
    (B) 30 miles
    (C) 35 miles
    (D) 40 miles

15. Sam wants to have carpet installed in his guest room that measures 9 feet wide and 12 feet long. Approximately, how much will it cost if the price of installation is $12.51 per square yard?

    (A) $150
    (B) $250
    (C) $300
    (D) $325

16. A number decreased by 372.6 gives the result 421.2. Find the number.

    (A) 742.6
    (B) 762.9
    (C) 793.8
    (D) 795.3

17. The interior angles of a convex pentagon are five consecutive numbers. Find the measure of the largest angle.

    (A) 110 degrees
    (B) 112 degrees
    (C) 114 degrees
    (D) 116 degrees

18. A right-angle triangle has a hypotenuse of 10 inches, and the height drawn from the right angle to the hypotenuse is 6 inches. Find the area of the triangle.

    (A) 6
    (B) 12
    (C) 18
    (D) 24

19. A square barn measures 42 feet on each side. A horse is tethered on an outside corner of the barn with a rope measuring 28 feet. How many square feet of land will the horse be able to graze?

    (A) 784 square feet
    (B) 890.75 square feet
    (C) 1,846.32 square feet
    (D) 2,461.76 square feet

20. A picture that measures 8 cm wide and 10 cm high is to be enlarged so that the height will be 25 cm. What will be the width of the enlargement?

    (A) 20 cm
    (B) 25 cm
    (C) 27 cm
    (D) 29 cm

21. Braided rope is on sale for $0.125 a foot. How many feet can you buy for a dollar?

    (A) 4 feet
    (B) 6 feet
    (C) 8 feet
    (D) 10 feet

22. Determine the circumference of a circle with radius of 17.

    (A) 105.55
    (B) 106.76
    (C) 107.23
    (D) 108.42

23. Two integers have a total of 65. 4 times the smaller is equal to the larger. Find the larger.

    (A) 50
    (B) 52
    (C) 54
    (D) 56

24. The area of a square is 144 square feet. Find the length of each side.

    (A) 12 feet
    (B) 14 feet
    (C) 16 feet
    (D) 20 feet

25. One number is twice another number. The sum of three times the smaller number and two times the larger number is 49. Find the smaller number.

    (A) 5
    (B) 7
    (C) 9
    (D) 11

26. The length of a rectangle is one less than twice its width. If the length is decreased by one and the width is increased by three, the area is increased by nineteen square units. Find the dimensions of the rectangle.

    (A) 4×8
    (B) 5×9
    (C) 6×9
    (D) 8×10

27. A line segment is 50 inches long. Divide this line segment into two parts that will have the ratio of 3 to 2. How long is the shortest segment of line?

    (A) 20 inches
    (B) 15 inches
    (C) 25 inches
    (D) 5 inches

28. Rod weighs 250 pounds. Three times Paul's weight is twice Rod's weight. How much does Paul weigh? Note: Round to the nearest full pound.

    (A) 150 pounds
    (B) 167 pounds
    (C) 171 pounds
    (D) 180 pounds

29. Michael has enough bricks to surface 125 square feet. He wants to build a rectangular patio that is 20 feet longer than it is wide. How wide should he make the patio?

    (A) 3 feet
    (B) 5 feet
    (C) 7 feet
    (D) 9 feet

30. If one root of the equation $2x^2 + 3x - k = 0$ is 6, what is the value of k?

    (A) 90
    (B) 42
    (C) 18
    (D) 10

Answer Key

PRACTICE TEST 5

Subtest 1—Paragraph Comprehension

1. B	4. A	7. B	10. D	13. D
2. C	5. D	8. D	11. C	14. D
3. D	6. B	9. C	12. A	15. D

Subtest 2—Word Knowledge

1. B	8. A	15. B	22. A	29. D
2. A	9. C	16. C	23. B	30. A
3. D	10. A	17. D	24. D	31. A
4. D	11. D	18. A	25. A	32. C
5. B	12. B	19. B	26. B	33. B
6. C	13. A	20. A	27. B	34. B
7. D	14. A	21. B	28. D	35. A

Subtest 3—Arithmetic Reasoning

1. B	7. D	13. A	19. C	25. B
2. C	8. C	14. A	20. A	26. B
3. C	9. B	15. A	21. C	27. A
4. C	10. B	16. C	22. B	28. B
5. A	11. C	17. A	23. B	29. B
6. A	12. C	18. D	24. A	30. A

Answer Explanations to Practice Test

SUBTEST 1—PARAGRAPH COMPREHENSION

1. **(B) democratic freedoms.** The author states that the great moments in history are made by those opposing tyranny and advancing freedom for the people.
2. **(C) an emperor.** Charles V was the emperor of the united kingdoms until he abdicated his throne in 1556..
3. **(D) France.** The "united kingdoms" included all of western continental Europe, except France and southern Italy.
4. **(A) territory.** In the context of the sentence, the word dominion is used to describe the amount of territory under Charles's control.
5. **(D) birds.** The room was a roosting place of hundreds of pigeons.
6. **(B) pleasant. The narrator found the sounds blending in the room to be pleasant.** This is the primary theme of the passage.
7. **(B) 54 percent.** If women comprise about 46 percent of the civilian labor force, the remaining 54 percent must be comprised of men.
8. **(D) 39.** Liquor cannot be sold between the hours of 1 A.M. and 6 A.M. Monday–Saturday (6 × 5 hours = 30), and between 1 A.M. and 10 A.M. on Sunday (9 hours).
9. **(C) emphasize the fit of organizational parts.** The first sentence of the passage states that organizations must achieve coherence among the component parts to function effectively.
10. **(D) warm temperatures.** The third sentence states that the bacterium that produces the toxin must be treated to temperatures that are just warm enough. The other options are not conditions necessary for the development of botulism toxin.
11. **(C) experimental.** In the context of the paragraph, the word *experimental* should be replaced with the word *proven.*
12. **(A) were the result of seeing the European polecat running loose.** The first sentence states that the rarely seen black-footed ferret is often confused with the common European polecat. The second sentence indicates that these two mammals resemble each other in some ways.
13. **(D) providing postal service.** Although providing postal service is an important government service, it is not an aspect of the fundamental function of government, as it is not protection of life and property against antisocial individuals within the country or enemies from without.
14. **(D) developing a new procedure for issuing supplies.** Non-repetitive office work and work that is primarily mental rather than manual are more difficult to measure. The other options are repetitive or manual operations.
15. **(D) the material needs of men and women are supplied by well-conducted businesses.** The last sentence states that when the nation's business is successfully carried on, it renders public service of the highest order. This is accomplished by supplying the material needs of men and women.

SUBTEST 2—WORD KNOWLEDGE

1. **(B) excellent.** Used as an adjective, *nonpareil* means having no equal or peerless.
2. **(A) incompetent.** Used as an adjective, *inapt* means awkward or clumsy.
3. **(D) intercede.** Used as a verb, *mediate* means to resolve or settle by working with conflicting parties.
4. **(D) Samaritan.** Used as a noun, *humanitarian* means one who is caring and giving.
5. **(B) irritate.** Used as a verb, *rankle* means to cause persistent irritation or annoyance.
6. **(C) aquatic.** Used as an adjective, *maritime* means of, relating to, or near the sea.
7. **(D) enthusiastic.** Used as a noun, *melodrama* means a play or film characterized by exaggerated emotions.
8. **(A) argumentative.** Used as an adjective, *litigious* means to show a trait to argue or disagree, even to the point of lawsuits.
9. **(C) fire.** Used as a noun, *conflagration* means a large, destructive fire.
10. **(A) speech.** Used as a noun, *harangue* means a long, pompous speech.
11. **(D) scene.** Used as a noun, *panorama* means an unbroken view of a surrounding area.
12. **(B) coward.** Used as a noun, *recreant* means someone who is craven or cowardly.
13. **(A) clock.** Used as a noun, *chronometer* means an exceptionally precise timepiece.
14. **(A) sticky.** Used as an adjective, *glutinous* means adhesive.
15. **(B) filter.** Used as a verb, *percolate* means to cause to pass through a porous substance or to filter.
16. **(C) sound.** Used as a noun, *dissonance* means a harsh, disagreeable combination of sounds.
17. **(D) seed.** Used as a noun, *kernel* means a grain or a seed.
18. **(A) brighten.** Used as a verb, *illuminate* means to light or brighten.
19. **(B) apparent.** In the context of this sentence, *discernible* means noticeable or apparent.
20. **(A) fatherhood.** In the context of this sentence, *paternity* means the state of being a father.
21. **(B) challenging.** In the context of this sentence, *formidable* means challenging, or tough.
22. **(A) ruined.** In the context of this sentence, *scuttled* means to destroy or defeat.
23. **(B) speech.** In the context of this sentence, *tirade* means a long, angry, censorious speech.
24. **(D) insult.** In the context of this sentence, *alienate* means to insult or offend.
25. **(A) pleasant.** In the context of this sentence, *benign* means pleasant or aesthetically pleasing.
26. **(B) candid.** In the context of this sentence, *forthright* means straightforward or truthful.
27. **(B) immune.** In the context of this sentence, *impervious* means indifferent or beyond caring.

28. **(D) gowns.** In the context of this *sentence*, kimono means a Japanese-style gown.
29. **(D) speech.** In the context of this sentence, *monologue* means a one-person speech or address.
30. **(A) alienated.** In the context of this sentence, *estranged* means separated, angry, or alienated.
31. **(A) painful.** In the context of this sentence, *grievous* means terrible, painful, or extensive.
32. **(C) impinge.** In the context of this sentence, *encroach* means to take advantage of, or impinge.
33. **(B) applicable.** In the context of this sentence, *germane* means applicable or relating to.
34. **(B) menacing.** In the context of this sentence, *ominous* means threatening or foreboding.
35. **(A) waved.** In the context of this sentence, *undulate* means to move in a wavy motion.

SUBTEST 3—ARITHMETIC REASONING

1. **(B) 3.**
   Let C = CIRCUMFERENCE
   Let R = RADIUS
   Given $C = 6\pi$
   Formula $C = 2\pi R$
   $C = 2\pi R$ // Circumference Formula
   $6\pi = 2\pi R$// Substitute 6π for C
   $R = 3$
2. **(C) 35.**
   $\frac{1}{5}x + x = 42$ // set up the equation
   $5*\frac{1}{5}x + 5x = 42*5$ // multiply both sides by 5
   $x + 5x = 210$
   $6x = 210$
   $x = 35$
3. **(C) 42 feet.**
   Let S = SHADOW (LAMP POST)
   Let H = HEIGHT (LAMP POST)
   Let s = shadow (tree)
   Let t = height (tree)
   Given S/H = s/t
   Given $H = 12$
   Given $S = 8$
   Given $s = 28$
   $8/12 = 28/t$ // Expand parentheses
   $8t = 12*28$
   $t = 42$

4. **(C) $142,222.**
   Let x = value of the estate
   Given: $\frac{x}{4}$ = amount to wife
   Given: $\frac{2x}{5}$ = amount to son
   Given: $\frac{x}{8}$ = amount to daughter
   Given $32,000 = amount to charity
   First, find the value of x:
   $\frac{10}{40} + \frac{16}{40} + \frac{5}{40} + \frac{x}{40} = 1$
   $\frac{31}{40} + \frac{x}{40} = 1$
   $x = 9$
   Solve:
   $\frac{16}{40}x = 32{,}000$
   $x = \$142{,}222$
5. **(A) 2.**
   Let P = PERIMETER
   Let S = SIDE
   Given $P = 8$
   $P = 4S$ // Square Perimeter Formula
   $8 = 4S$ // Substitute 8 for P
   $S = 2$
6. **(A) $15,737.50.**
   Let x = MSR price
   Given: $x - 20\%{*}x = \$12{,}590$ (purchase price)
   $x - 0.2x = \$12{,}590$
   $0.8x = \$12{,}590$
   $x = \frac{\$12{,}590}{0.8}$
   $x = \$15{,}737.50$
7. **(D) 44.**
   Let P = PERIMETER
   Let L = LENGTH
   Let W = WIDTH
   Given $P = 198$
   Given $\frac{L}{W} = \frac{5}{4}$
   Given $P = 2L + 2W$
   $\frac{L}{W} = \frac{5}{4}$
   $4L = 5W$
   $L = \frac{5W}{4}$
   $2\left(\frac{5W}{4}\right) + 2W = 198$
   $\frac{10W}{4} + 2W = 198$

$4.5W = 198$
$W = 44$

8. **(C) 18.**
Let R = RADIUS
Let D = DIAMETER
Given $R = 9$
$D = 2R$ // Diameter Formula
$D = 2*9$ // Substitute 9 for Radius
$D = 18$

9. **(B) 7.4 feet.**
Formula: Area = $\frac{1}{2}$*height × base
$37 = \frac{1}{2}(10)*b$ // substitute known values
$b = \frac{(37*2)}{10}$
$b = \frac{74}{10}$
$b = 7.4$ feet

10. **(B) 6936.26.**
Formula: Area = *pi* × radius^2
$a = \pi r^2$
$a = \pi 47^2$
$a = (3.14)*2209$
$a = 6936.26$ square inches

11. **(C) 9.**
Let A = AREA
Let B = BASE
Let H = HEIGHT
Given $A = 36$
Given $B = 8$
Given $A = \frac{BH}{2}$
$72 = BH$ // Substitute 36 for A
$72 = 8H$ // Substitute 8 for B
$H = 9$

12. **(C) 78.5.**
Formula: area = *pi* × radius^2
$a = \pi r^2$
Given: diameter = 10
Given: radius = $\frac{1}{2}$ diameter
$a = (3.14)5^2$
$a = (3.14)*25$
$a = 78.5$

13. **(A) 6 feet.**
Let A = AREA
Let S = SIDE
Given $A = 36$

$A = S^2$ // Square Area Formula
$36 = S^2$ // Substitute 36 for A
$S = 6$ // Solve for S

14. **(A) 24 miles.**
Formula: area = *pi* × radius^2
$a = \pi r^2$
$1808.64 = \pi r^2$ // substitute known values
$r^2 = \frac{1808.64}{3.14}$ // divide both sides by *pi*
$r^2 = 576$
$\sqrt{r^2} = \sqrt{576}$
$r = 24$ miles

15. **(A) \$150.**
Formula: Area = length × width
$a = lw$
Conversion: 9 feet = 9/3 yards = 3 yards
Conversion: 12 feet = 12/3 yards = 4 yards
$a = 3 \times 4$
$a = 12$ square yards
12 × \$12.51 = \$150.12
Round to \$150

16. **(C) 793.8.**
Let N = NUMBER
Given $N - 372.6 = 421.2$
$N = 793.8$

17. **(A) 110 degrees.**
Total interior angles for any polygon is $180(n-2)$, with n = the number of angles.
$180(n-2) = 540$ for 5 angles (pentagon)
Let x = the middle angle
Given: $x - 2$ = first angle
Given: $x - 1$ = second angle
Given: x = middle angle
Given: $x + 1$ = fourth angle
Given: $x + 2$ = fifth angle
Given: sum of all the angles is equal to $5x$
$x - 2 + x - 1 + x + x + 1 + x + 2 = 5x$
$x = 108$
$x + 2$ = largest angle, so $108 + 2 = 110$ degrees

18. **(D) 24.**
Formula: hypotenuse^2 is equal to height^2 plus base^2
$10^2 = 6^2 + b^2$
$100 = 36 + b^2$
$b^2 = 64$
$b = 8$ // base of the triangle is 8 inches
Formula: area is equal to $\frac{1}{2}$ of base × height

Answers–Practice Test 5

$a = \frac{1}{2}bh$

$a = \frac{1}{2}(8 \times 6)$ // substitute known values

$a = 24$

19. **(C) 1,846.32 square feet.**

As the horse is tied to a corner of the barn, it will be able to graze $\frac{3}{4}$ of a circle.

Formula: area = *pi* × radius^2

$a = \pi r^2$

$a = 3.14 \cdot 28^2$

$a = 3.14 \cdot 784$

$a = 2{,}461.76$

Let g = area grazed

$g = 0.75 \times a$

$g = 0.75 \times 2{,}461.76$

$g = 1{,}846.32$ square feet

20. **(A) 20 cm.**

Let W = ORIGINAL WIDTH

Let H = ORIGINAL HEIGHT

Let h = new height

Let w = new width

Given $\frac{W}{H} = \frac{w}{h}$

Given $W = 8$

Given $H = 10$

Given $h = 25$

$\frac{8}{10} = \frac{w}{25}$ // Expand parentheses

$8*25 = 10w$

$w = 20$

21. **(C) 8 feet.**

Divide the amount to spend by the price per foot: $1 \div 0.125 = 8$ feet.

22. **(B) 106.76.**

Let R = RADIUS

Given $R = 17$

Formula $C = 2\pi R$

$C = 2\pi R$ // Circumference Formula

$C = 2*17\pi$ // Substitute 17 for Radius

$C = 34\pi$

$C = 34*3.14$

$C = 106.76$

23. **(B) 52.**

Let L = LARGER

Let S = SMALLER

Given $S + L = 65$

Given $4S = L$

$4(65 - L) = L$ // Substitute 65–L for S

$L = 52$

24. **(A) 12 feet.**
Let A = AREA
Let S = SIDE
Given A = 144
$A = S^2$ // Square Area Formula
$144 = S^2$ // Substitute 144 for A
$S = 12$
25. **(B) 7.**
Let x = smaller number
Given: $2x$ = larger number
$3x + 2(2x) = 49$ // 3 times the smaller number plus 2 times the larger number equals 49
$3x + 4x = 49$
$7x = 49$
$x = 7$ // smaller number
26. **(B) 5 × 9.**
Let A = AREA
Let L = LENGTH
Let W = WIDTH
Given $L = 2W - 1$
Given $(L - 1)(W + 3) = LW + 19$
$LW + 3L - 1W - 3 = LW + 19$ // Expand parentheses
$3L - 1W - 3 = 19$
$3(2W - 1) - W - 3 = 19$ // Substitute $2W - 1$ for L
$6W - 3 - W - 3 = 19$
$5W - 3 = 22$
$W = 5$
$L = 9$ // Substitute $W = 5$ into $L = 2W - 1$
27. **(A) 20 inches.**
Let L = Longest line
Let S = Short line
Given $L + S = 50$
Given $L/S = 3/2$
$L/S = 3/2$ // Expand parentheses
$2L = 3S$
$L = 50 - S$ // Isolate N
$2(50 - S) = 3S$ // Substitute for N in $2N = 3D$
$100 - 2S = 3S$
$S = 20$ // Solve for D
$L = 30$ / Solve for N
28. **(B) 167 pounds.**
Let R = Rod's weight
Let P = Paul's weight
Formula: $3M = 2R$
Given $R = 250$
$3M = 2 \times 250$ // substitute known value for R
$3M = 500$
$M = 166.666$ (167 pounds)

Answers—Practice Test 5

29. **(B) 5 feet.**
Let A = AREA
Let L = LENGTH
Let W = WIDTH
Given $L = W + 20$
Given $A = 125$
$A = LW$ // Area formula
$125 = (W + 20)W$ // Substitute: $L = W + 20$
$W^2 + 20W - 125 = 0$
$W = (5, -25)$ // Solve for W
$W = 5$ // Reject negative width

30. **(A) 90.**
Substitute the root (known value of x) into the equation:
$2*6^2 + (3*6) - k = 0$
$90 - k = 0$
$k = 90$

CHAPTER 18

Practice Test for Navy OCS Applicants and Marine Corps/ Coast Guard Aviation Applicants 1

Navy and Marine Corps Aviation Selection Test Battery is used for all Navy Officer Candidate School applicants, as well as other Naval officer flight training candidates. The test is also used for Marine Corps and Coast Guard officers and officer applicants who desire to become commissioned as aviators.

The examination consists of six subtests totaling 176 questions that must be answered in 140 minutes.

Answer Sheet for Practice Test 6

Subtest 1—Math Skills

1 Ⓐ Ⓑ Ⓒ Ⓓ
2 Ⓐ Ⓑ Ⓒ Ⓓ
3 Ⓐ Ⓑ Ⓒ Ⓓ
4 Ⓐ Ⓑ Ⓒ Ⓓ
5 Ⓐ Ⓑ Ⓒ Ⓓ
6 Ⓐ Ⓑ Ⓒ Ⓓ
7 Ⓐ Ⓑ Ⓒ Ⓓ
8 Ⓐ Ⓑ Ⓒ Ⓓ
9 Ⓐ Ⓑ Ⓒ Ⓓ
10 Ⓐ Ⓑ Ⓒ Ⓓ
11 Ⓐ Ⓑ Ⓒ Ⓓ
12 Ⓐ Ⓑ Ⓒ Ⓓ
13 Ⓐ Ⓑ Ⓒ Ⓓ
14 Ⓐ Ⓑ Ⓒ Ⓓ
15 Ⓐ Ⓑ Ⓒ Ⓓ
16 Ⓐ Ⓑ Ⓒ Ⓓ
17 Ⓐ Ⓑ Ⓒ Ⓓ
18 Ⓐ Ⓑ Ⓒ Ⓓ
19 Ⓐ Ⓑ Ⓒ Ⓓ
20 Ⓐ Ⓑ Ⓒ Ⓓ
21 Ⓐ Ⓑ Ⓒ Ⓓ
22 Ⓐ Ⓑ Ⓒ Ⓓ
23 Ⓐ Ⓑ Ⓒ Ⓓ
24 Ⓐ Ⓑ Ⓒ Ⓓ
25 Ⓐ Ⓑ Ⓒ Ⓓ
26 Ⓐ Ⓑ Ⓒ Ⓓ
27 Ⓐ Ⓑ Ⓒ Ⓓ
28 Ⓐ Ⓑ Ⓒ Ⓓ
29 Ⓐ Ⓑ Ⓒ Ⓓ
30 Ⓐ Ⓑ Ⓒ Ⓓ

Subtest 2—Reading Skills

1 Ⓐ Ⓑ Ⓒ Ⓓ
2 Ⓐ Ⓑ Ⓒ Ⓓ
3 Ⓐ Ⓑ Ⓒ Ⓓ
4 Ⓐ Ⓑ Ⓒ Ⓓ
5 Ⓐ Ⓑ Ⓒ Ⓓ
6 Ⓐ Ⓑ Ⓒ Ⓓ
7 Ⓐ Ⓑ Ⓒ Ⓓ
8 Ⓐ Ⓑ Ⓒ Ⓓ
9 Ⓐ Ⓑ Ⓒ Ⓓ
10 Ⓐ Ⓑ Ⓒ Ⓓ
11 Ⓐ Ⓑ Ⓒ Ⓓ
12 Ⓐ Ⓑ Ⓒ Ⓓ
13 Ⓐ Ⓑ Ⓒ Ⓓ
14 Ⓐ Ⓑ Ⓒ Ⓓ
15 Ⓐ Ⓑ Ⓒ Ⓓ
16 Ⓐ Ⓑ Ⓒ Ⓓ
17 Ⓐ Ⓑ Ⓒ Ⓓ
18 Ⓐ Ⓑ Ⓒ Ⓓ
19 Ⓐ Ⓑ Ⓒ Ⓓ
20 Ⓐ Ⓑ Ⓒ Ⓓ
21 Ⓐ Ⓑ Ⓒ Ⓓ
22 Ⓐ Ⓑ Ⓒ Ⓓ
23 Ⓐ Ⓑ Ⓒ Ⓓ
24 Ⓐ Ⓑ Ⓒ Ⓓ
25 Ⓐ Ⓑ Ⓒ Ⓓ
26 Ⓐ Ⓑ Ⓒ Ⓓ
27 Ⓐ Ⓑ Ⓒ Ⓓ

Subtest 3—Mechanical Comprehension

1 Ⓐ Ⓑ Ⓒ Ⓓ
2 Ⓐ Ⓑ Ⓒ Ⓓ
3 Ⓐ Ⓑ Ⓒ Ⓓ
4 Ⓐ Ⓑ Ⓒ Ⓓ
5 Ⓐ Ⓑ Ⓒ Ⓓ
6 Ⓐ Ⓑ Ⓒ Ⓓ
7 Ⓐ Ⓑ Ⓒ Ⓓ
8 Ⓐ Ⓑ Ⓒ Ⓓ
9 Ⓐ Ⓑ Ⓒ Ⓓ
10 Ⓐ Ⓑ Ⓒ Ⓓ
11 Ⓐ Ⓑ Ⓒ Ⓓ
12 Ⓐ Ⓑ Ⓒ Ⓓ
13 Ⓐ Ⓑ Ⓒ Ⓓ
14 Ⓐ Ⓑ Ⓒ Ⓓ
15 Ⓐ Ⓑ Ⓒ Ⓓ
16 Ⓐ Ⓑ Ⓒ Ⓓ
17 Ⓐ Ⓑ Ⓒ Ⓓ
18 Ⓐ Ⓑ Ⓒ Ⓓ
19 Ⓐ Ⓑ Ⓒ Ⓓ
20 Ⓐ Ⓑ Ⓒ Ⓓ
21 Ⓐ Ⓑ Ⓒ Ⓓ
22 Ⓐ Ⓑ Ⓒ Ⓓ
23 Ⓐ Ⓑ Ⓒ Ⓓ
24 Ⓐ Ⓑ Ⓒ Ⓓ
25 Ⓐ Ⓑ Ⓒ Ⓓ
26 Ⓐ Ⓑ Ⓒ Ⓓ
27 Ⓐ Ⓑ Ⓒ Ⓓ
28 Ⓐ Ⓑ Ⓒ Ⓓ
29 Ⓐ Ⓑ Ⓒ Ⓓ
30 Ⓐ Ⓑ Ⓒ Ⓓ

Subtest 4–Spatial Apperception

1 Ⓐ Ⓑ Ⓒ Ⓓ Ⓔ
2 Ⓐ Ⓑ Ⓒ Ⓓ Ⓔ
3 Ⓐ Ⓑ Ⓒ Ⓓ Ⓔ
4 Ⓐ Ⓑ Ⓒ Ⓓ Ⓔ
5 Ⓐ Ⓑ Ⓒ Ⓓ Ⓔ
6 Ⓐ Ⓑ Ⓒ Ⓓ Ⓔ
7 Ⓐ Ⓑ Ⓒ Ⓓ Ⓔ
8 Ⓐ Ⓑ Ⓒ Ⓓ Ⓔ
9 Ⓐ Ⓑ Ⓒ Ⓓ Ⓔ
10 Ⓐ Ⓑ Ⓒ Ⓓ Ⓔ
11 Ⓐ Ⓑ Ⓒ Ⓓ Ⓔ
12 Ⓐ Ⓑ Ⓒ Ⓓ Ⓔ
13 Ⓐ Ⓑ Ⓒ Ⓓ Ⓔ
14 Ⓐ Ⓑ Ⓒ Ⓓ Ⓔ
15 Ⓐ Ⓑ Ⓒ Ⓓ Ⓔ
16 Ⓐ Ⓑ Ⓒ Ⓓ Ⓔ
17 Ⓐ Ⓑ Ⓒ Ⓓ Ⓔ
18 Ⓐ Ⓑ Ⓒ Ⓓ Ⓔ
19 Ⓐ Ⓑ Ⓒ Ⓓ Ⓔ
20 Ⓐ Ⓑ Ⓒ Ⓓ Ⓔ
21 Ⓐ Ⓑ Ⓒ Ⓓ Ⓔ
22 Ⓐ Ⓑ Ⓒ Ⓓ Ⓔ
23 Ⓐ Ⓑ Ⓒ Ⓓ Ⓔ
24 Ⓐ Ⓑ Ⓒ Ⓓ Ⓔ
25 Ⓐ Ⓑ Ⓒ Ⓓ Ⓔ

Subtest 5–Aviation/Nautical Information

1 Ⓐ Ⓑ Ⓒ Ⓓ Ⓔ
2 Ⓐ Ⓑ Ⓒ Ⓓ Ⓔ
3 Ⓐ Ⓑ Ⓒ Ⓓ Ⓔ
4 Ⓐ Ⓑ Ⓒ Ⓓ Ⓔ
5 Ⓐ Ⓑ Ⓒ Ⓓ Ⓔ
6 Ⓐ Ⓑ Ⓒ Ⓓ Ⓔ
7 Ⓐ Ⓑ Ⓒ Ⓓ Ⓔ
8 Ⓐ Ⓑ Ⓒ Ⓓ Ⓔ
9 Ⓐ Ⓑ Ⓒ Ⓓ Ⓔ
10 Ⓐ Ⓑ Ⓒ Ⓓ Ⓔ
11 Ⓐ Ⓑ Ⓒ Ⓓ Ⓔ
12 Ⓐ Ⓑ Ⓒ Ⓓ Ⓔ
13 Ⓐ Ⓑ Ⓒ Ⓓ Ⓔ
14 Ⓐ Ⓑ Ⓒ Ⓓ Ⓔ
15 Ⓐ Ⓑ Ⓒ Ⓓ Ⓔ
16 Ⓐ Ⓑ Ⓒ Ⓓ Ⓔ
17 Ⓐ Ⓑ Ⓒ Ⓓ Ⓔ
18 Ⓐ Ⓑ Ⓒ Ⓓ Ⓔ
19 Ⓐ Ⓑ Ⓒ Ⓓ Ⓔ
20 Ⓐ Ⓑ Ⓒ Ⓓ Ⓔ
21 Ⓐ Ⓑ Ⓒ Ⓓ Ⓔ
22 Ⓐ Ⓑ Ⓒ Ⓓ Ⓔ
23 Ⓐ Ⓑ Ⓒ Ⓓ Ⓔ
24 Ⓐ Ⓑ Ⓒ Ⓓ Ⓔ
25 Ⓐ Ⓑ Ⓒ Ⓓ Ⓔ
26 Ⓐ Ⓑ Ⓒ Ⓓ Ⓔ
27 Ⓐ Ⓑ Ⓒ Ⓓ Ⓔ
28 Ⓐ Ⓑ Ⓒ Ⓓ Ⓔ
29 Ⓐ Ⓑ Ⓒ Ⓓ Ⓔ
30 Ⓐ Ⓑ Ⓒ Ⓓ Ⓔ

Subtest 6–Aviation Supplemental Test

1 Ⓐ Ⓑ Ⓒ Ⓓ
2 Ⓐ Ⓑ Ⓒ Ⓓ Ⓔ
3 Ⓐ Ⓑ Ⓒ Ⓓ
4 Ⓐ Ⓑ Ⓒ Ⓓ
5 Ⓐ Ⓑ Ⓒ Ⓓ
6 Ⓐ Ⓑ Ⓒ Ⓓ Ⓔ
7 Ⓐ Ⓑ Ⓒ Ⓓ Ⓔ
8 Ⓐ Ⓑ Ⓒ Ⓓ
9 Ⓐ Ⓑ Ⓒ Ⓓ
10 Ⓐ Ⓑ Ⓒ Ⓓ
11 Ⓐ Ⓑ Ⓒ Ⓓ Ⓔ
12 Ⓐ Ⓑ Ⓒ Ⓓ
13 Ⓐ Ⓑ Ⓒ Ⓓ
14 Ⓐ Ⓑ Ⓒ Ⓓ Ⓔ
15 Ⓐ Ⓑ Ⓒ Ⓓ
16 Ⓐ Ⓑ Ⓒ Ⓓ
17 Ⓐ Ⓑ Ⓒ Ⓓ
18 Ⓐ Ⓑ Ⓒ Ⓓ
19 Ⓐ Ⓑ Ⓒ Ⓓ
20 Ⓐ Ⓑ Ⓒ Ⓓ Ⓔ
21 Ⓐ Ⓑ Ⓒ Ⓓ
22 Ⓐ Ⓑ Ⓒ Ⓓ
23 Ⓐ Ⓑ Ⓒ Ⓓ
24 Ⓐ Ⓑ Ⓒ Ⓓ
25 Ⓐ Ⓑ Ⓒ Ⓓ Ⓔ
26 Ⓐ Ⓑ Ⓒ Ⓓ
27 Ⓐ Ⓑ Ⓒ Ⓓ
28 Ⓐ Ⓑ Ⓒ Ⓓ
29 Ⓐ Ⓑ Ⓒ Ⓓ
30 Ⓐ Ⓑ Ⓒ Ⓓ Ⓔ
31 Ⓐ Ⓑ Ⓒ Ⓓ
32 Ⓐ Ⓑ Ⓒ Ⓓ Ⓔ
33 Ⓐ Ⓑ Ⓒ Ⓓ
34 Ⓐ Ⓑ Ⓒ Ⓓ Ⓔ

Subtest 1—Math Skills Test

Directions: The Math Skills subtest consists of 30 questions that must be answered in 25 minutes.

This subtest measures your knowledge of basic arithmetic and your ability to solve problems using mathematics. Read each question carefully and choose the response that best answers the question.

1. The Hair Palace gives a $5\frac{1}{2}$ percent discount to senior citizens. If Pam is 67 years old, and her hair restyling costs \$75, what is the amount of her bill once the discount is applied?

   (A) \$55.88
   (B) \$57.88
   (C) \$66.88
   (D) \$ 70.88

2. $2x(3xy + y)$ is equivalent to

   (A) $6xy + 2xy$
   (B) $6x^2y + 2xy$
   (C) $3xy + 2xy$
   (D) $3x^2y + xy$

3. Find the area of the shaded portion of the figure below

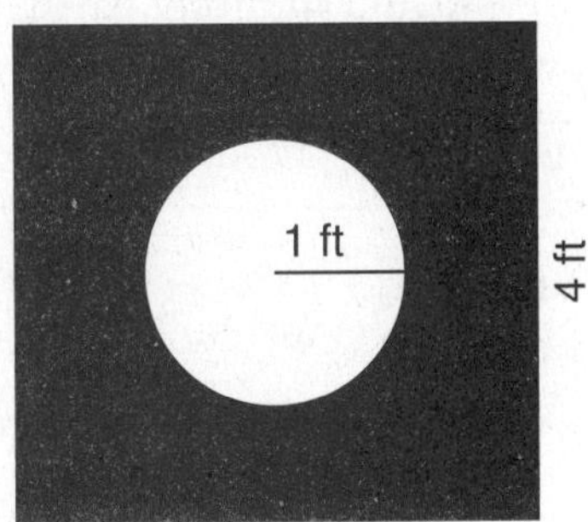

   (A) 10.57 square feet
   (B) 11.17 square feet
   (C) 12.86 square feet
   (D) 13.44 square feet

4. You are in charge of purchasing food for the annual Fourth of July picnic. If you purchase food items from whichever supplier will provide the item for the least cost, what would it cost for 400 cases of soda, 100 pounds of hotdogs, 150 pounds of hamburger, and 30 bags of potato chips?

Supplier	Soda	Hotdogs	Hamburger	Potato Chips
#1	\$3.50/ case	\$0.49/ pound	\$0.89/ pound	\$2.69/ bag
#2	\$3.89/ case	\$0.45/ pound	\$0.69/ pound	\$2.79/ bag
#3	\$3.55/ case	\$0.44/ pound	\$0.71/ pound	\$2.55/ bag
#4	\$3.57/ case	\$0.46/ pound	\$0.68/ pound	\$2.57/ bag

   (A) \$1,623.10
   (B) \$1,622.50
   (C) \$1,790.20
   (D) \$1,801.15

5. Yolanda invested \$500 in an investment account and received \$650 after three years. How much was her annual interest rate?

   (A) 6%
   (B) 8%
   (C) 10%
   (D) 12%

6. Susan can paint a room in 6 hours, while Tom can paint the same room in 5 hours. Working together, how long will it take them to paint the room?

   (A) 2.73 hours
   (B) 2.90 hours
   (C) 3.43 hours
   (D) 3.54 hours

7. $(5.37 \times 10^2) \times (2.54 \times 10^5) =$

   (A) 13.6398×10
   (B) 13.6398×10^{10}
   (C) 13.6398×10^3
   (D) 13.6398×10^7

8. Apply the Distributive Property and simplify the following: $-7(4x + 5) - 8$

 (A) $-28x + 43$
 (B) $28x - 43$
 (C) $-28x - 43$
 (D) $28x + 43$

9. $\frac{1}{2}x - \frac{1}{10} = \frac{1}{5}x + \frac{1}{2}$

 (A) 2
 (B) 4
 (C) 6
 (D) 8

10. What is the area of the shape below?

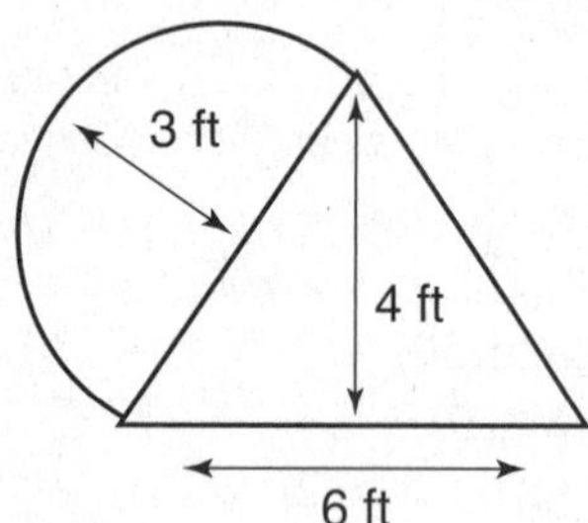

 (A) $4\pi + 12$ square feet
 (B) $6(\pi - 4)$ square feet
 (C) $\frac{9\pi}{2} + 12$ square feet
 (D) $6\pi - 24$ square feet

11. If each brick is 3 inches wide and 5 inches long, how many bricks would you need to build a wall that will measure 10 feet by 16 feet?

 (A) 940
 (B) 980
 (C) 1,302
 (D) 1,536

12. $(9i + 6)(3i - 7) =$

 (A) $54i - 21i$
 (B) $27i^2 - 45i - 42$
 (C) $18i^2 - 63i + 1$
 (D) $9i + 3i - 42$

13. Gravel is mixed with cement at a ratio of 5 parts of cement to 1 part of gravel. How many pounds of cement are there in 48 pounds of this mixture?

 (A) 20 pounds
 (B) 30 pounds
 (C) 40 pounds
 (D) 50 pounds

14. How much carpet would be necessary to cover a room that is 8 feet long and 6 feet wide?

 (A) 14 square feet
 (B) 20 square feet
 (C) 48 square feet
 (D) 60 square feet

15. A bakery specializes in peach and apple pies. Out of a batch of 26 pies, four are peach. What percent of the pies are peach?

 (A) 10.3 percent
 (B) 15.4 percent
 (C) 20.5 percent
 (D) 25.6 percent

16. Convert 6.39×10^5 to regular notation.

 (A) $(6.39)^5 \times 10$
 (B) 639,000
 (C) 639.10
 (D) 0.000639

17. A refrigerator costs $400 to purchase outright, or it can be rented for a non-refundable deposit of $50 and monthly payments of $25. After how many months would the cost of rental equal the purchase cost?

 (A) 10 months
 (B) 12 months
 (C) 14 months
 (D) 16 months

18. Courier charges for packages to a certain destination are 65 cents for the first 250 grams and 10 cents for each additional 100 grams or part thereof. What could be the weight in grams of a package for which the charge is $1.55?

    (A) 1155
    (B) 1145
    (C) 1040
    (D) 950

19. If $\frac{x}{y}$ is an integer, which of the following statements must be true?

    (A) Both x and y are integers.
    (B) x is an integer.
    (C) $x = ny$ where n is an integer.
    (D) $\frac{y}{x}$ is an integer.

20. The first term in a sequence is 1 and the second term is 5. From the third term on, each term is the average (arithmetic mean) of all preceding terms. What is the 25th term in the sequence?

    (A) 2.5
    (B) 3
    (C) 5
    (D) 25

21. $(3x + 2)(2x - 5) = ax^2 + kx + n$. What is the value of $a - n + k$?

    (A) 3
    (B) 8
    (C) 9
    (D) 10

22. What is the simplified result of following the steps below in order?

    (1) add $5y$ to $2x$
    (2) multiply the sum by 3
    (3) subtract $x + y$ from the product

    (A) $5x + 14y$
    (B) $5x + 16y$
    (C) $5x + 5y$
    (D) $6x + 4y$

23. What is the average of four tenths and five thousandths?

    (A) 25002
    (B) 2502
    (C) 0.225
    (D) 0.2025

24. Which of the following integers is not a prime number?

    (A) 3
    (B) 5
    (C) 7
    (D) 9

25. If $3^n = 9$, what is the value of 4^{n+1}?

    (A) 25
    (B) 30
    (C) 35
    (D) 64

26. If the ratio of $3x$ to $5y$ is 1:2, what is the ratio of x to y?

    (A) $\frac{1}{2}$
    (B) $\frac{2}{3}$
    (C) $\frac{3}{4}$
    (D) $\frac{5}{6}$

27. The floor area in a Navy warehouse measures 200 feet by 200 feet. What is the maximum safe floor load if the maximum weight the floor area can hold is 4,000 tons?

(A) 120 pounds per square foot
(B) 140 pounds per square foot
(C) 160 pounds per square foot
(D) 200 pounds per square foot

28. Assume that the U.S. Mint produces one million nickels a month. The total value of the nickels produced during a year is

(A) $50,000
(B) $60,000
(C) $550,000
(D) $600,000

29. There are 20 cigarettes in one pack and 10 packs of cigarettes in a carton. A certain brand of cigarette contains 12 mg of tar per cigarette. How many grams of tar are contained in one carton of these cigarettes? (1 gram = 1000 milligrams)

(A) .024 grams
(B) 0.24 grams
(C) 2.4 grams
(D) 24 grams

30. A certain governmental agency had a budget last year of $1,100,500. Its budget this year was 7 percent higher than that of last year. The budget for next year is 8 percent higher than this year's budget. Which one of the following is the agency's budget for next year?

(A) $1,117,600
(B) $1,161,600
(C) $1,261,700
(D) $1,271,700

Subtest 2—Reading Skills Test

Directions: The Reading Skills subtest consists of 27 questions, that must be answered in 25 minutes.

This subtest measures your reading comprehension level and basic vocabulary skills. Read each question carefully and choose the response that best answers the question.

Question 1 is based on the following paragraph.

"The earliest dynasty of the Counts of Holland—Dirks, Floris, and Williams—was a very remarkable one. Not only did it rule for an unusually long period, 922 to 1299, but in this long period without exception all the Counts of Holland were strong and capable rulers. The fiefs of the first two Dirks lay in what is now known as North Holland, in the district called Kennemerland. It was Dirk III who seized from the bishops of Utrecht some swampy land amidst the channels forming the mouth of the Meuse, which, from the bush which covered it, was named Holt-land (Holland or Wood-land). Here he erected, in 1015, a stronghold to collect tolls from passing ships. This stronghold was the beginning of the town of Dordrecht, and from here a little later the name Holland was gradually applied to the whole county. Of his successors the most illustrious was William II (1234 to 1256) who was crowned King of the Romans at Aachen, and would have received from Pope Innocent IV the imperial crown at Rome, had he not been unfortunately drowned while attempting to cross on horseback an ice-bound marsh."

1. William II failed to be crowned by the Pope because
   (A) he ruled unjustly.
   (B) he died.
   (C) he defied the Pope.
   (D) he wasn't married.

Question 2 is based on the following paragraph.

"In demographic terms, the salient feature of California is its diversity. One out of every four Californians has been born outside the United States. Into California has come the human, racial, ethnic, linguistic, and cultural richness of the planet itself. There is no people, no race, no cultural or linguistic tradition that is not in some way represented in California. In certain cases, in fact, California represents a major instance of a cultural tradition. There are more than a million Chinese-American Californians and a million and more Filipino-Americans. Los Angeles alone is one of the largest Mexican cities on the planet. The state also sustains major populations of Iranian, Armenian, Asian-Indian, Vietnamese, and other populations, the vast majority of them first-generation immigrants."

2. According to the above passage, what percent of Californians are born in the United States?

   (A) 25 percent
   (B) 50 percent
   (C) 75 percent
   (D) none of the above

3. Encumber most nearly means ____________.

   (A) encircle
   (B) relief
   (C) progress
   (D) impede

4. Inevitable most nearly means ____________.

   (A) utterly
   (B) unadvisable
   (C) unavoidable
   (D) unpredictable

5. Despite his reputation, his conversation with Betty was quite innocuous.

   (A) normal
   (B) harmless
   (C) perplexing
   (D) meaningful

6. The basic training recruits were required to assimilate an amazing amount of knowledge.

   (A) memorize
   (B) perform
   (C) demonstrate
   (D) absorb

Question 7 is based on the following paragraph.

"Victory is not measured by casualties inflicted, battles won or lost, or territory occupied, but by the achievement or failure to achieve political objectives. More than any other factor, political objectives (one's own and those of the enemy) shape war's scope and intensity. Military objectives and operations must support political objectives and be aligned with nonmilitary instruments of power."

7. A good title for the above passage would be

   (A) "The Importance of Superior Military Technology."
   (B) "War is an Instrument of National Policy."
   (C) "War is a Complex and Chaotic Endeavor."
   (D) "The Fundamental Nature of War."

Question 8 is based on the following paragraph.

"U.S. Armed Forces must always be ready to operate in smoothly functioning joint teams. Successful unified action across the range of military operations depends on unity of effort among all assigned, attached, and supporting forces. The Joint Force Commander should exploit the unique characteristics of forces that maximize the military effect to achieve strategic aims as rapidly as possible, while expending lives, minimizing costs, and achieving victory."

8. Which word in the above paragraph is incorrectly used?

   (A) unified
   (B) exploit
   (C) maintain
   (D) expending

9. The new vest was Teflon-plated, making it __________ to small projectiles.

   (A) hazardous
   (B) invulnerable
   (C) visible
   (D) irradiant

10. The incessant irritable noise from upstairs resulted in a __________ feeling among those in the room.

   (A) petulant
   (B) peaceful
   (C) harmonious
   (D) tranquil

Question 11 is based on the following paragraph.

"Leaders prepare for challenges through their career-long study and application of the art of leadership. Successful leaders generally exhibit common character traits and embrace experimental leadership principles. Leaders must strive to develop and hone their skills, build on expertise in their specialties, learn from others' experiences, and observe their environment."

11. Which word in the above paragraph is incorrectly used?

(A) hone
(B) career-long
(C) experimental
(D) environment

12. Replenish most nearly means ____________.

(A) complete
(B) refill
(C) makeshift
(D) trash

13. Diatribe most nearly means ____________.

(A) denunciation
(B) panic
(C) pragmatic
(D) problematic

Question 14 is based on the following paragraph.

"The sun set, and the chill dusk of autumn wrapped the yellow sedge, the dusty road, and the pines upon the horizon. The heavens were high and cold, and the night wind had a message from the north. But it was warm beneath the gum tree where the fire leaped and roared. In the light the nearer leaves of the surrounding trees showed in strong relief; beyond that copper fretwork all was blackness. Out of the dark came the breathing of the horses, fastened near the tobacco-cask, the croaking of frogs in a marshy place, and all the stealthy, indefinable stir of the forest at night. At times the wind brought a swirl of dead leaves across the ring of light, an owl hooted, or one of the sleeping dogs stirred and raised his head, then sank to dreams again. The tobacco-roller, weary from the long day's travel, wrapped himself in a blanket and slept in the lee of his thousand pounds of bright leaf, but the boy and the hunter sat late by the fire."

14. In the above passage, how many people are sleeping?

(A) one
(B) two
(C) three
(D) four

Question 15 is based on the following paragraph.

"Man-Afraid-of-His-Horse, then head chief of the Ogallalas, took counsel with Red Cloud in all important matters, and the young warrior rapidly advanced in authority and influence. In 1854, when he was barely thirty-five years old, the various bands were again encamped near Fort Laramie. A Mormon emigrant train, moving westward, left a footsore cow behind, and the young men killed her for food. The next day, to their astonishment, an officer with thirty men appeared at the Indian camp and demanded of old Conquering Bear that they be given up."

15. Red Cloud was born in ___________.

    (A) 1854
    (B) 1819
    (C) 1825
    (D) Cannot be determined from the above information.

16. Vassal most nearly means ___________.

    (A) nobleman
    (B) ship
    (C) slave
    (D) bucket

Question 17 is based on the following paragraph.

"Marked differences in caloric intakes exist across income and education subgroups over the whole range of intake levels, from light to moderate to high. When these differences are compared with differences in body fatness (as measured by Body Mass Index) across the same income and education groups, the patterns tend to match for men but not for women. For example, a greater share of low-income men consumes excessive calories and has BMIs in the obese range than high-income men. Among women, however, low incomes tend to be associated with high BMIs but lower caloric intakes. Determining the causes of disagreements between patterns of caloric intake and body fatness across socio-demographic groups may lead to a better understanding of the causes of disparities in overweight and obesity."

17. Which group tends to eat less, but has a higher Body Mass Index?

    (A) high-income men
    (B) low-income men
    (C) high-income women
    (D) low-income women

Question 18 is based on the following paragraph.

"Rwanda is a poor rural country with about 90% of the population engaged in (mainly subsistence) agriculture. It is the most densely populated country in Africa; landlocked with few natural resources and minimal industry. Primary foreign exchange earners are coffee and tea. The 1994 genocide decimated Rwanda's fragile economic base, severely impoverished the population, particularly women, and eroded the country's ability to attract private and external investment. However, Rwanda has made substantial progress in stabilizing and rehabilitating its economy to pre-1994 levels, although poverty levels are higher now. GDP has rebounded and inflation has been curbed."

18. Which of the following statements can be derived from the information in the above passage?

    (A) Rwanda is a province of South Africa.
    (B) poverty levels are higher than in the pre-1994 level.
    (C) Rwandan men are more impoverished than Rwandan women.
    (D) Rwanda has vast, unexploited natural resources.

19. The producer promised even more action in the __________ to the movie.

    (A) forerunner
    (B) aftermath
    (C) sequel
    (D) credits

20. <u>Prominent</u> most nearly means __________.

    (A) conspicuous
    (B) reliant
    (C) invisible
    (D) imaginative

Question 21 is based on the following paragraph.

"If they are to function effectively, organizations, like other systems, must achieve a natural harmony or coherence among their component parts. The structural and situational elements of an effective organization form themselves into a tightly knit, highly cohesive package. An organization whose parts are mismatched, however, cannot carry out its missions."

21. According to the passage, if managers are to design effective organizations, they need to

    (A) simplify organizational structures.
    (B) encourage greater specialization of labor.
    (C) emphasize the fit of organizational parts.
    (D) introduce more technological innovations.

Question 22 is based on the following paragraph.

"The English language is particularly rich in synonyms, and there is scarcely a language spoken among people that has not some representative in English speech. The spirit of the English-speaking peoples has subjugated these various elements to one idiom, making not a patchwork, but a composite language."

22. It can be truly stated that the English language

(A) has absorbed words from other languages.
(B) has few idiomatic expressions.
(C) has provided words for other languages.
(D) is difficult to translate.

Question 23 is based on the following paragraph.

"Honest people in one nation find it difficult to understand the viewpoints of honest people in another. Foreign ministries and their ministers exist for the purpose of explaining the viewpoints of one nation in terms understood by the ministries of another. Some of their most important work lies in this direction."

23. On the basis of this information, it may be stated that

(A) it is unusual for many people to share similar ideas.
(B) people of different nations may not consider matters in the same light.
(C) suspicion prevents understanding between nations.
(D) the chief work of foreign ministries is to guide relations between nations united by a common cause.

Question 24 is based on the following paragraph.

"One key person in a computer installation is a programmer, the man or woman who puts business and scientific problems into special symbolic languages that can be read by the computer. Jobs done by the computer range all the way from payroll operations to chemical process control, but most computer applications are directed toward management data. About half of the programmers employed by business come to their positions with college degrees; the remaining half are promoted to their positions from within the organization on the basis of demonstrated ability without regard to education."

24. Of the following, the most valid implication of the above passage is that the programmers in industry

(A) do not need a college degree to do programming work.
(B) must be graduates of a college or university.
(C) need professional training to advance.
(D) should be obtained only from outside the organization.

Question 25 is based on the following paragraph.

"It is important for every office to have proper lighting. Inadequate lighting is a common cause of fatigue and tends to create a dreary atmosphere in the office. Appropriate light intensity is essential for proper lighting. It is generally recommended that for "casual seeing" tasks such as in reception rooms or inactive file rooms, the amount of light be 30 foot-candles. For "ordinary seeing" tasks such as reading or for work in active file rooms and mail rooms, the recommended lighting is 100 foot-candles. For "very difficult seeing" tasks such as transcribing, accounting, and business machine use, the recommended lighting is 150 foot-candles."

25. For copying figures onto a payroll, the recommended lighting is

(A) less than 30 foot-candles.
(B) 30 foot-candles.
(C) 100 foot-candles.
(D) 150 foot-candles.

Question 26 is based on the following paragraph.

"The candidate's personal appearance is one factor that an interviewer may unconsciously overvalue. Of course, personal appearance may be relevant if the job is one involving numerous contacts with the public or with other people, but in most positions it is a matter of distinctly secondary importance. Other qualities that have no bearing on the job to be filled should also be discounted."

26. According to this passage

(A) a candidate should not be concerned about his or her appearance unless it is relevant to the job.
(B) there are many factors that should be considered during an interview even though they have no direct bearing on the job to be filled.
(C) in positions involving contact with the public, the personal appearance of the applicant is the most important factor to be considered.
(D) the personal appearance of a candidate should not be considered of primary importance when interviewing persons for most positions.

Question 27 is based on the following paragraph.

"The protection of life and property against antisocial individuals within the country and enemies from without is generally recognized to be the most fundamental activity of government."

27. Of the following choices, the one that is not an aspect of the fundamental function of government as described above is

(A) sending a delegation to a foreign country to participate in a disarmament conference.
(B) prosecuting a drug peddler who has been selling dope to schoolchildren.
(C) providing fire protection.
(D) providing postal service.

Subtest 3—Mechanical Comprehension

Directions: The Mechanical Comprehension subtest is comprised of 30 questions that must be answered in 15 minutes.

This subtest measures your ability to reason with and comprehend mechanical applications and simple rules of physics. Choose the answer that best answers the question.

1. Heat is a form of ____________.

   (A) calories
   (B) motion
   (C) energy
   (D) pressurization

2. On a standard day, at sea level, assuming static conditions, the speed of sound is

   (A) 1,100 feet per second.
   (B) 1,200 feet per second.
   (C) 1,300 feet per second.
   (D) 1,425 feet per second.

3. The following diagram depicts airflow around the wing of an aircraft. Most of the lift is caused by

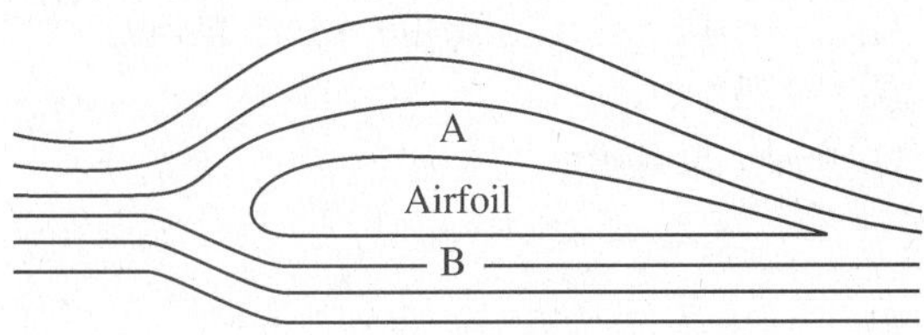

   (A) increased air pressure on the bottom side (side B).
   (B) increased air pressure on the top side (side A).
   (C) decreased air pressure on the bottom side (side B).
   (D) decreased air pressure on the top side (side A).

4. In the below diagram, which of the following statements is not true?

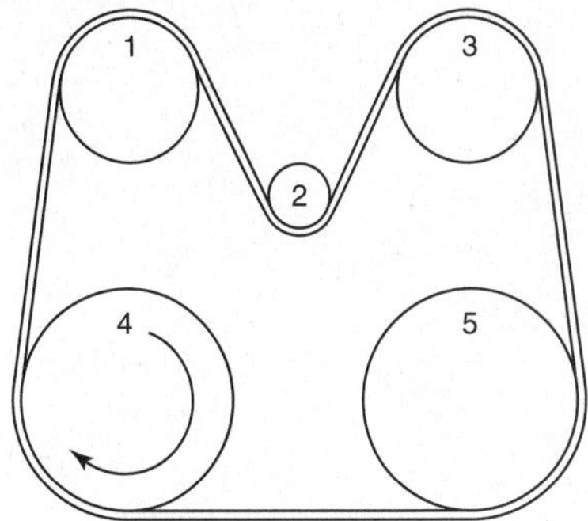

   (A) Pulley 2 would spin faster than Pulley 4.
   (B) Pulley 4 would spin faster than Pulley 3.
   (C) Pulley 1 would spin faster than Pulley 3.
   (D) Pulley 4 would spin faster than Pulley 5.

5. Which tool below is the best for cutting metal?

   (A) hacksaw
   (B) chain saw
   (C) rotary saw
   (D) handsaw

6. Which of the following is a type of lever?

   (A) elevator
   (B) seesaw
   (C) door hinge
   (D) electrical cord

7. Approximately how much force must be exerted to lift the box?

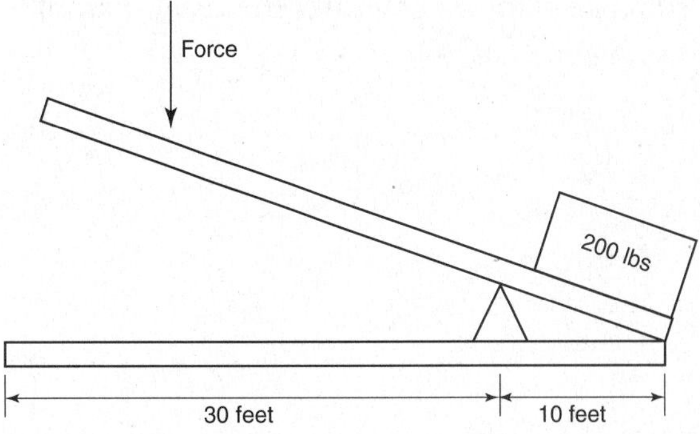

   (A) 67 pounds
   (B) 100 pounds
   (C) 250 pounds
   (D) 258 pounds

8. Which wrench would require more force to turn the bolt?

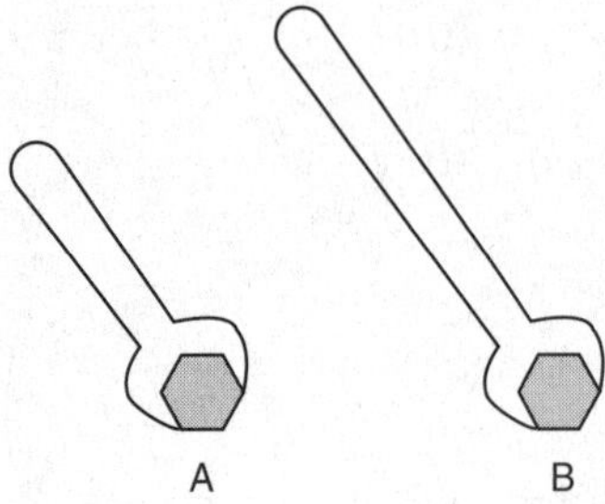

(A) Wrench A
(B) Wrench B
(C) No difference
(D) none of the above

9. In order to move the block five feet, how many feet of rope would have to be pulled?

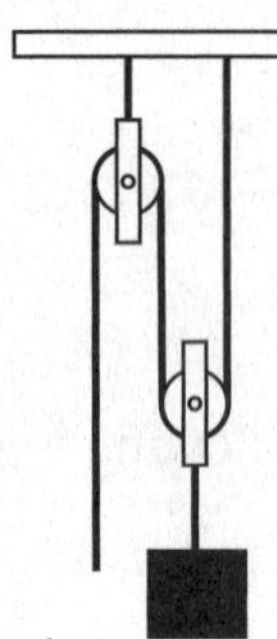

(A) 5
(B) 10
(C) 15
(D) 20

10. The number of cranks the crankshaft of a V-6 engine has is ____________.

(A) 2
(B) 4
(C) 6
(D) 8

11. Pulley A is the same size as Pulleys B and C, and twice the size of Pulley D. For each revolution made by Pulley C, how many revolutions will Pulley A make?

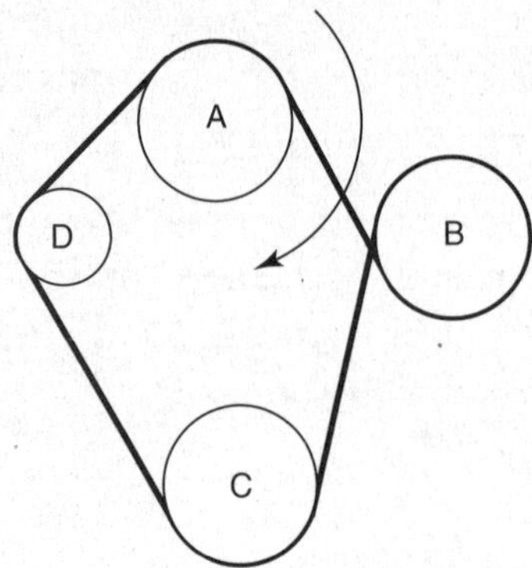

(A) 1
(B) 2
(C) 3
(D) 4

12. In order to lift a 100-pound load onto a dock five feet high, using only 25 pounds of force, how long of a ramp would have to be used?

(A) 5 feet
(B) 10 feet
(C) 15 feet
(D) 20 feet

13. One horsepower is equal to

(A) 33,000 foot-pounds of work per minute.
(B) 150 pounds of force in an hour.
(C) 950 psi.
(D) 17,500 ergs.

14. In the below diagram, how many pulleys are turning in a clockwise direction?

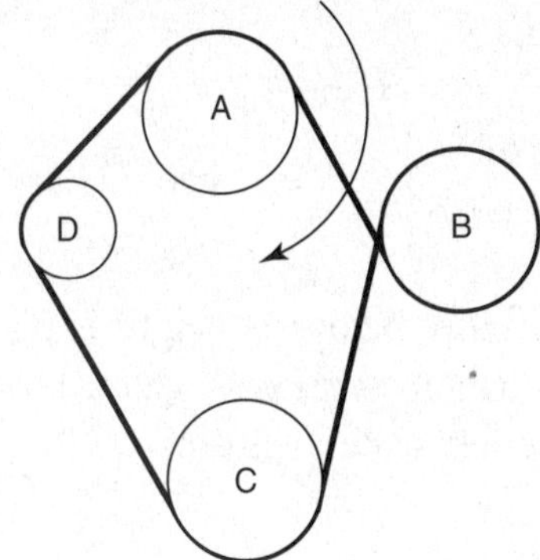

(A) 1
(B) 2
(C) 3
(D) 4

15. Wheel A has a diameter of 10 inches. Wheel B has a diameter of 25 inches. If both wheels revolve at the same speed, which wheel will travel the most distance in the same amount of time?

(A) Wheel A
(B) Wheel B
(C) same distance
(D) cannot determine

16. How many gears are turning in a counter-clockwise direction?

(A) 2
(B) 3
(C) 4
(D) 5

17. If Gear 1 revolves twice, how many times will Gear 2 revolve?

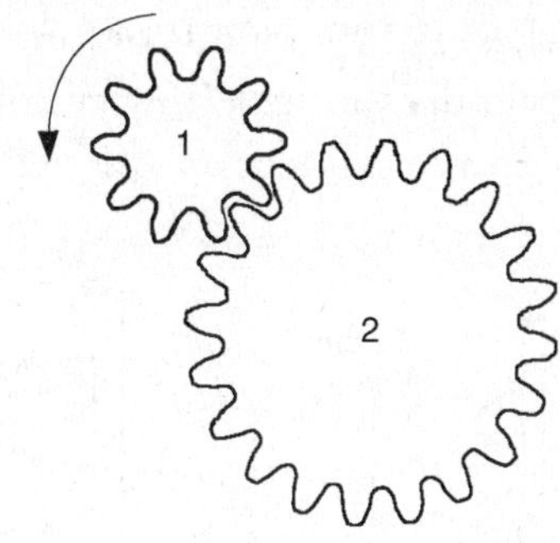

(A) 1
(B) 2
(C) 3
(D) 4

18. In the figure below, for each complete revolution of the cam, how many times will the valve open?

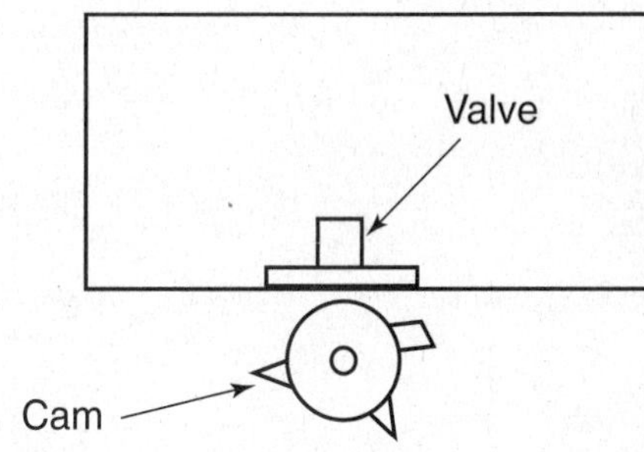

(A) 1
(B) 2
(C) 3
(D) 4

19. In the hydraulic system depicted below, the cylinder on the left has a diameter of 2 inches and the cylinder on the right has a diameter of 6 inches. If 100 pounds of force is applied to the cylinder on the left, what force will be exerted on the cylinder on the right?

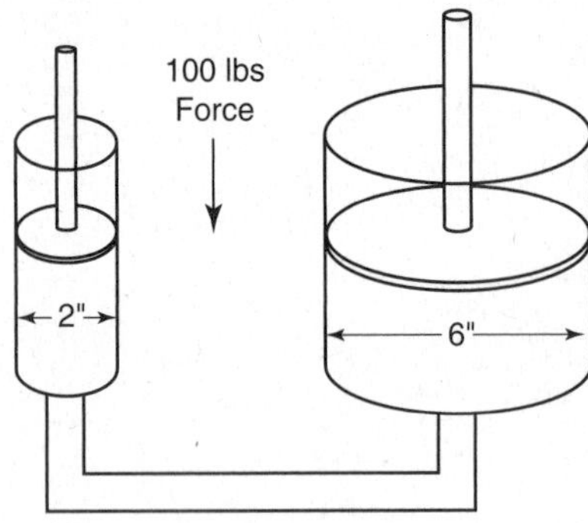

(A) 300 pounds
(B) 33.3 pounds
(C) 900 pounds
(D) 450 pounds

20. In the design below, which tank(s) will overfill?

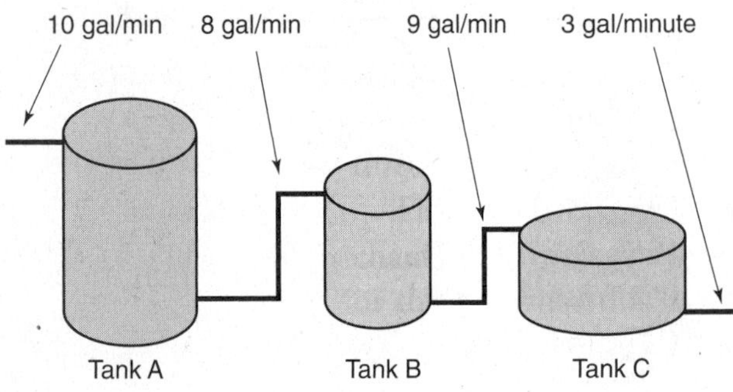

(A) Tank A
(B) Tank A and B
(C) Tank A and C
(D) Tank B and C

21. Which of the following are <u>not</u> parts of a braking system on an automobile?

(A) discs
(B) master cylinder
(C) axel
(D) wheels

22. In the figure below, a weight is placed on a board, balanced on two scales. How much will the left scale measure?

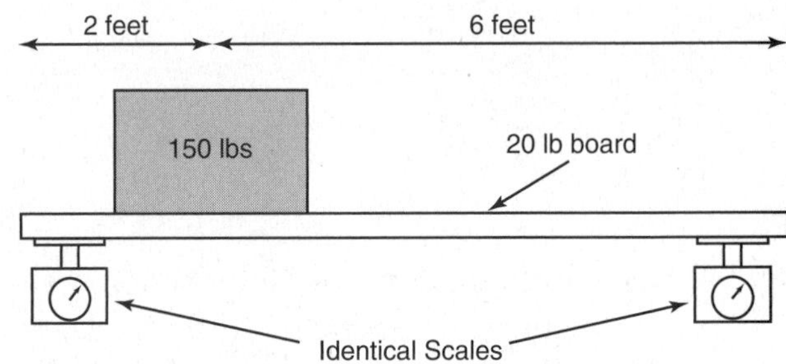

(A) 170 pounds
(B) 110 pounds
(C) 60 pounds
(D) 115 pounds

23. When a machine magnifies force, it is referred to as

(A) magnification factor.
(B) mechanical advantage.
(C) leverage factor.
(D) efficiency factor.

24. A <u>pitch</u> is

(A) the distance between the threads of a screw.
(B) the gap measurement of a spark plug.
(C) the angle measurement of a simple lever.
(D) one of the four basic measurements of force.

25. When an object is at equilibrium

    (A) its velocity does not change.
    (B) the object speeds up.
    (C) the object is at rest.
    (D) the object changes direction.

26. An example of a simple machine is

    (A) a door hinge.
    (B) light switch.
    (C) can opener.
    (D) all of the above

27. When a helium-filled balloon rises, the force responsible is ____________.

    (A) friction
    (B) air pressure
    (C) buoyancy
    (D) gravity

28. In physics, power can be defined as

    (A) work/time.
    (B) energy/efficiency.
    (C) leverage/mass.
    (D) friction/drag.

29. The force acting on an object dropped from a building is ____________.

    (A) buoyancy
    (B) elastic recoil
    (C) gravity
    (D) equilibrium

30. If you remove your foot from the gas pedal in your car, it will slowly coast to a stop. The force which causes this is ____________.

    (A) friction
    (B) gravity
    (C) velocity
    (D) magnitude

Subtest 4—Spatial Apperception

Directions: This subtest measures your ability to determine the position of an aircraft in flight in relation to the view a pilot would see when looking outside of the cockpit.

The subtest consists of 25 questions that must be answered in 10 minutes.

For each question, you will see a series of six pictures. The first picture will depict a view of the landscape that a pilot would see when looking out the front of the cockpit. You are to determine whether the aircraft is climbing, diving, banking, or in level flight, and choose the picture that best represents the same aircraft when viewed from the outside.

1.

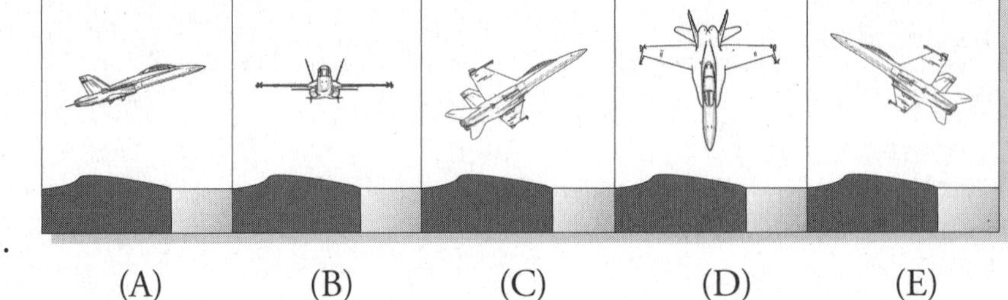

(A) (B) (C) (D) (E)

2.

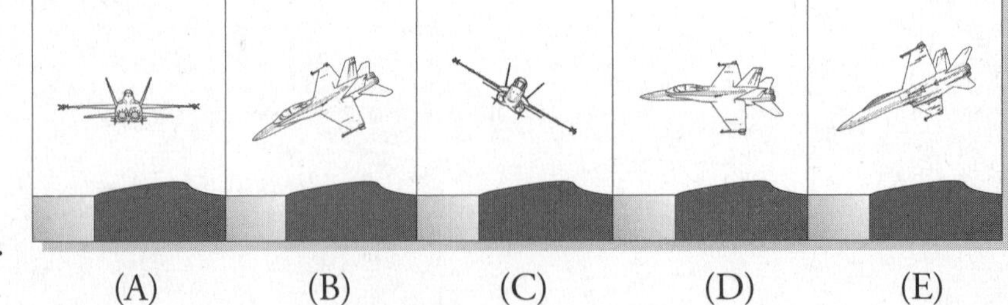

(A) (B) (C) (D) (E)

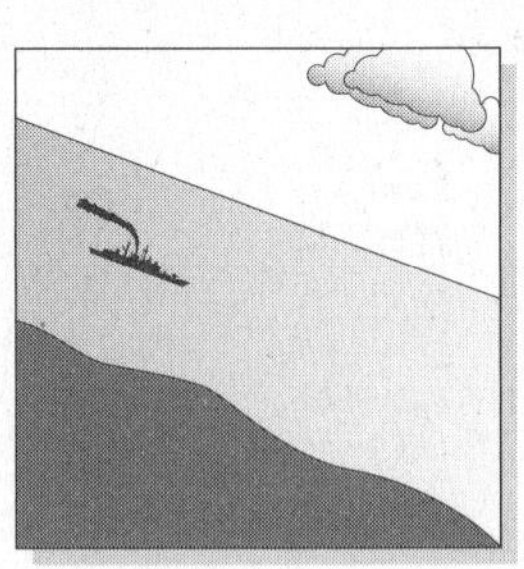

3.

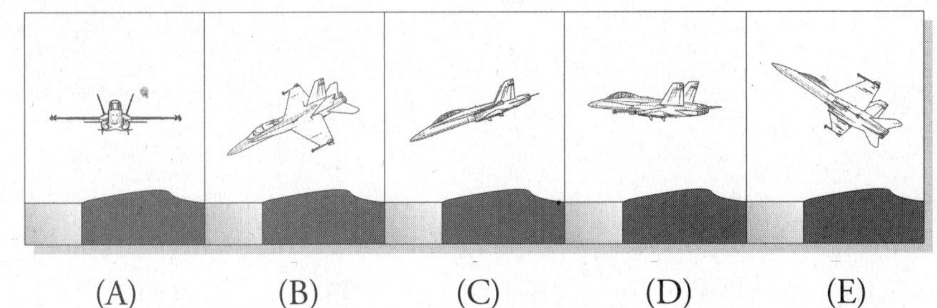

(A) (B) (C) (D) (E)

4.

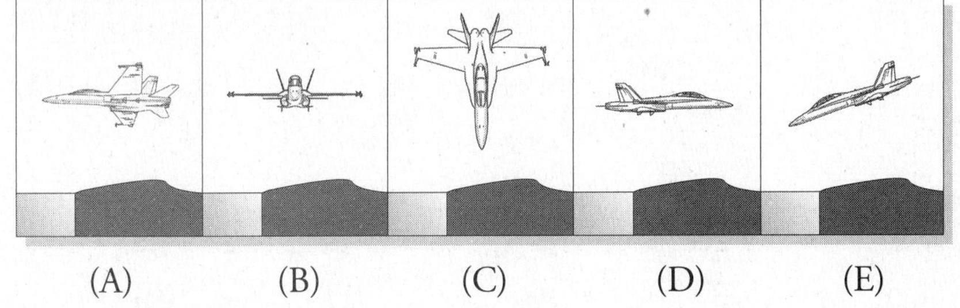

(A) (B) (C) (D) (E)

5.

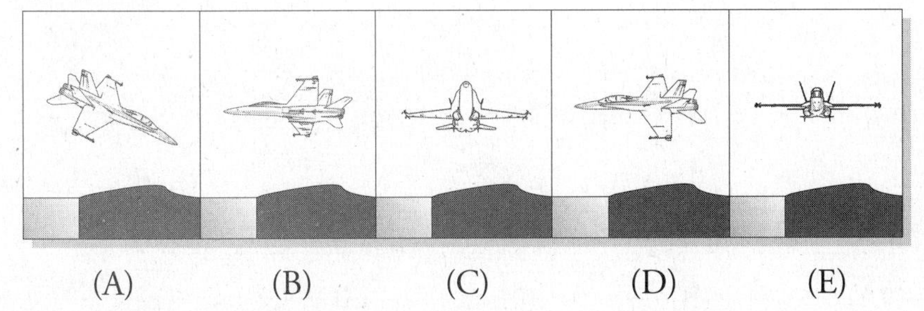

(A) (B) (C) (D) (E)

6.

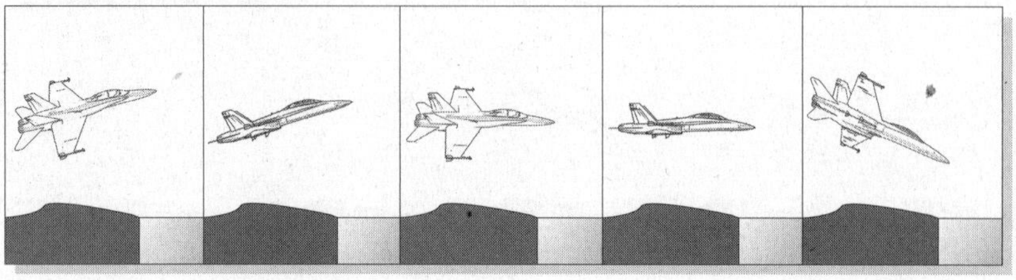

(A) (B) (C) (D) (E)

7.

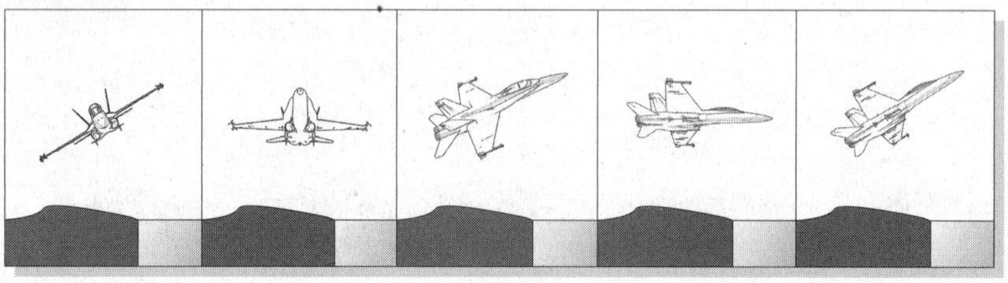

(A) (B) (C) (D) (E)

8.

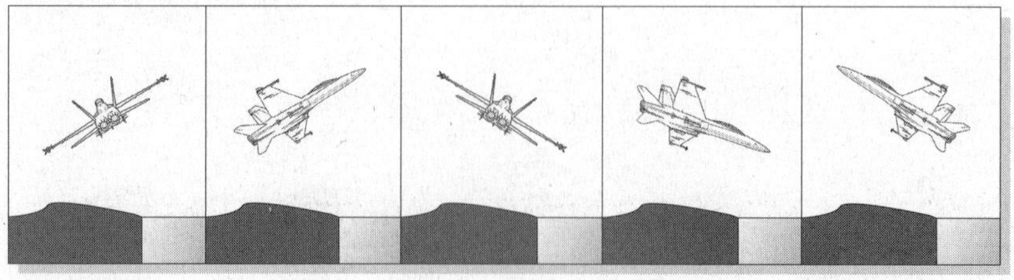

(A) (B) (C) (D) (E)

9.

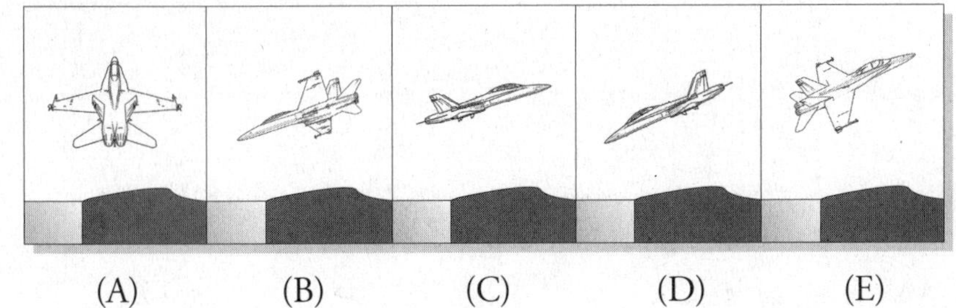

(A) (B) (C) (D) (E)

10.

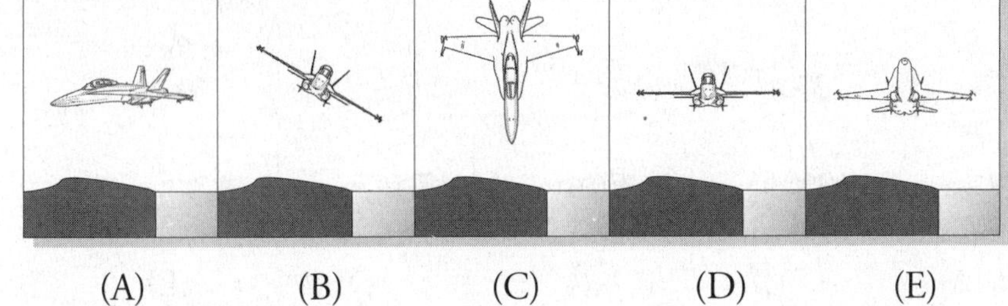

(A) (B) (C) (D) (E)

11.

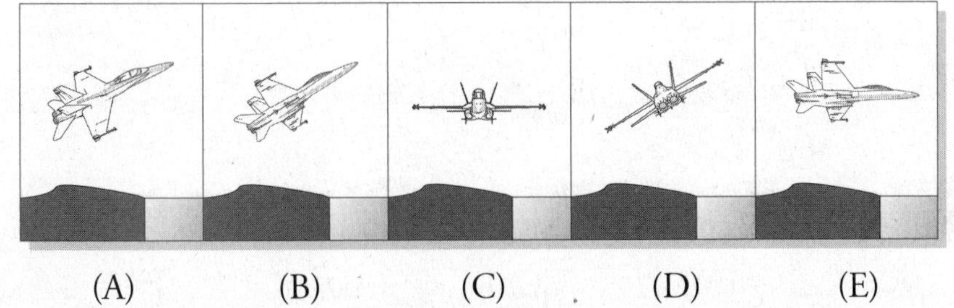

(A) (B) (C) (D) (E)

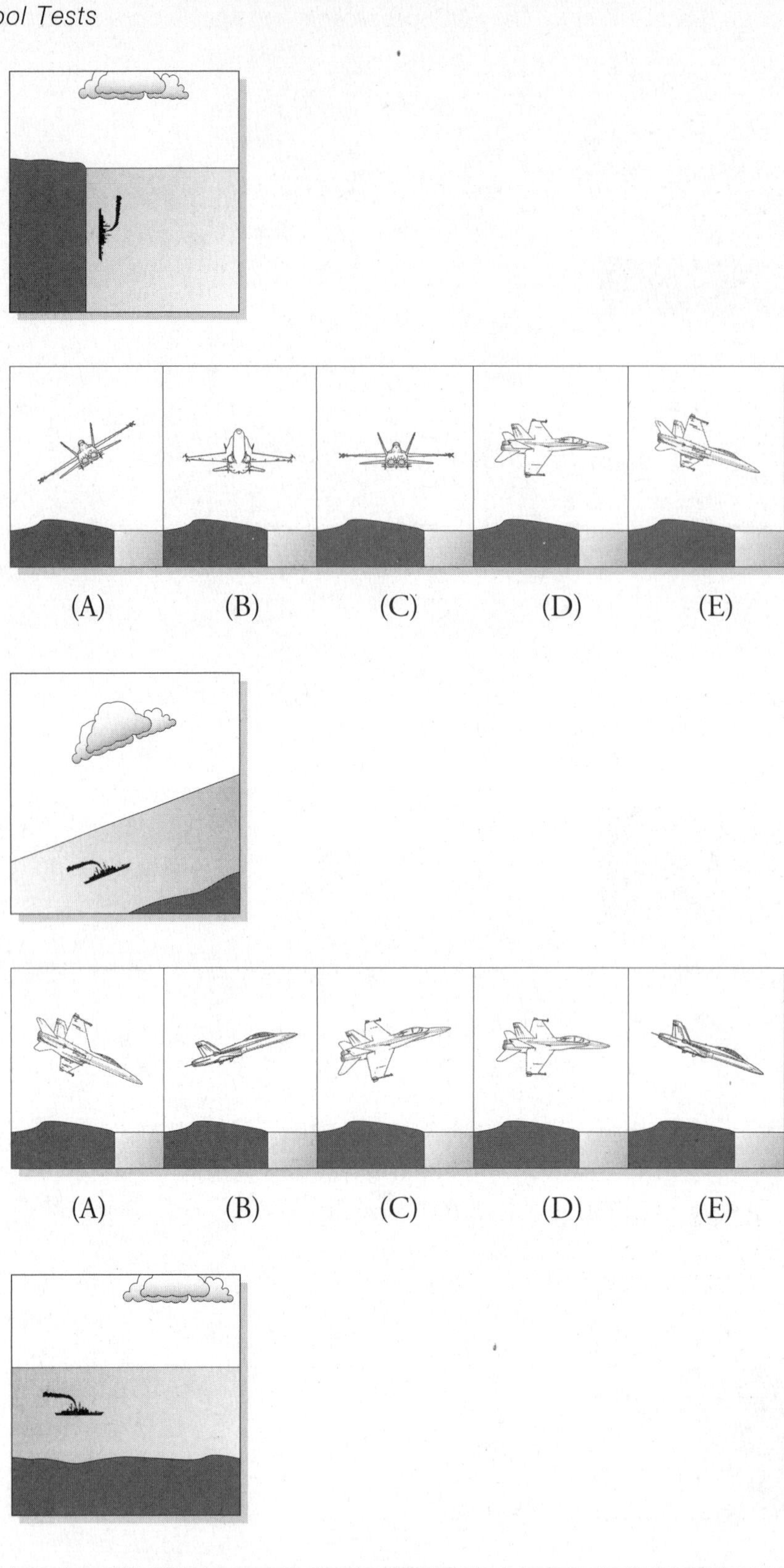

12.
(A)
(B)
(C)
(D)
(E)
13.
(A)
(B)
(C)
(D)
(E)
14.
(A)
(B)
(C)
(D)
(E)

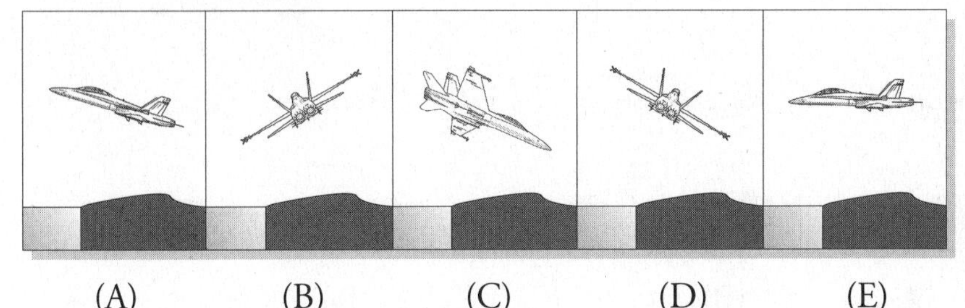

15.

(A) (B) (C) (D) (E)

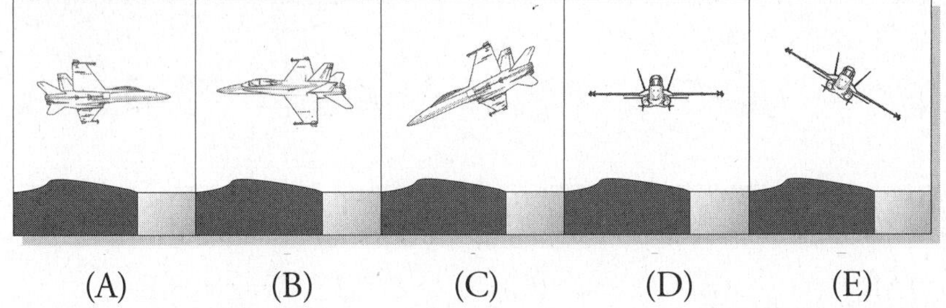

16.

(A) (B) (C) (D) (E)

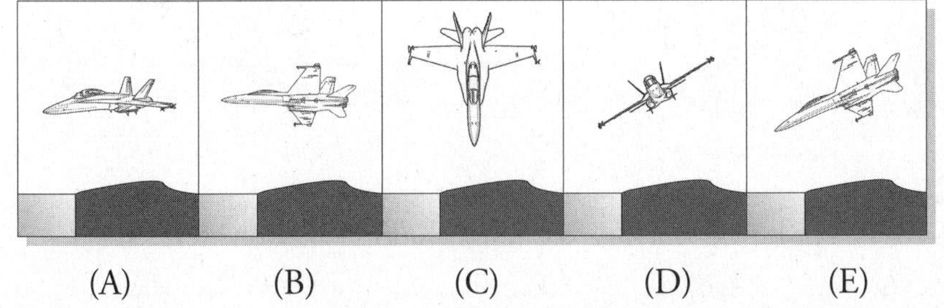

17.

(A) (B) (C) (D) (E)

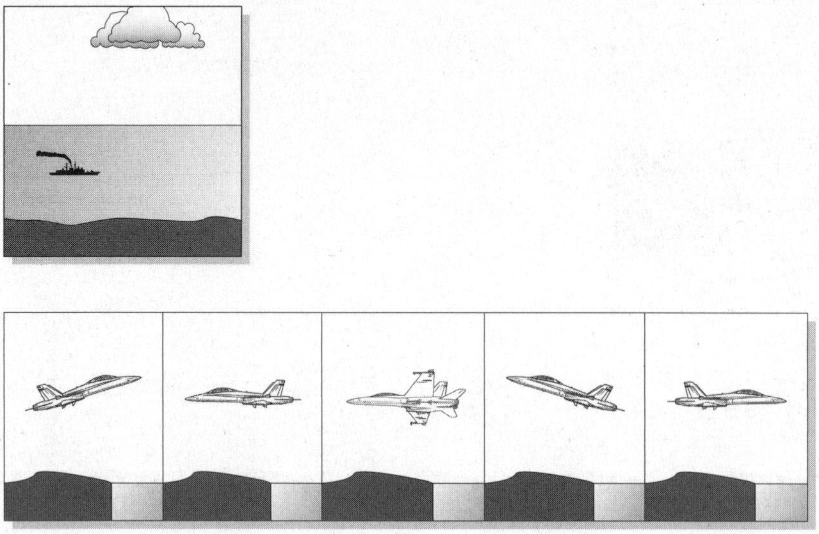

18.

(A) (B) (C) (D) (E)

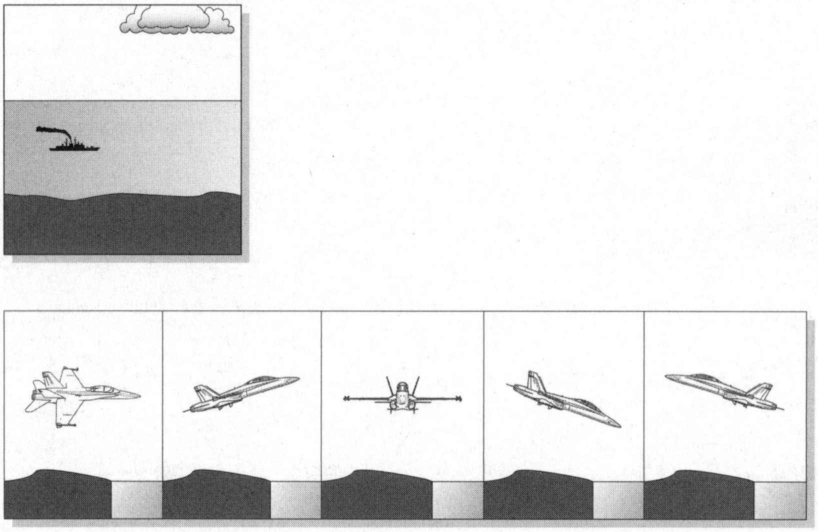

19.

(A) (B) (C) (D) (E)

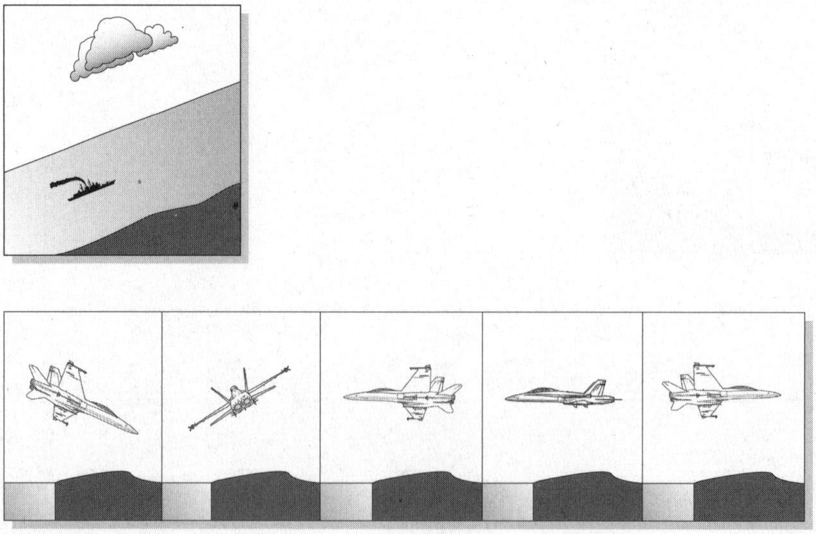

20.

(A) (B) (C) (D) (E)

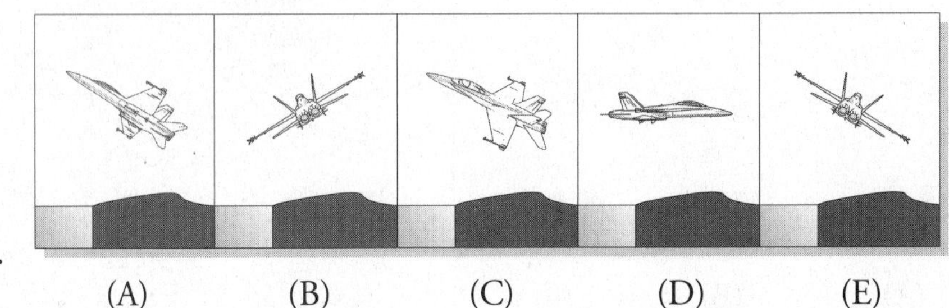

21.

(A) (B) (C) (D) (E)

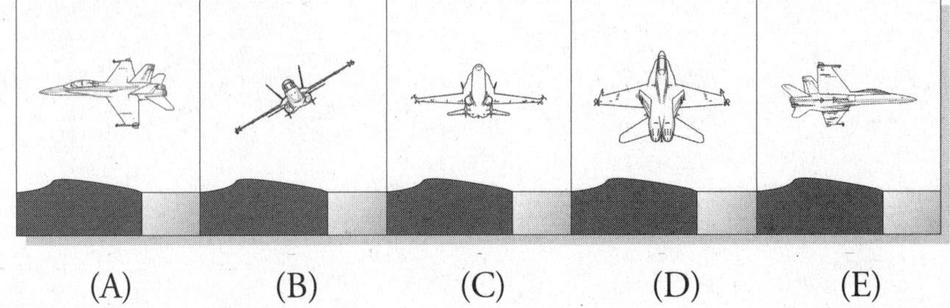

22.

(A) (B) (C) (D) (E)

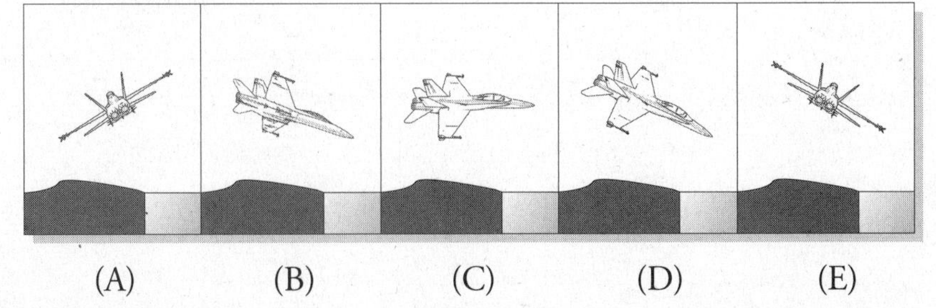

23.

(A) (B) (C) (D) (E)

24.

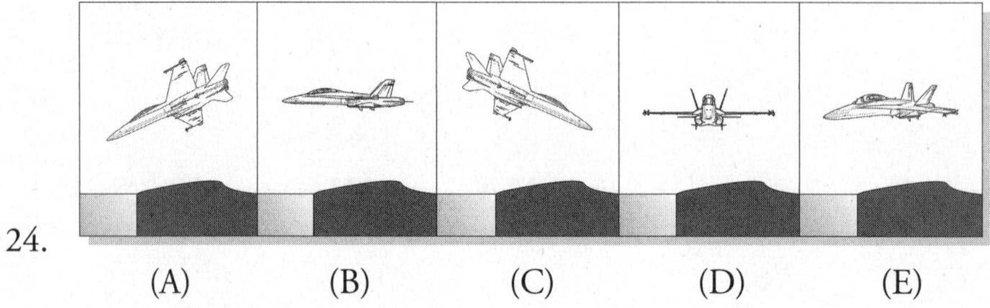

(A) (B) (C) (D) (E)

25.

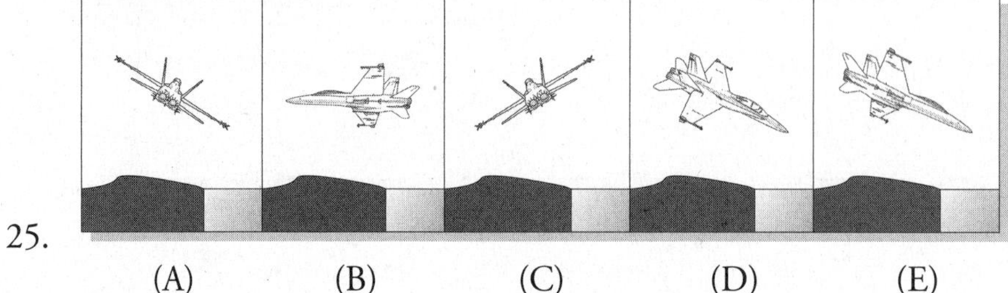

(A) (B) (C) (D) (E)

Subtest 5—Aviation/Nautical Information

Directions: This subtest measures your knowledge of general aviation principles and nautical information and terms, especially as it applies to naval nautical practices.

The subtest consists of 30 questions that must be completed in 15 minutes.

Choose the answer that best answers the question or completes the statement.

1. Two nautical miles are equal to __________.
   (A) 2 statute miles
   (B) 1.15 statute miles
   (C) 2.3 statute miles
   (D) 3 statute miles
   (E) 3.2 statute miles

2. "Zulu Time" refers to __________.
   (A) Pacific Standard Time (PST)
   (B) Eastern Standard Time (EST)
   (C) Daylight Savings Time
   (D) the time in Greenwich, England
   (E) the time on the Equator

3. An aircraft instructed to land on runway 23L would establish an approach heading of __________.
   (A) 023 degrees
   (B) 230 degrees
   (C) 23 feet AGL
   (D) 230 feet AGL
   (E) 23 feet level flight

4. Supersonic means
   (A) faster than the speed of light.
   (B) faster than 200 mph.
   (C) faster than the speed of sound.
   (D) cruise speed.
   (E) really loud.

5. What does the term "yaw" mean?
   (A) directional turning from the tail section
   (B) rate of descent
   (C) rate of climb
   (D) airspeed
   (E) bank

6. The compartment on a ship that serves as the kitchen is called the __________.
   (A) bulkhead
   (B) dining compartment
   (C) chow compartment
   (D) galley
   (E) plane-staff

7. The "IFF" on a military aircraft
   (A) indicates free flow of fuel.
   (B) indicates free flow of air into the jet engine compressor.
   (C) indicates rate of indicated free fall of a power-off glide.
   (D) indicates whether an aircraft is an enemy or an ally.
   (E) determines the flap positions.

8. An aircraft is flying straight and level at 15,000 feet at a constant airspeed of 180 knots, with a 3-degree nose up attitude. If the pilot applies thrust to bring the airspeed up to 200 knots, but applies no pressure to the stick, the aircraft will __________.
   (A) climb
   (B) descend
   (C) remain at a constant altitude
   (D) bank
   (E) stall

9. The control system that is used to relieve the pilot from having to maintain constant pressure on the flight controls is the __________.
   (A) pitch system
   (B) the gyroscopic system
   (C) the trim system
   (D) the parasitic system
   (E) the pitot static system

10. The right-hand side of the ship is known as __________.

    (A) the stern
    (B) the bow
    (C) the hull
    (D) the port side
    (E) the starboard side

11. Which of the following is not a primary flight control?

    (A) aileron
    (B) rudder
    (C) elevator
    (D) flaps
    (E) none of the above

12. What are the four forces that act on an aircraft in flight?

    (A) lift, bank, inertia, and gravity
    (B) bank, weight, inertia, and drag
    (C) lift, resistance, gravity, and drag
    (D) acceleration, drag, weight, and gravity
    (E) lift, thrust, weight, and drag

13. On an aircraft carrier, the lee helmsman

    (A) maintains the engines.
    (B) steers the ship.
    (C) acts as the Officer of the Day (OD).
    (D) controls the ship's speed.
    (E) serves as the principal assistant to the Captain.

14. In aircraft communications, when a flight is identified as "heavy," such as "Foxtrot 29er heavy, you are cleared to land on runway 28L," the word "heavy" means

    (A) more than $\frac{1}{2}$ full on fuel.
    (B) fully fueled.
    (C) more than 250,000 pounds of gross weight.
    (D) passengers on board.
    (E) unexpended munitions on board.

15. An aircraft on a heading of 300 degrees is heading __________.

    (A) northeast
    (B) southeast
    (C) east
    (D) west
    (E) northwest

16. On the ground, an aircraft is steered by

    (A) moving the stick or turning the yoke.
    (B) engine thrust.
    (C) pushing on the rudder peddles.
    (D) applying turning trim.
    (E) moving the ailerons.

17. A ship traveling at the rate of 10 knots will cover how many nautical miles in one hour?

    (A) 10 nautical miles
    (B) 8 nautical miles
    (C) 11.5 nautical miles
    (D) 5 nautical miles
    (E) 8.5 nautical miles

18. The body of a ship, excluding sails, masts, riggings, and yards is called the __________.

    (A) keel
    (B) hull
    (C) foreline
    (D) bulkhead
    (E) main stay

19. A minimally safe airspeed descent is principally used

    (A) for low-level flight patterns.
    (B) for normal landing approaches.
    (C) when flaps are inoperative.
    (D) on runways above sea level.
    (E) when clearing obstacles during landing.

20. The force indicated by the arrow in the below graphic represents __________.

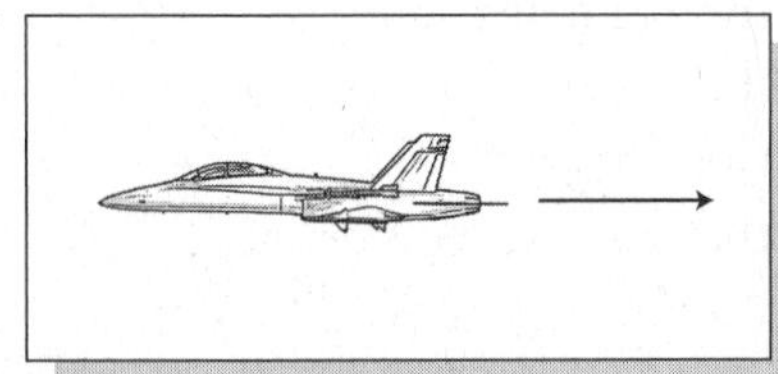

    (A) lift
    (B) drag
    (C) weight
    (D) thrust
    (E) none of the above

21. When entering a climb from level flight, the weight of the aircraft

    (A) results in increased drag.
    (B) results in decreased drag.
    (C) is directly perpendicular to the flight path.
    (D) results in increased angle of attack.
    (E) results in decreased angle of attack.

22. In Navy-speak, the term "Bravo Zulu" means

    (A) repeat.
    (B) is an expression of time.
    (C) well done.
    (D) ignore the last order.
    (E) report to the Captain.

23. The morning watch on a naval vessel occurs during the hours of

    (A) 8:00 A.M. and 12:00 noon.
    (B) 6:00 A.M. and 11:00 A.M.
    (C) 4:00 A.M. and 8:00 A.M.
    (D) 7:00 A.M. and 10:00 A.M.
    (E) 6:00 A.M. and 12:00 noon.

24. In creating lift, the relationship between the speed of the wind moving underneath the wing, compared to the speed of the wind moving over the wing can best be described as

    (A) the air moving over the wing moves faster than the air moving under the wing.
    (B) the air moving under the wing moves faster than the air moving over the wing.
    (C) the air moving under the wing moves at the same speed as the air moving over it.
    (D) the airflow moving over the wing stops.
    (E) the airflow moving under the wing stops.

25. Depressing the left rudder pedal would move the tail of the aircraft __________.

    (A) right
    (B) left
    (C) up
    (D) down
    (E) none of the above

26. Relative to the aircraft's speed over the ground, to maintain the same amount of lift, an aircraft must generally travel ____________ at 10,000 feet than it does at 1,000 feet.

    (A) slower
    (B) faster
    (C) the same speed
    (D) either (A) or (C)
    (E) either (B) or (C)

27. Turbulence is caused by

(A) convective air currents.
(B) obstructions to wind flow.
(C) wind shear.
(D) none of the above
(E) all of the above

28. Moving the control stick to the right or left affects which aircraft controls?

(A) flaps
(B) ailerons
(C) elevator
(D) vertical stabilizer
(E) trim tabs

29. On a ship, the "head" is

(A) the keel of the ship.
(B) the control room.
(C) the toilet.
(D) the Captain.
(E) the main sailing mast.

30. Flaps are generally used

(A) during takeoff.
(B) during landings.
(C) at high altitudes.
(D) during coordinated turns.
(E) both (A) and (B)

Subtest 6 – Aviation Supplemental Test

Directions: On this subtest you will experience a review of the previous five subtests. You may see questions that are exactly the same as questions you've previously answered; you may see questions that appear to be the same, but are slightly different; or you may see questions that are entirely different from those you answered previously. The results of this subtest are fed into a proprietary algorithm that affects the composite scores used for pilot and flight officer selections.

Read the questions carefully, then choose the response that best answers the question.

This subtest has 34 questions that must be answered in 25 minutes.

1. If each brick is 3 inches wide and 5 inches long, how many bricks would you need to build a wall that will measure 10 feet by 16 feet?

   (A) 1,536
   (B) 1,302
   (C) 980
   (D) 940

2. 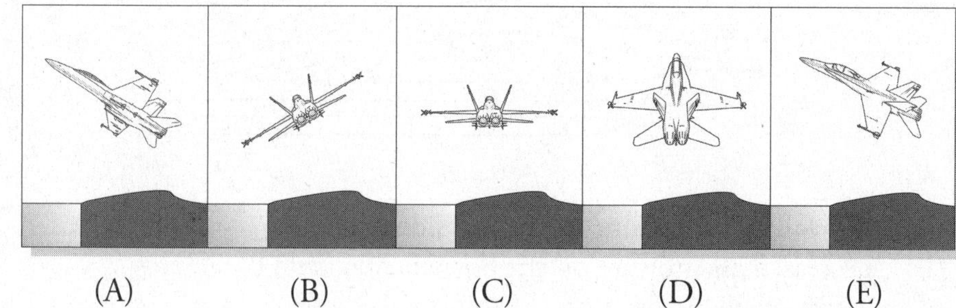

   (A) (B) (C) (D) (E)

3. The distance in miles around a circular course with a radius of 35 miles is __________. (use $pi = \frac{22}{7}$)

(A) 110 miles
(B) 156 miles
(C) 220 miles
(D) 440 miles

Question 4 is based on the following paragraph.

"The 20th century has been a time of amazing change for women. When the century began, women in the United States did not have even the fundamental human right to vote and were largely absent, save in stereotyped roles, from the American workplace including the Federal workplace. Today, women represent 42.8 percent of the permanent Federal workforce, compared to 46.4 percent in the Civilian Labor Force (CLF). The most important single factor in attracting and retaining women is direct, conscientious involvement by managers. Managers can identify where targeted recruiting efforts will best succeed and stimulate interest in public service careers. And at every phase of careers in public service, managers must mentor and lead their employees to obtain optimal results."

4. Men comprise about ________ of the civilian labor force.

(A) 46 percent
(B) 54 percent
(C) 50 percent
(D) 65 percent

5. The following diagram depicts airflow around the wing of an aircraft. Most of the lift is caused by

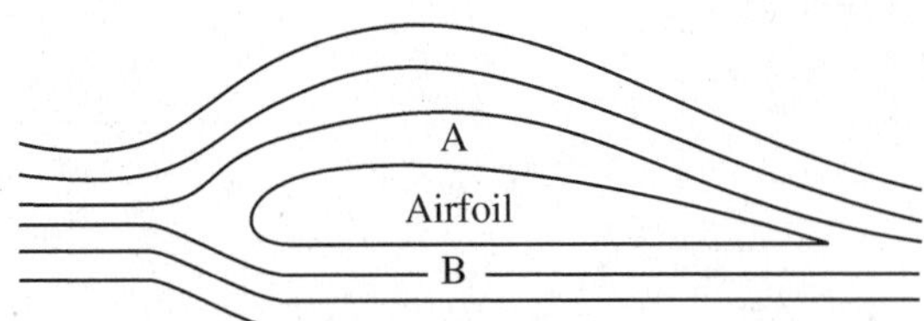

(A) decreased air pressure on the top side (side A).
(B) decreased air pressure on the bottom side (side B).
(C) increased air pressure on the top side (side A).
(D) increased air pressure on the bottom side (side B).

6.

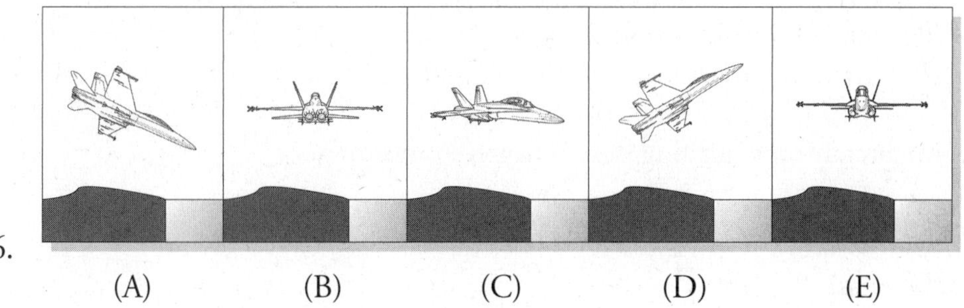

(A) (B) (C) (D) (E)

7.

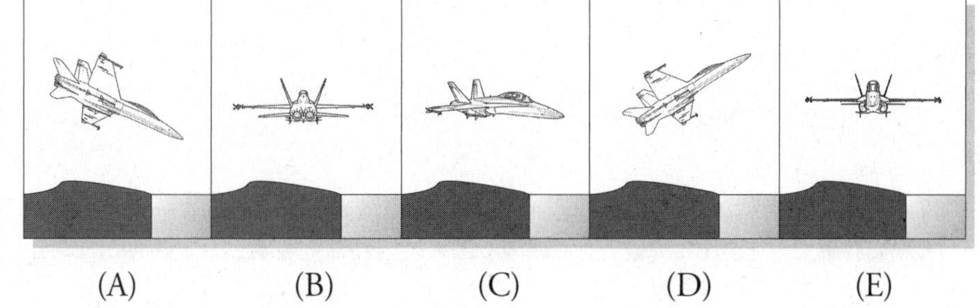

(A) (B) (C) (D) (E)

8. Dilated most nearly means

   (A) cleared
   (B) clouded
   (C) decreased
   (D) enlarged

9. The four aerodynamic forces acting on an airplane are

   (A) drag, gravity, power, and velocity.
   (B) drag, friction, power, and velocity.
   (C) drag, lift, thrust, and weight.
   (D) friction, power, velocity, and weight.

10. An aircraft on a heading of 090 degrees is heading __________.

    (A) north
    (B) south
    (C) east
    (D) west

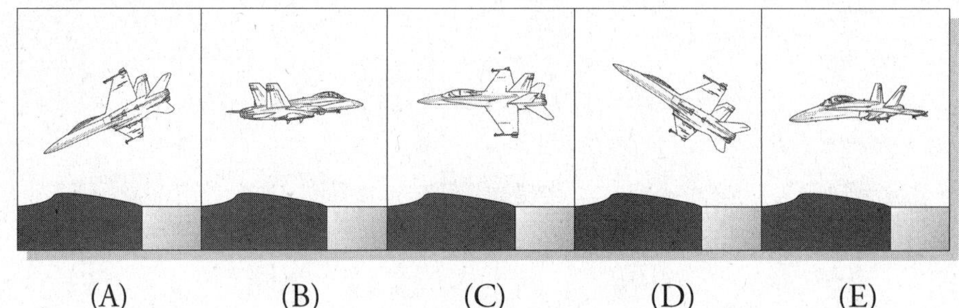

11. (A) (B) (C) (D) (E)

12. An athlete jogs 15 laps around a circular track. If the total distance jogged is 3 kilometers, what is the distance around the track?

    (A) 0.2 meters
    (B) 2 meters
    (C) 20 meters
    (D) 200 meters

13. A crate containing a tool weighs 12 pounds. If the tool weighs 9 pounds, 9 ounces, how much does the crate weigh?

    (A) 2 pounds, 7 ounces
    (B) 2 pounds, 9 ounces
    (C) 3 pounds, 3 ounces
    (D) 3 pounds, 7 ounces

14. 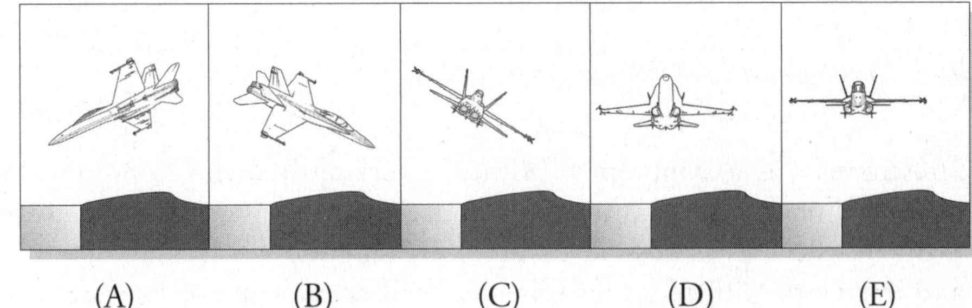

    (A) (B) (C) (D) (E)

15. The forenoon watch on a naval vessel occurs during the hours of

    (A) 8:00 A.M. and 12:00 noon.
    (B) 6:00 A.M. and 11:00 A.M.
    (C) 4:00 A.M. and 8:00 A.M.
    (D) 7:00 A.M. and 10:00 A.M.

16. If $3^n = 9$, what is the value of 4^{n+1}?

    (A) 35
    (B) 64
    (C) 52
    (D) 22

Question 17 is based on the following paragraph.

"Many factors must be considered when a police officer is deciding whether or not to make an arrest. If an arrest is not considered legal, it could mean that some evidence will not be allowed in court. An arrest made too early may tip off a suspect before evidence can be found. On the other hand, an officer must also realize that if an arrest is delayed too long, the suspect may run away or the evidence may be destroyed. In all cases, an arrest takes away from a person the very important right to liberty."

17. On the basis of the above passage, a judge may refuse to accept evidence of a crime if

    (A) it interfered with the suspect's right of liberty.
    (B) it was collected during an illegal arrest.
    (C) it was found before the suspect was tipped off.
    (D) it was found after the suspect was tipped off.

Question 18 is based on the following paragraph.

"Absenteeism is a symptom of difficult working or living conditions or of individual maladjustment. It can be controlled by eliminating or mitigating as many of its causes as possible and by increasing job satisfaction. Spot surveys and interviews with returning absentees will reveal some of the causes, while constant effort and ingenuity are necessary to find workable solutions since remedies are not universally applicable."

18. The passage above best supports the statement that

    (A) spot surveys and interviews are the proper cures for absenteeism.
    (B) individual maladjustment is the cause of lack of job satisfaction.
    (C) absenteeism will end as soon as all causes have been discovered.
    (D) absenteeism cures are not equally effective in all cases.

19. Moving the control stick to the right or left affects which of the following aircraft controls?

    (A) flaps
    (B) ailerons
    (C) elevator
    (D) vertical stabilizer

20.

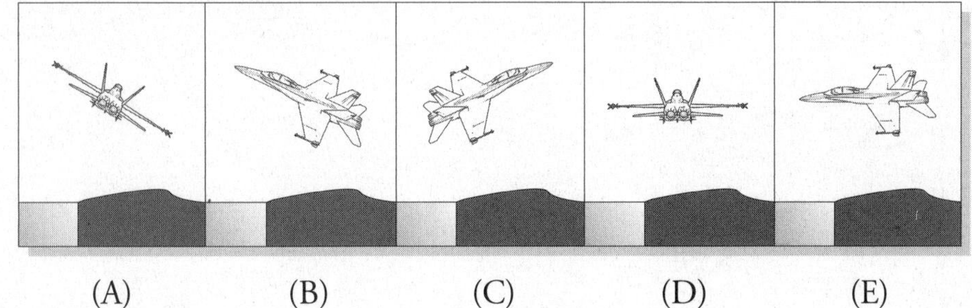

(A) (B) (C) (D) (E)

21. Nonpareil most nearly means __________.

(A) resourceful
(B) excellent
(C) trivial
(D) makeshift

22. Which wrench would require more force to turn the bolt?

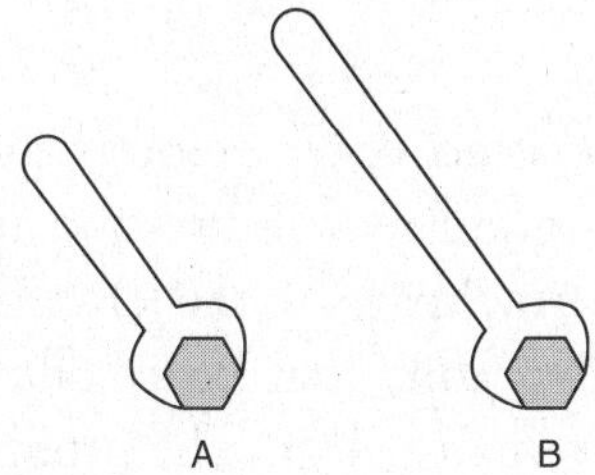

(A) Wrench A
(B) Wrench B
(C) no difference
(D) none of the above

23. 10^x divided by 10^y equals

(A) $10^{x/y}$
(B) 10^{xy}
(C) 10^{x+y}
(D) 10^{x-y}

24. Samantha worked 30 hours last week, earning $418. If she is paid $432 this week, how many hours will she have worked?

    (A) 31
    (B) 32
    (C) 33
    (D) 34

25.

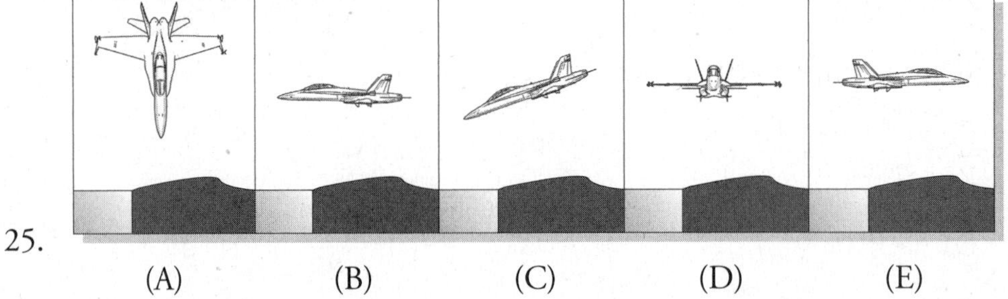

(A) (B) (C) (D) (E)

Question 26 is based on the following paragraph.

"The recipient gains an impression of a typewritten letter before beginning to read the message. Factors that provide for a good first impression include margins and spacing that are visually pleasing, formal parts of the letter that are correctly placed according to the style of the letter, copy that is free of obvious erasures and overstrikes, and transcript that is even and clear. The problem for the secretary is how to produce that first, positive impression."

26. According to the passage above, the addressee very quickly judges the quality of the typed letter by

    (A) counting the number of erasures and overstrikes.
    (B) looking at the spacing and cleanliness of the transcript.
    (C) measuring the margins to ascertain whether they are proper.
    (D) reading the date line and address for errors.

27. Using the 24–hour clock, 10:00 P.M. would be expressed as __________.

(A) 2100 hours
(B) 2200 hours
(C) 0800 hours
(D) 1800 hours

28. Two nautical miles is equal to __________.

(A) 2 statute miles
(B) 1.15 statute miles
(C) 2.3 statute miles
(D) 3 statute miles

29. An aircraft instructed to land on runway 14R would establish an approach heading of __________.

(A) 014 degrees
(B) 140 degrees
(C) 14 feet AGL
(D) 140 feet AGL

30. 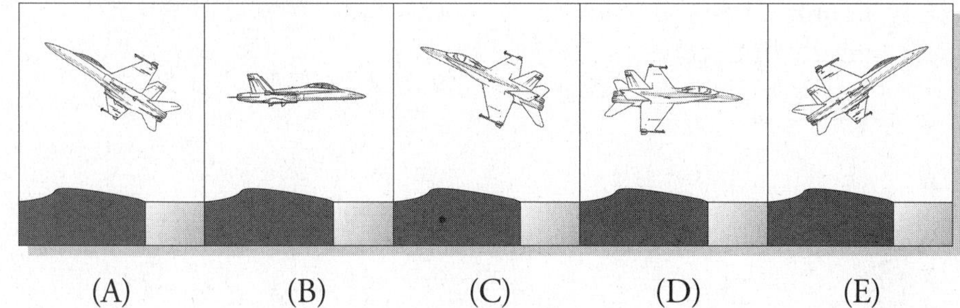

(A) (B) (C) (D) (E)

31. The sum of the angle measures of a hexagon is __________.

(A) 360°
(B) 540°
(C) 720°
(D) 900°

32.

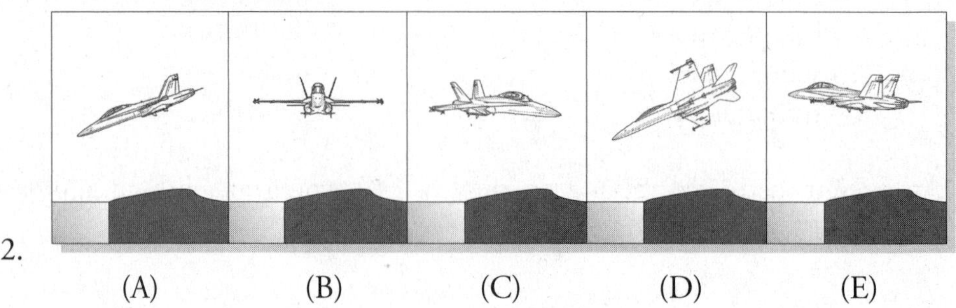

(A) (B) (C) (D) (E)

Question 33 is based on the following paragraph.

"The two systems of weights and measures are the English system and the metric system. The metric system was first adopted in France in 1795 and is now used in most countries of the world. The British recently changed their system of weights and measures to the metric system. However, in the United States, there has been much opposition to this change. It would cost billions of dollars to change all our weights and measures to the metric system."

33. The metric system is actually used
   (A) in all of Europe except Great Britain.
   (B) in almost all countries of the world.
   (C) in only a few countries.
   (D) mostly in Europe.

34.

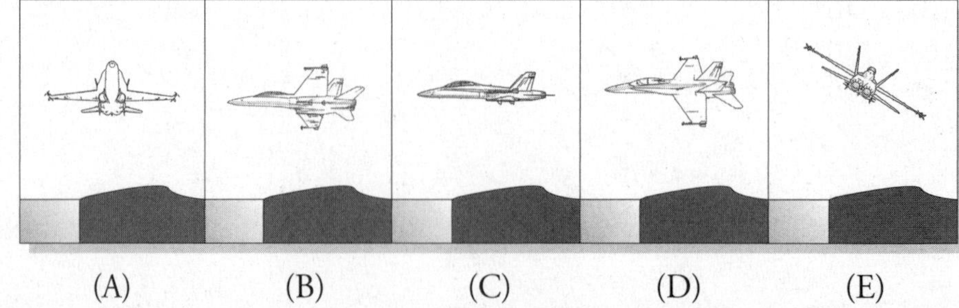

(A) (B) (C) (D) (E)

Answer Key

PRACTICE TEST 6

Subtest 1—Math Skills

1. D
2. B
3. C
4. B
5. C
6. A
7. D
8. C
9. A
10. C
11. D
12. B
13. C
14. C
15. B
16. B
17. C
18. B
19. C
20. B
21. A
22. A
23. D
24. D
25. D
26. D
27. D
28. D
29. C
30. D

Subtest 2—Reading Skills

1. B
2. C
3. D
4. C
5. B
6. D
7. B
8. D
9. B
10. A
11. C
12. B
13. A
14. A
15. B
16. C
17. D
18. B
19. C
20. A
21. C
22. A
23. B
24. A
25. D
26. D
27. D

Subtest 3—Mechanical Comprehension

1. C
2. A
3. D
4. B
5. A
6. B
7. A
8. A
9. C
10. C
11. B
12. D
13. A
14. C
15. B
16. B
17. A
18. C
19. C
20. C
21. C
22. B
23. B
24. A
25. A
26. D
27. C
28. A
29. C
30. A

Subtest 4—Spatial Apperception

1. A
2. C
3. B
4. C
5. D
6. B
7. E
8. D
9. D
10. B
11. D
12. C
13. C
14. A
15. B
16. A
17. E
18. E
19. D
20. C
21. A
22. B
23. D
24. E
25. A

Subtest 5–Aviation/Nautical Information

1. C	7. D	13. D	19. E	25. A
2. D	8. A	14. C	20. B	26. B
3. B	9. C	15. E	21. A	27. E
4. C	10. E	16. C	22. C	28. B
5. A	11. D	17. A	23. C	29. C
6. D	12. E	18. B	24. A	30. E

Subtest 6–Aviation Supplemental Test

1. A	8. D	15. A	22. A	29. B
2. C	9. C	16. B	23. D	30. D
3. C	10. C	17. B	24. A	31. C
4. B	11. B	18. D	25. B	32. E
5. A	12. D	19. B	26. B	33. B
6. C	13. A	20. A	27. B	34. D
7. E	14. E	21. B	28. C	

Answer Explanations to Practice Test

SUBTEST 1—MATH SKILLS

1. **(D) \$70.88.** First, change the percentage (5.5%) to a decimal (.055). Multiply by the amount of the original cost $.055 \times 75 = 4.12$. This is the amount of the discount. Finally, subtract this amount from the original price: $\$75.00 - 4.12 = \$70.88$.
2. **(B) $6x^2y + 2xy$.** $2x(3xy + y) = 2x(3xy) + 2x(y) = 6x^2y + 2xy$.
3. **(C) 12.86 square feet.** The area of the shaded portion is the area of the square minus the area of the circle. The area of the square is 16 square feet (4^2 or 4×4). The area of the circle is $\pi(r^2)$ or $\pi(1^2) = 3.14 \times 1$ or 3.14. The area of the shaded portion is $16 - 3.14 = 12.86$.
4. **(B) \$1,622.50.** Supplier #1 provides soda for the cheapest price. $\$3.50 \times 400 = \$1,400$. Supplier #3 provides hot dogs for the cheapest price. $\$0.44 \times 100 = \$44.00$. Supplier #4 provides hamburger for the cheapest price $\$0.68 \times 150 = \$102.00$. Supplier # 3 sells potato chips for the cheapest price. $\$2.55 \times 30 = \$76.50$. $\$1,400 + \$44.00 + \$102.00 + \$76.50 = \$1,622.50$
5. **(C) 10%.** Simple interest can be computed with the formula $I = Prt$, where I is the interest, P is the principle invested, r is the interest rate, and t is equal to time.

   $I = Prt$

   $150 = (500)r(3)$

   $150 = 1500r$

   $\frac{150}{1500} = r$

   $r = .10$

   $r = 10\%$
6. **(A) 2.73 hours.** Let x = the number of hours to paint the room together. In 1 hour Susan can do $\frac{1}{6}$ of the job, while Tom can do $\frac{1}{5}$ of the job.

   $\frac{1}{6}x + \frac{1}{5}x = 1$ (where 1 represents 100% of the job)

   $(\frac{1}{6} + \frac{1}{5})x = 1$

   $(\frac{5}{30} + \frac{6}{30})x = 1$

   $\frac{11}{30}x = 1$

   $x = \frac{30}{11}$

   $x = 2.73$ hours
7. **(D) 13.6398×10^7.** To multiply scientific notation, first multiply the base of both numbers ($5.37 \times 2.54 = 13.6398$). Next, add the exponents ($2 + 5 = 7$).
8. **(C) $-28x - 43$.**

   $-7(4x) - 7(5) - 8$

   $-28x - 35 - 8$

   $-28x - 43$

9. **(A) 2.**

$\frac{1}{2}x - \frac{1}{10} = \frac{1}{5}x + \frac{1}{2}$

$10(\frac{1}{2}x - \frac{1}{10}) = 10(\frac{1}{5}x + \frac{1}{2})$

$\frac{10}{2}x - \frac{10}{10} = \frac{10}{5}x + \frac{10}{2}$

$5x - 1 = 2x + 5$

$3x = 6$

$x = 2$

10. **(C) $\frac{9\pi}{2}$ + 12.**

The radius of the half-circle is 3 feet. That means that the length of the base of the triangle is 6 feet (twice the radius of the circle). The area of the triangle is $\frac{1}{2}bh$ or $\frac{1}{2}(4 \times 6) = 12$. The area of the circle is $\pi * r^2$, which is equal to 9π. But, we need $\frac{1}{2}$ of that, so it's $\frac{9\pi}{2}$. Adding the two together we get $\frac{9\pi}{2} + 12$.

11. **(D) 1,536.** To find the area of the brick wall, use the formula $A = lw$ (10 ft $\times$ 16 ft = 160 sq ft). Because the bricks are measured in inches, we convert 160 sq ft to sq in. There are 144 sq inches in a sq ft (160 $\times$ 144 = 23,040 sq in). Next determine the area of one brick (3 $\times$ 5 = 15 sq in). Divide that number into the area of the wall (23,040 ÷ 15 = 1,536 bricks).

12. **(B) $27i^2 - 45i - 42$.**

Use FOIL:

$(9i + 6)(3i - 7)$

$27i^2 - 63i + 18i - 42$

Simplify:

$27i^2 - 45i - 42$

13. **(C) 40 pounds.** Let x = number of pounds of cement. As a ratio, the problem can be stated as 5 parts is to 6 parts as x pounds is to 48 pounds:

$\frac{5}{6} = \frac{x}{48}$

$5 \times 48 = 6x$

$x = \frac{240}{6}$

$x = 40$

14. **(C) 48 square feet.** To determine the area of a rectangle, use the formula $A = lw$ (8 $\times$ 6 = 48).

15. **(B) 15.4 percent.** The equation is $\frac{x}{100} = \frac{4}{26}$.

$\frac{x}{100} = \frac{4}{26}$

$26x = 4 \times 100$

$26x = 400$

$x = \frac{400}{26}$

$x = 15.4$

16. **(B) 639,000.** To convert scientific notation to regulation notation, move the decimal place to the right the same number of spaces as the exponent (in this case, 5).
17. **(C) 14 months.** Let x = number of rental months needed to make the costs equal. This occurs when the purchase price (P) equals the rental cost (R), or $P = R$. We know that P = \$400, and $R = 50 + 25x$.
$R = 50 + 25x$
$400 = 50 + 25x$
$25x = 350$
$x = 14$ months
18. **(B) 1145.** The weight will be 250g plus (1.55 – 0.65)/0.10 units of 100g
250 + 900 = 1150
This is the maximum weight that can be sent at that price. But weights exceeding 250 + 800 will also get charged this amount (that is what the "part thereof" implies).
19. **(C) $x = ny$ where n is an integer.** Rearranging $\frac{x}{y} = n$, results in $x = ny$, which is therefore always true. In choice (A), x and y could both be equal fractions and $\frac{x}{y}$ would be an integer. Answer (D) does not need to be correct. Consider if $\frac{x}{y} = \frac{6}{3}$. Then $\frac{y}{x} = \frac{3}{6}$, which is not an integer.
20. **(B) 3.** After constructing the sequence, the pattern becomes obvious.
The average of 1 and 5 = 3.
The average of 1, 5, and 3 = 3.
The average of 1, 5, 3, and 3 = 3.
All subsequent terms = 3.
21. **(A) 3.** This is a quadratic equation. To find n, multiply the last terms in each set of parentheses together.
$(3x + 2)(2x - 5) = ax^2 + kx + n$
$6x^2 - 15x + 2x - 10 = ax^2 + kx + n$
$6x^2 - 13x - 10 = ax^2 + kx + n$
$a = 6$
$k = -13$
$n = -10$
Substitute and solve:
$a - n + k = 6 + 10 - 13 = 3$
22. **(A) $5x + 14y$.**
Step one: $2x + 5y$
Step two: $3(2x + 5y) = 6x + 15y$
Step three: $(6x + 15y) - (x + y) = 6x + 15y - x - y$
Simplify: $5x + 14y$
23. **(D) 0.2025.**
Four tenths = 0.4
Five thousandths = 0.005
The average is (0.4 + 0.005)/2 = 0.2025
24. **(D) 9.** A natural number that has no other factors except 1 and itself is a prime number. The number 9 is divisible by 1, 3, and 9.

25. **(D) 64.** $3^n = 9$; $n = 2$. $4^{n+1} = 4^{2+1} = 4^3 = 64$.
26. **(D)** $\frac{5}{6}$**.** $\frac{3x}{5y} = \frac{1}{2}$; $6x = 5y$; $6\frac{x}{y} = 5$; $\frac{x}{y} = \frac{5}{6}$.
27. **(D) 200 pounds per square foot.** 200 feet × 200 feet = 40,000 square feet of floor area; There are 2,000 pounds in a ton; 4,000 tons × 2,000 = 8,000,000 pounds; $\frac{8,000,000}{40,000} = 200$ pounds.
28. **(D) $600,000.** One million × 12 = 12 million = 12,000,000 (nickels per year); 12,000,000 × .05 = $600,000.00.
29. **(C) 2.4 grams.** There are 200 cigarettes in a carton (20 × 10 = 200). 12 mg × 200 = 2400 mg of tar in 200 cigarettes. 2400 mg = 2.4 grams.
30. **(D) $1,271,700.** $1,100,500 × .07 = $77,035; $1,100,500 + $77,035 = $1,177,535 = this year's budget. $1,177,535 × .08 = $94,203; $1,177,535 + $94,203 = $1,271,738 which is closest to option (D).

SUBTEST 2—READING SKILLS

1. **(B) he died.** The passage states that William would have received the imperial crown at Rome, except he drowned while attempting to cross an ice-bound marsh.
2. **(C) 75 percent.** One out of four (25 percent) Californians were born outside of the United States, which leaves 75 percent born inside of the United States.
3. **(D) impede.** Used as a verb, *encumber* means to impede with obstacles.
4. **(C) unavoidable.** Used as an adjective, *inevitable* means impossible to avoid or prevent.
5. **(B) harmless.** Used as an adjective, *innocuous* means having no adverse effect.
6. **(D) absorb.** Used as a verb, *assimilate* means to incorporate and absorb into the mind.
7. **(B) War is an Instrument of National Policy.** The primary focus of the passage is discussing war as a means of achieving political objectives.
8. **(D) expending.** In the context of the subject matter, it is obvious that the word *expending* should be replaced with the word *saving.*
9. **(B) invulnerable.** Used as an adjective, *invulnerable* means unable to be damaged or hurt, which relates to the context of the sentence.
10. **(A) petulant.** Used as a noun, petulant means irritating or annoyed, which is in context with the meaning of the sentence.
11. **(C) experimental.** In the context of the paragraph, the word *experimental* should be replaced with the word *proven.*
12. **(B) refill.** Used as an adjective, *replenish* means to fill again.
13. **(A) denunciation**. Used as a noun, *diatribe* means a bitter, abusive denunciation.
14. **(A) one.** The tobacco-roller is sleeping, while the boy and the hunter remain awake by the fire.
15. **(B) 1819.** According to the passage, Red Cloud was 35 years old in 1854.
16. **(C) slave.** Used as a noun, *vassal* means servant or slave.
17. **(D) low-income women.** According to the passage, low-income women took in fewer calories, but had a higher Body Mass Index.
18. **(B) poverty levels are higher than in the pre-1994 level.** This information can be derived from the fifth sentence.

19. **(C) sequel.** Used as a noun, *sequel* means a subsequent or additional part.
20. **(A) conspicuous.** Used as an adjective, *prominent* means highly visible, noticeable, or conspicuous.
21. **(C) emphasize the fit of organizational parts.** The first sentence of the passage states that organizations must achieve coherence among the component parts to function effectively.
22. **(A) has absorbed words from other languages.** The first sentence states that there is scarcely a language spoken among people that has not some representative in English speech.
23. **(B) people of different nations may not consider matters in the same light.** The first two sentences indicate that foreign ministries try to explain the viewpoints of one nation in terms understood by ministries of another in order to overcome the difficulty of one nation trying to understand the viewpoints of another.
24. **(A) do not need a college degree to do programming work.** The last sentence states that half of the programmers employed by business are promoted to their positions from within the organization without regard to education. This implies that a college degree is not needed to do programming work.
25. **(D) 150 foot-candles.** Copying figures onto a payroll is a "very difficult seeing" task for which the recommended lighting is 150 foot-candles.
26. **(D) the personal appearance of a candidate should not be considered of primary importance when interviewing persons for most positions.** The second sentence states that personal appearance is a matter of distinctly secondary importance in most positions.
27. **(D) providing postal service.** Although providing postal service is an important government service, it is not an aspect of the fundamental function of government as it is not protection of life and property against antisocial individuals within the country or enemies from without.

SUBTEST 3—MECHANICAL COMPREHENSION

1. **(C) energy.** Calorie is a unit of measurement for heat.
2. **(A) 1100 feet per second.** The speed of sound varies, however, with altitude, air density, and temperature.
3. **(D) decreased air pressure on the top side (side A).** Air flowing over the top creates a vacuum, while the air flowing over the bottom remains at approximately the same air pressure. The differences in pressure cause an upward lift.
4. **(B) Pulley 4 would spin faster than Pulley 3.** In a series of pulleys or gears, the larger the pulley or gear, the slower it will turn.
5. **(A) hacksaw.** The hacksaw is specifically designed to cut metal.
6. **(B) seesaw.** A seesaw is a plank, mounted on a fulcrum.
7. **(A) 67 pounds.** The formula is $w \times d = f \times d_2$. $(200 \times 10 = f \times 30)$.
   $2000 = 30f$
   $f = 66.66666$ pounds
8. **(A) Wrench A.** Because the handle is shorter, there is less leverage, and the wrench would require a greater application of force to turn than Wrench B.

9. **(C) 15.** There are three sections of rope, which means only $\frac{1}{3}$ of the force is required to lift the weight, but the rope must be pulled 3 times the height that the weight moves.
10. **(C) 6.** A V-6 engine has six pistons, and one crank per piston.
11. **(B) 2.** Pulleys A, B, and C will turn at the same rate. Because Pulley D is $\frac{1}{2}$ the size of the other pulleys, it will revolve two times for each revolution made by the other pulleys.
12. **(D) 20 feet.** In order to reduce the amount of force by a factor of 4, we would need a ramp 4 with a length of 4 times the distance of the height we wish to raise the weight.
13. **(A) 33,000 foot-pounds of work per minute**. One horsepower of force is equal to 33,000 foot-pounds of work performed in a one-minute time period.
14. **(C) four.** Pulleys A, C, and D are rotating clockwise, while Pulley B is rotating counterclockwise.
15. **(B) wheel B.** Assuming equal RPMs, the wheel with the largest diameter will travel the greatest distance in an equal amount of time.
16. **(B) 3.** Every other gear in a series revolves in the same direction.
17. **(A) 1**. Gear 1 has 10 teeth and gear 2 has 20 teeth.
18. **(C) 3.** The cam has three protruding points, each of which will open the valve.
19. **(C) 900 pounds.** The piston on the left is 2 inches in diameter (1-inch radius), while the piston on the right is 6 inches in diameter (3-inch radius). The area of the two pistons is $Pi * r^2$. The area of the left piston is therefore 3.14, while the area of the piston on the right is 28.26. The piston on the right is 9 times larger than the piston on the left. What that means is that any force applied to the left-hand piston will appear 9 times greater on the right-hand piston.
20. **(C) Tank A and C**. Both tanks have an inflow greater than their outflow.
21. **(C) axle.** While the axle supports the wheels, it is not part of the braking system. The master cylinder provides hydraulic force to press discs (or pads) against the wheels of a vehicle, making use of the force of friction to slow (or stop) the wheels.
22. **(B) 110 pounds.** $\frac{2}{3}$ of the weight of the block (100 lbs) will be supported by the left scale because the block is $\frac{2}{3}$ closer to the left than the right. The board is evenly placed, so each scale will support $\frac{1}{2}$ of its weight (10 lbs).
23. **(B) mechanical advantage.** When a machine magnifies force to make work easier, the magnification factor is termed mechanical advantage.
24. **(A) the distance between the threads of a screw**. Each time a screw makes one complete turn, it advances the distance of its pitch.
25. **(A) its velocity does not change.** An object at equilibrium may be at rest, but not necessarily so. When two or more forces act to cancel the effects of each other, velocity does not change and the condition is termed equilibrium.
26. **(D) all of the above**. A simple machine makes work easier.

27. **(C) buoyancy.** The force that acts in an upward direction on an object submerged in a liquid or gas is called buoyancy.
28. **(A) work/time.** In physics, power is the amount of work done per unit of time.
29. **(C) gravity.** Gravity is the force that causes objects to move toward the center of Earth.
30. **(A) friction.** The friction of the wheels against the road and the air against the vehicle causes the car to slow down, and ultimately come to a stop.

SUBTEST 4—SPATIAL APPERCEPTION

Question	Answer	Pitch	Bank	Direction
1.	A	Nose Up	Zero	Out to Sea
2.	C	Nose Up	Left	Out to Sea
3.	B	Nose Down	Left	Out to Sea
4.	C	Nose Down	Zero	Down the coastline
5.	D	Zero	Left	Out to Sea
6.	B	Nose Up	Zero	Out to Sea
7.	E	Nose Up	Left	Out to Sea
8.	D	Nose Down	Left	Out to Sea
9.	D	Nose Down	Zero	Out to Sea
10.	B	Zero	Left	Down the coastline
11.	D	Zero	Left	Up the coastline
12.	C	Zero	Zero	Up the coastline
13.	C	Nose Up	Right	Out to sea
14.	A	Nose Down	Zero	Out to sea
15.	B	Zero	Left	Up the coastline
16.	A	Zero	Left	Out to Sea
17.	E	Nose Down	Right	Out to Sea
18.	E	Zero	Zero	Out to sea
19.	D	Nose Down	Zero	Out to sea
20.	C	Zero	Right	Out to sea
21.	A	Nose Up	Right	Out to sea
22.	B	Zero	Right	Down the coastline
23.	D	Nose Down	Right	Out to sea
24.	E	Zero	Zero	45 degrees right of coastline
25.	A	Zero	Right	Up the coastline

SUBTEST 5—AVIATION/NAUTICAL INFORMATION

1. **(C) 2.3 statute miles.** A nautical mile is equal to 1.15 statute miles (2 × 1.15 = 2.3).
2. **(D) the time in Greenwich England**. Its official name is Coordinated Universal Time or UTC. This time zone had previously been called Greenwich Mean Time (GMT) but was replaced with UTC in 1972 as the official world time standard changed.
3. **(B) 230 degrees.** Runway numbers are associated with the compass direction that the runway is aligned with. 23L means a heading of 230 degrees (the "L" stands for the left-hand runway at airports with two runways aligned in the same direction). Runway 18 would indicate an approach heading of 180, runway 02, an approach heading of 020, etc.
4. **(C) faster than the speed of sound.** An aircraft is said to be going "supersonic" when it exceeds the speed of sound.
5. **(A) directional turning from the tail.** When an aircraft is "yawed," the nose displaces (turns) to the right or left in relation to the direction of flight.
6. **(D) galley.** Kitchens and eating areas on a ship are referred to as "galleys."
7. **(D) indicates whether an aircraft is an enemy or an ally.** IFF stands for "Identification Friend or Foe." It's a component that electronically communicates with other aircraft in the area to determine whether or not they are friendly forces.
8. **(A) climb.** The aircraft has a slight nose-up attitude, which is sufficient for level flight at 180 knots, and increase in airspeed will increase lift, causing the aircraft to climb.
9. **(C) the trim system.** They are designed to help minimize a pilot's workload by aerodynamically assisting movement and position of the flight control surface to which they are attached.
10. **(E) the starboard side.** The front of the ship is the bow, the rear of the ship is the stern, the left-hand side is port, and the right-hand side is starboard.
11. **(D) flaps.** Aircraft flaps are categorized as secondary flight controls.
12. **(E) lift, thrust, weight, and drag.** These are the four primary forces that affect an aircraft in flight.
13. **(D) controls the ship's speed.** The lee helmsman operates the engine order control, telling the engine room what speed to make.
14. **(C) more than 250,000 pounds of gross weight.** The term applies to very large cargo and passenger aircraft.
15. **(E) northwest.** 360 degrees is north, 90 degrees is east, 180 degrees is south, and 270 degrees is west. A heading of 300 falls between 270 and 360, so a heading of 300 would indicate a direction of north and west.
16. **(C) pushing on the rudder pedals.** When nose gear steering is engaged, and the aircraft is moving on the ground, pressing the rudder pedals causes the nose wheel to turn.
17. **(A) 10 nautical miles.** A knot is equivalent to one nautical mile per hour, or 1.15 statute miles per hour.
18. **(B) hull**. The hull is the main body of a ship.
19. **(E) when clearing obstacles during landing.** A minimum safe airspeed descent is a nose-high, power–assisted descent condition principally used for clearing obstacles during a landing approach to a short runway.

20. **(B) drag.** Drag is the force that resists forward motion of the aircraft.
21. **(A) results in increased drag.** When an airplane enters a climb, it changes its flight path from level flight to an inclined plane or climb attitude. In a climb, weight no longer acts in a direction perpendicular to the flight path. It acts in a rearward direction. This causes an increase in total drag.
22. **(C) well done.** It can also be combined with the "negative" signal, spoken or written NEGAT, to say "NEGAT Bravo Zulu," or "not well done."
23. **(C) 4:00 A.M. and 8:00 A.M.** The watch hours are:
Noon to 4:00 P.M. Afternoon watch
4:00 P.M. to 6:00 P.M. First dogwatch
6:00 P.M. to 8:00 P.M. Second dogwatch
8:00 P.M. to midnight. 1st night watch
Midnight to 4:00 A.M. Middle watch or midwatch
4:00 to 8:00 A.M. Morning watch
8:00 A.M. to noon. Forenoon watch
24. **(A) the air moving over the wing moves faster than the air moving under the wing.** This increased speed results in a lower air pressure over the wing, compared to the air pressure under the wing, and creates lift.
25. **(A) right.** Depressing the left rudder pedal would yaw the aircraft to the left. In other words, the tail would displace to the right, while the nose of the aircraft would displace to the left.
26. **(B) faster.** Air is less dense at higher altitudes, so the higher an aircraft flies, the faster it must travel (in relation to the ground) in order to produce the same amount of lift.
27. **(E) all of the above.** Convective air currents, obstructions to wind flow, and wind shear are all major causes of flight turbulence.
28. **(B) ailerons.** Moving the control stick to the left or right causes the ailerons to raise and lower, which results in the aircraft rotating on its horizontal axis (banking).
29. **(C) toilet.** The use of the term "head" to refer to a ship's toilet dates to at least as early as 1708, when Woodes Rogers (English privateer and Governor of the Bahamas) used the word in his book, *A Cruising Voyage Around the World.*
30. **(E) both (A) and (B).** Flaps are secondary flight controls that increase lift and drag. They are primarily used to increase lift during slower airspeeds for takeoffs and landings.

SUBTEST 6—AVIATION SUPPLEMENTAL TEST

1. **(A) 1,536.** To find the area of the brick wall, use the formula $A = lw$ (10 ft × 16 ft = 160 sq ft). Because the bricks are measured in inches, we convert 160 sq ft to sq in. There are 144 sq inches in a sq ft (160 × 144 = 23,040 sq in). Next determine the area of one brick (3 × 5 = 15 sq in). Divide that number into the area of the wall (23,040 ÷ 15 = 1,536 bricks).
2. **(C)** Zero pitch, zero bank, heading up the coastline.
3. **(C) 220 miles.** Circumference = *pi* × diameter; circumference = 22.6 × 69 = 220 miles.
4. **(B) 54 percent.** If women comprise about 46 percent of the civilian labor force, the remaining 54 percent must be comprised of men.

5. **(A) decreased air pressure on the top side (side A).** Air flowing over the top creates a vacuum, while the air flowing over the bottom remains at approximately the same air pressure. The differences in pressure causes an upward lift.
6. **(C)** Zero pitch, zero bank, heading 45 degrees left of the coastline.
7. **(E)** Nose up, zero bank, heading down the coastline.
8. **(D) enlarged.** Used as an adjective, *dilated* means having been widened; expanded.
9. **(C) drag, lift, thrust, and weight.** While the airplane is propelled through the air and sufficient lift is developed to sustain it in flight, there are four forces acting on the airplane. These are: thrust or forward force; lift or upward force; drag or rearward acting force; and weight or downward force.
10. **(C) east.** 360 degrees is north, 90 degrees is east, 180 degrees is south, and 270 degrees is west.
11. **(B)** Zero pitch, zero bank, heading 45 degrees right of the coastline.
12. **(D) 200 meters.** 3 kilometers = 3000 meters; $\frac{3000}{15} = 200$ meters.
13. **(A) 2 pounds, 7 ounces.** 12 pounds = 11 pounds, 16 ounces; weight of tool = 9 pounds, 9 ounces. 11 pounds, 16 ounces minus 9 pounds, 9 ounces = 2 pounds, 7 ounces.
14. **(E)** Zero pitch, zero bank, heading down the coastline.
15. **(A) 8:00 A.M. and 12:00 noon**. The watch hours are:
    Noon to 4:00 P.M. Afternoon watch
    4:00 P.M. to 6:00 P.M. First dogwatch
    6:00 P.M. to 8:00 P.M. Second dogwatch
    8:00 P.M. to midnight. 1st night watch
    Midnight to 4:00 A.M. Middle watch or mid watch
    4:00 to 8:00 A.M. Morning watch
    8:00 A.M. to noon. Forenoon watch
16. **(B) 64.** $3^n = 9$; $n = 2$. $4^{n+1} = 4^{2+1} = 4^3 = 64$.
17. **(B) it was collected during an illegal arrest.** The second sentence indicates that some evidence will not be allowed in court if an arrest is not considered legal.
18. **(D) absenteeism cures are not equally effective in all cases.** The passage states that absenteeism can be controlled, but not eliminated, by mitigating as many of its causes as possible and by increasing job satisfaction. However, remedies for absenteeism are not universally applicable.
19. **(B) ailerons.** Moving the control stick to the left or right causes the ailerons to raise and lower, which results in the aircraft rotating on its horizontal axis (banking).
20. **(A)** Zero pitch, right bank, heading up the coastline.
21. **(B) excellent.** Used as an adjective, *nonpareil* means having no equal or peerless.
22. **(A) wrench A.** Because the handle is shorter, there is less leverage, and the wrench would require a greater application of force to turn than Wrench B.
23. **(D) 10^{x-y}.** To divide powers of the same base, subtract the exponent of the denominator from the exponent of the numerator.

24. **(A) 31.**
Let D = DOLLARS
Let H = HOURS
Let d = dollars
Let h = hours
Given $D = 418$
Given $H = 30$
Given $d = 432$
Formula $\frac{D}{H} = \frac{d}{h}$
$Dh = Hd$ // Expand parentheses
$418h = 30(432)$
$418h = 12960$
$h = 31.0048$
25. **(B)** Zero pitch, zero bank, heading out to sea.
26. **(B) looking at the spacing and cleanliness of the transcript.** The second sentence lists the factors that provide for a good first impression. Spacing and cleanliness of the transcript are included. None of the other options is included among the factors that make for a good first impression.
27. **(B) 2200 hours.** The 24–hour clock consists of four numbers with 0000 as midnight, 0100 as 1:00 A.M., 0200 as 2:00 A.M., etc. 10:00 P.M. would be expressed as 2200.
28. **(C) 2.3 statute miles.** A nautical mile is equal to 1.15 statute miles ($2 \times 1.15 = 2.3$).
29. **(B) 140 degrees.** Runway numbers are associated with the compass direction that the runway is aligned with. 14R means a heading of 140 degrees (the "R" stands for the right-hand runway at airports with two runways aligned in the same direction). Runway 18 would indicate an approach heading of 180, runway 02, an approach heading of 020, etc.
30. **(D)** Zero pitch, right bank, heading out to sea.
31. **(C) 720°.** A hexagon has 6 sides. (Number of sides – 2) × 180 = sum of angles. $4 \times 180 = 720°$.
32. **(E)** Zero pitch, zero bank, heading out to sea.
33. **(B) in almost all countries of the world.** The second sentence indicates that the metric system is now used in most countries of the world.
34. **(D)** Zero pitch, left bank, heading out to sea.

CHAPTER 19

Practice Test for Navy OCS Applicants and Marine Corps/ Coast Guard Aviation Applicants 2

Navy and Marine Corps Aviation Selection Test Battery is used for all Navy Officer Candidate School applicants, as well as other Naval officer flight training candidates. The test is also used for Marine Corps and Coast Guard officers and officer applicants who desire to become commissioned as aviators.

The examination consists of six subtests, totaling 176 questions that must be answered in 140 minutes.

Answer Sheet for Practice Test 7

Subtest 1–Math Skills

1 Ⓐ Ⓑ Ⓒ Ⓓ	9 Ⓐ Ⓑ Ⓒ Ⓓ	17 Ⓐ Ⓑ Ⓒ Ⓓ	24 Ⓐ Ⓑ Ⓒ Ⓓ
2 Ⓐ Ⓑ Ⓒ Ⓓ	10 Ⓐ Ⓑ Ⓒ Ⓓ	18 Ⓐ Ⓑ Ⓒ Ⓓ	25 Ⓐ Ⓑ Ⓒ Ⓓ
3 Ⓐ Ⓑ Ⓒ Ⓓ	11 Ⓐ Ⓑ Ⓒ Ⓓ	19 Ⓐ Ⓑ Ⓒ Ⓓ	26 Ⓐ Ⓑ Ⓒ Ⓓ
4 Ⓐ Ⓑ Ⓒ Ⓓ	12 Ⓐ Ⓑ Ⓒ Ⓓ	20 Ⓐ Ⓑ Ⓒ Ⓓ	27 Ⓐ Ⓑ Ⓒ Ⓓ
5 Ⓐ Ⓑ Ⓒ Ⓓ	13 Ⓐ Ⓑ Ⓒ Ⓓ	21 Ⓐ Ⓑ Ⓒ Ⓓ	28 Ⓐ Ⓑ Ⓒ Ⓓ
6 Ⓐ Ⓑ Ⓒ Ⓓ	14 Ⓐ Ⓑ Ⓒ Ⓓ	22 Ⓐ Ⓑ Ⓒ Ⓓ	29 Ⓐ Ⓑ Ⓒ Ⓓ
7 Ⓐ Ⓑ Ⓒ Ⓓ	15 Ⓐ Ⓑ Ⓒ Ⓓ	23 Ⓐ Ⓑ Ⓒ Ⓓ	30 Ⓐ Ⓑ Ⓒ Ⓓ
8 Ⓐ Ⓑ Ⓒ Ⓓ	16 Ⓐ Ⓑ Ⓒ Ⓓ		

Subtest 2–Reading Skills

1 Ⓐ Ⓑ Ⓒ Ⓓ	8 Ⓐ Ⓑ Ⓒ Ⓓ	15 Ⓐ Ⓑ Ⓒ Ⓓ	22 Ⓐ Ⓑ Ⓒ Ⓓ
2 Ⓐ Ⓑ Ⓒ Ⓓ	9 Ⓐ Ⓑ Ⓒ Ⓓ	16 Ⓐ Ⓑ Ⓒ Ⓓ	23 Ⓐ Ⓑ Ⓒ Ⓓ
3 Ⓐ Ⓑ Ⓒ Ⓓ	10 Ⓐ Ⓑ Ⓒ Ⓓ	17 Ⓐ Ⓑ Ⓒ Ⓓ	24 Ⓐ Ⓑ Ⓒ Ⓓ
4 Ⓐ Ⓑ Ⓒ Ⓓ	11 Ⓐ Ⓑ Ⓒ Ⓓ	18 Ⓐ Ⓑ Ⓒ Ⓓ	25 Ⓐ Ⓑ Ⓒ Ⓓ
5 Ⓐ Ⓑ Ⓒ Ⓓ	12 Ⓐ Ⓑ Ⓒ Ⓓ	19 Ⓐ Ⓑ Ⓒ Ⓓ	26 Ⓐ Ⓑ Ⓒ Ⓓ
6 Ⓐ Ⓑ Ⓒ Ⓓ	13 Ⓐ Ⓑ Ⓒ Ⓓ	20 Ⓐ Ⓑ Ⓒ Ⓓ	27 Ⓐ Ⓑ Ⓒ Ⓓ
7 Ⓐ Ⓑ Ⓒ Ⓓ	14 Ⓐ Ⓑ Ⓒ Ⓓ	21 Ⓐ Ⓑ Ⓒ Ⓓ	

Subtest 3–Mechanical Comprehension

1 Ⓐ Ⓑ Ⓒ Ⓓ	9 Ⓐ Ⓑ Ⓒ Ⓓ	17 Ⓐ Ⓑ Ⓒ Ⓓ	24 Ⓐ Ⓑ Ⓒ Ⓓ
2 Ⓐ Ⓑ Ⓒ Ⓓ	10 Ⓐ Ⓑ Ⓒ Ⓓ	18 Ⓐ Ⓑ Ⓒ Ⓓ	25 Ⓐ Ⓑ Ⓒ Ⓓ
3 Ⓐ Ⓑ Ⓒ Ⓓ	11 Ⓐ Ⓑ Ⓒ Ⓓ	19 Ⓐ Ⓑ Ⓒ Ⓓ	26 Ⓐ Ⓑ Ⓒ Ⓓ
4 Ⓐ Ⓑ Ⓒ Ⓓ	12 Ⓐ Ⓑ Ⓒ Ⓓ	20 Ⓐ Ⓑ Ⓒ Ⓓ	27 Ⓐ Ⓑ Ⓒ Ⓓ
5 Ⓐ Ⓑ Ⓒ Ⓓ	13 Ⓐ Ⓑ Ⓒ Ⓓ	21 Ⓐ Ⓑ Ⓒ Ⓓ	28 Ⓐ Ⓑ Ⓒ Ⓓ
6 Ⓐ Ⓑ Ⓒ Ⓓ	14 Ⓐ Ⓑ Ⓒ Ⓓ	22 Ⓐ Ⓑ Ⓒ Ⓓ	29 Ⓐ Ⓑ Ⓒ Ⓓ
7 Ⓐ Ⓑ Ⓒ Ⓓ	15 Ⓐ Ⓑ Ⓒ Ⓓ	23 Ⓐ Ⓑ Ⓒ Ⓓ	30 Ⓐ Ⓑ Ⓒ Ⓓ
8 Ⓐ Ⓑ Ⓒ Ⓓ	16 Ⓐ Ⓑ Ⓒ Ⓓ		

Subtest 4—Spatial Apperception

1 Ⓐ Ⓑ Ⓒ Ⓓ Ⓔ	8 Ⓐ Ⓑ Ⓒ Ⓓ Ⓔ	14 Ⓐ Ⓑ Ⓒ Ⓓ Ⓔ	20 Ⓐ Ⓑ Ⓒ Ⓓ Ⓔ
2 Ⓐ Ⓑ Ⓒ Ⓓ Ⓔ	9 Ⓐ Ⓑ Ⓒ Ⓓ Ⓔ	15 Ⓐ Ⓑ Ⓒ Ⓓ Ⓔ	21 Ⓐ Ⓑ Ⓒ Ⓓ Ⓔ
3 Ⓐ Ⓑ Ⓒ Ⓓ Ⓔ	10 Ⓐ Ⓑ Ⓒ Ⓓ Ⓔ	16 Ⓐ Ⓑ Ⓒ Ⓓ Ⓔ	22 Ⓐ Ⓑ Ⓒ Ⓓ Ⓔ
4 Ⓐ Ⓑ Ⓒ Ⓓ Ⓔ	11 Ⓐ Ⓑ Ⓒ Ⓓ Ⓔ	17 Ⓐ Ⓑ Ⓒ Ⓓ Ⓔ	23 Ⓐ Ⓑ Ⓒ Ⓓ Ⓔ
5 Ⓐ Ⓑ Ⓒ Ⓓ Ⓔ	12 Ⓐ Ⓑ Ⓒ Ⓓ Ⓔ	18 Ⓐ Ⓑ Ⓒ Ⓓ Ⓔ	24 Ⓐ Ⓑ Ⓒ Ⓓ Ⓔ
6 Ⓐ Ⓑ Ⓒ Ⓓ Ⓔ	13 Ⓐ Ⓑ Ⓒ Ⓓ Ⓔ	19 Ⓐ Ⓑ Ⓒ Ⓓ Ⓔ	25 Ⓐ Ⓑ Ⓒ Ⓓ Ⓔ
7 Ⓐ Ⓑ Ⓒ Ⓓ Ⓔ			

Subtest 5—Aviation/Nautical Information

1 Ⓐ Ⓑ Ⓒ Ⓓ Ⓔ	9 Ⓐ Ⓑ Ⓒ Ⓓ Ⓔ	17 Ⓐ Ⓑ Ⓒ Ⓓ Ⓔ	24 Ⓐ Ⓑ Ⓒ Ⓓ Ⓔ
2 Ⓐ Ⓑ Ⓒ Ⓓ Ⓔ	10 Ⓐ Ⓑ Ⓒ Ⓓ Ⓔ	18 Ⓐ Ⓑ Ⓒ Ⓓ Ⓔ	25 Ⓐ Ⓑ Ⓒ Ⓓ Ⓔ
3 Ⓐ Ⓑ Ⓒ Ⓓ Ⓔ	11 Ⓐ Ⓑ Ⓒ Ⓓ Ⓔ	19 Ⓐ Ⓑ Ⓒ Ⓓ Ⓔ	26 Ⓐ Ⓑ Ⓒ Ⓓ Ⓔ
4 Ⓐ Ⓑ Ⓒ Ⓓ Ⓔ	12 Ⓐ Ⓑ Ⓒ Ⓓ Ⓔ	20 Ⓐ Ⓑ Ⓒ Ⓓ Ⓔ	27 Ⓐ Ⓑ Ⓒ Ⓓ Ⓔ
5 Ⓐ Ⓑ Ⓒ Ⓓ Ⓔ	13 Ⓐ Ⓑ Ⓒ Ⓓ Ⓔ	21 Ⓐ Ⓑ Ⓒ Ⓓ Ⓔ	28 Ⓐ Ⓑ Ⓒ Ⓓ Ⓔ
6 Ⓐ Ⓑ Ⓒ Ⓓ Ⓔ	14 Ⓐ Ⓑ Ⓒ Ⓓ Ⓔ	22 Ⓐ Ⓑ Ⓒ Ⓓ Ⓔ	29 Ⓐ Ⓑ Ⓒ Ⓓ Ⓔ
7 Ⓐ Ⓑ Ⓒ Ⓓ Ⓔ	15 Ⓐ Ⓑ Ⓒ Ⓓ Ⓔ	23 Ⓐ Ⓑ Ⓒ Ⓓ Ⓔ	30 Ⓐ Ⓑ Ⓒ Ⓓ Ⓔ
8 Ⓐ Ⓑ Ⓒ Ⓓ Ⓔ	16 Ⓐ Ⓑ Ⓒ Ⓓ Ⓔ		

Subtest 6—Aviation Supplemental Test

1 Ⓐ Ⓑ Ⓒ Ⓓ Ⓔ	10 Ⓐ Ⓑ Ⓒ Ⓓ	19 Ⓐ Ⓑ Ⓒ Ⓓ Ⓔ	27 Ⓐ Ⓑ Ⓒ Ⓓ
2 Ⓐ Ⓑ Ⓒ Ⓓ	11 Ⓐ Ⓑ Ⓒ Ⓓ	20 Ⓐ Ⓑ Ⓒ Ⓓ	28 Ⓐ Ⓑ Ⓒ Ⓓ
3 Ⓐ Ⓑ Ⓒ Ⓓ	12 Ⓐ Ⓑ Ⓒ Ⓓ	21 Ⓐ Ⓑ Ⓒ Ⓓ Ⓔ	29 Ⓐ Ⓑ Ⓒ Ⓓ
4 Ⓐ Ⓑ Ⓒ Ⓓ	13 Ⓐ Ⓑ Ⓒ Ⓓ	22 Ⓐ Ⓑ Ⓒ Ⓓ	30 Ⓐ Ⓑ Ⓒ Ⓓ
5 Ⓐ Ⓑ Ⓒ Ⓓ	14 Ⓐ Ⓑ Ⓒ Ⓓ	23 Ⓐ Ⓑ Ⓒ Ⓓ Ⓔ	31 Ⓐ Ⓑ Ⓒ Ⓓ
6 Ⓐ Ⓑ Ⓒ Ⓓ	15 Ⓐ Ⓑ Ⓒ Ⓓ Ⓔ	24 Ⓐ Ⓑ Ⓒ Ⓓ	32 Ⓐ Ⓑ Ⓒ Ⓓ Ⓔ
7 Ⓐ Ⓑ Ⓒ Ⓓ	16 Ⓐ Ⓑ Ⓒ Ⓓ	25 Ⓐ Ⓑ Ⓒ Ⓓ Ⓔ	33 Ⓐ Ⓑ Ⓒ Ⓓ Ⓔ
8 Ⓐ Ⓑ Ⓒ Ⓓ	17 Ⓐ Ⓑ Ⓒ Ⓓ Ⓔ	26 Ⓐ Ⓑ Ⓒ Ⓓ	34 Ⓐ Ⓑ Ⓒ Ⓓ Ⓔ
9 Ⓐ Ⓑ Ⓒ Ⓓ	18 Ⓐ Ⓑ Ⓒ Ⓓ		

Subtest 1—Math Skills Test

Directions: The Math Skills subtest consists of 30 questions that must be answered in 25 minutes.

This subtest measures your knowledge of basic arithmetic and your ability to solve problems using mathematics. Read each question carefully and choose the response that best answers the question.

1. $x^2y + xy^2 + 6x + 4 - (4x^2y + 3xy^2 - 2x + 5) =$

   (A) $2x^2 - 3xy - 5$
   (B) $6xy + 4x^2 + 1$
   (C) $-3x^2 - 2xy^2 + 8x - 1$
   (D) $-2xy + 4xy^2 + 7$

2. $5x + 7 = 6(x - 2) - 4(2x - 3)$. Find x.

   (A) 0
   (B) −1
   (C) 1
   (D) 2

3. In 2001, the death rate from heart attacks in the U.S. was 174.4 per 100,000. This was a $31\frac{3}{4}$ percent decrease from 1998. What was the death rate per 100,000 in 1998?

   (A) 150.3
   (B) 200.45
   (C) 255.53
   (D) 300.4

4. Tom and Kyle live 5 miles apart. If Tom leaves his house on a bicycle, heading for Kyle's house, traveling at 8 mph, and Kyle leaves his house, jogging at a rate of 7 mph, heading for Tom's house, how long will it take for them to meet?

   (A) 10 minutes
   (B) 15 minutes
   (C) 20 minutes
   (D) 25 minutes

5. The radius of a circle is increased by 5 inches. This increases its area by 155π square inches. What is the original radius of the circle?

   (A) 13 inches
   (B) 15 inches
   (C) 17 inches
   (D) 19 inches

6. $-x^2 - x + 30 = 0$. $x =$

   (A) 6, 5
   (B) −6, 5
   (C) −6, −5
   (D) 6, −5

7. A rectangle is one inch longer than it is wide. If the diameter of the rectangle is five inches, what are the dimensions of the rectangle?

   (A) 4 inches × 5 inches
   (B) 3 inches × 4 inches
   (C) 1 inch by 2 inches
   (D) 5 inches by 6 inches

8. The sum of two numbers is 10. Three times the smaller number plus 5 times the larger number equals 42. What is the larger number?

   (A) 4
   (B) 5
   (C) 6
   (D) 7

9. The final test in a course counts as one-fourth of the course grade. The average of four quizzes counts as the remaining three-fourths of the final grade. If a student's quiz scores are 61, 63, 65, and 83, what does she need to make on the final test to raise her average to 70?

   (A) 75
   (B) 76
   (C) 78
   (D) 79

10. The daily charge for a rental car is $18.00, plus 35 cents per mile driven. If the day's bill was $39.00, how far was the car driven?

(A) 40 miles
(B) 50 miles
(C) 60 miles
(D) 70 miles

11. Ensign Taggarty scored an average of 54 points per flight on the bombing range in his first five flights. Lieutenant Thompson scored an average of 59 points per flight on the bombing range during her first six flights. What is the average of points scored in all 11 flights?

(A) 54.3
(B) 55.4
(C) 56.7
(D) 57.3

12. The graph of $x^2 - y^2 - 3x + 4y - 5$ is which of the following?

(A) circle
(B) semicircle
(C) ellipse
(D) hyperbola

13. A new computer purchased for $2,800 depreciates at a rate of 22 percent per year. How much is the computer worth after 30 months?

(A) $1,505
(B) $1,603
(C) $1,691
(D) $1,703

14. What does the angle 480° equal in radian measure?

(A) $\frac{8\pi}{3}$
(B) $\frac{16\pi}{4}$
(C) $\frac{2\pi}{3}$
(D) $\frac{5\pi}{2}$

15. A gas station sets its gas price by raising the wholesale cost by 40 percent and adding $0.20. What must the wholesale price of gas be if the station is selling the gas for $3.00 per gallon?

(A) $1.50 per gallon
(B) $2.00 per gallon
(C) $1.75 per gallon
(D) $2.75 per gallon

16. $(3 \times 10^4) + (2 \times 10^2) + (4 \times 10) =$

(A) 302400
(B) 32400
(C) 30240
(D) 3240

17. Rod answers questions 74 to 125 inclusive on an English test. How many questions does he answer?

(A) 53
(B) 52
(C) 51
(D) 50

18. If x and y are integers, and $3x + 2y = 13$, which of the following could be the value of y?

(A) 0
(B) 1
(C) 2
(D) 3

19. If $n > 0$, which of the following <u>must</u> be true?

(A) $n^2 > 1$
(B) $n - n^2 < 0$
(C) $2n - 1 > 0$
(D) none of the above

20. If the slope of a line is $\frac{1}{2}$ and the y-intercept is 3, what is the x-intercept of the same line?

(A) 6
(B) $\frac{3}{2}$
(C) -6
(D) $-\frac{2}{3}$

21. Six people meet in the hallway after taking this exam. Each person shakes hands once with each other person present. How many handshakes take place?

    (A) 30
    (B) 21
    (C) 18
    (D) 15

22. If $x^2 - y^2 = 55$, and $x - y = 11$, then $y =$

    (A) 8
    (B) 5
    (C) 3
    (D) −3

23. In a casino with 30 people present, 17 people play poker, 19 people play blackjack, and two people do not play either game. How many people play both poker and blackjack?

    (A) 7
    (B) 8
    (C) 9
    (D) 10

24. $2x(3xy + y)$ is equivalent to

    (A) $6xy + 2xy$
    (B) $6x^2y + 2xy$
    (C) $3xy + 2xy$
    (D) $3x^2y + xy$

25. Solve for r: $\pi(r + 5)(r + 5) = 155\pi + \pi r^2$

    (A) 8
    (B) 10
    (C) 13
    (D) 15

26. The sum of the angle measures of a pentagon is ___________.

    (A) 360°
    (B) 540°
    (C) 720°
    (D) 900°

27. A Navy recruiting station enlisted 560 people. Of these, 25 percent were under 20 years old and 35 percent were 20 to 22 years old. How many of the recruits were over 22 years old?

    (A) 196
    (B) 224
    (C) 244
    (D) 280

28. Two office workers have been assigned to address 750 envelopes. One addresses twice as many envelopes per hour as the other. If it takes five hours for them to complete the job, what was the rate of the slower worker?

    (A) 50 envelopes per hour
    (B) 75 envelopes per hour
    (C) 100 envelopes per hour
    (D) 125 envelopes per hour

29. A pound of margarine contains four equal sticks. The wrapper of each stick has markings that indicate how to divide the stick into eight sections, each section measuring one tablespoon. If a recipe calls for four tablespoons of margarine, the amount to use is

    (A) $\frac{1}{16}$ lb.
    (B) $\frac{1}{8}$ lb.
    (C) $\frac{1}{4}$ lb.
    (D) $\frac{1}{2}$ lb.

30. If the weight of water is 62.4 pounds per cubic foot, the weight of the water that fills a rectangular container 6 inches by 6 inches by 1 foot is ___________.

    (A) 3.9 pounds
    (B) 7.8 pounds
    (C) 15.6 pounds
    (D) 31.2 pounds

Subtest 2—Reading Skills Test

Directions: The Reading Skills subtest consists of 27 questions that must be answered in 25 minutes.

This subtest measures your reading comprehension level and basic vocabulary skills. Read each question carefully and choose the response that best answers the question.

Question 1 is based on the following paragraph.

"He looked now and then at the bird which still preened itself on a little bough. When the shadows from the waving foliage fell upon its feathers it showed a bright purple, but when the sunlight poured through, it glowed a glossy blue. He did not know its name, but it was a brave bird, a gay bird. Now and then it ceased its hopping back and forth, raised its head and sent forth a deep, sweet, thrilling note, amazing in volume to come from so small a body. Had he dared to make a sound Robert would have whistled a bar or two in reply. The bird was a friend to one alone and in need, and its dauntless melody made his own heart beat higher. If a creature so tiny was not afraid in the wilderness why should he be!"

1. The bird in the forest made Robert feel ___________.

   (A) happy
   (B) sad
   (C) brave
   (D) melancholy

Question 2 is based on the following paragraph.

"It is clear that the general origin of poetry was due to two causes, each of them part of human nature. Imitation is natural to man from childhood, one of his advantages over the lower animals being this, that he is the most imitative creature in the world, and learns at first by imitation. And it is also natural for all to delight in works of imitation. The truth of this second point is shown by experience: though the objects themselves may be painful to see, we delight to view the most realistic representations of them in art, the forms for example of the lowest animals and of dead bodies. The explanation is to be found in a further fact: to be learning something is the greatest of pleasures not only to the philosopher but also to the rest of mankind, however small their capacity for it; the reason of the delight in seeing the picture is that one is at the same time learning—gathering the meaning of things, e.g. that the man there is so-and-so; for if one has not seen the thing before, one's pleasure will not be in the picture as an imitation of it, but will be due to the execution or colouring or some similar cause. Imitation, then, being natural to us—as also the sense of harmony and rhythm, the metres being obviously species of rhythms—it was through their original aptitude, and by a series of improvements for the most part gradual on their first efforts, that they created poetry out of their improvisations."

2. In the above passage, the author contends that one of the reasons man is superior to other animals is because

   (A) man is a natural philosopher.
   (B) only man can understand the delights of poetry.
   (C) man is capable of learning from his mistakes.
   (D) mimicking is natural to man.

Question 3 is based on the following paragraph.

"Father Percy Franklin, the elder of the two priests, was rather a remarkable-looking man, not more than thirty-five years old, but with hair that was white throughout; his grey eyes, under black eyebrows, were peculiarly bright and almost passionate; but his prominent nose and chin and the extreme decisiveness of his mouth reassured the observer as to his will. Strangers usually looked twice at him. Father Francis, however, sitting in his upright chair on the other side of the hearth, brought down the average; for, though his brown eyes were pleasant and pathetic, there was no strength in his face; there was even a tendency to feminine melancholy in the corners of his mouth and the marked droop of his eyelids."

3. Which of the following statements is <u>not</u> true?

   (A) Father Francis is a rather remarkable–looking man.
   (B) Father Franklin is about 35 years old.
   (C) Father Francis is younger than Father Franklin.
   (D) Father Franklin had black eyebrows and grey eyes.

4. <u>Henchman</u> most nearly means ___________.

   (A) adversary
   (B) teacher
   (C) follower
   (D) conspirator

5. <u>Juxtapose</u> most nearly means ___________.

   (A) apart
   (B) together
   (C) maintain
   (D) relax

6. <u>Magnitude</u> most nearly means ___________.

   (A) trivial
   (B) disregard
   (C) importance
   (D) small

7. In actuality, the provisions of the contract were quite clear.

 (A) clarity
 (B) pretense
 (C) essence
 (D) reality

8. The situation brought home to us the blunt verity of the military threat.

 (A) possibility
 (B) danger
 (C) truth
 (D) vernacular

9. Mr. Garrott's testimony was just a strategem to throw us off the track.

 (A) policy
 (B) plan
 (C) stigma
 (D) taciturn

10. There was clear evidence that he had a large part in inciting the workers to go on strike.

 (A) advising
 (B) urging
 (C) discouraging
 (D) planning

11. John's pitiless heart caused his wife to leave.

 (A) remorseful
 (B) empty
 (C) cold
 (D) merciless

12. Because of her behavior, Tammy was circumscribed to her room.

 (A) sent
 (B) allowed to go
 (C) carried
 (D) restricted

13. The rocket attack was an explicit violation of the cease-fire agreement.

 (A) definite
 (B) probable
 (C) possible
 (D) allowable

Questions 14 and 15 are based on the following paragraph.

"National military strategy describes the objectives, concepts, tasks, and capabilities necessary to implement the goals set for the military in the national security strategy. National military strategy evolves as the international environment, national strategy, and national military objectives change. This strategy lays the basis for applying military instruments at the strategic and operational levels of war. It requires responsive military forces to rapidly and decisively cope with diverse situations including nuclear and conventional threats; regional instability; proliferation of weapons of mass destruction; threats to unilateral peace-support operations; drug trafficking; terrorism; regional wars; and natural disasters. To execute flexible and selective engagement, military forces must not only be trained, organized, and equipped to fight, but they must also be ready to engage across the spectrum of peace, crisis, and conflict as part of any joint, combined, United Nations, or interagency force."

14. National military strategy

    (A) is an unchangeable, long-term plan.
    (B) may be changed only by Congress.
    (C) changes according to the current situation.
    (D) is reviewed annually by the NMS implementation committee.

15. National military strategy operates at the

    (A) operational level.
    (B) strategic level.
    (C) environmental level.
    (D) both (A) and (C)

Question 16 is based on the following paragraph.

"Leaders set a high standard for themselves and those around them. Followers will observe positive as well as negative characteristics and emulate them. Lack of self-discipline undermines a leader's authority, dilutes effectiveness, and ultimately, impairs the ability to perform the unit's mission. Especially in the profession of arms, a leader's actions must be beyond reproach if he or she is to be trusted—double standards and contradictory actions will permeate the entire organization. Regardless of how strongly leaders feel about themselves, it is the public's perception that counts and becomes the 'reality.'"

16. Which of the following statements is true?

    (A) Subordinates will mimic negative traits of their leaders.
    (B) Subordinates tend to copy only positive traits seen in their leaders.
    (C) Contradictory actions are usually ignored by subordinates.
    (D) It's more important how a leader feels about himself than what the public thinks.

Question 17 is based on the following paragraph.

"The sociologist, Harold Wilensky, asserts a profession begins when people 'start doing full-time the thing that needs doing' and then continue by establishing schools, setting standards, providing longer training, demanding commitment to the profession and the group, promoting and creating a professional association, and finally, establishing a code of ethics, eliminating internal competition, and protecting the client."

17. A profession requires

(A) natural talent.
(B) a professional association.
(C) limited training.
(D) an oath.

18. Extemporaneous most nearly means ___________.

(A) practiced
(B) relentless
(C) impromptu
(D) magnificent

19. Noxious most nearly means ___________.

(A) harmful
(B) sick
(C) tactless
(D) angry

20. Intrepid most nearly means ___________.

(A) careful
(B) sneaky
(C) tiresome
(D) brave

21. Myth most nearly means ___________.

(A) microscopic
(B) large
(C) lie
(D) person

22. Abase most nearly means ___________.

(A) floor
(B) wall
(C) degrade
(D) loosen

Question 23 is based on the following paragraph.

"In one form or another, data processing has been carried on throughout the entire history of civilization. In its most general sense, data processing means organizing data so that it can be used for a specific purpose—a procedure commonly known simply as "recordkeeping" or "paperwork." With the development of modern office equipment, and particularly with the introduction of computers, the techniques of data processing have become highly elaborate and sophisticated, but the basic purpose remains the same—turning raw data into useful information."

23. According to the above passage, the use of computers has

    (A) greatly simplified the clerical operations of an office.
    (B) had no effect on data processing.
    (C) led to more complicated systems for data handling.
    (D) made other modern office machines obsolete.

Question 24 is based on the following paragraph.

"In general, business forms are a reflection of work methods, operating procedures, and management know-how. If a company's forms constitute a simple, orderly plan showing clear and related purposes, there is reason to believe that its personnel know what they are doing and why, and may be giving fairly efficient service. If, on the other hand, its forms constitute an unintelligible tangle of red tape, it is pretty safe to assume that its methods and procedures are in much the same shape."

24. The passage best supports the statement that

    (A) an efficient system of business forms will result in an efficient business organization.
    (B) business forms used by a company should be continuously simplified and revised.
    (C) the best method for determining whether a company is successful is to study its business forms.
    (D) the business forms used by a company are a good indication of the efficiency of the company's operations.

Question 25 is based on the following paragraph.

"The function of business is to increase the wealth of the country and the value and happiness of life. It does this by supplying the material needs of men and women. When the nation's business is successfully carried on, it renders public service of the highest value."

25. The passage best supports the statement that

    (A) all businesses that render public service are successful.
    (B) business is the only field of endeavor that increases happiness.
    (C) human happiness is enhanced only by increasing material wants.
    (D) the material needs of men and women are supplied by well-conducted businesses.

Question 26 is based on the following paragraph.

"Inherent in all organized endeavors is the need to resolve the individual differences involved in conflict. Conflict may be either a positive or negative factor, since it may lead to creativity, innovation, and progress, on the one hand, or it may result, on the other hand, in a deterioration or even destruction of the organization. Thus, some forms of conflict are desirable, whereas others are undesirable and ethically wrong."

26. The word conflict as used in the above passage means most nearly ____________.

    (A) aggression
    (B) combat
    (C) competition
    (D) confusion

Question 27 is based on the following paragraph.

"The great events in history are those where, upon special occasions, a man or a people have made a stand against tyranny, and have preserved or advanced freedom for the people. Sometimes tyranny has taken the form of the oppression of the many by the few in the same nation, and sometimes it has been the oppression of a weak nation by a stronger one. The successful revolt against tyranny, the terrible conflict resulting in the emancipation of a people, has always been the favorite theme of the historian, marking as it does a step in the progress of mankind from a savage to a civilized state."

27. The author of this passage advocates

    (A) authoritative governments.
    (B) democratic freedoms.
    (C) religious expression.
    (D) documenting historical events.

Subtest 3—Mechanical Comprehension

Directions: The Mechanical Comprehension subtest is comprised of 30 questions that must be answered in 15 minutes.

This subtest measures your ability to reason with and comprehend mechanical applications and simple rules of physics. Choose the answer that best answers the question.

1. If valves A and D are open, and the other valves are closed, which tanks will fill with water?

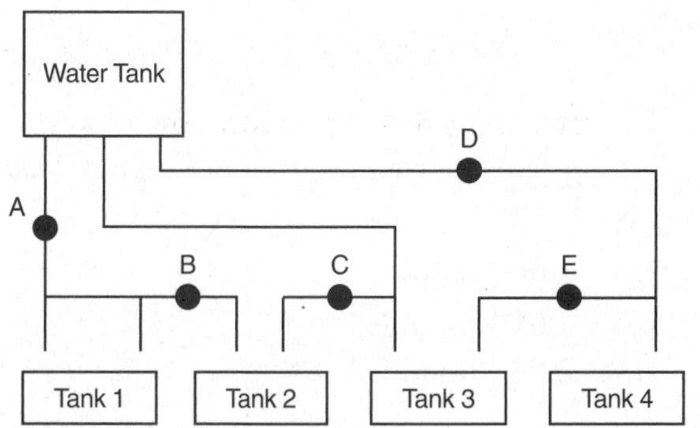

(A) 1, 3
(B) 1, 3, 4
(C) 1, 2, 3, 4
(D) 1, 2, 3

2. In which of the following is a force of friction necessary?

(A) When a ball is bouncing off a wall.
(B) When a drum skin is vibrating.
(C) When a rocket is taking off.
(D) When a car is accelerating.

3. How much force must be applied to point A in order to keep the bar level?

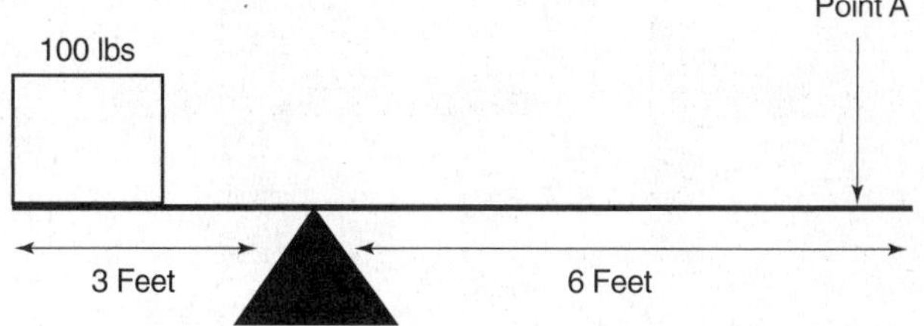

(A) 100 pounds
(B) 200 pounds
(C) 50 pounds
(D) 25 pounds

4. To move the weight up six inches, how much rope must be pulled?

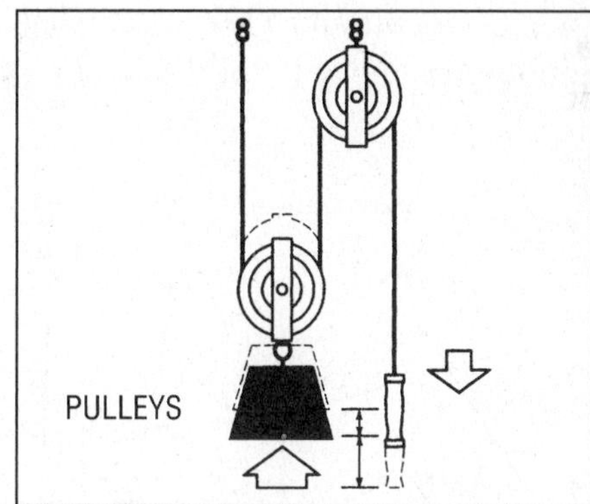

(A) 6 inches
(B) 1 foot
(C) 18 inches
(D) 3 inches

5. The driving gear is 10 inches in diameter and the driven gear is 20 inches in diameter. If the input torque is 500 pound-inches, what will the output torque be?

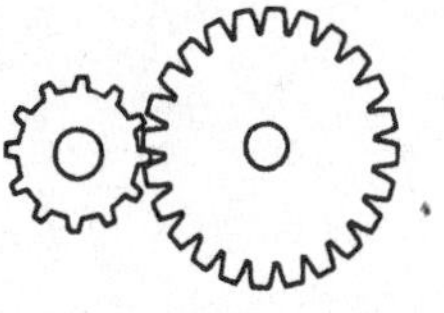

(A) 1,000 pound-inches
(B) 50 pound-inches
(C) 500 pound-inches
(D) 5,000 pound-inches

6. When moved horizontally, Gear B will mesh with

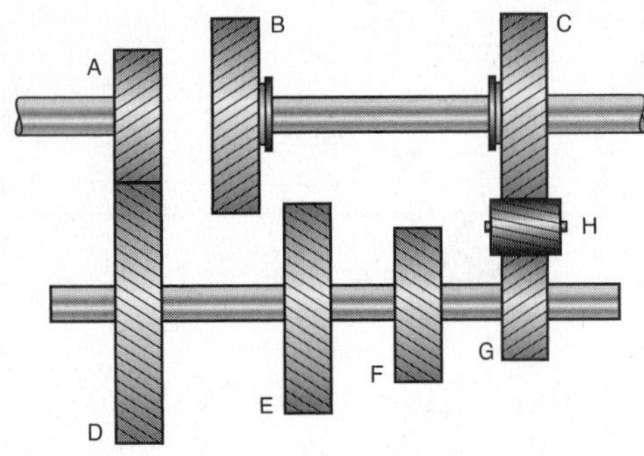

(A) gear E and F.
(B) gear A only.
(C) gear F only.
(D) gear E only.

7. If Pulley A is spinning clockwise, what directions are Pulley B and Pulley D spinning?

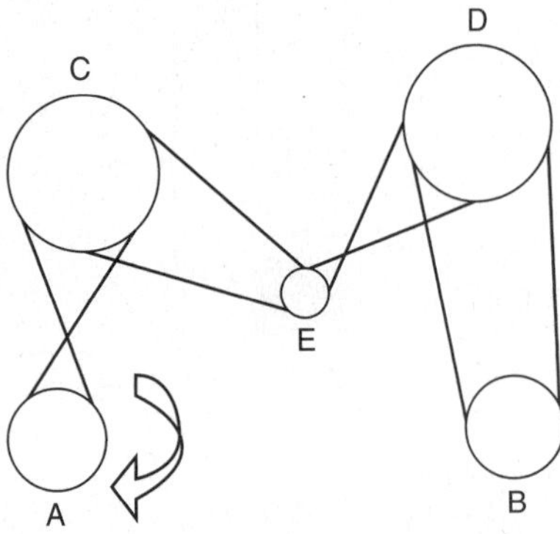

(A) clockwise, clockwise
(B) counterclockwise, clockwise
(C) counterclockwise, counterclockwise
(D) clockwise, counterclockwise

8. To lift the box with the least amount of force, at what point and direction should the force be applied?

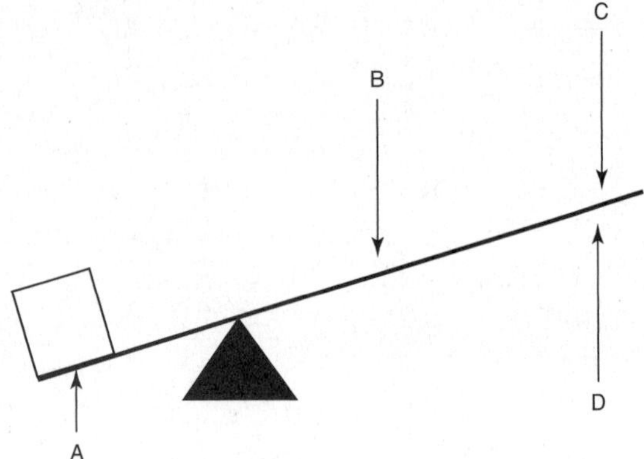

(A) A
(B) B
(C) C
(D) D

9. If a car weighs 8,000 pounds, how much weight is supported on each of its four tires?

(A) 8,000 pounds
(B) 6,000 pounds
(C) 4,000 pounds
(D) 2,000 pounds

10. The tool below is best utilized for

(A) cutting sheetrock.
(B) cutting plywood.
(C) cutting metal.
(D) cutting glass.

11. When the hand turns the driving shaft in the direction indicated, the driven shaft will turn

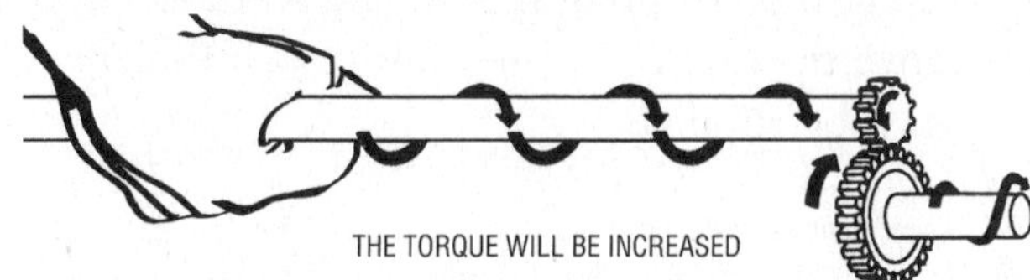

(A) faster.
(B) slower.
(C) at the same speed.
(D) This cannot be determined from the information provided.

12. If a single force acts on an object, the velocity of that object must ___________.

(A) accelerate
(B) decelerate
(C) change
(D) remain constant

13. An aircraft traveling at constant speed (with no change in direction or altitude) is in equilibrium with how many forces?

(A) 1
(B) 2
(C) 3
(D) 4

14. The spring attached to the lever below has a tension-strength of 30 lbs/inch. Approximately how far will the weight at the opposite end cause the spring to stretch?

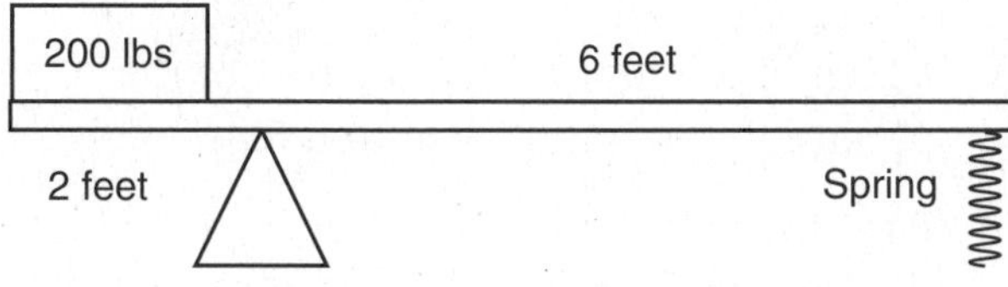

(A) one inch
(B) two inches
(C) three inches
(D) four inches

15. Safety glass is made by a process called __________.

(A) hardening
(B) blowing
(C) tempering
(D) molting

16. How much weight will register on the scale depicted in the diagram below?

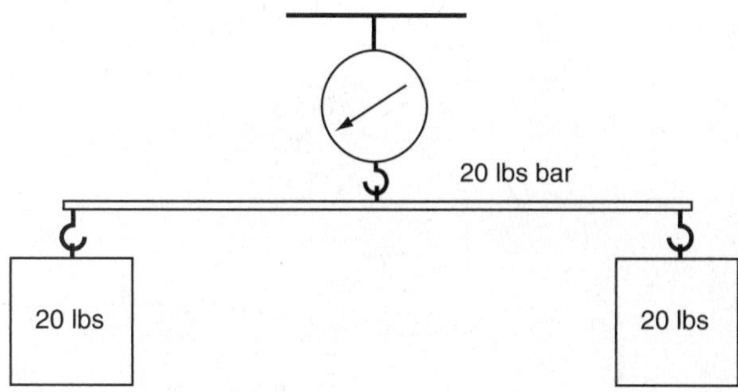

(A) 10 pounds
(B) 20 pounds
(C) 40 pounds
(D) 60 pounds

17. How many pounds of force will be required to lift the 120–pound weight shown in the diagram below?

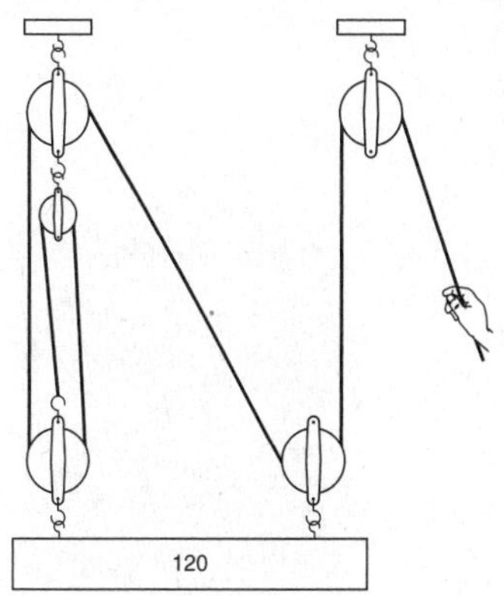

(A) 12
(B) 15
(C) 24
(D) 27

18. Which of the following is designed to be tightened by hand?

    (A) wingnut
    (B) wood screw
    (C) metal screw
    (D) bolt

19. If Pulley #1 is turning clockwise, how many pulleys in the below diagram will be rotating counterclockwise?

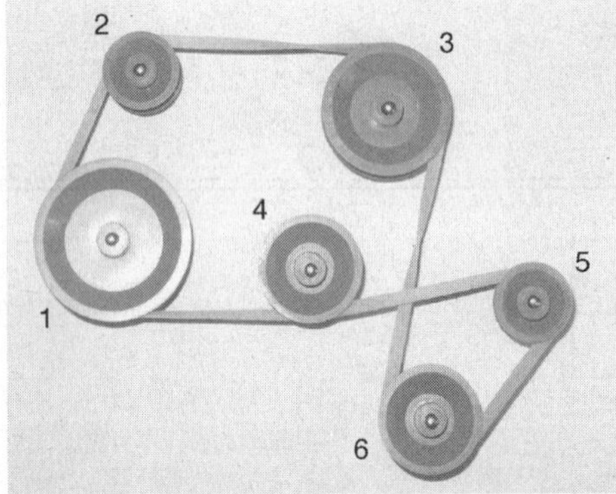

    (A) 0
    (B) 1
    (C) 2
    (D) 3

20. If the lower gear is turning in the direction indicated, which direction will the upper gear rotate?

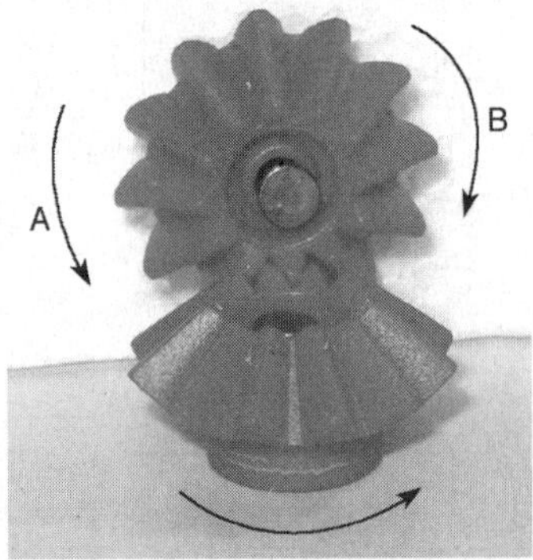

    (A) A
    (B) B
    (C) The upper gear will alternate directions.
    (D) This cannot be determined from the information provided.

21. Springs A and C have a tension strength of 5 pounds per inch, and Spring B has a tension strength of 10 pounds per inch. In order to move the block 3 inches, how much force must be applied?

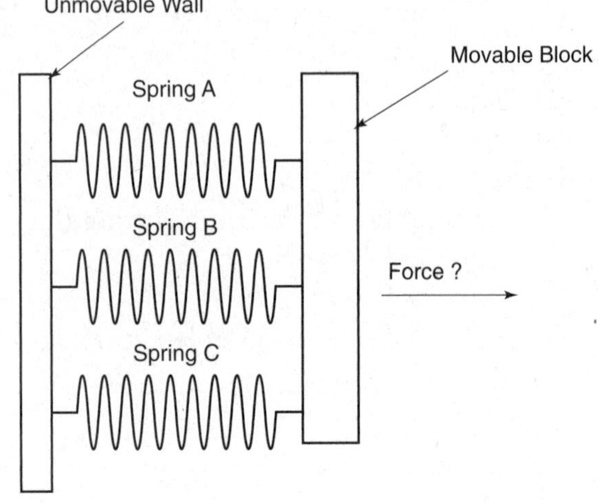

    (A) 5 pounds
    (B) 10 pounds
    (C) 30 pounds
    (D) 60 pounds

22. A large and a small ball of the same density are rolled toward one another at identical speeds. When the two balls collide, what will be the result?

    (A) Both balls will stop.
    (B) The large ball will be slowed, but continue to travel in the same direction.
    (C) The small ball will be propelled in the opposite direction.
    (D) both (B) and (C)

23. Which of the following is/are part of the suspension system on an automobile?

    (A) distributor
    (B) master cylinder
    (C) pistons
    (D) wheels

24. On which swing can the girl swing fastest?

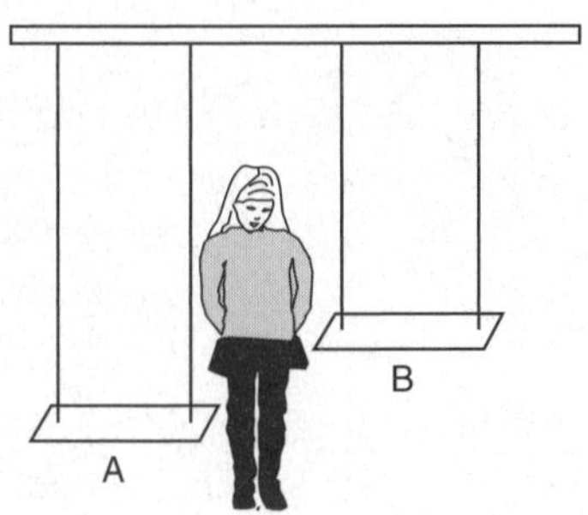

(A) swing A
(B) swing B
(C) no difference
(D) This cannot be determined from the information provided.

25. “Strap,” “spanner,” “torque,” and “stilson” are all types of ___________.

(A) wrenches
(B) saws
(C) vices
(D) screw drivers

26. How fast will gear D turn in relation to gear G?

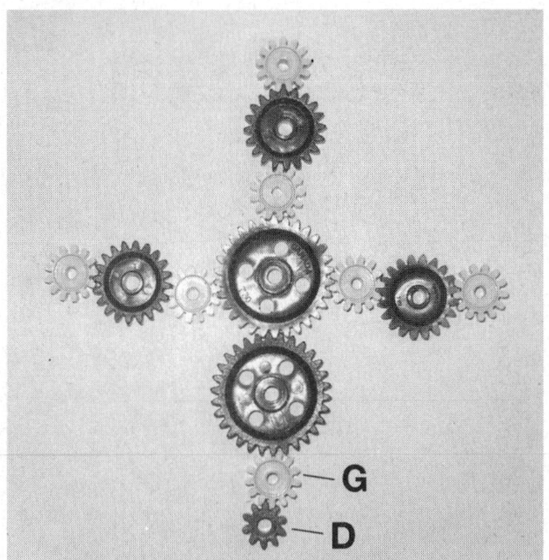

(A) Gear D will turn faster.
(B) Gear D will turn slower.
(C) Gear D and G will turn at the same speeds.
(D) This cannot be determined from the information provided.

27. Which of the following mechanical device is most likely to be found in a computer keyboard?

(A) lever
(B) spring
(C) pulley
(D) gear

28. Which of the following gauges would most likely be calibrated in PSI (pounds per square inch)?

(A) speedometer
(B) pressure gauge
(C) temperature gage
(D) depth gauge

29. The main purpose of a muffler on an automobile is to

(A) improve gas mileage.
(B) improve acceleration.
(C) reduce noise.
(D) comply with federal laws.

30. In the pulley system depicted below, how many pulleys will be rotating counterclockwise?

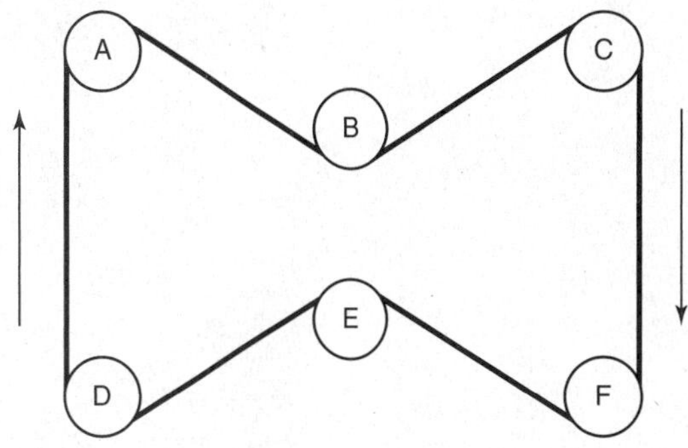

(A) 1
(B) 2
(C) 4
(D) 6

Subtest 4—Spatial Apperception

Directions: This subtest measures your ability to determine the position of an aircraft in flight, in relation to the view a pilot would see when looking outside of the cockpit.

The subtest consists of 25 questions that must be answered in 10 minutes.

For each question, you will see a series of six pictures. The first picture will depict a view of the landscape that a pilot would see when looking out the front of the cockpit. You are to determine whether the aircraft is climbing, diving, banking, or in level flight, and choose the picture that best represents the same aircraft when viewed from the outside.

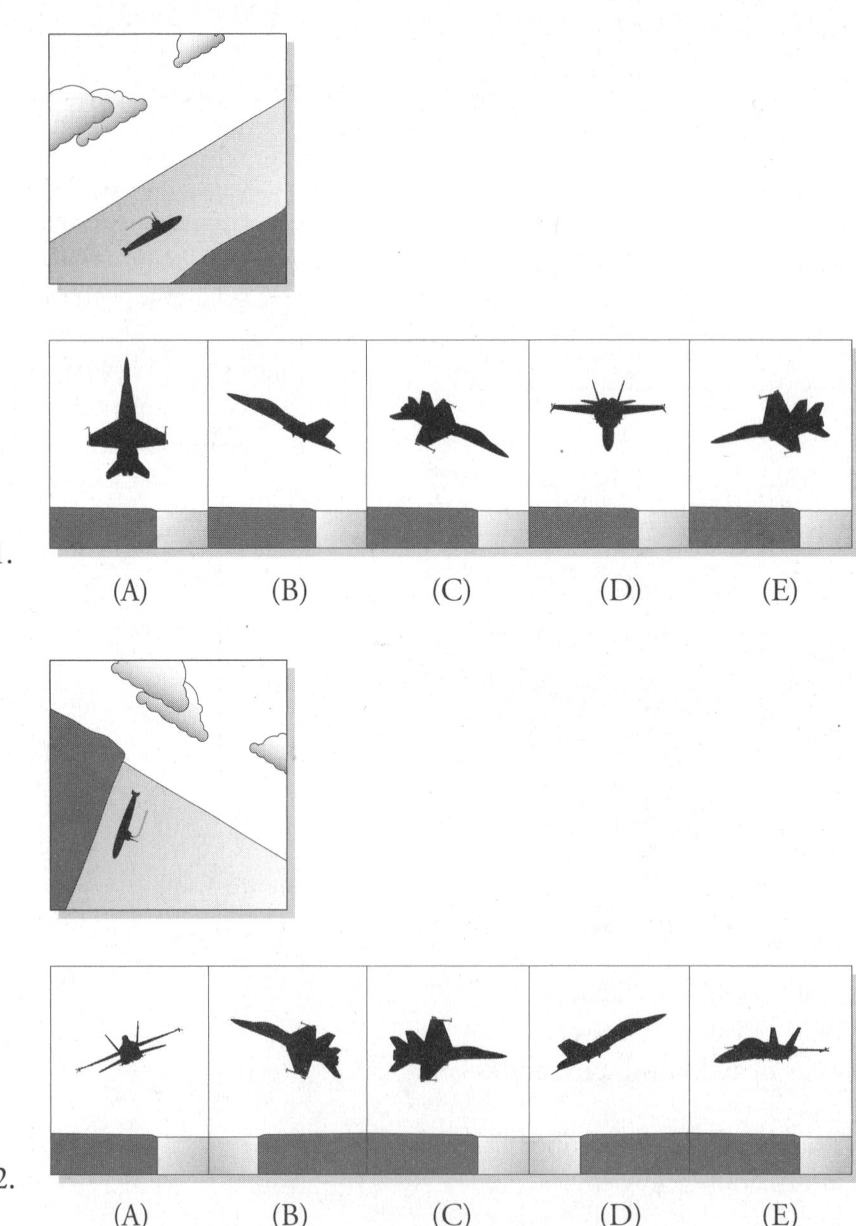

3.
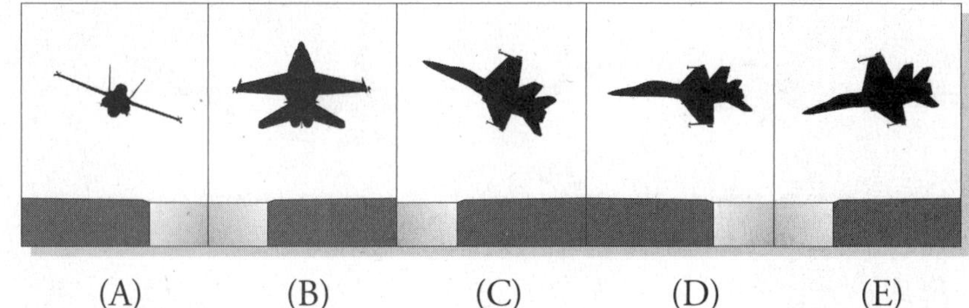
(A) (B) (C) (D) (E)

4.
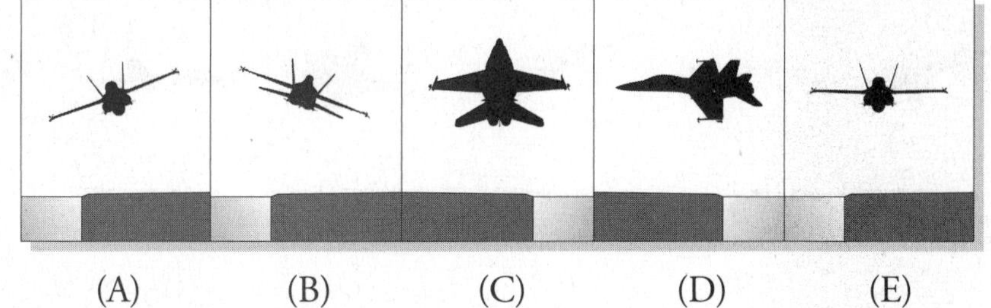
(A) (B) (C) (D) (E)

5.
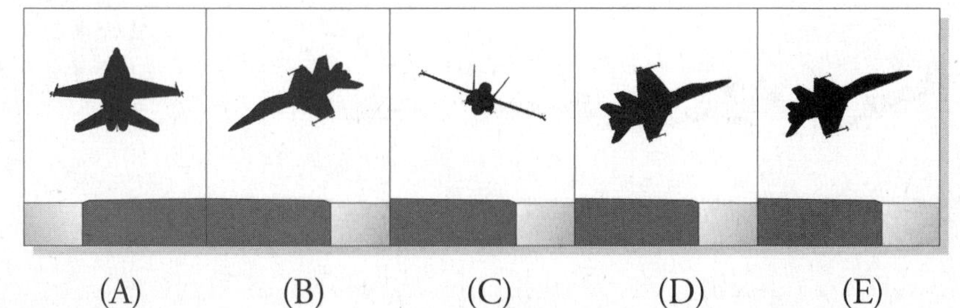
(A) (B) (C) (D) (E)

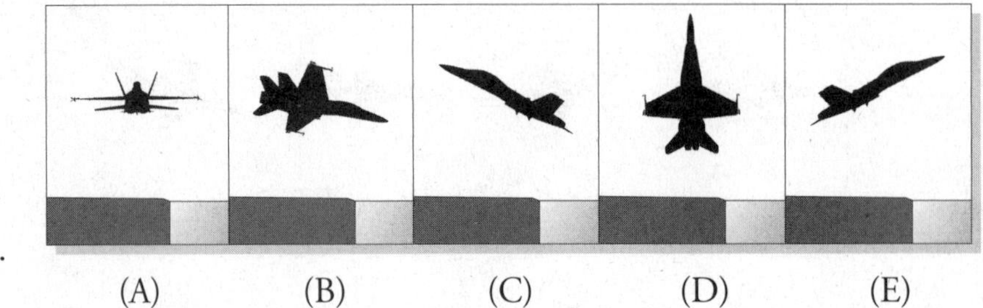

6. (A) (B) (C) (D) (E)

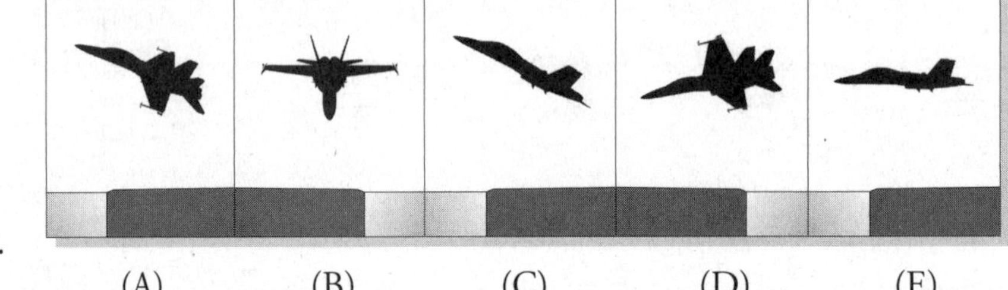

7. (A) (B) (C) (D) (E)

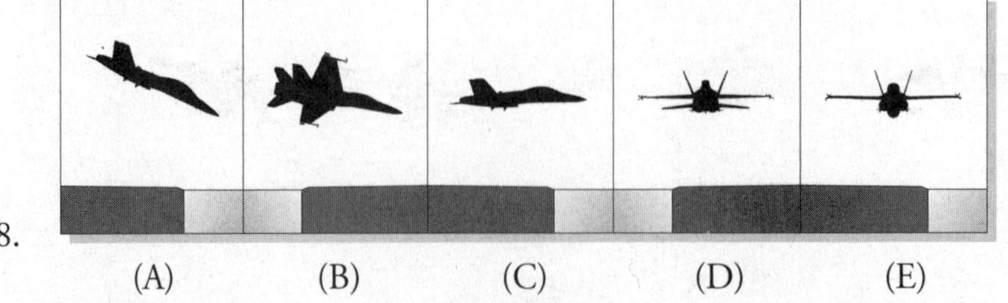

8. (A) (B) (C) (D) (E)

9.

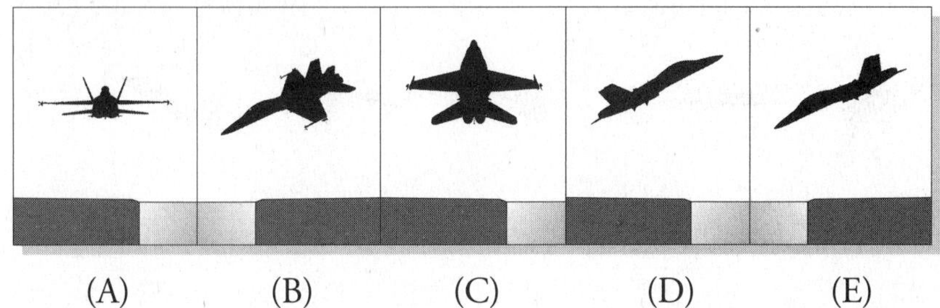

(A) (B) (C) (D) (E)

10.

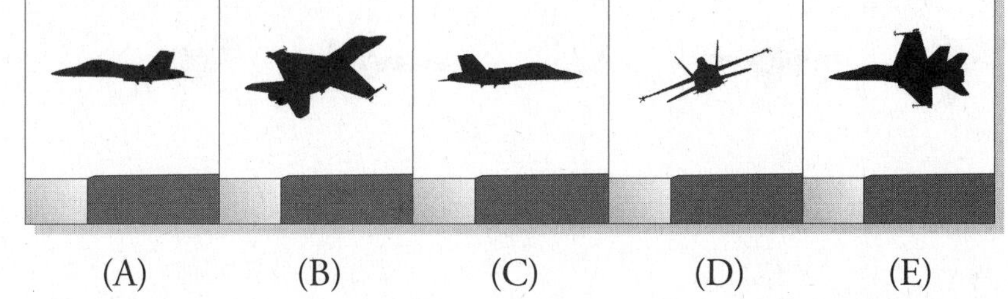

(A) (B) (C) (D) (E)

11.

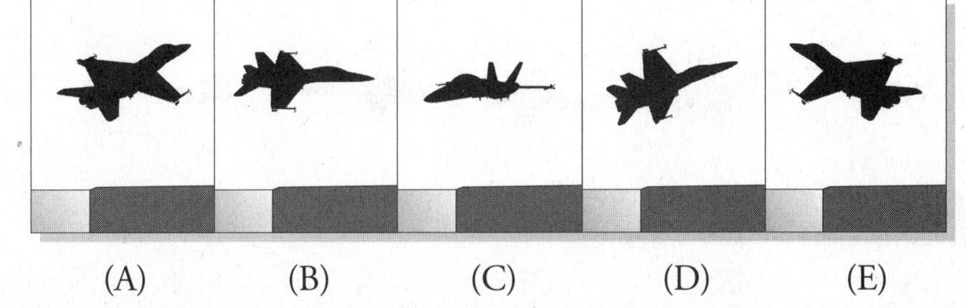

(A) (B) (C) (D) (E)

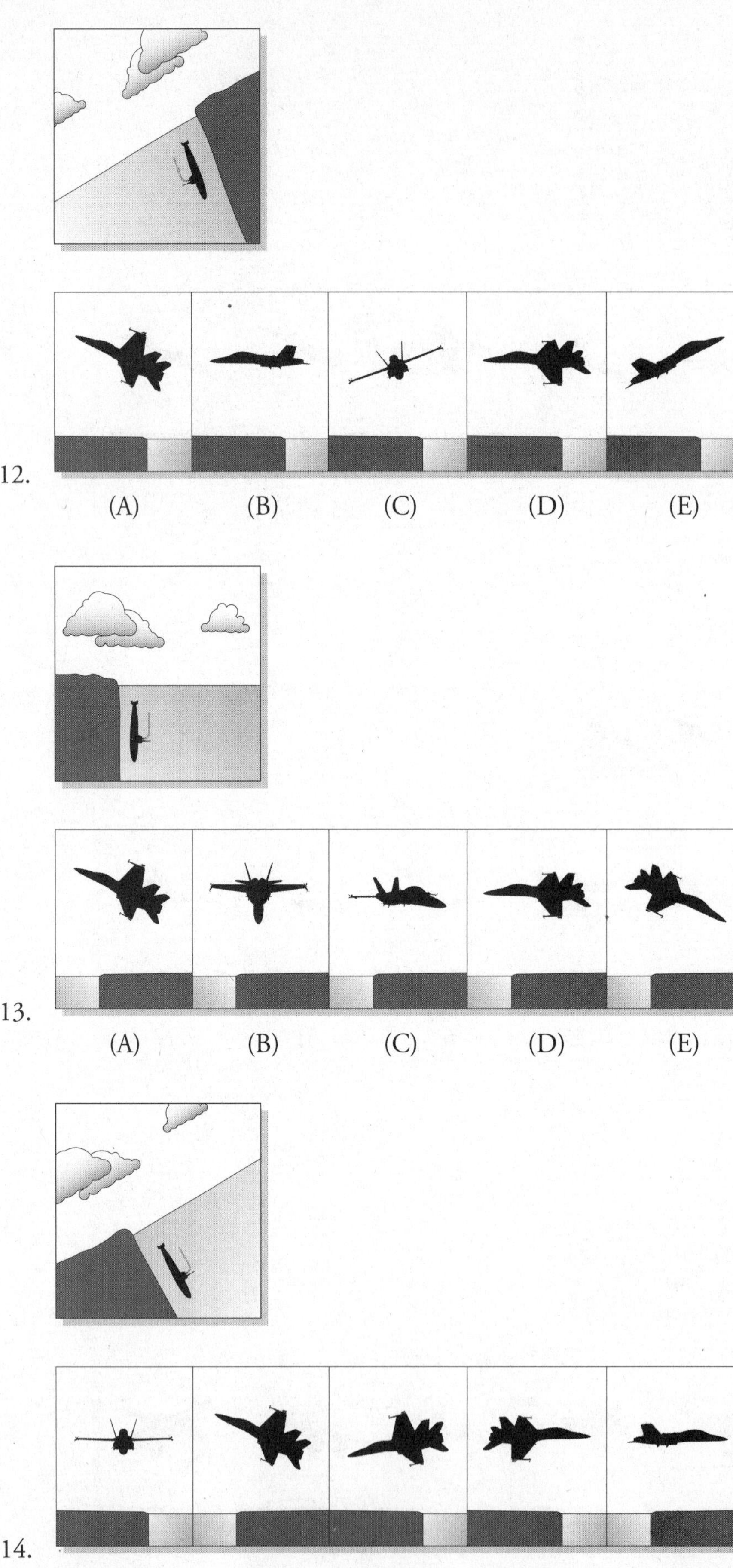
12.
(A)
(B)
(C)
(D)
(E)
13.
(A)
(B)
(C)
(D)
(E)
14.
(A)
(B)
(C)
(D)
(E)

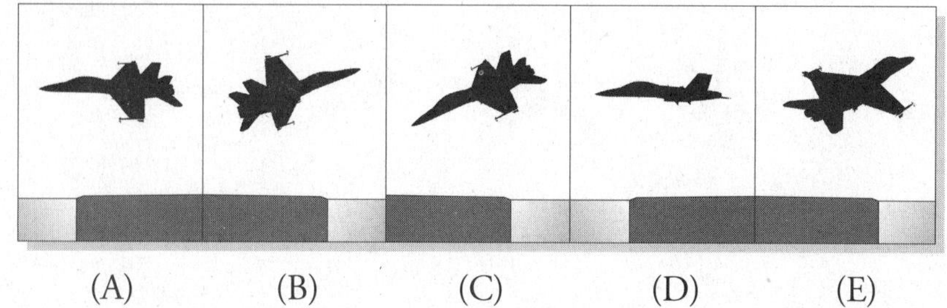

15. (A) (B) (C) (D) (E)

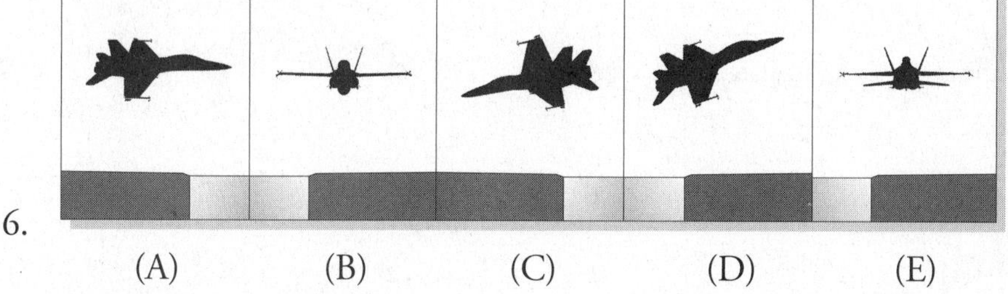

16. (A) (B) (C) (D) (E)

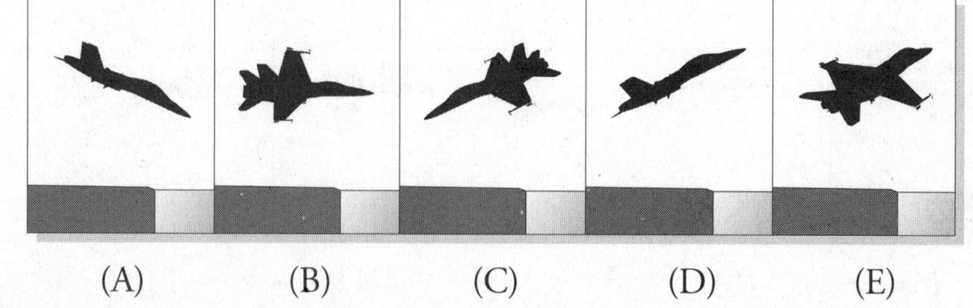

17. (A) (B) (C) (D) (E)

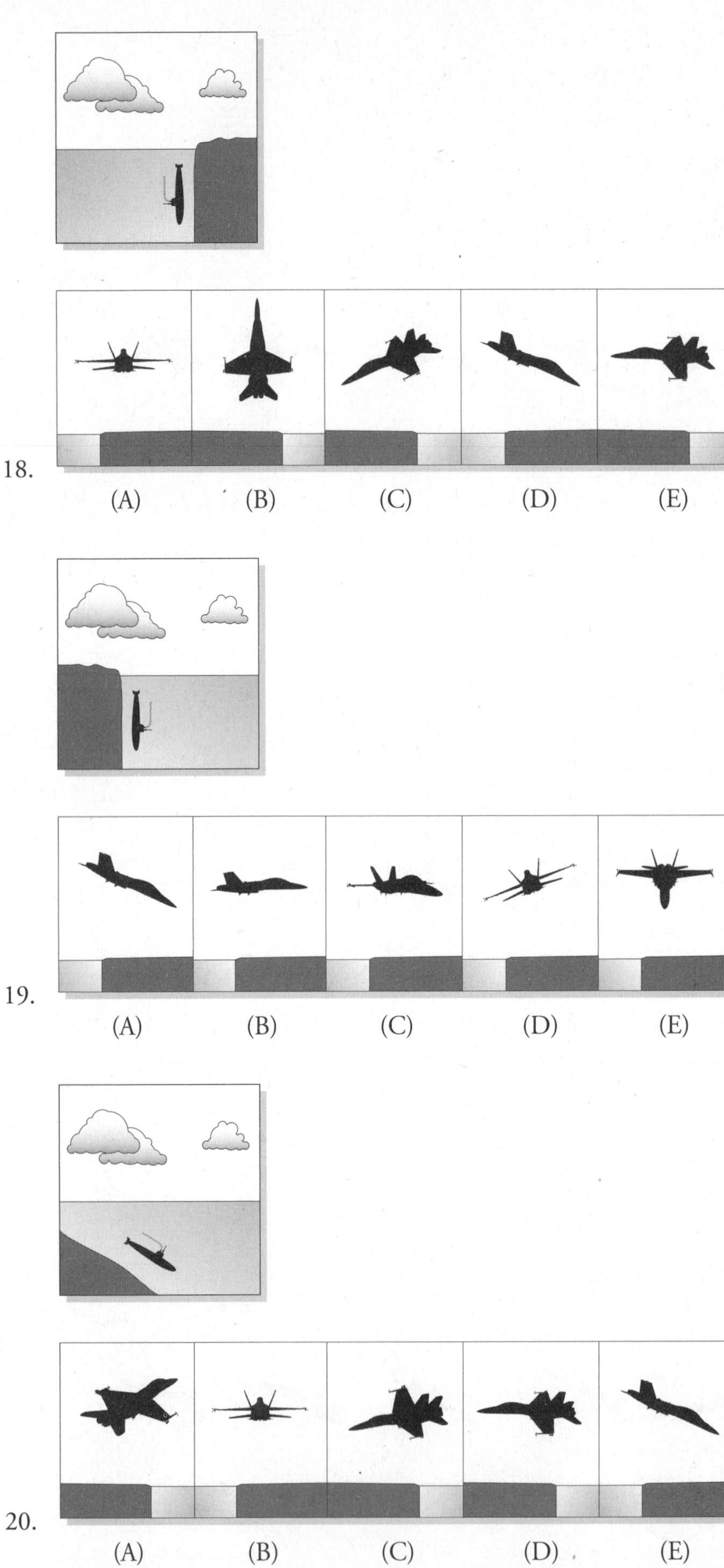
18.
(A)
(B)
(C)
(D)
(E)
19.
(A)
(B)
(C)
(D)
(E)
20.
(A)
(B)
(C)
(D)
(E)

21.
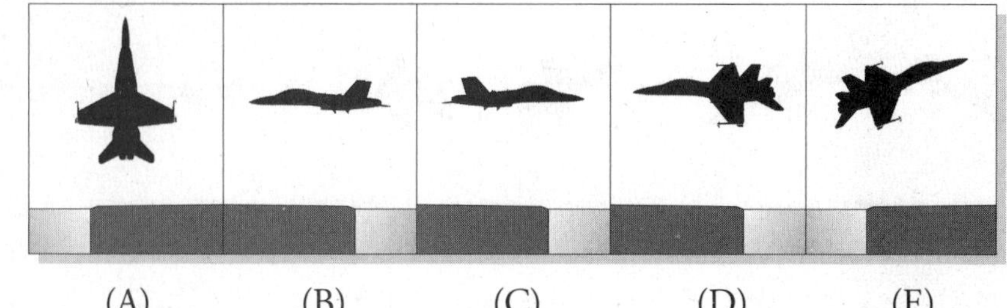
(A) (B) (C) (D) (E)

22.
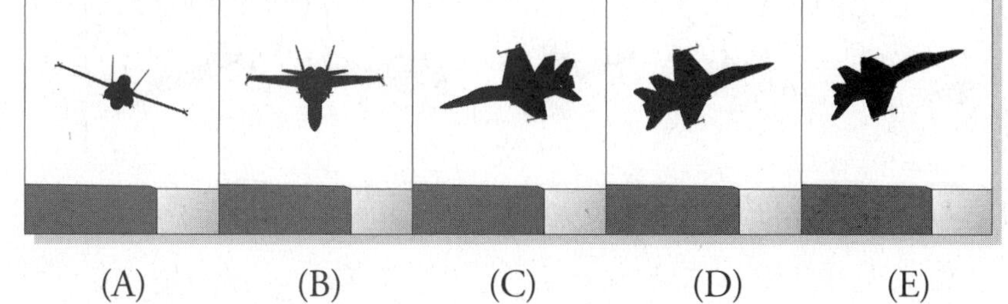
(A) (B) (C) (D) (E)

23.
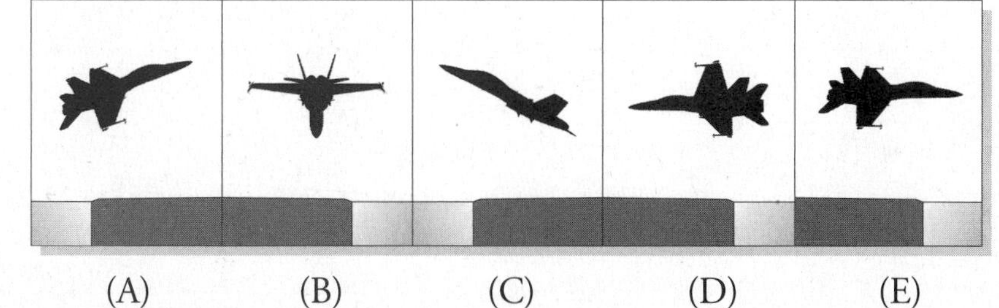
(A) (B) (C) (D) (E)

24.

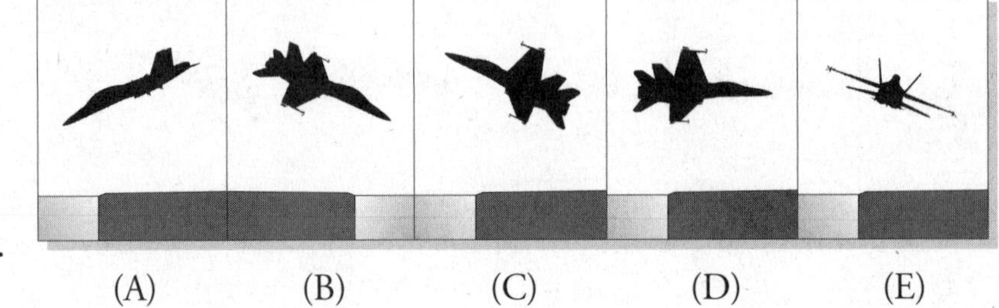

(A) (B) (C) (D) (E)

25.

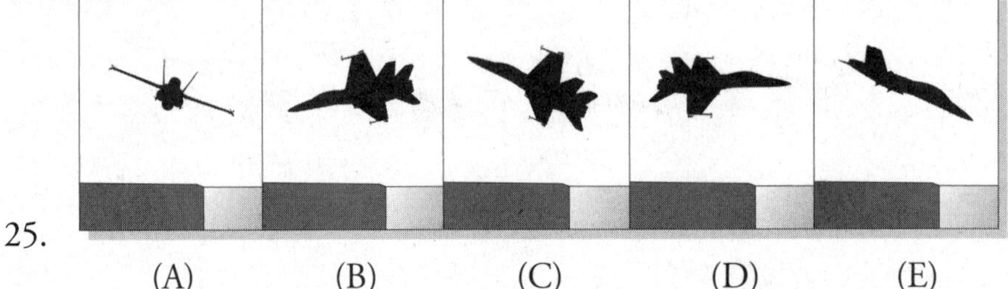

(A) (B) (C) (D) (E)

Subtest 5—Aviation/Nautical Information

Directions: This subtest measures your knowledge of general aviation principles and nautical information and terms, especially as it applies to Naval nautical practices.

The subtest consists of 30 questions that must be completed in 15 minutes.

Choose the answer that best answers the question or completes the statement.

1. If one end of a runway is numbered 27, what number would designate the other end of the same runway?

   (A) 27
   (B) 33
   (C) 09
   (D) 45
   (E) 18

2. For weight and balance computations, what is the standard weight that has been established for gasoline used in aircraft?

   (A) 5 lbs/gal
   (B) 12 lbs/gal
   (C) 3 lbs/gal
   (D) 7.6 lbs/gal
   (E) 6 lbs/gal

3. Using the 24–hour clock, 8:00 P.M. would be expressed as ___________.

   (A) 2100 hours
   (B) 2000 hours
   (C) 0800 hours
   (D) 1800 hours
   (E) 0600 hours

4. When a pilot applies forward pressure on the control stick, this causes the elevators to

   (A) move downward.
   (B) move upward.
   (C) extend.
   (D) retract.
   (E) return to the neutral position.

5. In the diagram below, the pilot has banked the aircraft

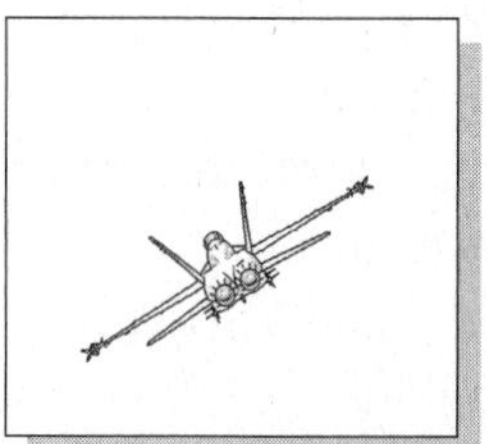

   (A) 30 degrees to the left.
   (B) 45 degrees to the left.
   (C) 60 degrees to the left.
   (D) 30 degrees to the right.
   (E) 45 degrees to the right.

6. In nautical navigation, speed is measured in

   (A) miles per hour.
   (B) range per standard.
   (C) knots.
   (D) bearing.
   (E) deviation.

7. Navigation lights installed on the port side of a vessel are ___________.

   (A) green
   (B) red
   (C) yellow
   (D) white
   (E) any color

8. A flashing green light directed to an aircraft on the ground indicates that the aircraft

   (A) is cleared for takeoff.
   (B) may cross the active runway.
   (C) is cleared to taxi.
   (D) must return to the terminal.
   (E) must contact the tower.

9. Which of the following <u>is not</u> a flight instrument?
   - (A) airspeed indicator
   - (B) vertical velocity indicator
   - (C) turn indicator
   - (D) altimeter
   - (E) fuel flow indicator

10. When taking off into a headwind, the result will be
    - (A) shorter takeoff distance and increased climb angle.
    - (B) shorter takeoff distance and decreased climb angle.
    - (C) longer takeoff distance and increased climb angle.
    - (D) longer takeoff distance and decreased climb angle.
    - (E) have no effect on aircraft performance.

11. At the airport depicted below, larger aircraft should request to land on which runways?

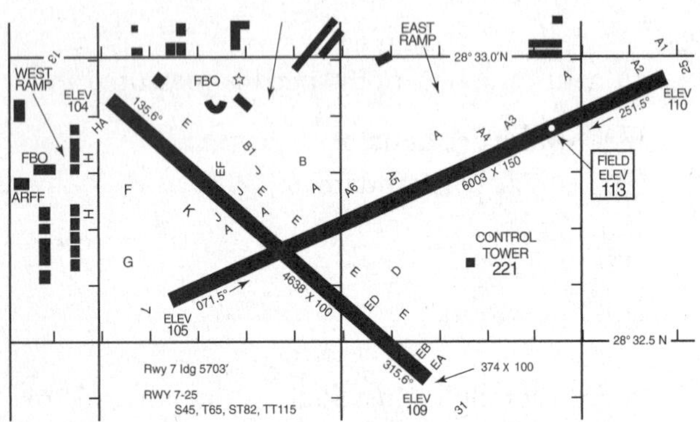

   - (A) 13 or 25
   - (B) 13 or 7
   - (C) 7 or 25
   - (D) 31 or 7
   - (E) 13 or 31

12. In the diagram depicted in question #11, the short runway is aligned in which direction?
    - (A) North-South direction
    - (B) East-West direction
    - (C) NW-SE direction
    - (D) NE-SW direction
    - (E) none of the above

13. What is a ship's windlass primarily used for?
    - (A) navigation
    - (B) cargo movement
    - (C) handling the anchor chain
    - (D) refueling
    - (E) calculating distance

14. An airplane wing is designed to produce lift resulting from relatively
    - (A) positive air pressure below and above the wing's surface.
    - (B) negative air pressure below the wing's surface and positive air pressure above it.
    - (C) positive air pressure below the wing's surface and negative air pressure above it.
    - (D) negative air pressure below and above the wing's surface.
    - (E) neutral air pressure below and above the wing's surface.

15. What is the difference between a steady red and a flashing red light signal from the tower to an aircraft approaching to land?
    - (A) Both light signals mean the same except the flashing red light requires a more urgent reaction.
    - (B) Both light signals mean the same except the steady red light requires a more urgent reaction.
    - (C) A steady red light signals to continue circling and a flashing red light signals that the airport is unsafe for landing.
    - (D) A steady red light signals to continue circling and a flashing red light signals to continue, but exercise extreme caution.
    - (E) A steady red light signals that the airport is unsafe and a flashing red light signals to use a different runway.

16. The propeller blades are curved on one side and flat on the other side to

    (A) increase its strength.
    (B) produce thrust.
    (C) provide proper balance.
    (D) reduce air friction.
    (E) reduce drag.

17. What makes an airplane turn?

    (A) centrifugal force
    (B) horizontal component of lift
    (C) rudder and aileron
    (D) rudder, aileron, and elevator
    (E) vertical component of lift

18. What is one advantage of an airplane said to be inherently stable?

    (A) The airplane will not spin.
    (B) The airplane will be difficult to stall.
    (C) The airplane will require less fuel.
    (D) The airplane will require less effort to control.
    (E) The airplane will not over-bank during steep turns.

19. If the elevator tabs on a plane are lowered, the plane will tend to

    (A) nose up.
    (B) nose down.
    (C) pitch fore and aft.
    (D) go into a slow roll.
    (E) wing over.

20. The pilot always advances the throttle during a __________.

    (A) nose dive
    (B) landing
    (C) turn
    (D) spin
    (E) climb

21. At sea, wind speed is generally measured using the __________.

    (A) Tangier scale
    (B) Beaufort scale
    (C) Regent scale
    (D) Monlop scale
    (E) Proto scale

22. If the clock on a ship sailing in time zone +3 reads 1600, what time would it be in Zulu time?

    (A) 1300
    (B) 1600
    (C) 1700
    (D) 1900
    (E) 0000

23. At the alarm, "Man Overboard," the first reaction should be to

    (A) throw life buoys over the side.
    (B) stop the ship.
    (C) locate the person.
    (D) idle the engines.
    (E) turn the ship around.

24. The International Date Line is located at the

    (A) 180th meridian.
    (B) 0 meridian.
    (C) 90th meridian.
    (D) 270th meridian.
    (E) none of the above

25. The pilot of an airplane can best detect the approach of a stall by the

    (A) increase in speed of the engine.
    (B) increase in pitch and intensity of the sound of the air moving past the plane.
    (C) increase in effectiveness of the rudder.
    (D) ineffectiveness of the ailerons and elevator.
    (E) decrease in pitch and intensity of the sound of the air moving past the plane.

26. It is ordinarily desirable to provide an unusually long flight strip at municipal airports for the take-off of
    (A) military planes in echelon.
    (B) heavily loaded ships in still air.
    (C) small airplanes in rainy weather.
    (D) any airplane across the wind.
    (E) airplanes that have high climbing speeds.

Questions 27 through 29 are based on the figure shown below:

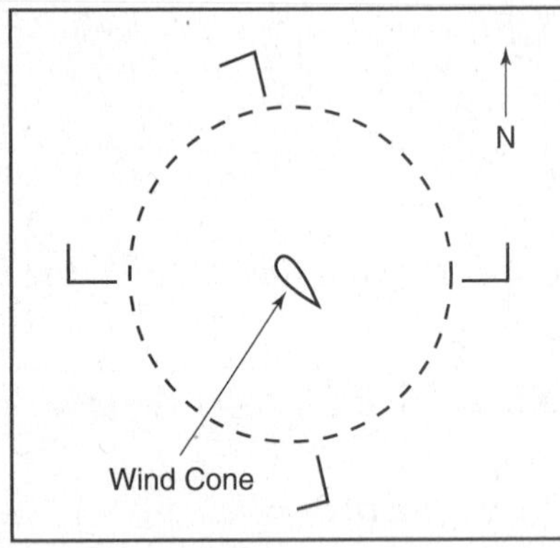

27. The segmented circle shown above indicates that the airport traffic is
    (A) left-hand for Runway 17 and right-hand for Runway 35.
    (B) right-hand for Runway 9 and left-hand for Runway 27.
    (C) right-hand for Runway 35 and right-hand for Runway 9.
    (D) left-hand for Runway 17 and right-hand for Runway 9.
    (E) left-hand for Runway 35 and right-hand for Runway 17.

28. The segmented circle indicates that a landing on Runway 27 will be with a
    (A) right-quartering headwind.
    (B) left-quartering headwind.
    (C) right-quartering tailwind.
    (D) left-quartering tailwind.
    (E) 90° crosswind.

29. Which runways and traffic pattern should be used as indicated by the wind cone in the segmented circle?
    (A) right-hand traffic on Runway 35 or left-hand traffic on Runway 27
    (B) left-hand traffic on Runway 35 or right-hand traffic on Runway 27
    (C) right-hand traffic on Runway 17 or left-hand traffic on Runway 9
    (D) left-hand traffic on Runway 17 or right-hand traffic on Runway 9
    (E) left-hand traffic on Runways 9 or 27

30. The line placed on an airspeed indicator to warn that operating above the indicated level is dangerous is colored ____________.
    (A) yellow
    (B) green
    (C) red
    (D) black
    (E) blue

Subtest 6—Aviation Supplemental Test

Directions: On this subtest you will experience a review of the previous five subtests. You may see questions that are exactly the same as questions you've previously answered; you may see questions that appear to be the same, but are slightly different; or you may see questions that are entirely different from those you answered previously. The results of this subtest are fed into a proprietary algorithm that affects the composite scores used for pilot and flight officer selections.

Read the questions carefully, then choose the response that best answers the question.

This subtest has 34 questions that must be answered in 25 minutes.

1. 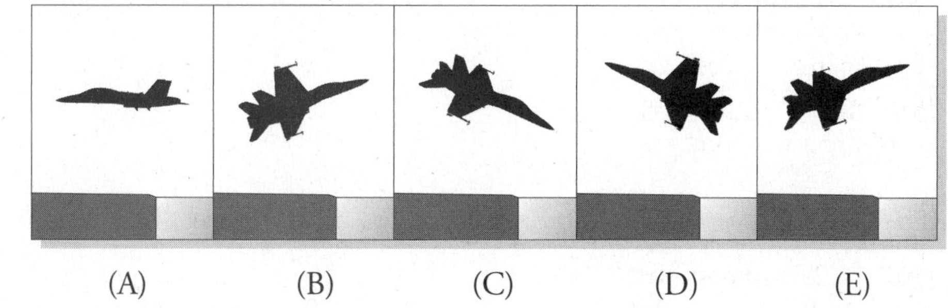

(A) (B) (C) (D) (E)

2. A rocket is fired straight up into the air with an initial velocity of 80 feet per second. The altitude (in feet) of the rocket at any given time during the acceleration phase can be determined by the polynomial $80x - 16x^2$, where x is equal to the number of seconds from lift-off. Assuming the rocket is still accelerating, find the altitude of the rocket 4 seconds after launch.
   (A) 15 feet
   (B) 33 feet
   (C) 52 feet
   (D) 64 feet

3. Two men agree to divide the profit on a business venture in the ratio of 4 to 7. If the total profit on the venture was $6,196, what was the share of the second man (the one with the larger share)?

   (A) $3942.91
   (B) $4003.23
   (C) $4129.40
   (D) $4232.39

4. Operation of modern airplanes is dependent upon the use of instruments. Instrument dials, displayed in the airplane's cockpit, are referred to as "flight instruments" or "engine instruments." Which one of the following is not a "flight instrument"?

   (A) airspeed indicator
   (B) altimeter
   (C) attitude indicator
   (D) tachometer

5. The time in Greenwich, England is referred to as

   (A) Coordinated Universal Time.
   (B) Zulu Time.
   (C) Standard Mean Time.
   (D) both (A) and (B)

6. On board a Naval vessel, if an officer tells you to "make a hole," she wants you to

   (A) clean your work area.
   (B) increase speed.
   (C) get out of the way.
   (D) fire a weapon.

7. The command used to place the rudder in line with the keel of the ship is

   (A) "align your rudder."
   (B) "stabilize the rudder."
   (C) "steady as she goes."
   (D) "rudder amidships."

8. Using the 24-hour clock, 6:00 P.M. would be expressed as

   (A) 2100 hours.
   (B) 2000 hours.
   (C) 0600 hours.
   (D) 1800 hours.

9. Juxtapose most nearly means ___________.

(A) apart
(B) together
(C) maintain
(D) relax

10. If there are red, green, and yellow marbles in a jar, and 20% of these marbles are either red or green, what are the chances of blindly picking a yellow marble out of the jar?

(A) 1 out of 3
(B) 1 out of 5
(C) 2 out of 3
(D) 4 out of 5

11. If Pulley #1 is turning clockwise, how many pulleys in the below diagram will be rotating counterclockwise?

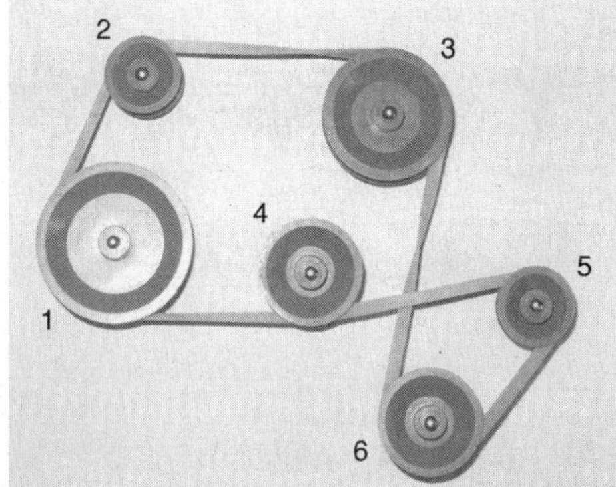

(A) 0
(B) 1
(C) 2
(D) 3

12. If x is an odd integer, which one of the following is an even integer?

(A) $2x + 1$
(B) $2x - 1$
(C) $x^2 - x$
(D) $x^2 + x - 1$

13. When a machine magnifies force, it is referred to as

(A) magnification multiple.
(B) mechanical factor.
(C) mechanical advantage.
(D) efficiency factor.

14. The device on an aircraft carrier that is used to help aircraft accelerate to the required takeoff speed is called the ___________.

    (A) thruster
    (B) pitot assembly
    (C) catapult
    (D) shotgun

15. 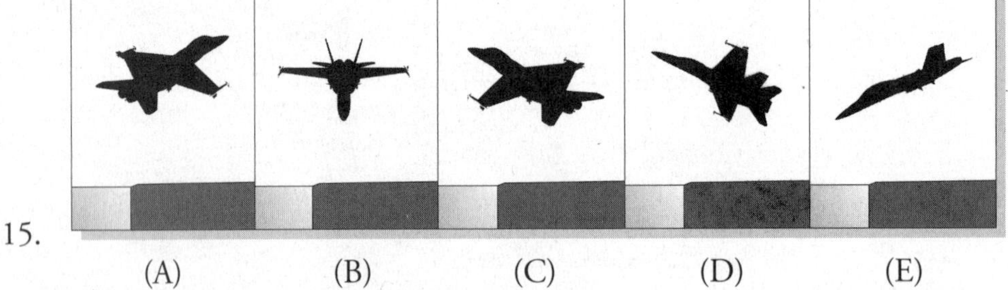

    (A) (B) (C) (D) (E)

Question 16 is based on the following paragraph.

"No matter how carefully planned or how painstakingly executed a sales letter or other mailing piece may be, unless it is sent to people selected from a good mailing list, it will be useless. A good mailing list is one consisting of the correct names and present addresses of bona fide prospects or customers."

16. The passage best supports the statement that

    (A) a good mailing list is more important than the sales letter.
    (B) a sales letter should not be sent to anyone who is not already a customer.
    (C) carefully planned letters may be wasted on poor mailing lists.
    (D) good sales letters do not depend on a good mailing list to be successful.

17. 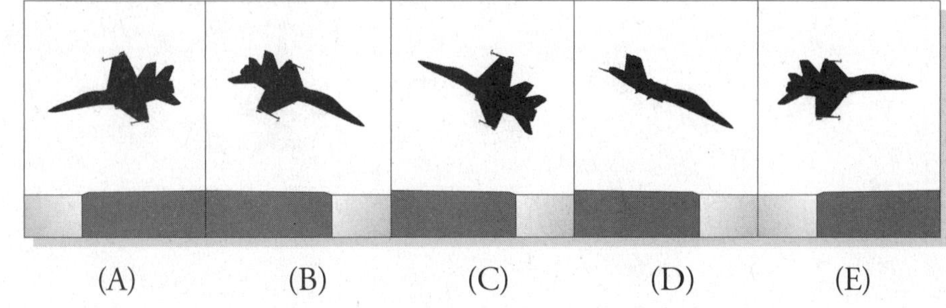

(A) (B) (C) (D) (E)

Question 18 is based on the following paragraph.

"In the metric system, the unit of length is the meter, which is one ten-millionth of the distance from the Equator to the North Pole. One kilometer (1,000 meters) is equal to $\frac{5}{8}$ of a mile. The meter is divided into smaller units, such as the centimeter ($\frac{1}{100}$ of a meter) or the millimeter ($\frac{1}{1,000}$ of a meter)."

18. The meter is actually equal to

(A) $\frac{1}{1,000,000}$ of the distance from the Equator to the North Pole.

(B) $\frac{1}{10,000,000}$ of the distance from the Equator to the North Pole.

(C) $\frac{1}{100,000,000}$ of the distance from the Equator to the North Pole.

(D) the distance from the Equator to the North Pole.

19. 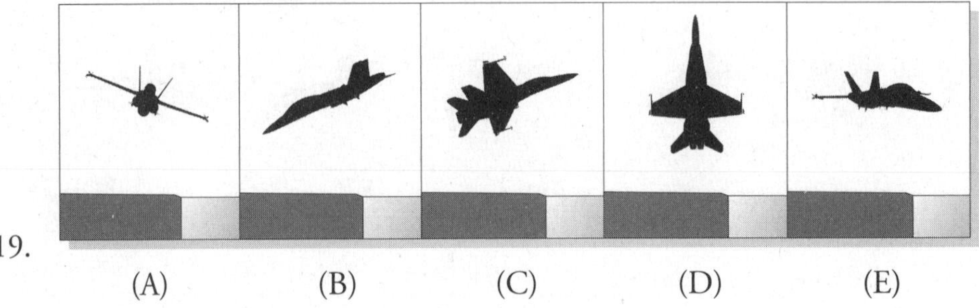

(A) (B) (C) (D) (E)

20. On an aircraft carrier, a “meatball” is

(A) the place where flight operations are controlled.
(B) a series of lights aiding the pilot in lining up for the landing.
(C) the forward edge of the takeoff platform.
(D) a sailor who constantly makes mistakes.

21. 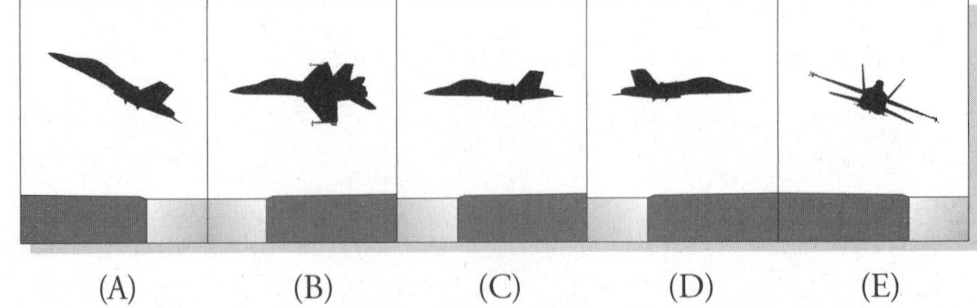

(A) (B) (C) (D) (E)

22. The graph of $x^2 - y^3 - 3x + 4y - 5$ is which of the following?
    (A) hyperbola
    (B) semicircle
    (C) ellipse
    (D) circle

23.
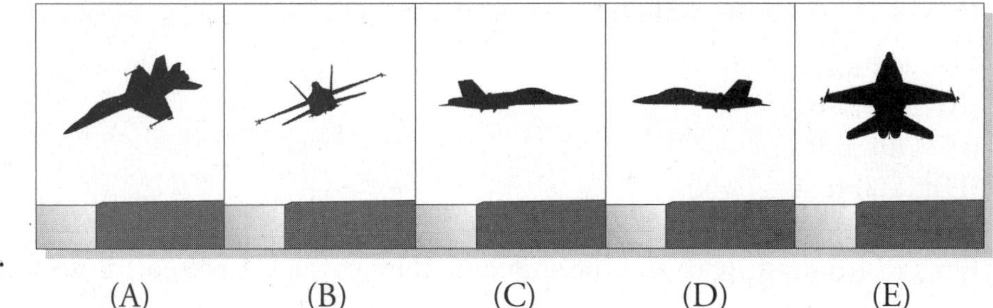
(A) (B) (C) (D) (E)

24. Recreant most nearly means ___________.
    (A) lazy
    (B) coward
    (C) priest
    (D) fireman

25.
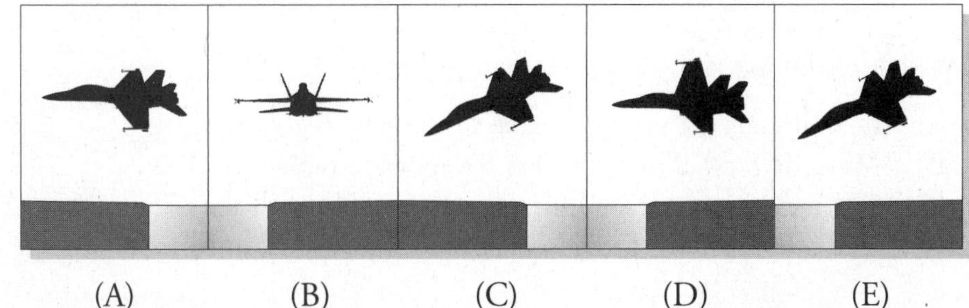
(A) (B) (C) (D) (E)

26. When forward pressure is applied to the elevator control

    (A) the nose will rotate up and the airspeed will decrease.
    (B) the nose will rotate up and the airspeed will increase.
    (C) the nose will rotate down and the airspeed will decrease.
    (D) the nose will rotate down and the airspeed will increase.

27. Convert 6.39×10^{-4} to regular notation

    (A) $(6.39)^5 \times 10$
    (B) 639,000
    (C) 639.10
    (D) 0.000639

28. A passenger plane can carry two tons of cargo. A freight plane can carry six tons of cargo. If an equal number of both kinds of planes are used to ship 160 tons of cargo and each plane carries its maximum cargo load, how many tons of cargo are shipped on the passenger planes?

    (A) 40 tons
    (B) 60 tons
    (C) 80 tons
    (D) 100 tons

29. On a scaled drawing of an office building floor, $\frac{1}{2}$ inch represents three feet of actual floor dimension. A floor that is actually 75 feet wide and 132 feet long would have which of the following dimensions on the scaled drawing?

    (A) 12.5 inches wide and 22 inches long
    (B) 17 inches wide and 32 inches long
    (C) 25 inches wide and 44 inches long
    (D) 29.5 inches wide and 52 inches long

Question 30 is based on the following paragraph.

"Air carriers had until Nov. 1987 to comply with a new regulation that required the installation of new fire-blocking layers on aircraft seat cushions. This marked the end of a three-year compliance schedule. Air carriers replaced 650,000 foam seat cushions on the U.S. fleet. FAA research found that the new material did a better job retarding burning and provided 40 to 60 seconds of additional time for aircraft evacuation. All existing seats in the U.S. fleet meet the improved standards."

30. Which of the following statements is not true?

    (A) U.S. aircraft are now safer due to the new regulation.
    (B) More than a half million seat covers were replaced.
    (C) Air carriers were given four years to comply with the regulation.
    (D) The new cushions provide for faster evacuations in times of emergency.

31. When a Naval vessel is under attack or battle is imminent, the ship's captain will generally order which of the following conditions?

    (A) attack positions
    (B) general quarters
    (C) alarm red
    (D) alarm yellow

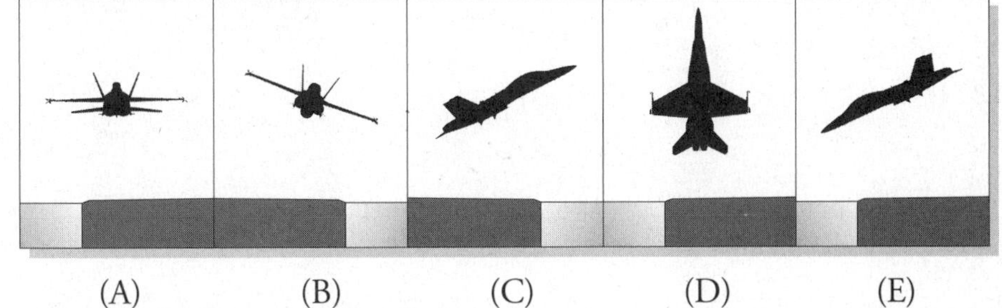

32. (A) (B) (C) (D) (E)

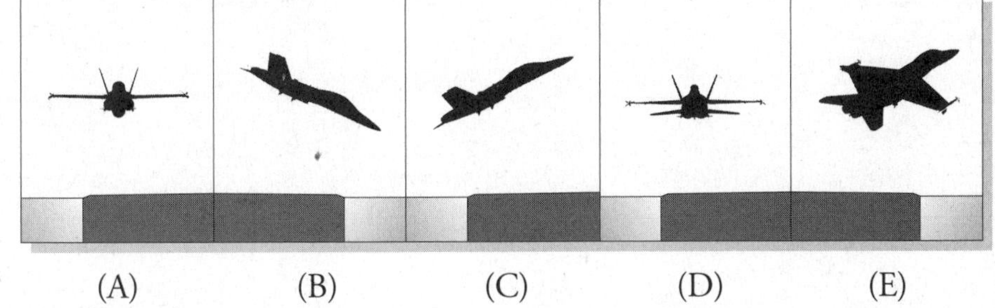

33. (A) (B) (C) (D) (E)

34.

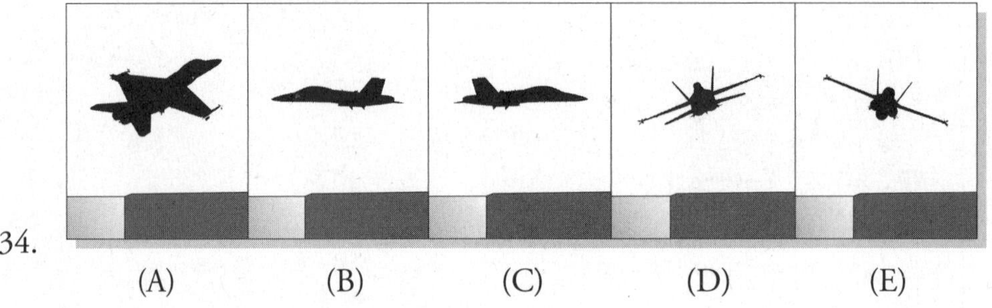

(A) (B) (C) (D) (E)

Answer Key

PRACTICE TEST 7

Subtest 1–Math Skills

1. C	7. B	13. A	19. D	25. C
2. B	8. C	14. A	20. C	26. B
3. C	9. B	15. B	21. D	27. B
4. C	10. C	16. C	22. D	28. A
5. A	11. C	17. B	23. B	29. B
6. B	12. D	18. C	24. B	30. C

Subtest 2–Reading Skills

1. C	7. D	13. A	19. A	25. D
2. D	8. C	14. C	20. D	26. C
3. A	9. B	15. D	21. C	27. B
4. C	10. B	16. A	22. C	
5. B	11. D	17. B	23. C	
6. C	12. D	18. C	24. D	

Subtest 3–Mechanical Comprehension

1. B	7. A	13. D	19. C	25. A
2. D	8. C	14. B	20. B	26. A
3. C	9. D	15. C	21. D	27. B
4. B	10. C	16. D	22. D	28. B
5. A	11. B	17. C	23. D	29. C
6. D	12. C	18. A	24. B	30. B

Subtest 4–Spatial Apperception

1. C	6. B	11. C	16. B	21. C
2. A	7. A	12. C	17. D	22. A
3. A	8. A	13. D	18. B	23. E
4. B	9. A	14. A	19. E	24. A
5. D	10. E	15. B	20. A	25. B

Subtest 5—Aviation/Nautical Information

1. C	7. B	13. C	19. A	25. D
2. E	8. C	14. C	20. E	26. B
3. B	9. E	15. C	21. B	27. E
4. A	10. A	16. B	22. D	28. A
5. A	11. C	17. B	23. A	29. B
6. C	12. C	18. D	24. A	30. C

Subtest 6—Aviation Supplemental Test

1. E	8. D	15. C	22. A	29. A
2. D	9. B	16. C	23. D	30. C
3. A	10. D	17. D	24. B	31. B
4. D	11. C	18. C	25. E	32. E
5. D	12. C	19. E	26. D	33. E
6. C	13. C	20. B	27. D	34. D
7. D	14. C	21. B	28. A	

Answer Explanations to Practice Test

SUBTEST 1—MATH SKILLS

1. **(C) $-3x^2 - 2xy^2 + 8x - 1$.**
   $x^2y + xy^2 + 6x + 4 - (4x^2y + 3xy^2 - 2x + 5) =$
   $x^2y + xy^2 + 6x + 4 - 4x^2y - 3xy^2 + 2x - 5 =$
   $x^2y - 4x^2y + xy^2 - 3xy^2 + 6x + 2x + 4 - 5 =$
   $(1-4)x^2y + (1-3)xy^2 + (6 + 2)x - 1 =$
   $-3x^2y - 2xy^2 + 8x - 1$
2. **(B) −1.**
   $5x + 7 = 6(x - 2) - 4(2x - 3)$
   $5x + 7 = 6x - 12 - 8x + 12$
   $5x + 7 = -2x$
   $7x + 7 = 0$
   $7x = -7$
   $x = -1$
3. **(C) 255.53.**
   Let x = death rate in 1998.
   $x - 31\frac{3}{4}\% = 174.4$
   $x - 0.3175x = 174.4$
   $x(1 - 0.3175) = 174.4$
   $0.6825x = 174.4$
   $x = \frac{174.4}{0.6825}$
   $x = 255.53$
4. **(C) 20 minutes.**
   The combined rates of Tom and Kyle are 15 mph (8 + 7 = 15).
   Let x = the number of hours until they meet.
   $15x = 5$ hours
   $x = \frac{5}{15}$
   $x = \frac{1}{3}$ hours, or 20 minutes.
5. **(A) 13 inches.**
   Let r = original radius. $R + 5$ equals the new radius.
   The formula $A = \pi r^2$ represents the original area. We know that the new area is 155π square inches larger than the original area, so $155\pi + A = \pi(r + 5)^2 = 155\pi + \pi r^2$.
   $\pi(r + 5)(r + 5) = 155\pi + \pi r^2$
   $\pi(r^2 + 10r + 25) = 155\pi + \pi r^2$
   $\pi r^2 + 10r\pi + 25\pi = 155\pi + \pi r^2$
   $10r\pi + 25\pi = 155\pi$
   $10r\pi = 130\pi$
   $r = \frac{130\pi}{10\pi}$
   $r = 13$

6. **(B) –6, 5.**
$-x^2 - x + 30 = 0$
$-(-x^2 - x + 30) = -0$
$x^2 + x - 30 = 0$
$(x + 6)(x - 5) = 0$
$x + 6 = 0$ and $x - 5 = 0$
$x = -6$, and $x = 5$
7. **(B) 3 inches × 4 inches.** The diagonal formula for a rectangle is $D^2 = L^2 + W^2$. We know that $D = 5$ and $L = W + 1$.
$D^2 = L^2 + W^2$.
$5^2 = (W + 1)^2 + W^2$
$25 = (W + 1)(W + 1) + W^2$
$25 = W^2 + 2W + 1 + W^2$
$25 = 2W^2 + 2W + 1$
$0 = 2W^2 + 2W - 24$
$\frac{1}{2}(0) = \frac{1}{2}(2W^2 + 2W - 24)$
$0 = W^2 + W - 12$
$0 = (W - 3)(W + 4)$
$W - 3 = 0$ and $W + 4 = 0$
$W = 3$ and $W = -4$ (–4 is not a possible solution)
$W = 3$, so the length $(W + 1) = 4$.
8. **(C) 6.** Let x = the smaller number. As the sum of the two numbers is 10, then the larger number is represented by $10 - x$.
$3x + 5(10 - x) = 42$
$3x + 50 - 5x = 42$
$-2x + 50 = 42$
$-2x = -8$
$x = \frac{-8}{-2}$
$x = 4$
As the smaller number (x) is equal to 4, the larger number ($10 - x$) is equal to 6.
9. **(B) 76.** Let x = final exam grade. The quiz average is 68.
$[\frac{(61 + 63 + 65 + 83)}{4} = 68]$.
$\frac{3}{4}$ of the quiz average (68) plus $\frac{1}{4}$ of the final exam (x) must equal 70.
$\frac{3}{4}(68) + \frac{1}{4}(x) = 70$
$51 + \frac{x}{4} = 70$
$\frac{x}{4} = 19$
$x = 4 \times 19$
$x = 76$
10. **(C) 60 miles.**
Let x = number of miles driven.
$39 = 18 + 0.35x$
$21 = 0.35x$

$\frac{21}{0.35} = x$

$x = 60$

11. **(C) 56.7 points.** Ensign Taggarty's total score is 270 points (5 × 54). Lieutenant Thompson's total score is 354 points (6 × 59).
(270 + 354)/11 = 56.7 points.
12. **(D) hyperbola.** As the x^2 and y^2 variables have different signs, the graph is a hyperbola.
13. **(A) $1,505.** The formula to compute value after depreciation is $V = O(1 - P)^T$, where V equals the value, O equals the original cost, P equals the percentage of depreciation, and T = the time (in years).
$V = O(1 - P)^T$
$V = 2{,}800(1 - 0.22)^{2.5}$
$V = 2{,}800(0.78)^{2.5}$
$V = 1{,}505$

14. **(A) $\frac{8\pi}{3}$.** π radians = 180°. To convert an angle to degrees, you multiply the angle by $\frac{\pi}{180}$.

$480 \times \frac{\pi}{180} =$

$\frac{480\pi}{180} =$

$\frac{8\pi}{3}$

15. **(B) $2.00 per gallon.** Let x = the wholesale price. Therefore, 40% of the wholesale price is $0.40x$. The retail price of the gas is the wholesale price plus 40% of the wholesale price plus $0.20.
$x + 0.40x + 0.20 = 3.00$
$1x + 0.40x + 0.20 = 3.00$
$1.4x + 0.2 = 3.00$
$1.4x = 2.80$
$x = \frac{2.80}{1.40}$
$x = 2.$
16. **(C) 30240.**
$2 \times 10^4 = 30{,}000$; $2 \times 10^2 = 200$; $4 \times 10 = 40$
30,000 + 200 + 40 = 30,240
17. **(B) 52.** To determine the number of questions answered, we need to take the difference and add one.
125 – 74 = 51.
51 + 1 = 52.
18. **(C) 2.** The fastest way to solve this is to substitute the possible answers for y in the equation and solve to see whether you get an integer value for x.

For example, for 1, we get $3x + 2 = 13$; $3x = 11$; $x = \frac{11}{3}$.

The correct answer is 2, as:
$3x + 2(2) = 13$
$3x = 13 - 4$

$3x = 9$

$x = \frac{9}{3}$

$x = 3$

19. **(D) none of the above.** n could be a positive fraction, a 1, or a fraction of a whole number greater than one.
If $n = 1$, then answer (A) is not correct $n^2 = 1$.
Likewise, if $n = 1$, then answer (B) is incorrect.
In answer (C), if $n = \frac{1}{2}$, then $2n - 1 = 0$, and again the statement is incorrect.
20. **(C) –6.** The equation for a straight line is $y = mx + c$, where m = slope and c = y-intercept.
Inserting the given values in this equation results in $y = \frac{x}{2} + 3$.
The x-intercept occurs where $y = 0$.
$0 = \frac{x}{2} + 3$
$-3 = \frac{x}{2}$
$-6 = x$
21. **(D) 15.** Imagine the first person of the six. He or she will have to shake hands with each of the other five. Now turn to the second person. He or she will have to shake with the other five, but he or she has already shaken with the first person. This means 4 new handshakes. The third person will have to shake with $5 - 2 = 3$ people, and so on. Total handshakes $= 5 + 4 + 3 + 2 + 1 = 15$.
22. **(D) –3.** $x^2 - y^2$ can be expressed as $(x + y)(x - y)$; since $x - y = 11$ we can write $(x + y)11 = 55$; therefore $x + y = 5$
Adding the two equations $x + y = 5$ and $x - y = 11$ we get $2x = 16$; $x = 8$.
Therefore $8 - y = 11$; $y = -3$
23. **(B) 8.** Since 2 do not play either, there are 28 people who play one game or the other. Let the number who play both be n.
Total (28) will be made up of only poker players $(17 - n)$, plus only blackjack players $(19 - n)$ and those who play both (n).
$28 = (17 - n) + (19 - n) + n$
$28 = 36 - n$
$n = 8$
24. **(B) $6x^2y + 2xy$.** $2x(3xy + y) = 2x(3xy) + 2x(y) = 6x^2y + 2xy$.
25. **(C) 13.**
$\pi(r + 5)(r + 5) = 155\pi + \pi r^2$
$\pi(r^2 + 10r + 25) = 155\pi + \pi r^2$
$\pi r^2 + 10r\pi + 25\pi = 155\pi + \pi r^2$
$10r\pi + 25\pi = 155\pi$
$10r\pi = 130\pi$
$r = \frac{130\pi}{10\pi}$
$r = 13$
26. **(B) 540°.** A pentagon has 5 sides. (Number of sides – 2) $\times$ 180 = sum of angles.

27. **(B) 224.** 25% + 35% = 60%. 60% were 22 years old or under 22 years of age. 40% were over 22 years old. 560 × .40 = 224.
28. **(A) 50 envelopes per hour.** Let x = number of envelopes addressed in 1 hour by slower worker. $2x$ = number of envelopes addressed in 1 hour by faster worker. $3x \times 5 = 750$; $15x = 750$; $x = 50$ envelopes per hour for slower worker.
29. **(B) $\frac{1}{8}$ lb.** Each stick of margarine = $\frac{1}{4}$ lb. Each stick consists of eight sections or tablespoons. Four sections or tablespoons = $\frac{1}{2}$ of $\frac{1}{4}$ lb = $\frac{1}{8}$ lb.
30. **(C) 15.6 pounds.** $\frac{1}{2} \times \frac{1}{2} \times 1 = \frac{1}{4}$ cu. ft.; $\frac{1}{4}$ of 62.4 = 15.6 pounds.

SUBTEST 2—READING SKILLS

1. **(C) brave.** "If a creature so tiny was not afraid in the wilderness why should he be!"
2. **(D) mimicking is natural to man.** The author contends that imitation is both natural to man and that mankind naturally delights in all works of imitation.
3. **(A) Father Francis is a rather remarkable looking man.** This statement is false, as the passage states that it is Father Franklin who is the more remarkable looking of the two.
4. **(C) follower.** Used as a noun, *henchman* means a trusted follower.
5. **(B) together.** Used as a verb, *juxtapose* means to place side-by-side.
6. **(C) importance.** Used as a noun, *magnitude* means degree of importance.
7. **(D) reality.** Used as a noun, *actuality* means the state or fact of being real.
8. **(C) truth.** Used as a noun, *verity* means the quality or condition of being true, factual, or real.
9. **(B) plan.** Used as a noun, *stratagem* means a clever, often underhanded scheme for achieving an objective.
10. **(B) urging.** Used as a verb, *incite* means to provoke or urge on.
11. **(D) merciless.** Used as an adjective, *pitiless* means having no pity or merciless.
12. **(D) restricted.** Used as a verb, *circumscribed* means restricted or confined.
13. **(A) definite.** Used as an adjective *explicit* means definite, or fully and completely defined.
14. **(C) changes according to the current situation.** National Military Strategy evolves as the international environment, national strategy, and national military objectives change.
15. **(D) both (A) and (C).** National military strategy lays the basis for applying military instruments at the strategic and operational levels of war.
16. **(A) subordinates will mimic negative traits of their leaders.** Followers will observe both the positive as well as negative characteristics and emulate them.
17. **(B) a professional association.** According to sociologist Harold Wilensky, one of the defining traits of a profession is the establishment of a professional association.
18. **(C) impromptu.** Used as an adjective, *extemporaneous* means done without much preparation or practice.
19. **(A) harmful.** Used as an adjective, *noxious* means harmful to life.

20. **(D) brave.** Used as an adjective, *intrepid* means resolutely courageous or fearless.
21. **(C) lie.** Used as a noun, *myth* means a narrative or story, presented as history, but not supported by facts or evidence.
22. **(C) degrade.** Used as a verb, *abase* means to lower in esteem or to degrade.
23. **(C) led to more complicated systems for data handling.** The third sentence states that the techniques of data processing have become highly elaborate and sophisticated with the introduction of computers.
24. **(D) the business forms used by a company are a good indication of the efficiency of the company's operations.** The passage states that proper business forms indicate a high degree of operational efficiency; improper business forms indicate probable inefficient operations.
25. **(D) the material needs of men and women are supplied by well-conducted businesses.** The last sentence states that when the nation's business is successfully carried on, it renders public service of the highest order. This is accomplished by supplying the material needs of men and women.
26. **(C) competition.** Conflict as used in the passage means competition that may be desirable or undesirable in an organization, depending upon whether it is a positive or negative factor in achieving organizational objectives.
27. **(B) democratic freedoms**. The author states that the great moments in history are made by those opposing tyranny and advancing freedom for the people.

SUBTEST 3—MECHANICAL COMPREHENSION

1. **(B) 1, 3, 4**. The arrangement of the valves would cause water to flow into tanks 1, 3, and 4.
2. **(D) when a car is accelerating.** The force causing a car to accelerate comes from the frictional force between the tires and the road.
3. **(C) 50 pounds**. The formula is $w \times d = f \times d_2$. $(100 \times 3 = f \times 6)$.
   $300 = 6f$
   $f = 50$ pounds
4. **(B) 1 foot**. The pulley system depicted gives a mechanical advantage of 2. While the force required to move the weight is cut in half, the amount of rope that must be moved is doubled.
5. **(A) 1,000 pound-inches.** Torque is multiplied in the same ratio as the size of the gears. The driving gear is 10 inches and the driven gear is 20 inches, giving us a ratio of 1:2.
6. **(D) gear E only.** Gear F is too small and gears A, D, C, G, and H are in constant mesh.
7. **(A) clockwise, clockwise**. If Pulley A is spinning clockwise, it will cause Pulley C to spin counterclockwise, which will cause Pulley E to spin counter clockwise, causing Pulley D to spin clockwise and Pulley B to spin clockwise.
8. **(C) Point C.** Point C would require the least amount of force because it is the farthest point from the fulcrum. Applying force at Point D would result in lowering the box, not raising it.
9. **(D) 2,000.** Each of the tires support an equal amount of weight.
   $\frac{8,000}{4} = 2,000$ pounds.

10. **(C) cutting metal.** The hacksaw is specifically designed to cut metal.
11. **(B) slower.** The gear on the driving shaft is significantly smaller in diameter than the gear on the driven shaft. This will result in an increase in torque, but a decrease in speed.
12. **(C) change.** If a single force acts on an object, the velocity of that thing must change.
13. **(D) 4.** The two vertical forces are gravity and lift, and the two horizontal forces are thrust and drag.
14. **(B) two inches.** The moment of the fulcrum created by the weight is 400 feet-lbs (200 lbs × 2 feet). Applying the same moment to the opposite end gives us the force applied to the spring $\frac{(400 \text{ feet-lbs})}{(5 \text{ feet})} = 66.6$ lbs. Applying 66.6 pounds of force to the spring with a stiffness of 30 lbs per inch (66.2 lbs/30 lbs/inch) = 2.2 inches.
15. **(C) tempering.** The process of making glass harder (less breakable) is called tempering.
16. **(D) 60 pounds**. The scale is supporting the complete weight of the 20-lb. bar, and the two 20-lb. weights.
17. **(C) 24.** There are five sections of rope supporting the weight, giving a mechanical advantage of 5. $\frac{120}{5} = 24$.
18. **(A) wing nut.** The other items listed are designed to be tightened with tools.
19. **(C) 2.** Pulleys #5 and #6 will be rotating counterclockwise.
20. **(B) Direction B.** Visualize the lower gear rotating very slowly and you will see that the movement of the teeth will result in the upper gear spinning clockwise.
21. **(D) 60 pounds.** Spring A has a tension strength of 5 lbs per inch. To stretch the spring 3 inches, 15 pounds of force is required (5 × 3). Apply the same formula to each spring and we arrive at a total amount of force of 60 pounds (5 × 3) + (10 × 3) + (5 × 3) = 60.
22. **(D) both (B) and (C).** Since the two balls have the same density, the larger ball has more mass. When the two balls collide, the ball with the most mass will be slowed, but will continue in the same direction. The ball with the lesser mass will be propelled backwards.
23. **(D) wheels.** The distributor is part of the electrical system, the master cylinder part of the breaking system, and the pistons are part of the engine.
24. **(B) swing B.** All things being equal, shorter pendulums swing faster than longer pendulums.
25. **(A) wrenches.** All of these are types of wrenches.
26. **(A) gear D will turn faster.** Gear D has 10 teeth, while gear G has 13. In a series of gears, the gear with the fewer teeth will turn faster.
27. **(B) spring.** The spring is used to push the key of the keyboard back into its original position, once pressure from the finger is removed.
28. **(B) pressure gage.** Pressure is normally measured in units of PSI.
29. **(C) reduce noise.** Part of the exhaust system, the main purpose of the muffler on a car is to reduce noise produced by the combustion process of the engine.
30. **(B) 2.** Pulleys B and E will rotate counterclockwise.

SUBTEST 4—SPATIAL APPERCEPTION

Question	Answer	Pitch	Bank	Direction
1.	C	Nose Down	Right	Out to sea
2.	A	Zero	Left	Up the coastline
3.	A	Nose Up	Right	Out to sea
4.	B	Zero	Right	Up the coastline
5.	D	Zero	Left	Out to sea
6.	B	Nose Down	Left	Out to sea
7.	A	Nose Up	Left	Out to sea
8.	A	Nose Down	Zero	Out to sea
9.	A	Zero	Zero	Up the coastline
10.	E	Zero	Right	Out to sea
11.	C	Zero	Zero	45 degrees right of coastline
12.	C	Zero	Right	Down the coastline
13.	D	Nose Down	Zero	Down the coastline
14.	A	Zero	Right	Up the coastline
15.	B	Nose Up	Left	Out to sea
16.	B	Zero	Zero	Down the coastline
17.	D	Nose Up	Zero	Out to sea
18.	B	Nose Up	Zero	Down the coastline
19.	E	Nose Down	Zero	Down the coastline
20.	A	Zero	Zero	45 degrees right of coastline
21.	C	Zero	Zero	Out to sea
22.	A	Zero	Left	Down the coastline
23.	E	Zero	Right	Out to sea
24.	A	Nose Down	Zero	Out to sea
25.	B	Nose Down	Right	Out to sea

SUBTEST 5—AVIATION/NAUTICAL INFORMATION

1. **(C) 09.** Runways are assigned numbers based on the magnetic compass direction of the runway. Runway 27 is a runway placed along the heading of 270 (west). The opposite direction would be heading 090 (east), and the runway would be numbered 09.
2. **(E) 6 lbs/gal.** The standard weight for gasoline for aircraft weight and balance computations is 6 pounds for every gallon of gasoline.
3. **(B) 2000 hours.** The 24 hour clock consists of four numbers with 0000 as midnight, 0100 as 1:00 A.M., 0200 as 2:00 A.M., etc. 8:00 P.M. would be expressed as 2000.
4. **(A) move downward.** The elevators would move downward, which pushes the aircraft's tail upward and the nose of the aircraft downward.
5. **(A) 30 degrees to the left.** Note the angle of the wings. The pilot has banked the aircraft 30 degrees to the left.
6. **(C) knots.** One knot is a speed of one nautical mile per hour.
7. **(B) red.** Port navigation lights are red, starboard navigation lights are yellow.
8. **(C) cleared to taxi.** A green light directed at an aircraft on the ground is a signal that the pilot is cleared to taxi.
9. **(E) fuel flow indicator.** The fuel flow indicator is categorized as an engine instrument. The other instruments listed are categorized as flight instruments.
10. **(A) shorter takeoff distance and increased climb angle.** A tailwind, on the other hand, would have the opposite effect, resulting in a longer takeoff distance and a decreased angle of climb.
11. **(C) 7 or 25.** Runways 7 and 25 are 6003 feet long. Runways 13 and 31 are only 4638 feet long.
12. **(C) NW-SE direction.** Runway 31 (compass heading 310) points to the northwest, and runway 13 (compass heading 130) is pointing to the southeast.
13. **(C) handling the anchor chain.** On a ship, the windlass is primarily designed to handle the anchor chain.
14. **(C) positive air pressure below the wing's surface and negative air pressure above the wing's surface.** The top of the wing is curved while the bottom is relatively flat. The air flowing over the top travels a little farther than the air flowing along the flat bottom. This means that the air on top must go faster. Hence, the pressure decreases, resulting in a lower pressure on top of the wing and a higher pressure below. The higher pressure then pushes (lifts) the wing up toward the lower pressure area.
15. **(C) a steady red light signals to continue circling and a flashing red light signals that the airport is unsafe for landing.** A steady red light from the tower to an aircraft in flight signals to continue circling; a flashing red light signals that the airport is unsafe for landing.
16. **(B) produce thrust.** The propeller blades, just like a wing, are curved on one side and straight on the other. As the propeller is rotated by the engine, forces similar to those on the wing "lift" in a forward direction and produce thrust.
17. **(B) horizontal component of lift.** The lift acting upward and opposing weight is called the vertical lift component. The lift acting horizontally and opposing inertia or centrifugal force is called the horizontal lift component. The horizontal lift component is the sideward force that forces the airplane from straight flight and causes it to turn.

18. **(D) the airplane will require less effort to control.** Stability is the inherent ability of a body, after its equilibrium is disturbed, to develop forces or moments that tend to return the body to its original position. The ability of the airplane to return, of its own accord, to its original condition of flight after it has been disturbed by some outside force (such as turbulent air) makes the airplane easier to fly and requires less effort to control.
19. **(A) nose up.** The elevator trim tab is a small auxiliary control surface hinged at the trailing edge of the elevators. The elevator trim tab acts on the elevators, which in turn act upon the entire airplane. A downward deflection of the trim tab will force the elevator upward, which will force the tail down and the nose up.
20. **(E) climb.** The thrust required to maintain straight and level flight at a given airspeed is not sufficient to maintain the same airspeed in a climb. Climbing flight takes more power than straight and level flight. Consequently, the engine power control must be advanced to a higher power setting.
21. **(B) Beaufort scale.** The Beaufort scale measures wind force.
22. **(D) 1900.** In time zone +3 add 3 hours to the local time to compute the time in Greenwich, which is Zulu time.
23. **(A) throw lifebuoys over the side.** This action should be accomplished immediately before any other action is taken.
24. **(A) 180th meridian.** The 180th meridian is also known as the International Date Line. Greenwich, England (the zone for Zulu time) is at the 0 meridian.
25. **(D) ineffectiveness of the ailerons and elevator.** The feeling of control pressures is very important in recognizing the approach of a stall. As speed is reduced, the "live" resistance to pressures on the controls becomes progressively less. Pressures exerted on the controls tend to become movements of the control surfaces, and the lag between those movements and the response of the airplane become greater until in a complete stall all controls can be moved with almost no resistance and with little immediate effect on the airplane.
26. **(B) heavily loaded ships in still air.** Heavily loaded ships require a longer ground roll and consequently much more space is required to develop the minimum lift necessary for takeoff. Similarly, takeoff in still air precludes a takeoff as nearly into the wind as possible to reduce ground roll. Accordingly, municipal airports have found it desirable to provide an unusually long flight strip to cope with such adverse takeoff factors.
27. **(E) left-hand for Runway 35 and right-hand for Runway 17.** 17-35 runs roughly north-south. 9-27 runs west-east. The traffic pattern indicators () show the direction of the turns when landing on the runways. A left-hand turn is required to land on Runways 9 and 35. A right-hand turn is required to land on Runways 17 and 27.
28. **(A) right-quartering headwind.** Runway 27 runs due west. When the wind blows through the large end of the wind cone, it causes the small end to stand out and point downward.
29. **(B) left-hand traffic on Runway 35 or right-hand traffic on Runway 27.** Runways 35 and 27 are the two most desirable ones for landing as both would be with a quartering headwind. Runway 35 takes left-hand traffic; Runway 27 takes right-hand traffic.
30. **(C) red.** The radical line indicating dangerous operating ranges on the airspeed indicator is colored red.

SUBTEST 6—AVIATION SUPPLEMENTAL TEST

1. **(E)** Nose up, right bank, heading out to sea.
2. **(D) 64 feet.**
   Let a = altitude of the rocket
   Formula: $a = 80x - 16^2$
   Given $x = 4$
   $a = (80*4) - 16*4^2$
   $a = 320 - 16*16$
   $a = 64$
3. **(A) $3942.91.**
   Let F = FIRSTMAN
   Let S = SECONDMAN
   Given $\frac{F}{S} = \frac{4}{7}$
   Given $F + S = 6196$
   $7F = 4S$ // Expand parentheses
   $F = 6196 - S$
   $4S = 7(6196 - S)$
   $4S = 43372 - 7S$
   $S = 3942.91$
4. **(D) tachometer.** The tachometer is an instrument for indicating speed at which the engine crankshaft is rotating. The other options are all flight instruments.
5. **(D) both (A) and (B).** Its official name is Coordinated Universal Time or UTC. This time zone had previously been called Greenwich Mean Time (GMT) but was replaced with UTC in 1972 as the official world time standard changed. U.S. Military personnel (especially those involved in aviation or ship operations) refer to it as Zulu Time.
6. **(C) get out of the way.** The term is used by anyone on official duty who is in a hurry. "Make a hole" means to clear out of the way.
7. **(D) "rudder amidships."**
8. **(D) 1800 hours.** The 24-hour clock consists of four numbers with 0000 as midnight, 0100 as 1:00 A.M., 0200 as 2:00 A.M., etc. 6:00 P.M. would be expressed as 1800.
9. **(B) together.** Used as a verb, *juxtapose* means to place side-by-side.
10. **(D) 4 out of 5.** If 20% are either red or green, 80% are yellow. The chance of blindly picking a yellow marble is 4 out of 5 (80%).
11. **(C) 2.** Pulleys #5 and #6 will be rotating counterclockwise.
12. **(C) $x^2 - x$.** Squaring an odd integer results in an odd integer. Subtracting an odd integer from it results in an even integer. Options A, B, and D remain odd.
13. **(C) mechanical advantage.** When a machine magnifies force to make work easier, the magnification factor is termed mechanical advantage.
14. **(C) the catapult.** The four steam-powered catapults thrust a 48,000-pound aircraft 300 feet, from zero to 165 miles per hour in two seconds. On each plane's nose gear is a T-bar that locks into the catapult's shuttle that pulls the plane down the catapult. The flight deck crew can launch two aircraft and land one every 37 seconds in daylight, and one per minute at night.

15. **(C)** Zero pitch, zero bank, heading 45 degrees left of the coastline.
16. **(C) carefully planned letters may be wasted on poor mailing lists.** The first sentence states that unless a sales letter is sent to people selected from a good mailing list, it will be useless.
17. **(D)** Nose down, zero bank, heading out to sea.
18. **(C)** $\mathbf{\frac{1}{1,000,000,000}}$ **of the distance from the Equator to the North Pole.** One ten-millionth is $\frac{1}{100,000,000}$.
19. **(E)** Zero pitch, zero bank, heading 45 degrees left of the coastline.
20. **(B) a series of lights aiding the pilot in lining up for the landing.** If the lights appear above the green horizontal bar of the "meatball," the pilot is too high. If it is below, the pilot is too low, and if the lights are red, the pilot is very low. If the red lights on either side of the amber vertical bar are flashing, it is a wave off.
21. **(B)** Zero pitch, left bank, heading out to sea.
22. **(A) hyperbola.** As the x^2 and y^2 variables have different signs, the graph is a hyperbola.
23. **(D)** Zero pitch, zero bank, heading out to sea.
24. **(B) coward.** Used as a noun, *recreant* means craven or cowardly.
25. **(E)** Nose down, left bank, heading down the coastline.
26. **(D) the nose will rotate down and the airspeed will increase.** Applying forward pressure to the control stick causes the nose of the aircraft to rotate down in relation to the pilot. As the nose rotates downward, airspeed will increase.
27. **(D) 0.000639.** To convert scientific notation to regulation notation, move the decimal place to the left (for a negative exponent), the same number of spaces as the exponent (in this case, 4).
28. **(A) 40 tons.** 2 tons + 6 tons = 8 tons carried by 1 passenger and 1 freight plane. $\frac{160}{8}$ = 20 pairs of passenger and freight planes needed. 20 passenger planes carrying 2 tons each = 40 tons of cargo.
29. **(A) 12.5 inches wide and 22 inches long.** $\frac{1}{2}$ inch on a scaled drawing = 3 feet of actual floor dimension. $\frac{75}{3} = 25\frac{1}{2}$ inches = 12.5 inches; $\frac{132}{3} = 44\frac{1}{2}$ inches = 22 inches.
30. **(C) Air carriers were given four years to comply with the regulation.** Air carriers were given only three years to comply.
31. **(B) general quarters.** This command is used to order personnel to their battle stations, on the double.
32. **(E)** Nose up, zero bank, heading up the coastline.
33. **(E)** Zero pitch, zero bank, heading up the coastline.
34. **(D)** Zero pitch, left bank, heading up the coastline.

Index

UNCLE SAM WANTS YOU—*to Succeed!* And BARRON'S Can Help

BARRON'S ASVAB
10th Edition with Optional CD-ROM

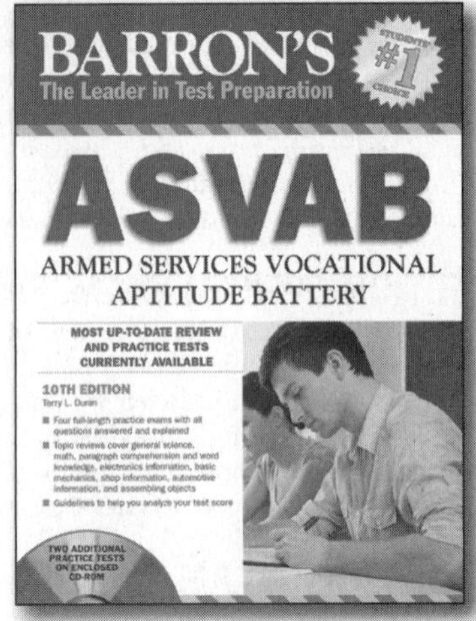

Terry L. Duran, Major, U.S. Army

The ASVAB test is required for recruits entering all branches of the U.S. Armed Forces. This test prep manual reviews all test areas: word knowledge, paragraph comprehension, math knowledge and reasoning, general science, electronics, basic mechanics, shop and automotive information. Also included is a diagnostic test and four practice ASVABs with questions and explained answers. An optional CD-ROM offers two additional tests with answers and automatic scoring.

Book: paper, ISBN: 978-0-7641-4793-7, $18.99, *Can$21.99*
Book w/CD-ROM: ISBN: 978-1-4380-7166-4, $29.99, *Can$34.50*

BARRON'S ASVAB FLASH CARDS
Armed Services Vocational Aptitude Battery

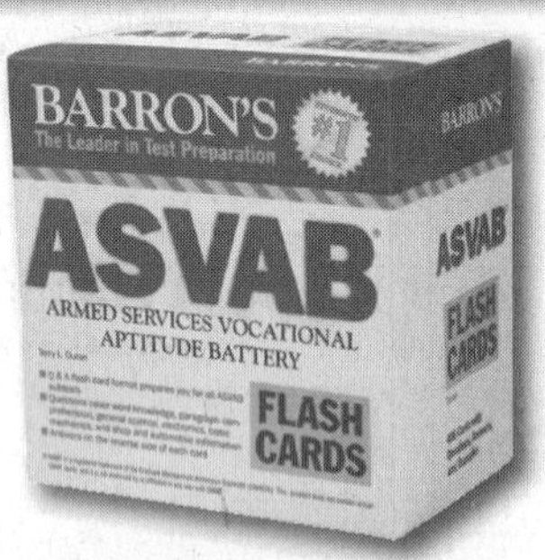

Terry L. Duran

This set of 400 flash cards prepares aspiring U.S. armed forces recruits for the required ASVAB test with questions and answers that cover all 19 subtests. Cards have a punch hole in one corner that accommodates a metal ring. The ring lets users arrange cards in any sequence that meets their study needs. The flash cards can be used alone or in tandem with Barron's ASVAB test prep manual described above.

400 Flash Cards, boxed: ISBN: 978-0-7641-9783-3, $18.99, *Can$22.99*

PASS KEY TO THE ASVAB
7th Edition

Terry L. Duran, Major, U.S. Army

This shorter version of Barron's full-size ASVAB test prep manual prepares U.S. Armed Forces recruits with features that include a diagnostic test and a complete practice exam with questions answered and explained. A detailed subject review covers all test subjects

Paperback, ISBN: 978-0-7641-4799-9, $9.99, *Can$11.50*

Barron's Educational Series, Inc.
250 Wireless Blvd.
Hauppauge, N.Y. 11788
Order toll-free: 1-800-645-3476

In Canada:
Georgetown Book Warehouse
34 Armstrong Ave.
Georgetown, Ontario L7G 4R9
Canadian orders: 1-800-247-7160

To order
Available at your local book store
or visit **www.barronseduc.com**

Prices subject to change without notice.

(#165) R 2/12